Simply C++

Deitel Books, Cyber Classrooms and Complete Training Courses
Published by Prentice Hall

Simply Series

Simply C++: An Application-Driven Tutorial Approach
Simply C#: An Application-Driven Tutorial Approach
Simply Visual Basic® .NET: An Application Driven
    Tutorial Approach
    (Visual Studio .NET 2002 Edition)

Simply Java™ Programming: An Application-Driven
    Tutorial Approach
Simply Visual Basic® .NET: An Application Driven
    Tutorial Approach
    (Visual Studio .NET 2003 Edition)

How to Program Series

Advanced Java™ 2 Platform How to Program
C How to Program, 4/E
C++ How to Program, 4/E
C# How to Program
e-Business and e-Commerce How to Program
Internet and World Wide Web How to Program, 3/E
Java™ How to Program, 6/E
Small Java™ How to Program, 6/E
Perl How to Program
Python How to Program
Visual Basic® 6 How to Program
Visual Basic® .NET How to Program, 2/E
Visual C++® .NET How to Program
Wireless Internet & Mobile Business How to Program
XML How to Program

.NET How to Program Series

C# How to Program
Visual Basic® .NET How to Program, 2/E
Visual C++® .NET How to Program

Visual Studio Series

C# How to Program
Getting Started with Microsoft® Visual C++® 6 with an Intro-
    duction to MFC
Simply C#: An Application-Driven Tutorial Approach
Simply Visual Basic® .NET: An Application- Driven Tutorial
    Approach (Visual Studio .NET 2002 Edition)
Simply Visual Basic® .NET: An Application- Driven Tutorial
    Approach (Visual Studio .NET 2003 Edition)
Visual Basic® 6 How to Program
Visual Basic® .NET How to Program, 2/E
Visual C++® .NET How to Program

For Managers Series

e-Business and e-Commerce for Managers

DEITEL® Developer Series

Java™ Web Services for Experienced Programmers
Web Services A Technical Introduction

Multimedia Cyber Classroom Series

C++ Multimedia Cyber Classroom, 4/E
C# Multimedia Cyber Classroom
e-Business and e-Commerce Multimedia Cyber Classroom
Internet and World Wide Web Multimedia
    Cyber Classroom, 2/E
Java™ 2 Multimedia Cyber Classroom, 5/E
Perl Multimedia Cyber Classroom
Python Multimedia Cyber Classroom
Visual Basic® 6 Multimedia Cyber Classroom
Visual Basic® .NET Multimedia Cyber Classroom, 2/E
Wireless Internet & Mobile Business Programming
    Multimedia Cyber Classroom
XML Multimedia Cyber Classroom

The Complete Training Course Series

The Complete C++ Training Course, 4/E
The Complete C# Training Course
The Complete e-Business and e-Commerce
    Programming Training Course
The Complete Internet and World Wide Web
    Programming Training Course, 2/E
The Complete Java™ 2 Training Course, 5/E
The Complete Perl Training Course
The Complete Python Training Course
The Complete Visual Basic® 6 Training Course
The Complete Visual Basic® .NET Training Course, 2/E
The Complete Wireless Internet &
    Mobile Business Programming Training Course
The Complete XML Programming
    Training Course

Computer Science Series

Operating Systems, 3/E

To follow the Deitel publishing program, please register for the free *DEITEL® BUZZ ONLINE* e-mail newsletter at:
    www.deitel.com/newsletter/subscribe.html

To communicate with the authors, send e-mail to:
    deitel@deitel.com

For information on Deitel Dive-Into ™ Series on-site training seminars, visit:
    www.deitel.com or write to deitel@deitel.com

For continuing updates on Prentice Hall/Deitel publications visit:
    www.deitel.com,
    www.prenhall.com/deitel or
    www.InformIT.com/deitel

Simply C++

H. M. Deitel
Deitel & Associates, Inc.

P. J. Deitel
Deitel & Associates, Inc.

D. R. Choffnes
Deitel & Associates, Inc.

C. L. Kelsey
Deitel & Associates, Inc.

PEARSON
Prentice Hall

Upper Saddle River, NJ 07458

Library of Congress Cataloging-in-Publication Data

On file

Vice President and Editorial Director, ECS: *Marcia J. Horton*
Senior Acquisitions Editor: *Kate Hargett*
Associate Editor: *Jennifer Cappello*
Assistant Editor: *Sarah Parker*
Editorial Assistant: *Michael Giacobbe*
Vice President and Director of Production and Manufacturing, ESM: *David W. Riccardi*
Executive Managing Editor: *Vince O'Brien*
Managing Editor: *Tom Manshreck*
Production Editor: *John F. Lovell*
Production Editor, Media: *Bob Engelhardt*
Production Assistant: *Asha Rohra*
Director of Creative Services: *Paul Belfanti*
A/V Production Editor: *Xiaohong Zhu*
Art Director: *Geoffrey Cassar*
Chapter Opener and Cover Artist: *Harvey M. Deitel, Shawn Murphy*
Interior Design: *Harvey M. Deitel, Jonathan Boylan, John Root*
Manufacturing Manager: *Trudy Pisciotti*
Manufacturing Buyer: *Lisa McDowell*
Marketing Manager: *Pamela Hersperger*
Marketing Assistant: *Barrie Reinhold*

© 2005 by Pearson Education, Inc.
Upper Saddle River, New Jersey 07458

The authors and publisher of this book have used their best efforts in preparing this book. These efforts include the development, research, and testing of the theories and programs to determine their effectiveness. The authors and publisher make no warranty of any kind, expressed or implied, with regard to these programs or to the documentation contained in this book. The authors and publisher shall not be liable in any event for incidental or consequential damages in connection with, or arising out of, the furnishing, performance, or use of these programs.

Many of the designations used by manufacturers and sellers to distinguish their products are claimed as trademarks and registered trademarks. Where those designations appear in this book, and Pearson Education, Inc. and the authors were aware of a trademark claim, the designations have been printed in initial caps or all caps. All product names mentioned remain trademarks or registered trademarks of their respective owners.

Printed in the United States of America

10 9 8 7 6 5 4 3 2 1

ISBN 0-13-142660-5

Pearson Education Ltd., *London*
Pearson Education Australia Pty. Ltd., *Sydney*
Pearson Education Singapore, Pte. Ltd.
Pearson Education North Asia Ltd., *Hong Kong*
Pearson Education Canada, Inc., *Toronto*
Pearson Educación de Mexico, S.A. de C.V.
Pearson Education–Japan, *Tokyo*
Pearson Education Malaysia, Pte. Ltd.
Pearson Education, Inc., *Upper Saddle River, New Jersey*

To my parents Albert and Susan,
for their profound love, support and encouragement
in all of my life's endeavors.

David

In loving memory of my father, David "Dave" L. Kelsey:

May the way you lived your life as a loving husband,
devoted father, dedicated businessman and faithful
friend be an inspiration to us all.

Christi

Brief Table of Contents

C ONTENTS

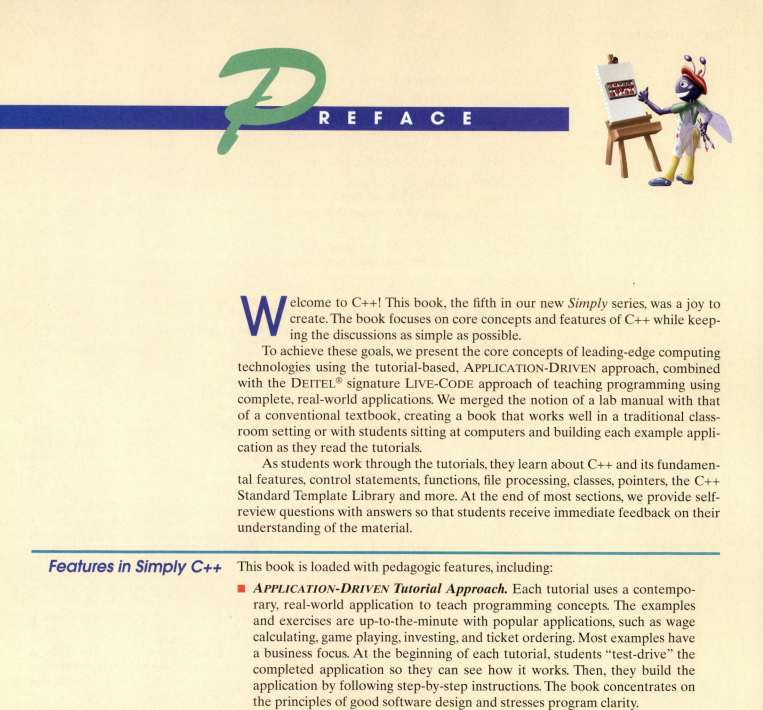

PREFACE

Welcome to C++! This book, the fifth in our new *Simply* series, was a joy to create. The book focuses on core concepts and features of C++ while keeping the discussions as simple as possible.

To achieve these goals, we present the core concepts of leading-edge computing technologies using the tutorial-based, APPLICATION-DRIVEN approach, combined with the DEITEL® signature LIVE-CODE approach of teaching programming using complete, real-world applications. We merged the notion of a lab manual with that of a conventional textbook, creating a book that works well in a traditional classroom setting or with students sitting at computers and building each example application as they read the tutorials.

As students work through the tutorials, they learn about C++ and its fundamental features, control statements, functions, file processing, classes, pointers, the C++ Standard Template Library and more. At the end of most sections, we provide self-review questions with answers so that students receive immediate feedback on their understanding of the material.

Features in Simply C++

This book is loaded with pedagogic features, including:

- **APPLICATION-DRIVEN *Tutorial Approach.*** Each tutorial uses a contemporary, real-world application to teach programming concepts. The examples and exercises are up-to-the-minute with popular applications, such as wage calculating, game playing, investing, and ticket ordering. Most examples have a business focus. At the beginning of each tutorial, students "test-drive" the completed application so they can see how it works. Then, they build the application by following step-by-step instructions. The book concentrates on the principles of good software design and stresses program clarity.

- **LIVE-CODE *Approach.*** This book contains many LIVE-CODE examples. Each tutorial ends with the complete, working application code and the students can run the application that they just created. We call this method of teaching and writing the **LIVE-CODE *Approach***. We feel that this approach is more effective than presenting only code snippets out of the context of a complete application.

- **Real-World Technologies.** This text incorporates today's technologies to develop useful applications. For example, we use the Unified Modeling Language™ (UML) to replace flowcharts—an older standard. The UML has become the preferred graphical modeling language for designing object-oriented applications. We use the UML to show the flow of control for several applications, so students gain practice reading the type of diagrams that are used in industry.

- **Full-Color Presentation.** This book is in full color so that students can see sample outputs as they might appear on a computer monitor. Also, we syntax color the C++ code, similar to the way C++ integrated development environments (IDEs) color the code in their editor windows. This way, students can match what they see in the book with what they see on their screens. Our syntax-coloring conventions are as follows:

```
comments appear in green
keywords appear in dark blue
literal values and constants appear in light blue
class, function and variable names and text appear in black
errors appear in red
```

■ *Object-Oriented Programming.* Object-oriented programming is the most widely employed technique for developing robust, reusable software, and C++ offers advanced object-oriented programming features. This book introduces students to defining classes and using objects, and lays a solid foundation for future programming courses.

■ *Debugging.* A **debugger** is a software program that allows you to analyze the behavior of your applications to locate logic errors. At the ends of several tutorials, we provide *Using the Debugger* sections in which you will learn to detect and remove logic errors by using the Visual Studio .NET debugger. Appendix A provides instructions for using the GNU debugger (GDB).

Notes to the Instructor

Focus of the Book

Our goal was clear: Produce a C++ textbook for introductory-level courses in computer programming for students with little or no programming experience. This book teaches computer programming principles and the C++ language, including input/output, data types, variables, pseudocode, algorithms, control statements, operators, functions, arrays, strings, classes, objects, inheritance, polymorphism, pointers, references, file processing, exceptions, templates, operator overloading and more. After mastering the material, students will be able to program in C++ and to employ its cross-platform capabilities. Note that this book is based on ANSI/ISO standard C++. All of the programs in the book will run on any ANSI/ISO C++ compliant compiler.

Lab Setup

Before you can compile and run the applications in this book, Microsoft's Visual C++ .NET, or an appropriate C++ development tool, must be installed. We discuss installing MS VC++ .NET in the *Before You Begin* section that follows this Preface. For computer labs in which students are not allowed to install software, instructors and system administrators must ensure that appropriate C++ software is installed on the lab computers in advance of the course.

Note Regarding the Platform We Used to Develop the Book

We assume that students are using Windows platform computers (Windows 2000 or Windows XP, in particular), so all directory names, instructions and sample screen captures appear in Windows format. However, the instructions and concepts presented work well on most computer platforms on which ANSI/ISO Standard C++ compilers are available, such as Linux and UNIX. [*Note:* All windows that show source code were created in VC++ .NET. © Copyright 1998–2002 Microsoft Corporation, All rights reserved. Used by permission.] If you have questions about using the VC++ .NET software, please refer to the documentation that comes with VC++ .NET or read our *Dive Into™ Series* publications, which are available on our Web site with the *Simply C++* resources at www.deitel.com/books/simplycpp1/index.html. The free *Dive-Into™ Series* publications help students and instructors familiarize themselves with various C++ development tools. These publications include: *Dive-Into™* Microsoft Visual C++® .NET, *Dive-Into™* GNU C++ on Linux, *Dive-Into™* GNU C++ with CygWin on Windows, *Dive-Into™* Microsoft Visual C++® 6 and *Dive-Into™* Borland C++ 5.5.

Objectives

Each tutorial begins with objectives that inform students of what to expect and gives them an opportunity, after reading the tutorial, to determine whether they have met the intended goals.

Outline

The tutorial outline enables students to approach the material in top-down fashion. Along with the tutorial objectives, the outline helps students anticipate future topics and set a comfortable and effective learning pace.

Example Applications (with Outputs)

We present C++ features in the context of complete, working C++ applications. We call this our LIVE-CODE approach. All examples are available on the CD that accompanies the book or as downloads from our Web site, www.deitel.com/books/simplycpp1/index.html.

Illustrations/Figures

An abundance of charts, line drawings and application outputs are included. The discussion of control statements, for example, is supported by carefully drawn UML activity diagrams. [*Note:* We do not teach UML diagramming as a program-development tool, but we do use UML diagrams to explain the precise operation of many of C++'s control statements.]

Programming Tips

Hundreds of programming tips help students focus on important aspects of application development. These tips and practices represent the best the authors have gleaned from a combined seven decades of programming and teaching experience.

Good Programming Practices highlight techniques that help students write applications that are clear, understandable and maintainable.

Students learning a language—especially in their first programming course—frequently make errors. Pointing out these *Common Programming Errors* in the text reduces the likelihood that students will make the same mistakes.

These tips describe aspects of C++ that prevent errors from getting into applications in the first place, which simplifies the testing and debugging process.

Teaching students to write clear and understandable applications is the most important goal for a first programming course. But students want to write applications that run the fastest, use the least memory, require the smallest number of keystrokes, etc. *Performance Tips* highlight opportunities for improving application performance.

Portability Tips

The *Portability Tips* provide insights into how C++ achieves its high degree of portability among different platforms.

Software Design Tips

The *Software Design Tips* highlight architectural and design issues that affect the construction of object-oriented software systems.

Skills Summary

Each tutorial includes a bullet-list-style summary of the new programming concepts presented. This reinforces key actions taken to build the tutorial's application.

544 Key Terms

Each tutorial includes a list of important terms defined in the tutorial. These terms also appear in the index and in a book-wide glossary, so the student can locate the terms and their definitions quickly.

192 Self-Review Questions and Answers

Self-review multiple-choice questions and answers are included after most sections to build students' confidence with the material and prepare them for the regular exercises. Students should be encouraged to attempt all the self-review exercises and check their answers.

358 Exercises (Solutions in Instructor's Manual)

Each tutorial concludes with exercises. Typical exercises include 10 multiple-choice questions, a "What does this code do?" exercise, a "What's wrong with this code?" exercise, three regular programming exercises and a programming challenge. [*Note:* In the "What does this code do?" and "What's wrong with this code?" exercises, we show only portions of the code in the text, but the instructor's manual contains full applications with outputs.] Several tutorials also include exercises that require students to use the C++ debugger to locate and fix logic errors in applications. Throughout the book, we make the assumption that the reader tries, or at least carefully reads, all of the exercises.

    The questions involve simple recall of important terminology and concepts, writing individual C++ statements, writing small portions of C++ applications and writing complete C++ functions, classes and applications. Every programming exercise uses a step-by-step methodology to guide the student. The solutions for the exercises are *available only to instructors* through their Prentice-Hall representatives. [*NOTE:* **Please do not write to us requesting the instructor's manual. Distribution of this publication is strictly limited to instructors teaching from the book. Instructors may obtain the solutions manual only from their regular Prentice Hall representatives. We regret that we cannot provide the solutions to professionals.**]

C++ Standard Library Reference Summaries

Each tutorial includes a summary of the classes, functions and other C++ Standard Library objects introduced in the tutorial. The summary includes a description of each library.

Index

The extensive index includes important terms both under main headings and as separate entries so that students can search for any term or concept by keyword. The code examples and the exercises are also included in the index. Every C++ source code application in the book is indexed under both the appropriate application and as a subindex item under "applications." We have also double-indexed features such as functions and classes. This makes it easier to find examples using particular features.

Simply C++ Ancillary Package

Simply C++ is accompanied by extensive ancillary materials for instructors, including the following:

- *Instructor's Resource CD (IRCD)* which contains the
    - *Instructor's Manual* with solutions to the end-of-tutorial exercises
    - *Test-Item File* of multiple-choice questions (approximately two per tutorial section)
    - *Customizable PowerPoint® Slides* containing all the code and figures in the text, and bulleted items that summarize the key points in the text

Companion Web Site

The *Companion Web Site* offers a *Syllabus Manager*, which helps instructors plan courses interactively and create online syllabi. Students also benefit from the functionality of the *Companion Web Site*. Book-specific resources for students include:

- Example source code
- Reference materials from the book appendices
- Tutorial objectives
- Tutorial outlines
- Programming tips from each tutorial

To access *Simply C++*'s *Companion Web Site*, visit www.prenhall.com/deitel.

PearsonChoices

Today's students have increasing demands on their time and money, and they need to be resourceful about how, when and where they study. Our publisher, Prentice Hall, is owned by Pearson Education, which has responded to that need by creating PearsonChoices to allow faculty and students to choose from a variety of textbook formats and prices.

SafariX WebBooks

SafariX Textbooks Online is a new service for college students looking to save money on required or recommended textbooks for academic courses. This secure WebBooks platform creates a new option in the higher education market; an additional choice for students alongside conventional textbooks and online learning services. By eliminating the costs relating to printing, manufacturing and retail distribution for the physical textbook, Pearson provides students with a WebBook at 50% of the cost of its conventional print equivalent.

SafariX WebBooks are viewed through a Web browser connected to the Internet. No special plug-ins are required and no applications need to be downloaded. Students simply log in, purchase access and begin studying. With SafariX Textbooks Online students will be able to search the text, make notes online, print out reading assignments that incorporate their professors' lecture notes and bookmark important passages they want to review later. They can navigate easily to a page number, reading assignment, or chapter. The Table of Contents of each WebBook appears in the left hand column alongside the text.

We are pleased to offer students the *Simply C++* SafariX WebBook available for January 2005 classes. Visit www.pearsonchoices.com for more information. Other Deitel titles available as SafariX WebBooks include *Small Java How to Program, 6/e* and *Java How to Program, 6/e*. Visit www.safarix.com/tour.html for more information.

Coming Soon: OneKey Powered by Course Compass, BlackBoard™ and WebCT™ Course Management Systems

OneKey is Prentice Hall's exclusive new resource that gives instructors and students access to the best online teaching and learning tools through one convenient Web site. OneKey enables instructors to prepare their courses effectively, present their courses more dramatically and assess students easily. An abundance of searchable presentation material together with practice activities and test questions—all organized by chapter or topic—helps to simplify course preparation.

Selected content from the Deitels' introductory programming language *Simply Series*, including *Simply C++*, will soon be available to integrate into various popular course management systems, including CourseCompass, Blackboard and WebCT. Course management systems help faculty create, manage and use sophisticated Web-based educational tools and programs. Instructors can save hours of inputting data by using Deitel course management systems content. Blackboard, CourseCompass and WebCT offer:

- **Features to create and customize an online course**, such as areas to post course information (e.g., policies, syllabi, announcements, assignments, grades, performance evaluations and progress tracking), class and student management tools, a gradebook, reporting tools, page tracking, a calendar and assignments.

- **Communication tools** to help create and maintain interpersonal relationships between students and instructors, including chat rooms, whiteboards, document sharing, bulletin boards and private e-mail.

- **Flexible testing tools** that allow an instructor to create online quizzes and tests from questions directly linked to the text, and that grade and track results effectively. All tests can be inputted into the gradebook for efficient course management. WebCT also allows instructors to administer timed online quizzes.

- **Support materials** for instructors are available in print and online formats.

In addition to the types of tools found in Blackboard and WebCT, CourseCompass from Prentice Hall includes:

- **CourseCompass course home page**, which makes the course as easy to navigate as a book. An expandable table of contents allows instructors to view course content at a glance and to link to any section.

- **Hosting on Prentice Hall's centralized servers**, which allows course administrators to avoid separate licensing fees or server-space issues. Access to Prentice Hall technical support is available.

- **"How Do I" online-support sections** are available for users who need help personalizing course sites, including step-by-step instructions for adding PowerPoint slides, video and more.

- **Instructor Quick Start Guide** helps instructors create online courses using a simple, step-by-step process.

To view free online demonstrations and learn more about these Course Management Systems, which support Deitel content, visit the following Web sites:

- Blackboard: www.blackboard.com and www.prenhall.com/blackboard

- WebCT: www.webct.com and www.prenhall.com/webct

- CourseCompass: www.coursecompass.com and www.prenhall.com/coursecompass

Acknowledgments

One of the great pleasures of writing a textbook is acknowledging the efforts of many people whose names may not appear on the cover, but whose hard work, cooperation, friendship and understanding were crucial to the production of the book. Many people at Deitel & Associates, Inc., devoted long hours to this project.

- Abbey Deitel, President
- Barbara Deitel, Chief Financial Officer

We would also like to thank the participants in the Deitel & Associates, Inc., College Internship Program who contributed to this book and its ancillaries: Tim Christensen, Jeffrey Peng and Eric Winokur.[1]

We are fortunate to have been able to work on this project with the talented and dedicated team of publishing professionals at Prentice Hall. We especially appreciate the extraordinary efforts of our Computer Science Editor, Kate Hargett and her boss and our mentor in publishing—Marcia Horton, Editorial Director of Prentice-Hall's Engineering and Computer Science Division. Tom Manshreck and Vince O'Brien managed the production of the book. John Lovell served as production editor. Geoff Cassar and Carole Anson worked on the cover design and Sarah Parker handled editorial responsibilities on the book's extensive ancillary package.

We wish to acknowledge the efforts of our reviewers and to thank Jennifer Capello of Prentice Hall, who managed the review process. The 21 reviewers from academia and industry adhered to a tight time schedule, these reviewers scrutinized the text and the applications, providing countless suggestions for improving the accuracy and completeness of the presentation. It is a privilege to have the guidance of such talented and busy professionals.

Simply C++ *Reviewers:*
Mark Andersen, Microsoft
Warren Bartlett, Florida Metropolitan University
Edward Brunjes, Miramar College
James Brzowski, University of Massachusetts at Lowell
Dharmesh Chauhan, Microsoft
Marg Chauvin, Palm Beach Community College
Mahesh Hariharan, Microsoft
Richard Holladay, San Diego Mesa College
Ravinder Kang, Highline Community College
Don Kostuch, Independent Consultant
Kriang Lerdsuwanakij, Siemens Limited Thailand (GCC Development team)
Ami Neiman, DeVry University, Fremont
Gavin Osborne, Saskatchewan Institute of Applied Science and Technology
Tom Pennings, Borland Software Corporation
Judy Scholl, Austin Community College
Ray Stephenson, Microsoft
William Tucker, Austin Community College
John Varghese, UBS Warburg
Jeff Welton, Microsoft
Ellen Williams, Atlantic Technical Center
Catherine Wyman, DeVry University, Phoenix

---

1. The Deitel & Associates, Inc. College Internship Program offers a limited number of salaried positions to college students majoring in Computer Science and Information Technology. Students work at our corporate headquarters in Maynard, Massachusetts full-time in the summers and (for those attending college in the Boston area) part-time during the academic year. We also offer full-time internship positions for students interested in taking a semester off from school to gain industry experience. For more information, please contact Abbey Deitel at deitel@deitel.com, visit our Web site, www.deitel.com and subscribe to our free e-mail newsletter at www.deitel.com/newsletter/subscribe.html.

We would sincerely appreciate your comments, criticisms, corrections and suggestions for improving this textbook. Please address all correspondence to:

```
deitel@deitel.com
```

We will respond promptly.

Well, that's it for now. Welcome to the exciting world of C++ programming. We hope you enjoy this first look at C++ applications development. Good luck!

```
Dr. Harvey M. Deitel
Paul J. Deitel
Dave Choffnes
Christi Kelsey
```

About the Authors

Dr. Harvey M. Deitel, Chairman and Chief Strategy Officer of Deitel & Associates, Inc., has 43 years experience in the computing field, including extensive industry and academic experience. Dr. Deitel earned B.S. and M.S. degrees from the Massachusetts Institute of Technology and a Ph.D. from Boston University. He worked on the pioneering virtual-memory operating-systems projects at IBM and MIT that developed techniques now widely implemented in systems such as UNIX, Linux and Windows XP. He has 20 years of college teaching experience and served as the Chairman of the Computer Science Department at Boston College before founding Deitel & Associates, Inc., with his son, Paul J. Deitel. He is the author or co-author of several dozen books and multimedia packages. With translations published in numerous foreign languages, Dr. Deitel's texts have earned international recognition. Dr. Deitel has delivered hundreds of professional seminars to major corporations, academic institutions, government organizations and various branches of the military.

Paul J. Deitel, CEO and Chief Technical Officer of Deitel & Associates, Inc., is a graduate of the Massachusetts Institute of Technology's Sloan School of Management, where he studied information technology. Through Deitel & Associates, Inc., he has delivered professional seminars to numerous industry and government clients and has lectured on C++ for the Boston Chapter of the Association for Computing Machinery. He and his father, Dr. Harvey M. Deitel, are the world's best-selling Computer Science textbook authors.

David R. Choffnes is a graduate of Amherst College *magna cum laude* with degrees in Physics and French. During his time at Amherst, he also completed significant course work in computer science. David contributed to *Simply Visual Basic .NET* and co-authored *Operating Systems, 3/e* with the Deitels. In his spare time, he designs Web sites and develops a content management system. David is the recipient of a Cabell Fellowship at Northwestern University, where he will pursue a Ph.D. in Computer Science beginning in the Fall of 2004.

Christiann L. Kelsey, Director of Business Development at Deitel & Associates, Inc., graduated from Purdue University with a degree in management and information systems. Christi has contributed to several Deitel & Associates, Inc. publications including *Wireless Internet & Mobile Business How to Program*; *Internet & World Wide Web How to Program, 3/e*; *Java How to Program, 6/e*; *Simply Visual Basic .NET 2003*; *Simply Java Programming*; *Simply C#* and many others. Christi is also responsible for the *Deitel® Buzz Online* e-mail newsletter and the Deitel Dive Into™ Series Corporate Training business.

About Deitel & Associates, Inc.

Deitel & Associates, Inc., is an internationally recognized corporate-training and content-creation organization specializing in computer programming languages, object technology and Internet/World Wide Web software technology education. Through its 28-year publishing partnership with Prentice Hall, Deitel & Associates, Inc. publishes leading-edge programming textbooks, professional books, interactive multimedia *Cyber Classrooms* and course management systems e-content.

To learn more about Deitel & Associates, Inc., its Prentice Hall publications and its worldwide Dive Into Series™ Corporate Training curriculum, see the last few pages of this book or visit:

    www.deitel.com

and subscribe to the free *Deitel® Buzz Online* e-mail newsletter at:

    www.deitel.com/newsletter/subscribe.html

Individuals wishing to purchase Deitel books, *Cyber Classrooms* and *Complete Training Courses* can do so through bookstores, or online booksellers and:

    www.deitel.com
    www.prenhall.com/deitel
    www.InformIT.com/deitel

Bulk orders by corporations and academic institutions should be placed directly with Prentice Hall. For ordering information, please visit:

    www.prenhall.com/deitel

The Deitel® Buzz Online e-Mail Newsletter

Our free e-mail newsletter includes links to articles and resources from our published books and upcoming publications, information on future publications, product-release schedules, information on corporate training, crossword puzzles using computing terminology and more. For quick opt-in registration, visit www.deitel.com/newsletter/subscribe.html.

Please follow the instructions in this section to ensure that your computer is set up properly before you begin this book.

Font and Naming Conventions

We use fonts to distinguish between Visual Studio .NET features (such as menu names and menu items) and other elements that appear in Visual Studio .NET. Our convention is to emphasize Visual Studio .NET features in a sans-serif bold **Helvetica** font (for example, **Properties** window) and to emphasize program text in a serif Lucida font (for example, private bool x = true).

Software Bundled with Simply C++

For the educational market only, this textbook is available in a "value pack" with the Microsoft® Visual C++ Standard Edition version 2003 integrated development environment as a free supplement. The standard edition is fully functional and is shipped on 5 CDs. There is no time limit for using the software. [*Note:* If you are a professional using this publication, you will have to purchase the necessary software to build and run the applications in this textbook.]

Hardware and Software Requirements to Run Visual C++ .NET 2003

To install and run Visual C++ .NET 2003, Microsoft recommends that PCs have these minimum requirements:

- Pentium II 450 MHz processor (Pentium III 600 MHz processor recommended)
- Microsoft Windows® Server 2003, Windows XP Professional, Windows XP Home Edition, Windows 2000 Professional (with Service Pack 3 or later), or Windows 2000 Server (with Service Pack 3 or later) operating system
- 160 megabytes for a Windows Server 2003 or Windows XP Professional computer; 96 MB for a Windows XP Home Edition or Windows 2000 Professional computer; 192 MB for a Windows 2000 Server computer
- 500 megabytes of space on the system drive and 1.5 gigabytes of space on the installation drive (additional 1.9 gigabytes of available space required for optional MSDN Library documentation)
- CD-ROM or DVD-ROM drive
- Super VGA monitor (1024 x 768 or higher-resolution display) with 256 colors

- Mouse or other Microsoft-compatible pointing device

- **You must install Microsoft's Internet Information Services (IIS) before installing Visual Studio .NET.**

This book assumes that you are using Windows 2000 or Windows XP, plus Microsoft's Internet Information Services (IIS). Additional setup instructions for Web servers and other software is available on our Web site along with the examples. [*Note:* This is copyrighted material. Feel free to use it as you study, but you may not republish any portion of it in any form without explicit permission from Prentice Hall and the authors.]

Monitor Display Settings

Simply C++ includes hundreds of screenshots of applications. Your monitor's display settings may need to be adjusted so that the screenshots in the book will match what you see on your computer screen as you develop each application. [*Note:* We refer to single-clicking with the left mouse button as **selecting**, or **clicking.** We refer to double-clicking with the left mouse button as **double clicking.**] Follow these steps to set your monitor display correctly:

1. Open the **Control Panel** and double click **Display**.
2. Click the **Settings** tab.
3. Click the **Advanced...** button.
4. In the **General** tab, make sure **Small Fonts** is selected; this should indicate that **96 dpi** is now the setting (if you already have this setting, you do not need to do anything else).
5. Click **Apply**.

Viewing File Extensions

Several screenshots in *Simply C++* display file names on a user's system, including the file extension of each file. Your settings may need to be adjusted to display file extensions. Follow these steps to set your machine to display file extensions:

1. In the **Start** menu, select **Programs** (**All Programs** in Windows XP), then **Accessories**, then **Windows Explorer**.
2. In the window that appears, select **Folder Options...** from the **Tools** menu.
3. In the dialog that appears, select the **View** tab.
4. In the **Advanced settings:** pane, uncheck the box to the left of the text **Hide file extensions for known file types** (**Hide extensions for known file types** in Windows XP). [*Note:* If this item is already unchecked, no action needs to be taken.]

Copying and Organizing Files

All the examples for *Simply C++* are included on the CD-ROM that accompanies this textbook. Follow the steps in the following box to copy the examples directory from the CD-ROM to your hard drive. We suggest that you work from your hard drive rather than your CD drive for two reasons: You cannot save your applications to the book's CD (the CD is read-only), and files can be accessed faster from a hard drive than from a CD. The examples from the book (and our other publications) are also available for download from the following Web sites:

```
www.deitel.com
www.prenhall.com/deitel
```

Screenshots in the following box might differ slightly from what you see on your computer, depending on whether you are using Windows 2000 or Windows XP. We used Windows XP to prepare the screenshots for this book.

Copying the Book Examples from the CD-ROM

1. ***Locating the CD-ROM drive.*** Insert the CD that accompanies *Simply C++* into your computer's CD-ROM drive. The window displayed in Fig. 1 should appear. If the page appears, proceed to *Step 3* of this box. If the page does not appear, proceed to *Step 2*.

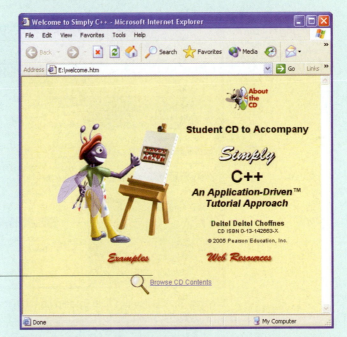

Click the **Browse CD Contents** link to access the CD's contents

Figure 1   Welcome page for *Simply C++* CD.

2. ***Opening the CD-ROM directory using My Computer.*** If the page shown in Fig. 1 does not appear, double click the **My Computer** icon on your desktop. In the **My Computer** window, double click your CD-ROM drive (Fig. 2) to access the CD's contents. Proceed to *Step 4*.

3. ***Opening the CD-ROM directory.*** If the page in Fig. 1 does appear, click the **Browse CD Contents** link to access the CD's contents.

4. ***Copying the Examples directory.*** Right click the `Examples` directory (Fig. 3), then select **Copy**. Next, go to **My Computer** and double click the `C:` drive. Select the **Edit** menu and select **Paste** to copy the directory and its contents from the CD to your `C:` drive.

    [*Note:* We save the examples to the `C:` drive and refer to this drive throughout the text. You may choose to save your files to a different drive based on your lab setup or personal preferences. If you are working in a computer lab, please see your instructor to confirm where the examples should be saved.]

(cont.)

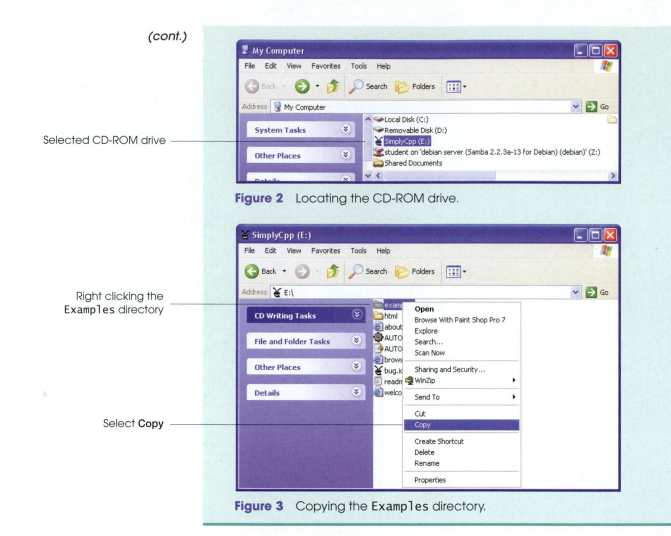

Figure 2 Locating the CD-ROM drive.

Figure 3 Copying the **Examples** directory.

The book example files you copied onto your computer from the CD are read-only. To access and modify these files, you must change this property. In the following box, you change the read-only property so that you can run and modify the examples.

Changing the Read-Only Property of Files	1. ***Opening the Properties dialog.*** Right click the **Examples** directory and select **Properties** from the menu. The **Examples Properties** dialog appears (Fig. 4).
	2. ***Changing the read-only property.*** In the **Attributes** section of this dialog, click the box next to **Read-only** to remove the check mark. Click **Apply** to apply the changes.
	3. ***Changing the property for all files.*** Clicking **Apply** will display the **Confirm Attribute Changes** window (Fig. 5). In this window, click the radio button next to **Apply changes to this folder, subfolders and files** and click **OK** to remove the read-only property for all the files and folders in the **Examples** directory.

(cont.)

Uncheck the
Read-only check box

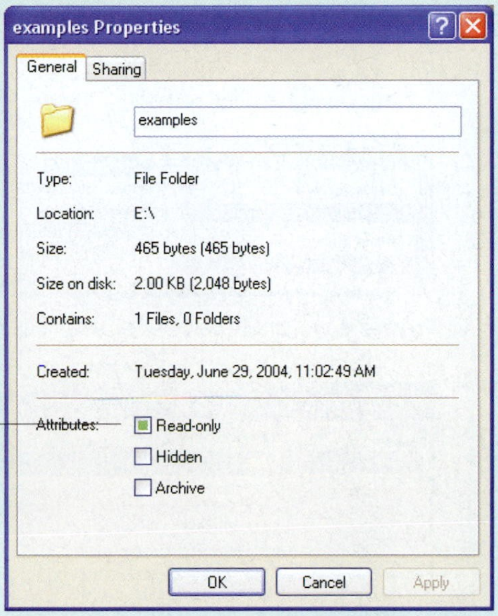

Figure 4 Removing the check in the **Read-only** check box.

Click this radio button to
remove the read-only
property for all the files

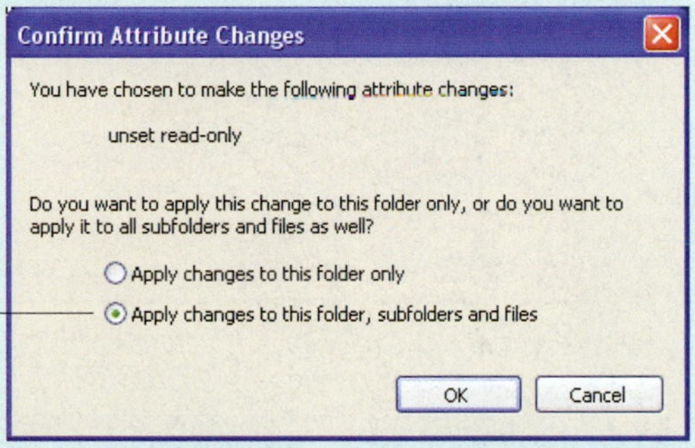

Figure 5 Removing read-only for all the files in the **Examples** directory.

As you work through this book, you will be developing your own applications. In the following box, you create a working directory on your C: drive in which you will save all of your applications.

Creating a Working Directory

1. *Selecting the drive.* Double click the **My Computer** icon on your desktop to access a list of your computer drives (Fig. 6). Double click the C: drive. The contents of the C: drive are displayed.

2. *Creating a new directory.* Select the **File** menu and, under the **New** submenu, select **Folder** (Fig. 7). A new, empty directory appears in your C: directory (Fig. 8). [*Note:* From this point onward, we use the > character to indicate the selection of a menu command. For example, we use the notation **File > Open** to indicate the selection of the **Open** command from the **File** menu.]

(cont.)

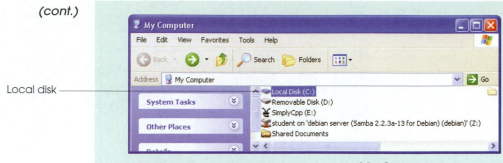

Local disk
My Computer
Local Disk (C:)
Removable Disk (D:)
SimplyCpp (E:)
Shared Documents

Figure 6 Computer drives listed under **My Computer**.

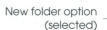

New folder option (selected)
Local Disk (C:)
New
Folder
Shortcut

Figure 7 Creating a new directory.

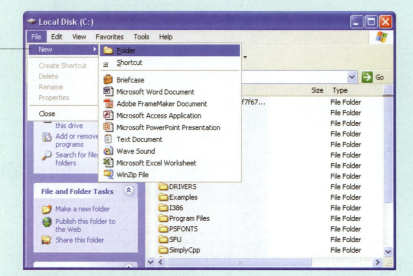

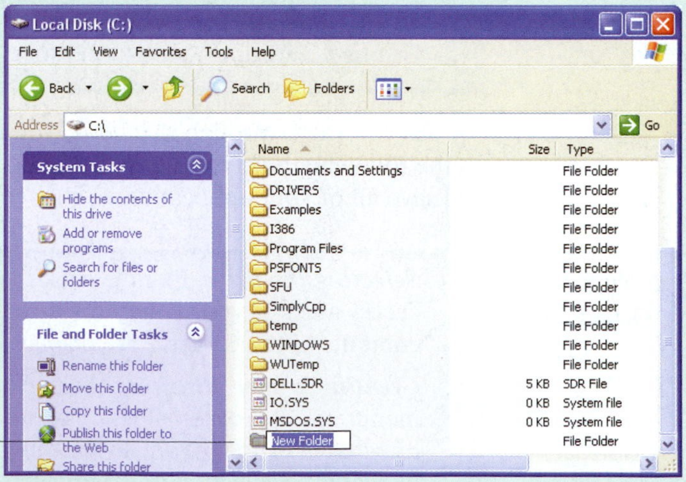

New directory
Local Disk (C:)
New Folder

Figure 8 New directory appears in the `C:` directory.

3. ***Naming the directory.*** Enter a name for the directory. We suggest that you choose a name that you recognize and remember. We chose `SimplyCPP` (Fig. 9). You can use this directory to save the examples from this book, your applications and your exercise solutions.

(cont.)

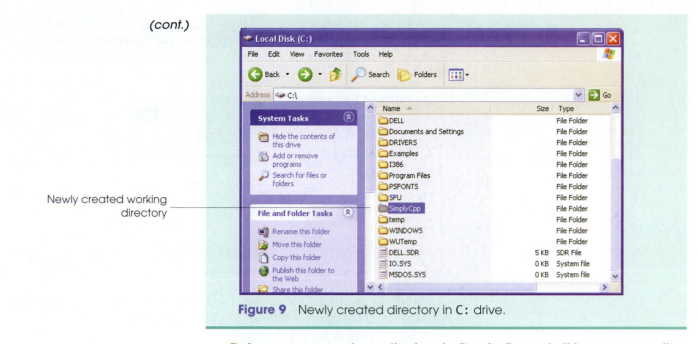

Newly created working directory

Figure 9 Newly created directory in C: drive.

Before you can run the applications in *Simply C++* or build your own applications, you should install a compiler such as Visual C++ .NET. Please note that this book is based on ANSI/ISO standard C++. All of the programs in the book will run on any ANSI/ISO C++ compliant compiler. The following boxes will guide you through this process.

Installing the Visual C++ .NET Prerequisites

1. ***Launching the installer.*** Insert the green disc labeled **Visual C++ .NET Disc 1** into your CD-ROM drive. The installer should appear after a brief loading period (Fig. 1.10). If it does not appear, proceed to *Step 2* of this box. Otherwise, proceed to *Step 4*.

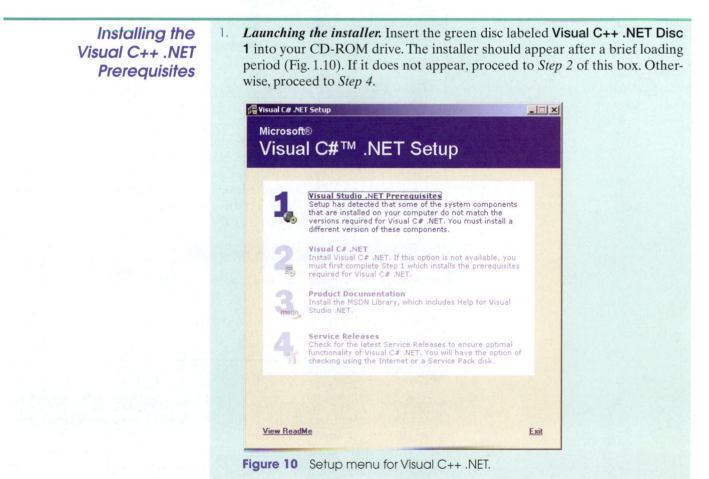

Figure 10 Setup menu for Visual C++ .NET.

(cont.)

2. ***Opening the CD-ROM directory using My Computer.*** If the dialog shown in Fig. 1.10 does not appear, double click the **My Computer** icon on your desktop. In the **My Computer** window, double click your CD-ROM drive (Fig. 11) to access the CD's contents.

Figure 11   Opening the CD-ROM directory.

3. ***Running the installer.*** Double click the `setup.exe` icon in the **VCSSTDD1** window to launch the installer (Fig. 12). The dialog in Fig. 1.10 should appear after a brief loading period.

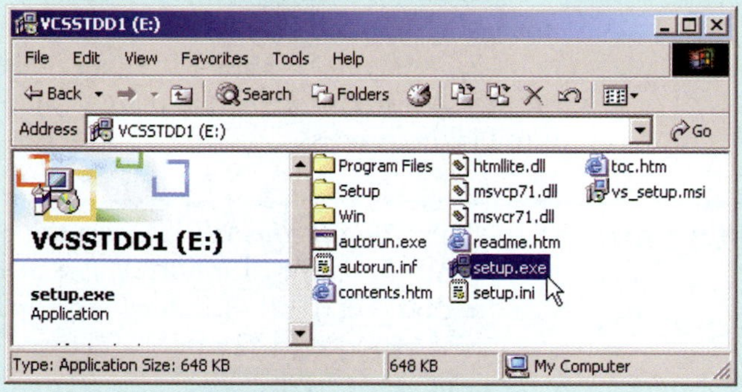

Figure 12   Running the installer.

4. ***Inserting the prerequisites disc.*** Before installing Visual C++ .NET, the installer must update certain software components on your system. Click the **Visual Studio .NET Prerequisites** link to begin this process. The installer will prompt you to insert the maroon disc labeled **Visual Studio .NET Prerequisites** (Fig. 13). [*Note:* The CD-ROM drive letter shown might be different on your system.] Insert the disc, then click **OK** to continue.

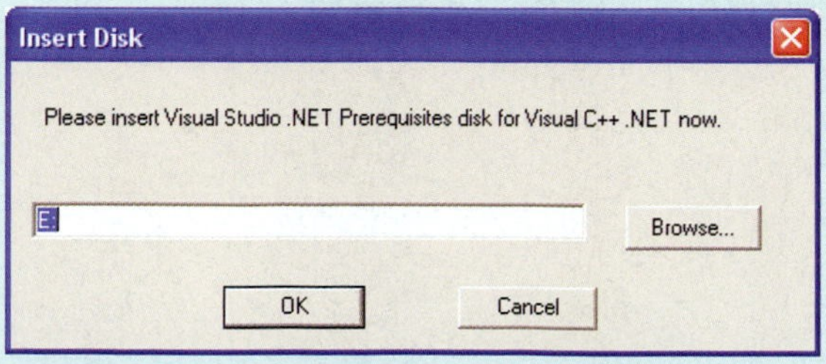

Figure 13   Inserting the prerequisites disc.

5. ***Accepting the license agreement.*** After a brief loading period, the **End User License Agreement** should appear (Fig. 14). Carefully read the license agreement. Click the **I agree** radio button, then click **Continue** to agree to the terms. [*Note:* If you choose not to accept the license agreement, the software will not install, and you will not be able to execute or create C++ applications.]

(cont.)

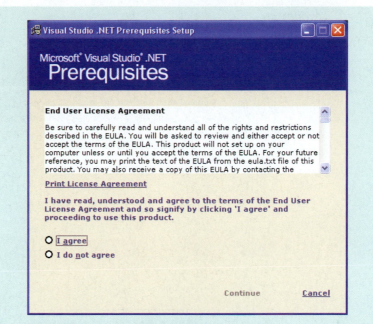

Figure 14 Prerequisites license agreement.

6. ***Installing the prerequisites.*** At this point, the installer will tell you which software components need to be updated (Fig. 15). [*Note:* The components in the list might be different on your system.] Click **Install Now!** to proceed with the installation.

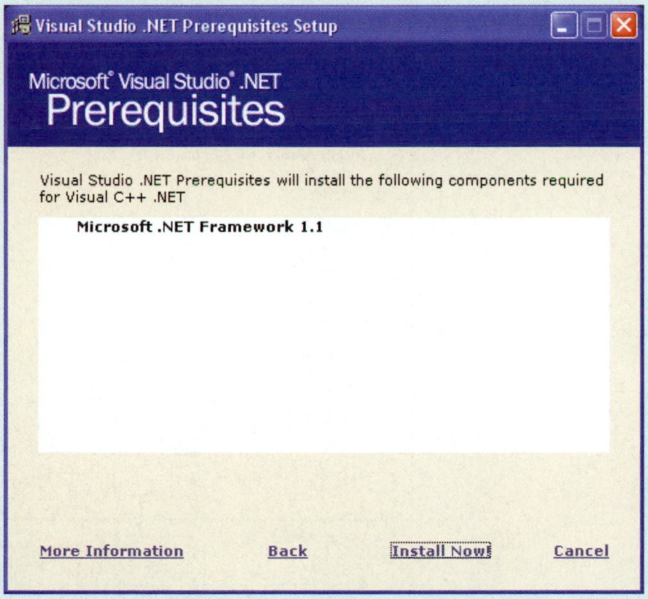

Figure 15 Listing the necessary prerequisites.

7. ***Automatic log on.*** Depending on which components require updates, your system might need to restart to complete the updates. If you have access to your system's password, click the **Automatically log on** check box and enter your password twice (to ensure it is entered correctly) (Fig. 16). If you do not, you can continue installing Visual Studio .NET, but you might need to contact your system administrator if prompted for a password during the installation. Click **Install Now!** to continue.

(cont.)

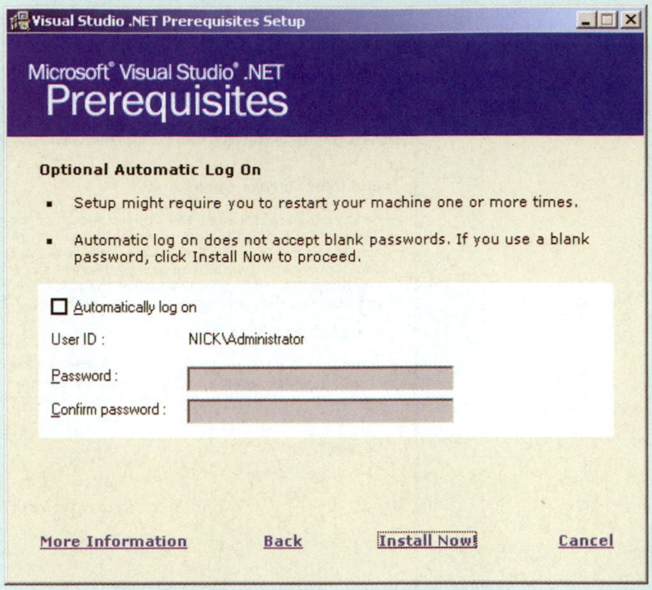

Figure 16   Automatic Log On dialog.

8. ***Finishing the installation***. The installer will now update your system. When it has finished, click **Done** to return to the main menu (Fig. 17).

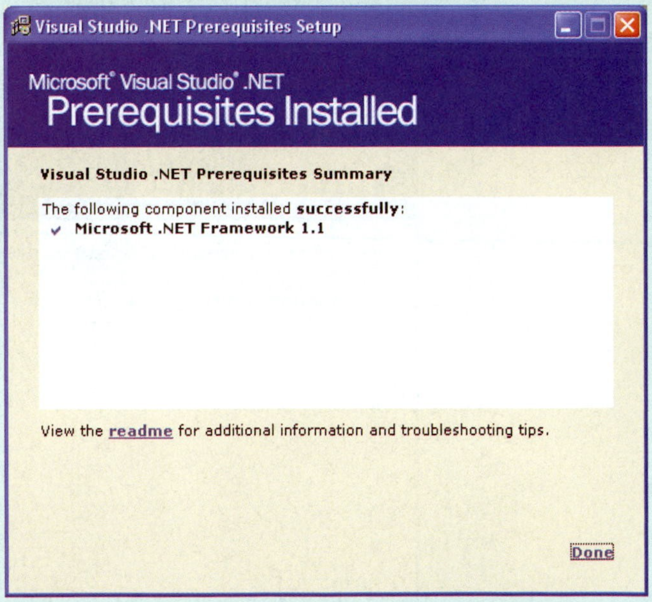

Figure 17   Finishing the prerequisites installation.

You are now ready to begin installing the main portion of the Visual C++ .NET software package. The following box will guide you through the necessary steps to complete this part of the installation.

Installing Visual C++ .NET

1. ***Beginning the installation.*** Click the **Visual C++ .NET** link to begin installing Visual C++ .NET (Fig. 18).

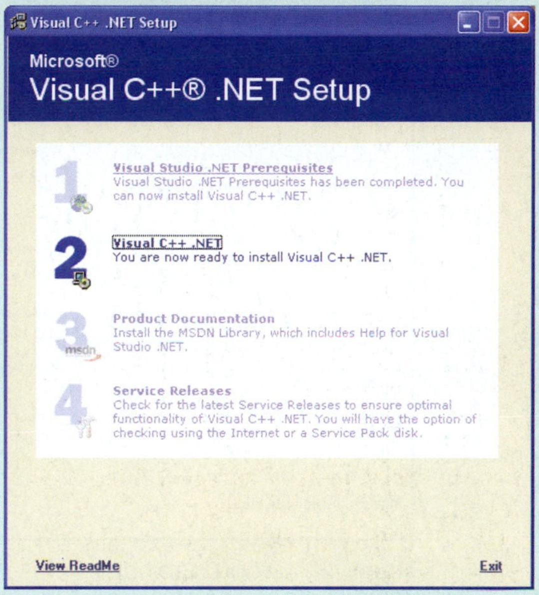

Figure 18   Visual C++ .NET installation.

2. ***Inserting the Visual C++ .NET disc.*** The installer will prompt you to insert the green disc labeled **Visual C++ .NET Disc 1** (Fig. 19). [*Note:* The CD-ROM drive letter shown might be different on your system.] Insert the disc, then click **OK** to continue.

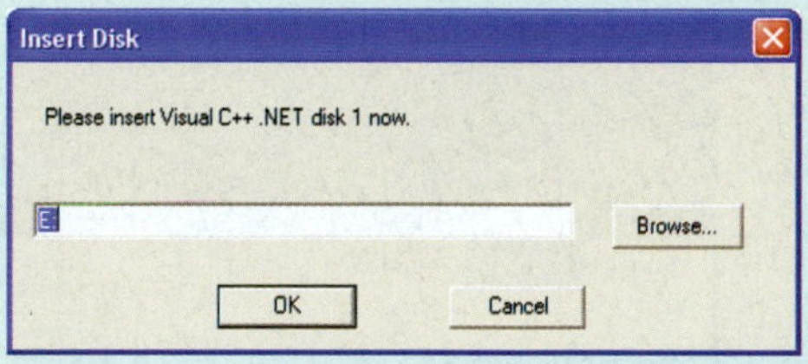

Figure 19   Inserting the Visual C++ .NET disc.

3. ***Accepting the license agreement and entering the product key.*** Carefully read the license agreement. Click the **I agree** radio button to agree to the terms (Fig. 20). [*Note:* If you choose not to accept the license agreement, the software will not install, and you will not be able to execute or create C++ applications.] Enter your product key (located in a yellow label on the back of your Visual C++ .NET CD case) and full name into the boxes provided. Click **Continue** to proceed. [*Note:* If you make a mistake when entering your product key, an error message will be displayed, and you will be asked to correct your information (Fig. 21).]

4. ***Selecting installation options.*** Select all the components of Visual C++ .NET Standard Edition (Fig. 22). You can also change the directory where Visual C++ .NET will be installed (though we recommend using the default location). After you have selected the desired options, click **Install Now!** to proceed. [*Note:* Sometimes the checkboxes will be checked, but will have a gray background. This indicates that only a portion of the feature selected will be installed. If this is the case, uncheck and recheck the box. Now, the background of the checkbox should be white, indicating that the entire feature will be installed.]

(cont.)

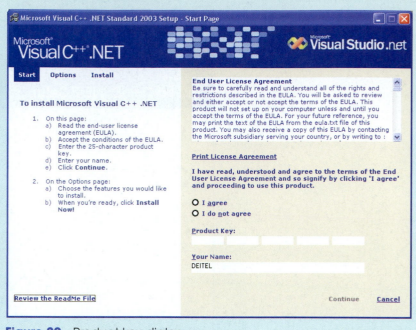

Figure 20 Product key dialog.

Figure 21 Invalid product key error message.

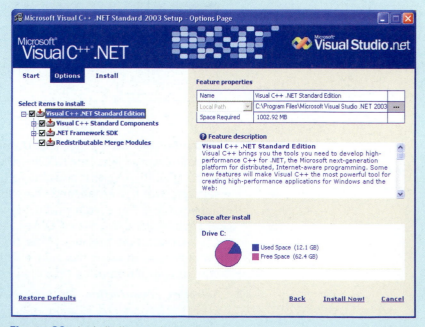

Figure 22 Installation options dialog.

5. ***Finishing the installation***. The installer will now begin copying the files required by Visual C++ .NET. Depending on your system, this process can take up to an hour. When it has finished, click **Done** to return to the main menu (Fig. 23).

(cont.)

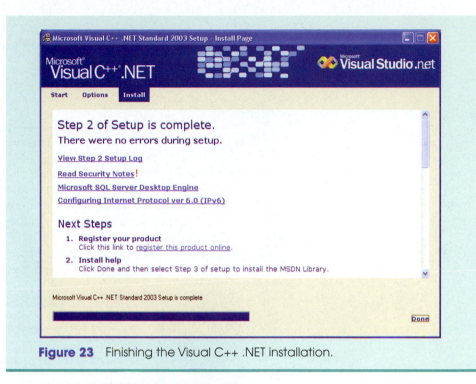

Figure 23   Finishing the Visual C++ .NET installation.

Next, you will install the Microsoft Developer Network (MSDN) Library, which contains detailed articles and tutorials on a wide range of topics, including C++ reference materials. The following box will guide you through this process.

Installing the MSDN Library

1. ***Beginning the installation.*** Click the **Product Documentation** link to begin installing the MSDN Library (Fig. 1.24).

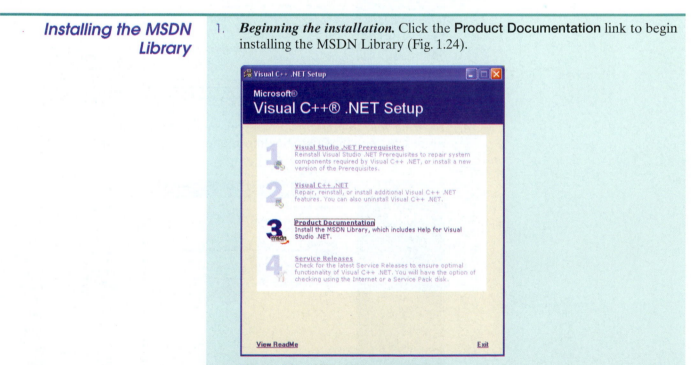

Figure 24   MSDN Library installation.

2. ***Inserting MSDN Library Disc 1.*** The installer will prompt you to insert the dark blue MSDN disc labeled **MSDN Library Disc 1** (Fig. 25). [*Note:* The CD-ROM drive letter shown might be different on your system.] Insert the disc, then click **OK** to continue.

(cont.)

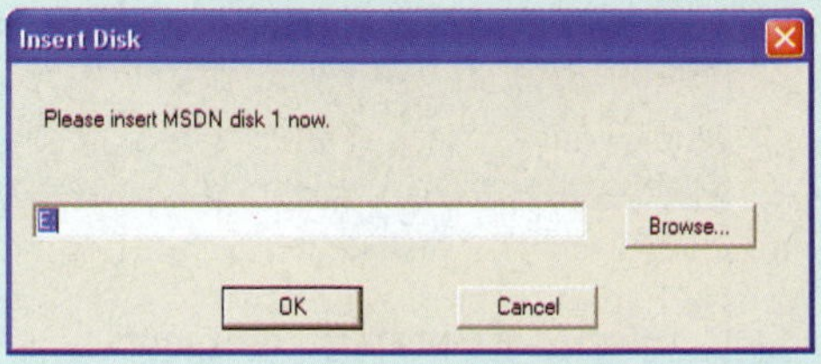

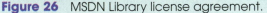

Figure 25   Inserting the first MSDN Library disc.

3. ***Accepting the license agreement.*** After a brief loading period, a dialog welcoming you to the **MSDN Library Setup Wizard** appears. Click **Next >** to proceed to the **License Agreement** dialog. Carefully read the license agreement. Click the **I accept the terms in the license agreement** radio button, then click **Next >** to agree to the terms (Fig. 26). [*Note:* If you choose not to accept the license agreement, the software will not install, and you will not be able to refer to the MSDN documentation for help using C++.]

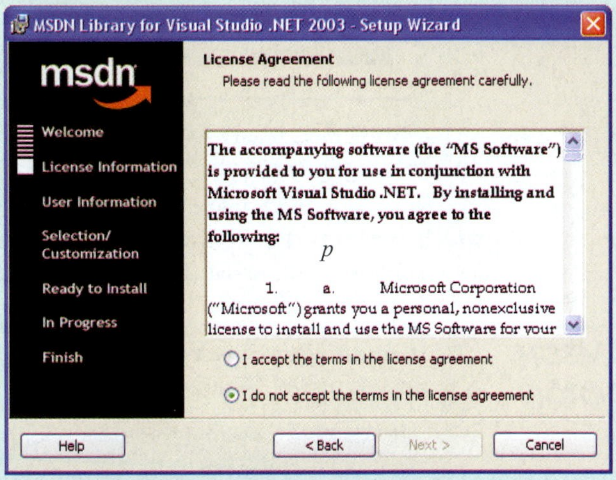

Figure 26   MSDN Library license agreement.

4. ***Entering your information.*** Enter your name and the name of your organization (if any) in the **Customer Information** dialog, then click **Next >** to continue (Fig. 27).

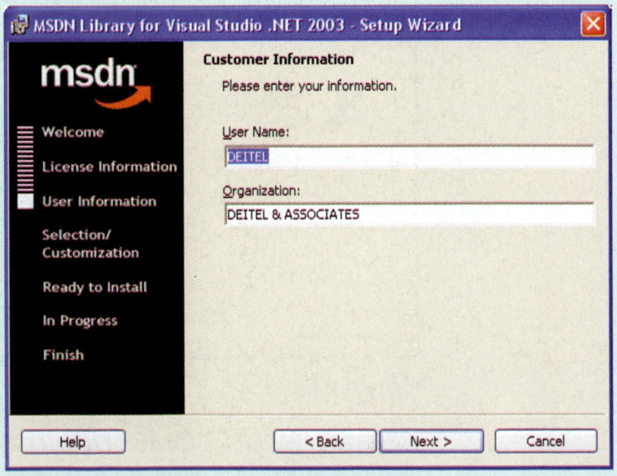

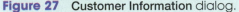

Figure 27   Customer Information dialog.

(cont.)

5. ***Selecting an installation type.*** Select an installation type from the list of choices. *[Note:* We recommend a **Full** installation if you have enough disk space, as you will be able to access all the MSDN articles without inserting the CD's in the future.] When you have made a selection, click **Next >** to continue (Fig. 28).

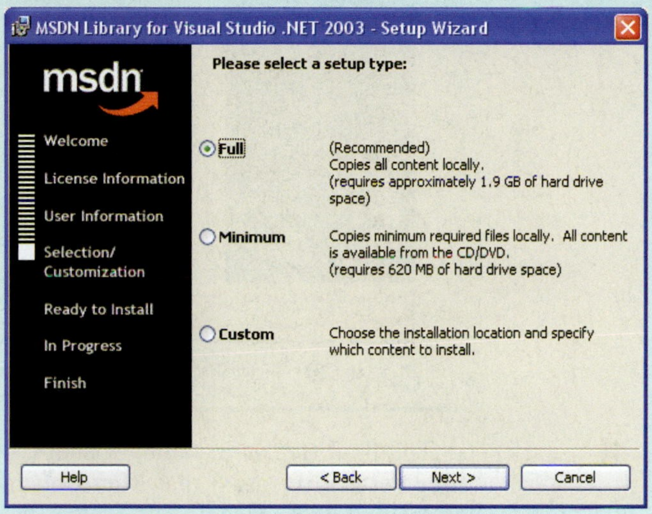

Figure 28   MSDN Library installation type.

6. ***Selecting a destination directory.*** Select the directory where you would like to install the MSDN Library (we recommend the default location). Click **Next >** to continue (Fig. 29).

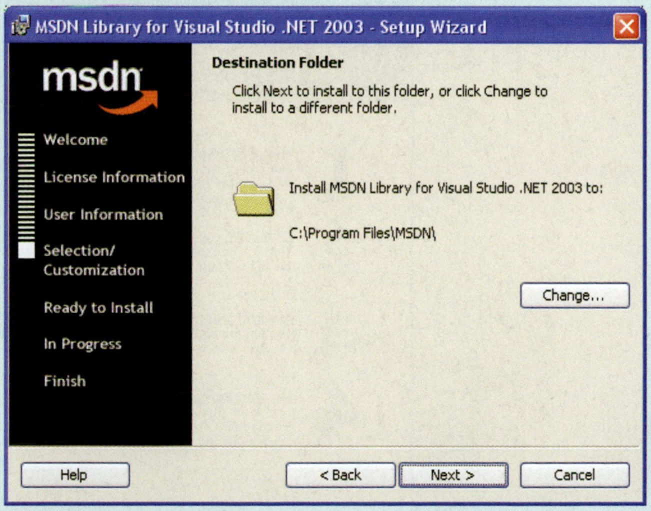

Figure 29   MSDN Library destination directory.

7. ***Finishing the installation.*** A dialog informing you that the MSDN Library is ready to install will appear. Click **Install** to begin the installation process. Depending on your system, this could take up to an hour to complete. During the installation, you will be prompted twice to insert the next disc in the series, much like Fig. 25. Insert the requested disc, then click **OK** to continue. When the installation is complete, click **Finish** to return to the main menu (Fig. 30).

(cont.)

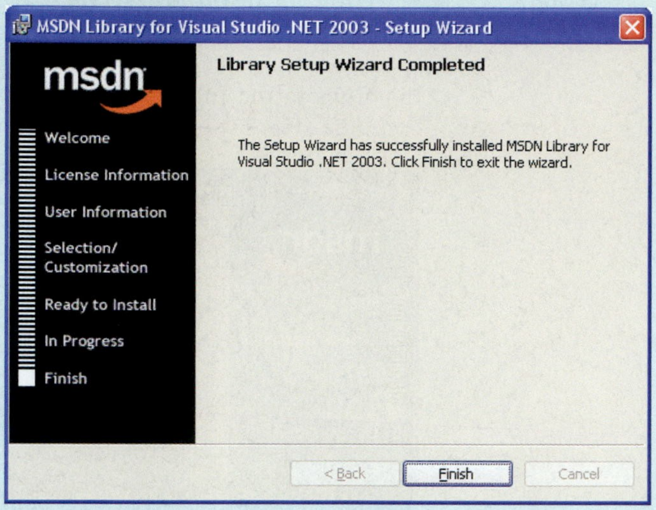

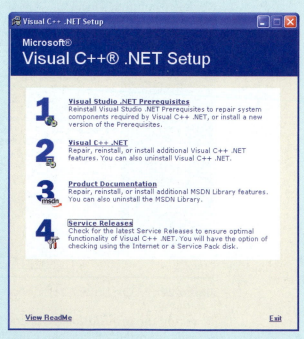

Figure 30 Finishing the MSDN Library installation.

The final step in installing Visual C++ .NET is to check for any updates (also called service releases) that Microsoft has released. The following box will guide you through this process.

Checking for Service Releases

1. ***Beginning the update check.*** Click the **Service Releases** link to begin the process of checking for updates to Visual C++ .NET (Fig. 31).

Microsoft®
Visual C++® .NET Setup

1 **Visual Studio .NET Prerequisites**
Reinstall Visual Studio .NET Prerequisites to repair system components required by Visual C++ .NET, or install a new version of the Prerequisites.

2 **Visual C++ .NET**
Repair, reinstall, or install additional Visual C++ .NET features. You can also uninstall Visual C++ .NET.

3 **Product Documentation**
Repair, reinstall, or install additional MSDN Library features. You can also uninstall the MSDN Library.

4 **Service Releases**
Check for the latest Service Releases to ensure optimal functionality of Visual C++ .NET. You will have the option of checking using the Internet or a Service Pack disk.

View ReadMe   Exit

Figure 31 Update check for Visual C++ .NET.

2. ***Connecting to the Internet.*** Make sure your system is connected to the Internet, then click the **Check for Service Releases on the Internet** link (Fig. 32). [*Note:* If you do not have an active Internet connection, you will receive an error repeatedly (Fig. 33), and you cannot complete this step. Click **Cancel** to return to the main menu.]

(cont.)

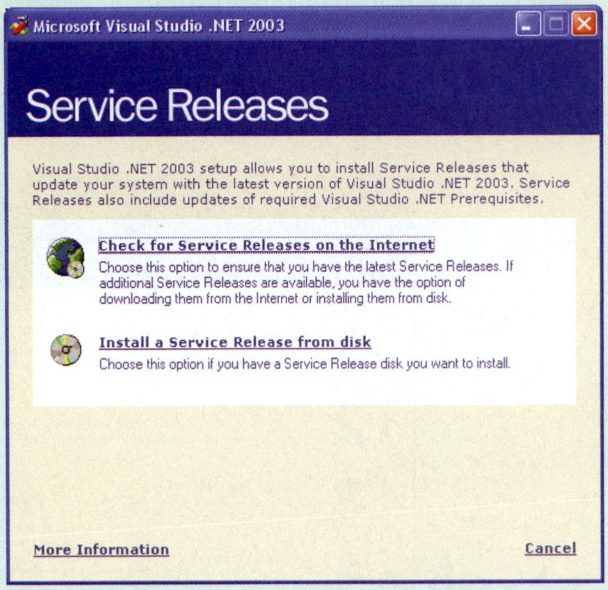

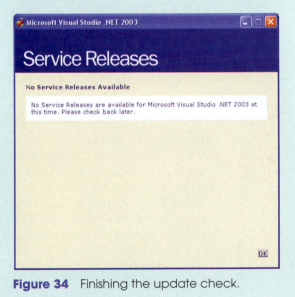

Figure 32 Connecting to the Internet to check for updates.

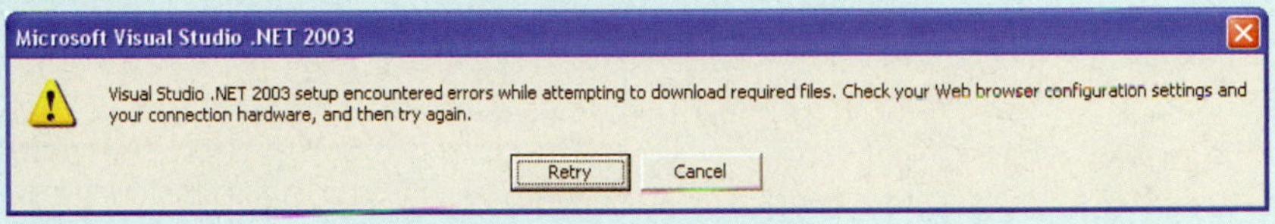

Figure 33 Error connecting to the Internet.

3. ***Finishing the update check.*** The installer will inform you if there are any updates to Visual C++ .NET (Fig. 34). If there are, select each item from the list to install it. [*Note:* If you are unsure how to proceed, contact your system administrator.] Once you have applied all the updates (or if there were none), click **OK** to return to the main menu.

Figure 34 Finishing the update check.

(cont.)

4. ***Finishing the installation.*** The main menu should now indicate that you have completed *Steps 1–4*. Click **Exit** to close the installer (Fig. 35). If prompted to check for Windows security updates, click **No** unless you are already comfortable with this procedure and authorized to do so on your system (Fig. 36).

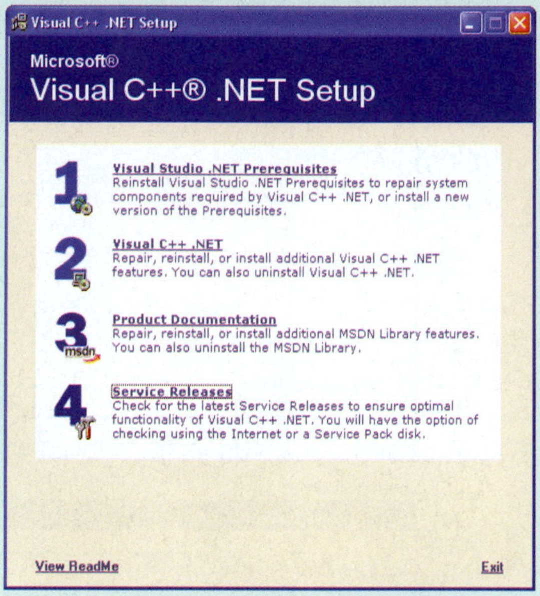

Figure 35 Finishing the installation.

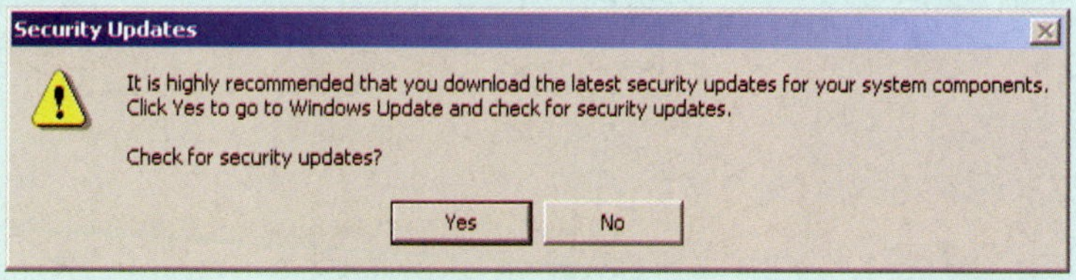

Figure 36 **Security Updates** dialog.

Before you begin to view and edit code, you should customize the way Visual Studio .NET displays and formats your code. Adding line numbers, adjusting tab sizes and setting fonts and colors will help you to navigate your code more easily.

Customizing the IDE

1. ***Open the IDE.*** Open Visual C++ .NET.

2. ***Displaying line numbers.*** In all of our programming discussions, we refer to specific code elements by line number. To help you locate where you will insert code in the examples, you need to enable Visual Studio .NET's capability to show line numbers in your code.

   Select **Tools > Options…**, and in the **Options** dialog that appears (Fig. 37), click the **Text Editor** folder icon. Then click the **C/C++** folder icon (Fig. 38) to expand the options for C++. If the arrow is not pointing to the **General** option after you click the **C/C++** folder, click **General** to display the page in Fig. 38. Locate the **Display** header. If the CheckBox next to **Line numbers** is not checked, click inside the box to add a check mark. If the box is already checked, you need not do anything; however, do not close the dialog.

(cont.)

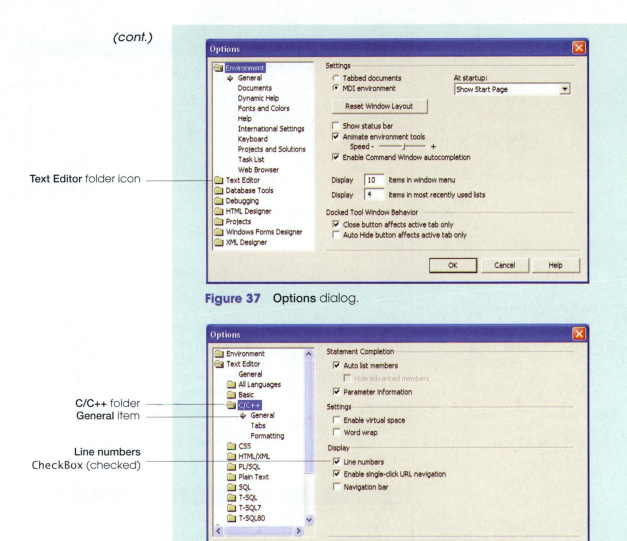

Text Editor folder icon

Figure 37   **Options** dialog.

C/C++ folder
General item

Line numbers
CheckBox (checked)

Figure 38   **General** settings page for the C++ text editor.

3. ***Setting the tab size.*** Just as you indent the first line of each paragraph when writing a letter, it is important to use proper spacing when writing code. Indenting code improves program readability. You can control indents with tabs. Click the **Tabs** item under the **C/C++** folder (Fig. 39). The **Smart** RadioButton, under the **Indenting** header, should be selected by default. If it is not, select the **Smart** RadioButton by clicking inside the white circle. Using this setting, Visual Studio .NET will indent code for you.

Set **Tab size:** to 3 and **Indent size:** to 3. The **Tab size:** setting indicates the number of spaces each tab character (inserted when you press the *Tab* key) represents. The **Indent size:** setting determines the number of spaces each indent inserted by Visual Studio .NET represents. Visual Studio .NET will now insert three spaces for you if you are using the **Smart** indenting feature; you can insert them yourself with one keystroke by pressing the *Tab* key.

Then, make sure the **Insert spaces** RadioButton is selected (Fig. 39), so Visual Studio .NET will insert three one-character spaces (instead of one tab character) to indent lines. If you select the **Keep tabs** RadioButton, each tab or indent will be represented by one tab character. We suggest you select the **Insert spaces** RadioButton.

(cont.)

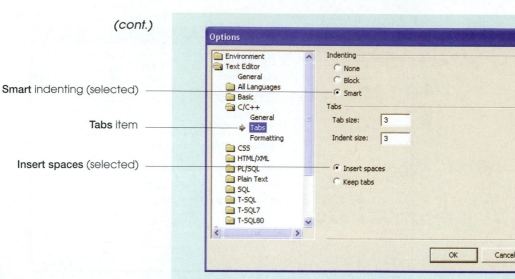

Smart indenting (selected) ——————

Tabs item ——————

Insert spaces (selected) ——————

Figure 39 Setting the **Tabs** options.

> **Good Programming Practice**
>
> You can change the font and color settings if you prefer a different appearance for your code. To remain consistent with this book (with the exception of the selected text colors), however, we recommend you do not change the default font and color settings.

4. ***Exploring fonts and colors.*** Click the **Environment** folder icon; then click the **Fonts and Colors** item. The screen that appears allows you to customize fonts and colors used to display code. Visual Studio .NET can apply colors and fonts to make it easier for you to read and edit code. In the book's examples, you will see code with the **Selected Text** background set to yellow for emphasis. The default setting for **Selected Text** is a blue background. You should use the default settings on your machine. If you need to reset your settings to the default for fonts and colors, click the **Use Defaults** Button (Fig. 40).

Fonts and Colors item ——————

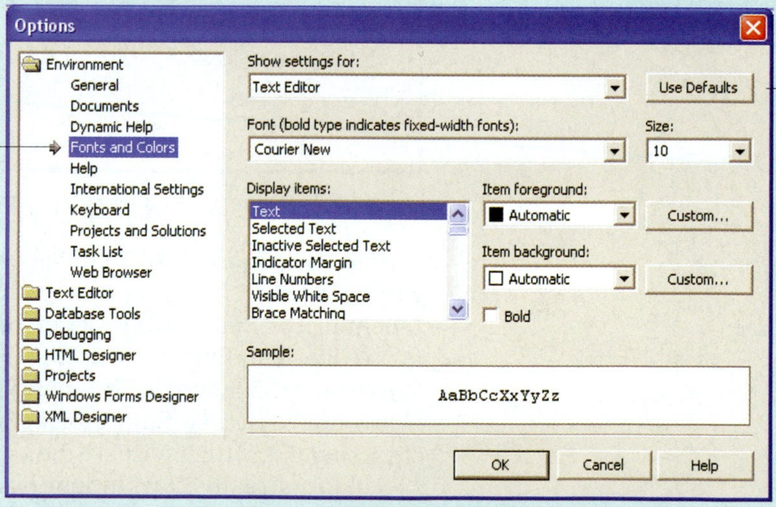

Use Defaults Button

Figure 40 Examining the **Fonts and Colors** page.

5. ***Applying your changes.*** Click the **OK** Button to apply your changes and dismiss the **Options** dialog.

You are now ready to begin your C++ studies with *Simply C++*. We hope you enjoy the book! You can reach us easily at deitel@deitel.com.

TUTORIAL

1

Car Payment Calculator and Guess the Number Applications

Introducing Computers, the Internet and C++ Programming

Welcome to C++! This book uses a straightforward, step-by-step tutorial approach to teach C++ programming fundamentals. We hope that you will be informed and entertained as you learn how to program in C++.

The core of the book teaches C++ using our **application-driven approach**, which provides step-by-step instructions for creating and interacting with useful, real-world computer applications. This approach, combined with our signature **live-code approach**, which shows dozens of complete, working C++ applications and depicts their outputs, will teach you basic programming skills. All of this book's examples are available on the accompanying CD-ROM and on our Web site, www.deitel.com.

Computer use is increasing in almost every field. In an era of rising costs, computing costs are actually decreasing dramatically because of rapid developments in both hardware and software technology. Silicon chip technology has made computing so economical that hundreds of millions of general-purpose computers are in use worldwide, helping people in business, industry, government and their personal lives.

Reading this text will start you on a challenging and rewarding educational path. If you'd like to communicate with us, send an e-mail to deitel@deitel.com, and we will respond promptly. For more information, visit our Web sites at www.deitel.com and www.prenhall.com/deitel, and subscribe to our newsletter at www.deitel.com/newsletter/subscribe.html.

1.1 What Is a Computer?

A **computer** is a device capable of performing computations and making logical decisions at speeds millions and even billions of times faster than humans can. For example, many of today's personal computers can perform billions of calculations per second. A person operating a desk calculator might require a lifetime to complete the same number of calculations that a powerful personal computer can perform in one second. Today's fastest **supercomputers** can perform hundreds of billions of calculations per second. Trillion-instructions-per-second computers are already functioning in research laboratories!

1

Computers process **data**, using sets of instructions called **computer programs**. These programs guide computers through orderly sets of actions that are specified by people known as **computer programmers**. **Object-oriented programming (OOP)** (which models real-world objects with software counterparts), available in C++ and other programming languages, is a significant breakthrough that can greatly enhance programmers' productivity. In this book, we generally use the term "application" instead of the term "program." An **application** is a program that performs a useful task. Most tutorials in this book present five object-oriented applications—one in the main example and four in the exercises. There are 104 applications in the book.

A computer is composed of various devices (such as the keyboard, screen, mouse, hard drive, memory, CD-ROM drive, DVD drive and processing units) that are known as **hardware**. The programs that run on a computer are referred to as **software**.

SELF-REVIEW   1. Computers process data, using sets of instructions called _____.

    a) hardware   b) computer programs

    c) processing units   d) programmers

2. The devices that make up a computer are called _____.

    a) hardware   b) software

    c) programs   d) applications

Answers: 1) b. 2) a.

1.2 Computer Organization

Computers can be thought of as being divided into six units:

1. **Input unit**. This "receiving" section of the computer obtains information (data and computer programs) from various **input devices**, such as the keyboard and the mouse. Other input devices include microphones (for recording speech to the computer), scanners (for scanning images) and digital cameras (for taking photographs and making videos).

2. **Output unit**. This "shipping" section of the computer takes information that the computer has processed and places it on various **output devices**, making the information available for use outside the computer. Output can be displayed on screens, played on audio/video devices, printed on paper and sent over a computer network (such as the Internet), among other things. Output also can be used to control other devices, such as robots used in manufacturing.

3. **Memory unit**. This rapid-access, relatively low-capacity "warehouse" section of the computer stores data temporarily while an application is running. The memory unit retains information that has been entered through input devices, so the information is immediately available for processing. To be executed, computer programs must be in memory. The memory unit also retains processed information until the information can be sent to output devices. Often, the memory unit is called either **memory** or **primary memory**. **Random access memory (RAM)** is an example of primary memory. Primary memory is usually **volatile**, which means that it is erased when the computer is turned off.

4. **Arithmetic and logic unit (ALU)**. The ALU is the "manufacturing" section of the computer. It performs calculations such as addition, subtraction, multiplication and division. It also makes decisions, allowing the computer to perform tasks such as determining whether two items stored in memory are equal or whether one is larger than the other.

5. **Central processing unit (CPU).** The CPU serves as the "administrative" section of the computer, supervising the operation of the other sections. The CPU alerts the input unit when information should be read into the memory unit, instructs the ALU when to use information from the memory unit in calculations and tells the output unit when to send information from the memory unit to various output devices. Today's computers often have several CPUs. A computer with several CPUs is called a **multiprocessor.**

6. **Secondary storage unit.** This unit is the long-term, high-capacity "warehouse" section of the computer. Secondary storage devices, such as hard disks, DVDs, CD-ROMs and floppy disks, normally hold programs and data that other units are not actively using; the computer then can retrieve this information when it is needed—hours, days, months or even years later. Information in secondary storage takes much longer to access than information in primary memory. However, secondary storage is much less expensive than primary memory. Unlike most forms of primary memory, secondary storage is **nonvolatile,** retaining information even when the computer is turned off.

SELF-REVIEW

1. The _____ is responsible for performing calculations and contains decision-making mechanisms.

    a) central processing unit   b) memory unit

    c) arithmetic and logic unit   d) output unit

2. Information stored in _____ is normally erased when the computer is turned off.

    a) primary memory   b) secondary storage

    c) CD-ROM drives   d) hard drives

Answers: 1) c. 2) a.

1.3 The Internet and the World Wide Web

In the late 1960s, ARPA—the Advanced Research Projects Agency of the Department of Defense—rolled out blueprints for networking the main computer systems of a group of ARPA-funded universities and research institutions. The computers were to be connected with communications lines operating at a then-stunning 56 Kbps (1 Kbps is equal to 1,024 bits per second or 128 characters of information per second), at a time when most people (of the few who even had networking access) were connecting over telephone lines to computers at a rate of 110 bits per second. (By contrast, today's communications lines transmit data at rates of millions or billions of bits per second.) Academic research was about to take a giant leap forward. ARPA proceeded to implement what quickly became called the **ARPANET**, the grandparent of today's **Internet**.

Things worked out differently from the original plan. Although the ARPANET enabled researchers to network their computers, its main benefit proved to be the capability for quick and easy communication via what came to be known as **electronic mail (e-mail)**. This is true even on today's Internet, with e-mail, instant messaging and file transfer allowing hundreds of millions of people worldwide to communicate with each other quickly, easily and economically.

The protocol (in other words, the set of rules) for communicating over the ARPANET became known as the **Transmission Control Protocol (TCP)**. TCP ensured that messages, consisting of pieces called "packets," were properly routed from sender to receiver and arrived intact.

In parallel with the early evolution of the Internet, organizations worldwide were implementing their own networks for both intraorganization (that is, within an organization) and interorganization (that is, between organizations) communication. A huge variety of networking hardware and software appeared. One challenge was to enable these different networks to communicate with each other. ARPA accomplished this by developing the **Internet Protocol (IP)**—which created a true "network of networks"—the current architecture of the Internet. The combined set of protocols is now commonly called **TCP/IP**.

Businesses rapidly realized that, by using the Internet, they could improve their operations and offer new and better services to their clients. Companies started spending large amounts of money to develop and enhance their Internet presence. This generated fierce competition among communications carriers and hardware and software suppliers to meet the increased infrastructure demand. As a result, **bandwidth**—the information-carrying capacity of communications lines—on the Internet has increased tremendously, while hardware costs have plummeted.

The **World Wide Web** (**WWW**) is a collection of hardware and software associated with the Internet that allows computer users to locate and view multimedia-based documents (documents with various combinations of text, graphics, animations, audios and videos) on almost any subject. In 1989, Tim Berners-Lee of CERN (the European Organization for Nuclear Research) began to develop a technology for sharing information by using "hyperlinked" text documents. Berners-Lee called his invention the **HyperText Markup Language (HTML)**. He also wrote communication protocols to form the backbone of his new hypertext information system, which he referred to as the World Wide Web.

In October 1994, Berners-Lee founded an organization, called the **World Wide Web Consortium** (**W3C**, `www.w3.org`), devoted to developing technologies for the World Wide Web. One of the W3C's primary goals is to make the Web universally accessible—regardless of a person's disabilities, language or culture.

The Internet and the World Wide Web are surely among humankind's most important and profound creations. In the past, most computer applications ran on computers that were not connected to one another. Today's applications can be written to communicate among the world's hundreds of millions of computers. The Internet mixes computing and communications technologies. It makes our work easier. It makes information instantly and conveniently accessible worldwide. It enables individuals and small businesses to get worldwide exposure. It is changing the way business is done. People can search for the best prices on virtually any product or service. Special-interest communities can stay in touch with one another. Researchers can be made instantly aware of the latest breakthroughs.

SELF-REVIEW

1. Today's Internet evolved from the _____, which was a Department of Defense project.

   a) ARPANET   b) HTML
   c) CERN   d) WWW

2. The combined set of protocols for communicating over the Internet is now commonly called _____.

   a) HTML   b) TCP/IP
   c) ARPA   d) TCP

Answers: 1) a. 2) b.

1.4 Machine Languages, Assembly Languages and High-Level Languages

Programmers write computer instructions in various programming languages. Some of these languages are directly understandable by computers, while others require intermediate translation steps. Although hundreds of computer languages are in use today, the diverse offerings can be divided into three general types:

1. Machine languages
2. Assembly languages
3. High-level languages

A computer can directly understand only its own **machine language**. As the "natural language" of a particular computer, machine language is defined by the computer's hardware design. Machine languages generally consist of streams of numbers (ultimately reduced to 1s and 0s) that instruct computers on how to perform their most elementary operations. Machine languages are **machine dependent**, which means that a particular machine language can be used on only one type of computer. The following section of a machine-language program, which adds *overtime pay* to *base pay* and stores the result in *gross pay*, demonstrates the incomprehensibility of machine language to humans:

```
+1300042774
+1400593419
+1200274027
```

As the popularity of computers increased, machine-language programming proved to be slow and error prone. Instead of using strings of numbers that computers could directly understand, programmers began using English-like abbreviations to represent the basic operations of the computer. These abbreviations form the basis of **assembly languages**. Translator programs called **assemblers** convert assembly-language programs to machine language at computer speeds. The following section of an assembly-language program also adds *overtime pay* to *base pay* and stores the result in *gross pay*, but presents the steps somewhat more clearly to human readers than the machine-language example:

```
load    basepay
add     overtimepay
store   grosspay
```

This assembly-language code is clearer to humans, but computers cannot understand it until the code is translated into machine language by an assembler program.

Although assembly languages enable programmers to write programs much more quickly than machine languages, assembly languages still require many instructions to accomplish even the simplest tasks. To speed up the programming process, programmers primarily use **high-level languages**, in which single program statements accomplish more substantial tasks. Translator programs called **compilers** convert high-level-language programs into one or more files containing machine language. After a program's high-level statements have been compiled, a **linker** program packages the machine-language files into one file that the computer can run. High-level languages enable programmers to write instructions that look almost like everyday English and that contain common mathematical notations. For example, a payroll application written in a high-level language might contain a statement such as

```
grossPay = basePay + overtimePay
```

From these examples, it is clear why programmers prefer high-level languages to either machine languages or assembly languages. C++ is one of the most popular high-level programming languages in the world, especially for implementing high performance applications. In the next section, you will learn about C++'s origins and benefits.

The process of compiling a substantial high-level language program into machine language can take a considerable amount of computer time. **Interpreter** programs were developed to execute high-level language programs directly, although much more slowly. Interpreters are popular in program-development environments, in which new features are being added and errors corrected. Once a program is fully developed, a compiled version can be produced to run more efficiently.

Some languages in use today are even closer to "spoken languages" like English. These languages, such as **SQL (Structured Query Language)**, are primarily used to manipulate information that is stored in organized collections of data called **databases**. For example, an automated teller machine (ATM) application that uses SQL might contain a statement such as

```
SELECT balance
    FROM AccountInformation
    WHERE accountNumber = "123456"
```

to obtain the balance for a specified account number, or a statement such as

```
UPDATE AccountInformation
    SET balance = 365.74
    WHERE accountNumber = "123456"
```

to update the balance for a specified account number.

SELF-REVIEW

1. The only programming language that a computer can directly understand is its own _____.

   a) high-level language   b) assembly language
   c) machine language   d) spoken language

2. Programs that translate high-level language programs into machine language are called _____.

   a) assemblers   b) compilers
   c) programmers   d) converters

   Answers: 1) c. 2) b.

1.5 C++

C++ evolved from C, which evolved from two previous languages, BCPL and B. BCPL was developed in 1967 by Martin Richards as a language for writing software and compilers for operating systems. Ken Thompson modeled many features in his language B after their counterparts in BCPL, using B to create early versions of the UNIX operating system at Bell Laboratories in 1970.

The C language was evolved from B by Dennis Ritchie at Bell Laboratories and was implemented originally in 1972. It initially became widely known as the development language of the UNIX operating system. Today, the majority of the code for general-purpose operating systems (e.g., those operating systems found in laptops, desktops, workstations and small servers) is written in C or C++.

C++, an extension of C, was developed by Bjarne Stroustrup in the early 1980s at Bell Laboratories. C++ provides a number of features that "spruce up" the C language, but more importantly, it provides capabilities for object-oriented programming. C++ is a hybrid language—it is possible to program in a C-like style, an object-oriented style or both.

SELF-REVIEW

1. _____ is an extension of C.

   a) Visual Basic   b) BCPL
   c) Machine Language   d) C++

2. Which of the following is true?

   a) C evolved from C++.
   b) C++ was originally designed to implement the first versions of UNIX.
   c) C++ provides capabilities for object-oriented programming.
   d) C++ is an assembly language.

   Answers: 1) d. 2) c.

1.6 Java

Perhaps the microprocessor revolution's most important contribution to date is that it made possible the development of personal computers, which now number in the hundreds of millions worldwide. Personal computers have profoundly impacted people's lives and the ways organizations conduct and manage their business.

Microprocessors are having a profound impact in intelligent consumer-electronic devices. Recognizing this, Sun Microsystems in 1991 funded an internal corporate research project code-named Green. The project resulted in the development of a C++-based language that its creator, James Gosling, called Oak after an oak tree outside his window at Sun. It was later discovered that there already was a computer language called Oak. When a group of Sun people visited a local coffee shop, the name Java was suggested, and it stuck.

The Green project ran into some difficulties. The marketplace for intelligent consumer-electronic devices did not develop in the early 1990s as quickly as Sun had anticipated. The project was in danger of being canceled. By sheer good fortune, the World Wide Web exploded in popularity in 1993, and Sun saw the immediate potential of using Java to add dynamic content and animations to Web pages. This breathed new life into the project.

Sun formally announced Java at a major conference in May 1995. Java generated immediate interest in the business community because of the phenomenal success of the World Wide Web. Java is now used to develop large-scale enterprise applications, to enhance the functionality of Web servers (the computers that provide the content we see in our Web browsers), to provide applications for consumer devices (such as cell phones, pagers and personal digital assistants) and for many other purposes. Current versions of C++, such as Microsoft's Visual C++ .NET, have similar capabilities.

SELF-REVIEW

1. The explosion of _____ helped to increase the initial popularity of Java.
   a) Visual Basic   b) C++
   c) C#   d) the World Wide Web

2. Java was released in 1995 by _____.
   a) Microsoft   b) Apple
   c) Sun Microsystems   d) Oracle

Answers: 1) d. 2) c.

1.7 Fortran, COBOL, Pascal and Ada

Although hundreds of high-level languages have been developed, only a few have achieved broad acceptance. IBM Corporation developed **Fortran** (FORmula TRANslator) in the mid-1950s to create scientific and engineering applications that require complex mathematical computations. Fortran is still widely used in the engineering community.

COBOL (COmmon Business Oriented Language) was developed in the late 1950s by a group of computer manufacturers in conjunction with government and industrial computer users. COBOL is used primarily for business applications that manipulate large amounts of data. A considerable portion of today's business software is still programmed in COBOL.

During the 1960s, software development efforts often ran behind schedule, costs greatly exceeded budgets and the finished products were unreliable. People began to realize that software development was a far more complex activity than they had imagined. Research intended to address these issues resulted in the evolution of **structured programming**—a disciplined approach to the creation of programs that are clear, correct and easy to modify.

One of the results of this research was the development of the **Pascal** programming language in the early 1970s. Pascal, named after the 17th-century mathematician and philosopher Blaise Pascal, was designed for teaching structured programming and rapidly became the preferred introductory programming language in most colleges. Unfortunately, the language lacked many features needed to make it useful in commercial, industrial and government applications. By contrast, C, which also arose from research on structured programming, did not have the limitations of Pascal, and professional programmers quickly adopted it.

The **Ada** programming language was developed under the sponsorship of the U.S. Department of Defense during the 1970s and early 1980s. The language was named after **Lady Ada Lovelace**, daughter of the poet Lord Byron. Lady Lovelace is generally credited with being the world's first computer programmer because of an application she wrote in the 1840s for the Analytical Engine mechanical computing device designed by Charles Babbage.

SELF-REVIEW

1. _____ was designed to teach structured programming in academic environments.

   a) C++   b) C
   c) Java   d) Pascal

2. _____ is generally credited as being the world's first computer programmer.

   a) Lord Byron   b) Dennis Ritchie
   c) Lady Ada Lovelace   d) Charles Babbage

3. _____, developed in the late 1950s, is still used to produce a considerable portion of today's business software.

   a) COBOL   b) Fortran
   c) Java   d) C

Answers: 1) d. 2) c. 3) a.

1.8 BASIC, Visual Basic, Visual C++ and .NET

The **BASIC** (Beginner's All-Purpose Symbolic Instruction Code) programming language was developed in the mid-1960s by Professors John Kemeny and Thomas Kurtz of Dartmouth College as a language for writing simple programs. BASIC's primary purpose was to familiarize novices with programming techniques. **Visual Basic** was introduced by Microsoft in 1991 to simplify the process of developing Microsoft Windows applications.

Visual Basic .NET is designed for Microsoft's recent programming platform, .NET. Earlier versions of Visual Basic provided object-oriented capabilities, but Visual Basic .NET offers enhanced object orientation and makes use of .NET's powerful library of reusable software components called the **Framework Class Library** (**FCL**).

The FCL is shared among Visual Basic, Visual C++, C# (a Microsoft language similar to Java that was developed expressly for .NET) and many other languages that Microsoft and other software vendors are making available for .NET. Visual C++ is a Microsoft implementation of C++ that includes Microsoft's own extensions to the language. We teach Visual C++ .NET in our textbook, *Visual C++ .NET How to Program.*

SELF-REVIEW

1. _____ is a programming language originally developed for Microsoft's .NET framework.

   a) C#   b) Java
   c) C++   d) Visual Basic

2. _____, developed in the 1960s, was created as a language to write simple programs and familiarize novices with programming techniques.

    a) BASIC   b) Fortran

    c) COBOL   d) C#

Answers: 1) a. 2) a.

1.9 Key Software Trend: Object Technology

As the benefits of structured programming were realized in the 1970s, improved software technology began to appear. However, it was not until object-oriented programming became widely used in the 1980s and 1990s that developers finally felt they had the necessary tools to improve the software development process dramatically.

What are objects, and why are they special? **Object technology** is a packaging scheme for creating meaningful software units. There are date objects, time objects, paycheck objects, invoice objects, automobile objects, people objects, audio objects, video objects, file objects, record objects and so on. In fact, almost any noun can be reasonably represented as a software **object**. Objects have **attributes** (also called **properties**), such as color, size and weight; and perform **actions** (also called **behaviors** or **functions**), such as moving, sleeping or drawing. **Classes** are types of similar objects. For example, all cars belong to the "car" class, even though individual cars may vary in make, model, color and options packages. A class specifies the general form of its objects, and the properties and actions available to an object depend on its class. An object is related to its class in much the same way as a building is related to its blueprint.

Before object-oriented languages appeared, **procedural programming languages** (such as Fortran, Pascal, BASIC and C) focused on actions (verbs) rather than objects (nouns). Using today's popular object-oriented languages, such as C++, Visual Basic .NET, Java and C#, programmers can program in an object-oriented manner that more naturally reflects the way in which they perceive the world. This has resulted in productivity gains.

With object technology, properly designed classes can be reused on future projects. Using libraries of classes can greatly reduce the amount of effort required to implement new applications. Some organizations report that such software reusability is not, in fact, the key benefit of object-oriented programming. Rather, they indicate that object-oriented programming tends to produce software that is more understandable because it is better organized and has fewer maintenance requirements.

Object orientation allows the programmer to focus on the "big picture." Instead of worrying about the minute details of how reusable objects are implemented, the programmer can focus on the behaviors and interactions of objects. A road map that showed every tree, house and driveway would be difficult, if not impossible, to read. When such details are removed and only the essential information (roads) remains, the map becomes easier to understand. In the same way, an application that is divided into objects is easy to understand, modify and update because it hides much of the detail. Object-oriented programming will probably be the key programming methodology for the next several decades.

SELF-REVIEW

1. _____ focuses on actions (verbs) rather than things (nouns).

    a) C#   b) Object-oriented programming

    c) Java   d) Procedural programming

2. In object-oriented programming, _____, which are in a sense like blueprints, are types of similar objects.

    a) classes   b) attributes

    c) behaviors   d) properties

Answers: 1) d. 2) a.

1.10 Compiling and Running C++ Applications

In this book's *For Students and Instructors: Important Information Before You Begin* section (which appeared before this tutorial), you installed Visual C++ .NET or an appropriate C++ compiler. In this section, you will learn how to run a C++ application in Visual C++ .NET. In the appendices and online at www.deitel.com, we also provide Dive Into™ publications containing instructions for compiling applications, using software including GCC and Borland C++ 5.5, and running applications in other environments, including Linux and CygWin.

Your compiler enables you to execute (that is, run) C++ applications. Throughout most of this text, you will focus on three types of files— **.cpp**, **.h** and **.exe** files. Files with the extensions **.cpp** (called **source code files**) and **.h** (called header files) store C++ statements written by you, the programmer. These statements indicate actions you would like your applications to perform. To execute an application, the statements stored in the **.cpp** file must first be converted into statements that your computer can understand. The process of converting statements from a high-level language like C++ into machine language is known as **compilation**. Files with the extension **.exe** are created after compiling and linking your source code. In Tutorial 2, you will learn how to compile your .cpp file and run an application. In the next section, you will test-drive two C++ applications.

The **Command Prompt** is a Windows program that lets you give the computer instructions by typing text at a prompt (**C:\>** in Fig. 1.1).

Figure 1.1 shows a **Command Prompt** window on a computer running Windows 2000. You can access the Windows 2000 **Command Prompt** window in the **Start > Programs > Accessories** menu. When the **Command Prompt** window is started, the beginning directory is **C:**. The **C:** typically refers to your computer's primary hard disk and the **** refers to the directory that contains all of the files stored on that disk.

Beginning directory for Windows 2000 ———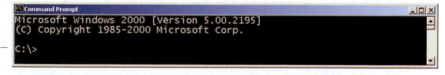

Figure 1.1   **Command Prompt** window in Windows 2000.

Figure 1.2 shows a **Command Prompt** window on a computer running Windows XP. You can access the Windows XP **Command Prompt** window in the **Start > All Programs > Accessories** menu. When the **Command Prompt** window is started, the beginning directory is **C:\Documents and Settings\Administrator**. **Administrator** is the user name on our computer. On your computer, **Administrator** will be replaced with your user name.

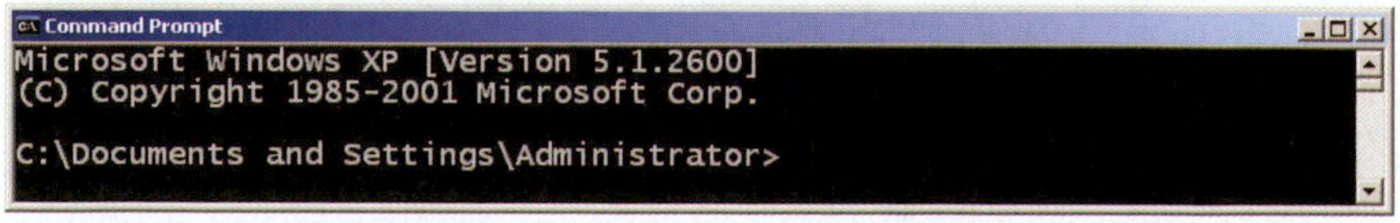

Beginning directory for Windows XP ———

Figure 1.2   **Command Prompt** window in Windows XP.

If you are running Windows 98 or Windows ME, your **Command Prompt** will be called the **MS-DOS Prompt** and your beginning directory may be different.

SELF-REVIEW   1. A _____ file contains the C++ statements written by you.

a) .cpp   b) .h

c) .exe   d) .compiler

2. The process of converting high-level language statements into machine language is known as _____.
   - a) transformation
   - c) mixing
   - b) execution
   - d) compilation

Answers: 1) d. 2) d.

1.11 Test-Driving the Car Payment Calculator and Guess the Number Applications

In this section, you will run two C++ applications, using our application-driven approach. In each subsequent tutorial, you will begin by "test-driving" an application—running the completed application. Then you will learn the C++ features you will need to build the application. Finally, you will "put it all together" and create your own working version of the application. You begin here in Tutorial 1 by running a "car payment calculator" application that calculates the amount a customer owes on a car loan given the initial down payment, the car price, the interest rate and the duration of the loan. (You will build this application in Tutorial 6.) You will also test-drive a game application that generates a random number. The player wins by guessing the number correctly. (This application is included as an exercise for you to build after completing Tutorial 12.)

In the following boxes, you will run and interact with each application. The elements and functionality you see in these applications are typical of what you will learn to program in this text. [*Note:* We use fonts to distinguish between features you see in a screen prompt (such as menu names) and elements that are not directly related to a screen prompt. Our convention is to emphasize screen features (such as the **File** menu) in a semibold **sans-serif Helvetica** font and to denote non-screen elements, such as file names (for example, `ProgramName.cpp`) in a `sans-serif Lucida` font. As you have already noticed, each term that is defined is set in heavy bold. Also, we have modified the color of the **Command Prompt** backgrounds throughout this text so that we may show input highlighting and callouts for new features.]

Test-Driving the Car Payment Calculator Application

1. ***Checking your setup.*** Read the *For Students and Instructors: Important Information Before You Begin* section to confirm that you have set up C++ properly on your computer and that you have copied the book's examples to your hard drive.

2. ***Locating the completed application.*** Open a **Command Prompt** window by selecting **Start > All Programs > Accessories > Command Prompt**. Change to your completed **Car Payment Calculator** application directory by typing `cd C:\Examples\Tutorial01\CarPayment`, then pressing *Enter* (Fig. 1.3). The command `cd` is used to change directories.

3. ***Running the Car Payment Calculator application.*** Type `CarPayment` in the **Command Prompt** window to run the application (Fig. 1.4). Typing the name of the application is all that is necessary to run it from the **Command Prompt**. Notice that you do not need to specify the `.exe` extension when using this command. [*Note:* On many systems, commands are case sensitive. It is important to type the name of this application with a capital "C" in "Car" and a capital "P" in "Payment". Otherwise, the application may not execute.]

Note that the current directory changed

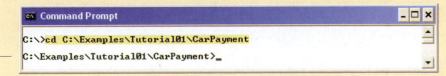

Figure 1.3   Changing to the **Car Payment Calculator** application's directory.

(cont.)

Executing the CarPayment application

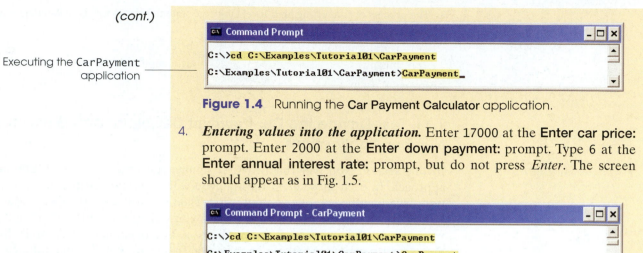

Figure 1.4   Running the **Car Payment Calculator** application.

4. ***Entering values into the application.*** Enter 17000 at the **Enter car price:** prompt. Enter 2000 at the **Enter down payment:** prompt. Type 6 at the **Enter annual interest rate:** prompt, but do not press *Enter*. The screen should appear as in Fig. 1.5.

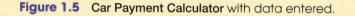

Figure 1.5   **Car Payment Calculator** with data entered.

5. ***Calculating the monthly payment amounts.*** Press *Enter* to input the value 6 into the application. The application displays in tabular format the monthly payment amounts for loan durations of 24, 36, 48 and 60 months (Fig. 1.6). In Tutorial 6, you will learn the programming concepts used to implement the **Car Payment Calculator** application.

Close box

Results displayed in tabular format

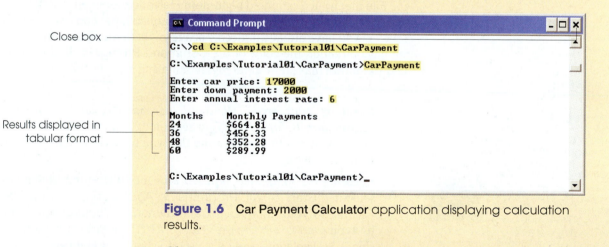

Figure 1.6   **Car Payment Calculator** application displaying calculation results.

6. ***Closing the Command Prompt window.*** Click the application's close box.

In the next test-drive section, you will be introduced to the **Guess the Number** game program, which generates a random number from 1 to 100 and prompts the user to guess the number using seven or fewer guesses. The user enters guesses at the **Enter guess:** prompt. If the guess is correct, the game ends. If the guess is not correct, the application indicates if the guess is higher or lower than the correct number. If the user has not guessed the number correctly after seven guesses, the application indicates that the user has no remaining guesses and displays the value of the number. [*Note:* The output values shown in the test-drive will vary each time you run the application because the computer chooses numbers at random.]

***Test-Driving the* Guess the Number Application**

Note that the current directory changed

Executing the GuessNumber application

Application displays whether your guess is too high or too low

1. ***Locating the completed application.*** Open a **Command Prompt** window by selecting **Start > All Programs > Accessories > Command Prompt**. Change to your completed **Guess the Number** application directory by typing cd C:\Examples\Tutorial01\GuessNumber, then pressing *Enter* (Fig. 1.7).

    ```
    c:\ Command Prompt                                           _ □ ×

    C:\>cd C:\Examples\Tutorial01\GuessNumber

    C:\Examples\Tutorial01\GuessNumber>_
    ```

    Figure 1.7   Changing to the **Guess the Number** application's directory.

2. ***Running the* Guess the Number *application.*** Now that you are in the directory that contains the application, type GuessNumber (Fig. 1.8) and press *Enter* to run the application.

    ```
    c:\ Command Prompt                                           _ □ ×

    C:\>cd C:\Examples\Tutorial01\GuessNumber

    C:\Examples\Tutorial01\GuessNumber>GuessNumber_
    ```

    Figure 1.8   Running the **Guess the Number** application.

3. ***Entering your first guess.*** At the **Enter guess:** prompt, enter the number 50 (Fig. 1.9).

    ```
    c:\ Command Prompt - GuessNumber                             _ □ ×

    C:\>cd C:\Examples\Tutorial01\GuessNumber

    C:\Examples\Tutorial01\GuessNumber>GuessNumber

    I'm thinking of a number from 1 to 100.
    Can you guess what it is in seven or fewer tries?

    Enter guess: 50_
    ```

    Figure 1.9   Entering an initial guess.

4. ***Entering another guess.*** The application displays "Too low...", meaning that the value you entered is below the number the application has chosen (Fig. 1.10). At the **Enter guess:** prompt, enter 75 (Fig. 1.10). This time the application displays "Too high...", because the value you entered is above the number the application has chosen.

    ```
    c:\ Command Prompt - GuessNumber                             _ □ ×

    I'm thinking of a number from 1 to 100.
    Can you guess what it is in seven or fewer tries?

    Enter guess: 50

    Too low...

    Enter guess: 75

    Too high...
    ```

    Figure 1.10   Entering a second guess and receiving feedback.

5. ***Entering additional guesses.*** Continue to play the game. Enter values until you guess the correct number—the application will display "Correct!" (Fig. 1.11)—or you enter seven unsuccessful guesses and the application displays "You have run out of guesses!" along with the correct number.

(cont.)

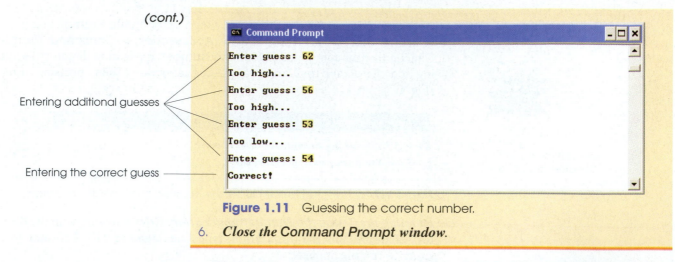

Entering additional guesses

Entering the correct guess

Figure 1.11 Guessing the correct number.

6. *Close the Command Prompt window.*

These are just two examples of the 100+ applications contained in this book. In the next tutorial, you will start learning how to program in C++ by writing your first lines of C++ code. We hope you enjoy learning how to build these applications and create applications of your own while learning how to program using C++.

1.12 Internet and Web Resources

The Internet and the Web give you access to an extraordinary collection of C++ resources. This section describes interesting and informative Web sites. Links to all these sites are provided on the CD included with this text and at www.deitel.com. Reference sections like this one are included throughout the book where appropriate.

www.deitel.com
Visit Deitel & Associates for *Simply C++* frequently asked questions (FAQs), links, errata, code downloads and Dive Into™ Series publications on using different C++ compilers and integrated development environments, such as Borland's C++, Microsoft Visual C++ and more.

www.prenhall.com/deitel
The Deitel & Associates page on the Prentice Hall Web site contains information about Deitel® publications and downloads.

www.softlord.com/comp
Visit this site to learn more about the history of computers.

www.elsop.com/wrc/h_comput.htm
This site also presents the history of computing. It provides links to discussions of famous people in the computer field, the evolution of programming languages and the development of operating systems.

www.w3.org/History.html
Visit this site for the history of the World Wide Web.

www.netvalley.com/intval.html
This site presents the history of the Internet.

www.ansi.org
The ANSI/ISO standards committee maintains the documentation and current specification for the C++ programming language.

www.cuj.com
This site provides a collection of resources, including articles, tutorials and code downloads, as well as quizzes and puzzles to test your C++ knowledge.

1.13 Wrap-Up

In this tutorial, you learned about how computers are organized. You studied the levels of programming languages and learned which kinds of languages, including C++, require translators. You also became familiar with other popular programming languages. You learned the importance of structured programming and object-oriented programming. You studied a brief history of the Internet and the World Wide Web and learned the history of the C++ programming language.

You took two working C++ applications out for a "test-drive." You were encouraged to explore several Web sites with additional information on this book, computers, the Internet, the Web and C++.

In the next tutorial, you will write your first C++ code in the context of a welcome application. You will continue to learn with our application-driven approach, in which you will see all C++ features in useful applications and in which you will, for each application,

1. study the user requirements,

2. test-drive a working version of the application,

3. learn the technologies you'll need to build the application yourself and

4. build your own working version of the application.

As you work through the book, if you have any questions about C++, send an e-mail to deitel@deitel.com, and we will respond promptly. We sincerely hope you enjoy learning C++ with *Simply C++*. Good luck!

KEY TERMS

Ada—A programming language, named after Lady Ada Lovelace, developed under the sponsorship of the U.S. Department of Defense in the 1970s and early 1980s.

arithmetic and logic unit (ALU)—The "manufacturing" section of the computer. The ALU performs calculations and makes decisions.

assembly language—A type of programming language that uses English-like abbreviations to represent the fundamental operations of the computer.

attribute—Another name for a property of an object.

bandwidth—The information-carrying capacity of communications lines, typically expressed in bits per second.

BASIC (Beginner's All-Purpose Symbolic Instruction Code)—A programming language developed in the mid-1960s by Professors Kemeny and Kurtz of Dartmouth College as a language for writing simple programs. Its primary purpose was to familiarize novices with programming techniques.

central processing unit (CPU)—The part of the computer's hardware that is responsible for supervising the operation of the other units of the computer.

class—The type of a group of similar objects. A class specifies the general format of its objects; the properties and actions available to an object depend on its class. An object is to its class much as a house is to its blueprint.

COBOL (COmmon Business Oriented Language)—A programming language developed in the late 1950s by a group of computer manufacturers in conjunction with government and industrial computer users. This language is used primarily for business applications that manipulate large amounts of data.

compiler—A translator program that converts high-level-language programs into machine language, so the programs may be executed on a computer.

computer—A device capable of performing computations and making logical decisions at speeds millions and even billions of times faster than the speeds at which human beings carry out those same tasks.

computer program—A set of instructions that guides a computer through an orderly series of actions to solve a problem.

computer programmer—A person who writes computer programs in programming languages.

.cpp file—The type of file in which programmers write the C++ code for an application; also called a "C++ source code file."

database—An organized collection of information.

.exe file—A Windows executable file. A .exe file is created by compiling the application's .cpp file and linking the compiler's output.

Fortran (FORmula TRANslator)—A programming language developed by IBM Corporation in the mid-1950s to create scientific and engineering applications that require complex mathematical computations.

Framework Class Library (FCL)—A powerful library of reusable software components developed for Microsoft's .NET platform. The FCL provides capabilities similar to the Java class library.

function—A portion of a C++ program that performs a task and possibly returns information when it completes that task.

hardware—The various devices that make up a computer, including the keyboard, screen, mouse, hard drive, memory, CD-ROM and DVD drives and processing units.

high-level language—A type of programming language in which a single program statement accomplishes a substantial task. High-level language instructions look almost like everyday English and contain common mathematical notations.

HyperText Markup Language (HTML)—A language for marking up information to share over the World Wide Web via hyperlinked text documents.

input unit—The "receiving" section of the computer that obtains information (data and computer programs) from various input devices, such as the keyboard and the mouse.

Internet—A worldwide computer network. Most people today access the Internet through the World Wide Web.

interpreter—A program that executes high-level language programs directly without the need for compiling those programs into machine language.

Lady Ada Lovelace—The person credited with being the world's first computer programmer, for work she did in the 1840s.

linker—A program that packages compiled code into a single executable file.

machine dependent language—A programming language that can be executed only on certain types of computers.

machine language—A computer's "natural" language, generally consisting of streams of numbers (1s and 0s) that tell the computer how to perform its most elementary operations.

memory unit—The rapid-access, relatively low-capacity "warehouse" section of the computer, which stores data temporarily while an application is running.

multiprocessor—A computer that contains more than one CPU.

object—A reusable software component that models a real world entity.

object technology—A packaging scheme for creating meaningful, reusable software units that focus on particular application areas. Examples of objects include date objects, time objects, paycheck objects and file objects.

output device—A device to which information that is processed by the computer can be sent.

output unit—The section of the computer that takes information the computer has processed and places it on various output devices, making the information available for use outside the computer.

Pascal—A programming language named after the 17th-century mathematician and philosopher Blaise Pascal. This language was designed to teach structured programming.

procedural programming language—A programming language (such as Fortran, Pascal, BASIC and C) that focuses on actions (verbs) rather than things or objects (nouns).

property—An object attribute, such as size, color or weight.

secondary storage unit—The long-term, high-capacity "warehouse" section of the computer.

software—The programs that run on computers.

source code file—A file with the extension .cpp that stores C++ code written by a programmer.

structured programming—A disciplined approach to creating programs that are clear, correct and easy to modify.

supercomputer—A computer that can perform hundreds of billions of calculations per second.

Transmission Control Protocol/Internet Protocol (TCP/IP)—The combined set of communications protocols for the Internet.

World Wide Web Consortium (W3C)—A forum through which individuals and companies cooperate to develop and recommend technologies for the World Wide Web.

World Wide Web (WWW)—A collection of hardware and software associated with the Internet that allows computer users to locate and view multimedia-based documents (such as documents with text, graphics, animations, audios and videos).

MULTIPLE-CHOICE QUESTIONS

1.1 The World Wide Web was developed _____.
a) by ARPA
b) at CERN by Tim Berners-Lee
c) before the Internet
d) as a replacement for the Internet

1.2 Files with the extension _____ store C++ source code written by programmers.
a) .java
b) .class
c) .exe
d) .cpp

1.3 Ada, Pascal and COBOL are examples of _____.
a) assembly languages
b) high-level languages
c) functions
d) C++ classes

1.4 _____ is an example of primary memory.
a) TCP
b) RAM
c) ALU
d) CD-ROM

1.5 C++ is an example of a(n) _____ language, in which single program statements accomplish more substantial tasks.
a) machine
b) assembly
c) high-level
d) None of the above.

1.6 The protocol primarily intended to create a "network of networks" is known as _____.
a) TCP
b) IP
c) OOP
d) FCL

1.7 _____ is one of the most widely used procedural programming languages.
a) C
b) C++
c) Java
d) Visual Basic .NET

1.8 A(n) _____ executes high-level languages directly.
a) compiler
b) linker
c) interpreter
d) object

1.9 The information-carrying capacity of communications lines is called _____.
a) networking
b) secondary storage
c) traffic
d) bandwidth

1.10 _____ is a disciplined approach to the creation of programs that are clear, correct and easy to modify.
a) Structured programming
b) TCP
c) Assembly programming
d) Secondary storage

EXERCISES   **1.11** Categorize each of the following items as either hardware or software:

a) CPU   b) Compiler

c) Input unit   d) Word-processing program

e) C++ program

1.12 Translator programs, such as assemblers and compilers, convert programs from one language (referred to as the source language) to another language (referred to as the target language). Determine which of the following statements are *true* and which are *false* (if the answer is *false*, explain why):

a) A compiler translates high-level-language programs into target-language programs.

b) An assembler translates source-language programs into machine-language programs.

c) A compiler translates source-language programs into target-language programs.

d) High-level languages are generally machine dependent.

e) A machine-language program requires translation before it can be run on a computer.

1.13 Computers can be thought of as being divided into six units.

a) Which unit can be thought of as "the boss" of the other units?

b) Which unit is the high-capacity "warehouse" and retains information even when the computer is powered off?

c) Which unit might determine whether two items stored in memory are identical?

d) Which unit obtains information from devices like the keyboard and mouse?

1.14 Expand each of the following acronyms:

a) W3C   b) TCP/IP

c) OOP   d) WWW

e) HTML

1.15 What are the advantages to using object-oriented programming techniques?

Objectives

In this tutorial, you will learn to:
- Read C++ code.
- Write a C++ statement that displays a message on the screen.
- Compile a C++ application.
- Execute an application.
- Use escape sequences.
- Locate and correct syntax errors.

Outline

Welcome Application

Introduction to C++ Programming

The C++ language facilitates a structured and disciplined approach to computer-program design. In this tutorial, you will use C++ programming to create a **Welcome** application. You will use C++'s output capabilities to display a message on the screen when the application is run. You will also learn the basic components of a C++ application by reading the source code. We will use examples to illustrate many important features of C++.

This tutorial also introduces you to programming in Visual Studio® .NET 2003. Visual Studio .NET is Microsoft's **Integrated Development Environment (IDE)** for creating and running applications written in several programming languages, including C++. You will learn how to add your application's source code file to a project, which enables you to compile the application. After you compile your application, you will learn how to run it from Visual Studio .NET so that you can verify that your application works correctly.

Finally, you will learn about syntax errors, which occur when code statements violate the grammatical rules of the programming language. You will introduce syntax errors into your application's source code and view the result when you attempt to compile your application. You will view the different messages issued by the compiler when syntax errors occur, and you will correct those errors so that your application will compile successfully.

2.1 Test-Driving the Welcome Application

The last tutorial introduced you to C++. In this tutorial, you will use C++ to build a simple **Welcome** application. Your application must meet the following requirements:

Application Requirements

*Develop a simple **Welcome** application that displays the greeting "Welcome to C++!" on the screen.*

You begin by test-driving the completed application. Then, you will learn the C++ technologies you will need to create your own version of this application.

Test-Driving the Welcome Application

1. ***Locating the completed application.*** Open the **Command Prompt** window by selecting **Start > All Programs > Accessories > Command Prompt**. Change to your completed **Welcome** application directory by typing cd C:\Examples\Tutorial02\CompletedApplication\Welcome, then pressing the *Enter* key (Fig. 2.1).

Figure 2.1   Locating the completed **Welcome** application.

2. ***Running the Welcome application.*** Type Welcome in the **Command Prompt** window and press the *Enter* key to run the application (Fig. 2.2). Figure 2.2 displays the result of executing the application—the application displays "Welcome to C++" on the screen. Note that the command prompt is displayed again after the program output. This indicates that the program has terminated and that the command prompt is ready to receive another command, such as to change the directory or to run another application.

```
C:\Examples\Tutorial02\CompletedApplication\Welcome>Welcome
Welcome to C++!

C:\Examples\Tutorial02\CompletedApplication\Welcome>_
```

Figure 2.2   Running the completed **Welcome** application.

3. ***Closing the Command Prompt window.*** Close the **Command Prompt** window by clicking its close button.

2.2 Compiling and Running the Template Welcome Application

In Tutorial 1, you learned that a C++ program's source code file (a file with the .cpp extension) must be compiled and linked to form an executable image before it can be run. In this section, you will learn how to compile and run the **Welcome** application in the Microsoft Visual Studio .NET environment.

In the appendices, we also provide instructions for compiling and running applications in other environments. If you are using the GNU Compiler Collection (GCC) toolset, instructions for compiling C++ applications are located in Appendix B. If you are using the Borland compiler, instructions for compiling C++ applications are located in Appendix C. If you are using the Metrowerks CodeWarrior IDE, instructions for compiling C++ applications are located in Appendix D.

The Visual Studio .NET IDE organizes applications into **projects** and **solutions**, which contain one or more projects. Large-scale applications can contain many projects, each of which performs a single, well-defined task (Fig. 2.3). In this book, each solution you build will contain only one project.

Figure 2.3 Solutions can contain one or more projects.

Creating a Project for the Welcome Application

1. *Copying the template to your working directory.* Copy the `C:\Examples\Tutorial02\TemplateApplication\Welcome` directory to your `C:\SimplyCpp` directory. In each tutorial, we will provide you with a partially completed application as a template file. We ask you to complete the applications using a copy of the template file, which you will place in your working directory (`C:\SimplyCpp`) so that later on you can replace the modified copy with the original, if necessary.

2. *Creating a new project.* If you have not already done so, start Visual Studio .NET by selecting **Start > All Programs > Microsoft Visual Studio .NET 2003 > Microsoft Visual Studio .NET 2003**. To create a new project, select **File > New > Project…**, causing the **New Project** dialog to display (Fig. 2.4).

Title bar (displaying **New Project**)

Visual C++ Projects directory (selected)

Project Types: pane

Location of the new project (your location may be different)

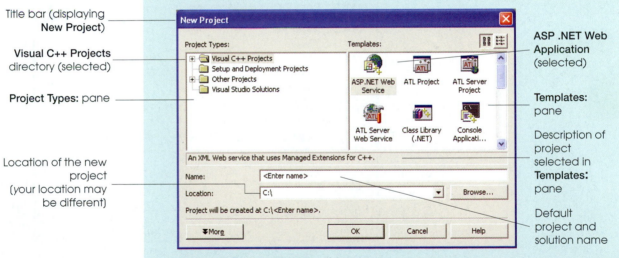

ASP .NET Web Application (selected)

Templates: pane

Description of project selected in **Templates:** pane

Default project and solution name

Figure 2.4 New Project dialog.

3. *Selecting the project type.* The Visual Studio .NET IDE allows you to choose from one of several project types. Click the **Visual C++ Projects** directory in the **Project Types:** pane (Fig. 2.4) to display the list of Visual C++ .NET project types in the **Templates:** pane. [*Note:* Depending on your version of Visual Studio .NET, the names and number of items shown in the **Project Types:** and **Templates:** panes could differ.]

4. *Selecting the template.* Select **Win32 Console Project**, which you will use to create a project that does not include any source code. We have provided you with the source code, which you will add to your project once it has been created.

5. *Changing the name of the project.* By default, the Visual Studio .NET IDE displays the text `<Enter name>` in the **Name:** field (Fig. 2.4). To rename the project, type `Welcome` in the **Name:** field (Fig. 2.5).

(cont.)

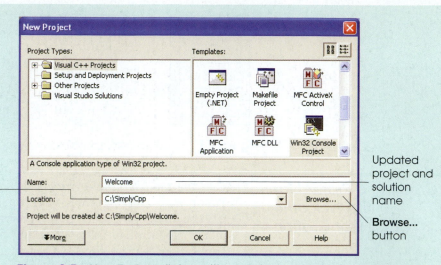

Updated project location

Updated project and solution name

Browse... button

Figure 2.5 **New Project** dialog with updated project information.

6. ***Changing the location of the project.*** Save this project in your SimplyCpp directory. To change the project's location, click the **Browse...** button (Fig. 2.5) to display the **Project Location** dialog (Fig. 2.6). In this dialog, locate your SimplyCpp directory, then click **Open**. After providing the project's name and location in the **New Project** dialog, click **OK**.

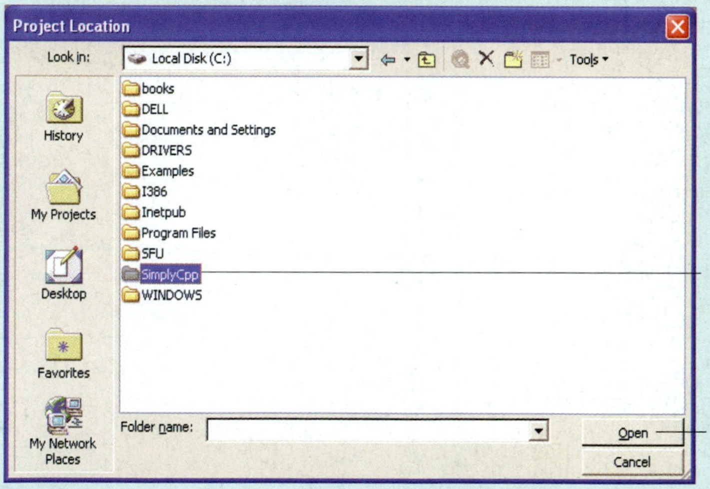

SimplyCpp directory (selected)

Open button

Figure 2.6 **Project Location** dialog.

7. ***Modifying the application settings.*** The **Win32 Application Wizard** dialog appears (Fig. 2.7). Click the **Application Settings** link on the left side of the dialog window.

8. ***Creating an empty project.*** In the **Win32 Application Wizard Application Settings** dialog, the **Console Application** radio button is selected by default (Fig. 2.8). To indicate that you want to create an empty project, click the **Empty Project** check box. Notice that a black check mark appears inside the box, indicating that it has been selected. Then click the **Finish** button to complete the **Win32 Application Wizard**. This creates a new solution named **Welcome** and a new project named **Welcome**. The **Solution Explorer** (Fig. 2.9) window displays the currently open solution and project and the files in your C++ application. If the **Solution Explorer** window does not appear, select **View > Solution Explorer**.

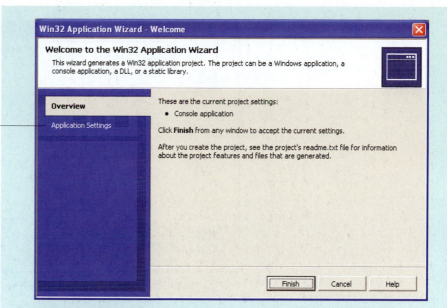

Application Settings link

Figure 2.7   **Win32 Application Wizard** dialog.

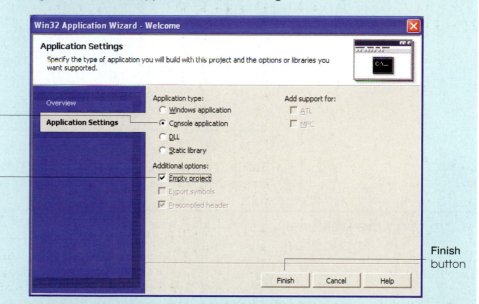

Console application
radio button
(selected)

Application Settings

Empty project check
box (selected)

Finish
button

Figure 2.8   **Application Settings** in the **Win32 Application Wizard** dialog.

Welcome solution
Welcome project
Source Files folder

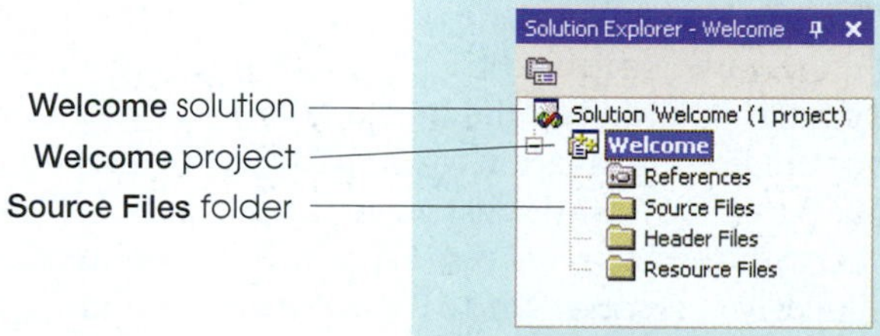

Figure 2.9   **Solution Explorer** window in Visual Studio .NET.

9. *Adding the Welcome.cpp source code file to your project.* Before you can compile the application, you must add its source code to the project. To add the Welcome.cpp source code file to your project, right click the **Source Files** folder and select **Add > Add Existing Item...**. The **Add Existing Item - Welcome** dialog should appear (Fig. 2.10). Click Welcome.cpp to select the file, then click **Open**. Welcome.cpp appears in the **Source Files** folder in the **Solution Explorer** (Fig. 2.11).

(cont.)

Welcome.cpp file
(selected)

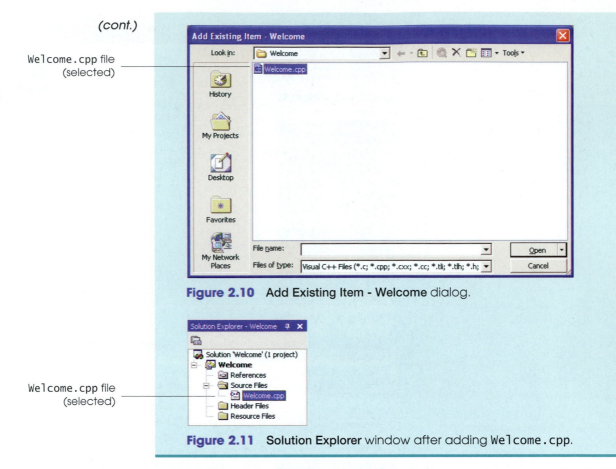

Figure 2.10 Add Existing Item - Welcome dialog.

Welcome.cpp file
(selected)

Figure 2.11 Solution Explorer window after adding Welcome.cpp.

You have now added the Welcome.cpp file to a solution and a project in Visual Studio .NET. In the next box, you will use Visual Studio .NET to compile the application, then view the files that are created as a result.

Compiling the Welcome Application

1. ***Opening your application's project directory.*** Locate the C:\Simply-Cpp\Welcome directory where the application is saved. Observe that Visual Studio .NET has created several files in your application's directory (Fig. 2.12). In addition to the Welcome.cpp source code file, the directory contains Welcome.ncb, Welcome.sln and Welcome.vcproj files. [*Note:* If your folder is set to show hidden files, then you will also see a Welcome.suo file that Visual Studio .NET created.]

   Recall that .cpp files, such as the Welcome.cpp file, are C++ source code files. These files must be compiled to translate the source code into machine code and linked so that you can run the machine code on your computer. The Welcome.ncb file contains information for *Intellisense,* an advanced feature in Visual Studio .NET that we will discuss in later tutorials. Welcome.sln is a **solution file** (a file with the .sln extension), which stores information about your solution. Similarly, Welcome.vcproj is a **Visual C++ project file** (a file with the .vcproj extension), which stores information regarding your project.

2. ***Compiling the application.*** In Visual Studio .NET, select the Welcome.cpp source code file by clicking the file in the **Solution Explorer** window. Then, select **Build > Build Solution**. The **Build > Build Solution** command will compile the C++ source code file and create a Welcome.exe file.

(cont.)

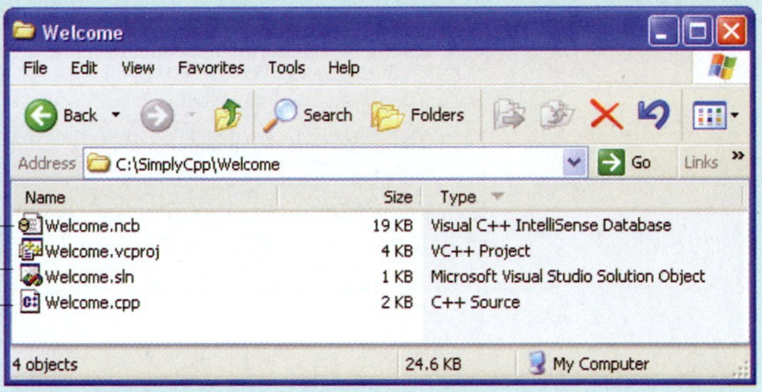

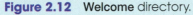

Source code (.cpp) file ———
Solution (.sln) file ———
Project (.vcproj) file ———

Figure 2.12   **Welcome** directory.

3. *Viewing the result of compilation.* Return to the `C:\SimplyCpp\Welcome` directory. Notice that the directory now contains a **Debug** directory (Fig. 2.13). Double click the **Debug** directory to display its contents (Fig. 2.14). The `Welcome.obj` file contains the machine code created by the compiler before linking. `Welcome.exe` is the executable file that you will use to run your application. This file is created when the object file is linked. The remaining files in the directory are files created by Visual Studio .NET to store information, such as debugging information, related to the compiled application. We introduce debugging later in this tutorial in Section 2.5.

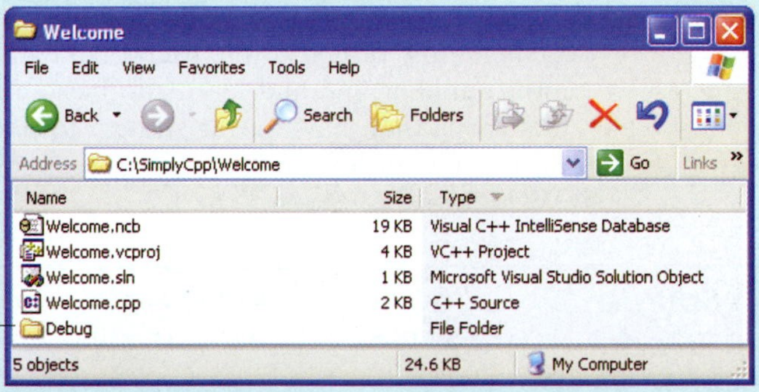

Newly created **Debug** directory ———

Figure 2.13   **Welcome** directory after compilation.

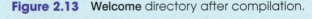

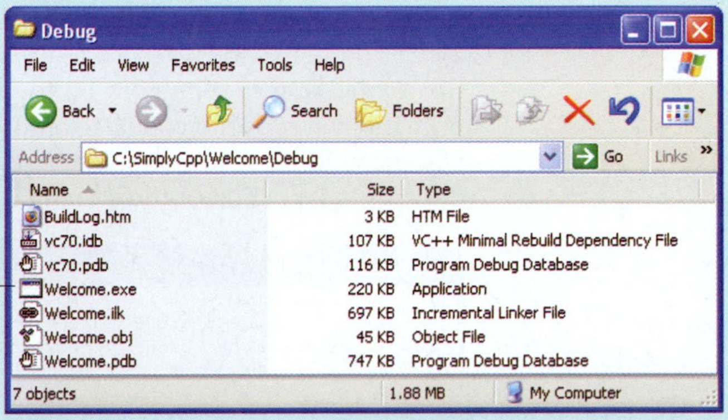

Newly created .exe file ———

Figure 2.14   Examining the contents of the **Debug** directory.

4. *Running the application.* In Visual Studio .NET, select **Debug > Start Without Debugging** to run your application. At this point, the application does not produce any output. The C++ applications you create will display text to the user and often retrieve input from the user before exiting. When the application terminates, the **Press any key to continue** prompt appears (Fig. 2.15). This prompt is generated by Visual Studio .NET.

(cont.)

Figure 2.15   Running the template **Welcome** application.

5. ***Closing the Command Prompt window.*** Close the **Command Prompt** window by pressing any key or by clicking its close button

---

SELF-REVIEW

1. A source code file has the _____ extension.
   a) .exe   b) .source
   c) .cpp   d) None of the above.

2. The _____ converts a .cpp file to machine code.
   a) debugger   b) compiler
   c) converter   d) loader

Answers: 1) c. 2) b.

2.3 Introduction to C++ Code

In this section, you develop your **Welcome** application. The application will display a single line of text to the user, then exit. You will examine the **Welcome** application template file and learn the basic components of a C++ program. C++ uses notations that may appear strange to nonprogrammers. In the following box you will take your first peek at C++ code. In Section 2.4, you will begin constructing the **Welcome** application.

Examining C++ Source Code

1. ***Viewing the Welcome application's template file source code.*** To open the Welcome.cpp source code file, double click the Welcome.cpp file in the **Solution Explorer** (Fig. 2.10) window.

   The code should look similar to Fig. 2.16, though each text editor and IDE will be different. [*Note:* All windows that show source code, like the one in Fig. 2.16, were created for this book in Microsoft Visual Studio .NET. 2003. You may choose to use a different text editor or IDE.] As you look at the application code in your editor, please keep in mind that you are seeing only a portion of the code. Also, to help you along in the early tutorials, we will provide most of the code for you. We will ask you to insert or modify only a small portion of the code in each application.

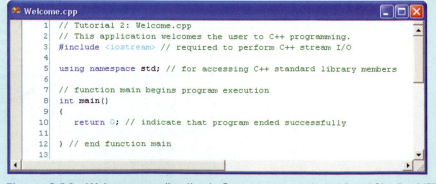

Figure 2.16   **Welcome** application's C++ source code in Visual Studio .NET.

(cont.)

2. ***Understanding comments.*** Lines 1 and 2 of Fig. 2.17 begin with two **forward-slash** characters (**//**), indicating that the remainder of each line is a **comment**. You insert comments in your applications to improve their readability. These comments explain your code so that you (and possibly other programmers) can understand it more easily. Comments also help you understand your code later, when you haven't looked at it for a while.

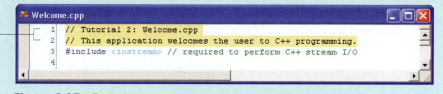

Full-line comments

Figure 2.17 Examining comments in the **Welcome** application's C++ source code in Visual Studio .NET.

Comments can be placed either in their own lines (these are called "**full-line comments**") or at the end of a line of code (these are called "**end-of-line comments**"). Many text editors display comments in green, as we do in this book. [*Note:* The comments in lines 1–2 are not in green because Visual Studio .NET unfortunately removes coloring when we highlight lines of code.]

The C++ compiler ignores comments, so they do not cause the computer to perform any actions when your applications run. Our convention is to use a comment in line 1 to indicate the tutorial number and file name. We use a comment in line 2 to describe the task performed by the application. You may choose a different commenting convention.

3. ***Understanding the `#include` preprocessor directive.*** C++ programs consist of pieces called classes and functions. You can program whatever pieces you need to form a C++ program. C++ programmers also take advantage of the existing classes and functions in the C++ Standard Library. Thus, there are really two parts to learning the C++ "world." The first is learning the C++ language itself; the second is learning how to use the classes and functions in the C++ Standard Library. Throughout the book, we discuss many of these classes and functions.

In this application, you will use the C++ Standard Library to display text on the screen. You could write your own code to display text—doing so would be quite complex. Instead of writing this code, you will direct the compiler to use code from the C++ Standard Library that provides display capabilities.

Line 3 (Fig. 2.18) is a **preprocessor directive**, which is a message to the C++ **preprocessor**. Lines that begin with **#** are processed by the preprocessor before the application is compiled. The C++ preprocessor obeys commands called preprocessor directives, which indicate that certain manipulations are to be performed on the source code before compilation. These manipulations usually specify other files to be compiled and linked to form an executable file. The preprocessor is invoked by the compiler before it converts the source code to machine language.

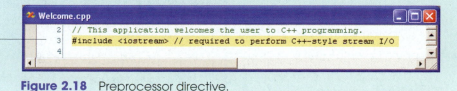

Preprocessor directive

Figure 2.18 Preprocessor directive.

Good Programming Practice

Place a blank line above a comment that is in a line by itself. The blank line makes the comment stand out and improves program readability.

Good Programming Practice

Comments written at the end of a line of code should be preceded by one or more spaces to enhance program readability.

(cont.)

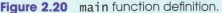

Common Programming Error

Forgetting to include the `<iostream>` file in a program that inputs data from the keyboard or outputs data to the screen causes the compiler to issue one or more error messages.

Line 3 uses the `#include` preprocessor directive, which notifies the preprocessor to include in the application the contents of the **input/output stream header file**, `<iostream>`. This file must be included for any application that outputs data to the screen or inputs data from the keyboard using C++-style stream input/output. As you observed in the box, *Test-Driving the Welcome Application*, the completed application outputs data to the screen. In the next section, you will provide this functionality. In the next tutorial, you will learn how to retrieve input that the user types at the keyboard.

Notice that line 4 is blank. When you press the *Enter* key to create a blank line, you create an example of a **whitespace character**—a character that does not appear as text when displayed. Other examples of whitespace characters are the space character and tab character. Whitespace characters generally are ignored by the compiler. Programmers often use whitespace characters to separate sections of code to improve readability.

4. ***Understanding the using directive.*** Line 5 (Fig. 2.19) contains a **using directive**, which is specified by including the `using` and `namespace` keywords, followed by the name of a namespace and a semicolon. In this case, the `using` directive specifies the `std` namespace (short for "standard"), which enables you to access technologies provided by the C++ Standard Library. Namespaces are an advanced C++ feature. For now, you should simply remember to include the `using namespace std` directive in all of your applications.

using directive —————

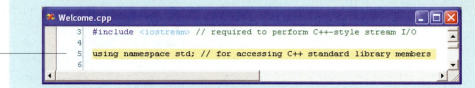

Figure 2.19 `using` directive.

5. ***Examining the main function definition.*** Line 7 (Fig. 2.20) is another full-line comment indicating that program execution begins from the next line. Line 8, which defines the **main** function, is a part of every C++ program. The parentheses after `main` indicate that `main` is a program building block called a **function**. C++ programs contain one or more functions, exactly one of which must be `main`. Your **Welcome** application contains only one function. C++ programs begin executing at the `main` function, the **entry point** of the application, even if `main` is not the first function in the program. The `int` keyword to the left of `main` indicates that `main` "returns" an integer (whole number) value. The operating system uses the value that `main` returns to determine whether the program terminated successfully. We will explain what it means for a function to "return a value" when we study functions in depth in Tutorial 10. For now, simply include the `int` keyword to the left of `main` in each of your programs. **Keywords** (or **reserved words**) are reserved for use by C++. Many text editors display keywords in blue, as we do in this book. We will discuss keywords in more detail in the next tutorial.

Function `main` header —————

Exiting the function using `return` —————

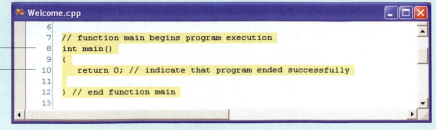

Figure 2.20 `main` function definition.

(cont.)

Good Programming Practice

Choose a convention for the size of an indent then uniformly apply that convention. The *Tab* key may be used to create indents, but tab stops may vary. We suggest using either 1/4-inch tab stops or (preferably) three spaces to form a level of indentation.

The **left brace**, **{**, (line 9) begins the **body** of every function. A corresponding **right brace**, **}**, (line 12) ends each function's body. The C++ `return` keyword (line 10) is one of several means we will use to exit a function. When the `return` statement is used at the end of `main`, as shown here, the value 0 indicates that the program has terminated successfully. In Tutorial 10, we discuss functions in detail, and the reasons for including this statement will become clear. For now, simply include this statement in each program, or the compiler may produce a warning on some systems.

Note that the statement

```
return 0;
```

is indented. Indenting statements in the body of a function makes your code easier to read. You should choose a convention for the size of an indent you prefer, then uniformly apply that convention. In this book, we use three spaces for each level of indentation.

SELF-REVIEW

1. A comment begins with _____.

   a) #   b) //

   c) \\   d) the `comment` keyword

2. Every C++ application must contain exactly one _____.

   a) `main` function   b) whitespace character

   c) preprocessor directive   d) header file

Answers: 1) b. 2) a.

2.4 Constructing the Welcome Application

In this section, you develop your **Welcome** application. You will write a C++ statement to display a message on the screen.

Most programs in C++ input and/or output data. Certain C++ functions take their input from **cin** (the **standard input stream object**; pronounced "see-in"), which is normally connected to the keyboard but can be connected to another device. Data is often output to **cout** (the **standard output stream object**; pronounced "see-out"), which is normally connected to the computer screen but can be connected to another device. When we say that a program prints a result, we normally mean that the result is displayed on a screen. Data may be output to other devices, such as disks and printers, and across computer networks such as the Internet.

In the following box, you will write your first C++ statement. This statement will display the message, "Welcome to C++!"

Displaying a Message Using cout

1. ***Opening the Welcome application's template file.*** If the **Welcome** application source code file is not currently open, locate the `Welcome.cpp` file and open it in your text editor or IDE.

2. ***Writing your own C++ statement.*** Insert line 10 of Fig. 2.21 into your application. [*Note:* To insert this statement, you will need to move the `return` statement to line 12 by placing the cursor to the left of the `return` statement and pressing *Enter* twice. You should not replace any code that already exists in the template file unless you are instructed to do so.]

(cont.)

Displaying a message ——

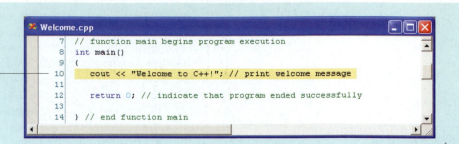

```
7    // function main begins program execution
8    int main()
9    {
10       cout << "Welcome to C++!"; // print welcome message
11
12       return 0; // indicate that program ended successfully
13
14   } // end function main
```

Figure 2.21 Inserting a C++ statement that displays text when executed.

Take a closer look at the first portion of the line of code you just inserted:

```
cout << "Welcome to C++!";
```

This line instructs the computer to display on the screen the **string** of characters contained between the quotation marks (Welcome to C++) using an **operator** (in this case, <<), which is a symbol that causes the application to display text. The text, starting at cout and including the << operator, the string "Welcome to C++!" and the **semicolon** (;), is called a **statement**. Most statements that you will write end with a semicolon (also known as the statement terminator). Line 10 of Fig. 2.21 is called an **executable statement** because the compiler uses it to generate code that performs an action when the application runs. Output and input in C++ are accomplished with **streams of characters**. When the preceding statement is executed, it sends the stream of characters Welcome to C++! to the standard output stream object—cout—which is normally "connected" to the screen.

The << operator is referred to as the **stream insertion operator**. The expressions on either side of the stream insertion operator are its **operands**. When this program executes, the value to the right of the operator, the **right operand**, is inserted in the object (the output stream, cout) to the left of the operator, the **left operand**. The stream insertion operator is known as a **binary operator**, because it has two operands. In this case, the operands are the string "Welcome to C++!" and cout, the output stream object. (Notice that the operator points in the direction in which the data goes. In this case, the operator points left, which is appropriate because the string "Welcome to C++!" is sent to the object to the left of the operator, cout). The characters of the right operand normally display exactly as they appear between the double quotes.

C++ code is **case sensitive**. This means that uppercase and lowercase letters are treated differently. For example, cout and cOut are considered to be different—using cOut in place of cout will cause an error that will prevent your program from compiling.

Recall from the previous section that the two forward slashes in line 10 of Fig. 2.21 begin a comment. In this case, the comment indicates that the statement you just entered displays a welcome message. Once again, comments are ignored by the compiler and do not perform any action when the program runs.

Common Programming Error

Forgetting the semicolon at the end of a statement results in an error when you compile your application.

Common Programming Error

Using incorrect capitalization for keywords and identifiers results in a compilation error.

3. *Saving the application.* Save your modified source code file. In most text editors and IDEs, this can be accomplished by selecting **File > Save**.

4. *Compiling the application.* Compile your application. If the compiler displays any errors, check your application carefully to ensure that you entered code exactly as shown in the preceding steps. [*Note:* From this point forward, you will be asked simply to compile your application. In Visual Studio .NET, select **Build > Build Solution** to compile your application. Refer to the appendices for compilation instructions for other environments.]

(cont.)

5. ***Running the application.*** Select **Debug > Start Without Debugging** to run your application. Figure 2.22 shows the result of running the updated application. Notice that there is no blank line between the program output and the **Press any key to continue** prompt inserted by Visual Studio .NET. In the next box, you will add code to insert a blank line between the program output and the output that follows (in this case, the **Press any key to continue** prompt). This helps the user to distinguish program output from output that follows.

> **▣ "c:\SimplyCpp\Welcome\Debug\Welcome.exe"**   ⬁ ⬜ ✕
>
> Welcome to C++!Press any key to continue_

Figure 2.22 **Welcome** application using `cout` to display text.

6. ***Close the Command Prompt window.***

In the preceding box, you wrote a C++ statement containing a string of characters (also known as a **string literal**, a **literal** or a **string constant**), consisting of words separated by space characters and punctuation. Notice that the compiler does not ignore the whitespace characters between the double quotation marks enclosing the string. Instead, these characters are displayed exactly as they appear between the double quotes. In the next box, you will add code to insert a character into the string that is displayed so that a blank line appears below the welcome message.

In C++, inserting a blank line into a string is not as simple as pressing *Enter* while the **cursor**—the current screen-position indicator—is located between the string's double quotes. In fact, it is an error to insert a newline character inside a string using *Enter*. For example, the statement:

```
cout << "Welcome
    to
    C++!";
```

Common Programming Error

Splitting a statement in the middle of a string is a syntax error.

would cause a syntax error when compiled. [*Note:* We use red to color C++ code that contains errors.] To enable programmers to insert newline characters into streams, C++ provides an **escape character**, the backslash (\). It indicates that a "special" character is to be output. When a backslash is encountered in a string of characters, the next character is combined with the backslash to form an **escape sequence**. Consider the following statement:

```
cout << "Welcome\n to\n C++!";
```

The escape sequence **\n** means **newline**. It causes the cursor to move to the beginning of the next line on the screen. In this case, the text

```
Welcome
to
C++!
```

would be displayed on the screen. Some other common escape sequences are listed in Fig. 2.23. Figure 2.24 shows several statements using escape characters and the result of executing those statements.

Escape Sequence	Description
\n	Newline. Positions the screen cursor at the beginning of the next line.
\t	Horizontal tab. Moves the screen cursor to the next tab stop.

Figure 2.23 Escape sequences. (Part 1 of 2.)

Escape Sequence	Description
\r	Carriage return. Positions the screen cursor at the beginning of the current line; does not advance to the next line.
\a	Alert. Sounds the system bell.
\\	Backslash. Used to print a backslash character.
\"	Double quote. Used to print a double quote character.

Figure 2.23 Escape sequences. (Part 2 of 2.)

Statement	Output
cout << "Welcome\nto\nC++!";	Welcome to C++!
cout << "Welcome to C++!\a\a\a";	Welcome to C++! *(followed by three beeps)*
cout << "Use \\n for a newline.";	Use \n for a newline.
cout << "\"This is quoted text.\"";	"This is quoted text."
cout << "\tWelcome to C++!";	Welcome to C++!
cout << "Welcome \rto C++!";	to C++!

Figure 2.24 Escape sequence examples.

Welcome to C++! can be displayed several ways. For example, Fig. 2.25 uses multiple stream insertion operators (lines 10–11), yet produces identical output (Fig. 2.26) to the application you created in the preceding box. This works because each stream-insertion statement resumes printing where the previous statement stopped printing. The first stream insertion prints Welcome, followed by a space; the second stream insertion begins printing on the same line immediately following the space. In general, C++ allows the programmer to express statements in a variety of ways. In the next box, you will insert a newline character into the output string.

> **Good Programming Practice**
>
> A lengthy statement may be spread over several lines. If a single statement must be split across lines, choose breaking points that make sense, such as after an operator. If a statement is split across two or more lines, indent all subsequent lines with one "level" of indentation.

Multiple stream insertion operators —

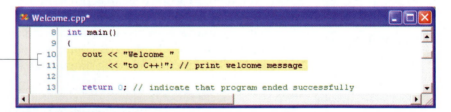

```
int main()
{

    cout << "Welcome "
        << "to C++!"; // print welcome message

    return 0; // indicate that program ended successfully
```

Figure 2.25 Welcome application using multiple stream insertion operators.

"c:\SimplyCpp\Welcome\Debug\Welcome.exe"

```
Welcome to C++!Press any key to continue_
```

Figure 2.26 Welcome application output.

Adding Newlines to the Welcome Application

1. *Opening the Welcome application's template file.* If the **Welcome** application source code file is not currently open, locate the Welcome.cpp file and open it in your text editor or IDE.

2. *Modifying the output statement.* Modify line 10 of your application as shown in Fig. 2.27. Notice that a newline escape sequence has been inserted at the beginning of the string and two have been appended to the end of the string to the right of the stream insertion operator (<<).

(cont.)

Appending a newline
to displayed text

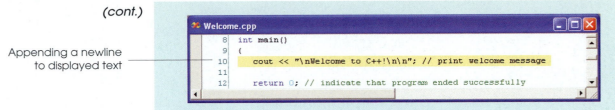

Figure 2.27   Inserting newlines.

3. *Saving the application.* Save your modified source code file.

4. *Compiling the application.* Compile your application. If the compiler displays any errors, check your application carefully to ensure that you entered the code exactly as shown in the preceding steps.

5. *Running the application.* Select **Debug > Start Without Debugging** to run your application. Figure 2.28 shows the result of the updated application running. Notice the blank line between the displayed message and the command prompt below it. This is the result of inserting two newlines (\n) in line 10 (Fig. 2.27).

```
"c:\simplycpp\welcome\debug\Welcome.exe"

Welcome to C++!

Press any key to continue_
```

Figure 2.28   **Welcome** application using a newline character.

6. *Close the Command Prompt window.*

Figure 2.29 presents the source code for the **Welcome** application. The lines of code that you added, viewed or modified in this tutorial are highlighted. [*Note:* Throughout each tutorial, we refer to "template" source code files and "template" applications. These references should not be confused with an advanced feature of the C++ programming language named "templates."]

Full-line comments describe the
application's purpose
Include the `iostream` header file

`using` directive provides
access to the `std` namespace

Define the `main` function

Print a welcome message

Exit the application

```cpp
1   // Tutorial 2: Welcome.cpp
2   // This application welcomes the user to C++ programming.
3   #include <iostream> // required to perform C++ stream I/O
4
5   using namespace std; // for accessing C++ Standard Library members
6
7   // function main begins program execution
8   int main()
9   {
10      cout << "\nWelcome to C++!\n\n"; // print welcome message
11
12      return 0; // indicate that program ended successfully
13
14   } // end function main
```

Figure 2.29 Code for the **Welcome** application.

SELF-REVIEW   1. Use _____ to print a message.

a) cin   b) cout

c) cprint   d) cwrite

2. Use _____ to print a double quote.

     a) "   b) ""

     c) \"   d) #"

Answers: 1) b. 2) c.

2.5 Compilation Errors

In this tutorial, you learned to compile the **Welcome** application. If you do not write your code correctly, your application will not compile, and errors will be displayed. Even after an application compiles correctly, it may still contain errors. **Debugging** is the process of locating and removing errors in an application. There are two types of errors—syntax errors and logic errors.

Compilation errors occur when the compiler detects mistakes in your source code. A **syntax error** is a compilation error that occurs when code statements violate the grammatical rules of the programming language. Examples of such errors include misspelling a word that is special to C++ and not placing a semicolon at the end of each statement that you added to your application in this tutorial. An application cannot be executed until all of its syntax errors are corrected—that is, until it compiles correctly.

Logic errors do not prevent your application from compiling successfully, but do cause your application to produce erroneous results when it runs. Most compiler vendors provide software called a **debugger**, which helps locate logic errors in your applications.

At the ends of several tutorials, we provide *Using the Debugger* sections, in which you will learn to detect and remove logic errors by using the Visual Studio .NET debugger. We also provide corresponding sections for other popular debuggers, such as the GNU debugger (gdb), in the appendices located at the end of the book or online at www.deitel.com.

During the compilation of a C++ application, any compilation errors appear in the **Output** window, along with a description of each error. Figure 2.30 displays the error message that appears in the **Output** window when the semicolon character is omitted from the end of line 12 of Fig. 2.29. Visual Studio .NET also arranges the information regarding errors in the **Task List** window (Fig. 2.31). In this case, the syntax error can be corrected by inserting the semicolon and recompiling. In this section, you will create some compilation errors, view the error messages from the compiler and fix the errors. In later *Using the Debugger* sections, you will actually use the debugger.

Missing semicolon at the end of the statement preceding line 12

```
Output                                                                  ☒
Build                                                                    ▼
  Compiling...
  Welcome.cpp
  Welcome.cpp(12) : error C2143: syntax error : missing ';' before 'return'
```

Figure 2.30   **Output** window listing a syntax error.

Location of error within the file

Description of error

Location of file containing error

```
Task List - 1 Build Error task shown (filtered)                          ☒
!  ✔  Description                              File                 Line
       Click here to add a new task
! ⬙ ☐ error C2143: syntax error : missing ';' before 'return'  c:\SimplyCpp\Welcome\Welcome.cpp  12
```

Figure 2.31   **Task List** window listing a syntax error.

Compilation Errors

1. **Opening the application.** If the **Welcome** application source code file is not currently open, locate the `Welcome.cpp` file and open it in your text editor or IDE.

2. **Creating your own compilation errors.** You will now create your own compilation errors, for demonstration purposes. Modify the escape sequences before the second double quote in line 10 and capitalize the `return` keyword in line 12 as shown in Fig. 2.32.

Two syntax errors

```
8   int main()
9   {
10      cout << "\nWelcome to C++!\"; // print welcome message
11
12      Return 0; // indicate that program ended successfully
13
```

Figure 2.32   Introducing two syntax errors into your code.

3. **Compiling the application.** Compile your application by selecting **Build > Build Solution**. Figure 2.33 shows the error messages generated by the compiler. [*Note:* Visual Studio .NET saves any changes to your application's source code file before compiling it.]

Number of errors displayed in task list title bar

Description of the errors including file name and line number

Task List - 4 Build Error tasks shown (filtered)

✔	Description	File	Line
	Click here to add a new task		
	error C2001: newline in constant	c:\SimplyCpp\Welcome\Welcome.cpp	10
	error C2146: syntax error : missing ';' before identifier 'Return'	c:\SimplyCpp\Welcome\Welcome.cpp	12
	error C2065: 'Return' : undeclared identifier	c:\SimplyCpp\Welcome\Welcome.cpp	12
	error C2143: syntax error : missing ';' before 'constant'	c:\SimplyCpp\Welcome\Welcome.cpp	12

Figure 2.33   Syntax error messages generated by the compiler.

4. **Locating the first compilation error.** Each error that the compiler finds is accompanied by the file name (`Welcome.cpp`), the line number, a description of the error and the function in which the error occurs. In this case, the compiler notified you that it found errors in lines 10 and 12.

The error in line 10 occurs because each string must begin and end with a double quote character. After you inserted a backslash before the second double quote character, the compiler read the escape sequence \", indicating that a double quote is to be inserted as a character in the string that is displayed. Accordingly, the color of the text in the remainder of line 10 changed to cyan (Fig. 2.34)—indicating the string has not been terminated. Because the string was not terminated after the second double quote, the compiler did not recognize the semicolon in line 10 and issued an error message when it encountered a newline character at the end of the line. Note that, because the compiler may generate multiple error messages for a single error, fixing one error often eliminates many error messages. The compiler also issued an error for a missing semicolon when it reached line 12.

Syntax error creates unterminated string (displayed in cyan)

Figure 2.34   Syntax error causes remainder of line 10 be displayed in cyan.

(cont.)

> Note that C++ compilers read your source code file in order from the first line to the last line. As a result, it is common for the compiler to detect a statement containing a compilation error only after beginning to read the next statement. In this case, the compiler issued a message indicating a missing semicolon in line 12 (error C2146 of Fig. 2.33), but the semicolon is actually missing in line 10. When the compiler issues a message regarding a syntax error on a particular line, inspect your code to determine whether the line indeed contains a syntax error. If you cannot find an error on the specified line, the syntax error is probably located in a previous statement.
>
> The last two errors indicate that your program contains an undeclared identifier called `Return` in line 12. You will learn about identifiers in the next tutorial. For now, recall that C++ is case sensitive, therefore the `return` keyword must be spelled using only lowercase characters.

5. ***Fixing the compilation errors.*** Now that the compiler has indicated the location of your compilation errors, go back to the source code and correct the errors you created in *Step 2*. Recompile your application, which should now compile correctly.

6. ***Close the Visual Studio .NET IDE.***

SELF-REVIEW

1. Upon finding a syntax error in an application, the compiler will notify the user of an error by giving the user _____.
   a) the line number of the error
   b) the correct code to fix the error
   c) a brief description of the error
   d) Both a and c.

2. Syntax errors occur for many reasons, such as when a(n) _____.
   a) application terminates unexpectedly
   b) word is spelled incorrectly
   c) application produces erroneous results
   d) Both b and c.

Answers: 1) d. 2) b.

2.6 Wrap-Up

This tutorial introduced you to programming in C++. You learned how to create an application that displays a message to the user.

In creating your **Welcome** application, you learned basic components of C++ programs, such as `#include` preprocessor directives, `using` directives, function `main` and return values. You used the input/output stream header file to use predefined C++ technologies that enable you to display text. You learned that `cout` is an output stream, typically connected to the user's screen, that can be used to display text. You displayed text using a string of characters and the stream insertion operator (`<<`). You formatted your text by including the newline escape character in your string. Finally, you learned how to locate and correct syntax errors when compiling your application's source code.

In the next tutorial, you will continue learning how to use C++'s built-in input/output stream objects. In particular, you will create an application that can accept user inputs, perform arithmetic calculations with these inputs and display the result.

SKILLS SUMMARY

Compiling an Application
- In Visual Studio .NET, select **Build > Build Solution**.

Running an Application
- In Visual Studio .NET, select **Debug > Start Without Debugging**.

Creating Applications Quickly and Efficiently

■ Include C++ Standard Library files and reuse predefined classes, functions and objects, such as cout.

Displaying Text on the Screen

■ Use cout, the output stream object, followed by the stream insertion operator (<<) and the string of characters (enclosed in double quotes) to be displayed.

Inserting a Newline Character Into an Output Stream

■ Use the newline escape sequence, \n.

Inserting Comments in the Code

■ Begin the comment with two forward-slash characters (//). Then, insert text that describes what is happening in the code so you can understand the code better. A comment can be placed either on its own line or at the end of a line of code.

Locating and Fixing Syntax Errors

■ Locate syntax errors by reading the compiler output, describing the source file name and line number where syntax errors were found.

■ Understand the description of the syntax error and correct the error appropriately.

■ After fixing a syntax error, always recompile the application. The compiler might find additional errors that were not identified earlier.

KEY TERMS

 # (preprocessor operator)—An operator that must begin each statement that is processed by the C++ preprocessor.

binary operator—An operator that requires two operands.

body of a function—The group of statements contained inside a function. The body of a function begins with a left brace, {, and ends at the corresponding right brace, }.

case sensitive—A property of a programming language that distinguishes between uppercase and lowercase letters in code.

cin (the standard input stream)—An object that has the ability to retrieve keyboard input from the user.

comment—Text in a source code file that increases code readability by explaining the code. Comments are ignored by the compiler.

compilation error—An error detected by the compiler, such as a syntax error. Also called a compile-time error.

cout (the standard output stream)—An object that has the ability to display text.

cursor—The current screen-position indicator. When an application displays text, the next character is displayed at the cursor, and the cursor is advanced to the position just after the end of the character. When the user inputs text at the keyboard, the next character that is entered is typically displayed at the cursor, and the cursor is advanced to the position just after the end of the character.

debugger—Software that allows you to monitor the execution of your applications to locate and remove logic errors.

debugging—The process of locating and correcting errors in an application.

end-of-line comment—A comment that appears at the end of a line, following a statement or definition.

entry point—The location in an application's source code where execution begins. In C++, the entry point for an application is the main function.

escape character (\)—The character that begins an escape sequence.

escape sequence—The combination of an escape character and the character that immediately follows. An escape sequence temporarily changes the way a stream of characters is processed, causing characters such as tabs, newlines and carriage returns to be printed or causing actions such as sounding the system bell.

executable statement—A statement that performs an action, such as displaying text on the screen.

forward slash character (/)—Two consecutive forward slash characters indicate that the remainder of the line is a comment.

full-line comment—A comment that starts at the beginning of a line.

function—A program building block consisting of a name, return type, comma-separated list of parameter declarations (if any) and executable statements enclosed in curly braces.

input/output stream header file `<iostream>`—A file that provides basic stream input/output services. This file must be included to use objects such as `cout` and `cin`.

integrated Development Environment (IDE)—An application that allows a programmer to create, run and debug applications.

keyword—A word that is reserved for use by C++ and cannot be used to create your own identifiers. See also "reserved word."

left brace ({)—A symbol that indicates the beginning of a block of code, such as a function body.

left operand—An expression that appears on the left side of a binary operator.

literal—A sequence of characters within double quotes.

logic error—An error that does not prevent your application from compiling successfully, but does cause your application to produce erroneous results.

main—The function that every C++ application executes first when started. Every C++ application must have exactly one `main` function.

newline character (/n)—A character that moves the cursor to the beginning of the next line. This character can be used to prepare the application to display text on the next line or to insert blank lines into an output stream (when several newlines appear back to back).

operand—An expression that is combined with an operator (and possibly other expressions) to perform a task (such as addition, comparison or stream insertion).

operator—A symbol (or pair of symbols) that causes an application to perform a task by applying the operator to its operands.

preprocessor—A program that performs manipulations on the application's source code file(s), such as including C++ Standard Library files, before the compiler's translation phase begins.

preprocessor directive—A message to the compiler's preprocessor. Preprocessor directives can be used, for example, to include source code from other files. This enables you to incorporate functions and services provided by those files in your applications.

project—The group of files containing source code and any instructions for building your application.

reserved word—A word that is reserved for use by C++ and cannot be used to create your own identifiers. See also "keyword."

right brace(})—A symbol that indicates the end of a block of code, such as a function body.

right operand—An expression that appears on the right side of a binary operator.

semicolon (;)—The character used to indicate the end of a C++ statement.

solution—A file containing one or more projects.

solution file—A file with the `.sln` extension. These files are created by Visual Studio .NET when you create a solution, and they store information about your solution.

statement—Code that instructs the computer to perform a task. Most statements end with a semicolon (;) character. Most applications consist of many statements.

stream insertion operator (<<)—The operator that sends characters to a stream object such as `cout`. The stream object must be specified to the left of the operator; the characters must be placed to the right of the operator.

stream of characters—A sequence of characters passed to a stream object such as `cout` or input from a stream object such as `cin`.

string—A sequence of characters.

string constant—A sequence of characters within double quotes.

string literal—A sequence of characters within double quotes.

syntax error—An compilation error that occurs when code violates the grammatical rules of a programming language. Syntax errors are detected by the compiler.

using directive—A directive that notifies the compiler that the application will use services from the specified namespace.

Visual C++ project file—A file with the .vcproj extension. These files are created by Visual Studio .NET, and they store information regarding your project.

whitespace character—A newline, space or tab character. Whitespace characters generally are ignored by the compiler.

USER INTERFACE DESIGN GUIDELINES

Displaying Text

■ Displayed text should convey meaningful messages to the user. Text that prompts a user for input should clearly indicate the required input format. Text that displays results should describe the result.

C++ LIBRARY REFERENCE

`iostream` Provides access to the basic services required for all stream-I/O operations.

■ *Objects*

cout—Displays text on the screen. Text is displayed using the stream insertion operator (<<).

MULTIPLE-CHOICE QUESTIONS

2.1 Use the _____ object to display text on the screen.

    a) `screen`   b) `cout`

    c) `output`   d) `iostream`

2.2 To compile an application in Visual Studio .NET, select _____.

    a) **File > Compile Solution**   b) **Build > Compile Solution**

    c) **Build > Build Solution**   d) **Compile > Build Solution**

2.3 _____ must begin the body of every function.

    a) A newline character   b) The `int` keyword

    c) A `return` statement   d) A left brace ({)

2.4 Syntax errors in a C++ application _____.

    a) can cause subtle errors when the application runs   b) prevent the application from compiling correctly

    c) are ignored by the compiler   d) are detected after the application has been compiled

2.5 Files with a .obj extension contain _____.

    a) source code   b) an executable image

    c) machine code   d) preprocessor information

2.6 Operator << is the _____ operator.

    a) stream insertion   b) stream extraction

    c) display   d) `cout`

2.7 The _____ escape sequence sounds the system bell.

    a) \b   b) \a

    c) \sb   d) None of the above.

2.8 To run an application using Visual Studio .NET, select _____.

    a) **Run > Start Without Debugging**   b) **Build > Start**

    c) **Debug > Start Without Debugging**   d) **Run > Start**

2.9 A _____ is an example of whitespace character.

    a) tab   b) space

    c) newline   d) All of the above.

2.10 The _____ escape sequence places the cursor at the beginning of the current line.

a) \n

b) \r

c) \t

d) \b

EXERCISES

2.11 *(Alarm Application)* Many universities provide computer networks that enable multiple users to access information on the local area network (LAN) and on the Internet. To increase security, the system will log off a user if that user has been inactive for a significant period of time. Suppose the system administrator wants the system to warn the user before logging off. In this exercise, you will create an application that displays a message to the user and sounds the system bell three times to indicate that the user will be logged off in one minute (Fig. 2.35).

Figure 2.35 Alarm application output for completed application.

a) *Copying the template to your working directory.* Copy the directory `C:\Examples\Tutorial02\Exercises\Alarm` to your `C:\SimplyCpp` directory. If you are not using Visual Studio .NET, skip to *Step c.*

b) *Creating a new project.* If you have not already done so, start Visual Studio .NET. To create a new project, select **File > New > Project...**, causing the **New Project** dialog to display. Click the **Visual C++ Projects** folder in the **Project Types:** pane to display the list of Visual C++ .NET project types in the **Templates:** pane. Select **Win32 Console Project** from the **Templates:** pane. In the **Win32 Application Wizard**, click the **Application Settings** link, select the **Empty project** check box, then click **Finish**. Name the project `Alarm`. Save this project in your `SimplyCpp` directory. Then add the existing source code file, `Alarm.cpp`, which is located in the `C:\SimplyCpp\Alarm` directory.

c) *Opening the template file.* Open the `Alarm.cpp` file in your text editor or IDE.

d) *Displaying a message to the user.* Before sounding the system bell, you should display a warning message to the user. After line 9 in the template code, insert a statement to display a newline and the message, `"Warning: You have been inactive for over 30 minutes."`. Do not terminate the statement yet. Insert a second stream insertion operator on the next line of your application's source code to display the text, `"You will be logged out in one minute."` This text should be displayed on a new line, using the newline escape sequence. Two newlines should be inserted after this message is displayed. Remember to terminate the second line of your statement with a semicolon.

e) *Sounding the system bell.* To sound the system bell, display a string that consists of three alert escape sequences.

f) *Save your modified source code file.*

g) *Compile the completed application.*

h) *Running the completed application.* Select **Debug > Start Without Debugging** to run your application. Compare the program output to the one shown in Fig. 2.35 to ensure that you displayed the message to the user correctly. [*Note:* Depending on the system you are using, you may not hear the computer's system bell or the three bells may sound so quickly that you may hear the system bell sound only once when the application runs.]

i) *Close the Command Prompt window.*

j) *Close your text editor or IDE.*

2.12 *(Table of Powers Application)* Throughout this book, you will be asked to create C++ applications that display tables of values. In this exercise, you will use the tab and newline escape sequences to display a table of the squares and cubes of the numbers from zero to 5 (Fig. 2.36). In a later tutorial, you will modify the application to calculate the values displayed in Fig. 2.36.

```
 "c:\SimplyCpp\TableOfPowers\Debug\TableOfPowers.exe"

Number  Square  Cube
0       0       0
1       1       1
2       4       8
3       9       27
4       16      64
5       25      125

Press any key to continue_
```

Figure 2.36 Table of Powers application output.

a) ***Copying the template to your working directory.*** Copy the directory C:\Examples\ Tutorial02\Exercises\TableOfPowers to your C:\SimplyCpp directory. If you are not using Visual Studio .NET, skip to *Step c.*

b) ***Creating a new project.*** If you have not already done so, start Visual Studio .NET. To create a new project, select **File > New > Project...**, causing the **New Project** dialog to display. Click the **Visual C++ Projects** folder in the **Project Types:** pane to display the list of Visual C++ .NET project types in the **Templates:** pane. Select **Win32 Console Project** from the **Templates:** pane. In the **Win32 Application Wizard**, click the **Application Settings** link, select the **Empty project** check box, then click **Finish**. Name the project TableOfPowers. Save this project in your SimplyCpp directory. Then add the existing source code file, TableOfPowers.cpp, which is located in the C:\SimplyCpp\TableOfPowers directory.

c) ***Opening the template file.*** Open the TableOfPowers.cpp file in your text editor.

d) ***Displaying the table header.*** When displaying a table of values, each column of values typically is separated by at least one tab character. You should always begin the table with a header, which is a line of text that labels each column, so that the user can identify the contents of each column. In this application, the first column will display a number, the second column will display its square and the third column will display its cube. Display a line of text containing the words number, square and cube, separated by tab escape sequences. Terminate the output string with a newline escape sequence.

e) ***Displaying the values.*** For the first row of values, display three zeros, each separated by tab escape sequences. Terminate the output string with a newline escape sequence. For the next five rows, use the values in Fig. 2.36, separating each value by a tab escape sequence and ending each output string with a newline escape sequence. Add a second newline escape sequence to the last output string.

f) ***Save your modified source code file.***

g) ***Compile the completed application.***

h) ***Running the completed application.*** Select **Debug > Start Without Debugging** to run your application. Compare the output of your completed **Table of Powers** application with the output shown in Fig. 2.36 to ensure that you wrote your application correctly.

i) ***Close the Command Prompt window.***

j) ***Close your text editor or IDE.***

2.13 *(Restaurant Survey Application)* In the next tutorial, you will learn how to create applications that retrieve input that the user types at the keyboard. To improve ease of use, many C++ applications include a numbered list of options, called a menu, from which users choose. Instead of typing the name of an option, the user simply enters the option's number. For example, many restaurants allow you to place an order using a number corresponding to a particular menu item. In this exercise, you display a menu of options for a restaurant (Fig. 2.37). In later tutorials, you will create applications that respond to the user's selection.

Figure 2.37 Restaurant Survey application output.

a) *Copying the template to your working directory.* Copy the directory C:\Examples\ Tutorial02\Exercises\RestaurantSurvey to your C:\SimplyCpp directory. If you are not using Visual Studio .NET, skip to *Step c.*

b) *Creating a new project.* If you have not already done so, start Visual Studio .NET. To create a new project, select **File > New > Project...**, causing the **New Project** dialog to display. Click the **Visual C++ Projects** folder in the **Project Types:** pane to display the list of Visual C++ .NET project types in the **Templates:** pane. Select **Win32 Console Project** from the **Templates:** pane. In the **Win32 Application Wizard**, click the **Application Settings** link, select the **Empty project** check box, then click **Finish**. Name the project RestaurantSurvey. Save this project in your SimplyCpp directory. Then add the existing source code file, RestaurantSurvey.cpp, which is located in the C:\SimplyCpp\RestaurantSurvey directory.

c) *Opening the template file.* Open the RestaurantSurvey.cpp file in your text editor or IDE.

d) *Displaying the menu header.* Before displaying the menu, you should display a message instructing the user to select one of the options that will follow. Use a cout statement to display a blank line followed by the message, "Select a menu option", followed by a newline escape sequence.

e) *Displaying the first menu option.* Each menu item should consist of the option's number and a description of the option. The options should be presented in increasing numerical order. In this case, the first option is a hamburger. Therefore, display the message "1 - Hamburger" and insert a newline escape sequence to terminate the line.

f) *Displaying the remaining menu options.* The second menu option is "Hot dog." Display the option number followed by its description, as you did in *Step e.* Similarly, display the third option, "Salad." Finally, display the fourth option, which is "Exit." Each option should appear on its own line. Finally, on a new line, display a question mark (?), followed by a space. This is where the user will type input to make a selection. In the next tutorial, you will learn how to read the user's response from the keyboard.

g) *Save your modified source code file.*

h) *Compile the completed application.*

i) *Running the completed application.* Select **Debug > Start Without Debugging** to run your application. Compare the output of your completed **Restaurant Survey** application with the output shown in Fig. 2.37 to ensure that you wrote your application correctly.

j) *Close the* **Command Prompt** *window.*

What does this code do? ▶ **2.14** What does the following code do? In particular, what does it display?

```
1   // Exercise 2.14: WDTCD.cpp
2   // What does this code do?
3   #include <iostream> // required to perform C++ stream I/O
4
5   using namespace std; // for accessing C++ Standard Library members
6
7   // function main begins program execution
```

```
 8   int main()
 9   {
10      cout << "\n  *\n ***\n*****\n ***\n  *\n\n";
11
12      return 0; // indicate that program ended successfully
13
14   } // end function main
```

What's wrong with this code? ▶ **2.15** The following code segment should display a table listing an item for sale in the first column and the item's price in the second column (Fig. 2.38).

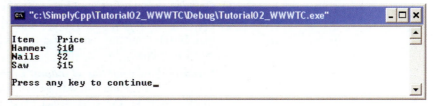

Figure 2.38 Correct application output.

Find the error(s) in the following code:

```
 1   // Exercise 2.15: WWWTC
 2   // This application displays prices for certain items
 3   #include <iostream> // required to perform C++ stream I/O
 4
 5   using namespace std; // for accessing C++ Standard Library members
 6
 7   // function main begins program execution
 8   int main()
 9   {
10      cout << "Item\tPrice";
11      cout << "Hammer\t$10";
12      cout << "Nails\t$2";
13      cout << "Saw\t$15";
14
15      return 0; // indicate that program ended successfully
16
17   } // end function main
```

Programming Challenge ▶ **2.16** *(Enhanced Welcome Application)* The **Welcome** application you created in this tutorial displayed plain text. A series of symbols (such as asterisks) can be used to display simple graphics. In this application, you will modify the **Welcome** application to display a message containing a border, centered text and the word "C++" displayed using asterisks (Fig. 2.39).

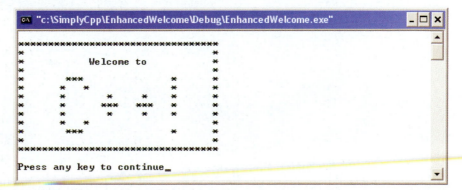

Figure 2.39 Enhanced **Welcome** application output.

a) ***Copying the template to your working directory.*** Copy the directory `C:\Examples\Tutorial02\Exercises\EnhancedWelcome` to your `C:\SimplyCpp` directory. If you are not using Visual Studio .NET, skip to *Step c.*

b) ***Creating a new project.*** If you have not already done so, start Visual Studio .NET. To create a new project, select **File > New > Project...**, causing the **New Project** dialog to display. Click the **Visual C++ Projects** folder in the **Project Types:** pane to display the list of Visual C++ .NET project types in the **Templates:** pane. Select **Win32 Console Project** from the **Templates:** pane. In the **Win32 Application Wizard**, click the **Application Settings** link, select the **Empty project** check box, then click **Finish**. Name the project `EnhancedWelcome`. Save this project in your `SimplyCpp` directory. Then add the existing source code file, `Welcome.cpp`, which is located in the `C:\SimplyCpp\EnhancedWelcome` directory.

c) ***Opening the template file.*** Open the `Welcome.cpp` file in your text editor or IDE.

d) ***Creating the top border.*** The first line of output should be the top border for your text. In the template code, insert a `cout` statement that displays a newline, then 34 asterisks followed by a newline.

e) ***Creating the second line of output.*** To create the left and right borders, each output line should begin and end with an asterisk. Also, each output line must be exactly 34 characters wide. The second line of output does not contain any text, so the line should output an asterisk, followed by 32 spaces, an asterisk and a newline escape sequence (in that order).

f) ***Displaying "Welcome to."*** To center the text "Welcome to," display 11 spaces after the first asterisk before displaying "Welcome to." Remember to insert a newline at the end of every line you display.

g) ***Displaying "C++"*** Display a line containing only the left and right borders. Then use the next seven lines of output to create the "C++" out of asterisks, as shown in Fig. 2.39. Then, display a line containing only the left and right borders. Display the bottom border, which should appear exactly as the top border from *Step d*. Finally, display two newlines.

h) ***Save your modified source code file.***

i) ***Compile the completed application.***

j) ***Running the completed application.*** Select **Debug > Start Without Debugging** to run your application. Compare the output of your completed Welcome application with the output shown in Fig. 2.39 to ensure that you wrote your application correctly.

k) ***Close the Command Prompt window.***

l) ***Close your text editor or IDE.***

m) ***(Optional) Using a single statement to display the welcome message.*** Try displaying the entire welcome message using a single statement. Note that your statement may continue on multiple lines of source code when you use multiple stream insertion operators.

Objectives

In this tutorial, you will learn to:
- Define variables.
- Enable your applications to accept input that the user types at the keyboard.
- Use arithmetic operators.
- Use `cin` to store user input in an `int`.
- Apply basic memory concepts using variables.
- Use the precedence rules of arithmetic operators.
- Set breakpoints to debug applications.

Outline

Inventory Application

Introducing Variables, Input, Memory Concepts and Arithmetic

This tutorial introduces fundamentals of C++ programming to create an application with which users can interact. You will learn programming concepts as you add functionality (with C++ code) to the **Inventory** application. The term **functionality** describes the tasks an application can perform. In this tutorial, you will examine **stream input**, which enables your application to read data that a user types at the keyboard. You will also learn how C++ stores and manipulates information to produce meaningful results, such as calculating and displaying the product of two numbers.

3.1 Test-Driving the Inventory Application

In this tutorial, you will create an **Inventory** application that calculates the number of textbooks received at a college bookstore. This application must meet the following requirements:

Application Requirements

A college bookstore receives cartons of textbooks. In a shipment, each carton contains the same number of textbooks. The inventory manager wants to use a computer to calculate the total number of textbooks arriving at the bookstore for each shipment, from the number of cartons and the number of textbooks in each carton. The inventory manager will enter the number of cartons received and the fixed number of textbooks in each carton for each shipment; the application then will calculate the total number of textbooks in a shipment.

In the sections that follow, you will write code that makes your **Inventory** application multiply the number of cartons by the number of textbooks per carton and display the result—that is, the total number of textbooks received—using variables to perform arithmetic calculations. You will study memory concepts to help you better understand how applications run on computers. You begin by test-driving the completed application. Then, you will learn the additional C++ capabilities you will need to create your own version of this application.

***Test-Driving the
Completed Inventory
Application***

1. ***Locating the completed application.*** Open the **Command Prompt** window by selecting **Start > All Programs > Accessories > Command Prompt**. Change to your **Inventory** application directory by typing `cd C:\Examples\ Tutorial03\CompletedApplication\Inventory`, then pressing *Enter*. [*Note:* From this point forward, we will no longer tell you to press *Enter* after each command you type in the **Command Prompt** window.]

2. ***Running the Inventory application.*** Type `Inventory` in the **Command Prompt** window to run the application. Enter 3 at the **Enter the number of cartons in shipment:** prompt and enter 15 at the **Enter the number of items per carton:** prompt (Fig. 3.1).

```
Command Prompt - Inventory                                      _ □ ×

C:\Examples\Tutorial03\CompletedApplication\Inventory>Inventory

Enter the number of cartons in shipment: 3
Enter the number of items per carton: 15_
```

Figure 3.1   **Inventory** application with quantities entered.

3. ***Calculating the total number of items received.*** After you enter 15 at the **Enter items per carton:** prompt, the application multiplies the two numbers you entered and displays 45 as the result (Fig. 3.2).

```
Command Prompt                                                  _ □ ×

C:\Examples\Tutorial03\CompletedApplication\Inventory>Inventory

Enter the number of cartons in shipment: 3
Enter the number of items per carton: 15

The total number of items is: 45

C:\Examples\Tutorial03\CompletedApplication\Inventory>_
```

Result of calculation ⎯⎯⎯⎯⎯⎯

Figure 3.2   Calculating the total in the **Inventory** application.

4. ***Close the Command Prompt window.***

3.2 Variables

A **variable** is an area in the computer's memory that holds data, such as numbers, dates, and times. Each variable used in C++ corresponds to exactly one type of information. For example, a variable that stores a number cannot be used to store a name (or any other text).

In C++, all variables must be **defined** before they are used in an application. All variable **definitions** include the variable's **type**, which specifies the kind of data a variable stores, and an optional **initialization value**, which specifies the beginning value stored in the variable. In this tutorial, you study the **int** type, which you use to define **integer** variables—that is, variables whose values must be whole numbers.

In the following box, you will learn to define variables. A variable name must be a valid **identifier**, which is a sequence of characters consisting of letters, digits and underscores (_). Identifiers cannot begin with a digit and cannot contain spaces. Examples of valid identifiers are `Welcome1`, `label_Value`, `outputString` and `_total`. The sequence of characters `7welcome` is not a valid identifier because it begins with a digit, and `input field` is not a valid identifier because it contains a space. Recall that C++ is case sensitive—that is, uppercase and lowercase letters are distinct—so `a1` and `A1` are different valid identifiers.

**Good Programming
Practice**

Use only letters and digits in your variable names.

Using Variables in the Inventory Application

1. *Copying the template to your working directory.* Copy the C:\Examples\ Tutorial03\TemplateApplication\Inventory directory to your C:\SimplyCpp directory.

2. *Opening the Inventory application's solution file.* If you are using Visual Studio .NET, browse to your C:\SimplyCpp\Inventory directory and double click the **Inventory** application's solution file, Inventory.sln, to open it. Otherwise, skip to the next step. [*Note:* In the remaining tutorials, we will simply ask you to open the application's source code file. If you are using Visual Studio .NET, you should open the solution file, then open the source code file from the **Solution Explorer.**]

3. *Opening the Inventory application's template source code file.* Open the template source code file Inventory.cpp.

4. *Adding variable definitions to function main.* Add lines 11–14 of Fig. 3.3 to the main function. Lines 12–14 are definitions, which begin with each variable's type—in this case, int. The int keyword indicates that the variable being defined will store only integer values (whole numbers such as 919, 0 and –11). The words cartons, items and result are the variables' names.

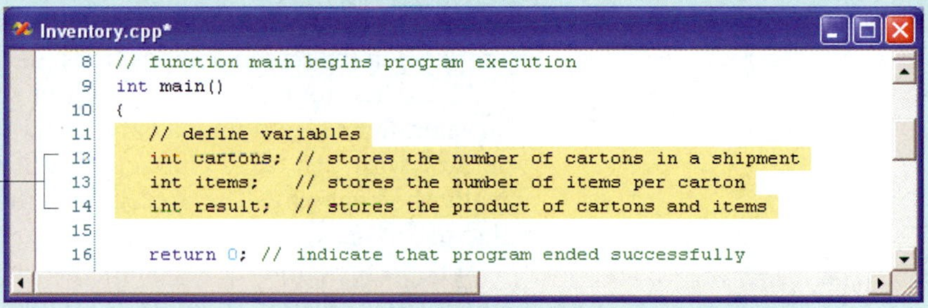

Variable definitions ——

```
 8    // function main begins program execution
 9    int main()
10    {
11        // define variables
12        int cartons; // stores the number of cartons in a shipment
13        int items;   // stores the number of items per carton
14        int result;  // stores the product of cartons and items
15
16        return 0; // indicate that program ended successfully
```

Figure 3.3 Defining variables in the main function.

5. *Save the application.*

You just learned that variables of the int type are whole numbers. Variables of the **double** type store numbers with a decimal point. These are called **floating-point numbers**, and they hold values such as 2.3456, 0.0 and –845.4680. Variables of the double type can hold much larger (and much smaller) values than variables of the int type. Types already defined in C++, such as int, are known as **primitive types**. Primitive type names are also keywords. The 14 primitive types are listed in Fig. 3.4. Recall that keywords are reserved for use by C++, so keywords cannot be used as identifiers. (A complete list of C++ keywords is presented in Appendix F.)

Primitive types				
bool	float	long int	unsigned char	unsigned short int
char	int	signed char	unsigned int	void
double	long double	short int	unsigned long int	

Note that long int is synonymous with long; short int is synonymous with short.

Figure 3.4 C++ primitive types.

SELF-REVIEW

1. The name of a variable must be a _____.

    a) keyword   b) valid identifier

    c) Both a and b.   d) Neither a nor b.

2. Types already defined in C++, such as `int`, are known as _____ types.
    a) built-up   b) existing
    c) defined   d) primitive

Answers: 1) b. 2) d.

3.3 Performing Stream Input Using `cin`

In Section 2.4, you learned that C++ applications use `cin`, the input stream object, to read data that the user enters at the keyboard. In this section, you will use `cin` and the **stream extraction operator, >>**, to obtain two integers typed by a user at the keyboard. Then you will write code so that your application computes the product of these values and outputs the result using `cout`.

The code

```
int integer1;                   // define an integer variable
cout << "Enter first integer: "; // prompt user for an integer
cin >> integer1;                // read an integer into a variable
```

prompts the user to enter the first integer, then uses `cin` to read an `int` value typed at the keyboard and place it in the `integer1` variable. The first statement defines `int` variable `integer1`. The second statement uses `cout` to print the string `Enter first integer:` on the screen and positions the cursor after the space following the colon.

The third statement uses the input stream object, `cin`, and the stream extraction operator, `>>`, to obtain a value from the keyboard. Using the stream extraction operator with `cin` takes character input from the standard input stream, which is usually the keyboard. The preceding statement is often pronounced as, "`cin` *gives* a value to `integer1`" or simply "`cin` *inputs* a value *into* `integer1`."

When the computer executes the preceding statement, it waits for the user to enter a value for the `integer1` variable. The user responds by typing an integer, then pressing *Enter* to send the integer to the application. The application then assigns this number (or value) to the `integer1` variable. Any subsequent references to `integer1` in this application will use this same value.

You should be careful when using the stream extraction operator, `>>`, with an `int` operand. If the value that the user enters does not represent an integer value, an error occurs that may cause your program to produce incorrect results. You will learn how to write code that prevents such errors when we discuss exceptions in Tutorial 20.

You will now prompt the user for the number of cartons in a shipment and the number of items per carton. You will use `cin` to place the values typed by the user at the prompts into the `cartons` and `items` variables. After performing the tasks in the following box, you will complete the **Inventory** application by inserting code that calculates the product of the cartons and items and displays the result.

Reading User Input Using `cin`

Good Programming Practice

We suggest that you insert a space character after the colon or question mark, so that the user input is clearly separated from the program output. This makes your application easier to use because the user can distinguish between your application's output and the values that the user inputs at the prompt.

1. ***Opening the Inventory application's template file.*** If the template file is not already open, open it in your text editor or IDE.

2. ***Prompting the user for input and placing the value in a variable.*** Insert lines 16–18 of Fig. 3.5.

    Line 17 of Fig. 3.5 displays the string `Enter the number of cartons in shipment:`, followed by a space character. Unlike the message you displayed in the **Welcome** application in Tutorial 2, this string does not end with a newline character. Note that our convention is to end each input prompt with a colon or question mark, followed by a space, to indicate that the user should input a value. When the user types a value at the keyboard, each input character will appear on the screen at the cursor.

(cont.)

Prompt user for number of cartons

Place value entered by user in the `cartons` variable

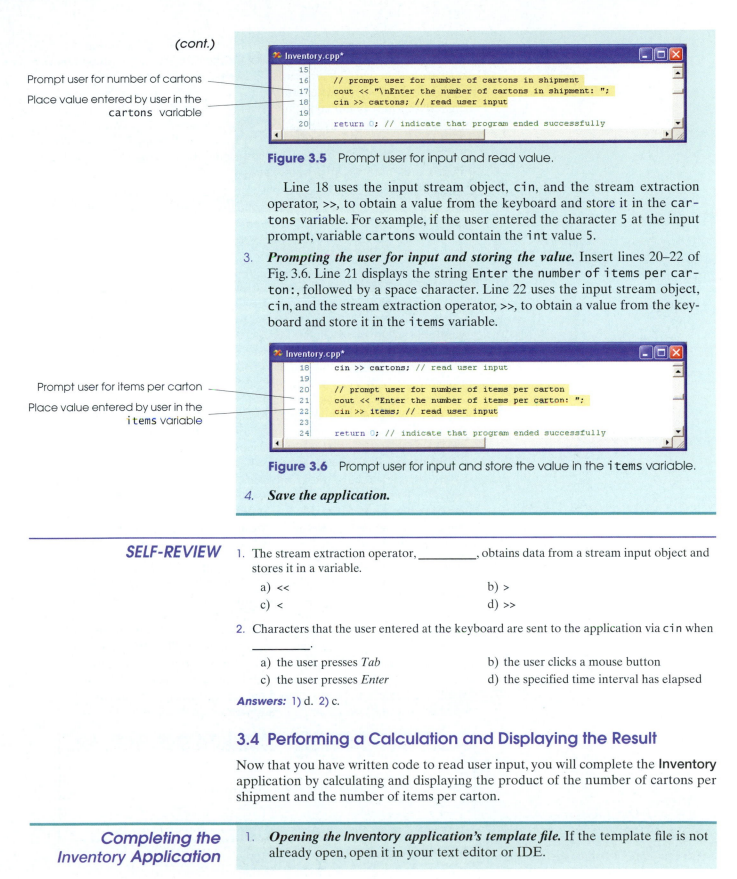

Figure 3.5   Prompt user for input and read value.

Line 18 uses the input stream object, `cin`, and the stream extraction operator, `>>`, to obtain a value from the keyboard and store it in the `cartons` variable. For example, if the user entered the character 5 at the input prompt, variable `cartons` would contain the `int` value 5.

3. ***Prompting the user for input and storing the value.*** Insert lines 20–22 of Fig. 3.6. Line 21 displays the string `Enter the number of items per carton:`, followed by a space character. Line 22 uses the input stream object, `cin`, and the stream extraction operator, `>>`, to obtain a value from the keyboard and store it in the `items` variable.

Prompt user for items per carton

Place value entered by user in the `items` variable

Figure 3.6   Prompt user for input and store the value in the `items` variable.

4. ***Save the application.***

SELF-REVIEW

1. The stream extraction operator, _____, obtains data from a stream input object and stores it in a variable.

   a) `<<`   b) `>`

   c) `<`   d) `>>`

2. Characters that the user entered at the keyboard are sent to the application via `cin` when _____.

   a) the user presses *Tab*   b) the user clicks a mouse button

   c) the user presses *Enter*   d) the specified time interval has elapsed

Answers: 1) d. 2) c.

3.4 Performing a Calculation and Displaying the Result

Now that you have written code to read user input, you will complete the **Inventory** application by calculating and displaying the product of the number of cartons per shipment and the number of items per carton.

Completing the Inventory Application

1. ***Opening the Inventory application's template file.*** If the template file is not already open, open it in your text editor or IDE.

(cont.)

2. ***Using variables to perform a calculation.*** Insert lines 24–25 of Fig. 3.7. The statement in line 25 multiplies the value of the `int` variable `cartons` by the value of the `int` variable `items` and assigns the result to the `result` variable, using the **assignment operator, =**. The statement is read as "`result` *is assigned* the value of `cartons` times `items`." The statement may also be read as "`result` *gets* the value of `cartons` times `items`." Most calculations are performed in assignment statements. When a variable appears in a calculation, the current value of that variable is used in the calculation. This calculation does not modify `cartons` or `items`.

Multiply the integer values and store the result in `result`

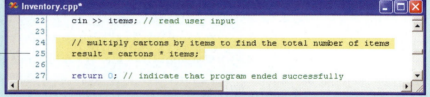

Figure 3.7 Using multiplication in the **Inventory** application.

Let's take a closer look at line 25. The expression `cartons * items` appears to the right of the = operator. In this expression, the asterisk (*) is known as the **multiplication operator**. It multiplies two numeric values and returns their product. These values can be variables, such as `cartons` and `items`, or numeric constants, such as 3 and 15.0. In algebra, you would typically represent multiplication with the middle dot operator, as in 3 · 15. However, the middle dot operator is not available on computer keyboards, so most programming languages use the asterisk character (*) instead. [*Note:* You can still perform addition, subtraction and division with the +, - and / operators, respectively.]

When line 25 executes, the expression to the right of the assignment operator (=) is evaluated first. Then, the assignment operator copies the value of the expression on its right side into the variable on its left side. If the user enters 3 and 15 at the two input prompts, line 25 assigns the value 45 (3 * 15) to the `result` variable.

3. ***Displaying the result of the calculation.*** Insert lines 27–29 of Fig. 3.8. Line 28 displays descriptive text that labels the result with the string "The total number of items is: ", then displays the value of the `result` variable. Before the statement is terminated, line 29 inserts two newline characters using **endl** (`endl` is an abbreviation for "end line")—a so-called **stream manipulator**. The `endl` manipulator outputs a newline, then "flushes the output buffer." This simply means that, on some systems where outputs accumulate in the machine until there are enough to "make it worthwhile" to display on the screen, `endl` forces any accumulated outputs to be displayed at that moment. You will learn more about stream manipulators in Tutorial 4.

Display the result

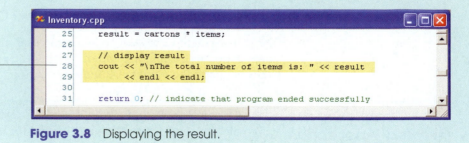

Figure 3.8 Displaying the result.

(cont.)

Note that the preceding statement outputs multiple values of different types. The stream insertion operator "knows" how to output each piece of data. Using multiple stream insertion operators (<<) in a single statement is referred to as **concatenating**, (or **chaining** or **cascading**) stream insertion operations. Thus, it is unnecessary to have multiple output statements to display multiple pieces of data, but it is allowed.

4. *Save, compile and run the application.* Figure 3.9 shows the output from running the application. When you enter data at both input prompts (use 5 and 10, respectively), the application will multiply the two numbers entered and display the result (50). [*Note:* Select **Debug > Start Without Debugging** to run your application in Visual Studio .NET.]

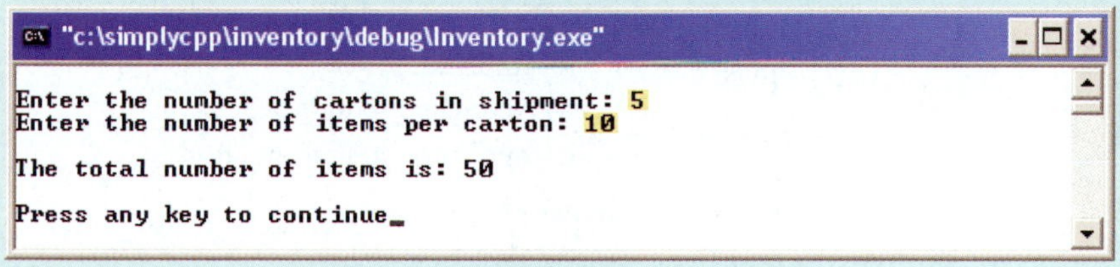

```
"c:\simplycpp\inventory\debug\Inventory.exe"                          _□×

Enter the number of cartons in shipment: 5
Enter the number of items per carton: 10

The total number of items is: 50

Press any key to continue_
```

Figure 3.9 Executing the completed **Inventory** application.

5. *Close the Command Prompt window.*

Figure 3.10 presents the source code for the **Inventory** application. The lines of code that you added, viewed or modified in this tutorial are highlighted.

```cpp
1   // Tutorial 3: Inventory.cpp
2   // Calculates the number of items in a shipment based on the number
3   // of cartons received and the number of items per carton.
4   #include <iostream> // required to perform C++ stream I/O
5
6   using namespace std; // for accessing C++ Standard Library members
7
8   // function main begins program execution
9   int main()
10  {
11      // define variables
12      int cartons; // stores the number of cartons in a shipment
13      int items;   // stores the number of items per carton
14      int result;  // stores the product of cartons and items
15
16      // prompt user for number of cartons in shipment
17      cout << "\nEnter the number of cartons in shipment: ";
18      cin >> cartons; // read user input
19
20      // prompt user for number of items per carton
21      cout << "Enter the number of items per carton: ";
22      cin >> items; // read user input
23
24      // multiply cartons by items to find the total number of items
25      result = cartons * items;
26
27      // display result
28      cout << "The total number of items is: " << result
29          << endl << endl;
30
```

Use the **int** keyword to define variables inside a function (lines 12–14)

Assigns user input to variables (lines 18, 22)

Calculate a result (line 25)

Figure 3.10 **Inventory** application code. (Part 1 of 2.)

```
31        return 0; // indicate that program ended successfully
32
33    } // end function main
```

Figure 3.10 **Inventory** application code. (Part 2 of 2.)

3.5 Memory Concepts

Variable names—such as cartons, items and result—correspond to actual locations in the computer's memory. Every variable has a **name**, **type**, **size** and **value**. In the **Inventory** application code listing in Fig. 3.10, when the stream extraction statement (line 18)

```
cin >> cartons;
```

executes, the value entered at the input prompt is converted to a value of the int type. This int value is placed into the memory location to which the name cartons has been assigned. When the user enters 12 at the **Enter cartons per shipment:** prompt, the stream extraction operator converts the user input to an int and places this int value into the cartons location, as shown in Fig. 3.11.

cartons	12

Figure 3.11 Memory location showing name and value of variable cartons.

Whenever a value is placed in a memory location, this value replaces the value previously stored in that location. The previous value is overwritten (lost). Thus, the process of writing to a memory location is said to be **destructive**.

Each primitive type in Fig. 3.4 has a size—that is, a number of bytes in memory used to store a value of that type. For instance, an int is typically stored in four bytes of memory and is capable of representing values in the range −2,147,483,648 to +2,147,483,647.

Suppose the user enters 10 at the **Enter items per carton:** prompt. Line 22 of Fig. 3.10

```
cin >> items;
```

converts the user input to an int and places this int value 10 into the items location. Memory then appears as shown in Fig. 3.12.

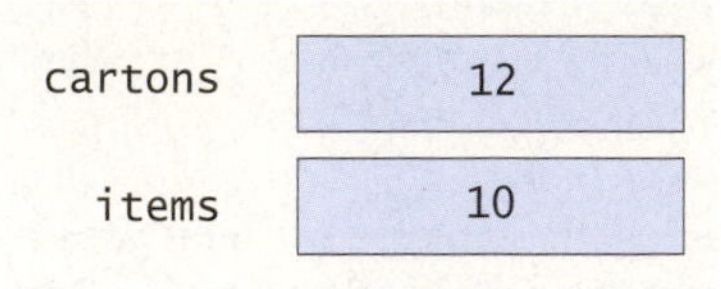

cartons	12
items	10

Figure 3.12 Memory locations after assigning values to cartons and items.

The next statement, line 25, multiplies these values and places their total into the `result` variable. The statement

```
result = cartons * items;
```

performs the multiplication and replaces (that is, overwrites) `result`'s previous value. After `result` is calculated, the memory appears as shown in Fig. 3.13. Note that the values of `cartons` and `items` appear exactly as they did before they were used in the calculation of `result`. Although these values were used when the computer performed the calculation, they were not overwritten. This illustrates that when a value is read from a memory location, the process is **nondestructive** (meaning that the value is not changed).

cartons	12
items	10
result	120

Figure 3.13   Memory locations after a multiplication operation.

1. When a value is placed into a memory location, the value _____ the previous value in that location.

   a) copies
   b) replaces
   c) adds itself to
   d) moves

2. When a value is read from memory, that value is _____.

   a) overwritten
   b) replaced with a new value
   c) moved to a new location in memory
   d) not changed

Answers: 1) b. 2) d.

3.6 Arithmetic

Most applications perform arithmetic calculations. In this tutorial, you performed the arithmetic multiplication operation by using the multiplication operator (`*`). The **arithmetic operators** are summarized in Fig. 3.14. Note the use of various special symbols that are not used in algebra. For example, the **asterisk** (`*`) indicates multiplication, the **percent sign** (`%`) represents the **remainder** (or **modulus**) **operator**, which will be explained shortly, and the **forward slash** (`/`) represents division.

All arithmetic operators in Fig. 3.14 are binary operators, each requiring two operands. For example, the expression `sum + value` contains the binary operator `+` and the two operands `sum` and `value`. C++ also provides **unary operators**, which are operators that take only one operand. For example, unary versions of plus (`+`) and minus (`–`) are provided so that programmers can write expressions such as `+9` (a positive number) and `–19` (a negative number). [*Note:* Unary plus is rarely used because numbers are positive by default.]

C++ operation	Arithmetic operator	Algebraic expression	C++ expression
Addition	+	$f + 7$	`f + 7`
Subtraction	–	$p - c$	`p - c`
Multiplication	*	bm	`b * m`

Figure 3.14   Arithmetic operators. (Part 1 of 2.)

| Division | / | x / y or $\dfrac{x}{y}$ or $x \div y$ | x / y |
| Remainder | % | $r \bmod s$ | r % s |

Figure 3.14   Arithmetic operators. (Part 2 of 2.)

Integer division takes two integer operands and yields an integer quotient. For example, the expression 7 / 4 evaluates to 1, and the expression 17 / 5 evaluates to 3. Note that any fractional part of the integer division result is discarded (this is called **truncating**)—no rounding occurs. When floating-point numbers (numbers with decimal points) are used with the division operator, the result is a floating-point number. For example, the expression 7.0 / 4.0 evaluates to 1.75 and the expression 17.0 / 5.0 evaluates to 3.4.

The remainder operator, %, yields the remainder after division. For example, the expression x % y yields the remainder after x is divided by y. Thus, 7 % 4 yields 3, and 17 % 5 yields 2. This operator can be used only with integer operands. The remainder operator can be applied to several interesting problems, such as discovering whether one number is a multiple of another. For example, if a and b are numbers, a % b yields 0 if a is a multiple of b. 8 % 3 yields 2, so 8 is not a multiple of 3. But 8 % 2 and 8 % 4 each yield 0, because 8 is a multiple of both 2 and 4.

Arithmetic expressions in C++ must be written in **straight-line form** so that you can type them into a computer. For example, the division of 7.1 by 4.3 is not written

$$\frac{7.1}{4.3}$$

but in straight-line form, as 7.1 / 4.3.

Parentheses are used in C++ expressions in the same manner as in algebraic expressions. For example, to multiply a times the quantity $b + c$, you write

```
a * ( b + c )
```

C++ applies the operators in arithmetic expressions in a precise sequence determined by its **rules of operator precedence,** which are generally the same as those followed in algebra. These rules enable C++ to apply operators in the correct order. Figure 3.15 lists these rules in order.

Let's consider several expressions in light of the rules of operator precedence. Each example lists an algebraic expression and its C++ equivalent.

Rules of operator precedence

1. *Parentheses are applied first*. If an expression contains nested parentheses, the innermost pair is evaluated first. If there are several pairs of parentheses "on the same level" (that is, not nested), they are evaluated left to right.

2. *Unary plus (+) and minus (–) are applied next*. If an expression contains several unary plus and minus operators, these operators are applied from right to left.

3. *Multiplication (*), division (/) and remainder (%) are applied next*. If an expression contains several multiplication, division and remainder operations, these operators are applied from left to right.

4. *Addition (+) and subtraction (–) are applied next*. If an expression contains several addition and subtraction operations, these operators are applied from left to right.

4. *Assignment (=) is applied last*. This operator has the lowest precedence so far. If an expression contains several assignment operators, these operators are applied from right to left.

Figure 3.15   Rules of operator precedence.

The following calculates the average of three numbers:

Algebra: $m = \dfrac{(a + b + c)}{3}$

C++:   m = (a + b + c) / 3

As in algebra, parentheses can be used to group expressions for evaluation purposes. The parentheses in the preceding expression are required, because division has higher precedence than addition. The entire quantity (a + b + c) is to be divided by 3. If the parentheses are omitted, you obtain a + b + c / 3, which evaluates as

$$a + b + \dfrac{c}{3}$$

producing an incorrect result (this is an example of a logic error). Also note that assignment to the m variable occurs last, after the addition.

The following is the equation of a straight line:

Algebra: $y = mx + b$

C++:   y = m * x + b

No parentheses are required. The multiplication is applied first because multiplication has a higher precedence than addition. The assignment occurs last because it has a lower precedence than multiplication and addition. Note that

$$y = mx + b$$

would be a logic error, because mx in C++ is a valid name for a single variable — mx does not mean "m times x" as it does in algebra.

To develop a better understanding of the rules of operator precedence, consider how the expression $y = ax^2 + bx + c$ is evaluated:

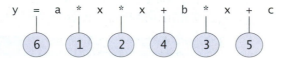

The circled numbers under the statement indicate the order in which C++ applies the operators. In C++, x^2 is represented as x * x, because there is no exponentiation operator. Also, note that the assignment operator is applied last because it has a lower precedence than any of the arithmetic operators.

As in algebra, it is acceptable to place unnecessary parentheses in an expression to make the expression easier to read — these parentheses are called **redundant parentheses**. For example, the preceding assignment statement might use redundant parentheses to emphasize terms:

    y = (a * x * x) + (b * x) + c

Good Programming Practice

The use of redundant parentheses in complex arithmetic expressions can make the expressions easier to read.

SELF-REVIEW

1. Arithmetic expressions in C++ must be written _____ to facilitate entering expressions into the computer.

   a) using parentheses   b) on multiple lines
   c) in straight-line form   d) None of the above.

2. The expression to the right of the assignment operator (=) is always evaluated _____ the assignment occurs.

   a) before   b) after
   c) at the same time   d) None of the above.

Answers: 1) c. 2) a.

3.7 Using the Debugger: Breakpoints

In Section 2.5, you learned that there are two types of errors—syntax errors and logic errors—and you learned how to eliminate syntax errors from your code.

Logic errors (also called **bugs**) do not prevent the application from compiling successfully, but do cause the application to produce erroneous results when it runs. Most C++ compiler vendors provide software called a debugger, which, as discussed in Tutorial 2, allows you to monitor the execution of your applications to locate and remove logic errors.

The debugger will be one of your most important application development tools. You begin your study of the debugger by learning about **breakpoints**, which are markers that can be set at any executable line of code. When application execution reaches a breakpoint, execution pauses, allowing you to examine the values of variables and ensure that there are no logic errors. For example, you can examine the value of a variable that stores the result of a calculation to ensure that the calculation was performed correctly. (You will learn about this in greater detail in Tutorial 4.) Note that setting a breakpoint at a line of code that is not executable (such as a comment) causes the debugger to pause execution at the next executable statement that occurs after that line. You will use breakpoints and various debugger commands to examine the values of the variables defined in the main function.

Recall that we use the Visual Studio .NET debugger in each tutorial's *Using the Debugger* section. We provide corresponding sections for other popular debuggers, such as the GNU debugger (gdb), in the appendices located at the end of the book or online at www.deitel.com.

Using the Debugger: Breakpoints

1. ***Enabling the debugger.*** The debugger is enabled by default. If it is not enabled, you have to change the settings of the *Solution Configuration* ComboBox. To do this, click the ComboBox's down arrow (Fig. 3.16) to access the *Solution Configuration* ComboBox, then select **Debug**. The IDE toolbar will display **Debug** in the *Solution Configuration* ComboBox.

Down arrow

Solution Configuration ComboBox

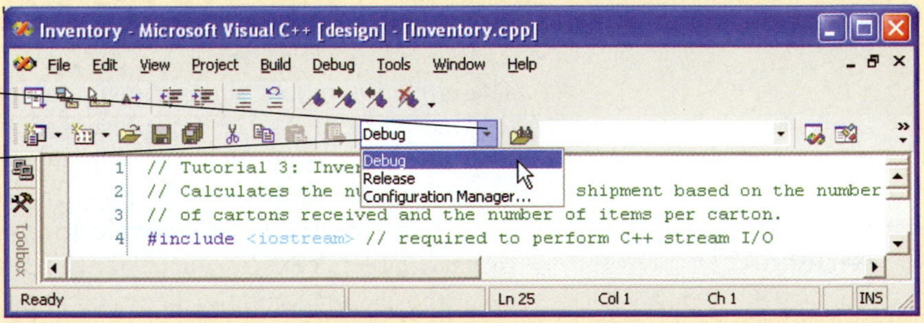

Figure 3.16 Setting *Solution Configuration* to **Debug**.

2. ***Inserting breakpoints in Visual Studio .NET.*** To insert a breakpoint in Visual Studio .NET, either click inside the **margin indicator bar** (the gray margin indicator at the left of the code window in Fig. 3.17) next to the line of code at which you wish to break or right click that line of code and select **Insert Breakpoint**. You can set as many breakpoints as necessary. Set breakpoints at lines 25 and 28 of your code. A solid maroon circle appears where you clicked, indicating that a breakpoint has been set (Fig. 3.17). When the application runs, it suspends execution at any line that contains a breakpoint. The application is said to be in **break mode** when the debugger pauses the application's execution. Breakpoints can be set before running an application, in break mode and while an application is running.

(cont.)

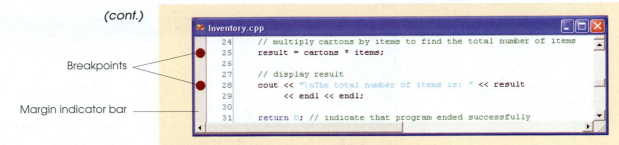

Breakpoints

Margin indicator bar

Figure 3.17   Setting two breakpoints.

3. ***Beginning the debugging process.*** After setting breakpoints in the code editor, select **Build > Build Solution** to compile the application, then select **Debug > Start** to begin the debugging process. During debugging of a C++ application, a **Command Prompt** window appears (Fig. 3.18), allowing application interaction (input and output). Enter 10 and 7 at the prompts. After you enter the second value, the title bar of the IDE will display **[break]** (Fig. 3.19), indicating that the IDE is in break mode.

```
c:\SimplyCpp\Inventory\Debug\Inventory.exe

Enter the number of cartons in shipment: 7
Enter the number of items per carton: 10_
```

Figure 3.18   **Inventory** application running.

Title bar displays **[break]**

```
Inventory - Microsoft Visual C++ [break] - [Inventory.cpp]
 File   Edit   View   Project   Build   Debug   Tools   Window   Help
```

Figure 3.19   Title bar of the IDE displaying **[break]**.

4. ***Examining application execution.*** Application execution suspends at the first breakpoint, and the IDE becomes the active window (Fig. 3.20). The **yellow arrow** to the left of line 25 indicates that this line contains the next statement to execute.

```
Inventory.cpp
  22        cin >> items; // read user input
  23
  24        // multiply cartons by items to find the total number of items
  25        result = cartons * items;
  26
  27        // display result
```

Yellow arrow

Next executable statement

Figure 3.20   Application execution suspended at the first breakpoint.

5. ***Using the Continue command to resume execution.*** To resume execution, select **Debug > Continue**. The application executes until it stops at the next breakpoint, lines 28–29. Notice that the breakpoint that you set at line 28 in *Step 2* has moved to line 29 in Fig. 3.21. This is because the debugger moves breakpoints to the end of an executable statement. Also notice that when you place your mouse pointer over the variable name `result`, the value that the variable stores is displayed in a ***Quick Info*** box (Fig. 3.21). In a sense, you are peeking inside the computer at the value of one of your variables. As you'll see, this can help you spot logic errors in your applications.

(cont.)

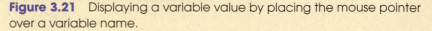

Quick Info box displays the `result` variable's value

Figure 3.21 Displaying a variable value by placing the mouse pointer over a variable name.

6. *Setting a breakpoint at the return statement.* Set a breakpoint at line 31 in the source code by clicking in the margin indicator bar to the left of line 31 (Fig. 3.22). This will prevent the application from closing immediately after displaying its result. If you do not set this breakpoint, you will not be able to view the application's output before the console window closes.

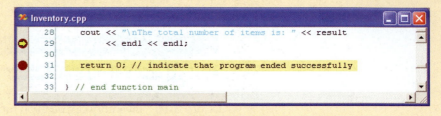

Figure 3.22 Setting a breakpoint at line 31 prevents the application from exiting immediately after displaying its result.

7. *Continuing application execution.* Use the **Debug > Continue** command to execute lines 28–29. The application displays the result of its calculation (Fig. 3.23). When there are no more breakpoints at which to suspend execution, the application will execute to completion and the **Command Prompt** window will close.

```
c:\SimplyCpp\Inventory\Debug\Inventory.exe

Enter the number of cartons in shipment: 7
Enter the number of items per carton: 10

The total number of items is: 70
```

Figure 3.23 Application output.

8. *Disabling a breakpoint.* To **disable a breakpoint**, right click a line of code on which a breakpoint has been set and select **Disable Breakpoint**. The disabled breakpoint is indicated by a hollow maroon circle (Fig. 3.24). Disabling rather than removing a breakpoint allows you to re-enable the breakpoint (by clicking inside the hollow circle) in an application. This also can be done by right clicking the line marked by the hollow maroon circle and selecting **Enable Breakpoint**.

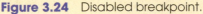

Disabled breakpoint

Figure 3.24 Disabled breakpoint.

(cont.)

> 9. ***Removing a breakpoint.*** To remove a breakpoint that you no longer need, right click a line of code on which a breakpoint has been set and select **Remove Breakpoint**. You also can remove a breakpoint by clicking the maroon circle in the margin indicator bar.
>
> 10. ***Finishing application execution.*** Select **Debug > Continue** to execute the application to completion.
>
> 11. ***Save the application.***
>
> 12. ***Close the Visual Studio .NET IDE.***

In this section, you learned how to enable the debugger and set breakpoints so that you can examine the results of code while an application is running. You also learned how to continue execution after an application suspends execution at a breakpoint and how to disable and remove breakpoints.

SELF-REVIEW

1. A breakpoint cannot enter break mode at a line containing a(n) _____.

    a) full-line comment   b) executable line of code

    c) assignment statement   d) arithmetic statement

2. When application execution suspends at a breakpoint, the next statement to be executed is the statement _____ the breakpoint.

    a) before   b) after

    c) at   d) None of the above.

Answers: 1) a. 2) c.

3.8 Web Resources

Please take a moment to visit each of these Web sites.

`www.cplusplus.com`
This site contains C++ news, tutorials and resources.

`www.cppreference.com`
This site includes a reference manual for the C++ programming language and the C++ Standard Template Library (STL).

`www.cpp-home.com`
This site contains C++ news, technical discussions, code and tutorials.

`www.cprogramming.com`
This site contains provides tutorials, tools, links and other resources for C++.

`www.research.att.com/~bs/C++.html`
This site, maintained by C++'s creator, Bjarne Stroustrup, offers C++ articles, frequently asked questions about the language and links to other C++ resources.

`msdn.microsoft.com/visualc`
This site contains resources for programmers using Visual C++ .NET.

3.9 Wrap-Up

In this tutorial, you used variables, arithmetic operators, the stream input object, `cin`, and the stream extraction operator, `>>`, to build your **Inventory** application. Your application prompted the user for two values, stored them in variables, calculated their product and displayed the result.

After learning briefly about the stream input object, `cin`, and how to store user input in variables using the stream extraction operator, you wrote code to perform a simple multiplication calculation and display the result to the user. You also used comments to improve the readability of your code.

You learned about memory concepts, including how variables are read and written. You will apply these concepts to the applications that you will build in later tutorials, which rely heavily on variables. You learned how to perform arithmetic in C++ and you studied the rules of operator precedence to help ensure that your mathematical expressions evaluate correctly. Finally, you learned how to insert, disable and remove breakpoints in the debugger using Visual Studio .NET. Breakpoints allow you to pause application execution so you can examine variable values. This capability will help you find and fix logic errors in your applications. You can find the corresponding section for other debuggers, such as the GNU debugger (gdb) in the appendices or online at www.deitel.com.

In the next tutorial, you will design an application that calculates wages using input values that can be floating-point values. You will learn pseudocode, an informal language that can help you design your applications. You will use debugger commands and windows to evaluate C++ expressions and change the values of variables in your application.

SKILLS SUMMARY

Defining a Variable

- Specify a variable type, such as `int` or `double`, for each variable.
- Use a valid identifier, which is a series of characters consisting of letters, digits and underscores, as a variable name.

Obtaining User Input from the Keyboard

- Use the stream input object, `cin`, and the stream extraction operator, `>>`. For example, the following expression places the integer typed at the keyboard in `int` variable `input`:

```
cin >> input;
```

Reading a Value from a Memory Location

- Use the variable's name on the right side of an assignment statement, such as `result = product`, or in an expression, such as `items * cartons`.

Replacing a Value in a Memory Location

- Use the variable name, followed by the assignment operator (=), followed by an expression giving the new value.
- Use an input stream (such as `cin`), followed by the stream extraction operator (>>), followed by the variable name.

Representing Positive and Negative Numbers

- Use the unary versions of plus (+) and minus (−).
- You typically can omit the unary version of plus because C++ assumes a number is positive if it is not preceded by a unary minus.

Performing Arithmetic Operations

- Write arithmetic expressions in C++ in straight-line form.
- Use the rules of operator precedence to determine the order in which operators will be applied.
- Use the + operator to perform addition.
- Use the − operator to perform subtraction.
- Use the * operator to perform multiplication.
- Use the / operator to perform division.
- Use the % operator to calculate the remainder after division.
- Use the = operator to assign the results of a calculation to a variable.
- Use parentheses, (), to force the order of evaluation to occur in the sequence you desire.

Running an Application through the Debugger

- In Visual Studio .NET, select **Debug > Start**.

Setting a Breakpoint

- Click the margin indicator bar (the gray margin indicator at the left of the code window) next to the line at which you wish to break or right click a line of code and select **Insert Breakpoint**.

Resuming Application Execution after Entering Break Mode

- Select **Debug > Continue**.

Disabling a Breakpoint

- Right click a line of code containing a breakpoint and select **Disable Breakpoint**.

Removing a Breakpoint

- Right click a line of code containing a breakpoint and select **Remove Breakpoint**.
- You also can remove a breakpoint by clicking the maroon circle in the margin indicator bar.

Enabling a Breakpoint

- Enable a disabled breakpoint by clicking inside the hollow circle in the margin indicator bar.
- You also can enable a disabled breakpoint by right clicking the line marked by the hollow maroon circle and selecting **Enable Breakpoint**.

KEY TERMS

arithmetic operators—The +, -, *, / and % operators, used for performing calculations.

assignment operator—The assignment operator, =, copies the value of the expression on its right side into the variable on its left side.

asterisk (*)—An arithmetic operator that indicates multiplication.

break mode—The debugger mode the application is in when execution stops at a breakpoint.

breakpoint—A marker that can be set in the debugger at any executable line of source code, causing the application to pause when it reaches the specified line. One reason to set a breakpoint is to be able to examine the values of variables at that point in the application's execution.

bug—A flaw in an application (sometimes called a logic error) that prevents the application from executing correctly.

concatenating stream insertion operators—Occurs when multiple stream insertion operators (<<) are used in a single statement. The operands do not have to be of the same type because the stream insertion operator "knows" how to place values of different types into the output stream. Also called chaining, or cascading, stream insertion operators.

define a variable—Specify the type and name of a variable to be used in an application.

definition of a variable—Code that specifies the name and type of a variable.

destructive operation—The process of writing to a memory location in which the previous value is overwritten or lost.

disable a breakpoint (Visual Studio .NET)—Action that prevents the debugger from breaking at a breakpoint. A disabled breakpoint is displayed as a hollow maroon circle in the margin indicator bar, enabling you to reenable the breakpoint easily by clicking inside the circle.

double type—A type that is used to store floating-point numbers.

endl stream manipulator—A stream manipulator that places a newline in the output stream and flushes the buffer so that any text in the output stream object is displayed immediately.

forward slash (/)—The arithmetic operator that indicates division.

floating-point number—A number with a decimal point, such as 2.3456, 0.0 and -845.4680.

functionality—The tasks or actions an application can execute.

identifier—A series of characters consisting of letters, digits, underscores or dollar signs used to name application units such as variables and functions.

initialization value—The beginning value of a variable.

integer—A whole number, such as 919, -11 or 0.

int type—A type that stores integer values.

margin indicator bar (Visual Studio .NET)—A margin in the IDE where breakpoints are displayed.

modulus operator (%)—An arithmetic operator that calculates the remainder after an integer division.

multiplication operator—The asterisk (*) used to multiply its two numeric operands, calculating their product as a result.

name of a variable—The identifier used in an application to access or modify a variable's value.

nondestructive operation—The process of reading from a memory location, which does not modify the value in that location.

operator precedence—See "rules of operator precedence."

primitive type—A type already defined in C++. The primitive types are `bool`, `char`, `int`, `short int`, `long int`, `float`, `double`, `long double`, `signed char`, `unsigned char`, `unsigned short int`, `unsigned int`, `unsigned long int` and `void`.

***Quick Info* box (Visual Studio .NET)**—The box that displays the value of a variable when the mouse pointer hovers over that variable.

redundant parentheses—Extra parentheses used in calculations to clarify the order in which calculations are performed. Such parentheses can be removed without affecting the results of the calculations.

remainder operator (%)—An arithmetic operator that calculates the remainder after an integer division.

rules of operator precedence—The rules that determine the precise order in which operators are applied in an expression.

size of a variable—The number of bytes required to store a value of the variable's type. For example, an `int` is typically stored in four bytes of memory and a `double` is typically stored in eight bytes.

straight-line form—The manner in which arithmetic expressions must be written so they can be typed in C++ code.

stream extraction operator (>>)—An operator that obtains data from the left operand (a stream input object, such as `cin`) and places that data in the variable to the right of the operand. When `cin` is the left operand, the stream extraction operator reads data entered at the keyboard.

stream input—Occurs when the stream of characters that the user types at the keyboard is sent to the application.

stream manipulator—An object that modifies a stream object (such as `cout`). The `endl` stream manipulator places a newline character in the output stream and flushes the stream buffer.

truncating in integer division—Any fractional part of an integer division result is discarded.

type of a variable—Specifies the kind of data that can be stored in a variable and the range of values that can be stored.

unary operator—An operator (such as unary + or unary -) with only one operand.

value of a variable—The piece of data that is stored in a variable's location in memory.

variable—A location in the computer's memory where a value can be stored for use by an application.

yellow arrow in the debugger (Visual Studio .NET)—The arrow that appears in the margin indicator bar to the left of the next statement to execute.

C++ LIBRARY REFERENCE

`iostream` Provides access to the basic services required for all stream-I/O operations.

- *Objects*

  `cin`—This object reads characters entered at the keyboard. Text is sent to the application when the user presses *Enter* and placed in a variable using the stream extraction operator, `>>`.

  `cout`—Displays text on the screen. Text is displayed using the stream insertion operator (`<<`).

- *Stream manipulator*

  `endl`—This object places a newline into the output stream and flushes the stream's buffer so that all text stored in the output stream object is displayed immediately.

USER INTERFACE DESIGN GUIDELINES

Displaying an Input Prompt

- To indicate that the user should input a value, you should end each input prompt with a colon or question mark followed by a space. The colon or question mark indicates that the program expects the user to enter a value. The space character after the colon or question mark separates user input from the program output.

MULTIPLE-CHOICE QUESTIONS

3.1 Parentheses that are added to an expression simply to make it easier to read are known as _____ parentheses.

  a) necessary   b) redundant

  c) embedded   d) nested

3.2 The _____ operator performs division.

  a) \   b) /

  c) %   d) *

3.3 Every variable has a _____.

  a) name   b) type

  c) Both of the above.   d) Neither of the above.

3.4 In C++, use _____ to force the order of evaluation of operators.

  a) parentheses   b) variables

  c) the debugger   d) memory

3.5 If an expression contains several multiplication, division and remainder operators, they are performed from _____.

  a) right to left   b) left to right

  c) Both of the above.   d) Neither of the above.

3.6 Reading a value from a variable is a _____ process.

  a) destructive   b) nondestructive

  c) overwriting   d) None of the above.

3.7 The _____ character is the multiplication operator.

  a) asterisk (*)   b) forward-slash (/)

  c) semicolon (;)   d) None of the above.

3.8 When the debugger suspends program execution at a breakpoint, the application is said to be in _____ mode.

  a) run   b) debug

  c) stop   d) break

3.9 Variables used to store integer values should be defined with the _____ keyword.

  a) `integer`   b) `int`

  c) `intVariable`   d) `Int`

3.10 The _____ feature in Visual Studio .NET allows you to "peek into the computer" and look at the value of a variable.

  a) *Value Info*   b) *Variable Info*

  c) *Quick Info*   d) *Peek Info*

EXERCISES

3.11 *(Inventory Application Enhancement)* Enhance the **Inventory** application to include a prompt at which the user can enter the number of shipments received in a week (Fig. 3.25). Assume every shipment has the same number of cartons (each of which has the same number of items), and modify the code so that the **Inventory** application uses the number of shipments in its calculation.

Figure 3.25   Enhanced **Inventory** application output.

a) *Copying the template to your working directory.* Copy the `C:\Examples\Tutorial03\Exercises\InventoryEnhancement` directory to your `C:\SimplyCpp` directory.

b) *Opening the template source code.* Open the `Inventory.cpp` file in your text editor or IDE.

c) *Defining a variable to store the number of shipments this week.* After line 14, insert a statement that defines an `int` variable `shipment`.

d) *Displaying the Enter shipments this week: input prompt.* After line 24, insert a blank line for readability and a full-line comment in line 26. Then insert a statement in line 27 that displays text prompting the user to enter the number of shipments this week. Be sure that the output string includes a space after the colon. Because the characters that the user types should appear on the same line as the prompt, do not send a newline or `endl` stream manipulator to `cout`.

e) *Retrieving user input from the keyboard.* After line 27, insert a statement that places in the `int` variable `shipment` the value that the user types at the keyboard.

f) *Calculating the result.* Modify the statement in line 31 that assigns the value of `int` variable `result`. The statement should assign the product of the number of cartons, items and shipments to `result`. Modify the full-line comment above line 31 to accurately describe the modified calculation.

g) *Save, compile and run the completed application.* Compare the output of your completed **Inventory** application with the output shown in Fig. 3.25 to ensure that you modified the application correctly.

3.12 *(Simple Encryption Application)* This application uses a simple technique to encrypt a number. Encryption is the process of modifying data so that only those intended to receive the data can undo the changes and view the original data. The user inputs the number to be encrypted—this is often called the "plain text" value. The application then multiplies the number by 7 and adds 5 to encrypt the original number—this new value is often called the "cipher text" value. The application displays the encrypted number, as shown in Fig. 3.26. A user who receives the encrypted number and who knows the encryption algorithm could determine the original number (25) by subtracting 5 from 180 (to get 175) and dividing by 7 to get 25. Reconstructing the original number from the encrypted number is called decryption.

Figure 3.26   Result of completed **Simple Encryption** application.

a) *Copying the template to your working directory.* Copy the `C:\Examples\Tutorial03\Exercises\SimpleEncryption` directory to your `C:\SimplyCpp` directory.

b) *Opening the template file.* Open the `SimpleEncryption.cpp` file in your text editor or IDE.

c) *Defining variables to store user input and program output.* Before line 10, insert a full line comment indicating that you are defining variables. Below that statement, define `int` variable `plainText`, which stores the value that the user enters. On the next line, define `int` variable `cipherText`, which will store the encrypted value.

d) *Prompting the user to enter a number and storing the value entered at the keyboard.* Insert a blank line after line 12 for readability. Line 14 should contain a full-line comment describing the following statements. Then, use lines 15–16 to prompt the user for a value using `cout` and place the value entered at the keyboard in variable `plainText` using `cin`.

e) *Calculating the encrypted number.* Insert a blank line after line 16 for readability. Use lines 18–19 to insert a comment and a statement that multiplies the number stored in variable `plainText` by 7 and adds 5, then stores the result in `int` variable `cipherText`.

f) *Displaying the encrypted number.* Insert a blank line after line 19 for readability. In line 21, display the encrypted number preceded by descriptive text that labels the value you are displaying. Before terminating the statement, be sure to place the `endl` stream manipulator in `cout`. Use line 20 for a full-line comment describing this statement.

g) *Save, compile and run the completed application.* Type 25 at the **Enter number to encrypt:** prompt. Ensure that the encrypted value 180 is displayed.

3.13 *(Temperature Conversion Application)* Write an application that converts a Celsius temperature, *C*, to its equivalent Fahrenheit temperature, *F*. Figure 3.27 displays the completed application. Use the following formula:

$$F = \frac{9}{5}C + 32$$

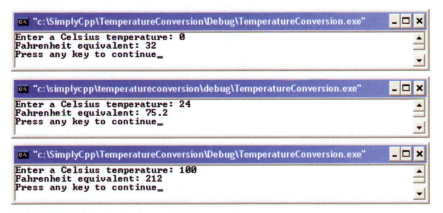

Figure 3.27 Completed **Temperature Conversion** application.

a) *Copying the template to your working directory.* Copy the `C:\Examples\Tutorial03\Exercises\TemperatureConversion` directory to your `C:\SimplyCpp` directory.

b) *Opening the template file.* Open the `TemperatureConversion.cpp` file in your text editor or IDE.

c) *Defining a variable to store user input.* After line 10, insert a full-line comment and a statement that defines `double` variable `celsius`, which will store the value that the user enters at the keyboard.

d) *Prompting the user for input and storing the value entered at the keyboard.* Insert a blank line after line 13 for readability. In line 14, include a full-line comment. In the next line, insert a statement that prompts the user for a Celsius temperature. In line 16, use `cin` to place the value entered at the keyboard in variable `celsius`.

e) *Converting the Celsius temperature to Fahrenheit and displaying the result.* Insert a statement that performs the conversion calculation and assigns the result to the `double` variable `fahrenheit` as follows:

```
double fahrenheit = 9.0 / 5.0 * celsius + 32;
```

Finally, insert a statement that displays the value of `fahrenheit` as shown in Fig. 3.27.

f) *Save, compile and run the completed application.* Type 24 at the **Enter a Celsius temperature:** prompt. Ensure that the converted value 75.2 is displayed.

What does this code do? ▶   **3.14** This code modifies values `number1`, `number2` and `result`. What are the final values?

```
1   // Exercise 3.14: WDTCD.cpp
2   // What does this code do?
3   #include <iostream> // required to perform C++ stream I/O
4
5   using namespace std; // for accessing C++ Standard Library members
6
7   // function main begins program execution
8   int main()
9   {
10     int number1;
11     int number2;
12     int result;
13
14     number1 = 5 * ( 4 + 6 );
15     number2 = 2 * 2;
16     result = number1 / number2;
17
18     cout << "\nNumber one = " << number1 << endl;
19     cout << "Number two = " << number2 << endl;
20     cout << "Result = " << result << endl;
21
22     return 0 ; // indicate the program ended correctly
23
24  } // end function main
```

What's wrong with this code? ▶   **3.15** Find the error(s) in the following code, which uses variables to perform a calculation.

```
1   // Exercise 3.15: WWWTC.cpp
2   // This code uses variables to perform several calculations
3   #include <iostream> // required to perform C++ stream I/O
4
5   using namespace std; // for accessing C++ Standard Library members
6
7   // function main begins program execution
8   int main()
9   {
10     int number1;
11     int number2;
12     int result;
13
14     number1 = ( 4 * 6 - 4 ) / ( 10 % 4 - 2 );
15     number2 = ( 16 / 3 ) - 2 * 6 + 1;
16     result = number1 - number2;
17
18     cout << "Result = " << result << endl;
19
20     return 0; // indicate that program ended correctly
21
22  } // end function main
```

Using the Debugger ▶   **3.16** *(Average Three Numbers)* You have just written an application that takes three numbers as input, stores the three numbers in variables and finds the average of the numbers. Then, the output is displayed (see Fig. 3.28, which displays the incorrect output). You soon realize, however, that the number displayed is not the average, but rather a number that does not make sense given the input. Use the debugger to help locate and remove this error.

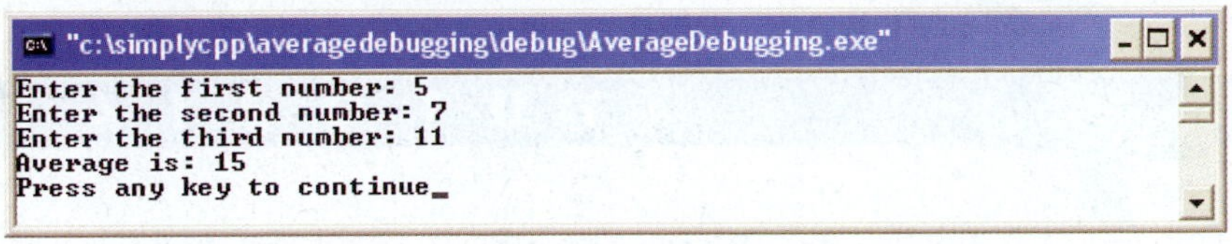

Figure 3.28 Average Three Numbers application.

a) *Copying the template to your working directory.* Copy the C:\Examples\ Tutorial03\Exercises\AverageDebugging directory to your C:\SimplyCpp directory.

b) *Running the application.* Run the **Average Three Numbers** application, located in the directory C:\SimplyCpp\AverageDebugging. Type 5, 7 and 11 at the input prompts. View the output to observe that it is incorrect. The average of these three numbers should be 7 in integer arithmetic. (Recall from Section 3.6 that integer division yields an integer result.)

c) *Compile the application for debugging.* If you are not using Visual Studio, make sure to specify the compiler option that includes debugging information.

d) *Start the debugger.* In Visual Studio .NET, this is accomplished by selecting **Debug > Run**.

e) *Setting breakpoints.* Set breakpoints in the main function at lines 28 and 31. Run the application again and use the debugger to help find the logic error(s). Type 5, 7 and 11 at the three input prompts. The program will stop executing at the first breakpoint. After inspecting variable values, continue execution until the next breakpoint. Then, inspect the values of the variables number1, number2, number3 and result.

f) *Finding and correcting the error(s).* Once you have found the logic error(s), open Average.cpp in your text editor or IDE. Modify the code in the main function so that it correctly calculates the average of three numbers and test the application again.

Programming Challenge ▶

3.17 *(Digit Extraction)* Complete an application that allows the user to input a five-digit number. Your application should then separate the number into its individual digits and display on a separate line each digit, preceded by descriptive text identifying the digit (Fig. 3.29).

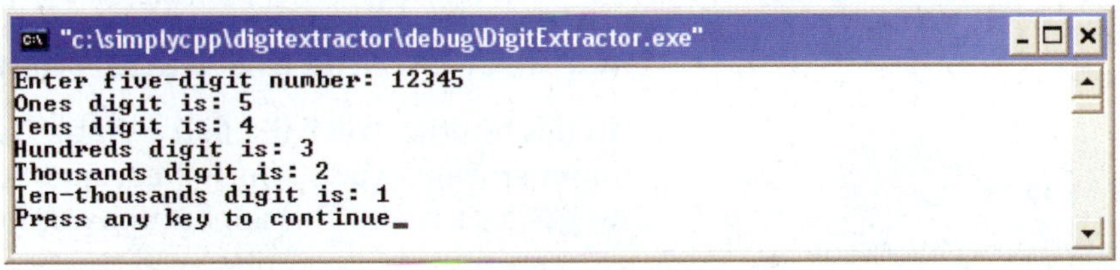

Figure 3.29 Digit Extractor application output.

a) *Copying the template to your working directory.* Copy the C:\Examples\Tutorial03\Exercises\DigitExtractor directory to your C:\SimplyCpp directory.

b) *Defining a variable to store user input.* All the code you need to write should go inside the main function, which is defined in lines 8–12 of the template file DigitExtractor.cpp. Start writing your code after line 9 in the file. Define a variable to store user input, including appropriate comments.

c) *Prompting the user for and storing a number.* Prompt the user for a number and use cin to place the value in the variable you defined in the preceding step.

d) *Display each digit separately.* [*Hint:* You can use the % operator to extract the ones digit from a number. For instance, 12345 % 10 is 5. You can use division (/) to "peel off" digits from a number. For instance, 12345 / 10 is 1234. This allows you to treat the 4 in 12345 as a ones digit. Now you can isolate the 4 by using the % operator. Apply this technique to the rest of the digits.]

e) *Save, compile and run the completed application.* Type 12345 at the **Enter five-digit number:** prompt. Ensure that the output appears as shown in Fig. 3.29.

4 TUTORIAL

Objectives

In this tutorial, you will learn to:
- Use basic problem-solving techniques.
- Use control statements.
- Use pseudocode as an application development tool.
- Use the `if` and `if...else` selection statements to choose between alternative actions.
- Use the assignment operators.
- Define constants to contain values that do not change as an application executes.
- Use the debugger's **Watch** window to evaluate expressions.
- Use the debugger's **Locals** window to change variable values during program execution.

Outline

Wage Calculator Application

Introducing Algorithms, Pseudocode and Program Control

Before you write an application, it is essential to have a thorough understanding of the problem you need to solve. This will help you carefully plan your approach to finding a solution. When writing an application, it is equally important to recognize the types of building blocks that are available and to use proven application-construction principles. In this tutorial, you will learn the theory and principles of **structured programming**. Structured programming is a technique for organizing program control to help you develop applications that are easy to understand, debug and modify. The techniques presented are applicable to most high-level languages, including C++.

4.1 Test-Driving the Wage Calculator Application

In this tutorial, you will build a **Wage Calculator** application that enables you to input an employee's hourly wage and hours worked to calculate the employee's wages for a week. This application must meet the following requirements:

Application Requirements

A payroll company calculates the gross earnings per week of employees. Employees' weekly salaries are based on the number of hours they work and their hourly wages. Create an application that accepts this information and calculates the employee's total (gross) earnings. The application assumes a standard work week of 40 hours. The wages for 40 or fewer hours are calculated by multiplying the employee's hourly salary by the number of hours worked. Any time worked over 40 hours in a week is considered "overtime" and earns time and a half. Salary for time and a half is calculated by multiplying the employee's hourly wage by 1.5 and multiplying the result of that calculation by the number of overtime hours worked. The total overtime earned is added to the user's gross earnings for the regular 40 hours of work to calculate the total earnings for that week.

This application calculates gross wages from an employee's hourly wage and hours worked per week. If an employee has worked 40 or fewer hours, the employee is paid the regular hourly wage. If the employee has worked more than the standard 40-hour work week, the employee is paid time and a half for the extra hours. In this tutorial, you will learn a programming tool known as a **control statement** that allows you to make this distinction and perform different calculations based on different user inputs. You begin by test-driving the completed **Wage Calculator** application. Then, you will learn the additional C++ capabilities you will need to create your own version of this application.

Test-Driving the Wage Calculator Application

1. *Locating the completed application.* Open the **Command Prompt** window by selecting **Start > Programs > Accessories > Command Prompt**. Change to your completed **Wage Calculator** application directory by typing cd C:\Examples\Tutorial04\CompletedApplication\WageCalculator.

2. *Running the Wage Calculator application.* Type WageCalculator in the **Command Prompt** window to run the application (Fig. 4.1).

Figure 4.1 Running the **Wage Calculator** application.

3. *Enter the employee's hourly wage.* Enter **10** (for $10) at the **Enter hourly wage:** prompt, then press *Enter*. The application will prompt you for the number of hours worked in a particular week (Fig. 4.2).

```
Command Prompt - WageCalculator                              _ □ ×

C:\Examples\Tutorial04\CompletedApplication\WageCalculator>WageCalcula
tor

Enter hourly wage: 10
Enter hours worked this week: _
```

Figure 4.2 Entering data in the **Wage Calculator** application.

4. *Enter the number of hours the employee worked.* Enter **45** at the **Enter hours worked this week:** prompt, then press *Enter*.

5. *Calculate the employee's gross earnings.* The result (**$475.00**) is displayed in the **Gross wages:** output field, and the application exits (Fig. 4.3). Notice that the employee's wages for one week are the sum of the wages for the standard 40-hour work week (40 * 10, or $400) and the overtime pay (5 * 10 * 1.5, or $75).

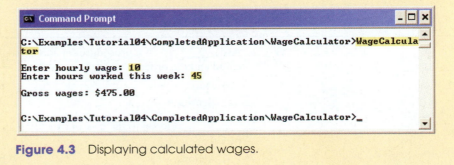

Figure 4.3 Displaying calculated wages.

(cont.)

6. ***Running the Wage Calculator application again.*** The **Wage Calculator** application also accepts input values that are not whole numbers. Type WageCalculator in the **Command Prompt** window. Enter 12.50 at the **Enter hourly wage:** prompt and enter 50.5 at the **Enter hours worked this week:** prompt. The result ($696.88) is displayed in the **Gross wages:** output field, and the application exits (Fig. 4.4).

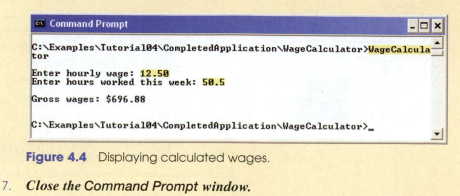

Figure 4.4 Displaying calculated wages.

7. ***Close the Command Prompt window.***

4.2 Algorithms

Computing problems can be solved by executing a series of actions in a specific order. A procedure for solving a problem, in terms of:

1. the **actions** to be executed and

2. the **order** in which these actions are to be executed

is called an **algorithm**. The following example demonstrates the importance of correctly specifying the order in which the actions are to be executed. Consider the "rise-and-shine algorithm" followed by one junior executive for getting out of bed and going to work: (1) get out of bed, (2) take off pajamas, (3) take a shower, (4) get dressed, (5) eat breakfast and (6) carpool to work. This routine prepares the executive for a productive day at the office.

However, suppose that the executive performs the same steps in a slightly different order: (1) get out of bed, (2) take off pajamas, (3) get dressed, (4) take a shower, (5) eat breakfast and (6) carpool to work. In this case, our junior executive shows up for work soaking wet!

Program control refers to the task of executing an application's statements in the correct order. In this tutorial, you will begin to investigate C++'s program-control capabilities.

SELF-REVIEW

1. A(n) _____ is a procedure for solving a problem in terms of the actions to be executed and the order in which these actions are to be executed.

   a) chart   b) control statement
   c) algorithm   d) ordered list

2. _____ refer(s) to the task of executing an application's statements in the correct order.

   a) Actions   b) Program control
   c) Control statements   d) Input/output

Answers: 1) c. 2) b.

4.3 Poeudocode

Pseudocode is an informal language that helps you develop algorithms. The pseudocode you will learn is particularly useful for developing algorithms that will be converted to structured programming portions of C++ applications. Pseudocode resembles everyday English; it is convenient and user-friendly, but it is not an actual programming language.

Pseudocode statements are not executed on computers. Rather, pseudocode helps you "think out" an application before attempting to write it in a programming language, such as C++. In this tutorial, you will see several examples of pseudocode. We will use pseudocode in each of the remaining tutorials.

The style of pseudocode that you will learn consists solely of characters, so you can create and modify pseudocode conveniently by using your text editor. A carefully prepared pseudocode program can be easily converted to a corresponding C++ application. Much of this conversion is as simple as replacing pseudocode statements with their C++ equivalents. Let's look at an example of a pseudocode statement:

Software Design Tip

Pseudocode helps you conceptualize an application during the application design process. Pseudocode statements can be converted to source code at a later point.

Assign 0 to the counter

This pseudocode statement specifies an easy-to-understand task. You can put several such statements together to form an algorithm that can be used to meet application requirements. When the pseudocode algorithm has been completed, you can then convert pseudocode statements to their equivalent C++ statements. The pseudocode statement above, for instance, can be converted to the following C++ statement:

```
counter = 0;
```

Pseudocode normally describes only **executable statements**, which are the actions that are performed when the corresponding C++ application is run. One type of programming statement that is not executable is a definition, such as

```
int counter;
```

which informs the compiler of `counter`'s type and instructs the compiler to reserve space in memory for this variable. This definition does not cause any action (such as input, output or a calculation) to occur when the application executes, so you would not include this definition in the pseudocode.

SELF-REVIEW

1. _____ is an artificial and informal language that helps programmers develop algorithms.
   a) Pseudocode   b) C++-Speak
   c) Notation   d) Executable

2. Pseudocode _____.
   a) usually describes only definitions   b) is executed on computers
   c) usually describes only executable lines d) usually describes definitions and
      of code   executable lines of code

Answers: 1) a. 2) c.

4.4 Control Statements

Normally, statements in an application are executed one after another in the order in which they are written. This is called **sequential execution**. However, C++ allows you to specify that the next statement to be executed might not be the next one in sequence. A **transfer of control** occurs when the next statement to be executed does not come immediately after the currently executing statement. This is common in computer applications.

All applications can be written in terms of only three forms of control: **sequence**, **selection** and **repetition**. Unless directed to act otherwise, the computer executes C++ statements sequentially—that is, one after the other in the order in which they appear in the application. The **activity diagram** in Fig. 4.5 illustrates two statements that execute in sequence. In this case, two calculations are performed in order. The activity diagram presents a graphical representation of the algorithm.

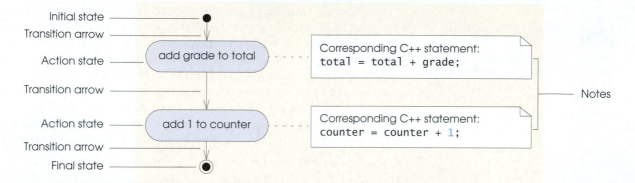

Figure 4.5 Sequence statement activity diagram.

Activity diagrams are part of the **Unified Modeling Language (UML)**—an industry standard for modeling software systems graphically. An activity diagram models the **activity** (also called the **workflow**) of a portion of a software system. An activity might include a portion of an algorithm, such as the sequence of two statements in Fig. 4.5. Activity diagrams are composed of special-purpose symbols, such as **action-state symbols** (rectangles with their left and right sides replaced with arcs curving outward), **diamonds** and **small circles**. These symbols are connected by **transition arrows**, which represent the flow of the activity. Figure 4.5 does not include any diamond symbols—these will be used in activity diagrams later in this tutorial.

Like pseudocode, activity diagrams help programmers develop and represent algorithms. Activity diagrams clearly show how control statements operate.

The activity diagram contains two **action states**, which represent actions to perform (Fig. 4.5). Each action state contains an **action expression**—for example, "add grade to total" or "add 1 to counter"—which specifies a particular action to perform. Action expressions are similar to pseudocode. The arrows in the activity diagram, called transition arrows, represent **transitions**, which indicate the order in which the actions represented by the action states occur. The application that implements the activities illustrated by Fig. 4.5 first adds `grade` to `total`, then adds `1` to `counter`.

The **solid circle** located at the top of the activity diagram represents the activity's **initial state**—the beginning of the workflow, before the application performs the activities. The **solid circle surrounded by a hollow circle** that appears at the bottom of the activity diagram represents the **final state**—the end of the workflow, after the application performs its activities.

Notice in Fig. 4.5 the rectangles with the upper-right corners folded over. These look like sheets of paper and are called **notes** in the UML. Notes are like comments in C++ applications—they are explanatory remarks that describe the purpose of symbols in the diagram. Figure 4.5 uses UML notes to show the C++ code that the programmer might associate with each action state in the activity diagram. A **dotted line** connects each note to the element that the note describes. Activity diagrams normally do not show the C++ code that implements the activity, but we use notes here to show you how the diagram relates to C++ code.

C++ provides three types of **selection statements**, which you will learn in this tutorial and in Tutorial 9. The `if` statement is a **single-selection statement** because it selects or ignores a single action to execute. The `if...else` statement is called a

double-selection statement because it selects between two different actions. The switch statement (discussed in Tutorial 9) is called a **multiple-selection statement** because it selects among many different actions or sequences of actions.

C++ provides three types of **repetition statements**—while, do...while and for—to execute statements in an application repeatedly. The while repetition statement is covered in Tutorial 6, do...while is covered in Tutorial 7 and for is covered in Tutorial 8. The words if, else, switch, while, do and for are all C++ keywords—Appendix F includes a complete list of C++ keywords. Most of C++'s keywords and their uses are discussed throughout this book.

C++ control statements are **single-entry/single-exit control statements**—each has one entry point and one exit point. Such control statements make it easy to build applications—the control statements are "attached" to one another by "connecting" the exit point of one control statement to the entry point of the next. This is accomplished simply by placing the control statements one after the other in a program. This is similar to stacking building blocks, so we call it **control-statement stacking**. The only other way to connect control statements is through **control-statement nesting**, whereby one control statement is placed inside another (we show an example in Section 4.6). Thus, algorithms in C++ applications are constructed from only three forms of control (sequence, selection and repetition) combined in only two ways (stacking and nesting). This is a model of simplicity.

SELF-REVIEW

1. Three types of program control in C++ applications are _____.
   a) sequence, nesting and repetition   b) stacking, selection and repetition
   c) sequence, selection and repetition   d) sequence, selection and nesting

2. The process of application statements executing one after another in the order in which they are written is called _____.
   a) transfer of control   b) sequential execution
   c) workflow   d) None of the above.

Answers: 1) c. 2) b.

4.5 if Selection Statement

A selection statement chooses among alternative courses of action in an application. The **if** selection statement performs (selects) an action based on a condition. A **condition** (also referred to as a **boolean expression**) is an expression with a true or false value that is used to make a decision. A condition is evaluated (that is, tested) to determine whether its value is true or false. If the condition evaluates to true, the action specified by the if statement will execute. If the condition evaluates to false, the action specified by the if statement will be skipped. For example, suppose that the passing grade on a test is 60 (out of 100). The pseudocode statement

> *If student's grade is greater than or equal to 60*
>   *Display "Passed"*

determines whether the condition "student's grade is greater than or equal to 60" is true or false. If the condition is true, then "Passed" is displayed, and the next pseudocode statement in order is "performed." (Remember that pseudocode is not a real programming language, so pseudocode "programs" do not actually execute on computers.) If the condition is false, the display statement is ignored, and the next pseudocode statement in order is performed.

The preceding pseudocode *if* statement may be written in C++ as

```
if ( studentGrade >= 60 )
{
    cout << "Passed";
}
```

Error-Prevention Tip

Always using braces in an if state-ment helps prevent their accidental omission when the if statement's body contains more than one state-ment.

Good Programming Practice

Indent the body of if statements to improve readability.

Common Programming Error

It is a syntax error to add spaces between the symbols in the ==, !=, >= and <= operators (as in ! =, > =, < =).

Common Programming Error

Reversing the symbols in the !=, >= and <= operators (as in =!, =>, =<) is a syntax error.

Common Programming Error

Using the assignment operator, =, when the equality operator, ==, is intended can lead to subtle logic errors.

Notice that the C++ code corresponds closely to the pseudocode, demonstrating the usefulness of pseudocode as a program-development tool. The body of an if state-ment can specify a single action or a sequence of actions (that is, many statements). The body of the if statement contains a statement that displays the string "Passed" on the screen. The braces, which define a **block** of program code, are required only when the body of an if statement contains more than one statement. The left brace symbol, {, begins a block, and the right brace symbol, }, closes the block. We suggest, however, that you always use braces to delimit the body of an if statement. To avoid omitting one or both of the braces, some programmers type the beginning and ending braces of a block even before typing the individual state-ments in the braces.

Notice the indentation of the statement in the body of the if statement. Such indentation makes it easier for you and others to read your application code. Recall that C++ compilers ignore whitespace, such as spaces, tabs and newlines used for indentation and vertical spacing, unless the whitespace is contained in strings.

The condition in the parentheses after the if keyword

```
studentGrade >= 60
```

determines whether the statement(s) in the body of the if statement will execute. If the condition is true, the body of the if statement executes. If the condition is false, the body does not execute. Conditions in if statements can be formed by using the **equality operators** and **relational operators**, which are summarized in Fig. 4.6. The relational operators have a higher level of precedence than the equality operators. Appendix C contains the complete operator precedence chart.

Algebraic equal-ity or relational operators	C++ equality or relational operators	Example of C++ condi-tion	Meaning of C++ condition
Relational operators			
>	>	x > y	x is greater than y
<	<	x < y	x is less than y
≥	>=	x >= y	x is greater than or equal to y
≤	<=	x <= y	x is less than or equal to y
Equality operators			
=	==	x == y	x is equal to y
≠	!=	x != y	x is not equal to y

Figure 4.6 Equality and relational operators.

Figure 4.7 uses a UML activity diagram to illustrate the single-selection if statement. This diagram contains what is perhaps the most important symbol in an activity diagram—the diamond, or **decision symbol**, which indicates that a decision is to be made. Note the two expressions in square brackets above or next to the arrows leading from the decision symbol—these are called **guard conditions**. Each transition arrow emerging from a decision symbol has a guard condition. If a partic-ular guard condition is true, the workflow enters the action state to which that tran-sition arrow points. For example, in Fig. 4.7, if the grade is greater than or equal to 60, the application displays "Passed," then transitions to the final state of this activ-ity. If the grade is less than 60, the application immediately transitions to the final state without displaying a message (because the grade was a failing grade—59 or less). Only one guard condition associated with a particular decision symbol can be true at once.

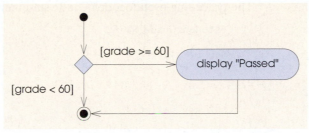

Figure 4.7 if single-selection statement UML activity diagram.

Note that the if statement diagrammed in Fig. 4.7 is a single-entry/single-exit statement. The UML activity diagrams for the remaining control statements also contain (aside from small circle symbols and transition arrows) only action-state symbols, indicating actions to be performed, and diamond symbols. Representing control statements in this way emphasizes the **action/decision model of programming**.

SELF-REVIEW

1. Which of the following if statements correctly displays that a student received an A on an exam if the score was 90 or above?

    a) ```
       if (studentGrade != 90)
       {
           cout << "Student received an A";
       }
       ```

    b) ```
       if ( studentGrade > 90 )
       {
           cout << "Student received an A";
       }
       ```

    c) ```
       if (studentGrade <= 90)
       {
           cout << "Student received an A";
       }
       ```

    d) ```
       if ( studentGrade >= 90 )
       {
           cout << "Student received an A";
       }
       ```

2. The _____ symbol is not a C++ operator.

    a) *   b) !=

    c) <>   d) %

Answers: 1) d. 2) c.

4.6 if...else Selection Statement

As you have learned, the if selection statement performs an indicated action (or sequence of actions) only when the condition evaluates to true; otherwise, the action (or sequence of actions) is skipped. The **if...else** selection statement performs an action (or sequence of actions) if a condition is true and performs a different action (or sequence of actions) if the condition is false. For this reason, if...else is known as a double-selection statement. For example, the pseudocode statement

> If student's grade is greater than or equal to 60
>   Display "Passed"
> Else
>   Display "Failed"

displays "Passed" if the student's grade is greater than or equal to 60, but displays "Failed" if the student's grade is less than 60. In either case, after output occurs, the next pseudocode statement in sequence is "performed."

The preceding pseudocode *if...else* statement may be written in C++ as

```
if ( studentGrade >= 60 )
{
    cout << "Passed";
}
else
{
    cout << "Failed";
}
```

Good Programming Practice

Indent both body statements of an if...else statement to improve readability.

Note that the body of the **else** clause is indented so that it lines up with the indented body of the if clause. A standard indentation convention should be applied consistently throughout your applications. It is difficult to read code that does not use uniform spacing conventions. The if...else selection statement follows the same general syntax as the if statement. The else keyword and any related statements are placed following the end of the if statement's body.

Figure 4.8 uses a UML activity diagram to illustrate the flow of control in the preceding if...else double-selection statement. Once again, note that (besides the initial state, transition arrows and final state) the only symbols in the activity diagram represent action states and decisions. In this example, the grade is either less than 60 or greater than or equal to 60. If the grade is less than 60, the application displays "Failed". If the grade is greater than or equal to 60, the application displays "Passed". We continue to emphasize this action/decision model of computing.

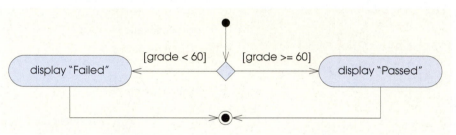

Figure 4.8 if...else double-selection statement UML activity diagram.

Nested if...else statements test for multiple conditions by placing if...else statements inside other if...else statements. For example, the pseudocode in Fig. 4.9 will display "A" for exam grades greater than or equal to 90, "B" for grades in the range 80–89, "C" for grades in the range 70–79, "D" for grades in the range 60–69 and "F" for all other grades.

```
if student's grade is greater than or equal to 90
    Display "A"
else
    If student's grade is greater than or equal to 80
        Display "B"
    else
        If student's grade is greater than or equal to 70
            Display "C"
        else
            If student's grade is greater than or equal to 60
                Display "D"
            else
                Display "F"
```

Figure 4.9 Pseudocode for an application that displays a student's grades.

The pseudocode in Fig. 4.9 may be written in C++ as shown in Fig. 4.10. If studentGrade is greater than or equal to 90, the first condition evaluates to true and the statement cout << "A"; is executed. Notice that, with a value for studentGrade

Common Programming Error

Following an `else` clause with another `else` or `else if` clause is a syntax error.

Good Programming Practice

If there are several levels of indentation, each level should be indented further to the right by the same amount of space.

greater than or equal to 90, the remaining three conditions would also evaluate to `true`. These conditions, however, are never evaluated, because they are placed within the `else` portion of the outer `if...else` statement. Because the first condition is `true`, all statements within the `else` clause of the outer `if...else` statement are skipped. Now assume `studentGrade` contains the value 75. The first condition evaluates to `false`, so the program will execute the statements within the first `else` clause. This `else` clause also contains an `if...else` statement, with the condition `studentGrade >= 80`. This condition evaluates to `false`, causing the statements in the second `else` clause to execute. This `else` clause contains yet another `if...else` statement, with the condition `studentGrade >= 70`. This condition is `true`, causing the statement `cout << "C";` to execute. The `else` clause of this `if...else` statement is then skipped.

```cpp
if ( studentGrade >= 90 )
{
   cout << "A";
}
else
   if ( studentGrade >= 80 )
   {
      cout << "B";
   }
   else
      if ( studentGrade >= 70 )
      {
         cout << "C";
      }
      else
         if ( studentGrade >= 60 )
         {
            cout << "D";
         }
         else
         {
            cout << "F";
         }
```

Figure 4.10   C++ code converted from the pseudocode in Fig. 4.9.

C++ programmers, when writing nested `if...else` statements such as the one in Fig. 4.10, often use the format shown in Fig. 4.11.

```cpp
if ( studentGrade >= 90 )
{
   cout << "A";
}
else if ( studentGrade >= 80 )
{
   cout << "B";
}
else if ( studentGrade >= 70 )
{
   cout << "C";
}
else if ( studentGrade >= 60 )
{
   cout << "D";
}
else
{
   cout << "F";
}
```

Figure 4.11   Nested `if...else` statements with alternative indentation.

The nested if...else statements in Fig. 4.10 and Fig. 4.11 are equivalent, but the latter format is preferred by some programmers because it avoids deep indentation of the code. Such deep indentation often leaves little room on a line, forcing statements to be split and decreasing code readability. Some programmers feel that the code in Fig. 4.10 better emphasizes the nesting of the if...else statements.

SELF-REVIEW

1. if...else is a _____-selection statement.

   a) single   b) double

   c) triple   d) nested

2. Placing an if...else statement inside another if...else statement is an example of _____.

   a) nesting if...else statements   b) stacking if...else statements

   c) creating sequential if...else statements   d) None of the above.

Answers: 1) b. 2) a.

4.7 Constructing the Wage Calculator Application

Now you will build your **Wage Calculator** application by using the if...else statement, which will allow you to calculate regular wages and include overtime pay based on the number of hours worked. The following pseudocode describes the basic operation of the **Wage Calculator** application that calculates and displays the employee's pay when the user enters the hourly wage and number of hours worked per week.

> *When the user inputs the hourly wage and the number of hours worked*
>
> > *If the number of hours worked is less than or equal to 40 hours*
> > > *Gross wages equals hours worked times hourly wage*
> >
> > *Else*
> > > *Gross wages equals 40 times hourly wage plus*
> > > > *hours above 40 times hourly wage times 1.5*
> >
> > *Display gross wages*

Figure 4.12 Pseudocode for the **Wage Calculator** application.

Before developing each application, you take it for a test drive. Here you interact with the application via the keyboard and begin to understand the purpose of the application. You also learn the input/output (I/O) operations that will be required to obtain user input and display results. For the remainder of this textbook, you will use pseudocode to aid your application development. Pseudocode describes the algorithm—that is, the actions to be performed and the order in which those actions should be performed. As you read the pseudocode, you will see that there are specific actions to perform, such as "Calculate gross wages," "Input the hourly wage" and "Display gross wages."

The following box guides you through the process of defining the variables you'll need to calculate the employee's wages. You will use these variables to store values input by the user. Then, you will use those variables in an if...else statement to compute the employee's gross wages. Finally, your program will display the gross wages.

Implementing the Wage Calculator

1. ***Copying the template to your working directory.*** Copy the `C:\Examples\Tutorial04\TemplateApplication\WageCalculator` directory to your `C:\SimplyCpp` directory.

2. ***Open the Wage Calculator application's template source code file.***

(cont.)

3. ***Locating the main function.*** In this example, the `main` function calculates the gross wages when the user enters the hourly wage and hours worked. Lines 10–14 of Fig. 4.13 show the function containing only a `return` statement. Next, you will write the code for this function so that your application will calculate and display the gross wages.

Initial `main` function

```
WageCalculator.cpp
 9   // function main begins program execution
10   int main()
11   {
12      return 0; // indicate that program ended successfully
13
14   } // end function main
```

Figure 4.13   `main` function (containing only a `return` statement).

Notice the comments in lines 9 and 14. In lines 11 and 14, the "{" and "}" symbols indicate the body of the `main` function. The comment after the "}" symbol documents the end of the function.

4. ***Defining variables and obtaining inputs from the user.*** This application uses the primitive type `double`. The **double** type is used to represent floating-point numbers (that is, numbers with decimal points). Because an employee's hourly wage and hours worked are often fractional numbers, the `int` data type is not appropriate for this application. Insert lines 12–22 of Fig. 4.14 into `main`. The statements in lines 13–14 define `double` variables `hourlyWage` and `hoursWorked`. The statements in lines 17–18 prompt the user for the hourly wage and input into the `hourlyWage` variable the value the user enters at the keyboard. The statements in lines 21–22 input into the `hoursWorked` variable the value the user enters at the keyboard.

Define variables to store user input

Prompt user for hourly wage and input result into the `hourlyWage` variable

Prompt user for hours worked and input result into the `hoursWorked` variable

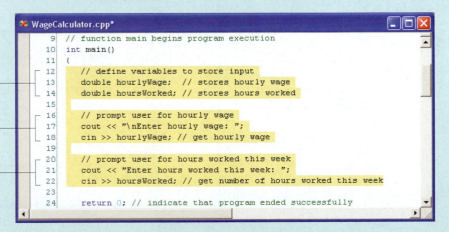

```
WageCalculator.cpp*
 9   // function main begins program execution
10   int main()
11   {
12      // define variables to store input
13      double hourlyWage;  // stores hourly wage
14      double hoursWorked; // stores hours worked
15
16      // prompt user for hourly wage
17      cout << "\nEnter hourly wage: ";
18      cin >> hourlyWage; // get hourly wage
19
20      // prompt user for hours worked this week
21      cout << "Enter hours worked this week: ";
22      cin >> hoursWorked; // get number of hours worked this week
23
24      return 0; // indicate that program ended successfully
```

Figure 4.14   Assigning user input to variables.

5. ***Defining a constant.*** Add lines 24–26 of Fig. 4.15 to the `main` function. Line 26 contains a **constant**—a variable whose value cannot be changed after its initial definition. Constants are defined by preceding the data type with the **const** keyword. In this case, you initialize the HOUR_LIMIT constant to contain the maximum number of hours worked before mandatory overtime pay (40.0). Notice that, by convention, you capitalize the constant's name to emphasize that it is a constant.

Line 26 demonstrates that C++ allows you to define a variable so that it appears close to where it is first used. However, many programmers prefer to group all of a function's variable definitions in the first lines of the function's body.

(cont.)

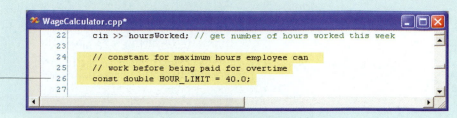

Constant definition ———

Figure 4.15   Creating a constant.

Good Programming Practice

Capitalize all letters in a constant's name to make the constant stand out in the application. Separate each word in the name of a constant with an underscore to make the identifier easier to read.

6. ***Defining a variable to store the gross wages.*** Add lines 28–29 of Fig. 4.16 to `main`. Line 29 defines the variable `wages`, which you will use to store the employee's gross wages for the week (after your application calculates the gross wages).

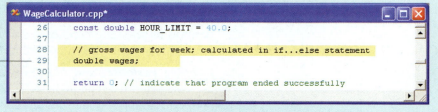

Define `double` variable `wages` ———

Figure 4.16   Defining a variable of the `double` type.

Software Design Tip

Although C++ allows variables to be defined throughout the body of a function, many C++ programmers prefer to group all variable definitions at the top of a function body. Such programmers feel that this makes applications easier to read and maintain.

7. ***Determining wages based on hours worked.*** Add lines 31–45 of Fig. 4.17 to the `main` function. This `if...else` statement determines whether the employee worked overtime and calculates the gross wages accordingly.

`if...else` statement to calculate wages ———

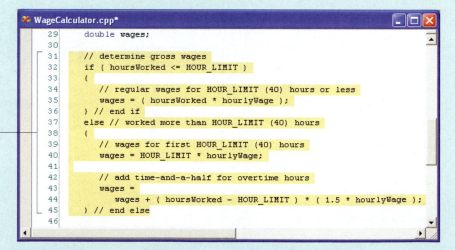

Figure 4.17   `if...else` statement that calculates gross wages.

Line 32 determines whether the value stored in `hoursWorked` is less than or equal to `HOUR_LIMIT` (40.0, specified in line 26). If so, line 35 calculates the product of `hoursWorked` and `hourlyWage` and assigns the result to `wages`.

If, on the other hand, `hoursWorked` is greater than `HOUR_LIMIT`, then execution proceeds to the `else` part of the `if...else` statement in lines 37–45. Line 40 computes the wages for the hours worked up to the limit set by `HOUR_LIMIT` (that is, 40.0) and assigns the result to `wages`. Lines 43–44 calculate the user's overtime pay and add it to the wages calculated in line 40. The expression in line 44 first determines the user's overtime hours (by using the calculation `hoursWorked - HOUR_LIMIT`), then multiplies the overtime hours by the product of 1.5 times the user's hourly wage. The overtime pay is then added to the value of `wages`, and the result is assigned to `wages`.

Good Programming Practice

Place a blank line above and below each `if...else` statement to help make your applications more readable. In general, do this for all control statements.

(cont.)

8. ***Displaying the result.*** Insert lines 47–48 of Fig. 4.18 in the `main` function. Line 48 displays the label `"Gross wages: $"` followed by the value in the variable `wages`.

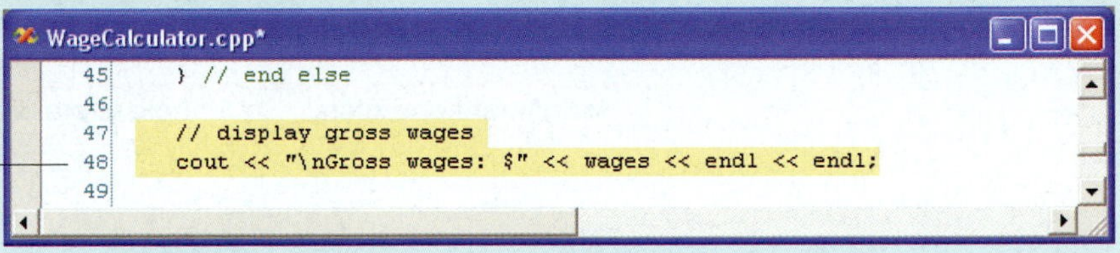

Displaying output ———

```
45         } // end else
46
47         // display gross wages
48         cout << "\nGross wages: $" << wages << endl << endl;
49
```

Figure 4.18 Displaying gross wages.

9. ***Save, compile and run the application.*** Figure 4.19 shows the updated application running. Notice that the output in Fig. 4.19 is not yet formatted as a proper dollar amount (that is, including the trailing decimal point followed by two zeros) as it should be in the completed application. You will learn how to format the dollar amount properly in Section 4.9.

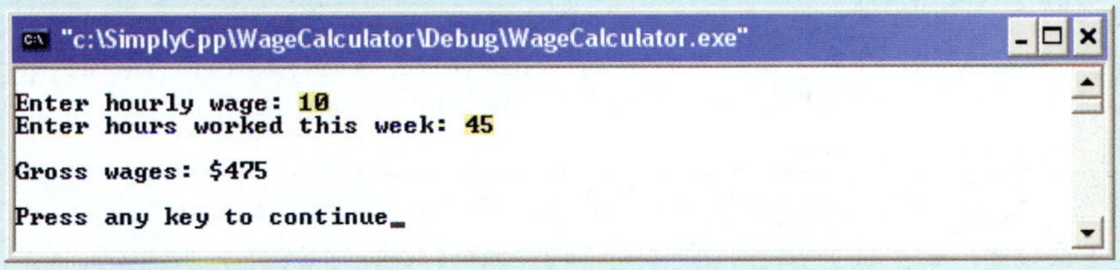

Displaying unformatted number ———

```
"c:\SimplyCpp\WageCalculator\Debug\WageCalculator.exe"

Enter hourly wage: 10
Enter hours worked this week: 45

Gross wages: $475

Press any key to continue_
```

Figure 4.19 Updated application displaying unformatted number.

10. ***Close the*** Command Prompt ***window.***

1. The `double` type can be used to store _____.

   a) letters and digits   b) numbers with decimal points

   c) strings   d) None of the above.

2. Constants are defined with the _____ keyword.

   a) `fixed`   b) `constant`

   c) `final`   d) `const`

Answers: 1) b. 2) d.

4.8 Assignment Operators

C++ provides several **assignment operators** for abbreviating assignment statements. For example, the statement

```
value = value + 3;
```

which adds 3 to the value in the variable `value`, can be abbreviated with the addition assignment operator, +=, as

```
value += 3;
```

The **addition assignment operator (+=)** adds the value of its right operand to the current value of its left operand and stores the result in the left operand. Any statement of the form

   variable = *variable operator expression*;

in which the same variable appears on both sides of the assignment operator and *operator* is one of the binary operators +, -, ^, /, or % (or others we will discuss later in the text), can be written in the form

   variable operator= *expression*;

C++ provides assignment operators for several binary operators, including +, -, *, / and %. When an addition assignment statement is evaluated, the expression to the right of the operator is evaluated first only if it has a higher level of precedence than the assignment operator. Figure 4.20 includes the arithmetic assignment operators, sample expressions using these operators and explanations.

Assignment operators	Sample expression	Explanation	Assigns to c
	Assume c = 4		
+=	c += 7	c = c + 7	11
-=	c -= 3	c = c - 3	1
*=	c *= 4	c = c * 4	16
/=	c /= 2	c = c / 2	2
%=	c %= 3	c = c % 3	1

Figure 4.20 Arithmetic assignment operators.

Next, you will learn how to abbreviate your overtime wages calculation with the += operator. When you run the application again, you will notice that the application runs the same as before.

Using the Addition Assignment Operator

1. *Open the Wage Calculator application's source code file.*

2. *Using the addition assignment operator.* Replace lines 43–44 of Fig. 4.17 with lines 43–44 of Fig. 4.21. The new statement uses the addition assignment operator, making it unnecessary to include the wages variable in both the left and right operands of the assignment. The statement still performs the same action—the overtime pay for the employee is calculated and added to the regular wages earned.

Addition assignment operator ——

```
WageCalculator.cpp*
42        // add time-and-a-half for overtime hours
43        wages +=
44           ( hoursWorked - HOUR_LIMIT ) * ( 1.5 * hourlyWage );
45     } // end else
```

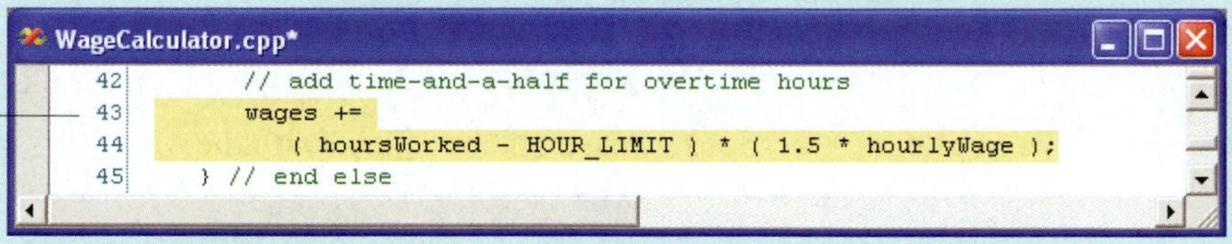

Figure 4.21 Using the addition assignment operator in a calculation.

3. *Save, compile and run the application.* Verify that the application produces the correct output.

4. *Close the Command Prompt window.*

SELF-REVIEW

1. The *= operator _____.
   a) adds the value of its right operand to the value of its left operand and stores the result in its left operand
   b) creates a new variable and assigns the value of the right operand to that variable
   c) multiplies the value of its left operand by the value of its right operand and assigns the result to its left operand
   d) None of the above.

2. If the x variable contains the value 5, what value will x contain after the expression x -= 3 is executed?
   a) 3   b) 5
   c) 7   d) 2

Answers: 1) c. 2) d.

4.9 Formatting Numbers

There are several ways to format output in C++. In this section, you will use the **stream manipulators** setprecision and fixed to control how text displays. Modifying the appearance of text for display purposes is called text **formatting**. Consider the following example.

```
cout << fixed << setprecision( 2 );
```

The **fixed** stream manipulator indicates that floating-point values should be output in so-called **fixed-point format**, as opposed to **scientific notation**. For example, the number 1,234.56 would be displayed as 1234.56 using fixed-point format and displayed as 1.23456e+003 (shorthand for 1.23456×10^3) in scientific notation. Specifying fixed-point formatting also forces the decimal point and several trailing zeros to display, even if the value is a whole number amount, such as 88.00. Without the fixed-point formatting option, your application would display such a value as 88 without the trailing zeros and without the decimal point.

The **setprecision** stream manipulator sets the **precision**, which is the number of digits to the right of the decimal point. For example, the call setprecision(2) indicates that a variable of numeric type should be printed with two digits of precision. Thus, when the preceding statement is followed by the statement

```
cout << 1234.5678;
```

the program will display the value 1234.57. When specifying fixed-point format, the printed value is rounded to the indicated number of decimal positions, although the value in memory remains unaltered. For example, after setprecision(2) the values 87.946 and 67.543 are output as 87.95 and 67.54, respectively. Note that the effects of the fixed and setprecision stream manipulators persist until the application terminates or until the application encounters a stream manipulator that changes the output format for floating-point numbers.

The setprecision(2) call is referred to as a **parameterized stream manipulator** because it contains a parameter (2). Programs that use these must contain the preprocessor directive

```
#include <iomanip>
```

Note that endl and fixed are **nonparameterized stream manipulators** and do not require the <iomanip> header file to be included. If the precision is not specified, floating-point values are normally output with six digits of precision—this is called **default precision**.

Recall that your **Wage Calculator** application does not display the result of its calculation with the appropriate decimal places that you saw when test-driving the application. Next, you will learn how to apply number formatting to the value displayed for the user so that the value displays in currency format.

Formatting the Gross Wages

1. *Open the Wage Calculator application's source code file.*

2. *Including the <iomanip> header file.* Add line 6 of Fig. 4.22. Line 6 uses the #include preprocessor directive to include the **<iomanip>** header file. This enables the setprecision stream manipulator, which you will use in the next step. Using the setprecision stream manipulator without including the <iomanip> header file is a syntax error.

(cont.)

The `<iomanip>` header file declares the `setprecision` stream manipulator

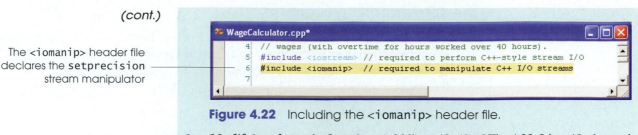

Figure 4.22 Including the `<iomanip>` header file.

3. **Modifying the main function.** Add lines 48–49 of Fig. 4.23. Line 49 places the `fixed` and `setprecision( 2 )` stream manipulators in `cout`, causing it to display each floating-point value with at least one digit (sometimes the digit 0) to the left of the decimal point and exactly two digits to the right of the decimal point. The formatted number is rounded to the nearest hundredth.

The `fixed` and `setprecision` stream manipulators cause `cout` to display numeric values accurate to two decimal places

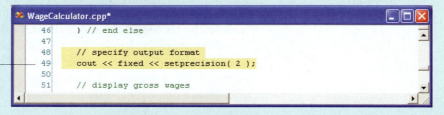

Figure 4.23 Using the `fixed` and `setprecision` stream manipulators to display the gross wages with two digits of precision to the right of the decimal point.

4. **Save, compile and run the application.** Figure 4.24 shows the completed application running and producing a number properly formatted as a dollar amount.

Displaying formatted number

```
"c:\SimplyCpp\WageCalculator\Debug\WageCalculator.exe"

Enter hourly wage: 10
Enter hours worked this week: 45

Gross wages: $475.00

Press any key to continue_
```

Figure 4.24 Completed application displaying formatted wages.

5. **Close the Command Prompt window.**

Figure 4.25 shows the completed source code of the **Wage Calculator** application. The lines of code that you added, viewed or modified in this tutorial are highlighted. In lines 31–47, notice the use of blank lines above and below the `if...else` statement. Such vertical spacing makes the application easier to read.

```
1    // Tutorial 4: WageCalculator.cpp
2    // This application inputs the hourly wage and number of hours
3    // worked for an employee, then calculates the employee's gross
4    // wages (with overtime for hours worked over 40 hours).
5    #include <iostream> // required for C++ stream I/O
6    #include <iomanip>  // required to manipulate C++ I/O streams
7
8    using namespace std; // for accessing C++ Standard Library members
9
10   // function main begins program execution
11   int main()
12   {
```

Figure 4.25 **Wage Calculator** application completed source code. (Part 1 of 2.)

Define **double** variables to store fractional values

```
13      // define variables to store input
14      double hourlyWage;  // stores hourly wage
15      double hoursWorked; // stores hours worked
16
17      // prompt user for hourly wage
18      cout << "\nEnter hourly wage: ";
19      cin >> hourlyWage; // get hourly wage
20
21      // prompt user for hours worked this week
22      cout << "Enter hours worked this week: ";
23      cin >> hoursWorked; // get number of hours worked this week
24
25      // constant for maximum hours employee can
26      // work before being paid for overtime
27      const double HOUR_LIMIT = 40.0;
28
29      // gross wages for week; calculated in if...else statement
30      double wages;
31
32      // determine gross wages
33      if ( hoursWorked <= HOUR_LIMIT )
34      {
35          // regular wages for HOUR_LIMIT (40) hours or less
36          wages = hoursWorked * hourlyWage;
37      } // end if
38      else // worked more than HOUR_LIMIT (40) hours
39      {
40          // wages for first HOUR_LIMIT (40) hours
41          wages = HOUR_LIMIT * hourlyWage;
42
43          // add time-and-a-half for overtime hours
44          wages +=
45              ( hoursWorked - HOUR_LIMIT ) * ( 1.5 * hourlyWage );
46      } // end else
47
48      // specify output format
49      cout << fixed << setprecision( 2 );
50
51      // display gross wages
52      cout << "\nGross wages: $" << wages << endl << endl;
53
54      return 0; // indicate that program ended successfully
55
56  } // end function main
```

The **const** keyword specifies that HOUR_LIMIT is a constant

Variable to store gross wages

Begin **if...else** statement

End **if** part of **if...else** statement and begin **else** part; **else** body executes when condition in line 33 evaluates to **false**

Assign to left operand the result of adding left and right operands
End **else** part of **if...else**

Format result as a dollar amount

Figure 4.25 Wage Calculator application completed source code. (Part 2 of 2.)

SELF-REVIEW   1.   The <iomanip> header file is required to access _____.

a) the stream output object, cout   b) nonparameterized stream manipulators

c) parameterized stream manipulators   d) the stream input object, cin

2.   The _____ stream manipulator of <iomanip> can display numeric values in a special format, such as with two digits to the right of the decimal point.

a) setfixed   b) setprecision

c) precision   d) fixedprecision

Answers: 1) c. 2) b.

4.10 Using the Debugger: The Watch and Locals Windows

Visual C++ .NET includes several debugging features that are accessible when an application is started with debugging enabled. As you learned in Section 3.7, the *Quick Info* features allows you to examine the value of a variable. In this section, you will learn how to use the **Watch** window to examine the value of more complex expressions. You will also use the **Locals** window to assign new values to variables while your application is running.

Using the Debugger: The Watch and Locals Windows

1. *Opening the Wage Calculator application in Visual Studio .NET.* Open your completed application, located at `C:\SimplyCpp\WageCalculator\WageCalculator.sln`.

2. *Inserting breakpoints.* Set a breakpoint at line 23 in the source code by clicking in the margin indicator bar to the left of line 23 (Fig. 4.26). Set another breakpoint at line 36 of the code by clicking in the margin indicator bar to the left of line 36.

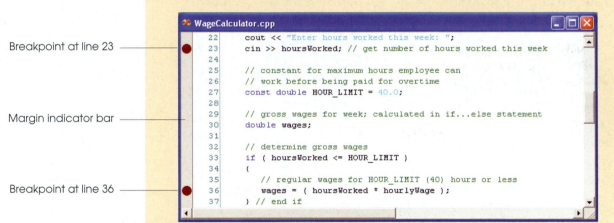

Breakpoint at line 23

Margin indicator bar

Breakpoint at line 36

Figure 4.26 Setting breakpoints at lines 23 and 36.

3. *Starting debugging.* Compile your application by selecting **Build > Build Solution**. Then select **Debug > Start**. This will start your application in debugging mode. Type 12 at the **Enter hourly wage:** prompt (Fig. 4.27).

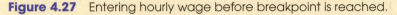

Figure 4.27 Entering hourly wage before breakpoint is reached.

4. *Suspending program execution.* Press *Enter* so that your application reads the value you just entered. This will cause the application to execute until the breakpoint at line 23. When the application reaches line 23, Visual C++ .NET suspends program execution and switches the application into break mode (Fig. 4.28). At this point, the statement in line 19 (Fig. 4.25) has input in the `hourlyWage` variable the hourly wage that you entered (12), the statement in line 22 has displayed a prompt for the hours worked this week and the statement in line 23 is the next statement that will be executed.

(cont.)

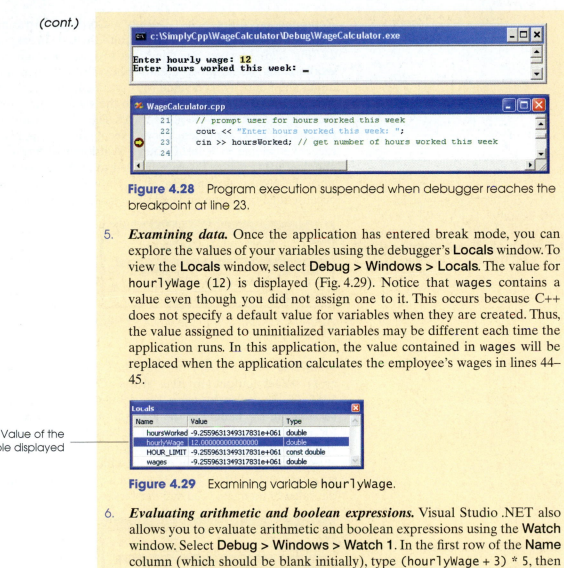

Figure 4.28 Program execution suspended when debugger reaches the breakpoint at line 23.

5. ***Examining data.*** Once the application has entered break mode, you can explore the values of your variables using the debugger's **Locals** window. To view the **Locals** window, select **Debug > Windows > Locals**. The value for `hourlyWage` (12) is displayed (Fig. 4.29). Notice that `wages` contains a value even though you did not assign one to it. This occurs because C++ does not specify a default value for variables when they are created. Thus, the value assigned to uninitialized variables may be different each time the application runs. In this application, the value contained in `wages` will be replaced when the application calculates the employee's wages in lines 44–45.

Value of the
`hourlyWage` variable displayed

Figure 4.29 Examining variable `hourlyWage`.

6. ***Evaluating arithmetic and boolean expressions.*** Visual Studio .NET also allows you to evaluate arithmetic and boolean expressions using the **Watch** window. Select **Debug > Windows > Watch 1**. In the first row of the **Name** column (which should be blank initially), type `(hourlyWage + 3) * 5`, then press *Enter*. Notice that the **Watch** window can evaluate arithmetic expressions. In this case, it displays the value `75.0` (Fig. 4.30). In the next row of the **Name** column in the **Watch** window, type `hourlyWage == 3`, then press *Enter*. This expression determines whether the value contained in `hourlyWage` is 3. Expressions containing the `==` symbol are treated as boolean expressions, stored by the **bool** type. A true value is specified in C++ code by using the **true** keyword; a false value is specified in C++ code by using the **false** keyword. The value returned is `false` (Fig. 4.30), because `hourlyWage` does not currently contain the value 3.

Evaluating an
arithmetic expression

Evaluating a **bool** expression

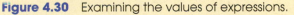

Figure 4.30 Examining the values of expressions.

(cont.)

7. ***Resuming execution.*** Select **Debug > Continue** to resume execution. The application will continue to execute until the next breakpoint at line 36. Line 23 (Fig. 4.26) executes, enabling you to enter a value at the **Enter hours worked this week:** prompt. Enter the value 40, then press *Enter*. Line 23 inputs the hours worked value (40) into hoursWorked. Line 27 defines constant HOUR_LIMIT and initializes it to the value (40.0). Line 30 defines variable wages to contain the gross wages. The if condition in line 33 evaluates to true, so the if statement's body executes and the application is once again suspended at line 36. Select **Debug > Windows > Locals.** The updated hoursWorked value is now displayed in red to indicate that it has been modified since the last breakpoint (Fig. 4.31). The value in hourlyWage is not in red because it has not been updated since the last breakpoint.

Values of the hoursWorked and HOUR_LIMIT variables displayed in red ⎯⎯

Figure 4.31   Displaying the value of the variables in the **Wage Calculator** application.

8. ***Modifying values.*** Based on the values input by the user (12 and 40), the gross wages output by the **Wage Calculator** application should be $480.00. However, by using the debugger, you can change the values of variables in the middle of the application's execution. This can be valuable for experimenting with different values and for locating logic errors in applications. You can use the **Locals** window to change the value of a variable. In the **Locals** window, click the **Value** field in the hoursWorked row to select the value 40.0. Type 35.0, then press *Enter*. The debugger changes the value of hoursWorked and displays its new value in red (Fig. 4.32).

Value modified in the debugger ⎯⎯

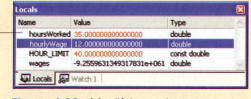

Figure 4.32   Modifying values.

9. ***Setting a breakpoint at the return statement.*** Set a breakpoint at line 54 in the source code by clicking in the margin indicator bar to the left of line 54 (Fig. 4.33). This will prevent the application from closing immediately after displaying its result. If you do not set this breakpoint, you will not be able to view the application's output before the console window closes.

Breakpoint at line 54 ⎯⎯

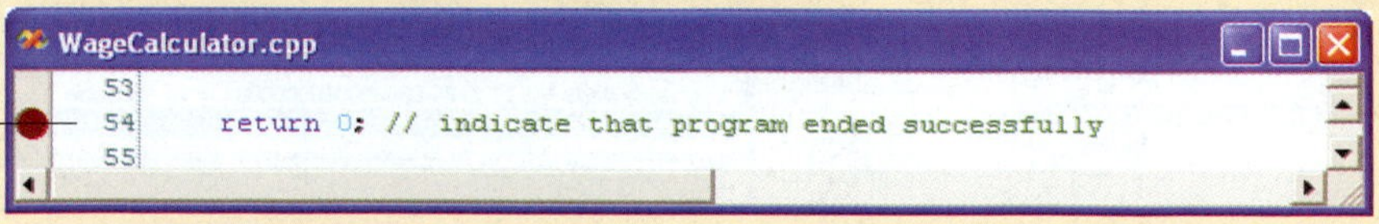

```
53
54        return 0; // indicate that program ended successfully
55
```

Figure 4.33   Setting a breakpoint at line 54 prevents the application from exiting immediately after displaying its result.

(cont.)

10. ***Viewing the application result.*** Select **Debug > Continue** to continue program execution. Function `main` executes until the `return` statement on line 54 and displays the result. Notice that the result is $420.00 (Fig. 4.34). This shows that the previous step changed the value of `hoursWorked` from the user input value (40) to 35.0.

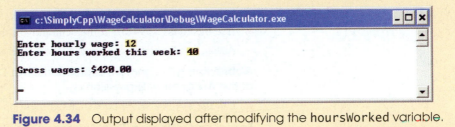

Figure 4.34 Output displayed after modifying the `hoursWorked` variable.

11. ***Stopping the debugging session.*** Select **Debug > Stop Debugging**.

12. ***Close the Visual Studio .NET IDE.***

SELF-REVIEW

1. You can examine the value of an expression by using the debugger's _____ window.

   a) **Autos**   b) **Locals**
   c) **Watch**   d) **Output**

2. You can modify the value of a variable by using the debugger's _____ window.

   a) **Output**   b) **Locals**
   c) **Watch**   d) **Value**

Answers: 1) c. 2) b.

4.11 Wrap-Up

In this tutorial, you learned techniques for solving programming problems. You were introduced to algorithms, pseudocode, the UML and control statements. You were shown different types of control statements and when each might be used.

You began by test-driving an application that used an `if...else` statement to determine an employee's gross wages. You learned the `if` and `if...else` control statements and studied UML activity diagrams that showed the decision-making processes of these statements. You were introduced to boolean expressions, which can be created using relational or equality operators. You saw how these expressions are used in control statements to control program execution.

You formatted program output by using `<iomanip>` stream manipulators `setprecision` and `fixed`. These stream manipulators allowed you to cause floating-point numbers to be displayed in currency format. You also learned how to abbreviate mathematical statements containing the same variable on both sides of an operator by using the arithmetic assignment operators. In the *Using the Debugger* section, you learned how to use the **Watch** window to examine the value of an expression and how to use the **Locals** window to change the value of a variable.

In the next tutorial, you will learn how to use characters and strings to retrieve input from the user. You will also study the logical operators, which give you more expressive power for forming the conditions in your control statements.

SKILLS SUMMARY   **Choosing Among Alternate Courses of Action**

■ Use the `if`, `if...else` or nested `if...else` control statements.

Conceptualizing the Application Before Using C++

■ Use pseudocode.

Understanding the Flow of Control in Control Statements

■ Review the text's discussions of the control statement's corresponding UML activity diagram.

Performing Comparisons in Conditions

■ Use the equality (== and !=) and relational (<, <=, > and >=) operators.

Creating a Constant

■ Use the const keyword at the beginning of the variable's definition.

■ Assign a value to the constant in the definition.

Abbreviating Assignment Expressions That Contain the Same Variable on Both Sides of the Assignment Expression

■ Use the +=, -=, *=, /= and %= assignment operators.

Formatting a Floating-Point Number As Currency

■ Use the fixed stream manipulator to force the number to be displayed using fixed-point notation.

■ Use stream manipulator setprecision (declared in the <iomanip> header file) with an argument of 2 to display exactly two digits to the right of the decimal point.

Examining Expression Values During Program Debugging

■ Use the debugger to set a breakpoint and examine expressions using the **Watch** window.

Modifying Data During Program Debugging

■ Use the debugger to set a breakpoint and modify variable values using the **Locals** window.

KEY TERMS

action/decision model of programming—Representing control statements as *actions* to be performed and *decisions* to be made. In a UML activity diagram, actions are represented by action-state symbols and decisions are represented by diamond symbols.

action expression (in the UML)—An expression used in an action state within a UML activity diagram to specify a particular action to perform.

action state (in the UML)—An action (represented by an action-state symbol) to perform in a UML activity diagram.

action-state symbol (in the UML)—A rectangle with its left and right sides replaced with arcs curving outward that represents an action to perform in a UML activity diagram.

activity diagram (in the UML)—A UML diagram that models the activity (also called the workflow) of a portion of a software system.

addition assignment operator (+=)—An operator that adds the value of its right operand to the current value of its left operand and stores the result in the left operand.

algorithm—A procedure for solving a problem, specifying the actions to be executed and the order in which these actions are to be executed.

assignment operator—A symbol used for abbreviating assignment expressions that contain the same variable on both sides of the assignment expression.

block—A set of statements that is enclosed in curly braces ({ and }).

bool type—A type that stores either the value true or the value false.

boolean expression—An expression with a true or false value that is used to make a decision.

condition— A bool expression (that is, an expression that evaluates to either true or false value) that is used to make a decision.

const keyword—The keyword that precedes the data type in a definition of a constant.

constant—A variable whose value cannot be changed after its initialization in its definition.

control statement—A program statement (such as if, if...else, switch, while, do...while or for) that specifies the flow of control (that is, the order in which statements execute).

control-statement nesting—Placing one control statement in the body of another control statement.

control-statement stacking—Setting control statements in sequence. The exit point of one control statement is "connected" to the entry point of the next control statement in sequence.

decision symbol (in the UML)—The diamond-shaped symbol in a UML activity diagram that indicates a decision is to be made.

default precision—The precision with which C++ prints floating-point values by default. Normally, these values are displayed with six digits of precision.

diamond (in the UML)—The symbol (also known as the decision symbol) in a UML activity diagram that indicates a decision is to be made. [*Note:* In a later tutorial, you will learn that this symbol serves two purposes in the UML.]

dotted line (in the UML)—A UML activity diagram symbol that connects each UML-style note with the element that the note describes.

double type—A type that can represent numbers with decimal points.

double-selection statement—The if...else statement; it selects between two different actions or sequences of actions.

else clause—The block of code that is executed if the condition specified by the if part of the if...else statement is false.

equality operators—The == (is equal to) and != (is not equal to) operators, which compare two values.

executable statement—A statement that has its effect, such as performing an action or making a decision, when the statement is encountered as the program runs. Comments are not executable statements; assignment statements, input/output statements, return statements and control statements are executable statements.

false—One of the two possible values for an expression of type bool; the other is true.

final state (in the UML)—A solid circle surrounded by a hollow circle (a "bullseye") in a UML activity diagram. It represents the end of the workflow after an application segment performs its activities.

fixed-point format—The format that displays floating-point values with a decimal point after the value's ones digit, followed by the specified number of digits to the right of the decimal point.

fixed stream manipulator—Stream manipulator that causes floating-point values to be displayed using fixed-point notation (rather than scientific notation).

formatting—Modifying the appearance of text for display purposes.

guard condition (in the UML)—A condition contained in square brackets that must be associated with a transition arrow leading from a decision symbol in a UML activity diagram. The guard condition associated with a particular transition must be true for the workflow to continue along that path.

if statement—The if single-selection statement performs an action (or sequence of actions) based on a condition.

if...else statement—The if...else double-selection statement performs an action (or sequence of actions) if a condition is true and performs a different action (or sequence of actions) if the condition is false.

initial state (in the UML)—The beginning of the workflow in a UML activity diagram before the application performs the activities. The initial state is represented by a small solid circle.

<iomanip> header file—The header file that declares parameterized stream manipulators, such as setprecision, that enable the programmer to manipulate displayed text.

Locals window (in the debugger)—A debugger window that can be used to change the value of a variable at a breakpoint while an application is running.

multiple-selection statement—The switch statement; a statement that chooses among many different actions by evaluating an integer expression.

nonparameterized stream manipulator—A stream manipulator that does not specify any parameters, such as endl and fixed.

nested statement—A statement that is placed inside the body of another control statement.

note (in the UML)—An explanatory remark (represented by a rectangle with a folded upper-right corner) describing the purpose of a symbol in a UML activity diagram. A dotted line connects each note to the item it describes.

parameterized stream manipulator—A stream manipulator that requires an argument, such as setprecision(2). Programs that use parameterized stream manipulators must include the <iomanip> header file.

precision—The accuracy with which a number is printed to a display or stored in memory.

program control—The task of determining the next program statement to execute.

pseudocode—An informal language that helps programmers develop algorithms.

relational operators—The < (less than), > (greater than), <= (less than or equal to) and >= (greater than or equal to) operators, which compare two values.

repetition statement—A control statement that might cause an application to execute statements multiple times. C++ provides the while, do…while and for repetition statements.

scientific notation—A numeric format that represents a floating-point number as the product of a value between 1 (inclusive) and 10 (exclusive) and a power of 10. For example, the value 12345.67 is written as 1.234567×10^4 in scientific notation.

selection statement—A control statement that selects among alternative courses of action. C++ provides the if, if…else and switch selection statements.

sequential execution—This occurs when an application's statements are executed in the order in which they appear.

setprecision stream manipulator—The parameterized stream manipulator that sets the number of digits of precision when displaying floating-point values.

single-entry/single-exit control statement—Each control statement has one entry point and one exit point.

single-selection statement—The if statement; it selects or ignores a single action or sequence of actions.

small circle (in the UML)—A UML activity diagram symbol that represents either the activity's initial or its final state.

solid circle (in the UML)—A UML activity diagram symbol that represents the activity's initial state.

solid circle surrounded by a hollow circle (in the UML)—A UML activity diagram symbol that represents the activity's final state.

stream manipulator—An object that modifies the display characteristics of the output stream in which it is placed.

structured programming—A technique for organizing program control to help you develop applications that are easy to understand, debug and modify.

transfer of control—This occurs when the next statement to be executed in an application does not come immediately after the currently executing statement.

transition (in the UML)—A change from one action state to another that is represented by a transition arrow in a UML activity diagram.

transition arrow (in the UML)—A UML activity diagram symbol that represents a change from one action state to another.

true—One of the two possible values for a bool type; the other is false.

UML (Unified Modeling Language)—An industry standard for modeling software systems graphically.

Watch window (in the debugger)—A debugger window that is used to examine the values of variables and expressions.

workflow—The activity of a portion of a software system.

C++ LIBRARY REFERENCE

iomanip Provides access to parameterized stream manipulators.

- *Stream manipulators*

    fixed—This stream manipulator specifies that floating-point numbers should be printed using fixed-point notation (as opposed to scientific notation).

    setprecision—This stream manipulator specifies that numeric values should be printed using the specified number of digits to the right of the decimal point. The argument to setprecision determines the number of digits that are displayed to the right of the decimal point when a floating-point value is printed.

4.1 The _____ operator returns `false` if the left operand is greater than the right operand.

a) `==`

b) `<`

c) `<=`

d) All of the above.

4.2 A _____ occurs when an executed statement does not directly follow the previously executed statement in the written application.

a) transition

b) flow

c) logic error

d) transfer of control

4.3 A variable or an expression can be examined in the _____ debugger window.

a) **Watch**

b) **Output**

c) **View**

d) **Display**

4.4 The `if` statement is called a _____ statement because it selects or ignores one action (or sequence of actions).

a) single-selection

b) multiple-selection

c) double-selection

d) repetition

4.5 The three types of program control are sequence, selection and _____.

a) reduction

b) decision

c) branching

d) repetition

4.6 In an activity diagram, a rectangle with curved sides represents _____.

a) a complete algorithm

b) a comment

c) an action

d) the termination of the application

4.7 The body of an `if` statement that contains multiple statements is placed in _____.

a) `()`

b) `[]`

c) `<>`

d) `{}`

4.8 A variable of the `bool` type can be assigned either the value _____ or the value _____.

a) `true`, `false`

b) `off`, `on`

c) `one`, `zero`

d) `yes`, `no`

4.9 A variable whose value cannot be changed after its initial definition is called a _____.

a) `double`

b) constant

c) standard

d) `bool`

4.10 The _____ operator assigns to the left operand the result of adding the left and right operands.

a) `+`

b) `=+`

c) `+=`

d) `+ =`

4.11 *(Currency Converter Application)* Develop an application that functions as a currency converter as shown in Fig. 4.35. The user provides a number at the **Enter dollars to convert:** prompt and selects a currency name (as a number) from a menu of options. After the user enters the currency selection, the application should convert the specified amount into the indicated currency and display it. If the user enters an invalid currency selection, the application should simply display the dollar amount that the user entered. Your application should be able to convert currency amounts from dollars to Euros, Yen and Pesos, using the following exchange rates: 1 Dollar = 0.8 Euros, 109 Yen and 11 Pesos. [*Note:* Currency exchange rates are constantly changing. There are many online sites where you can view current exchange rates, including `finance.yahoo.com/m3`, `www.x-rates.com` and `www.rubicon.com/passport/currency/currency.html`.]

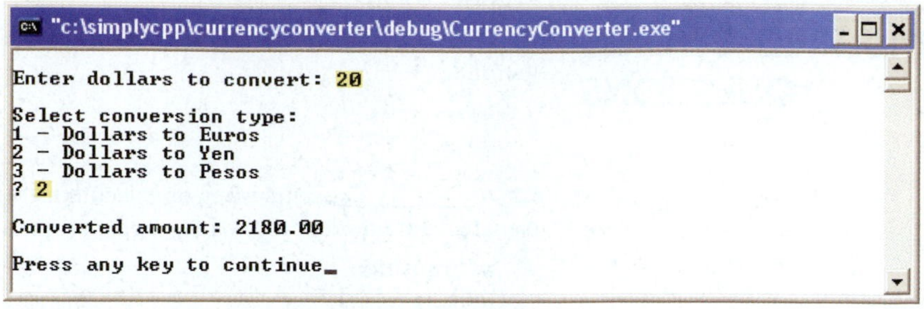

```
c:\simplycpp\currencyconverter\debug\CurrencyConverter.exe

Enter dollars to convert: 20

Select conversion type:
1 - Dollars to Euros
2 - Dollars to Yen
3 - Dollars to Pesos
? 2

Converted amount: 2180.00

Press any key to continue_
```

Figure 4.35 Currency Converter application output.

a) *Copying the template to your working directory.* Copy the C:\Examples\ Tutorial04\Exercises\CurrencyConverter directory to your C:\SimplyCpp directory.

b) *Opening the template file.* Open the CurrencyConverter.cpp file in your text editor or IDE.

c) *Including the <iomanip> header file.* In line 4, add an #include preprocessor directive that includes the <iomanip> header file. This will enable you to use the setprecision stream manipulator to display currency values with exactly two digits of precision to the left of the decimal point.

d) *Defining variables to contain user input.* In line 11 of the main function, add a comment indicating that the next two lines contain variable definitions. In line 12, define a double variable amount to contain the dollar value that the user inputs. In line 13, define a variable response as the int type that will contain the user's menu selection.

e) *Obtaining the user input.* Insert a cout statement that prompts the user for the number of dollars to convert, as shown in Fig. 4.35. Then insert a statement that uses cin to input the user response into variable amount.

f) *Obtaining the currency name.* Add a cout statement that displays a menu of options to the user, as shown in Fig. 4.35. Then insert a statement that uses cin to store the user response in variable response.

g) *Performing the currency conversion.* Next, you will use a nested if...else statement to determine which currency the user entered, then perform the appropriate conversion. Insert a nested if...else statement with three conditions. In the first condition, use the expression response == 1, which evaluates to true if the user selected 1, the menu option corresponding to euros. If this condition is true, the body of this if statement should convert the dollars to euros by multiplying amount by 0.8 and assigning the result to amount. Otherwise, in the nested if statement, test the condition response == 2. If this condition is true, the body of this if statement will convert the dollars to yen by multiplying amount by 109 and assigning the result to amount. Finally, if the first two conditions are false, the third nested if statement should test the condition response == 3. If this condition is true, the body of this if statement should convert the dollars to pesos by multiplying amount by 11 and assigning the result to amount.

h) *Displaying the result.* Add a statement that inserts the fixed and setprecision (with an argument of 2) stream manipulators into cout as you did in the **Wage Calculator** application (Fig. 4.23, line 49). Finally, insert a statement that uses cout to display a label for the converted amount, followed by a colon, a space and the result.

i) *Save, compile and run the completed application.* Type 20.00 at the **Enter dollars to convert:** prompt and select option 2 (Yen) from the menu by entering 2 at the menu's prompt. Ensure that the converted value 2180.00 displays. Run the application again, type 20.00 at the **Enter dollars to convert:** prompt and select option 1 (Euros) from the menu by entering 1 at the menu's prompt. Ensure that the converted value 16.00 displays. Run the application again, type 20.00 at the **Enter dollars to convert:** prompt and select option 3 (Pesos) from the menu by entering 3 at the menu's prompt. Ensure that the converted value 220.00 displays. Finally, run the application once more, type 20.00 at the **Enter dollars to convert:** prompt and enter any number at the menu's prompt. Notice that the application simply displays the dollar amount if an incorrect option is selected from the menu.

j) *Close the Command Prompt window.*

4.12 *(Expanded Wage Calculator that Performs Tax Calculations)* Develop an application that calculates an employee's wages as shown in Fig. 4.36. The user enters the hourly wage and number of hours worked per week. Then the application displays the user's gross wages, Federal taxes (the amount deducted for Federal taxes) and net wages (the difference between the gross wages and the Federal tax amount). Assume overtime wages are 1.5 times the hourly wage and Federal withholding taxes are 15% of gross earnings. [*Note:* The calculation for actual Federal withholding taxes is more complicated. See www.irs.gov/newsroom/article/0,,id=109817,00.html for more information.]

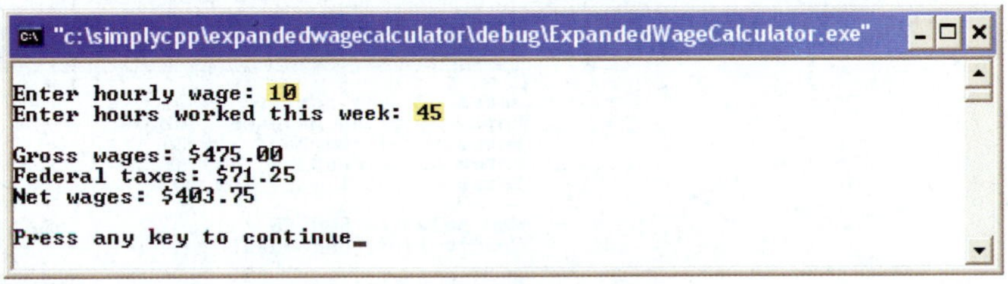

Figure 4.36   Expanded **Wage Calculator** application output.

a) *Copying the template to your working directory.* Copy the C:\Examples\ Tutorial04\Exercises\ExpandedWageCalculator directory to your C:\Simply-Cpp directory.

b) *Opening the template file.* Open the WageCalculator.cpp file in your text editor or IDE.

c) *Modifying the main function.* Add the code for *Steps d* and *e* to main (lines 10–56).

d) *Calculating and displaying the Federal taxes deducted.* After line 52, insert a statement that defines a constant double variable—TAX_RATE—and initializes it to 0.15, which represents 15%. On the next line, insert a statement that defines double variable federalTaxes and assigns to it the product of wages and TAX_RATE. The result is the amount that will be deducted for Federal taxes from the gross wages. Note that the cout statement provided in the template file in line 49 ensures that numeric values displayed by cout are formatted properly. It also causes any cout statements that appear after in your application's main function after line 49 to format numbers as specified in line 49. Use a cout statement to label the output as Federal taxes and display the value.

e) *Calculating and displaying the employee's net wages.* Insert a statement that subtracts federalTaxes from wages to calculate the employee's net wages. Use a cout statement to label the output as net wages and display the value, as shown in Fig. 4.36.

f) *Save, compile and run the completed application.* Type 10 at the **Enter hourly wage:** prompt and type 45 at the **Enter hours worked this week:**. Ensure that the results appear as shown in Fig. 4.36.

g) *Close the Command Prompt window.*

4.13 *(Credit Checker Application)* Develop an application (as shown in Fig. 4.37) that a credit manager can use to determine whether a department store customer has exceeded the credit limit on a charge account. For each customer, the credit manager enters an account number (an int), a balance at the beginning of the month (a double), the total of all items charged this month (a double), the total of all credits applied to the customer's account this month (a double) and the customer's allowed credit limit (a double). The application should input each of these facts, calculate the new balance (= *beginning balance + charges – credits*), display the new balance and determine whether the new balance exceeds the customer's credit limit. If the customer's credit limit is exceeded, the application should display a message informing the manager of this fact.

a) *Copying the template to your working directory.* Copy the C:\Examples\ Tutorial04\Exercises\CreditChecker directory to your C:\SimplyCpp directory.

b) *Opening the template file.* Open the CreditChecker.cpp file in your text editor or IDE.

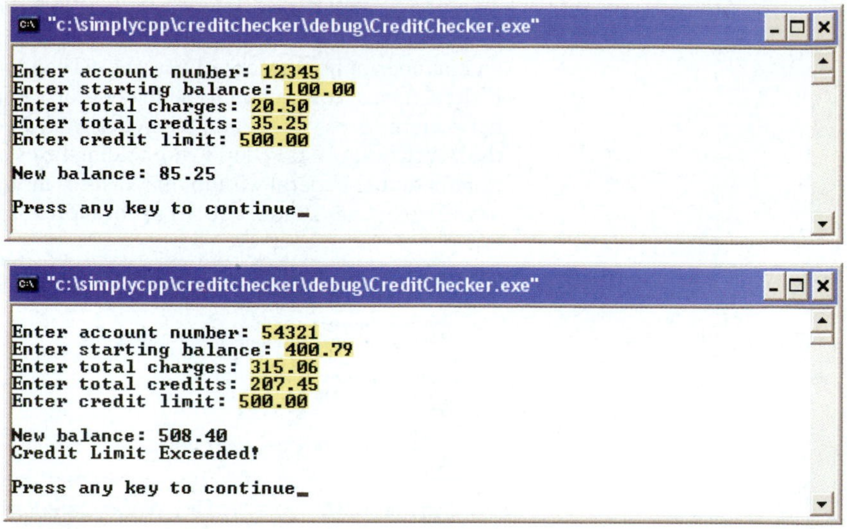

Figure 4.37 Credit Checker application output.

c) *Coding the main function.* Add the code for *Steps d* through *g* to function main (lines 10–14).

d) *Defining variables.* Starting in line 12, insert a statement that defines an int variable accountNumber to contain the account number entered by the user. Then insert statements that define four double variables—startBalance, totalCharges, totalCredits and creditLimit.

e) *Obtaining the user input.* Use cout and cin in five pairs of statements that prompt the user for and input the account number, starting balance, total charges, total credits and credit limit (Fig. 4.37). Input the values entered at each of these prompts in the accountNumber, startBalance, totalCharges, totalCredits and creditLimit, variables respectively.

f) *Calculating and displaying the new balance.* Define a fifth double variable called newBalance to contain the new balance in the account after the charges and credits have been applied. Calculate the new balance by adding the total charges to the starting balance and subtracting the credits. Assign the result to newBalance. Insert the fixed and setprecision stream manipulators into cout, as you did in Fig. 4.23. Display a label and value for newBalance.

g) *Determining if the credit limit has been exceeded.* Insert an if statement that determines whether the new balance exceeds the specified credit limit. If so, display "Credit Limit Exceeded!" on a new line.

h) *Save, compile and run the completed application.* Use the values shown in the two sample outputs of Fig. 4.37 to ensure that your application performs the credit check correctly.

i) *Close the Command Prompt window.*

What does this code do? ▶   **4.14** Assume that the user enters the value 27 at the **Enter your age:** prompt. Determine what is displayed by the following code:

```
1   // Exercise 4.14: WDTCD.cpp
2   // What does this code do?
3   #include <iostream> // required for C++ stream I/O
4
5   using namespace std; // for accessing C++ Standard Library members
6
7   // function main begins program execution
8   int main()
9   {
10      int age;
```

```
11
12        cout << "\nEnter your age: ";
13        cin >> age;
14
15        if ( age < 0 )
16        {
17           cout << "Enter a value greater than or equal to zero." << endl;
18        } // end if
19        else if ( age < 13 )
20        {
21           cout << "Child" << endl;
22        } // end else if
23        else if ( age < 20 )
24        {
25           cout << "Teenager" << endl;
26        } // end else if
27        else if ( age < 30 )
28        {
29           cout << "Young Adult" << endl;
30        } // end else if
31        else if ( age < 65 )
32        {
33           cout << "Adult"  << endl;
34        } // end else if
35        else
36        {
37           cout << "Senior Citizen" << endl;
38        } // end else
39
40        cout << endl;
41
42        return 0; // indicate that program ended successfully
43
44     } // end function main
```

What's wrong with this code? ▶

4.15 The following code segment should display "AM" if the hour is a value in the range 0–11 and should display "PM" if the hour is a value in the range 12–23. For any other hour value, the code segment should display "Time Error". Find the error(s) in the following code:

```
1     // Exercise 3.15: WWWTC.cpp
2     // Application displays "AM" if hour is in the range of 0-11 and
3     // "PM" if hour is in the range of 12-23. Any other value causes
4     // an error message to be displayed.
5     #include <iostream> // required for C++ stream I/O
6
7     using namespace std; // for accessing C++ Standard Library members
8
9     // function main begins program execution
10    int main()
11    {
12       int hour = 14;
13
14       if ( hour >= 0 )
15       {
16          if ( hour < 12 )
17          {
18             cout << "\nAM" << endl;
19
```

```
20            } // end if
21
22         } // end if
23         else
24         {
25            cout << "\nTime Error" << endl;
26
27         } // end else
28         else if ( hour >= 12 )
29         { // end if
30            if ( hour < 24 )
31            {
32               cout << "\nPM" << endl;
33
34            } // end if
35
36         } // end else if
37
38         return 0; // indicate program ended successfully
39
40   } // end function main
```

Using the Debugger ▶

4.16 *(Grade Converter Application)* The **Grade Converter** application is supposed to input an integer grade between 0 and 100 from the user and display the corresponding letter grade. For values 90–100 the application should display **A**; for 80–89 the application should display **B**; for 70–79 the application should display **C**; for 60–69 the application should display **D**; and for grades from 0–59, the application should display **F**. However, when you run the application you will notice that the application incorrectly displays **B** for the value 90; the application should display **A** for this value. Follow the steps below to locate and fix the logic error. Fig. 4.38 shows the incorrect output when the value 90 is input.

```
"c:\simplycpp\gradeconverter\debug\GradeConverter.exe"

Enter numeric grade: 90
Grade is: B
Press any key to continue_
```

Figure 4.38 Incorrect output for **Grade Converter** application output.

a) *Copying the template to your working directory.* Copy the C:\Examples\Tutorial04\Exercises\Debugger\GradeConverter directory to your C:\SimplyCpp directory.

b) *Opening the Grade Converter application's solution file.* Open the GradeConverter.sln file in Visual Studio .NET.

c) *Compiling the Grade Converter application.* Select **Build > Build Solution** to compile the **Grade Converter** application.

d) *Setting breakpoints.* Set breakpoints at lines 22 and 26 by clicking the margin indicator to the left of those lines.

e) *Running the application in the debugger.* Select **Debug > Start**. Type 90 at the **Enter grade (0-100):** prompt, then press *Enter*.

f) *Locating the logic error.* Use the debugger's **Watch** window and the **Debug > Continue** command to help you locate the logic error. When you continue execution from the breakpoint at line 22, notice that execution continues to line 26, which is in the next if statement. If the program logic is implemented correctly, the main function should terminate after line 22 executes. Stop debugging by selecting **Debug > Stop Debugging**. Locate lines 22–26 in the application and fix the logic error.

g) *Save, compile and run the completed application.* Select **Debug > Start**. Set a breakpoint at the return statement in line 41 to prevent the application from exiting immediately after displaying its result. Test the program again with the value 90 to ensure that the application displays the correct letter grade (**A**).

h) *Close the Visual Studio .NET IDE.*

Programming Challenge ▶

4.17 *(Encryption Application)* A company that transmits data over the telephone is concerned that its phones might be tapped. All its data is transmitted as four-digit int values. The company has asked you to write an application that encrypts its data so that the data may be transmitted more securely. Encryption is the process of transforming data into a form that can be recognized only by the intended receiver. Your application should read a four-digit integer input by the user and encrypt the information as described in the steps of this exercise (Fig. 4.39).

Figure 4.39 Encryption application output.

a) *Copying the template to your working directory.* Copy the C:\Examples\ Tutorial04\Exercises\Encryption directory to your C:\SimplyCpp directory.

b) *Opening the template file.* Open the Encryption.cpp file in your text editor or IDE.

c) *Coding the main function.* Add the code for *Steps d* through *f* to function main (lines 8–12).

d) *Defining a variable to contain user input.* In lines 10–11, insert a full-line comment followed by a definition for an int variable number that will store user input. Then use cout to prompt the user to enter a 4-digit integer, followed by a statement using cin to input the value that the user enters into the number variable.

e) *Extracting the digits from the user input.* Use the programming techniques you used to solve Exercise 3.17 to insert statements that extract the digits from int variable number. Assign the digits of number to the int variables digit1, digit2, digit3 and digit4, respectively.

f) *Encrypting each digit and display the encrypted results.* Replace each digit by performing the calculation *(the sum of that digit plus 7) modulo 10*. We use the term modulo (mod, for short) to indicate that you are to use the remainder (%) operator. Swap the first digit with the third, and swap the second digit with the fourth. Display a label for the encrypted digits, then display each digit separated by a space character (Fig. 4.39). [*Note:* Once a number is encrypted, it will need to be decrypted in the future. You might consider how to write an application that will decrypt these values.]

g) *Save, compile and run the completed application.* Use the values shown in the sample output of Fig. 4.39 to ensure that your application performs the encryption correctly.

h) *Close the Command Prompt window.*

T U T O R I A L

5

Dental Payment Application

Introducing Logical Operators, chars and strings

Many C++ applications allow users to select different actions to perform based on what the user types at the keyboard. In the preceding tutorial, you used simple conditions to determine the **Wage Calculator**'s output. In this tutorial, you will use **logical operators** in your application to make more complex decisions in response to user input.

In earlier tutorials, your applications stored user input as numbers using primitive types, such as int and double. However, these primitive types can store only numbers, which makes them inappropriate for storing many other forms of user input, such as names, dates and other text. In this tutorial, you will learn how to store keyboard input as single characters or strings of characters, which can include letters, numbers and symbols such as dollar signs, whitespace characters, punctuation marks and escape sequences.

5.1 Test-Driving the Dental Payment Application

Dentists perform many different procedures on their patients, and they frequently use computers to prepare their bills. In this tutorial, you will develop the **Dental Payment** application. This application must meet the following requirements:

Application Requirements

A dentist has asked you to create an application that employees can use to bill patients. Your application must allow the user to enter the patient's name and specify which services were performed during the visit. The application should allow the user to specify whether a cleaning, cavity filling or x-ray was performed. Your application will then calculate the total charges, given that a cleaning costs $35, a cavity filling costs $150 and an x-ray costs $85. If a user attempts to calculate the total of a bill without specifying any services or entering the patient's name, an error message should be displayed.

You begin by test-driving the completed application. Then, you will learn the additional C++ capabilities you will need to create your own version of this application.

Test-Driving the Dental Payment Application

1. *Locating the completed application.* Open the **Command Prompt** window by selecting **Start > All Programs > Accessories > Command Prompt**. Change to the completed **Dental Payment** application directory by typing cd C:\Examples\Tutorial05\CompletedApplication\DentalPayment.

2. *Attempting to calculate a total without entering input.* Type DentalPayment in the **Command Prompt** window to run the application (Fig. 5.1). Press *Enter* at the **Enter patient name:** prompt without entering a name. Notice that an error message displays, indicating that you must enter a name (Fig. 5.2).

```
Command Prompt - DentalPayment                                    _ □ ×

C:\>cd C:\Examples\Tutorial05\CompletedApplication\DentalPayment

C:\Examples\Tutorial05\CompletedApplication\DentalPayment>DentalPaymen
t

Enter patient name: _
```

Figure 5.1   **Dental Payment** application before input is entered.

```
Command Prompt                                                    _ □ ×

Enter patient name:
Error: You must enter a name

C:\Examples\Tutorial05\CompletedApplication>_
```

Error message

Figure 5.2   Error message displays when no patient name is entered.

3. *Entering a name without selecting services.* Type DentalPayment in the **Command Prompt** window to run the application again. Type Bob Green at the **Enter patient name:** prompt. Indicate that no services were performed by entering n (short for "no") at each of the three remaining prompts (Fig. 5.3). Notice that an error message appears, indicating that you must select at least one service.

```
Command Prompt                                                    _ □ ×

C:\Examples\Tutorial05\CompletedApplication>DentalPayment
Enter patient name: Bob Green
Was cleaning performed (y = yes, n = no)? n
Was cavity filling performed (y = yes, n = no)? n
Was an x-ray performed (y = yes, n = no)? n

Error: Select at least one service

C:\Examples\Tutorial05\CompletedApplication>_
```

Error message

Figure 5.3   Error message displays when no services are selected.

4. *Selecting the cleaning and x-ray services.* Run the application once more. Type Bob Green at the **Enter patient name:** prompt. To indicate that cleaning was performed, type y (short for "yes") at the **Was cleaning performed (y = yes, n = no)?** prompt. To indicate that a cavity filling was not performed, type n at the **Was cavity filling performed (y = yes, n = no)?** prompt. Finally, to indicate that an x-ray was performed, type y at the **Was an x-ray performed (y = yes, n = no)?** prompt. This causes the application to calculate and display the total cost of the services performed during the dentist visit (Fig. 5.4).

(cont.)

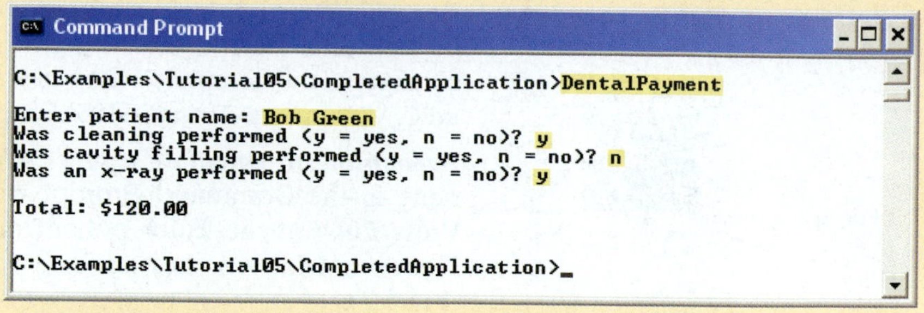

Figure 5.4 **Dental Payment** application with input entered and total cost of services displayed.

5. *Close the Command Prompt window.*

5.2 Constructing the Dental Payment Application

Now you will build your **Dental Payment** application by using variables that store whether services were performed as individual characters and a variable that stores the patient name as a string of characters. The pseudocode in Fig. 5.5 describes the basic operation of the **Dental Payment** application. Recall that pseudocode is an informal language that helps programmers develop algorithms.

> Prompt for and input a patient name
>
> If the user has not entered a patient name
>   Display error message
> Else
>   Prompt for and input selected services
>
>   If user has not selected any services
>   Display error message
>   Else
>   If Cleaning was selected
>   Add the cost of a cleaning to the total
>
>   If Cavity Filling was selected
>   Add the cost of a cavity filling to the total
>
>   If X-Ray was selected
>   Add the cost of an x-ray to the total
>
>   Display the total cost of services in dollar format

Figure 5.5 Pseudocode for the **Dental Payment** application.

First, your application will prompt the user for four inputs: the patient's name, whether cleaning was performed, whether a cavity filling was performed and whether an x-ray was taken. Then, your application will display the total cost of services in dollar format.

5.3 Introduction to chars and strings

In this section, you will learn how to use the **char** primitive data type to store individual characters. You will then learn how to store strings of characters in a `string` object.

Defining and Using chars

The definition

```
char grade;
```

creates a variable of the `char` type named `grade`. The value of a variable of the `char` type is a **character constant** (or **character literal**), which is a single character or escape sequence within single quotes. Character constants include letters (such as `'A'` and `'d'`), digits (such as `'5'` and `'0'`), special characters (such as `','`—the comma—`'$'` and `'*'`), whitespace characters (such as `' '`—a space) and escape sequences (such as `'\n'`—the newline character).

Character constants can be used in assignment statements, such as

```
grade = 'A';
```

which assigns the character `'A'` to `grade`. Character constants can also be used in boolean expressions, such as:

```
if ( grade == 'A' )
{
   cout << "Excellent!";
}
```

When this statement is executed, the text `Excellent!` is displayed if `grade` contains the character `'A'`.

Characters normally are stored in variables of the `char` type; however, an important feature of C++ is that characters can be stored in any integer data type because they are represented as integers (for the `char` data type, typically a value in the range 0–255) in the computer. Thus, we can treat a character either as an integer or as a character, depending on its use. For example, the statements

```
int charValue = 'A'; // assign the integer value of 'A' to charValue
cout << "The character (A) has the value "
     << charValue << endl;
```

prints the character A and its integer value as follows:

```
The character (A) has the value 65
```

The integer 65 is the character `'A'`'s numerical representation in the computer. Many computers today use the **ASCII (American Standard Code for Information Interchange)** character set, in which 65 represents the uppercase letter `'A'`, 97 represents the lowercase letter `'a'` and 48 represents the digit `'0'`. A list of the ASCII characters and their decimal values is presented in Appendix D.

Defining and Using `strings`

The **`string`** class (defined in the C++ Standard Library) enables you to create objects that store strings of characters. You have already used strings of characters to display text in each of the applications you have created. `string` objects enable you to store such strings of characters in a variable.

To access the features of the `string` class, you must insert the preprocessor directive

```
#include <string>
```

into your code, which includes the **`<string>` standard library header file**. A `string` object can be defined as follows

```
string month = "March";  // assign string "March" to month
```

The preceding statement defines the `month` variable, which creates `string` object `month`. The statement then assigns to that `string` object the value `"March"`. Note that you cannot assign an `int` or a `char` to a `string` in a `string` definition. For example, the definitions

```
string error1 = 'c'; // Error: string cannot be initialized with a char
string error2 = 22; // Error: string cannot be initialized with an int
```

Common Programming Error

Attempting to convert an `int` or `char` to a `string` using an assignment in a definition is a syntax error.

result in syntax errors. However, assigning a single character to a `string` object is permitted in an assignment statement, as in

```
string string1; // define string string1
string1 = 'n'; // assignment allowed after string1 is created
```

The second assignment has the same effect as

```
string string1 = "n";
```

Your **Dental Payment** application will store the patient's name in a `string` object. The application will also use a `char` to determine which services were performed. In the following box, you will include the `<string>` standard library header file and define variables that you will use to store user input.

Including the `<string>` Header File and Defining Variables

1. ***Copying the template to your working directory.*** Copy the `C:\Examples\Tutorial05\TemplateApplication\DentalPayment` directory to your `C:\SimplyCpp` directory.

2. ***Open the Dental Payment application's template source code file.*** Open the template file `DentalPayment.cpp` in your text editor or IDE.

3. ***Including the `<string>` header file.*** Insert line 6 of Fig. 5.6. Including the `<string>` header file enables you to create `string` objects and call functions defined in the `string` class.

The `<string>` header file enables access to classes and functions defined in the `string` class

```
DentalPayment.cpp
4  #include <iostream> // required to perform C++ stream I/O
5  #include <iomanip>  // required for parameterized stream manipulators
6  #include <string>   // required to access string functions
7
8  using namespace std; // for accessing C++ Standard Library members
```

Figure 5.6   Including the `<string>` standard library header file.

4. ***Defining variables to store user input.*** Add lines 13–17 of Fig. 5.7. Line 14 defines `string` variable `patient`, which will store the patient's name. Lines 15–17 define `char` variables `cleaning`, `filling` and `xRay`, each of which will store a character that determines whether cleaning, cavity-filling or X-ray services were performed, respectively. The value of each of these variables is initialized to `'n'`, indicating that the service has not been performed.

Define the variables that store user input

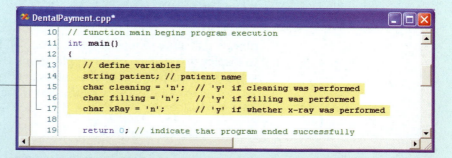

```
DentalPayment.cpp*
10  // function main begins program execution
11  int main()
12  {
13      // define variables
14      string patient; // patient name
15      char cleaning = 'n';  // 'y' if cleaning was performed
16      char filling = 'n';   // 'y' if filling was performed
17      char xRay = 'n';      // 'y' if whether x-ray was performed
18
19      return 0; // indicate that program ended successfully
```

Figure 5.7   Defining variables of the `char` and `string` types.

5. ***Save the application.***

As you learned in Tutorial 3 and Tutorial 4, the stream extraction operator (`>>`) can place numeric user input in `int` and `double` variables. Similarly, the stream extraction operator can place a single character typed at the keyboard in a `char` variable. The statements

```
char inputCharacter; // define char variable inputCharacter
cin >> inputCharacter; // place user input in inputCharacter
```

place a single character typed at the keyboard in char variable inputCharacter. If the user typed the letter c, inputCharacter would store the character 'c', which is 99 in the ASCII character set. If the user typed the number 5, inputCharacter would store the character '5'. When the user enters a digit, the computer does not store the integer value in inputCharacter, but rather the ASCII value for the character. (In the case of '5', the ASCII value is 53, as indicated in Appendix D.)

The stream extraction operator can also place a string of characters in a string object. The statements

```
string string1; // define string variable string1
cin >> string1; // store user input in string1
```

reads a string from the keyboard. When using the stream extraction operator to read a stream of characters, input is **delimited** (that is, terminated) by whitespace characters. For example, if the user entered the name Bob Green at the input prompt in the preceding statement, cin would give the value "Bob" to string1. Input terminates at the space between "Bob" and "Green" because the space character is a delimiter. The last name "Green" is not lost. The next input from the keyboard, such as

```
string string2; // define string variable string2
cin >> string2; // store user input in string2
```

would read "Green" into string2.

In the following box, you will use the **getline** function (defined in the <string> header) to read streams of characters that the user types at the keyboard. The getline function accepts an input stream (such as cin) as its first parameter and a string as its second parameter. The statements

```
string string1; // define string variable string1
getline( cin, string1 ); // place a line of user input in string1
```

define string variable string1 and place in string1 the characters entered at the keyboard (using cin). When your application calls the getline function as shown in the preceding example, the delimiter is the newline character, so input terminates when the user presses *Enter*. This enables your application to store multiple names (such as a first and last name, separated by spaces) in one string object using one function call. If the user entered the name Bob Green at the input prompt in the preceding example, cin would input the value "Bob Green" into string1.

Retrieving User Input and Displaying the Result

1. ***Prompting the user for and inputting the patient's name.*** Add lines 19–21 of Fig. 5.8 to your application. Be sure to include all blank lines and comments as shown in Fig. 5.8 to improve code readability. Line 20 displays a blank line using a newline (\n), then displays the input prompt **Enter patient name:**.

Prompt the user for the patient's name and input the response into the string variable patient

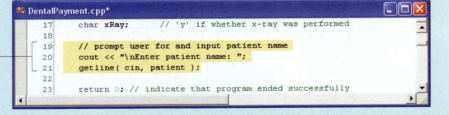

Figure 5.8 Prompting the user for the patient name and using the getline function to input the name into a string.

(cont.)

Line 21 calls the `getline` function with arguments `cin` and `patient`. When executed, this statement inputs characters from `cin` into `string` variable `patient` until a newline is encountered. In general, this statement will input into `patient` *all* the characters that the user types at the input prompt before pressing *Enter*. The newline character, however, is not placed in `patient`. Unlike the `getline` function, the expression `cin >> patient` would input only the characters entered before the application encounters *any* whitespace character, including the space character.

2. ***Prompting the user for and inputting the services performed.*** Add lines 23–31 of Fig. 5.9 to your application. Line 24 prompts the user to enter a character indicating whether cleaning was performed. The application is designed to accept a single character— `'y'` if the answer is "yes" and `'n'` if the answer is "no." Notice that the input prompt displays the input values that the application accepts and their corresponding meanings (y = yes, n = no). In line 25, `cin` inputs the first character that the user enters into `cleaning`.

Good Programming Practice

If your C++ application accepts limited input values, you should display prompts that clearly indicate those limits.

Prompt the user for and input services performed

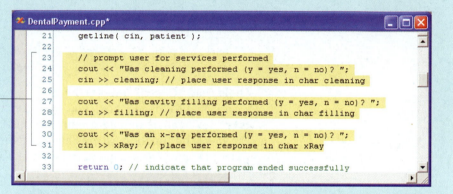

```
21      getline( cin, patient );
22
23      // prompt user for services performed
24      cout << "Was cleaning performed (y = yes, n = no)? ";
25      cin >> cleaning; // place user response in char cleaning
26
27      cout << "Was cavity filling performed (y = yes, n = no)? ";
28      cin >> filling; // place user response in char filling
29
30      cout << "Was an x-ray performed (y = yes, n = no)? ";
31      cin >> xRay; // place user response in char xRay
32
33      return 0; // indicate that program ended successfully
```

Figure 5.9 Prompting the user for and inputting responses for services performed.

Similar to lines 24–25, line 27 prompts the user to enter a character indicating whether a cavity filling was performed, and line 28 inputs a single character from `cin` into `char` variable `filling`. Likewise, line 30 prompts the user to enter a character indicating whether an x-ray was performed, and line 31 inputs a single character from `cin` into `char` variable xRay. Note that if the user enters "yes" at the first input prompt, `cleaning` will contain the character `'y'`, `filling` the character `'e'` and xRay the character `'s'`. This occurs because the stream extraction operation inputs one character at a time from the input stream when the right operand is a `char`.

3. ***Calculating the total.*** Add lines 33–51 of Fig. 5.10. Line 33 defines the `total` variable, which stores the total charges for the patient as a `double`. This variable is initialized to `0.0`. Lines 36–51 define three `if` statements that determine which services were performed. Each `if` statement's condition uses the equality operator (`==`) to determine whether the value stored in each `char` variable is `'y'` (yes). The body of each `if` statement adds the dollar value of the service to `total`. For example, the first `if` statement (lines 36–39) adds 35 to `total` (line 38) only if `cleaning` contains `'y'` (line 36).

4. ***Displaying the total in dollar format.*** Add lines 53–57 of Fig. 5.11. Line 54 inserts the `fixed` stream manipulator in `cout` so that floating-point values are displayed using fixed-point notation. The statement also inserts the parameterized stream manipulator `setprecision( 2 )` in `cout`, which causes floating-point values to be displayed with two digits of precision to the right of the decimal point.

Good Programming Practice

Use newlines to separate your application's input prompts from the application's results.

(cont.)

Define **double** variable **total** and initialize its value to **0.0**

If a service was performed, add its cost to **total**

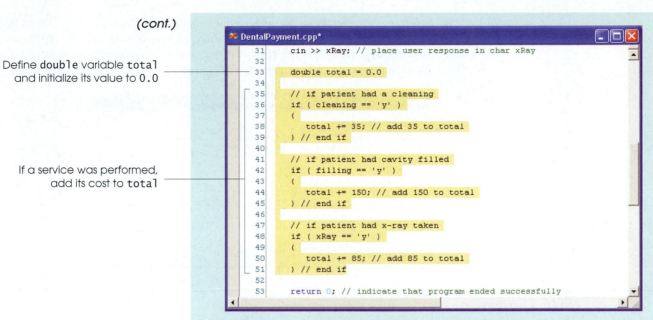

```
    31        cin >> xRay; // place user response in char xRay
    32
    33        double total = 0.0;
    34
    35        // if patient had a cleaning
    36        if ( cleaning == 'y' )
    37        {
    38           total += 35; // add 35 to total
    39        } // end if
    40
    41        // if patient had cavity filled
    42        if ( filling == 'y' )
    43        {
    44           total += 150; // add 150 to total
    45        } // end if
    46
    47        // if patient had x-ray taken
    48        if ( xRay == 'y' )
    49        {
    50           total += 85; // add 85 to total
    51        } // end if
    52
    53        return 0; // indicate that program ended successfully
```

Figure 5.10 Determining the total cost for the patient's visit.

Display **total** as currency

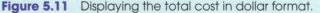

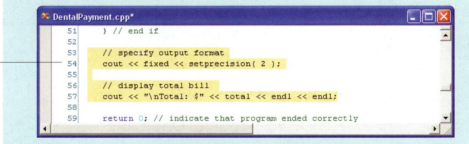

```
    51        } // end if
    52
    53        // specify output format
    54        cout << fixed << setprecision( 2 );
    55
    56        // display total bill
    57        cout << "\nTotal: $" << total << endl << endl;
    58
    59        return 0; // indicate that program ended correctly
```

Figure 5.11 Displaying the total cost in dollar format.

Line 57 uses **cout** to insert a newline to separate the application's output from its input. The newline is followed by descriptive text (**Total:**), a space character, a dollar sign and the value of **total**, formatted with two positions to the left of the decimal point. The **endl** stream manipulators place two newlines in the output stream.

5. *Save, compile and run the application.* Leave the patient name blank and enter **n** (for "no") at each of the subsequent prompts. Figure 5.12 shows the application output. Notice that the user is not required to enter a name or select any services. If no services are selected, the bill displays the value **$0.00**. In the next section, you will modify your application so that it displays an error message if the user does not enter a name or select any services.

Application calculates a bill of **$0.00** when no services are selected

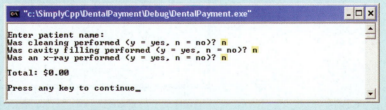

```
Enter patient name:
Was cleaning performed (y = yes, n = no)? n
Was cavity filling performed (y = yes, n = no)? n
Was an x-ray performed (y = yes, n = no)? n

Total: $0.00

Press any key to continue_
```

Figure 5.12 Application output with no patient name entered and no services selected.

(cont.)   6. ***Selecting services*** Run the application again. This time, enter y at the **Was cleaning performed (y = yes, n = no)?** prompt. Notice that the application now displays **$35.00** as the total (Fig. 5.13). Run the application several times, each time selecting different combinations of services to see the different totals.

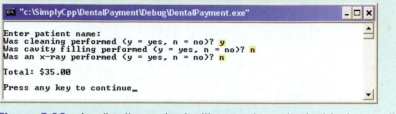

Figure 5.13 Application output with a service selected, but no patient name entered.

7. ***Close the Command Prompt window.***

SELF-REVIEW   1. _____ is not a character literal.

    a) `'5'`   b) `'a'`

    c) `'\n'`   d) None of the above.

2. By default, the _____ function extracts characters from an input stream until a new-line is encountered.

    a) `readline`   b) `inputline`

    c) `getline`   d) `getstring`

Answers: 1.) d. 2.) c.

5.4 Logical Operators

When you test-drove the completed application, a message was displayed if the user attempted to calculate the total charges without entering a patient name or without specifying which services were performed. In the following box, you will learn how to add code that determines whether the user entered a patient name. Later in this section, you will add code that determines whether at least one service is selected.

Displaying a Message If a Patient Name Is Not Entered

1. ***Adding an `if` statement to the `main` function.*** An error message should display if the user does not enter the patient's name. Add lines 23–27 of Fig. 5.14 to the `main` function. Be sure to include a blank line after the closing brace of the `if` statement for readability.

Verify that a patient name was entered ⎯⎯⎯

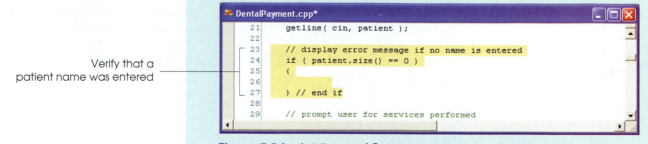

```
21        getline( cin, patient );
22
23        // display error message if no name is entered
24        if ( patient.size() == 0 )
25        {
26
27        } // end if
28
29        // prompt user for services performed
```

Figure 5.14 Adding an `if` statement to the `main` function.

(cont.)

Recall that line 21 places the characters typed at the keyboard (except for the newline) in the `patient` variable. If the user did not type any characters before pressing *Enter*, `patient` will contain the **empty string ("")**, which is a `string` value that contains no characters.

Line 24 calls `string` function **size**, which returns the number of characters in the `string` on which it is called. Note the use of the dot (`.`) between the `string` object's name, `patient`, and the name of the function that accesses the number of characters in the `string`, `size()`. The dot, known as the **member-access operator**, enables you to access data and functions that "belong" to the object to the left of the operator. You will learn more about objects and the member-access operator in Tutorial 15.

Line 24 tests whether data was entered at the **Enter patient name:** prompt. If the user doesn't enter any text, the `patient.size()` function returns the value 0, the expression `patient.size() == 0` evaluates to `true` and the body of the `if` statement executes. You will add the body of this `if` statement in the next step.

2. ***Adding code to display an error message.*** Add lines 26–27 of Fig. 5.15 to the body of the `if` statement you created in the previous step. Line 27 displays an error message indicating the user must enter a patient name.

Add an error message ────────────

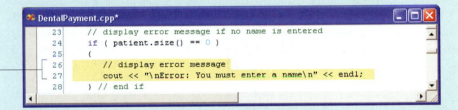

```
23     // display error message if no name is entered
24     if ( patient.size() == 0 )
25     {
26         // display error message
27         cout << "\nError: You must enter a name\n" << endl;
28     } // end if
```

Figure 5.15 Displaying an error message to the users.

3. ***Adding an `else` part to the `if` statement.*** If the condition in line 24 of Fig. 5.15 is `true` (that is, the user has omitted some required information), then the function should not execute the code that calculates the bill. You can prevent that code from executing by changing the `if` statement in lines 24–28 of Fig. 5.15 into an `if...else` statement. Add lines 29–30 and line 67 of Fig. 5.16 into the function. Also, lines 31–65, which are now in the body of the `else`, should be indented one more level to the right for readability. (Remember, the compiler ignores this indentation, so your application runs the same regardless of how it's indented.) The body of the `else` will now execute only if the user enters a name at the **Enter patient name:** prompt.

4. ***Save, compile and run the application.*** Figure 5.17 shows the updated application running. Notice that you do not have to select any services, but you must enter a name at the **Enter patient name:** prompt. If you do not enter a name, the error message in Fig. 5.17 displays. If none of the services is selected but a name is entered, the total for the bill will display $0.00 (Fig. 5.18). Later in this section, you will modify the code to determine whether the user has selected any services.

(cont.)

else statement ────

Right brace to
end the `else` statement ────

```
28    } // end if
29    else // otherwise, do calculations
30    {
31        // prompt user for services performed
32        cout << "Was cleaning performed (y = yes, n = no)? ";
33        cin >> cleaning; // place user response in char cleaning
34
35        cout << "Was cavity filling performed (y = yes, n = no)? ";
36        cin >> filling; // place user response in char filling
37
38        cout << "Was an X-ray performed (y = yes, n = no)? ";
39        cin >> xRay; // place user response in char xRay
40
41        double total = 0.0; // sum of all services performed
42
43        // if patient had a cleaning
44        if ( cleaning == 'y' )
45        {
46            total += 35; // add 35 to total
47        } // end if
48
49        // if patient had cavity filled
50        if ( filling == 'y' )
51        {
52            total += 150; // add 150 to total
53        } // end if
54
55        // if patient had x-ray taken
56        if ( xRay == 'y' )
57        {
58            total += 85; // add 85 to total
59        } // end if
60
61        // specify output format
62        cout << fixed << setprecision( 2 );
63
64        // display total bill
65        cout << "\nTotal: $" << total << endl;
66
67    } // end else
68
69    return 0; // indicate that program ended successfully
```

Figure 5.16   Adding an `else` part to an `if` statement.

```
"c:\SimplyCpp\DentalPayment\Debug\DentalPayment.exe"
Enter patient name:
Error: You must enter a name
Press any key to continue_
```

Figure 5.17   Application output without a name entered.

User must now enter a name ────

Application calculates a bill of
$0.00 when a name is entered
but no services are selected ────

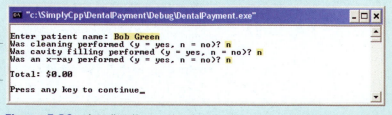
```
"c:\SimplyCpp\DentalPayment\Debug\DentalPayment.exe"
Enter patient name: Bob Green
Was cleaning performed (y = yes, n = no)? n
Was cavity filling performed (y = yes, n = no)? n
Was an x-ray performed (y = yes, n = no)? n

Total: $0.00

Press any key to continue_
```

Figure 5.18   Application output with a name entered, but without any
services selected.

5. **Close the Command Prompt window.**

So far, you have studied only **simple conditions**, such as `count <= 10`,
`total > 1000` and `number != value`. Each selection statement that you have used

evaluated only one condition with one of the relational (or comparison) operators (<, >, <=, >=) or one of the equality operators (== and !=).

To handle multiple conditions more efficiently, C++ provides logical operators that can be used to form **complex conditions**, or conditions that combine multiple simple conditions. The logical operators are **&& (logical AND)**, **|| (logical OR)** and **! (logical negation)**. After you learn about logical operators, you will use them to create a complex condition in your **Dental Payment** application to confirm service selections.

Using Logical AND (&&)

Suppose that you wish to ensure that two conditions are *both* true in an application before choosing a certain path of execution. In that case, you can use the logical && operator as follows:

```
if ( gender == 'F' && age >= 65 )
{
    seniorFemales += 1;
}
```

This if statement contains two simple conditions. The condition gender == 'F' determines whether a person is female, and the condition age >= 65 determines whether a person is a senior citizen. The if statement then considers the combined condition

```
gender == 'F' && age >= 65
```

This condition is true if and only if *both* of the simple conditions are true, meaning that gender contains the value 'F' *and* age contains a value greater than or equal to 65. When this combined condition is true, the count of seniorFemales is incremented by 1. However, if either or both of the simple conditions are false, the application skips the increment and proceeds to the statement following the if statement. The readability of the preceding combined condition can be improved by adding redundant (that is, unnecessary) parentheses:

```
( gender == 'F' ) && ( age >= 65 )
```

Figure 5.19 illustrates the outcome of using the && operator with two bool expressions. The table lists all four possible combinations of true and false values for *expression1* and *expression2*, which represent the left operand and the right operand, respectively. Such tables are called **truth tables**. C++ evaluates to true or false expressions with relational operators, equality operators and logical operators.

expression1	expression2	expression1 && expression2
false	false	false
false	true	false
true	false	false
true	true	true

Figure 5.19 Truth table for the && operator.

Using Logical OR (||)

Now let's consider the || operator. Suppose that you wish to ensure that *either or both* of two conditions are true before you choose a certain path of execution. You would use the || operator as in the following if statement:

```
if ( semesterAverage >= 90 || finalExam >= 90 )
{
    cout << "Student grade is A." << endl;
}
```

This statement also contains two simple conditions. The condition `semester-Average >= 90` is evaluated to determine whether the student deserves an "A" in the course because of an outstanding performance throughout the semester. The condition `finalExam >= 90` is evaluated to determine whether the student deserves an "A" in the course because of an outstanding performance on the final exam. The `if` statement then considers the combined condition

```
( semesterAverage >= 90 || finalExam >= 90 )
```

and assigns the student an "A" if either or both of the conditions are true, meaning that the student performed well during the semester, performed well on the final exam or both. Note that the text `"Student grade is A."` is displayed unless both of the conditions are false. Figure 5.20 provides a truth table for the `||` operator. Note in Appendix C that the `&&` operator has a higher precedence than the `||` operator.

expression1	expression2	expression1 || expression2
false	false	false
false	true	true
true	false	true
true	true	true

Figure 5.20 Truth table for the `||` operator.

An expression containing the `&&` operator is evaluated only until it is known whether the condition is true or false. For example, evaluation of the expression

```
( gender == 'F' ) && ( age >= 65 )
```

stops immediately if `gender` is not equal to `'F'` (which would mean the entire expression is false). In this case, the evaluation of the second expression is irrelevant—once the first expression is known to be false, the whole expression must be false. Evaluation of the second expression occurs if and only if `gender` is equal to `'F'` (which would mean that the entire expression could still be true if the condition `age >= 65` is true).

Similarly, an expression containing `||` is evaluated only until it is known whether the condition is true or false. For example, evaluation of the expression

```
if ( semesterAverage >= 90 || finalExam >= 90 )
```

stops immediately if `semesterAverage` is greater than or equal to 90 (which would mean the entire expression is true). In this case, the evaluation of the second expression is irrelevant—once the first expression is known to be true, the whole expression must be true.

This way of evaluating logical expressions can require fewer operations, therefore taking less time. This performance feature for the evaluation of `&&` and `||` expressions is called **short-circuit evaluation**.

Using Logical Negation (!)

C++'s `!` (logical negation, also called logical NOT or logical complement) operator enables a programmer to "reverse" the meaning of a condition. Unlike the logical operators `&&` and `||`, each of which combines two expressions (that is, these are all binary operators), the logical negation operator is a unary operator, requiring only one operand. The logical negation operator is placed before a condition to choose a path of execution if the original condition (without the logical negation operator) is false. The logical negation operator is demonstrated by the following `if` statement:

```
if ( !( grade == value ) )
{
   cout << "They are not equal!" << endl;
}
```

In this case, the body of the `if` executes if `grade` is not equal to `value`. The parentheses around the condition `grade == value` are necessary, because the logical negation operator (`!`) has a higher precedence than the equality operator. For clarity, most programmers prefer to write

```
!( grade == value )
```

as

```
( grade != value )
```

Figure 5.21 provides a truth table for the logical negation operator. Next, you will modify your **Dental Payment** application to use a complex logical expression to determine whether any of the services are selected.

expression	! expression
false	true
true	false

Figure 5.21   Truth table for the `!` (logical negation) operator.

Using Logical Operators in Complex Expressions

1. ***Inserting a complex expression into the `main` function.*** Insert lines 41–46 of Fig. 5.22. Lines 42–43 define a more complex logical expression than those you have used so far in this book. Notice the use of **&&**. Each expression, which determines if a service has not been selected, needs to be `true` for the entire expression inside the `if` statement to evaluate to `true`. The body of the `if` statement is executed only if the entire expression evaluates to `true`.

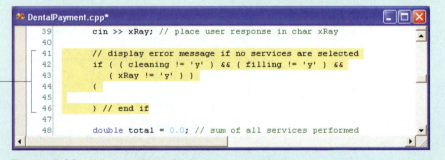

Insert a complex expression

```
39        cin >> xRay; // place user response in char xRay
40
41        // display error message if no services are selected
42        if ( ( cleaning != 'y' ) && ( filling != 'y' ) &&
43            ( xRay != 'y' ) )
44        {
45
46        } // end if
47
48        double total = 0.0; // sum of all services performed
```

Figure 5.22   Using multiple **&&** logical operators.

2. ***Displaying an error message.*** Insert lines 45–46 of Fig. 5.23. Now that your application tests whether a service has been selected, you should modify your `if` statement so that it becomes an `if...else` statement to prevent the application from calculating the bill if no services are selected.

Add an error message to the body of the `if` statement

```
41        // display error message if no services are selected
42        if ( ( cleaning != 'y' ) && ( filling != 'y' ) &&
43            ( xRay != 'y' ) )
44        {
45            // display error message
46            cout << "\nError: Select at least one service\n" << endl;
47        } // end if
48
49        double total = 0.0; // sum of all services performed
```

Figure 5.23   Displaying an error message if no services are selected.

(cont.) 3. ***Adding an `else` part to the `if` statement.*** Add lines 48–49 and line 75 of Fig. 5.24. Also, lines 50–74, which are now in the body of the `else`, should be indented one more level to the right for readability. The body of the `else` will now execute only if the user indicates that a service was performed. Modify the comments in lines 75 and 77 as shown in Fig. 5.24 to help distinguish between the nested `if...else` statement and the outer `if...else` statement.

Add an `else` statement ⟶

Right brace to end the nested `else` statement ⟶

```
46         cout << "\nError: Select at least one service\n" << endl;
47      } // end if
48      else // otherwise, do calculation
49      {
50         double total = 0.0; // sum of all services performed
51
52         // if patient had a cleaning
53         if ( cleaning == 'y' )
54         {
55            total += 35; // add 35 to total
56         } // end if
57
58         // if patient had cavity filled
59         if ( filling == 'y' )
60         {
61            total += 150; // add 150 to total
62         } // end if
63
64         // if patient had x-ray taken
65         if ( xRay == 'y' )
66         {
67            total += 85; // add 85 to total
68         } // end if
69
70         // specify output format
71         cout << fixed << setprecision( 2 );
72
73         // display total bill
74         cout << "\nTotal: $" << total << endl << endl;
75      } // end inner else
76
77   } // end outer else
78
```

Figure 5.24 Adding an `else` part to the nested `if` statement.

4. ***Save, compile and run the application.*** Figure 5.25 shows the completed application running. Notice that the user must enter a name and select at least one service before the application will display the total bill. Otherwise, an error message is displayed. The application appears the same as in the test-drive. (You have finally corrected the weakness from your earlier implementation of the **Dental Payment** application.) Figure 5.26 shows the completed application running with correct input.

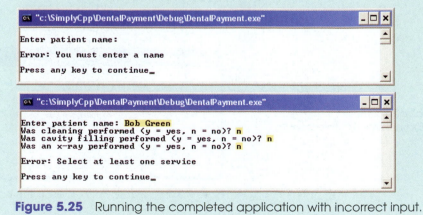

Figure 5.25 Running the completed application with incorrect input.

(cont.)

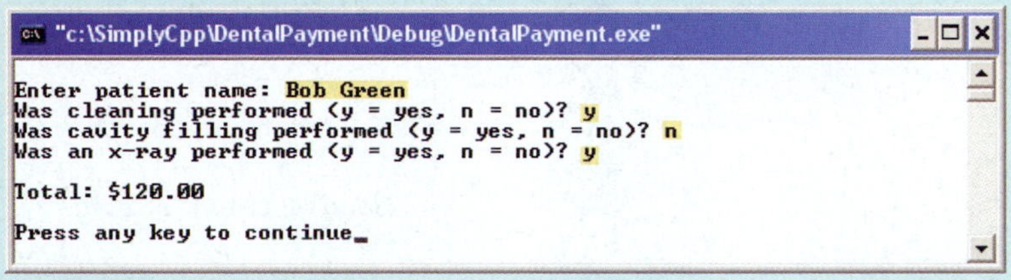

Figure 5.26 Running the completed application with correct input.

5. ***Close the Command Prompt window.***

Figure 5.27 presents the source code for the **Dental Payment** application. The lines of code that you added, viewed or modified in this tutorial are highlighted.

```
1   // Tutorial 5: DentalPayment.cpp
2   // This application calculates the total cost of the bill for a
3   // patient at a dental office.
4   #include <iostream> // required to perform C++ stream I/O
5   #include <iomanip>  // required for parameterized stream manipulators
6   #include <string>   // required to access string functions
7
8   using namespace std; // for accessing C++ Standard Library members
9
10  // function main begins program execution
11  int main()
12  {
13     // define variables
14     string patient; // patient name
15     char cleaning = 'n';  // 'y' if cleaning was performed
16     char filling = 'n';   // 'y' if filling was performed
17     char xRay = 'n';      // 'y' if x-ray was performed
18
19     // prompt user for and input patient name
20     cout << "\nEnter patient name: ";
21     getline( cin, patient );
22
23     // display error message if no name is entered
24     if ( patient.size() == 0 )
25     {
26        // display error message
27        cout << "\nError: You must enter a name\n" << endl;
28     } // end if
29     else // otherwise, do calculations
30     {
31        // prompt user for services performed
32        cout << "Was cleaning performed (y = yes, n = no)? ";
33        cin >> cleaning; // place user response in char cleaning
34
35        cout << "Was cavity filling performed (y = yes, n = no)? ";
36        cin >> filling; // place user response in char filling
37
38        cout << "Was an x-ray performed (y = yes, n = no)? ";
39        cin >> xRay; // place user response in char xRay
40
41        // display error message if no services are selected
42        if ( ( cleaning != 'y' ) && ( filling != 'y' ) &&
43           ( xRay != 'y' ) )
44        {
```

Define variables — lines 14–17
Obtain patient name — lines 20–21
Call **string** function **size** and determine whether the user entered a name — line 24
Use multiple logical operators to determine whether any services were selected — lines 42–43

Figure 5.27 Code for the **Dental Payment** application. (Part 1 of 2.)

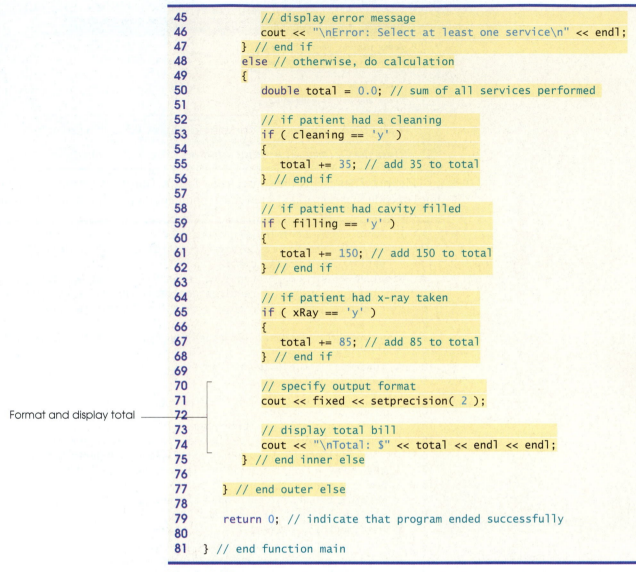

```
45              // display error message
46              cout << "\nError: Select at least one service\n" << endl;
47          } // end if
48          else // otherwise, do calculation
49          {
50              double total = 0.0; // sum of all services performed
51
52              // if patient had a cleaning
53              if ( cleaning == 'y' )
54              {
55                  total += 35; // add 35 to total
56              } // end if
57
58              // if patient had cavity filled
59              if ( filling == 'y' )
60              {
61                  total += 150; // add 150 to total
62              } // end if
63
64              // if patient had x-ray taken
65              if ( xRay == 'y' )
66              {
67                  total += 85; // add 85 to total
68              } // end if
69
70              // specify output format
71              cout << fixed << setprecision( 2 );
72
73              // display total bill
74              cout << "\nTotal: $" << total << endl << endl;
75          } // end inner else
76
77      } // end outer else
78
79      return 0; // indicate that program ended successfully
80
81  } // end function main
```

Format and display total — lines 70–74 bracketed

Figure 5.27   Code for the **Dental Payment** application. (Part 2 of 2.)

5.5 Wrap-Up

In this tutorial, you used `chars` and `strings` to store user input in your **Dental Payment** application. You learned that the value of a variable of the `char` type is a character constant (or character literal), which is a single character or escape sequence within single quotes. Characters normally are stored in variables of the `char` type; however, an important feature of C++ is that characters can be stored in any integer data type. Each `char`'s integer value corresponds to its ASCII code. You also learned that the stream extraction operator can place user input into character data types in addition to numerical data types.

You included the `<string>` standard library header file in your application so that you could create a `string` object to store the patient's name. You used the `getline` function to store an entire line of characters, including whitespace, delimited by a newline. You also called the `size` function on a `string` object to determine the number of characters it contained. You used several `if` statements nested in an `if...else` statement to calculate the cost of the dental visit or display an error message if the user was missing input.

You learned to use the logical AND (&&) operator when both conditions must be true for the complex condition to be true—if either condition is false, the complex condition is false. You also learned that the logical OR (||) operator requires at least one of its conditions to be true for the complex condition to be true—if both conditions are false, the complex condition is false. The logical NOT (!) operator reverses the `bool` result of a condition—`true` becomes `false`, and `false` becomes `true`. You used the && and || operators to form a complex expression.

In the next tutorial, you will learn more about C++'s control statements. In particular, you will use repetition statements, which allow the programmer to specify that an action or a group of actions should be performed many times.

SKILLS SUMMARY

Storing User Input as a char

- Use a `char` variable to the right of the stream extraction operator.

Storing a Line of User Input

- Use the `getline` function to store all characters, including whitespace, encountered before a newline.

Determining the Number of Characters in a `string`

- Call the `size` function on a `string` by preceding the function call with the variable name and the member-access operator (`.`).

Combining Multiple Conditions

- Use the logical operators to form complex conditions by combining simple ones.

KEY TERMS

ASCII (American Standard Code for Information Interchange)—A character set, popular in personal computers and data communication systems, that stores characters as one byte.

char type—The primitive type used to store character values.

character constant—Another name for a character literal.

character literal—The value of a variable of the `char` type, represented by a character within single quotes, such as `'A'`, `'d'`, `'*'`, `'.'`, `' '` and the like.

complex condition—A condition that combines multiple simple conditions.

delimit—Terminate. The stream extraction operator delimits input at whitespace characters.

empty string ("")—A `string` value that does not contain any characters.

getline function—A function that places characters from the specified input stream into the specified `string` object until a newline is reached.

logical AND (&&) operator—A logical operator used to ensure that two conditions are both `true` before choosing a path of execution. It performs short-circuit evaluation.

logical negation (!) operator—A logical operator that enables a programmer to reverse the meaning of a condition: A `true` condition, when logically negated, becomes `false`, and a `false` condition, when logically negated, becomes `true`.

logical operators—The operators (&&, || and !) that can be used to form complex conditions by combining simple ones.

logical OR (||) operator—A logical operator used to ensure that either or both of two conditions are `true` before a path of execution is chosen. It performs short-circuit evaluation.

member-access operator (.)—An operator that enables access to data and functions that belong to the object to the left of the operator.

short-circuit evaluation—The evaluation of the right operand in && and || expressions occurs only if the condition to the left of the && in an expression is true or the condition to the left of the || in an expression is false.

simple condition—A condition that contains one boolean expression.

size function of the string class—A function that returns the number of characters (as an int) in the string on which it is called.

<string> header file—The header file that declares classes and functions that store and manipulate strings.

string object—An object that stores a string of characters.

truth table—A table that displays the truth value of a logical operator for each possible combination of true and false values of its operand(s).

USER INTERFACE GUIDELINES

Displaying Input Prompts

- If your C++ application accepts limited input values, you should display prompts that clearly indicate those limits.
- Use newlines to separate your application's input prompts from the application's results.

C++ LIBRARY REFERENCE

string Declares classes and functions that store and manipulate strings.

- *Object*

  string—This object stores a string of characters.

- *Functions*

  size—This function returns the number of characters (as an int) in the string on which it is called.

  getline—This function places characters from the specified input stream into the specified string object until a newline is reached. For example, the statements

  ```
  string string1;
  getline( cin, string1 );
  ```

  cause the application to read from cin an entire line of text and store it in string variable string1.

MULTIPLE-CHOICE QUESTIONS

5.1 Which of the following statements contains a syntax error?
a) int charValue = 'A';
b) string singleCharacter = 'z';
c) char newCharacter = '\n';
d) None of the above.

5.2 The first argument to the getline function is _____.
a) an input stream
b) a string object
c) a delimiter
d) a char variable

5.3 The _____ function returns the number of characters in the string on which it is called.
a) width
b) getwidth
c) size
d) getsize

5.4 The _____ operator accesses data and functions that "belong" to the object to the left of the operator.
a) .
b) !
c) &&
d) ||

5.5 The _____ header file declares classes and functions that store and manipulate strings.
a) <iostream>
b) <iostring>
c) <strmanip>
d) <string>

5.6 The && operator _____.

    a) performs short-circuit evaluation   b) is a comparison operator

    c) evaluates to false if both operands are true

    d) None of the above.

5.7 The stream extraction operator terminates input when a _____ is encountered.

    a) space   b) newline

    c) tab   d) All of the above.

5.8 The condition *expression1* && *expression2* evaluates to true when _____.

    a) *expression1* is true and *expression2* is false

    b) *expression1* is false and *expression2* is true

    c) both *expression1* and *expression2* are true

    d) both *expression1* and *expression2* are false

5.9 The condition *expression1* || *expression2* evaluates to false when _____.

    a) *expression1* is true and *expression2* is false

    b) *expression1* is false and *expression2* is true

    c) both *expression1* and *expression2* are true

    d) both *expression1* and *expression2* are false

5.10 The condition !*expression1* && *expression2* evaluates to true when _____.

    a) *expression1* is true and *expression2* is false

    b) *expression1* is false and *expression2* is true

    c) both *expression1* and *expression2* are true

    d) Both a and b.

EXERCISES

5.11 (*Enhanced Dental Payment Application*) Because the char value 'y' differs from the character 'Y', the **Dental Payment** application from this tutorial will display an error message if the user enters Y at any of the input prompts. Modify the **Dental Payment** application so that it accepts uppercase and lowercase letters as input (Fig. 5.28).

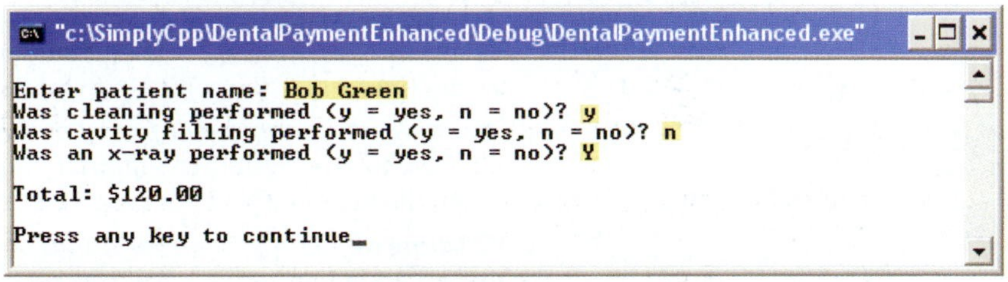

Figure 5.28   Enhanced **Dental Payment** application.

    a) *Copying the template to your working directory.* Copy the C:\Examples\ Tutorial05\Exercises\DentalPaymentEnhanced directory to your C:\SimplyCpp directory.

    b) *Opening the template source code file.* Open the DentalPayment.cpp file in your text editor or IDE.

    c) *Using boolean operators to support uppercase letters.* The if statement beginning in line 42 specifies a condition that prevents the body of the if statement from executing if the user enters y at any of the input prompts. Modify that condition so that an error message is not displayed if the user enters y or Y at any of the input prompts. Use redundant parentheses and break the expression across three lines to improve readability.

    d) *Adding the cost of each service to the total.* Modify the if statements in lines 54–69 so the cost of a service is added to the total if the user enters y or Y at the corresponding input prompt.

e) *Save, compile and run the completed application.* Test each calculation to ensure that you implemented the function properly. Make sure the functionality for each of the services works properly, both the existing services and the services you added in this exercise.

f) *Close the Command Prompt window.*

5.12 (*Modified Dental Payment Application*) Modify the **Dental Payment** application from this tutorial to include additional services (Fig. 5.29). The fluoride service costs $50, a root canal costs $225 and the user is allowed to select exactly one "other" service. If the "other" service is selected, the application should prompt the user for the cost of that service and add the cost to the total. Add the proper functionality (using `if` statements) to determine whether any of the new services are selected and, if so, add the price of the service to the total bill. As in the original application, which requires the user to enter a lowercase y to select a service, an error message should be displayed if the patient's name is missing or if none of the services is selected.

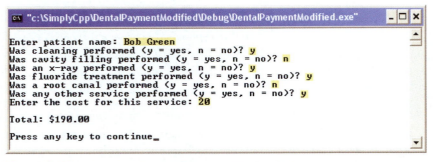

Figure 5.29 Modified **Dental Payment** application.

a) *Copying the template to your working directory.* Copy the `C:\Examples\Tutorial05\Exercises\DentalPaymentModified` directory to your `C:\SimplyCpp` directory.

b) *Opening the template source code file.* Open the `DentalPayment.cpp` file in your text editor or IDE.

c) *Defining additional variables.* In lines 18–20, insert three `char` variable definitions, `fluoride`, `rootCanal` and `other`, to store a character that determines whether the fluoride, root canal or other service was performed, respectively. Initialize their values to `'n'`. In line 21, insert a definition for the `double` variable `otherCost`, which stores the cost for the "other" services performed.

d) *Creating an input prompt for a fluoride treatment.* In lines 45–46, insert statements that ask the user whether a fluoride treatment was performed, as shown in Fig. 5.29. Store the user's response in `char` variable `fluoride`.

e) *Creating an input prompt for a root canal.* In lines 48–49, insert statements that ask the user whether a root canal was performed, as shown in Fig. 5.29. Store the user's response in `char` variable `rootCanal`.

f) *Creating an input prompt for an "other" services and an input prompt to store the cost of the other services.* In lines 51–52, insert statements that ask the user whether any other services were performed, as shown in Fig. 5.29. Store the user's response in `char` variable `other`. If the user enters y (for yes), the application should prompt the user for the cost of the service. In lines 54–60, insert an `if` statement that determines whether the user entered `'y'`. The body of the `if` statement should prompt the user for the cost of the "other" service and place the user response in the `otherCost` variable.

g) *Modifying the bill calculation.* Modify the `if` statement that starts in line 63 to check if the user has not entered a name and/or selected any services. Also add code that determines whether any new services are selected. This can be done using `if` statements that are similar to the ones already in the application. Use the `if` statements to update the total bill amount.

h) *Save, compile and run the completed application.* Test each calculation to ensure that you implemented your code properly. Make sure the functionality for each of the services works correctly, both the existing services and the services you added in this exercise.

i) *Close the Command Prompt window.*

5.13 (*Grade Average Application*) Write an application that inputs three letter grades, and displays their average, as shown in Fig. 5.30. The application should use a four-point scale to calculate the grade point average (GPA): 4 for an A, 3 for a B, 2 for a C, 1 for a D and 0 for an F. Your application should display A for the average grade if the GPA is greater than 3.5, B if the GPA is greater than 2.5, C if the GPA is greater than 1.5, D if the GPA is greater than 0.5 and F otherwise. For simplicity, your application should accept only upper-case letter grades.

```
"c:\simplycpp\gradeaverage\debug\GradeAverage.exe"          - □ ×

Enter first grade: A
Enter second grade: B
Enter third grade: C

Average grade is: B

Press any key to continue_
```

Figure 5.30 Grade Average application output.

a) *Copying the template to your working directory.* Copy the C:\Examples\Tutorial05\Exercises\GradeAverage directory to your C:\SimplyCpp directory.

b) *Opening the template file.* Open the GradeAverage.cpp file in your text editor or IDE.

c) *Defining chars to store user input.* In the main function, define char variables firstGrade, secondGrade and thirdGrade to store the letter grades that the user inputs. Then define double variables total and average to store the total numeric grade and the average numeric grade, respectively. Initialize total to 0.0.

d) *Inputting three letter grades.* Insert statements that prompt the user for three letter grades. The first letter should be stored in firstGrade, the second in secondGrade and the third in thirdGrade.

e) *Adding functionality to the convertToNumericGrade function.* Note that the template source code file already contains calls to the convertToNumericGrade function from the main function. In this step, you will code the functionality for convertToNumericGrade. In the convertToNumericGrade function, replace the statement in line 11 with a series of nested if...else statements that determine which character was entered. If the character is 'A', the function should return the value 4. In this case, the body of the if statement should contain the statement

```
return 4;
```

If the character is 'B', the function should return the value 3 using the statement,

```
return 3;
```

Use this technique to return the proper values for each of the other possible letter grades. If the user enters an invalid letter grade, the function should return 0.

f) *Calculating and displaying the average grade.* After the calls to the convertToNumericGrade function in the main function, insert code that finds the average of the three numeric grades. Then use nested if...else statements to display the appropriate letter grade that corresponds to the average numeric grade.

g) *Save, compile and run the completed application.* Test the application by using various sets of grades and calculating their average.

h) *Close the Command Prompt window.*

What does this code do? ▶   **5.14** What does this code do?

```cpp
1  // Exercise 5.14: WDTCD.cpp
2  // What does this code do?
3  #include <iostream>  // required to perform C++ stream I/O
4  #include <string>    // required to access string functions
5
6  using namespace std; // for accessing C++ Standard Library members
```

```
 7
 8    // function main begins program execution
 9    int main()
10    {
11       string name;
12       int grade = 0;
13
14       cout << "\nEnter student name: ";
15       getline( cin, name );
16
17       cout << "Enter student grade: ";
18       cin >> grade;
19
20       if ( ( name.size() == 0 ) ||
21          !( ( grade > 0 ) && ( grade <= 100 ) ) )
22       {
23          cout << "\nError: Enter a grade in the range 0-100.\n" << endl;
24       } // end if
25
26       return 0; // indicate that program ended successfully
27
28    } // end function main
```

What's wrong with this code? ▶   **5.15** Find the error(s) in the following code, which is supposed to prompt the user to input a name (which may contain a space character), then display an error message if no text was entered at the input prompt.

```
 1    // Exercise 5.15: WWWTC.cpp
 2    // This application prints an error message if no name is entered.
 3    #include <iostream>   // required to perform C++ stream I/O
 4    #include <string>     // required to access string functions
 5
 6    using namespace std; // for accessing C++ Standard Library members
 7
 8    // function main begins program execution
 9    int main()
10    {
11
12       string name;
13
14       cout << "\nEnter name: ";
15       cin >> name;
16
17       if name.size( 0 )
18       {
19          cout << "\nError: Enter a name\n" << endl
20       } // end if
21
22       return 0; // indicate that program ended successfully
23
24    } // end function main
```

Using the Debugger ▶   **5.16** (*Sibling Survey Application*) The **Sibling Survey** application prompts the user for the number of siblings, the number of sisters and the number of brothers. If the sum of the number of brothers and sisters does not equal the number of siblings, an error message is displayed. Otherwise, the application displays a message indicating whether the number of brothers or sisters is greatest. While testing this application, you noticed that the application does not display the expected message in response to the number of siblings that you entered. Use your debugger to find and correct the logic error(s) in the code. Figure 5.31 shows the correct output for the application.

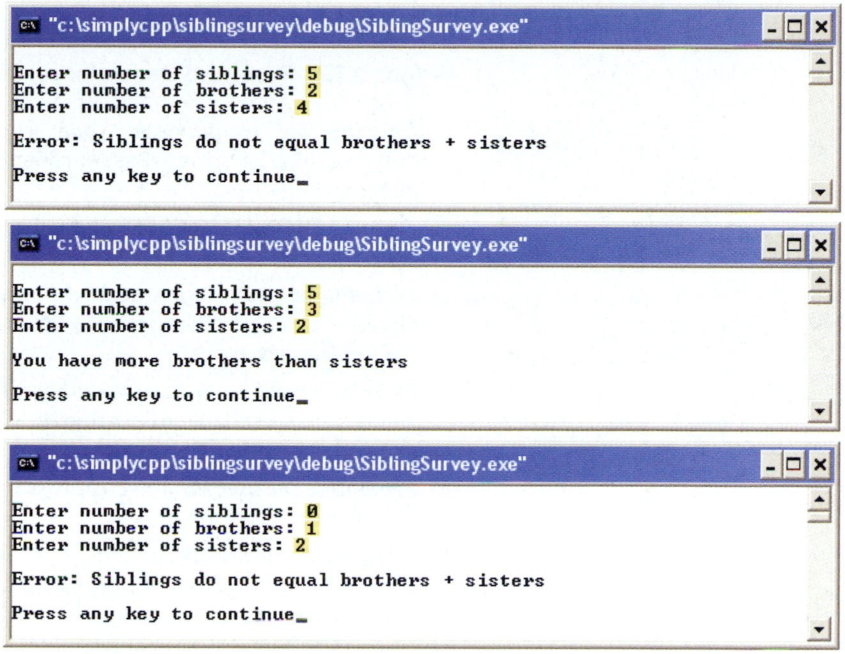

Figure 5.31 Correct output for the **Sibling Survey** application.

a) *Copying the template to your working directory.* Copy the C:\Examples\ Tutorial05\Exercises\Debugger\SiblingSurvey directory to your C:\Simply-Cpp directory.

b) *Opening the Command Prompt window and changing directories.* Open the **Command Prompt** window by selecting **Start > All Programs > Accessories > Command Prompt**. Change to your working directory by typing cd C:\SimplyCpp\Debugger\SiblingSurvey.

c) *Running the application.* Test the application several times using different values at each input prompt each time you run the application. Notice that when you enter valid values, an error message is displayed.

d) *Start the debugger.* Compile your application for use with your debugger, then start your application in the debugger.

e) *Finding and correcting the error(s).* Use the debugging skills learned in previous tutorials to determine where the application's logic errors exist. You should begin by setting breakpoints at each of the conditions in the application's if statements. Then run the application, input values and inspect the value of each variable to determine whether it makes sense to execute the body of the if statement if its condition evaluates to true. Modify the application so that it displays the correct output.

f) *Save, compile and run the corrected application.* Test the application using various values at the input prompts to ensure that the application works correctly.

g) *Close the debugger.*

Programming Challenge ▶

5.17 (*Password Generator Application*) Write an application that generates a password from a five-character string that the user enters (Fig. 5.32). The application should generate the password by reversing the order of the string and subtracting 15 from each character's ASCII code. If the user enters a string that does not contain exactly five characters, the application should display an error message and exit.

Figure 5.32 Password Generator application output.

a) *Copying the template to your working directory.* Copy the `C:\Examples\Tutorial05\Exercises\PasswordGenerator` directory to your `C:\SimplyCpp` directory.

b) *Opening the template file.* Open the `PasswordGenerator.cpp` file in your text editor or IDE.

c) *Including the `<string>` standard library header file.* In line 5, insert a preprocessor directive to include the `<string>` standard library header file so that you can access the `string` class.

d) *Defining variables to store user input.* In lines 12–14, insert a full-line comment and define `string` variable `plainText` to store user input, and `char` variable `password`, to contain a password character.

e) *Prompting the user for a five-character `string`.* In lines 16–18, prompt the user for a five-character `string`.

f) *Generating a password.* In lines 21–24, include the `if` part of an `if...else` statement. The `if` part should determine whether the `string` has five characters. If not, the body of the `if` statement should display an error message. The `else` part of the `if...else` statement should generate a password. First, display descriptive text for the password. To generate the password, you must modify each character of user input individually. To access each character of the `string` `plainText`, you will use `string` function `at`. When you call the `at` function, you must specify the position of the character that you want to access. The first character in a string is located at position 0, the second at position 1, the third and position 2 and so on. For example, the expression `plainText.at( 1 )` returns the second character in the `string`. For each character in `plainText`, subtract 15 from the current character and assign the result to `password`. Use `cout` to display the value contained in `password`. Recall that C++ allows such manipulations of `chars` because they are stored as integers. Start with the last plain text character, which can be accessed by calling `plainText.at( 4 )`. For each character in `plainText`, modify the integer value of the character, assign the result to `password` and display it. After displaying the last password character, insert two `endl` stream manipulators in `cout`.

g) *Save, compile and run the completed application.* Test the application to ensure that the correct password is generated and that the application displays an error message when the user does not enter a five-character `string`.

h) *Close the* Command Prompt *window.*

Objectives

In this tutorial, you will learn to:
- Use the `while` repetition statement to execute statements repeatedly.
- Use counter-controlled repetition.
- Use the increment and decrement operators.
- Use the `setw` and `left` stream manipulators.

Outline

Car Payment Calculator Application

Introducing the `while` Repetition Statement

This tutorial continues the discussion of control statements that began in Tutorial 4. You will learn to use repetition statements, which are control statements that repeat actions while a condition remains true. In your daily life, you perform many repetitive tasks based on conditions. For example, each time you turn a page in this book (while there are more pages to read), you are repeating the simple task of turning a page, based on the condition that there are more pages to read.

The ability to perform tasks repeatedly is an important part of application development. Repetition statements are used to represent repetitive tasks in many types of applications. In this tutorial, you will learn to use the `while` repetition statement and include it in the **Car Payment Calculator** application that you will build. Later tutorials will introduce additional repetition statements.

6.1 Test-Driving the Car Payment Calculator Application

In this tutorial, you will build a **Car Payment Calculator** application that displays monthly payments for loan lengths of two, three, four and five years. The following problem statement requires an application that repeats a calculation four times—you will use a repetition statement to solve this problem. This application must meet the following requirements:

Application Requirements

Typically, banks offer car loans for periods ranging from two to five years (24 to 60 months). Borrowers repay the loans in monthly installments. The amount of each payment is based on the length of the loan, the amount borrowed and the interest rate. Create an application to allow the customer to enter the price of a car, the down payment amount and the annual interest rate of the loan. The application should display the loan's duration in months and the monthly payments for two-, three-, four- and five-year loans. The variety of payment options allows the user to easily compare the loan options and choose the most appropriate payment plan. The results should be displayed in tabular format.

You begin by test-driving the completed application. Then, you will learn the additional C++ capabilities you will need to create your own version of this application.

Test-Driving the Car Payment Calculator Application

1. ***Locating the completed application.*** Open the **Command Prompt** window by selecting **Start > All Programs > Accessories > Command Prompt**. Change to your completed **Car Payment Calculator** application directory by typing cd C:\Examples\Tutorial06\CompletedApplication\CarPayment.

2. ***Running the Car Payment Calculator application.*** Type CarPayment in the **Command Prompt** window to run the application (Fig. 6.1). Enter 16900 at the **Enter car price:** prompt. Enter 6000 at the **Enter down payment:** prompt. Enter 7.5 at the **Enter annual interest rate:** prompt. The screen should appear as in Fig. 6.2.

```
Command Prompt - CarPayment

C:\>cd C:\Examples\Tutorial06\CompletedApplication\CarPayment

C:\Examples\Tutorial06\CompletedApplication\CarPayment>CarPayment

Enter car price: _
```

Figure 6.1   **Car Payment Calculator** application before data has been entered.

```
Command Prompt - CarPayment

C:\Examples\Tutorial06\CompletedApplication\CarPayment>CarPayment

Enter car price: 16900
Enter down payment: 6000
Enter annual interest rate: 7.5_
```

Figure 6.2   **Car Payment Calculator** application after data has been entered.

3. ***Calculating the monthly payment amounts.*** The application displays the monthly payment amounts in tabular format (Fig. 6.3). You will use a `while` repetition statement and the `setw` stream manipulator to produce the output that is displayed.

Results displayed in tabular format —

```
Command Prompt

C:\Examples\Tutorial06\CompletedApplication\CarPayment>CarPayment

Enter car price: 16900
Enter down payment: 6000
Enter annual interest rate: 7.5

Months      Monthly Payments
24          $490.50
36          $339.06
48          $263.55
60          $218.41

C:\Examples\Tutorial06\CompletedApplication\CarPayment>_
```

Figure 6.3   **Car Payment Calculator** application displaying calculation results.

4. ***Close the Command Prompt window.***

6.2 `while` Repetition Statement

A **repetition statement** repeats actions while a condition remains true. For example, if you go to the grocery store with a list of items to purchase, you go through the list until you have added each item to your shopping cart. This process is described by the following pseudocode statements:

> While there are still items on my shopping list
>   Add an item to my shopping cart
>   Cross the item off my list

These statements describe the repetitive actions that occur during a shopping trip. The condition, "There are still items on my shopping list" can be true or false. If it is true, then the actions, "Add an item to my shopping cart" and "Cross the item off my list" are performed in sequence. These actions execute repeatedly while the condition remains true. The statements indented in this repetition statement constitute its body. When the last item on the shopping list has been purchased and crossed off the list, the condition becomes false. At this point, the repetition terminates, and the first statement after the repetition statement executes. In the shopping example, you would most likely proceed to the checkout station.

As an example of a **while** repetition statement, consider an application segment designed to find the first power of 3 greater than 50.

```
int product = 3;

while ( product <= 50 )
{
    product *= 3;
}
```

The application segment initializes the `product` variable to 3. The condition in the `while` statement, `product <= 50`, is referred to as the **loop-continuation condition**. While the loop-continuation condition remains `true`, the `while` statement iterates (that is, executes its body repeatedly). When the loop-continuation condition becomes `false`, the `while` statement finishes executing, and `product` contains the first power of 3 larger than 50. Let's examine the execution of the preceding code in detail.

When the application enters the `while` statement, the value of `product` is 3. Each time the loop executes, `product` is multiplied by 3, successively taking on the values 3, 9, 27 and 81. When `product` becomes 81, the condition in the `while` statement, `product <= 50`, evaluates to `false`. When the repetition ends, the final value of `product` is 81, which is indeed the first power of 3 greater than 50. Application execution continues with the next statement after the repetition statement. Note that, if a `while` statement's condition is initially `false`, the body statements are not performed, and your application simply continues executing with the next statement after the right curly brace that ends the body of the `while` loop. Also note that if the loop-continuation condition never becomes `false`, the `while` statement will not stop executing. This is called an **infinite loop**. The following box describes each step as the preceding repetition statement executes.

Common Programming Error

Provide in the body of every `while` statement an action that eventually causes the loop-continuation condition to become false. If you do not, the repetition statement never terminates, causing an error called an infinite loop. (*Note:* To terminate an application containing an infinite loop, click in the **Command Prompt** window, hold the *Ctrl* key and press the letter *c*.)

Executing the while Repetition Statement

1. The application defines the `product` variable and sets its value to 3.

2. The flow of control enters the `while` repetition statement.

3. The loop-continuation condition is checked. The condition evaluates to `true` (`product` is 3, which is less than or equal to 50), so the application executes the `while` loop's body.

4. The number (currently 3) stored in `product` is multiplied by 3, and the result is assigned to `product`; `product` now contains 9.

5. The loop-continuation condition is checked. The condition evaluates to `true` (`product` is 9, which is still less than or equal to 50), so the application executes the `while` loop's body again.

6. The number (currently 9) stored in `product` is multiplied by 3, and the result is assigned to `product`; `product` now contains 27.

(cont.) 7. The loop-continuation condition is checked. The condition evaluates to `true` (`product` is 27, which is still less than or equal to 50), so the application executes the `while` loop's body again.

8. The number (currently 27) stored in `product` is multiplied by 3, and the result is assigned to `product`; `product` now contains 81.

9. The loop-continuation condition is checked. The condition evaluates to `false` (`product` is now 81, which is not less than or equal to 50), so the application exits the `while` statement and continues execution at the first statement after the right curly brace that ends the body of the `while` loop.

The UML activity diagram of Fig. 6.4 illustrates the flow of control in the preceding `while` repetition statement. The action state represents the action in which the value of `product` is multiplied by 3.

Figure 6.4 introduces the UML's **merge symbol**. The merge symbol joins two flows of activity into one flow of activity. The UML **diamond symbol** is used as both the merge symbol and the decision symbol. In this diagram, the merge symbol joins the transitions from the initial state and the action state, so they both flow into the decision that determines whether the loop's body statement should execute. In this case, the UML diagram enters its action state when the loop-continuation condition (also called the guard condition) `product <= 50` is true.

Although the UML represents both the decision symbol and the merge symbol with the diamond shape, the symbols can be distinguished by the number of "incoming" and "outgoing" transition arrows. A decision symbol has one transition arrow pointing to the diamond and two (or more) transition arrows pointing from the diamond to indicate possible transitions from that point. In addition, each transition arrow pointing from a decision symbol has a guard condition next to it. A merge symbol has two (or more) transition arrows pointing to the diamond and only one transition arrow pointing from the diamond to indicate multiple activity flows merging to continue the activity. None of the transition arrows associated with a merge have guard conditions.

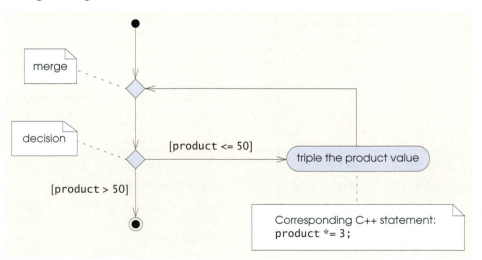

Figure 6.4   `while` repetition statement UML activity diagram.

The activity diagram in Fig. 6.4 clearly shows the repetition. The transition arrow emerging from the action state points back to the merge from which the activity transitions into the decision, creating a **loop**. The guard conditions are tested each time the loop iterates (executes its body) until the guard condition `product > 50` becomes true. At this point, the `while` loop terminates, and control passes to the next statement in the application following the loop.

1. The body of a `while` statement executes _____.

   a) at least once   b) never

   c) while its condition remains true   d) while its condition remains false

2. The UML represents both the merge symbol and the decision symbol as _____.

   a) rectangles with rounded sides   b) diamonds

   c) small black circles   d) ovals

Answers: 1) c. 2) b.

6.3 Increment and Decrement Operators

The process of **incrementing** a variable by one is so common in computer applications that C++ has a specific operator for this purpose, **++**. Similarly, C++ provides an operator, **--**, to subtract one from a variable, which is called **decrementing** a variable. These operators are called the **unary increment operator** (**++**) and the **unary decrement operator** (**--**). These operators are summarized in Fig. 6.5.

An application can increment the value of a variable called `counter` by 1 using the increment operator, **++**, rather than either of the following expressions:

```
counter = counter + 1
counter += 1
```

An increment or decrement operator that is prefixed to (placed before) a variable is referred to as the **preincrement** or **predecrement** operator. An increment or decrement operator that is postfixed to (placed after) a variable is referred to as the **postincrement** or **postdecrement** operator.

Operator	Called	Sample expression	Explanation
++	preincrement	++counter	Increment counter by 1, then use the new value of counter in the expression in which counter resides.
++	postincrement	counter++	Use the current value of counter in the expression in which counter resides, then increment counter by 1.
--	predecrement	--counter	Decrement counter by 1, then use the new value of counter in the expression in which counter resides.
--	postdecrement	counter--	Use the current value of counter in the expression in which counter resides, then decrement counter by 1.

Figure 6.5 Increment and decrement operators.

Good Programming Practice

Place unary operators next to their operands with no intervening spaces.

Preincrementing (or predecrementing) a variable causes the value of the variable to be incremented (decremented) by 1, after which the new value of the variable is used in the expression in which it appears. For example, if `counter` is 5, the statement

```
cout << ++counter;
```

adds one to `counter` and stores the result (6) in `counter`, then displays the new value of `counter` (6).

Postincrementing (or postdecrementing) the variable causes the current value of the variable to be used in the expression in which it appears, after which the variable's value is incremented (decremented) by 1. For example, if counter is 5, the statement

```
cout << counter++;
```

displays the current value of counter (5), then adds one to counter and stores the result (6) in counter.

It is important to note that when incrementing or decrementing a variable in a statement by itself, as in

```
++counter;
```

or

```
counter++;
```

the preincrement and postincrement (and similarly the predecrement and postdecrement) forms have the same effect. It is only when a variable appears in the context of a larger expression that preincrementing and postincrementing (and similarly predecrementing and postdecrementing) the variable have different effects.

SELF-REVIEW

1. Assuming a = 3, the values of variables a and b after the assignment b = a-- are _____, respectively.

   a) 3 and 3   b) 2 and 3
   c) 3 and 2   d) 2 and 2

2. Assuming c = 5, the values of variables c and d after the assignment d = ++c are _____, respectively.

   a) 5 and 6   b) 6 and 6
   c) 5 and 5   d) 6 and 5

Answers: 1) b. 2) b.

6.4 Constructing the Car Payment Calculator Application

Now that you have learned the while repetition statement, you are ready to construct your **Car Payment Calculator** application. The pseudocode in Fig. 6.6 describes the basic operation of the **Car Payment Calculator** application.

Initialize the loan length to two years
Prompt the user for and input the car price, down payment and annual interest rate
Calculate the loan amount
Calculate the monthly interest rate

While the loan length is less than or equal to five years
    Calculate the number of months
    Calculate the monthly payment based on the loan amount, monthly interest rate and loan length in months
    Display the result (in tabular format)
    Increment the loan length by one year

Figure 6.6   Pseudocode for the **Car Payment Calculator** application.

Now that you have test-driven the **Car Payment Calculator** application and studied its pseudocode representation, you will begin building the application by writing code that defines variables and retrieves user input. Later in this section, you will learn how to use the setw stream manipulator to output your results in tabular format.

Defining Variables and Retrieving User Input

1. *Copying the template to your working directory.* Copy the C:\Examples\Tutorial06\TemplateApplication\CarPayment directory to your C:\SimplyCpp directory.

2. *Opening the Car Payment Calculator application's template source code file.* Open the template file CarPayment.cpp in your text editor or IDE.

3. *Defining variables.* Insert lines 22–28 (Fig. 6.7) to define the variables that you will use in your **Car Payment Calculator** application. The years and months variables store the length of the loan in years and in months, respectively. The calculation requires the length in months, but the loop-continuation condition will use the number of years. The monthlyPayment variable (line 25) stores the calculation result. The calculation is based on user input that specifies the car's price, the customer's down payment and the annual interest rate. These inputs will be stored in the price (line 26), downPayment (line 27) and interestRate (line 28) variables, respectively. Lines 26–27 indicate that the price and downPayment variables are of the int type, so the car price and down payment must be entered as whole number values.

Define variables to store user input and calculated values →

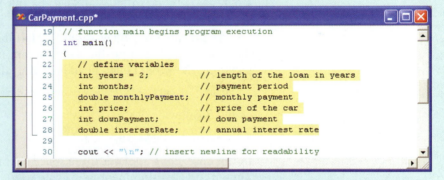

```
19    // function main begins program execution
20    int main()
21    {
22        // define variables
23        int years = 2;             // length of the loan in years
24        int months;                // payment period
25        double monthlyPayment;     // monthly payment
26        int price;                 // price of the car
27        int downPayment;           // down payment
28        double interestRate;       // annual interest rate
29
30        cout << "\n"; // insert newline for readability
```

Figure 6.7 Define variables that are used in the **Car Payment Calculator**.

4. *Prompting the user for and inputting values.* Insert lines 30–39 (Fig. 6.8) to prompt the user for and input values for the car price, the down payment and the annual interest rate. Lines 32–33 prompt the user for the car price and input the value entered at the keyboard in int variable price. Similarly, lines 35–36 prompt the user for the down payment and input the value entered at the keyboard in int variable downPayment. Finally, lines 38–39 prompt the user for the annual interest rate (percentage) and input the value typed at the keyboard in double variable interestRate.

Prompt user for and input the car price, down payment and annual interest rate →

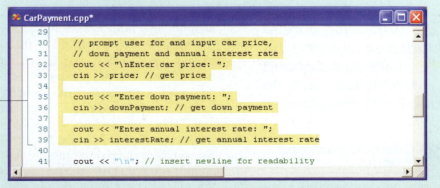

```
29
30        // prompt user for and input car price,
31        // down payment and annual interest rate
32        cout << "\nEnter car price: ";
33        cin >> price; // get price
34
35        cout << "Enter down payment: ";
36        cin >> downPayment; // get down payment
37
38        cout << "Enter annual interest rate: ";
39        cin >> interestRate; // get annual interest rate
40
41        cout << "\n"; // insert newline for readability
```

Figure 6.8 Prompt user for and input car price, down payment and annual interest rate.

5. *Save the application.*

In Tutorial 4, you learned how to use the `setprecision` parameterized stream manipulator to format floating-point values. In this section, you will use the **setw** parameterized stream manipulator (which is made accessible by including the `<iomanip>` header file) to display your application's output in tabular format. In the statement

```
cout << "Payment: $" << setw( 10 ) << monthlyPayment;
```

the manipulator `setw( 10 )` specifies that the next value output to `cout` (in this case, `monthlyPayment`) should appear in a field of width 10, meaning that `cout` displays the value with at least 10 character positions. If the output value is less than 10 character positions wide, the value is **right justified** in the field (that is, aligned to the right side of the field) by default. Thus, if `monthlyPayment` contained the value `1234.56` the preceding example would display

```
Payment: $    1234.56
```

Because the value `1234.56` contains seven characters (six digits plus the decimal point), the `setw( 10 )` manipulator causes `cout` to precede the value with three blanks so that the total number of characters in the field is 10. If the value to be output is more than 10 characters wide, the field width is extended to the right to accommodate the entire value.

To indicate that values should be **left justified** (that is, aligned to the left side of the field), simply output the **left** stream manipulator (which can be accessed by including the `<iostream>` header). For example, the statement

```
cout << left << "Payment: $" << setw( 10 ) << monthlyPayment;
```

would display

```
Payment: $1234.56
```

In this case, `cout` appends three space characters to the right of the value `1234.56`. Thus, if the next statement to execute was

```
cout << "(including interest)";
```

the screen would display

```
Payment: $1234.56    (including interest)
```

In the following box, you will use the `setw` and `left` stream manipulators to display a formatted header for the table of values that your **Car Payment Calculator** application will generate. This box also guides you through converting the annual interest rate to the monthly interest rate and shows you how to calculate the amount of the loan.

Displaying a Table Header, Calculating the Loan Amount and Monthly Interest Rate and Formatting Output

 Good Programming Practice

Use table headers to improve readability when you are displaying tabular data.

1. **Displaying a table header.** For clarity, you will add a line of text at the top of the output—called a **header**—that introduces the information being displayed. Insert lines 41–43 of Fig. 6.9 into the `main` function. The `setw` stream manipulator (line 42) creates a field of width 10 and the `left` stream manipulator left justifies the string `Months` in that field. Line 43 inserts the string `Monthly Payments` in the output stream, then inserts a newline using the `endl` stream manipulator.

   Due to the call to `setw`, the string `"Monthly Payments"` is displayed 10 characters to the right of the start of `"Months"`. As a result, this table header creates two columns—the first begins at the leftmost character position and the second starts 10 characters to the right of that position. Note that the field width specified with `setw` applies *only* to the next value that is output; however, the `left` stream manipulator applies to all output until that format is changed (or the application terminates).

(cont.)

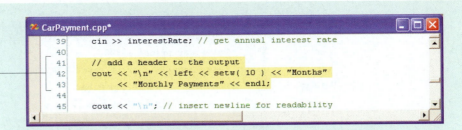

Displaying a table header using the `setw` and `left` stream manipulators

Figure 6.9   Formatting output using the `setw` and `left` stream manipulators.

2. *Calculating the loan amount and monthly interest rate.* The application computes the loan amount by subtracting the down payment from the price. Add lines 45–47 of Fig. 6.10 to `main` to calculate the amount borrowed (line 46) and the monthly interest rate (line 47).

Error-Prevention Tip

The `left` stream manipulator applies to all output until that format is changed (or the application terminates). To right justify values in fields after inserting the `left` stream manipulator, insert the `right` stream manipulator (which we will discuss in Tutorial 14).

Calculate the loan amount and monthly interest rate

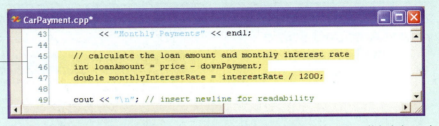

Figure 6.10   Determining the amount borrowed and the monthly interest rate.

Notice that line 47 divides the interest rate by 1200 to obtain the floating-point equivalent of the monthly interest rate. This is equivalent to taking the interest rate percentage input by the user and dividing it by 100 to get the corresponding floating-point annual interest rate, and then dividing by 12 to obtain the monthly interest rate. For example, if the annual interest rate is 5%, dividing 5.0 by 100 produces the corresponding floating-point rate (0.05) of the annual interest rate, and dividing the floating-point value of the annual interest rate by 12 produces the monthly interest rate. Because these calculations occur only once, they are placed before the `while` statement. The `loanAmount` and `monthlyInterestRate` variables will be used in the calculation of monthly payments, which you will add to your application shortly.

Common Programming Error

Dividing two int values when the result should be a floating-point value is a logic error. For example, the expression 5 / 100 yields 0 because C++ performs integer division and truncates the resulting value (from 0.05 to 0).

3. *Formatting floating-point values.* The application formats the results with two positions to the left of the decimal point. Add lines 49–50 of Fig. 6.11 to `main` to format `cout` to display the monthly payments.

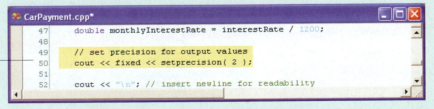

Use `fixed` and `setprecision` to format the output as dollar amounts

Figure 6.11   Displaying the result in currency format.

4. *Save, compile and run the application.* Enter 16900 at the **Enter car price:** prompt. Enter 6000 at the **Enter down payment:** prompt. Enter 7.5 at the **Enter annual interest rate:** prompt. Figure 6.12 shows the updated application running. Notice that the application displays a header before exiting.

(cont.)

```
"c:\SimplyCpp\CarPayment\Debug\CarPayment.exe"

Enter car price: 16900
Enter down payment: 6000
Enter annual interest rate: 7.5

Months    Monthly Payments

Press any key to continue_
```

Table header ——

Figure 6.12 Displaying a table header.

5. *Close the Command Prompt window.*

The following box adds a `while` statement to the application to calculate the monthly payments for loans of two, three, four and five years.

Calculating the Monthly Payment Amounts with a `while` Repetition Statement

1. *Setting the loop-continuation condition.* Add lines 52–56 of Fig. 6.13 to the `main` function.

Insert the `while` statement ——

```
CarPayment.cpp*
50        cout << fixed << setprecision( 2 );
51
52        // process loans of 2, 3, 4 and 5 years
53        while ( years <= 5 )
54        {
55
56        } // end while
57
58        cout << "\n"; // insert newline for readability
```

Figure 6.13 Adding the `while` statement.

Recall that the shortest loan in this application lasts two years, so you initialized `years` to 2 in line 23 (Fig. 6.7). The loop-continuation condition (`years <= 5`) in line 53 of Fig. 6.13 specifies that the `while` statement executes while `years` remains less than or equal to the maximum length of the loan (5). This loop is an example of **counter-controlled repetition**. This technique uses a variable called a **counter** (in this case, `years`) to control the number of times that a set of statements will execute. Counter-controlled repetition also is called **definite repetition**, because the number of repetitions is known before the loop begins executing. In this example, repetition terminates when the counter (`years`) exceeds 5.

2. *Calculating the payment period.* Add lines 55–56 of Fig. 6.14 to the body of the `while` repetition statement to calculate the number of payments (that is, the length of the loan in months). The number of months changes as the length of the payment period changes, so the calculation result changes with each iteration of the loop. The `months` variable will have the values 24, 36, 48 and 60, on successive iterations of the loop.

Determine the number of months in a loan period ——

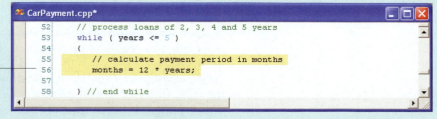

```
CarPayment.cpp*
52        // process loans of 2, 3, 4 and 5 years
53        while ( years <= 5 )
54        {
55            // calculate payment period in months
56            months = 12 * years;
57
58        } // end while
```

Figure 6.14 Converting the loan duration from years to months.

(cont.)   3.   ***Calculating the monthly payment.*** Add lines 58–60 of Fig. 6.15 to the `while` repetition statement immediately after the code you just entered. Lines 59–60 use the `calculateMonthlyPayment` function to calculate the user's monthly payment. This function is provided for you in the template code. The function returns a `double` value that specifies the monthly payment amount on a loan for a constant interest rate (`monthlyInterestRate`), a given time period (`months`) and a given loan amount (`loanAmount`). Lines 59–60 pass to `calculateMonthlyPayment` the interest rate, the number of months and the amount borrowed. The assignment operator (=) in line 59 assigns to the `monthlyPayment` variable the `double` value returned by the `calculate-MonthlyPayment` function.

Calculate the monthly payment —————

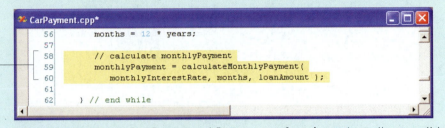

```
56          months = 12 * years;
57
58          // calculate monthlyPayment
59          monthlyPayment = calculateMonthlyPayment(
60             monthlyInterestRate, months, loanAmount );
61
62       } // end while
```

Figure 6.15   The `calculateMonthlyPayment` function returns the monthly payment.

4.   ***Displaying the monthly payment amount.*** Add lines 62–64 of Fig. 6.16 to the `while` repetition statement. The number of monthly payments and the monthly payment amounts are displayed beneath the header. Line 63 uses the `left` and `setw( 10 )` stream manipulators to left justify the value of the `months` variable in a field of width 10. A dollar sign followed by the value of the `monthlyPayment` variable is displayed. Note that the value of the `monthlyPayment` variable is displayed with two positions to the left of the decimal point due to the `fixed` and `setprecision` variable in line 50 (Fig. 6.11). Note that the value in `int` variable `months` is not displayed with two positions to the left of the decimal point because `fixed` and `setprecision` format only floating-point values.

Display the monthly payment —————

```
60             monthlyInterestRate, months, loanAmount );
61
62          // insert result into output stream
63          cout << left << setw( 10 ) << months
64             << "$" << monthlyPayment << endl;
65
66       } // end while
```

Figure 6.16   Displaying the number of months and the amount of each monthly payment.

5.   ***Incrementing the counter variable.*** Add line 66 of Fig. 6.17 before the closing brace of the `while` statement. Line 66 uses the `++` operator to increment the counter variable (`years`). The `years` variable will be incremented until it equals 6. Then, the loop-continuation condition (`years <= 5`) will evaluate to `false`, terminating the repetition.

6.   ***Save, compile and run the application.*** Figure 6.18 shows the result of executing the application.

7.   ***Close the Command Prompt window.***

(cont.)

Increment the `years` counter

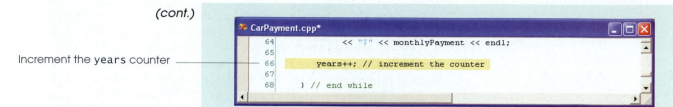

Figure 6.17 Incrementing the counter.

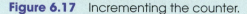

```
Enter car price: 16900
Enter down payment: 6000
Enter annual interest rate: 7.5

Months     Monthly Payments
24         $490.50
36         $339.06
48         $263.55
60         $218.41

Press any key to continue_
```

Figure 6.18 Output from the completed application.

Figure 6.19 presents the source code for the **Car Payment Calculator** application. The lines of code that you added, viewed or modified in this tutorial are highlighted.

```cpp
1   // Tutorial 6: CarPayment.cpp
2   // Calculate different billing plans for a car loan.
3   #include <iostream> // required to perform C++ stream I/O
4   #include <iomanip>  // required for parameterized stream manipulators
5   #include <cmath>    // required to use the C++ math library functions
6
7   using namespace std; // for accessing C++ Standard Library members
8
9   // calculate monthly payment
10  double calculateMonthlyPayment( double monthlyInterestRate,
11     int months, int loanAmount )
12  {
13     double base = pow( 1 + monthlyInterestRate, months );
14
15     return loanAmount * monthlyInterestRate / ( 1 - ( 1 / base ) );
16
17  } // end function calculateMonthlyPayment
18
19  // function main begins program execution
20  int main()
21  {
22     // define variables
23     int years = 2;          // length of the loan in years
24     int months;             // payment period
25     double monthlyPayment;  // monthly payment
26     int price;              // price of the car
27     int downPayment;        // down payment
28     double interestRate;    // annual interest rate
29
30     // prompt user for and input car price,
31     // down payment and annual interest rate
32     cout << "Enter car price: ";
33     cin >> price; // get price
```

Define variables

Figure 6.19 Car Payment Calculator application code. (Part 1 of 2.)

Prompt for and input car price, down payment and annual interest rate

Display a table header

Calculate the loan amount and monthly interest

Format floating-point values as currency

Begin a `while` statement

Call the `calculateMonthlyPayment` function to get the monthly payment

Display the monthly payment

Increment the counter

Right brace closes the `while` statement

```cpp
34
35       cout << "Enter down payment: ";
36       cin >> downPayment; // get down payment
37
38       cout << "Enter annual interest rate: ";
39       cin >> interestRate; // get annual interest rate
40
41       // add a header to the output
42       cout << left << setw( 10 ) << "Months"
43            << "Monthly Payments" << endl;
44
45       // calculate the loan amount and monthly interest rate
46       int loanAmount = price - downPayment;
47       double monthlyInterestRate = interestRate / 1200;
48
49       // set precision for output values
50       cout << fixed << setprecision( 2 );
51
52       // process loans of 2, 3, 4, and 5 years
53       while ( years <= 5 )
54       {
55          // calculate payment period in months
56          months = 12 * years;
57
58          // calculate monthlyPayment
59          monthlyPayment = calculateMonthlyPayment(
60             monthlyInterestRate, months, loanAmount );
61
62          // insert result into output stream
63          cout << left << setw( 10 ) << months
64               << "$" << monthlyPayment << endl;
65
66          years++; // increment the counter
67
68       } // end while
69
70       cout << "\n"; // insert newline for readability
71
72       return 0; // indicate that program ended successfully
73
74    } // end function main
```

Figure 6.19   Car Payment Calculator application code. (Part 2 of 2.)

SELF-REVIEW   1. Counter-controlled repetition is also called _____ because the number of repetitions is known before the loop begins executing.

   a) definite repetition   b) known repetition
   c) sequential repetition   d) counter repetition

2. The line of text that is added to a table to clarify the information that will be displayed in tabular format is called a _____.

   a) title   b) starter
   c) header   d) clarifier

Answers: 1) a. 2) c.

6.5 do...while Repetition Statement

The **do...while** repetition statement is similar to the while statement—each iterates while its loop-continuation condition is true. In the while statement, the loop-continuation condition is tested at the beginning of the loop, before the body of the loop is performed. The do...while statement evaluates the loop-continuation condition *after* the loop body is performed. Therefore, in a do...while statement, the loop body always executes at least once. Recall that a while statement executes only if its loop-continuation condition is true, so it is possible that the body of a while statement will never execute. When a do...while statement terminates, execution continues with the first statement after the do...while statement.

Common Programming Error

An infinite loop occurs when the loop-continuation condition in a do...while repetition statement never becomes false.

Error-Prevention Tip

Make sure each do...while loop body contains code that eventually makes the loop-continuation condition become false.

To illustrate the do...while repetition style, consider the example of packing a suitcase: Before you begin packing, the suitcase is empty. You will always pack at least one item in the suitcase. You place an item in the suitcase, then determine whether the suitcase is full. As long as the suitcase is not full, you continue to put items in the suitcase. (Assume for the purpose of this example that you are attempting to pack more items than the suitcase will hold and that no item is larger than the suitcase.) For an example of a do...while statement, consider the following application segment that displays the numbers 1 through 3:

```
int counter = 1;

do
{
    cout << counter << endl;
    counter++;
}
while ( counter <= 3 );
```

The application segment initializes the counter to 1. The loop-continuation condition in the do...while statement is counter <= 3. The do...while statement executes its body once, then loops (executing repeatedly) while the loop-continuation condition is true. The do...while contains a block comprised of two statements. The first places the value of the counter (and a newline) in cout. The second statement increments the value of counter. When the loop-continuation condition becomes false (that is, when counter becomes greater than 3), the do...while statement terminates, having displayed the numbers 1 through 3, each on a separate line. The following box describes each step as the preceding repetition statement executes.

Executing the do...while Repetition Statement

1. The application defines the counter variable and sets its value to 1.
2. The flow of control enters the do...while repetition statement.
3. The number stored in counter (currently 1) is inserted into cout (along with a newline).
4. The value of counter is increased by 1; counter now contains 2.
5. The loop-continuation condition is checked. The condition evaluates to true (counter is less than or equal to 3), so the application executes the statements contained in the do...while statement.
6. The number stored in counter (currently 2) is inserted into cout (along with a newline).
7. The value of counter is increased by 1; counter now contains 3.
8. The loop-continuation condition is checked. The condition evaluates to true (counter is less than or equal to 3), so the application executes the statements contained in the do...while statement.
9. The number stored in counter (currently 3) is inserted into cout (along with a newline).

(cont.)

10. The value of `counter` is increased by 1; `counter` now contains 4.

11. The loop-continuation condition is checked. The condition evaluates to `false` (`counter` is not less than or equal to 3), so the application exits the do...while statement.

12. Execution continues with the next statement after the do...while statement.

Error-Prevention Tip

Including a final value in the condition of a repetition statement (and choosing the appropriate relational operator) can reduce the occurrence of off-by-one errors. For example, in a **do...while** statement used to print the values 1–10, the loop-continuation condition should be `counter <= 10`, rather than `counter < 10` (which is an off-by-one error) or `counter < 11` (which is correct, but less clear).

An **off-by-one error** (a type of logic error) occurs when a loop executes for one more or one fewer iteration than is necessary. Such logic errors are introduced into applications when you provide incorrect loop-continuation conditions. For example, the do...while statement discussed in this section should loop three times. If the condition is incorrectly stated as `counter < 3` or `counter <= 2`, the application would display only 1 and 2. The most frequent causes of off-by-one errors are including an incorrect relational operator (such as the less than sign in `counter < 3`) or an incorrect final value for a loop counter (such as the 2 in `counter <= 2`) in the condition of any repetition statement.

Figure 6.20 illustrates the UML activity diagram for the preceding do...while statement. This diagram makes it clear that the loop-continuation guard condition (`[counter <= 3]`) is not checked until after the loop enters the action state at least once. Recall that action states can include one or more C++ statements executed one after the other (sequentially) as in the preceding example. When you use do...while statements in building your applications, you will provide the appropriate action states and guard conditions for your application.

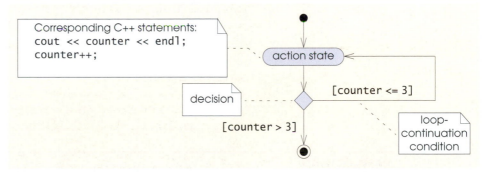

Figure 6.20   do...while repetition statement UML activity diagram.

In the following box, you will convert the **Car Payment Calculator**'s while repetition statement into a do...while repetition statement.

Converting a while Statement to a do...while Statement

1. ***Converting a `while` statement to a `do...while` statement.*** Modify line 53 and lines 68–69 of Fig. 6.21. Note that a semicolon must appear after the condition in line 69 and that the comments have been modified to reflect the updated code.

2. ***Save, compile and run the application.*** Figure 6.22 shows the result of executing the application. Note that the output is identical to Fig. 6.18.

3. ***Close the Command Prompt window.***

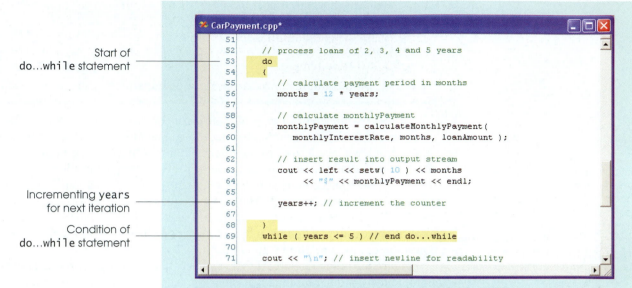

Start of
do...while statement

Incrementing `years`
for next iteration

Condition of
do...while statement

Figure 6.21 **Car Payment Calculator** using a do...while repetition statement.

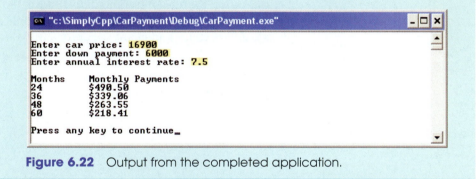

Figure 6.22 Output from the completed application.

SELF-REVIEW

1. The do...while statement tests the loop-continuation condition _____.
   a) after the loop body executes
   b) before the loop body executes
   c) Both of the above.
   d) Neither of the above.

2. An infinite loop occurs when the loop-continuation condition in a do...while statement _____.
   a) never becomes `true`
   b) never becomes `false`
   c) is `false`
   d) is tested repeatedly

Answers: 1) a. 2) b.

6.6 Wrap-Up

In this tutorial, you began using repetition statements. You used the `while` statement to repeat actions in an application, depending on a loop-continuation condition. The `while` repetition statement executes as long as its loop-continuation condition is true. When the loop-continuation condition becomes false, the repetition terminates. An infinite loop occurs if the condition never becomes false. You studied a UML activity diagram that explained how this statement executes.

You learned about counter-controlled repetition, in which a repetition statement uses a counter variable to precisely count the number of iterations. You used a repetition statement to develop your **Car Payment Calculator** application, in which you calculated the monthly payments for a given loan amount and a given interest rate for loan durations of two, three, four and five years. In your **Car Payment Calculator** application, you used the `setw` and `left` stream manipulators to display several payment options on a car loan in tabular format.

Finally, you modified your **Car Payment Calculator** so that it used the `do...while` repetition statement. You studied a UML activity diagram that explained how this statement executes. The `do...while` repetition statement executes as long as its loop-continuation condition is `true`. This statement always executes its body at least once. When the loop-continuation condition becomes `false`, the repetition terminates. An infinite loop occurs if the loop-continuation condition never becomes `false`. You observed that the **Car Payment Calculator** application produced the same results as the version that used the `while` repetition statement.

In the next tutorial, you will learn sentinel-controlled repetition. The **Car Payment Calculator** application demonstrated one common use of repetition statements—performing a calculation for several different values. The next application introduces another common application of repetition statements—summing and averaging a series of numbers.

SKILLS SUMMARY

Displaying Values in Tabular Format

- Use the `setw` stream manipulator to specify the width of each column. By default, output will be right justified.
- To left justify output, use the `left` stream manipulator.

Repeating Actions in an Application

- Use a repetition statement (such as the `while` statement) that depends on the `true` or `false` value of a loop-continuation condition.

Executing a Repetition Statement for a Known Number of Repetitions

- Use counter-controlled repetition, which uses a counter variable to determine the number of times that a set of statements will execute.

Using the `while` Repetition Statement

- This repetition statement repeatedly executes its body statements while its loop-continuation condition is `true`.
- An infinite loop occurs if the condition never becomes `false`.

Looping with the `do...while` Repetition Statement

- Insert a `do...while` statement in your code and place in its body the statements that you want to execute at least once. The loop will iterate while its loop-continuation condition remains `true`.
- Place the loop-continuation condition in the parentheses after the `while` at the end of the loop body.
- Place a semicolon (;) after the closing right parenthesis of the condition.

KEY TERMS

counter—A variable often used to determine the number of times a block of statements in a loop will execute.

counter-controlled repetition—A technique that uses a counter variable to determine the number of times that a block of statements will execute. It is also called definite repetition.

decrementing a variable—The process of subtracting one from an integer variable.

definite repetition—See counter-controlled repetition.

diamond symbol (in the UML)—The UML symbol that represents the decision symbol or the merge symbol, depending on how it is used.

do...while repetition statement—A control statement that executes a set of body statements while the loop-continuation condition is `true`. The condition is tested after the loop body executes, so the body statements always execute at least once.

header—A line of text at the top of a table that clarifies the information being displayed.

incrementing a variable—The process of adding one to an integer variable.

infinite loop—A logical error in which a repetition statement never terminates.

left-justified output—Output that is aligned to the left side of a field.

left stream manipulator—A nonparameterized stream manipulator that causes output to be left justified in a field specified by stream manipulator `setw`.

loop—Another name for a repetition statement. A loop repeatedly executes its body until its continuation condition becomes false.

loop-continuation condition—The condition used in a repetition statement (such as `while` or `do...while`) that enables repetition to continue while the condition is `true`, but that causes repetition to terminate when the condition becomes `false`.

merge symbol—A symbol (in the shape of a diamond) in the UML that joins two flows of activity into one flow of activity. A merge symbol has two (or more) transition arrows pointing to the diamond and only one transition arrow pointing from the diamond to indicate multiple activity flows merging to continue the activity. None of the transition arrows associated with a merge have guard conditions.

off-by-one error—The kind of logic error that occurs when a loop executes for one more or one fewer iteration than is intended.

repetition statement—Allows the programmer to specify that an action or actions should be repeated, depending on the value of a condition.

right-justified output—Output that is aligned to the right side of a field.

setw stream manipulator—A parameterized stream manipulator that indicates that (only) the next value should appear in a field of the specified width. If the output value is less than the specified width, the value is right justified in the field by default. If the value to be output is greater than the specified width, the field is expanded to the right to the appropriate width.

unary postdecrement operator (--)—Subtracts one from an integer variable. The variable is used to evaluate the expression containing the variable, then is decremented.

unary postincrement operator (++)—Adds one to an integer variable. The variable is used to evaluate the expression containing the variable, then is incremented.

unary predecrement operator (--)—Subtracts one from an integer variable. The variable is decremented, then is used to evaluate the expression containing the variable.

unary preincrement operator (++)—Adds one to an integer variable. The variable is incremented, then is used to evaluate the expression containing the variable.

while repetition statement—A control statement that executes a set of body statements while its loop-continuation condition is `true`.

USER INTERFACE DESIGN GUIDELINES

Displaying Output in Tabular Format

- Use table headers to improve readability when you are displaying tabular data.

C++ LIBRARY REFERENCE

`iostream` This header file provides access to the basic services required for all stream-I/O operations.

- *Objects*

    `cin`—This object reads characters entered at the keyboard. Text is sent to the application when the user presses *Enter* and placed in a variable using the stream extraction operator, `>>`.

    `cout`—This object displays text on the screen. Text is displayed using the stream insertion operator (`<<`).

- *Stream manipulators*

    `endl`—This object places a newline into the output stream and flushes the stream's buffer so that all text stored in the output stream object is displayed immediately.

    `fixed`—This stream manipulator specifies that floating-point numbers should be printed using fixed-point notation (as opposed to scientific notation).

    `left`—This object causes values to be left justified in a field. The stream into which `left` is inserted remains left justified until the application terminates or until the stream's justification is changed, whichever comes first.

iomanip This header file provides access to parameterized stream manipulators.

■ *Stream manipulators*

setprecision—This stream manipulator specifies that numeric values should be printed using the specified number of digits to the right of the decimal point. The argument to setprecision determines the number of digits that are displayed to the right of the decimal point when a floating-point value is printed.

setw—This stream manipulator indicates that (only) the next value should appear in a field of the specified width. If the value to be output is less than the specified width, the value is right justified in the field by default. If the value to be output is greater than the specified width, the field is expanded to the right to the appropriate width.

MULTIPLE-CHOICE QUESTIONS

6.1 If the value that is output after a setw stream manipulator establishes a field width contains more characters than the field width specified, _____.

a) a syntax error occurs   b) the value is truncated
c) the field expands to the right to accom-   d) a runtime error occurs
   modate the value

6.2 The _____ statement executes until its loop-continuation condition becomes false.

a) while   b) if
c) until   d) if...else

6.3 A(n) _____ loop occurs when a condition in a while statement never becomes false.

a) indefinite   b) undefined
c) nested   d) infinite

6.4 A _____ is a variable that helps control the number of times that a set of statements will execute.

a) repeater   b) counter
c) loop   d) repetition control statement

6.5 The _____ stream manipulator is required to left justify text inside a field.

a) leftjustify   b) justify
c) left
d) None of the above. Text is left justified by default.

6.6 In a UML activity diagram, a(n) _____ symbol joins two flows of activity into one flow of activity.

a) merge   b) combine
c) action state   d) decision

6.7 The UML decision and merge symbols can be distinguished by _____.

a) the number of flowlines entering   b) whether or not the flowlines have guard
   or exiting the symbol   conditions
c) Both a and b.   d) Neither of the above.

6.8 The _____ header file is required to use the setw stream manipulator.

a) <iostream>   b) <string>
c) <iomanip>   d) None of the above.

6.9 The _____ statement predecrements int variable counter.

a) ++counter;   b) --counter;
c) counter++;   d) counter--;

6.10 Counter-controlled repetition also is called _____.

a) infinite repetition   b) unlimited repetition
c) limited repetition   d) definite repetition

EXERCISES

6.11 *(Table of Powers Application)* Write an application that displays a table of numbers from 1 to an upper limit, along with the square and cube of each number. The user should specify the upper limit, and the results should be displayed as in Fig. 6.23.

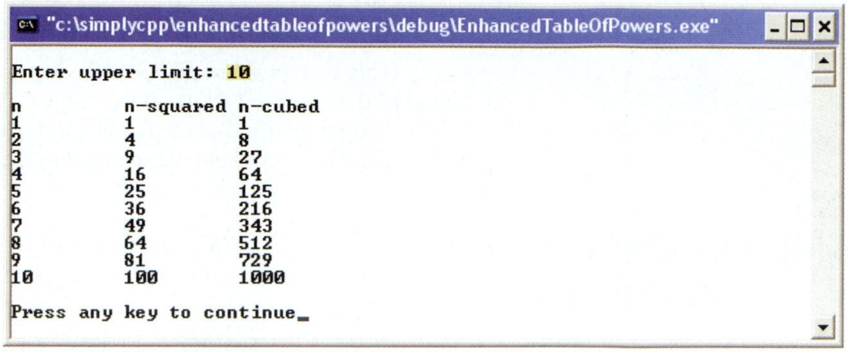

Figure 6.23 Table of Powers application output.

a) *Copying the template to your working directory.* Copy the C:\Examples\Tutorial06\Exercises\EnhancedTableOfPowers directory to your C:\SimplyCpp directory.

b) *Opening the template source code file.* Open the TableOfPowers.cpp file in your text editor or IDE.

c) *Defining a variable to store the loop counter and limit.* In the main function, define int variable counter and initialize its value to 1. Then, define int variable limit to store the limit specified by the user at the input prompt.

d) *Retrieve user input.* Add code to the main function that prompts the user for the limit and places the value typed at the keyboard in the limit variable.

e) *Adding a header to the table.* Add a statement to main that uses cout to display a header. The header should provide the descriptive text "n", "n-squared" and "n-cubed" for three columns. Columns should be 10 characters wide and each string should be left justified.

f) *Calculating the powers from 1 to the specified upper limit.* Add a while statement to main that calculates the square and the cube of each number from 1 to the limit, inclusive. Use cout to display a line of text containing the current counter value, its square and its cube. Each value should be left justified inside its 10-character field. [*Note:* The square of a number is the number multiplied by itself. The cube of a number is the square of the number times the number.]

g) *Incrementing counter in the while statement.* Remember to increment the counter each time through the loop.

h) *Save, compile and run the application.* Type an integer value at the **Enter upper limit:** prompt. Ensure that the output resembles Fig. 6.23.

i) *Close the Command Prompt window.*

6.12 *(Mortgage Calculator Application)* A bank offers mortgages that can be repaid in 10, 15, 20, 25 or 30 years. Write an application that allows a user to enter the amount of the mortgage and the annual interest rate. The application then displays a table of the mortgage length in years together with the monthly payment as shown in Fig. 6.24.

a) *Copying the template to your working directory.* Copy the C:\Examples\Tutorial06\Exercises\MortgageCalculator directory to your C:\SimplyCpp directory.

b) *Opening the template source code file.* Open the MortgageCalculator.cpp file in your text editor or IDE.

c) *Defining variables required to determine monthly payments.* In main, define int variable years and initialize its value to 10. Also, define int variable months, double variable monthlyPayment, int variable amount, double variable annualRate and double variable monthlyRate

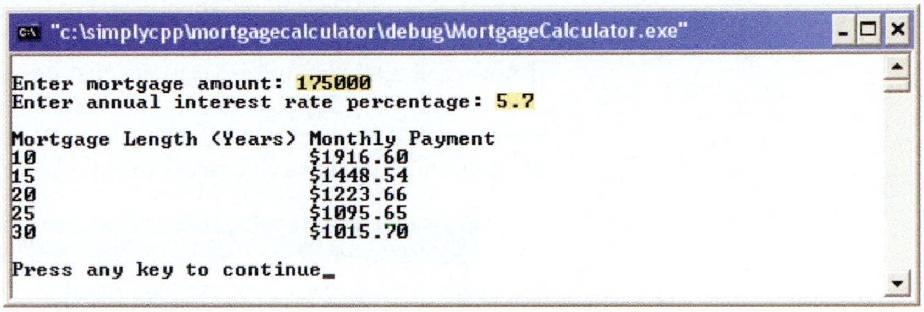

Figure 6.24 Mortgage Calculator application output.

d) *Copying the template to your working directory.* Copy the C:\Examples\ Tutorial06\Exercises\MortgageCalculator directory to your C:\SimplyCpp directory.

e) *Opening the template source code file.* Open the MortgageCalculator.cpp file in your text editor or IDE.

f) *Defining variables required to determine monthly payments.* In main, define int variable years and initialize its value to 10. Also, define int variable months, double variable monthlyPayment, int variable amount, double variable annualRate and double variable monthlyRate

g) *Obtaining the user input and converting the annual interest rate to the monthly interest rate.* Add statements to main that prompt the user for and input the mortgage amount in amount. Add another pair of statements that prompts the user for and inputs the annual interest rate in annualRate. To convert the annual interest rate from a percent value into its double equivalent, divide the annual rate by 100. Then, you should divide the annual rate by 12 to obtain the monthly rate. To perform this operation, divide annualRate by 1200 and input the result in monthlyRate.

h) *Displaying a header.* Add a statement that displays the column headers "Mortgage Length (Years)" and "Monthly Payment". Use the setw and left stream manipulators to ensure that the first column is 24 characters wide and that the text is left justified inside the field.

i) *Formatting cout to display floating-point values.* Add a statement to main that inserts the fixed and setprecision stream manipulators into cout so that cout displays floating-point values with two positions to the left of the decimal point.

j) *Using a while repetition statement.* Add a while statement to main that calculates five monthly payment options for the user's mortgage. Each option has a different number of years that the mortgage can last. For this exercise, the while statement will iterate over the following sequence of values: 10, 15, 20, 25 and 30.

k) *Converting the length of the mortgage from years to months.* In the while statement, add a statement that converts the number of years to months (by multiplying years by 12).

l) *Calculating the monthly payments for five different mortgages.* On the next line in the while statement, call the calculateMonthlyPayment function (provided for you in the template source code) to compute the monthly payments. Pass to this function the monthly interest rate, the number of months in the mortgage and the mortgage amount. Assign the result of the function call to monthlyPayment.

m) *Displaying the results.* Use cout to display the length of the mortgage (in years) in the first column and the monthly payment in the second column of the table. You will need to use setw to ensure that the first column's width is 24 characters.

n) *Incrementing counter in the while statement.* Remember to increment the years by 5 each time through the loop.

o) *Save, compile and run the application.* Use the values in Fig. 6.24 to test your application to ensure that it runs correctly.

p) *Close the Command Prompt window.*

6.13 (*Enhanced Password Generator Application*) Modify your **Password Generator** application from Exercise 5.17 so that it uses a single `while` repetition statement to produce the password. Recall that the application generates a password from a five-character string that the user enters (Fig. 6.25). The application should generate the password by reversing the order of the string and subtracting 15 from each character's ASCII code. If the user enters a string that contains more than five characters, the application should display an error message and exit.

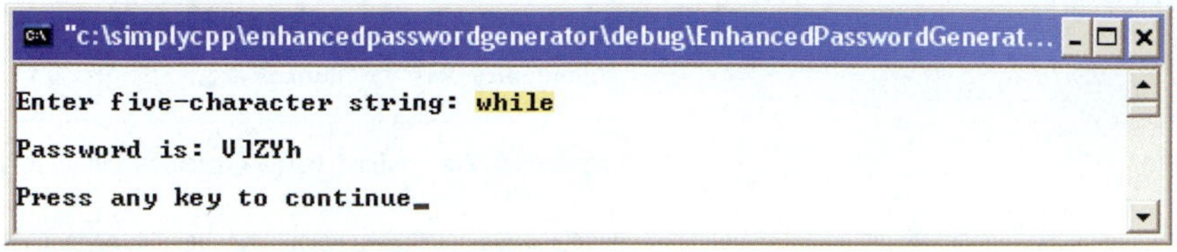

Figure 6.25 **Password Generator** application output.

a) *Copying the completed Exercise 5.17 solution to your working directory.* Copy the `C:\Examples\Tutorial06\Exercises\EnhancedPasswordGenerator` directory to your `C:\SimplyCpp` directory. If you have not completed Exercise 5.17, do so before continuing to the next step. When you have completed Exercise 5.17, copy your `C:\SimplyCpp\PasswordGenerator\PasswordGenerator.cpp` file to `C:\Simply-Cpp\EnhancedPasswordGenerator`.

b) *Opening the template source code file.* Open the `PasswordGenerator.cpp` file in your text editor or IDE.

c) *Define a counter variable.* After line 14, define an `int` variable `counter` to store the value of the counter. Initialize its value to 4.

d) *Using a `while` repetition statement to reduce redundant code.* The `else` part of the `if...else` statement contains pairs of statements that differ only by the argument to `string` function `at`. Use a `while` statement to iterate over the integer values of `counter` from 4 to 0, inclusive. The body of the `while` statement should display the modified version of the character located at the position in `string plainText` specified by `counter`. Before ending the body of the `while` repetition statement, be sure to decrement the counter value to prevent an infinite loop. After the `while` statement, place the `endl` stream manipulator in `cout` to display a newline.

e) *Save, compile and run the completed application.* Test the application to ensure that the correct password is generated and that the application displays an error message when the user does not enter a five-character string.

f) *Close the Command Prompt window.*

What does this code do? ▶ **6.14** What is the result of the following code?

```
1   // Exercise 6.14: WDTCD.cpp
2   // What does this code do?
3   #include <iostream> // required to perform C++ stream I/O
4
5   using namespace std; // for accessing C++ Standard Library members
6
7   // function main begins program execution
8   int main()
9   {
10     // define variables
11     int x = 1;
12     int mysteryValue = 1;
13
14     while ( x < 6 )
15     {
16        mysteryValue *= x;
17        x++;
18     } // end while
```

```
19
20        cout << "\nMystery value: " << mysteryValue << endl << endl;
21
22        return 0; // indicate the program ended successfully
23
24    } // end function main
```

What's wrong with this code? ▶   **6.15** Find the error(s) in the following code:

a) Assume that the variable counter is defined and initialized to 1. The loop should sum the numbers from 1 to 100.

```
■ "c:\simplycpp\tutorial06\exercises\wwwtca\debug\WWWTCa.exe"       _□×

Total: 5050

Press any key to continue_
```

```
 1    // Exercise 6.15a: WWWTCa.cpp
 2    // This application displays the total of the sum of numbers from
 3    // 1 to 100.
 4    #include <iostream>   // required to perform C++ stream I/O
 5
 6    using namespace std; // for accessing C++ Standard Library members
 7
 8    // function main begins program execution
 9    int main()
10    {
11        // define variables
12        int counter = 1;
13        int total = 0;
14
15        while ( counter <= 100 )
16        {
17            total += counter;
18
19        } // end while
20
21        counter++;
22
23        cout << "\nTotal: " << total << endl << endl;
24
25        return 0; // indictate the program ended successfully
26
27    } // end function main
```

b) Assume that the variable counter is defined and initialized to 1000. The following loop should iterate from 1000 to 1.

```
■ "c:\simplycpp\tutorial06\exercises\wwwtcb\debug\WWWTCb.exe"       _□×

1000
999
998
997
996
995
994
993
992
```

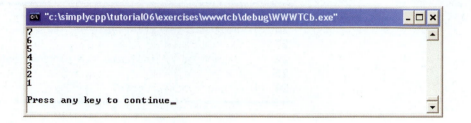

```
1   // Exercise 6.15b: WWWTCb.cpp
2   // This application displays every number from 1000 to 1
3   // in descending order
4   #include <iostream>  // required to perform C++ stream I/O
5
6   using namespace std; // for accessing C++ Standard Library members
7
8   // function main begins program execution
9   int main()
10  {
11     // define variables
12     int counter = 1000;
13
14     cout << endl;
15
16     while ( counter > 0 )
17     {
18        cout << counter << endl;
19        counter++;
20
21     } // end while
22
23     cout << endl; // insert newline for readability
24
25     return 0; // indicate that program ended successfully
26
27  } // end function main
```

    c) Assume that the variable counter is defined and initialized to 1. The loop should execute five times to display the final result, 12345.

```
     "c:\simplycpp\tutorial06\exercises\wwwtcc\debug\WWWTCc.exe"    - □ ×
12345
Press any key to continue_
```

```
1   // Exercise 6.15c: WWWTCc.cpp
2   // This application displays the number 12345
3   #include <iostream>  // required to perform C++ stream I/O
4
5   using namespace std; // for accessing C++ Standard Library members
6
7   // function main begins program execution
8   int main()
9   {
10     // define variables
11     int counter = 1;
12
```

```
13      cout << endl;
14
15      do
16      {
17         cout << counter;
18         counter++;
19      }
20      while ( counter < 5 ) // end do...while
21
22      cout << endl << endl;
23
24      return 0; // indicate that program ended successfully
25
26  } // end function main
```

Using the Debugger ▶

6.16 (*Odd Numbers Application*) The **Odd Numbers** application should display all the odd integers from one through the number input by the user. Figure 6.26 displays the correct output for the application. In this exercise, you will use the debugger to find and fix the error(s) in the application.

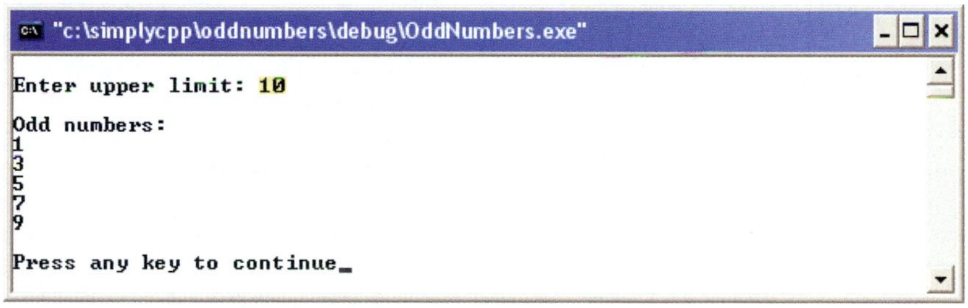

```
"c:\simplycpp\oddnumbers\debug\OddNumbers.exe"

Enter upper limit: 10

Odd numbers:
1
3
5
7
9

Press any key to continue_
```

Figure 6.26 Correct output for the **Odd Numbers** application.

a) *Copying the template to your working directory.* Copy the C:\Examples\Tutorial06\Exercises\Debugger\OddNumbers directory to your C:\SimplyCpp directory.

b) *Opening the Command Prompt window and changing directories.* Open the **Command Prompt** window by selecting **Start > All Programs > Accessories > Command Prompt**. Change to your working directory by typing cd C:\SimplyCpp\Debugger\OddNumbers.

c) *Running the application.* Run the application by typing OddNumbers. Enter a value at the **Enter upper limit:** prompt. Notice that no output occurs. This is because the application contains an infinite loop.

d) *Closing the running application.* Close the running application by holding the *Ctrl* key and pressing *C*.

e) *Opening the template file.* Open the OddNumbers.cpp file in the Visual Studio .NET IDE.

f) *Compiling the Odd Numbers application.* Select **Build > Build Solution** to compile the **Odd Numbers** application.

g) *Setting a breakpoint.* Set a breakpoint at line 24.

h) *Running the application in the debugger.* Run the **Odd Numbers** application by selecting **Debug > Start**. Type 10 at the **Enter upper limit:** prompt. The application will enter break mode at line 24.

i) *Locating the logic error.* Use the IDE's *Quick Info* feature to examine the values of variables counter and limit. The values should be 1 and 10, respectively. Use the **Debug > Continue** command to continue execution from the breakpoint at line 24. This causes one iteration of the loop to be performed; the application then enters break mode again at line 24. Use the debugger's IDE's *Quick Info* feature to examine the values of the `counter` and `limit` variables again. The values should be 2 and 10, respectively. However, the value of `counter` is still 1 and the value of `limit` is now 11. If necessary, use **Continue** and *Quick Info* several more times to determine the problem in the code.

j) *Fixing the error in the code.* Open the `OddNumbers.cpp` file in your IDE, scroll to lines 21–31, locate the error in the code and fix the error.

k) *Save, compile and run the application.* Test the application again by entering an integer at the **Enter upper limit:** prompt.

l) *Close the Command Prompt window and IDE.*

Programming Challenge ▶

6.17 *(Histogram Application)* One interesting application of computers is the drawing of bar charts, often called histograms, to help the user conveniently visualize data. Write an application that allows the user to enter three numbers (Fig. 6.27). For each number entered, your application should display a line containing that number of adjacent asterisks. For example, if the user enters 7, your application should display *******.

Figure 6.27   Histogram application output.

a) *Copying the template to your working directory.* Copy the `C:\Examples\Tutorial06\Exercises\Histogram` directory to your `C:\SimplyCpp` directory.

b) *Opening the template source code file.* Open the `Histogram.cpp` file in your text editor or IDE.

c) *Defining variables required to store the counter value and user input.* In `main`, define `int` variables `first`, `second` and `third` to store the values that the user enters. Also, define `int` variable `counter` to store the counter value and initialize it to 1.

d) *Obtaining user input.* Add statements that prompt the user for and input three integer values, as shown in Fig. 6.27. Store the values in variables `first`, `second` and `third`.

e) *Displaying a header for the histogram.* Add a statement that displays the descriptive text `Histogram:` followed by a newline.

f) *Using a while repetition statement to display a line of asterisks.* Insert a `while` repetition statement that iterates over each value from 1 to the value of variable `first`. The body of the `while` statement should display a single asterisk (without inserting a newline) and increment `counter`. After the `while` statement terminates, your application should reset the value of `counter` to 1 and display a newline character so that the next group of asterisks appears on the next line.

g) *Using while repetition statements to display the remaining lines of asterisks.* Insert two more `while` repetition statements similar to the one you wrote in *Step f*, but each time iterating over the values from 1 to the value of `second` and `third`, respectively. After each `while` statement terminates, reset the value of `counter` to 1 and insert a newline character. [*Note:* It is not necessary to reset the value of `counter` after the last `while` statement executes.]

h) *Save, compile and run the application.* Use the values in Fig. 6.27 to test your application to ensure that it runs correctly.

i) *Close the Command Prompt window and IDE.*

Objectives

In this tutorial, you will learn to:
- Use sentinel-controlled repetition to obtain an indefinite number of user inputs.
- Convert values from one primitive C++ type to another.
- Identify and prevent fatal logic errors.

Outline

Class Average Application

Introducing Sentinel-Controlled Repetition

This tutorial continues our discussion of repetition statements. In the previous tutorial, you examined the while repetition statement, which tests a loop-continuation condition before performing the statement(s) in the body of the loop. You also learned the do...while repetition statement, which performs its loop-continuation test after performing the loop body statements. You used these statements to perform counter-controlled repetition.

In some applications, however, you will not know the number of times that the repetition statement must iterate before program execution. This tutorial introduces **sentinel-controlled repetition**, a technique that enables an application to repeat an action until the user enters a special value, called a **sentinel value**, indicating that repetition should terminate. You will learn how to convert integer values to floating-point values, which will allow you to store user input as integers and perform calculations that result in floating-point values.

7.1 Test-Driving the Class Average Application

This application must meet the following requirements:

> **Application Requirements**
>
> *A teacher regularly gives quizzes to a class of students. The grades on these quizzes are integers in the range 0 to 100 (0 and 100 are each valid grades). The teacher would like you to develop an application that computes the class average for a quiz. The teacher should be able to enter an arbitrary number of grades. When the teacher enters the value –1 to signal the end of input, the application should display the class average.*

The class average is equal to the sum of the grades divided by the number of students who took the quiz. The algorithm for solving this problem on a computer is to input each of the grades until the end of input is signaled with the value –1, total the grades, perform the averaging calculation and display the result.

You begin by test-driving the completed application. Then, you will learn the additional C++ capabilities you will need to create your own version of this application.

Test-Driving the Class Average Application

1. *Locating the completed application.* Open the **Command Prompt** window by selecting **Start > All Programs > Accessories > Command Prompt**. Change to your completed **Class Average** application directory by typing cd C:\Examples\Tutorial07\CompletedApplication\ClassAverage.

2. *Running the Class Average application.* Type ClassAverage in the **Command Prompt** window to run the application (Fig. 7.1). The application prompts the user to enter a grade.

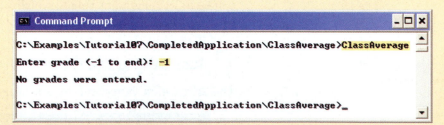

```
Command Prompt - ClassAverage                                    _ □ ×
C:\>cd C:\Examples\Tutorial07\CompletedApplication\ClassAverage
C:\Examples\Tutorial07\CompletedApplication\ClassAverage>ClassAverage
Enter grade (-1 to end): _
```

Figure 7.1 Running the completed **Class Average** application.

3. *Entering quiz grades.* Enter 85 as the first quiz grade at the input prompt (Fig. 7.2). The value entered is used in the average calculation. The application displays the input prompt from a loop, so after you enter a grade, the application displays another input prompt at which you can enter the next grade. This continues until you enter the value -1, at which point the average is calculated. The **Class Average** application uses -1 as a special value called a sentinel value (also called a **signal value**, a **dummy value** or a **flag value**) to indicate "end of data entry." If no grades have been input when the user enters the value -1, an error message is displayed (Fig. 7.3).

```
Command Prompt - ClassAverage                                    _ □ ×
C:\>cd C:\Examples\Tutorial07\CompletedApplication\ClassAverage
C:\Examples\Tutorial07\CompletedApplication\ClassAverage>ClassAverage
Enter grade (-1 to end): 85
Enter grade (-1 to end): _
```

Figure 7.2 Entering grades in the **Class Average** application.

```
Command Prompt                                                   _ □ ×
C:\Examples\Tutorial07\CompletedApplication\ClassAverage>ClassAverage
Enter grade (-1 to end): -1
No grades were entered.

C:\Examples\Tutorial07\CompletedApplication\ClassAverage>_
```

Figure 7.3 Error message displayed when no grades are entered.

4. *Repeat* **Step 3** *nine times.* Enter the nine other grades shown in Fig. 7.4. Notice that the average of the 10 grades is displayed after entering the sentinel value (-1).

5. *Close the* **Command Prompt** *window.*

(cont.)

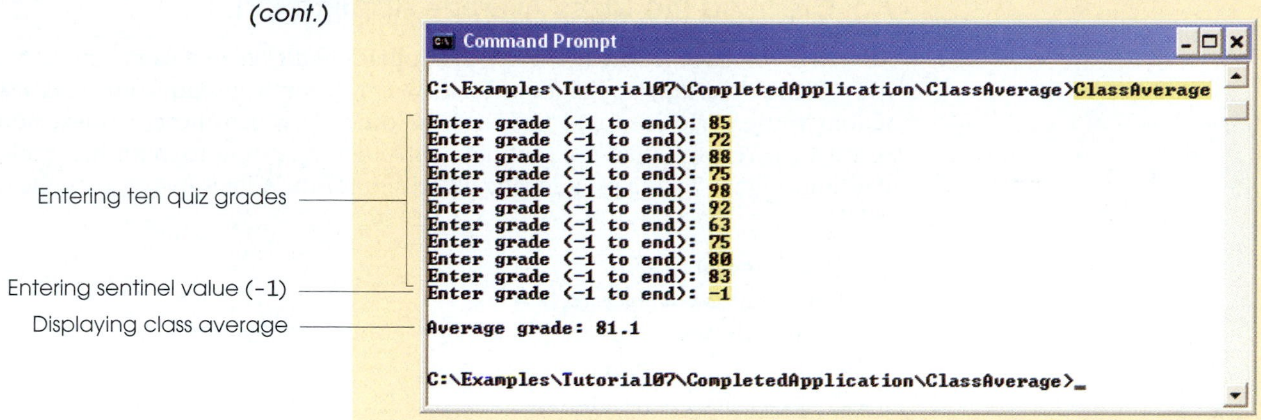

Entering ten quiz grades

Entering sentinel value (−1)

Displaying class average

Figure 7.4 **Class Average** application after 10 grades and the sentinel value have been entered.

7.2 Sentinel-Controlled Repetition

In the **Class Average** application, you will use a `while` repetition statement to input each grade until the last grade has been entered. In Tutorial 6, the **Car Payment Calculator** used counter-controlled repetition to execute the body of its `while` statement exactly four times (for loan durations of two, three, four and five years). You specified the initial and final values of the control variable, `years`, in the source code and none of the user input altered the value of `years`. In this tutorial's problem statement, the number of grades that the user will enter during the application's execution is not specified. The application must process an arbitrary number of grades. How can the application determine when to stop the grade input? How will it know when to calculate and print the class average?

One way to solve this problem is to use a sentinel value. The user types each grade that should be averaged. The user then types the sentinel value to indicate that the last grade has been entered. Sentinel-controlled repetition is often called **indefinite repetition** because the number of repetitions is not known before the loop begins executing.

Common Programming Error

Choosing a sentinel value that is also a legitimate data value is a logic error.

Clearly, the sentinel value must be chosen so that it cannot be confused with an acceptable input value. Grades on a quiz are normally non-negative integers in the range 0 to 100, so −1 is an acceptable sentinel value for this application. Thus, the **Class Average** application could process successfully this stream of inputs: 95, 96, 75, 74, 89 and −1. The application would then compute and print the class average for the grades 95, 96, 75, 74 and 89. The sentinel value (in this case -1) will not enter into the averaging calculation.

SELF-REVIEW

1. In _____ repetition, the repetition statement specifies the number of times that the loop will iterate. An example of _____ repetition is sentinel-controlled repetition.

   a) definite, indefinite   b) infinite, indefinite

   c) defined, undefined   d) None of the above.

2. A sentinel value is also called a _____.

   a) signal value   b) dummy value

   c) flag value   d) All of the above.

Answers: 1) a. 2) d.

7.3 Creating the Class Average Application

Now that you have learned sentinel-controlled repetition, you can begin to develop your **Class Average** application. First, you will study pseudocode that lists the actions to be performed and indicates the order in which those actions should be performed. You will then use sentinel-controlled repetition to input the grades one at a time. Figure 7.5 is a pseudocode algorithm for the **Class Average** application.

> Set the total to zero
> Set the grade counter to zero
> Prompt the user for and input the first grade from the keyboard
>
> While the value entered is not -1
>   Add the grade to the total
>   Add one to the grade counter
>   Prompt the user for and input the next grade from the keyboard
>
> If the value of the counter is zero
>   Display a message indicating that no grades were entered
>
> Else
>   Calculate the class average by dividing the total by the counter value
>   Display the class average

Figure 7.5   Pseudocode for the **Class Average** application.

Notice that the application does not execute the body of the `while` loop if the user enters the value −1 as the first grade. In this case, the counter value will remain zero, so the `if` part of the `if...else` statement executes, displaying an error message. If the application were to attempt to calculate the class average, the application would divide by zero, the result of which is undefined in mathematics. Thus, we ensure that the application does not attempt to divide by zero—normally a **fatal logic error** that, if undetected, would cause the application to fail (often called **"bombing"** or **"crashing"**).

Now that you have formulated an algorithm for building the **Class Average** application, you can begin adding functionality to the template application. The following box guides you through retrieving user input from the keyboard.

Common Programming Error

An attempt to divide by zero normally causes a fatal error.

Entering a Grade in the Class Average Application

1. *Copying the template to your working directory.* Copy the `C:\Examples\Tutorial07\TemplateApplication\ClassAverage` directory to your `C:\SimplyCpp` directory.

2. *Opening the Class Average application's template source code file.* Open the template source code file `ClassAverage.cpp` in your text editor or IDE.

3. *Defining variables used in the class-average calculation.* Insert lines 11–14 of Fig. 7.6 in the `main` function. Line 12 defines `int` variable `total` and initializes its value to 0. Line 13 defines and initializes to 0 variable `gradeCount`, which will be used to store the number of grades that the user has entered. It is important that variables used as totals and counters have appropriate initial values before they are used. Otherwise, errors such as incorrect results infinite loops or division by zero, may occur. The `grade` variable (defined in line 14) will be used to store each grade as it is input by the user.

4. *Displaying an input prompt and retrieving a grade.* Add lines 16–18 of Fig. 7.7 to `main`. Line 17 displays an input prompt. Line 18 inputs the next grade into `int` variable `grade`.

5. *Save the application.*

(cont.)

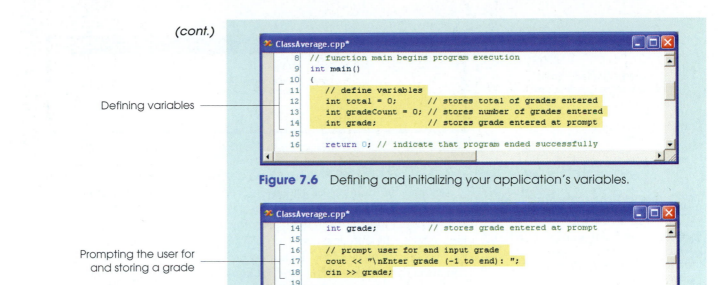

Defining variables ⟶

Figure 7.6 Defining and initializing your application's variables.

Prompting the user for
and storing a grade ⟶

Figure 7.7 Getting the grade input.

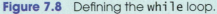

Error-Prevention Tip

The value contained in a variable
before it is initialized is undefined. Initialize counters and totals before
they are used to help prevent logic
errors.

You have added the code to input a single grade. Next, you will use a `while`
loop to input grades until the user enters the sentinel value, -1.

Inputting Multiple Grades

1. ***Creating a `while` loop to input grades until encountering the sentinel value.***
   Your application should accept grades until the user enters the value -1 at
   the input prompt. Add lines 20–23 of Fig. 7.8. The condition in line 20 indicates that the loop will repeat until `grade` equals -1.

`while` statement repeats until the
sentinel value (-1) is input ⟶

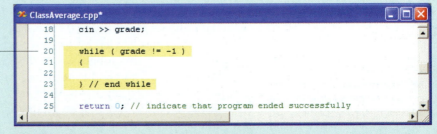

Figure 7.8 Defining the `while` loop.

2. ***Adding each grade to the total.*** Add lines 22–23 of Fig. 7.9 to the body of the
   `while` loop. Line 22 adds to the `total` variable the last grade that was input
   by the user, contained in `grade`. Line 23 increments the `gradeCount` variable, which contains the number of grades that have been entered. This
   value will be used to calculate the class average after the `while` loop terminates. These statements occur in the `while` loop, so they will be executed
   only after a valid grade has been entered. When the `while` loop terminates,
   `total` will contain the sum of the grades entered, and `gradeCount` will contain the number of grades entered.

(cont.)

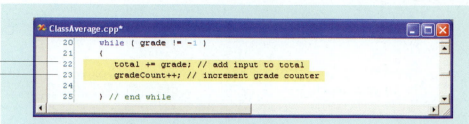

Adding `grade` to `total`
Incrementing `gradeCount`

Figure 7.9 Adding each grade to the total and incrementing the counter.

Good Programming Practice

Clearly indicating the sentinel value in your input prompts ensures that the user will know how to terminate input properly.

3. ***Prompting the user for the next grade.*** After updating the sum of the grades and the number of grades entered, the application should prompt the user for the next grade. Add lines 25–27 of Fig. 7.10 to the body of the `while` loop. Line 26 prompts the user for the next grade, and line 27 inputs into `grade` the integer that the user enters. When program execution reaches line 28 of Fig. 7.10, the application evaluates the loop-continuation condition (`grade != -1`) in line 20 of Fig. 7.9. When the user enters the sentinel value (`-1`), this condition will evaluate to `false` and the repetition will end. Otherwise, having updated `total` and `gradeCount`; the application will prompt the user for another grade.

Prompting the user for and storing the next grade

```
ClassAverage.cpp*
23        gradeCount++; // increment grade counter
24
25        // prompt user for and input next grade
26        cout << "Enter grade (-1 to end): ";
27        cin >> grade;
28     } // end while
```

Figure 7.10 Prompting the user for and storing the next grade.

4. ***Checking for division by zero.*** If the user enters `-1` at the first input prompt (lines 17–18 of Fig. 7.7), the loop-continuation condition in line 20 will evaluate to `false`, and the application will not execute the body of the `while` loop. As a result, the `total` and `gradeCount` variables will contain their initial values—both 0 (lines 12–13 of Fig. 7.7). The class average calculation divides `total` by `gradeCount`, which would result in division by zero, causing the application to fail. Add lines 30–34 of Fig. 7.11 after the `while` loop. The condition in line 31 determines whether the value contained in `gradeCount` is 0. If the condition evaluates to `true`, a message is displayed indicating that no grades have been entered. In the next box, you will write the `else` part of this `if...else` statement, which will calculate and display the class average.

Error-Prevention Tip

When performing division by an expression whose value could be zero, explicitly test for this possibility and handle it appropriately in your program (such as by printing an error message) rather than allowing the fatal error to occur.

Determining whether grades were entered

Indicating that no grades were entered

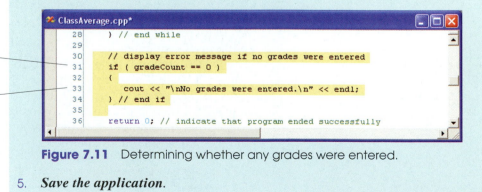

Figure 7.11 Determining whether any grades were entered.

5. ***Save the application.***

When the computer accesses data, it needs to know the type of the data for the data to make sense. Imagine that you are purchasing a book from an online store that ships internationally. You notice that the price for the book is 20, but no currency is associated with the price—it could be dollars, euros, pesos, yen or some other currency. Without this information, it is impossible to know the true cost of the book. Therefore, it is important to know what type of currency is being used. If the currency is different from the one you normally use, you will need to perform a conversion to get the correct price of the book.

These types of conversions occur in applications as well. The computer determines the type of a value and converts that value into the type that is needed for a certain operation. **Implicit conversions** (also called **promotions**) are those performed by C++ without requiring any extra code. For example, you are allowed to assign an `int` value to a `double` variable without writing code that tells the application to do the conversion. When an attempted conversion doesn't make sense, such as assigning the `string` value `"hello"` to an `int` variable, a compilation error occurs. Figure 7.12 lists C++'s primitive types; each primitive type in the list can be implicitly converted (or promoted) to any type that appears above it in the list. For example, a `float` value can be promoted to a `double` or a `long double`. The primitive types that are indented in Fig. 7.12 are not discussed in this book.

Primitive type	
`long double`	
`double`	
`float`	
`unsigned long int`	(synonymous with `unsigned long`)
`long int`	(synonymous with `long`)
`unsigned int`	(synonymous with `unsigned`)
`int`	
`unsigned short int`	(synonymous with `unsigned short`)
`short int`	(synonymous with `short`)
`unsigned char`	
`char`	
`signed char`	
`bool`	(`false` becomes 0, `true` becomes 1)

Figure 7.12 Promotion hierarchy for C++ primitive types.

Only certain conversions are allowed. The types listed at the top of the list are "larger" types, in that they can store a wider range of values than the types lower in the list. For example, `char` values can be promoted to `int` values. A `char` variable can store values in the range –128 to 127, while an `int` variable can store numbers in the approximate range –2.1 billion to +2.1 billion (on most systems). This means that any `char` value can be assigned to an `int` variable without losing any data.

When specifying a conversion that changes a value of a "larger" type to a value of a "smaller" type, you should specify an **explicit conversion** (or **cast**). C++ provides the **unary cast operator** to accomplish this task. The expression

```
static_cast< double >( operand )
```

uses the cast operator to create a temporary floating-point copy of its operand. Cast operators are available for every primitive data type. The **static_cast operator** is formed by following the `static_cast` keyword with angle brackets (< and >) around a data type name.

According to Fig. 7.12, you should explicitly convert `double` values to `int` values (because information could be lost). [*Note:* Many C++ compilers issue a warning when implicit conversions could result in information being lost. These warnings do not prevent your applications from compiling.] For example, if `intValue` is of the `int` type and `doubleValue` is of the `double` type, you can write

```
intValue = static_cast< int >( doubleValue );
```

Error-Prevention Tip

Avoid casting from a larger data type to a smaller one where possible, because doing so can result in a loss of information.

without causing a compiler warning or compilation error. Note that the value stored in `doubleValue` may lose some precision when it is cast to an `int`. If there is a fractional part of `doubleValue`, it will be truncated. For example, the `double` value `76.5432` is truncated to `76` when cast to an `int` value. Also, the conversion from a `double` to an `int` may be entirely meaningless if the `double` value is outside the range of values stored by an `int`. For example, because an `int` typically cannot represent values larger than 2.1 billion, it is meaningless to convert the `double` value 4 trillion to an `int`. In the following box, you will add code that uses an explicit conversion to calculate the class average and display the result.

Calculating and Displaying the Class Average

1. *Calculating the class average*. Add lines 35–40 of Fig. 7.13 to the `main` function. Line 35 begins the `else` part of the `if...else` statement that you started writing in the preceding box. This ensures that the average calculation is performed only if at least one grade has been entered.

Explicitly cast total to a `double` value to produce a floating-point result

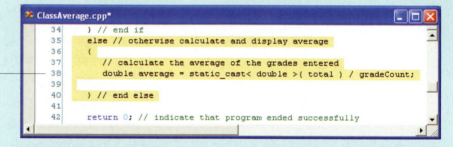
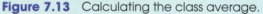

Figure 7.13 Calculating the class average.

To average the sum of all of the grades, you must divide the value in `int` variable `total` by the number of grades (contained in `int` variable `grade-Count`). Recall from Section 3.6 that integer division yields integer results—any fractional part is truncated. In this case, you would like a more accurate floating-point result (such as `81.1` in Fig. 7.4). To produce a floating-point calculation with integer values, you must use the cast operator to create temporary floating-point values for the calculation.

Line 38 calculates the average by creating a temporary floating-point copy of `total`, using the `static_cast` operator. The temporary value is divided by `gradeCount` (the number of grades entered). The calculation now consists of a floating-point value (the temporary `double` version of `total`) divided by the integer `gradeCount`. The floating-point result of the division in line 38 is stored as a `double` in the `average` variable.

2. *Formatting and displaying the result*. Add lines 40–42 of Fig. 7.14 to the `main` function. Line 41 inserts the `fixed` and `setprecision` stream manipulators in `cout` so that floating-point values are displayed with one digit of precision. Line 42 displays the value of the `average` variable.

3. *Save, compile and run the application*. Figure 7.15 shows the completed application running. Test the application to ensure that it runs as it did in the test drive.

4. *Close the Command Prompt window*.

(cont.)

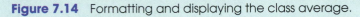

```
 38            double average = static_cast< double >( total ) / gradeCount;
 39
 40            // format output and display the average
 41            cout << fixed << setprecision( 1 );
 42            cout << "\nAverage grade: " << average << endl << endl;
 43         } // end else
 44
 45         return 0; // indicate that program ended successfully
```

Format and display the average

Figure 7.14 Formatting and displaying the class average.

```
"c:\simplycpp\classaverage\debug\ClassAverage.exe"

Enter grade (-1 to end): 85
Enter grade (-1 to end): 72
Enter grade (-1 to end): 88
Enter grade (-1 to end): 75
Enter grade (-1 to end): 98
Enter grade (-1 to end): 92
Enter grade (-1 to end): 63
Enter grade (-1 to end): 75
Enter grade (-1 to end): 80
Enter grade (-1 to end): 83
Enter grade (-1 to end): -1

Average grade: 81.1

Press any key to continue_
```

Figure 7.15 Completed **Class Average** application.

Figure 7.16 presents the source code for the **Class Average** application. The lines of code that you added, viewed or modified in this tutorial are highlighted.

```
 1   // Tutorial 7: ClassAverage.cpp
 2   // This application enables user calculate the average of grades.
 3   #include <iostream> // required to perform C++ stream I/O
 4   #include <iomanip>  // required for parameterized stream manipulators
 5
 6   using namespace std; // for accessing C++ Standard Library members
 7
 8   // function main begins program execution
 9   int main()
10   {
11      // define variables
12      int total = 0;        // stores total of grades entered
13      int gradeCount = 0;   // stores number of grades entered
14      int grade;            // stores grade entered at prompt
15
16      // prompt user for and input grade
17      cout << "\nEnter grade (-1 to end): ";
18      cin >> grade;
19
20      while ( grade != -1 )
21      {
22         total += grade; // add input to total
23         gradeCount++;    // increment grade counter
24
25         // prompt user for and input next grade
26         cout << "Enter grade (-1 to end): ";
27         cin >> grade;
28      } // end while
29
```

Define variables

Prompt user for and store grade

Repeat until the sentinel value is entered

Add grade to the total and increment the grade counter

Prompt user for and store next grade

Figure 7.16 **Class Average** application code. (Part 1 of 2.)

If no grades have been entered, display error message and avoid division by zero.

Explicitly cast **total** to a **double** value to produce a floating-point result

Format and display the class average

```
30      // display error message if no grades were entered
31      if ( gradeCount == 0 )
32      {
33         cout << "\nNo grades were entered.\n" << endl;
34      } // end if
35      else // otherwise calculate and display average
36      {
37         // calculate the average of the grades entered
38         double average = static_cast< double >( total ) / gradeCount;
39
40         // format output and display the average
41         cout << fixed << setprecision( 1 );
42         cout << "\nAverage grade: " << average << endl << endl;
43      } // end else
44
45      return 0; // indicate that program ended successfully
46
47   } // end function main
```

Figure 7.16 Class Average application code. (Part 2 of 2.)

SELF-REVIEW

1. The _____ operator converts its operand to the type specified in parentheses.

   a) type   b) converter

   c) convert   d) cast

2. When a value is converted from one type to another without loss of information, it is called _____.

   a) elevation   b) explicit conversion

   c) promotion   d) crashing

Answers: 1) d. 2) c.

7.4 Wrap-Up

In this tutorial, you learned how to perform sentinel-controlled repetition. You used the `while` statement to implement repetition in your **Class Average** application. In addition, you learned how to convert between numeric types by using a cast operator.

Sentinel-controlled repetition is often called indefinite repetition because the number of repetitions is not known before the loop begins executing. The user types the sentinel value to indicate that there is no more data to be entered. As a result, the sentinel value must be chosen in such a way that it cannot be confused with an acceptable input value.

You also learned that division by zero at runtime can lead to errors that, if undetected, would cause the application to fail. You wrote code that prevented your application from dividing by zero. In the next tutorial, you will continue studying repetition statements and learn how to use the `for` repetition statement, which is particularly useful for counter-controlled repetition.

SKILLS SUMMARY

Performing Sentinel-Controlled Repetition

- Select a sentinel value that cannot be confused with an acceptable input value. Ensure that the sentinel value does not enter into the application's calculation.

- Retrieve input in a repetition structure (such as `while` or `do...while`). The loop-continuation condition should evaluate to `false` when the sentinel value is encountered.

Converting an `int` Variable's Value to a `double`

■ Use the `static_cast< double >` cast operator, using the integer variable's name as the argument. For example, the expression

```
static_cast< double >( intValue )
```

creates a temporary floating-point copy of the value of `intValue`.

Understanding Implicit Conversion

■ Values of certain primitive types can be converted to values of other primitive types. A temporary value of the appropriate type is created, but the original value remains unchanged.

■ The promotion hierarchy is listed in Fig. 7.12. Values of a particular data type can be implicitly converted to a value of any type that appears higher in the figure.

KEY TERMS

"bombing"—Occurs when an application encounters a fatal logic error, causing the application to terminate unexpectedly.

cast operator (unary)—The unary operator (`static_cast`) that converts its operand to the type placed within its associated angle brackets.

"crashing"—See bombing.

dummy value—See sentinel value.

explicit conversion—The type conversion that occurs when the programmer uses the cast operator to change the type of a value. An operation that converts a "larger" type to a "smaller" type can be dangerous because information can be lost.

fatal logic error—An error that causes an application to terminate unexpectedly—for example, division by zero.

flag value—See sentinel value.

implicit conversion—The type conversion that occurs when the compiler performs promotion. For example, when a `double` value is divided by an `int` value, the compiler will implicitly convert the `int` value to a `double`. Implicit conversions are "safe" in the sense that no information is lost when a value is converted.

indefinite repetition—See sentinel-controlled repetition.

promotion—A type conversion where the value of a variable is stored in an equal or larger number of bytes to perform a calculation. Promotion changes only the type and size of the variable, not the value of the variable.

sentinel value—A special value that indicates that the application should terminate repetition.

sentinel-controlled repetition—A technique that causes an application to repeat an action until it encounters the sentinel value. This technique should be used when the number of repetitions is not known before the application runs.

signal value—See sentinel value.

`static_cast` operator—See cast operator.

unary cast operator—See cast operator.

USER INTERFACE DESIGN GUIDELINES

Sentinel-Controlled Repetition

■ Clearly indicating the sentinel value in your input prompts ensures that the user will know how to terminate input properly.

MULTIPLE-CHOICE QUESTIONS

7.1 The expression _____ creates a temporary `double` copy of `int` variable `intValue`.

a) `static_cast< double >( intValue )`   b) `static_cast< intValue >( double )`

c) `static_cast( double )< intValue >`   d) `static_cast( intValue )< double >`

7.2 A value is promoted when its type is converted from a(n) _____ to a(n) _____.

a) `double, int`   b) `long, char`

c) `int, double`   d) `int, bool`

7.3 Sentinel-controlled repetition terminates when _____.

a) the application terminates
b) the sentinel value is encountered
c) the user enters -1
d) None of the above.

7.4 A(n) _____ results when an application attempts to divide by zero.

a) infinite loop
b) sentinel value
c) off-by-one error
d) fatal logic error

7.5 Assuming that variables `value1` and `value2` are both declared as `int`s, which of the following statements causes the result of the calculation to be truncated?

a) `double result = static_cast< double >( value 1 ) / value2`
b) `double result = value2 + static_cast< double >( value 1 )`
c) `double result = value1 / value2`
d) All of the above.

7.6 A _____ is not required for sentinel-controlled repetition.

a) dummy value
b) final value
c) counter
d) None of the above.

7.7 Sentinel-controlled repetition is also called _____ repetition.

a) definite
b) indefinite
c) infinite
d) Both b and c.

7.8 Fatal logic errors _____.

a) are detected by the compiler
b) cause the application to crash
c) can be caused by division by zero
d) Both b and c.

7.9 When a `double` containing the value `2.718` is cast to an `int`, the `int` will contain the value _____.

a) 2.7
b) 3
c) 2
d) A `double` cannot be cast to an `int`.

7.10 When an `int` is divided by a `double`, the result is _____.

a) a double value
b) an int value
c) a syntax error
d) a fatal logic error

EXERCISES

7.11 (*Modified Class Average Application*) The **Class Average** application of Fig. 7.16 has a deficiency. The application does not check whether the user entered a valid value (an integer between 0 and 100). Modify the **Class Average** application as in Fig. 7.17, so that the application displays an error message if an invalid grade has been entered. If the grade is invalid, the application should discard the value and prompt the user for the next grade (the invalid value should not enter the average calculation).

```
"c:\simplycpp\modifiedclassaverage\debug\ModifiedClassAverage.exe"

Enter grade (-1 to end): 78
Enter grade (-1 to end): 63
Enter grade (-1 to end): 99
Enter grade (-1 to end): 106

Input error: Please enter a grade between 0 and 100 or -1 to end.

Enter grade (-1 to end): 55
Enter grade (-1 to end): 87
Enter grade (-1 to end): -20

Input error: Please enter a grade between 0 and 100 or -1 to end.

Enter grade (-1 to end): -1

Average grade: 76.4

Press any key to continue_
```

Figure 7.17 Modified **Class Average** application.

a) *Copying the template to your working directory.* Copy the C:\Examples\ Tutorial07\Exercises\ModifiedClassAverage directory to your C:\SimplyCpp directory.

b) *Opening the template source code file.* Open the ClassAverage.cpp file in your text editor or IDE.

c) *Modifying the while loop.* Insert an if statement just after the opening brace of the while statement that begins in line 20. The condition of the if statement should evaluate to true if the user entered a grade between 0 and 100, inclusive. Move lines 22–23 of Fig. 7.16 inside the body of this if statement.

d) *Adding an else part to the if statement.* Add an else part to the if statement that you created in *Step c.* The body of the else part will execute only if the user enters an invalid grade. Your application should display an error message as shown in Fig. 7.17.

e) *Save, compile and run the application.* Test the application to ensure that it runs correctly by entering invalid grades. Make sure that once you enter the sentinel value, the application calculates the average of only valid grades.

f) *Close the Command Prompt window.*

7.12 *(Enhanced Currency Converter Application)* In Exercise 4.11, you created an application that converted a dollar value to a value in another currency. Use sentinel-controlled repetition to modify the application in Exercise 4.11 so that the user can enter multiple values to convert before exiting the application (Fig. 7.18). The user provides a number at the **Enter dollars to convert:** prompt or enters the sentinel value -1 to exit. If the user entered a valid value, a menu of options is displayed. After the user enters the currency selection, the application should convert the specified amount into the indicated currency and display it. If the user enters an invalid currency selection, the application should display an error message and prompt the user for input again. Your application should be able to convert currency amounts from dollars to euros, yen and pesos, using the following exchange rates: 1 dollar = 0.8 euros, 109 yen and 11 pesos. [*Note:* Currency exchange rates are constantly changing. There are many online sites where you can view current exchange rates, including finance.yahoo.com/m3, www.x-rates.com and www.rubicon.com/passport/currency/ currency.html.]

```
"c:\SimplyCpp\EnhancedCurrencyConverter\Debug\EnhancedCurrencyConvert...

Enter dollars to convert (-1 to end): 20.00
Select conversion type:
1 - Dollars to Euros
2 - Dollars to Yen
3 - Dollars to Pesos
? 2
Converted amount: 2180.00

Enter dollars to convert (-1 to end): 40.50
Select conversion type:
1 - Dollars to Euros
2 - Dollars to Yen
3 - Dollars to Pesos
? 1
Converted amount: 32.40

Enter dollars to convert (-1 to end): 35.00
Select conversion type:
1 - Dollars to Euros
2 - Dollars to Yen
3 - Dollars to Pesos
? 4

Input error: Please select a valid menu option.

Enter dollars to convert (-1 to end): -1

Press any key to continue_
```

Figure 7.18 Enhanced **Currency Converter** application output.

a) *Copying the completed exercise to your working directory.* Copy the C:\Examples\Tutorial07\Exercises\EnhancedCurrencyConverter directory to your C:\SimplyCpp directory. Then, copy the file C:\SimplyCpp\CurrencyConverter\CurrencyConverter.cpp to your C:\SimplyCpp\EnhancedCurrencyConverter directory. If you have not completed Exercise 4.11, follow the steps in Exercise 4.11 before copying the file.

b) *Opening the source code file.* Open the CurrencyConverter.cpp file in your text editor or IDE.

c) *Modifying the Enter dollars to convert: prompt.* Modify the **Enter dollars to convert:** prompt so that it displays the text, **Enter dollars to convert (-1 to end):**, clearly indicating the application's sentinel value.

d) *Adding a sentinel-controlled repetition statement.* Modify the application's variable definitions so that both variables are initialized to 0. Immediately following the **Enter dollars to convert (-1 to end):** prompt, insert a while statement. The loop-continuation condition should evaluate to false when amount is -1. This will enable the user to enter multiple dollar values to convert with a single execution of the application. The closing brace for the while statement should appear immediately before the return statement. To improve readability, add a level of indentation to the statements now contained in the body of the while loop.

e) *Prompting the user for the next value.* Immediately before the closing brace of the while loop, insert statements that prompt the user for the next value and store the value entered at the keyboard in variable amount.

f) *Validating user input.* Use an if...else statement to display the converted amount only if the user enters a valid selection from the menu of currency-conversion options. Otherwise, the application should display an error message and prompt the user for the next value to convert.

g) *Save, compile and run the completed application.* Test the application to ensure that it runs correctly. Type 20.00 at the **Enter dollars to convert (-1 to end):** prompt and select option 2 (Yen) from the menu by entering 2 at the menu's prompt. Ensure that the converted value 2180.00 displays. Run the application again, type 20.00 at the **Enter dollars to convert (-1 to end):** prompt and select option 1 (Euros) from the menu by entering 1 at the menu's prompt. Ensure that the converted value 16.00 displays. Run the application again, type 20.00 at the **Enter dollars to convert (-1 to end):** prompt and select option 3 (Pesos) from the menu by entering 3 at the menu's prompt. Ensure that the converted value 220.00 displays. Finally, run the application once more, type 20.00 at the **Enter dollars to convert (-1 to end):** prompt and enter any number at the menu's prompt. Notice that the application does not display the dollar amount if an incorrect option is selected from the menu.

h) *Close the Command Prompt window.*

7.13 *(Enhanced Class Average Application)* Modify the **Class Average** application of Fig. 7.16 so that it accepts letter grades as input. The application should use the value 95 for an A, 85 for a B, 75 for a C, 65 for a D and 55 for an F. When the user enters the letter Q (or q), the application should display the numeric class average and exit (Fig. 7.19).

```
c:\simplycpp\enhancedclassaverage\debug\EnhancedClassAverage.exe

Enter letter grade (q to end): A
Enter letter grade (q to end): b
Enter letter grade (q to end): c
Enter letter grade (q to end): A
Enter letter grade (q to end): B
Enter letter grade (q to end): C
Enter letter grade (q to end): D
Enter letter grade (q to end): q

Average grade: 82.1

Press any key to continue_
```

Figure 7.19 Enhanced **Class Average** application.

a) *Copying the template to your working directory.* Copy the C:\Examples\ Tutorial07\Exercises\EnhancedClassAverage directory to your C:\SimplyCpp directory.

b) *Opening the template source code file.* Open the ClassAverage.cpp file in your text editor or IDE.

c) *Redefining the grade variable.* Modify line 14 so that grade is defined as the char type. This causes cin to read a single character in lines 18 and 27.

d) *Modifying the input prompts.* Modify the input prompts in lines 17 and 26. The prompt should read, "Enter letter grade (q to end): ".

e) *Modifying the while loop.* Modify the loop-continuation condition in line 20. The condition should evaluate to false when the user enters an uppercase or lowercase "q."

f) *Adding the grade value to the total.* Replace line 22 with a set of nested if...else statements that add the corresponding value of the letter grade to the total. For example, if the user entered an uppercase or lowercase "a," the application should add 95 to total. If the user enters an invalid letter grade (such as x), display an error message. Note, however, that the error message should not be displayed if the user enters the sentinel value, q.

g) *Save, compile and run the application.* Test the application to ensure that it runs correctly by entering uppercase and lowercase grades. Make sure that once you enter the sentinel value, the application correctly calculates the average the grades you entered.

h) *Close the Command Prompt window.*

What does this code do? ▶   **7.14** What is the result of the following code?

```
1   // Exercise 7.14: WDTCD.cpp
2   // What does this code do?
3   #include <iostream>  // required to perform C++ stream I/O
4
5   using namespace std; // for accessing C++ Standard Library members
6
7   // function main begins program execution
8   int main()
9   {
10      // define variables
11      int y;
12      int x = 0;
13
14      cout << "\nEnter positive integer (-1 to end): ";
15      cin >> x;
16
17      while (x != -1 )
18      {
19         y = x * x;
20
21         cout << "Result: " << y << endl;
22
23         cout << "\nEnter positive integer (-1 to end): ";
24         cin >> x;
25      } // end while
26
27      cout << "\n"; // insert newline for readability
28
29      return 0; // indicate that program ended successfully
30
31   } // end function main
```

What's wrong with this code? ▶   **7.15** Find the error(s) in the following code. This code should display the sum of all numbers that the user enters.

```cpp
1   // Exercise 7.15: WWWTC.cpp
2   // This application displays the sum of the numbers
3   // input by the user
4   #include <iostream>  // required to perform C++ stream I/O
5
6   using namespace std; // for accessing C++ Standard Library members
7
8   // function main begins program execution
9   int main()
10  {
11     // define variables
12     int total = 0;
13     int value = 0;
14
15     do
16     {
17        cout << "\nEnter a positive integer (-1 to end): ";
18        cin >> value;
19
20        total += value;
21
22     }
23     while ( total != -1 ) // end do...while
24
25     cout << "\nSum is: " << total << endl;
26
27     return 0; // indicate that program ended successfully
28
29  } // end function main
```

Using the Debugger ▶

7.16 (*Account Balance Application*) The **Account Balance** application helps the user balance a checkbook by inputting the user's starting balance, then allowing the user to enter a series of credits (increases to the balance) and debits (decreases to the balance) on the account. After the user has entered all credits and debits, the account balance is displayed. While testing the application, you notice that it does not execute correctly. Use the debugger to find and correct the logic error(s) in the application. Figure 7.20 displays the correct output for the **Account Balance** application.

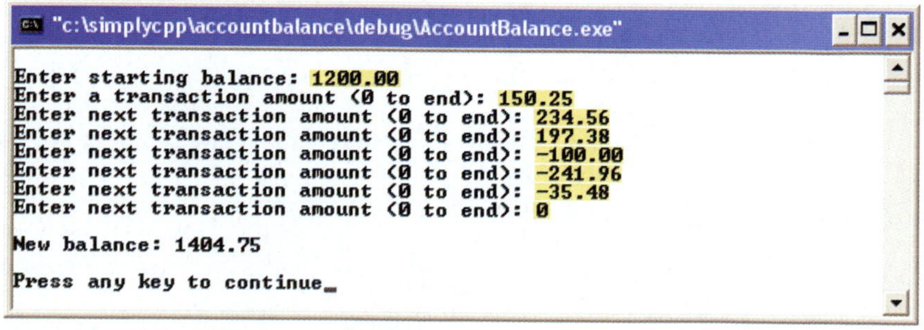

Figure 7.20 Correct output for the **Account Balance** application.

a) *Copying the template to your working directory.* Copy the C:\Examples\Tutorial07\Exercises\Debugger\AccountBalance directory to your C:\SimplyCpp directory.

b) *Compile and run the application.* Enter the values as shown in Fig. 7.20. Notice that the application does not terminate when you enter 0 at the **Enter transaction amount (0 to end):** prompt.

c) *Close the application.*

d) *Start the debugger.* Compile your application for use with your debugger, then start your application in the debugger.

e) *Opening the template file.* Open the AccountBalance.cpp file in your text editor or IDE.

f) *Finding and correcting the error(s).* Use the debugging skills learned in previous tutorials to locate the logic error(s) in the main function. Set a breakpoint in the while statement that enables you to examine the value of the credit variable. After you locate the logic error, modify the code so that the application exits the while statement when the user enters 0. Run the application again, using the input values from Fig. 7.20. Notice that the application does not calculate the correct result. Use breakpoints to at each assignment statement to ensure that the correct assignments and calculations are being performed. When you find the remaining logic errors, modify the code so that the application displays the correct results.

g) *Save, compile and run the completed application.* Test the application to ensure that it runs correctly. Use several different inputs to ensure the resulting account balance is correct for each input value.

h) *Close the Command Prompt window.*

Programming Challenge ▶ **7.17** *(Arithmetic Calculator Application)* Write an application that allows users to enter two numbers that can then be added or multiplied (Fig. 7.21). Users should enter each number at an input prompt, then enter the operand at a third input prompt. The application should then display the result of the desired calculation and display a prompt asking the user whether the application should continue. If the user enters either an uppercase or lowercase "n," the application should exit. Otherwise, the application should prompt the user for the next calculation.

```
"c:\simplycpp\arithmeticcalculator\debug\ArithmeticCalculator.exe"

Enter first operand: 5
Enter second operand: 10
Enter operator (+ or *): +
Sum is: 15

Would you like to enter another set of values (y = yes, n = no)? y

Enter first operand: 10
Enter second operand: 5
Enter operator (+ or *): *
Product is: 50

Would you like to enter another set of values (y = yes, n = no)? y

Enter first operand: 5
Enter second operand: 10
Enter operator (+ or *): /

Improper operand. Enter * for multiplication and + for addition.

Would you like to enter another set of values (y = yes, n = no)? n

Press any key to continue_
```

Figure 7.21 Arithmetic Calculator application.

a) *Copying the template to your working directory.* Copy the C:\Examples\ Tutorial07\Exercises\ArithmeticCalculator directory to your C:\SimplyCpp directory.

b) *Opening the template source code file.* Open the ArithmeticCalculator.cpp file in your text editor or IDE.

c) *Defining variables.* After line 10, define int variables value1 and value2 to store the operands for the calculation. Then define char variable operation to store the operator that the user enters and char variable response to store the user's response to the prompt to continue entering values or exit the application. Initialize response's value to 'y' (short for "yes"). This will ensure that the application will prompt the user for at least one calculation. (As you will see in the next step, the sentinel value is the letter n.)

d) *Inserting a while loop to perform sentinel-controlled repetition.* After defining the variables that your application will use, insert a while repetition statement. The loop-continuation condition should evaluate to `false` if `response` contains either the uppercase or lowercase "n" character.

e) ***Prompting the user for and storing the operands and operator.*** Inside the `while` loop, use `cout` and `cin` to prompt the user for and store the first operand (in `value1`), the second operand (in `value2`) and the operator (in `operation`).

f) ***Performing the calculation and displaying the result.*** After the code you entered in *Step e* (and still inside the `while` loop), use a nested `if...else` statement to perform the appropriate calculation and display the result. The condition for each `if` statement should determine the value contained in `operation`. If the value contained in `operation` is not a plus sign (+) or an asterisk (*), the application should display an error message indicating that an invalid operator was specified.

g) ***Prompting the user to continue.*** Before the closing brace of the `while` loop, display a prompt asking the user whether the application should continue (Fig. 7.21). Store the user's response in `char` variable `response`.

h) ***Save, compile and run the completed application.*** Test the application to ensure that it runs correctly. Use various inputs, and make sure each result is correct. Also make sure that the application exits when you enter n at the prompt that you coded in *Step g*.

i) ***Close the Command Prompt window.***

Objectives

In this tutorial, you will learn to:

- Execute statements repeatedly with the `for` repetition statement.
- Use the math library to execute common mathematical functions.

Outline

Interest Calculator Application

Introducing the *for Repetition Statement and the Math Library*

A s you learned in Tutorial 6, applications are often required to repeat actions. Using a `while` or a `do...while` statement allows you to specify a loop-continuation condition and test that condition either before entering the loop or after executing the body of the loop. In the **Car Payment Calculator** application, you used a counter to determine the number of times the loop should iterate. The use of counters in repetition statements is so common that C++ provides an additional control statement specially designed for counter-controlled looping—the `for` repetition statement. In this tutorial, you will use the `for` repetition statement to create an **Interest Calculator** application.

8.1 Test-Driving the Interest Calculator Application

The **Interest Calculator** application calculates the balance in your savings account after you begin with a certain amount of money and are paid a certain interest rate for a certain amount of time. You specify the principal amount (the initial amount of money in the account), the annual interest rate and the number of years for which interest will be calculated. The application then displays the amount of money you will have on deposit at the end of each year for the duration of time that the money is on deposit. The application must meet the following requirements:

Application Requirements

You are considering investing $1000.00 in a savings account that yields 5% interest, and you want to forecast how your investment will grow. Assuming that you will leave all interest earned on deposit, develop an application that will calculate and display the amount of money in the account at the end of each year over a period of n years. To compute these amounts, use the following formula:

$$a = p(1 + r)^n$$

where

p is the original amount of money invested (the principal)
r is the annual interest rate (for example, 0.05 is equivalent to 5%)
n is the number of years (for example, n = 10 for 10 years)
a is the amount on deposit at the end of the nth year.

You begin by test-driving the completed application. Then, you will learn the additional C++ capabilities you will need to create your own version of this application.

Test-Driving the Interest Calculator Application

1. ***Locating the completed application.*** Open the **Command Prompt** window by selecting **Start > All Programs > Accessories > Command Prompt**. Change to your **Interest Calculator** application directory by typing `cd C:\Examples\Tutorial08\CompletedApplication\InterestCalculator`.

2. ***Running the Interest Calculator application.*** Type `InterestCalculator` in the **Command Prompt** window to run the application (Fig. 8.1). The user is prompted to enter the principal (the amount invested), the annual interest rate and the number of years for the deposit. Once the user enters this information, the amount on deposit for each year is displayed.

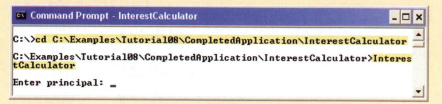

Figure 8.1 Running the completed **Interest Calculator** application.

3. ***Entering a principal value.*** Once the application is running, enter a value at the **Enter principal:** prompt. Input 1000 as specified in the application requirements.

4. ***Entering an interest-rate value.*** Next, enter a value at the **Enter interest rate:** prompt. The interest rate specified was 5%, in the problem statement, so enter 5.

5. ***Selecting the duration of the investment.*** Now you should choose the number of years for which you want to calculate the amount in the savings account. In this case, enter 10.

6. ***Calculating the amount.*** The amount of money in your account at the end of each year during a period of 10 years will be displayed (Fig. 8.2).

```
Command Prompt                                          _ □ ×
C:\Examples\Tutorial08\CompletedApplication\InterestCalculator>Interes
tCalculator

Enter principal: 1000
Enter interest rate: 5
Enter number of years for deposit: 10

Year          Amount on Deposit
1             $1050.00
2             $1102.50
3             $1157.63
4             $1215.51
5             $1276.28
6             $1340.10
7             $1407.10
8             $1477.46
9             $1551.33
10            $1628.89

C:\Examples\Tutorial08\CompletedApplication\InterestCalculator>_
```

Displaying the result in tabular format

Figure 8.2 Completed **Interest Calculator** application output.

7. ***Close the Command Prompt window.***

8.2 Essentials of Counter-Controlled Repetition

This section uses the `while` repetition statement introduced in Tutorial 6 to formalize the elements required to perform counter-controlled repetition. There are four essential elements of counter-controlled repetition. They are

1. the **name** of the **control variable** (or loop counter) that is used to determine whether the loop continues to iterate.

2. the **initial value** of the control variable.

3. the **increment** (or **decrement**) by which the control variable is modified during each iteration of the loop (that is, each time the loop is performed).

4. the condition that tests for the **final value** of the control variable (to determine whether looping should continue).

Figure 8.3 contains the `while` repetition statement from Tutorial 6's completed **Car Payment Calculator** application. Recall that this application calculates and displays monthly car payments over periods of two through five years. The counter for that `while` statement was represented by the `years` variable; for simplicity, we call the variable `counter` in Fig. 8.3.

```
 1   int counter = 2; // repetition counter
 2
 3   // format floating-point output with two digits of precision
 4   cout << fixed << setprecision( 2 );
 5
 6   while ( counter <= 5 )
 7   {
 8      months = 12 * counter; // calculate payment period
 9
10      // get monthly payment
11      monthlyPayment = calculateMonthlyPayment(
12         monthlyInterest, months, loanAmount );
13
14      // display result
15      cout << months << left << setw( 10 ) << "$" << monthlyPayment
16         << endl;
17
18      counter++; // increment counter
19
20   } // end while
```

Figure 8.3 Examining counter-controlled repetition using a `while` statement.

This example uses the four elements of counter-controlled repetition as follows.

1. The definition in line 1 *names* the control variable (`counter`), indicating that it is of the `int` data type.

2. The definition in line 1 also includes an *initialization*, which sets the variable to an initial value of 2.

3. Line 18 *increments* the control variable `counter` by 1 for each iteration of the loop.

4. The condition in the `while` statement (line 6) tests whether the value of the control variable is less than or equal to 5, meaning that 5 is the *final value* for which the condition is `true`. The loop terminates when the control variable exceeds 5 (that is, when `counter` has a value of 6).

SELF-REVIEW

1. The control variable's _____ is one of the four essential elements of counter-controlled repetition.

   a) final value   b) initial value

   c) increment (or decrement)   d) All of the above.

2. What element of counter-controlled repetition specifies how the control variable is modified during each iteration of the loop?

   a) name   b) initial value

   c) increment (or decrement)   d) final value

Answers: 1) d. 2) c.

8.3 Introducing the for Repetition Statement

The **for repetition statement** conveniently specifies all four elements essential to counter-controlled repetition, making it easier for you to write code to perform counter-controlled repetition. To help solidify your understanding of this new repetition statement, we will replace the `while` statement of Fig. 8.3 with an equivalent `for` statement (Fig. 8.4).

```
1   // format floating-point output with two digits of precision
2   cout << fixed << setprecision( 2 );
3
4   for ( int counter = 2; counter <= 5; counter++ )
5   {
6      months = 12 * counter; // calculate payment period
7
8      // get monthly payment
9      monthlyPayment = calculateMonthlyPayment(
10        monthlyInterest, months, loanAmount );
11
12     // display value
13     cout << months << left << setw( 10 ) << "$" << monthlyPayment
14        << endl;
15
16  } // end for
```

Good Programming Practice

Vertical spacing above and below control statements and indentation within control statements enhance program readability.

Figure 8.4   Code segment for the **Car Payment Calculator** application that demonstrates the `for` statement.

Let's examine this `for` repetition statement. The `for` statement's first line (including the **for** keyword and everything in parentheses after for)—line 4 of Fig. 8.4—is informally called the **for statement header**, or simply the **for header**. The `for` header specifies all four essential elements of counter-controlled repetition. Figure 8.5 takes a closer look at the `for` header of Fig. 8.4. Notice that the `for` statement "does it all"—it specifies each of the items needed for counter-controlled repetition with a control variable. [*Note:* You do not need to define the counter variable (using the `int` keyword) before the `for` statement. It can be done within the header as shown in Fig. 8.5. If the counter variable is defined this way, however, it will only exist within the bounds of the `for` statement. If the counter variable needs to be accessed after the `for` statement, it will need to be defined before the `for` statement.]

```
for keyword        Initial value of the control variable        Increment (or decrement)
                                                                  of the control variable

        for ( int counter = 2; counter <= 5; counter++ )

              Control variable name              Final value of the control variable
```

Figure 8.5 for header components.

The two required semicolons divide the for header into three expressions. The first expression specifies the name and initial value of the control variable counter (in this case, int counter = 2). The second expression specifies the loop-continuation condition (in this case, counter <= 5). The last expression specifies the increment (the amount by which counter is modified each time the for body is executed—in this case, 1). The line should be read *"for each value of counter starting at 2 and ending at 5, do the following statements then add one to counter."* The following box describes how the for statement in Fig. 8.4 executes.

Executing the for Repetition Statement

1. The application defines int variable counter and sets its initial value to 2.
2. The loop-continuation condition is checked. The condition evaluates to true (counter is 2, which is less than or equal to 5), so the application executes the statements in the for loop's body.
3. The value of counter is increased by 1; counter now contains 3.
4. The loop-continuation condition is checked. The condition evaluates to true (counter is 3, which is less than or equal to 5), so the application executes the statements in the for loop's body.
5. The value of counter is increased by 1; counter now contains 4.
6. The loop-continuation condition is checked. The condition evaluates to true (counter is 4, which is less than or equal to 5), so the application executes the statements in the for loop's body.
7. The value of counter is increased by 1; counter now contains 5.
8. The loop-continuation condition is checked. The condition evaluates to true (counter is 5, which is less than or equal to 5), so the application executes the statements in the for loop's body.
9. The value of counter is increased by 1; counter now contains 6.
10. The loop-continuation condition is checked. The condition evaluates to false (counter is 6, which is not less than or equal to 5), so the application exits the for loop.

Error-Prevention Tip

Although the value of the control variable can be changed in the body of a for loop, avoid doing so, because this practice can lead to subtle errors.

Common Programming Error

Counter-controlled loops should not be controlled with floating-point variables. Floating-point variables are represented only approximately in the computer's memory, possibly resulting in imprecise counter values and inaccurate tests for termination that could lead to logic errors.

The initial value, final value and increment (or decrement) portions of a for statement can contain arithmetic expressions. For example, if a = 2 and b = 10, the header

```
for ( int i = a; i <= 4 * a * b; i += ( b / a ) )
```

is equivalent to the header

```
for ( int i = 2; i <= 80; i += 5 )
```

If the loop-continuation condition is initially false (for example, if the initial value of control variable i is 5 and the loop-continuation condition is i <= 4), the for's body is not performed. Instead, execution proceeds with the first statement after the for statement.

Common Programming Error

Using an increment expression that does not modify the control variable's value (such as **counter + 1** when **counter++** or **counter += 1** should be used) normally causes an infinite loop.

The control variable frequently is displayed or used in calculations in the **for** loop, but it does not have to be. It is common to use the control variable only to control repetition and not use it within the loop.

The UML activity diagram of Fig. 8.6 illustrates the **for** statement of Fig. 8.4. This activity diagram is similar to that of the **while** statement (Fig. 6.4). Notice that the UML diagram shows that the initialization occurs only once and that incrementing occurs *after* each execution of the body statement. Also note that, besides small circles and flowlines, the activity diagram contains only rounded rectangle symbols and small diamond symbols. The rounded rectangle symbols are filled with the actions, and the flowlines coming out of the small diamond symbols are labeled with the appropriate guard conditions for this algorithm.

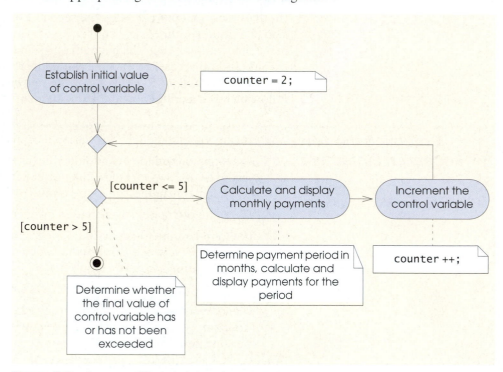

Figure 8.6   **for** repetition statement UML activity diagram.

SELF-REVIEW   1. The value before the first semicolon in a **for** statement typically specifies the _____.

   a) initial value of the counter variable   b) final value of the counter variable
   c) increment   d) number of times the statement iterates

2. The first line of the **for** repetition statement is informally known as the **for** _____.

   a) body   b) header
   c) counter   d) expression

Answers: 1) a. 2) b.

8.4 Examples Using the **for** Statement

The following examples demonstrate ways to vary the control variable in a **for** statement. In each case, you are provided with the appropriate **for** header:

■ Vary the control variable from 1 to 100 in increments of 1.

```
for ( int i = 1; i <= 100; i++ )
```

■ Vary the control variable from 100 to 1 in increments of –1 (that is, decrements of 1). Notice that when counting downwards, the loop-continuation condition, i >= 1, now uses the relational operator >=.

```
for ( int i = 100; i >= 1; i-- )
```

■ Vary the control variable from 7 to 77 in increments of 7.

```
for ( int i = 7; i <= 77; i += 7 )
```

■ Vary the control variable from 20 to 2 in increments of -2 (that is, decrements of 2).

```
for ( int i = 20; i >= 2; i -= 2 )
```

■ Vary the control variable over the sequence of the following values: 2, 5, 8, 11, 14, 17, 20.

```
for ( int i = 2; i <= 20; i += 3 )
```

■ Vary the control variable over the sequence of the following values: 99, 88, 77, 66, 55, 44, 33, 22, 11, 0.

```
for ( int i = 99; i >= 0; i -= 11 )
```

SELF-REVIEW

1. Which of the following is an appropriate for header to vary the control variable over the following sequence of values: 25, 20, 15, 10, 5?

   a) `for ( int i = 5; i <= 25; i += 5 )`
   b) `for ( int i = 25; i >= 5; i -= 5 )`
   c) `for ( int i = 5; i <= 25; i -= 5 )`
   d) `for ( int i = 25; i >= 5; i += 5 )`

2. Which of the following statements describes what the following for header does?

   ```
   for ( int i = 81; i <= 102; i++ )
   ```

   a) Vary the control variable from 81 to 102 in increments of 1.
   b) Vary the control variable from 81 to 102 in increments of 0.
   c) Vary the control variable from 102 to 81 in increments of -1.
   d) Vary the control variable from 81 to 101 in increments of 1.

Answers: 1) b. 2) a.

8.5 Constructing the Interest Calculator Application

Now you will build your **Interest Calculator** application by using cin to gather input and a for statement to calculate the value of the investment after each year. The pseudocode in Fig. 8.7 describes the basic operation of the **Interest Calculator** application, which executes after the user enters all information requested by the input prompts.

> Prompt the user for and input the principal, interest rate and years
> Display a table header
>
> For each year, starting at 1 and ending with the number of years entered
>   Calculate and display the year
>   Calculate and display the current value of the investment

Figure 8.7 Pseudocode for the **Interest Calculator** application.

You will write code to retrieve input from the user. Then you will add functionality to your application using a for statement. Now that you have test-driven the **Interest Calculator** application and studied its pseudocode representation, you will begin building your own **Interest Calculator** application by defining variables and retrieving user input.

Defining Variables and Retrieving Input

1. *Copying the template application to your working directory.* Copy the `C:\Examples\Tutorial08\TemplateApplication\InterestCalcula-tor` directory to your `C:\SimplyCpp` directory.

2. *Opening the Interest Calculator application's template source code file.* Open the template source code file `InterestCalculator.cpp` in your text editor or IDE.

3. *Defining variables.* Insert lines 11–14 of Fig. 8.8 to define the variables that you will use in your **Interest Calculator** application. Line 12 defines `double` variable `principal` to store the principal amount on deposit. Line 13 defines `double` variable `rate` to store the annual interest rate. Line 14 defines `int` variable `years` to store the number of years that the principal is on deposit.

Define variables to store user input

```
InterestCalculator.cpp*
 8    // function main begins program execution
 9    int main()
10    {
11        // define variables
12        double principal; // principal
13        double rate;      // interest rate
14        int years;        // investment duration
15
16        cout << "\n"; // insert newline for readability
```

Figure 8.8 Defining variables to store the principal, interest rate and investment duration.

4. *Prompting the user for and inputting values.* Insert lines 16–25 (Fig. 8.9) to prompt the user for and input values for the principal, interest rate and investment duration. Lines 18–19 prompt the user for the value of the principal and input the value entered at the keyboard into `double` variable `principal`. Similarly, lines 21–22 prompt the user for the annual interest rate percentage and input the value entered at the keyboard into `double` variable `rate`. Finally, lines 24–25 prompt the user for the number of years that the principal will be on deposit and input the value typed at the keyboard into `int` variable `years`.

Prompt the user for and input the principal, interest rate and investment duration

```
InterestCalculator.cpp*
14        int years;        // investment duration
15
16        // prompt the user for and input principal, interest rate
17        // and investment duration
18        cout << "\nEnter principal: ";
19        cin >> principal; // get principal
20
21        cout << "Enter interest rate: ";
22        cin >> rate; // get interest rate
23
24        cout << "Enter number of years for deposit: ";
25        cin >> years; // get years for deposit
26
27        cout << "\n"; // insert newline for readability
```

Figure 8.9 Prompting the user for and inputting the principal, interest rate and investment duration.

5. *Save the application.*

The **Interest Calculator** application displays the results of its calculations in tabular format. In the following box, you will write code to display a table header and format floating-point values with two positions to the right of the decimal point.

Displaying a Table Header and Formatting Output

1. ***Displaying a table header.*** Add lines 27–29 of Fig. 8.10 to your code. This statement displays a table header with descriptive text that identifies two columns. The first column, titled `Year`, displays values that are left justified (due to the `left` stream manipulator in line 28) in a field that is 10 characters wide (due to `setw( 10 )`, also in line 28). The second column is titled `Amount on Deposit`.

```
InterestCalculator.cpp*
25        cin >> years; // get years for deposit
26
27        // display header for yearly balances
28        cout << "\n" << left << setw( 10 ) << "Year"
29           << "Amount on Deposit" << endl;
30
31        cout << "\n"; // insert newline for readability
```

Displaying a table header

Figure 8.10   Displaying a table header.

2. ***Formatting floating-point numbers.*** Add lines 31–32 of Fig. 8.11 to your code. Line 32 uses the `fixed` and `setprecision` stream manipulators to format floating-point numbers as with two positions to the right of the decimal point.

```
InterestCalculator.cpp*
29           << "Amount on Deposit" << endl;
30
31        // set the format for displaying dollar values
32        cout << fixed << setprecision( 2 );
33
34        cout << "\n"; // insert newline for readability
```

Formatting floating-point numbers

Figure 8.11   Formatting floating-point numbers.

3. ***Save the application.***

Now that you have displayed a table header and used stream manipulators to format output, you will use a `for` statement to calculate and display the value of the investment at the end of each year. You will also learn to use the **pow** function to perform exponentiation. The pow function is declared in the **math library**, which is accessed by including the **<cmath> header file**, which provides functions to perform common arithmetic calculations, such as exponentiation, square roots and trigonometry. [*Note:* Unlike other programming languages, C++ does not provide an exponentiation operator.]

Calculating the Annual Balance with a for Statement

1. ***Creating an empty for statement.*** Add lines 34–38 of Fig. 8.12 to `main`. The `for` header in line 35 initializes control variable `count` to 1. The `for` statement's loop-continuation condition (`count <= years`) specifies that the body will execute once for each year up to the value of `year`, varying the control variable `count` from 1 to `year` in increments of 1.

2. ***Including the <cmath> standard library header file.*** Insert line 5 of Fig. 8.13. The `#include <cmath>` preprocessor directive enables your application to access functions provided by the `<cmath>` standard library header file.

(cont.)

Empty **for** statement

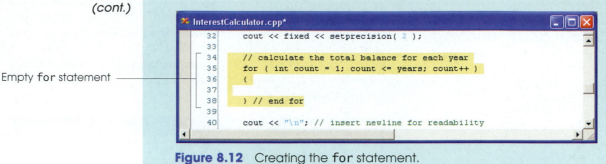

Figure 8.12 Creating the **for** statement.

Including **<cmath>**

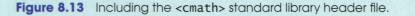

Figure 8.13 Including the **<cmath>** standard library header file.

3. ***Performing the interest calculation.*** Add lines 38–40 of Fig. 8.14 to the body of your **for** statement. Lines 39–40 perform the calculation from the formula

$$a = p \ (1 + r)^n$$

where *a* is **amount**, *p* is **principal**, *r* is (**rate** / 100) and *n* is the number of years.

Line 40 calls the pow function, which performs exponentiation. pow takes two arguments—the first specifies the value that will be raised to a power, and the second specifies the power to which the first argument will be raised. For instance, pow(4, 2) is used to represent the expression 4^2, which evaluates to 16.

Using **<cmath>** function **pow** to calculate the amount on deposit after the specified number of years

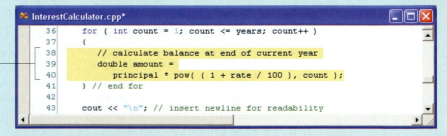

Figure 8.14 Calculating amount on deposit after specified number of years.

Line 40 also performs the $(1 + r)^n$ portion of the formula. The first argument to pow is (1 + rate / 100), representing the (1 + *r*) portion of the formula. The division by 100 converts the input (which is in percentage format, like the 5 in 5%) into a decimal value (like 0.05) that can be used in the interest calculation. The second argument to pow, count, represents the power that (1 + rate / 100) is raised to (the *n* in the preceding formula).

When the computer executes line 40, the pow function performs the exponentiation calculation with the supplied arguments. After completing the calculation, the result is returned and multiplied by the value in principal. The product of these two values is then assigned to double variable amount, defined in line 39.

(cont.)

4. ***Inserting the result of the calculation into cout.*** Add lines 42–43 of Fig. 8.15 to your `for` statement. These lines display the year and the amount on deposit at the end of that year. The `setw` stream manipulator specifies that the value of the counter (that is, the current year of the investment) should be displayed in a field of width 10. The value is left justified due to the `left` stream manipulator, which is now in line 29. The next value, a dollar sign (`"$"`), is output after the 10-character field, followed by the value `amount` displayed with two positions to the right of the decimal point.

   After the body of the loop is performed, execution reaches the right brace, which is now in line 44. The counter (`count`) is incremented by 1, and the loop begins again with the loop-continuation test in the `for` header (line 36). The `for` statement executes until the control variable exceeds the number of years specified by the user.

Displaying the amount on deposit for each year

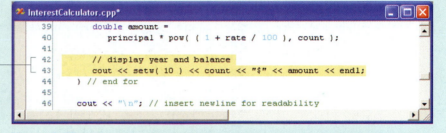

Figure 8.15 Displaying the amount on deposit for each year.

5. ***Save, compile and run the application.*** Figure 8.16 shows the completed application running. Use the values displayed in Fig. 8.16 to test your application to ensure that it runs correctly.

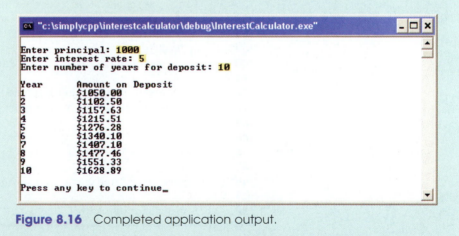

Figure 8.16 Completed application output.

6. ***Close the Command Prompt window.***

Figure 8.17 presents the source code for your **Interest Calculator** application. The lines of code that you added, viewed or modified are highlighted.

Include the `<cmath>` standard library header file

```
1   // Tutorial 8: InterestCalculator.cpp
2   // Calculate the total value of an investment.
3   #include <iostream> // required to perform C++ stream I/O
4   #include <iomanip> // required for parameterized stream manipulators
5   #include <cmath>    // required to use the C++ math library functions
6
```

Figure 8.17 **Interest Calculator** application code. (Part 1 of 2.)

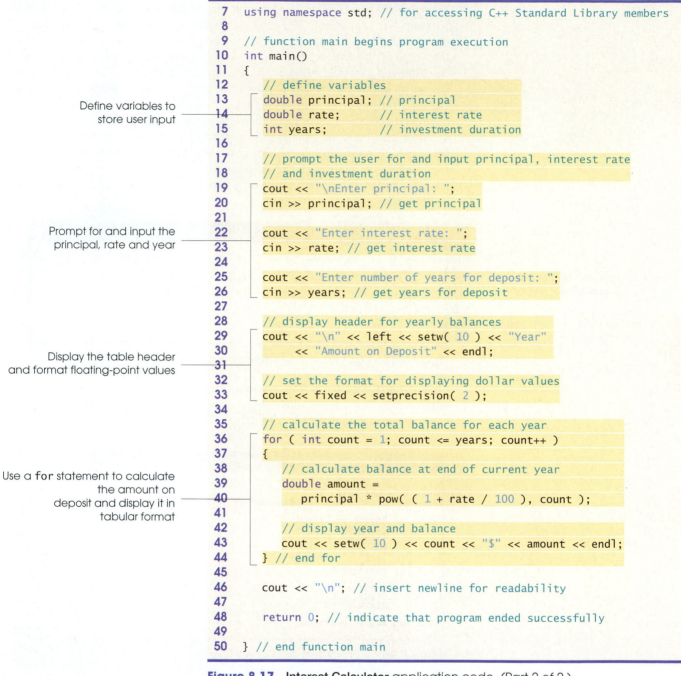

Define variables to store user input

Prompt for and input the principal, rate and year

Display the table header and format floating-point values

Use a **for** statement to calculate the amount on deposit and display it in tabular format

```cpp
 7    using namespace std; // for accessing C++ Standard Library members
 8
 9    // function main begins program execution
10    int main()
11    {
12       // define variables
13       double principal; // principal
14       double rate;        // interest rate
15       int years;          // investment duration
16
17       // prompt the user for and input principal, interest rate
18       // and investment duration
19       cout << "\nEnter principal: ";
20       cin >> principal; // get principal
21
22       cout << "Enter interest rate: ";
23       cin >> rate;  // get interest rate
24
25       cout << "Enter number of years for deposit: ";
26       cin >> years; // get years for deposit
27
28       // display header for yearly balances
29       cout << "\n" << left << setw( 10 ) << "Year"
30          << "Amount on Deposit" << endl;
31
32       // set the format for displaying dollar values
33       cout << fixed << setprecision( 2 );
34
35       // calculate the total balance for each year
36       for ( int count = 1; count <= years; count++ )
37       {
38          // calculate balance at end of current year
39          double amount =
40             principal * pow( ( 1 + rate / 100 ), count );
41
42          // display year and balance
43          cout << setw( 10 ) << count << "$" << amount << endl;
44       } // end for
45
46       cout << "\n"; // insert newline for readability
47
48       return 0; // indicate that program ended successfully
49
50    } // end function main
```

Figure 8.17   **Interest Calculator** application code. (Part 2 of 2.)

SELF-REVIEW

1. The _____ header file provides access to functions that perform common arithmetic calculations, such as exponentiation and trigonometry.

    a) <math>   b) <cmath>

    c) <pow>   d) <cpow>

2. The expression _____ calculates 2^8.

    a) pow(2, 8)   b) 2 ^ 8

    c) pow(8, 2)   d) Both b and c.

Answers: 1) b. 2) a.

8.6 Wrap-Up

In this tutorial, you learned that the essential elements of counter-controlled repetition are the name of a control variable, the initial value of the control variable, the increment (or decrement) by which the control variable is modified each time through the loop and the condition that tests the final value of the control variable. You then explored the `for` repetition statement, which combines these essentials of counter-controlled repetition in its header.

After becoming familiar with the `for` repetition statement, you changed the **Car Payment Calculator** application's `while` statement into a `for` statement. You then built an **Interest Calculator**, after analyzing its pseudocode. In the **Interest Calculator**'s main function, you used the pow function from the `<cmath>` standard library to calculate the value of the user's investment over time.

In the next tutorial, you will learn to use the `switch` multiple-selection statement. You have learned that the `if...else` selection statement can be used in code to select among multiple courses of action, depending on the value of a condition. You will see that a `switch` multiple-selection statement can save development time and improve code readability if the number of conditions is large. You will use a `switch` multiple-selection statement to build an **Income Tax Calculator** application.

SKILLS SUMMARY

Using the `for` Repetition Statement

- Specify the initial value of the control variable before the first semicolon in the `for` header.
- Specify the loop-continuation condition after the first semicolon.
- Specify the increment (or decrement) after the second semicolon.
- Use curly braces ({ and }) to delineate the body of the `for` repetition statement.

Performing Exponentiation

- Call the pow function, which you can access by including the `<cmath>` standard library header file.
- Pass as the first argument to pow the value that is to be raised to a power.
- Pass as the second argument to pow the value of the power.

KEY TERMS

`<cmath>` header file—This header file provides access to functions that perform common arithmetic calculations.

control variable—A variable used to control the number of iterations of a counter-controlled loop.

final value of a control variable—The last value a control variable will hold before a counter-controlled loop terminates.

`for` keyword—The keyword that begins each `for` statement.

`for` statement header/`for` header—The first line in a `for` statement. The `for` header specifies all four essential elements of counter-controlled repetition—the name of a control variable, the initial value, the increment or decrement value and the final value.

`for` repetition statement—A repetition statement that conveniently handles the details of counter-controlled repetition. The `for` statement header specifies all four elements essential to counter-controlled repetition.

increment (or decrement) of a control variable—The amount by which the control variable's value changes during each iteration of the loop.

initial value of a control variable—The value a control variable will hold when counter-controlled repetition begins.

math library—A standard library that provides functions to perform common arithmetic calculations.

name of a control variable—The identifier used to reference the control variable of a loop

pow function—A function of the `<cmath>` standard library that performs exponentiation. The first argument specifies the value that will be raised to a power; the second argument specifies the power to which the first argument will be raised.

C++ LIBRARY REFERENCE

cmath This header provides access to functions that perform common arithmetic calculations.

■ *Function*

pow—This function performs exponentiation. The first argument specifies the value that will be raised to a power, and the second argument specifies the power to which the first argument will be raised.

MULTIPLE-CHOICE QUESTIONS

8.1 Which of the following is not a valid increment (or decrement) of the control variable in a for repetition statement header?

a) i *= 10;

b) i++;

c) i + 1;

d) i -= 1;

8.2 _____ is typically used to determine whether a for loop continues to iterate.

a) The initial value of the control variable

b) The right brace

c) The left brace

d) The final value of the control variable

8.3 In a for loop, the control variable is incremented (or decremented) _____.

a) after the body of the loop executes

b) before the body of the loop executes

c) while the loop-continuation condition is false

d) while the body of the loop executes

8.4 The _____ is not an essential element for counter-controlled repetition.

a) name of a control variable

b) for statement

c) final value

d) increment (or decrement)

8.5 The for header _____ can be used to vary the control variable over the odd numbers between 1 and 10.

a) for (int i = 1; i <= 10; i += 1)

b) for (int i = 1; i <= 10; i += 2)

c) for (int i = 1; i <= 10; i -= 1)

d) for (int i = 1; i <= 10; i -= 2)

8.6 The body of the for loop with the header for (int i = 0; i <= 50; i += 5) will be executed _____ times.

a) 50

b) 10

c) 11

d) None of the above.

8.7 The <cmath> standard library provides functions that _____.

a) perform exponentiation

b) format floating-point numbers

c) perform trigonometric calculations

d) Both a and c.

8.8 The for header _____ will cause an application to enter an infinite loop.

a) for (int i = 1; i == 10; i += 1)

b) for (int i = 8; i >= 1; i += 2)

c) for (int i = 20; i <= 10; i -= 1)

d) for (int i = 4; i <= 8; i += 2)

8.9 The body of the for loop with the header for (int i = 1; i <= 10; i -= 1) will be executed _____ times.

a) a very large number of

b) 9

c) 10

d) 11

8.10 The _____ function returns the value of one number raised to the power of another number.

a) power

b) exponent

c) pow

d) exp

EXERCISES   **8.11** *(Validating Input to the Interest Calculator Application)* Enhance the **Interest Calculator** application you built in this tutorial with error checking. Test whether the user has entered valid values for the principal and interest rate. If the user enters an invalid value, display an error message. Invalid values include a principal that is less than zero, an interest rate that is less than zero or greater than 10 (percent) and an investment duration that is less than or equal to zero. Figure 8.18 demonstrates the application handling invalid input.

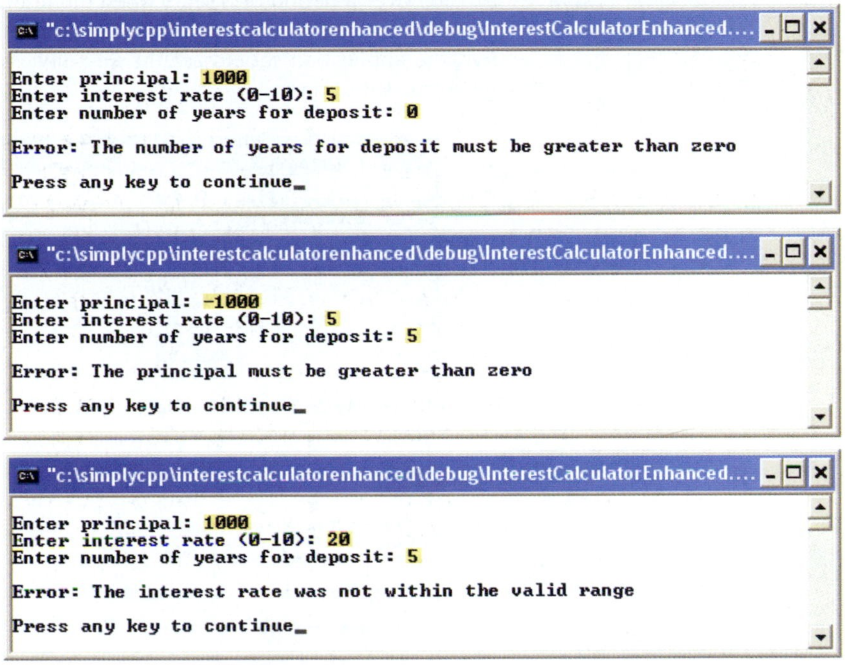

Figure 8.18   Interest Calculator application with error checking.

a) *Copying the template to your working directory.* Copy the `C:\Examples\Tutorial08\Exercises\InterestCalculatorEnhanced` directory to your `C:\SimplyCpp` directory.

b) *Opening the template source code file.* Open the `InterestCalculator.cpp` file in your text editor or IDE.

c) *Modifying* `main` *to handle invalid input.* After line 27, enter the `if` part of a series of nested `if...else` statements that will determine whether the user entered valid input. The condition of this `if` statement should test whether `rate` is not between 0 and 10. If the condition is `true`, the body of the `if` statement should display an error message indicating that the user entered an invalid interest rate. Modify the prompt in line 22 to display the valid range of input.

d) *Inserting an* `else if` *statement.* After the code you entered in *Step c*, insert an `else if` statement that determines whether the principal is less than or equal to 0. If this condition is `true`, the application should display an error message.

e) *Inserting a second* `else if` *statement.* After the code you entered in *Step d*, insert a second `else if` statement that determines whether the investment duration is less than 1. If this condition is `true`, the application should display an error message.

f) *Performing the calculation.* The application should calculate and display the amount on balance each year only if the user entered valid inputs. Place the code in lines 28–44 of Fig. 8.17 inside an `else` statement directly following the second `else if` statement to ensure that this occurs.

g) *Save, compile and run the application.* Input a principal value, interest rate and number of years. Make sure all your input is valid. View the results to ensure that the correct number of years is displayed and that the initial deposit results are correct. Now, modify your input values so that you are entering invalid input. Make sure that the appropriate error messages are displayed.

h) *Close the Command Prompt window.*

8.12 *(Present Value Calculator Application)* A bank wants to show its customers how much they would need to invest to achieve a specified financial goal (future value) in 5, 10, 15, 20, 25 or 30 years. Users must provide their financial goal (the amount of money desired after the specified number of years has elapsed), the interest rate and the length of the investment in years. Create an application that calculates and displays the principal needed to achieve the user's financial goal. Your application should allow the user to invest money for 5, 10, 15, 20, 25 or 30 years. For example, if a customer wants to reach the financial goal of $15,000 over a period of 5 years when the interest rate is 6.6%, the customer would need to invest $10,896.96 as shown in Fig. 8.19. If the specified number of years is not a multiple of five, the application should use the next lowest multiple of five as the upper bound for the investment duration.

```
"c:\simplycpp\presentvalue\debug\PresentValue.exe"

Enter future value: 15000
Enter interest rate: 6.6
Enter years (5 - 30): 30

Duration (Years) Initial Deposit
5                $10896.96
10               $7916.24
15               $5750.87
20               $4177.80
25               $3035.02
30               $2204.83

Press any key to continue_
```

```
"c:\simplycpp\presentvalue\debug\PresentValue.exe"

Enter future value: 15000
Enter interest rate: 6.6
Enter years (5 - 30): 35

Error: Enter an investment duration between 5 and 30 years

Press any key to continue_
```

Figure 8.19 Present Value Calculator application output.

a) *Copying the template to your working directory.* Copy the C:\Examples\Tutorial08\Exercises\PresentValue directory to your C:\SimplyCpp directory.

b) *Opening the template source code file.* Open the PresentValue.cpp file in your text editor or IDE.

c) *Including the <cmath> standard library header file and defining variables.* Because you will use the pow function in this application, you must include the <cmath> standard library header file. Insert an #include preprocessor directive after line 5 to include <cmath>. To store user input, define int variable futureValue, double variable rate and int variable years in main after line 12.

d) *Prompting the user for and storing input.* Prompt the user for the future value, annual interest rate and investment duration as shown in Fig. 8.19. Store the future value in futureValue, the annual interest rate in rate and the investment duration in years.

e) *Determining whether the user entered a valid investment duration.* After retrieving user input, insert the if part of an if...else statement that will determine whether the user entered an investment duration that is not between 5 and 30, inclusive. If this condition is true, your application should display an error message (Fig. 8.19).

f) *Displaying a table header and formatting output.* Immediately after the closing brace for your if statement, insert an else part to the if...else statement. The code in the else part will execute only if the user has entered a valid investment duration. Use the left and setw stream manipulators to display a table header as shown in Fig. 8.19. The first column should be 17 characters wide. Then, use the fixed and setprecision stream manipulators to format floating-point values with two positions to the left of the decimal point.

g) *Writing a for statement header.* Insert a for statement header. Before the first semicolon, define and initialize the counter variable to 5. Before the second semicolon, enter a loop-continuation condition that will cause the `for` statement to loop until `counter` has reached the number of years specified by the user. After the second semicolon, enter the increment of `counter` so that the `for` statement executes for every fifth year.

h) *Calculating present values.* You will now calculate the amount needed to achieve the future value for each five-year interval. To do this, you will need to implement the following formula within the `for` statement:

$$p = a / (1 + r)^n$$

where

    p is the amount needed to achieve the future value
    r is the annual interest rate
    n is the number of years
    a is the future value amount (the amount the user would like to have after n years)

In the body of the `for` statement, use the `pow` function (as well as the variables you defined in *Step c*) to calculate the present value needed for the current number of years. Store this value in `double` variable `amount`. Use two lines for clarity. Then use `cout` to display the current number of years in a field of width 10, followed by a dollar sign and the present value. Use two lines for clarity.

i) *Save, compile and run the application.* Input a future value, interest rate and number of years. View the results to ensure that the correct number of years is displayed, and that the initial deposit results are correct.

j) *Close the* Command Prompt *window.*

8.13 *(Compound Interest: Comparing Rates Application)* Write an application that calculates the amount of money in an account after 10 years for interest rates of 5%–10%, inclusive (Fig. 8.20). For this application, users must provide the initial principal.

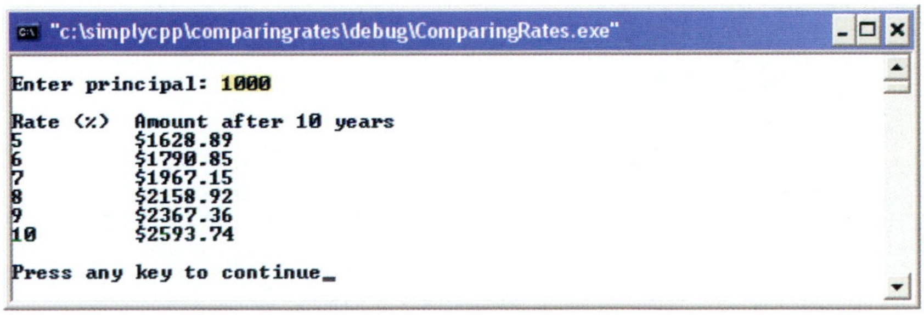

Figure 8.20   Comparing Rates application output.

a) *Copying the template to your working directory.* Copy the C:\Examples\Tutorial08\Exercises\ComparingRates directory to your C:\SimplyCpp directory.

b) *Opening the template source code file.* Open the ComparingRates.cpp file in your text editor or IDE.

c) *Including the <cmath> standard library header file and defining variables.* Because you will use the pow function in this application, you must include the <cmath> standard library header file. Insert an #include preprocessor directive after line 5 to include <cmath>. To store the principal that user inputs, define double variable principal in main after line 12.

d) *Prompting the user for and storing the principal.* Insert a statement that prompts the user for the principal. Store the value typed at the keyboard in the principal variable.

e) *Displaying a table header and formatting output.* Use the `left` and `setw` stream manipulators to display a table header as shown in Fig. 8.20. The first column should be 10 characters wide. Then use the `fixed` and `setprecision` stream manipulators to format floating-point values with two positions to the left of the decimal point.

f) *Writing a for statement header.* Write a for statement header that iterates over interest rate values from 5–10%, inclusive, in increments of 1%. Before the first semicolon, define and initialize the rate variable (which will be used as your counter) to

5. Before the second semicolon, enter a loop-continuation condition that will cause the **for** statement to loop until the counter has reached 10. After the second semicolon, enter the increment of the counter so that the **for** statement executes for every integer rate percentage from 5 to 10.

g) ***Calculating the amount after 10 years.*** You will now calculate the amount on deposit after 10 years, for different interest rates. To do this, you will need to implement the following formula within the **for** statement:

$$a = p\,(1 + r)^{n}$$

where

p is the original amount invested (the principal)
r is the annual interest rate
n is the number of years
a is the investment's value at the end of the nth year.

In lines 30–31, use the pow function (as well as the variable `principal`) to calculate the amount on deposit in 10 years with the **for** statement's current interest rate. Be sure to divide rate by `100.0` before adding the result to 1, so that the result is a double. Use two lines for clarity. Then use `cout` to display the current number of years in a field of width 10, followed by a dollar sign and the value of the investment. Use two lines for clarity.

h) ***Save, compile and run the application.*** Input a principal value. View the results to ensure that the correct rate percentages are displayed and that the future value results are correct.

i) ***Close the Command Prompt window.***

What does this code do? ▶   **8.14** What is the output when the following code executes?

```
1   // Exercise 8.14: WDTCD.cpp
2   // What does this code do?
3   #include <iostream> // required to perform C++ stream I/O
4   #include <cmath>    // required to use the C++ math library functions
5
6   using namespace std; // for accessing C++ Standard Library members
7
8   // function main begins program execution
9   int main()
10  {
11     // define variables
12     int power = 5;
13     int number = 10;
14
15     cout << endl;
16
17     for ( int counter = 1; counter <= power; counter++ )
18     {
19        cout << pow( number, counter ) << endl;
20     } // end for
21
22     cout << "\n"; // insert newline for readability
23
24     return 0; // indicate that the program ended successfully
25
26  } // end main
```

What's wrong with this code? ▶   **8.15** Identify and correct the error(s) in each of the following:

a) This code should display all integers from 100 to 1 in decreasing order.

```
1   // Exercise 8.15a: WWWTCa.cpp
2   // Application that displays every number from 100 to 1 in
3   // decreasing order.
4   #include <iostream> // required to perform C++ stream I/O
5
6   using namespace std; // for accessing C++ Standard Library members
7
8   // function main begins program execution
9   int main()
10  {
11     cout << endl;
12
13     for ( int counter = 100; counter >= 1; counter++ )
14     {
15        cout << counter << endl;
16     } // end for
17
18     cout << "\n"; // insert newline for readability
19
20     return 0; // indicate that the program ended successfully
21
22  } // end main
```

b) The following code should display a table of integers and the cube of those integers for the values in the range 1–10, inclusive.

```
1   // Exercise 8.15b: WWWTCb.cpp
2   // Application that displays a table of integers and the cube of
3   // those integers for the values in the range 1-10, inclusive.
4   #include <iostream> // required to perform C++ stream I/O
5   #include <iomanip>  // required for parameterized stream manipulators
6   #include <cmath>    // required to use the C++ math library functions
7
8   using namespace std; // for accessing C++ Standard Library members
9
10  // function main begins program execution
11  int main()
12  {
13     cout << left << "Value" << "Value cubed" << endl;
14
15     for ( int counter = 1; counter >= 10; counter++ )
16     {
17        cout << counter << pow( 3, counter ) << endl;
18     } // end for
19
20     return 0; // indicate that program ended successfully
21
22  } // end main
```

Using the Debugger ▶   **8.16** (*Savings Calculator Application*) The **Savings Calculator** application calculates the amount that the user will have on deposit after one year. The application gets the initial amount on deposit from the user, and assumes that the user will add $100 to the account every month for the entire year. No interest is added to the account. While testing the application, you noticed that the amount calculated by the application was incorrect. Use the debugger to locate and correct any logic error(s). Figure 8.21 displays the correct output for this application.

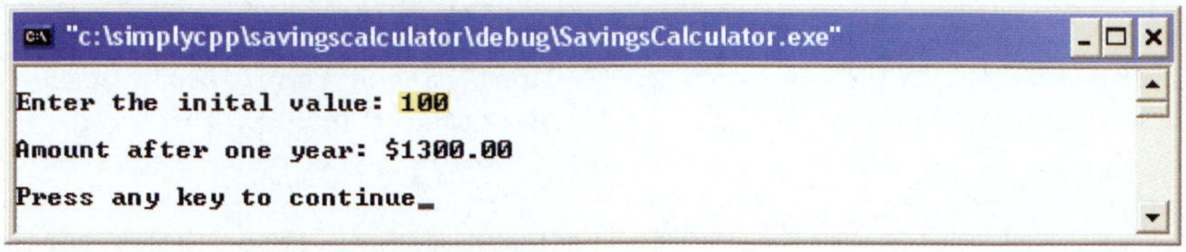

Figure 8.21 Correct output for the **Savings Calculator** application output.

a) *Copying the template to your working directory.* Copy the C:\Examples\Tutorial08\Exercises\Debugging\SavingsCalculator directory to your C:\SimplyCpp directory.

b) *Opening the template source code file.* Open the SavingsCalculator.cpp file in your text editor or IDE.

c) *Compile and run the application.* Enter 100 as the starting amount. Notice that the amount after one year is 1200, whereas the correct output should be 1300 (Fig. 8.21).

d) *Compile your application with debugging enabled.*

e) *Starting the debugger.* Run the application in the debugger.

f) *Finding and correcting the error(s).* Use the debugging skills that you learned in previous tutorials to determine where the application's logic errors exist. Modify the application so that it displays the correct value.

g) *Save, compile and run the application.* Test the application using several different inputs, and make sure the resulting savings output is correct.

h) *Close the Command Prompt window.*

Programming Challenge ▶

8.17 *(Pay Raise Calculator Application)* Develop an application that computes the amount of money an employee makes each year over a user-specified number of years. Assume the employee receives a pay raise once every year. The user specifies in the application the initial weekly salary, the amount of the raise (in percent per year) and the number of years for which the amounts earned will be calculated. The application should run as shown in Fig. 8.22.

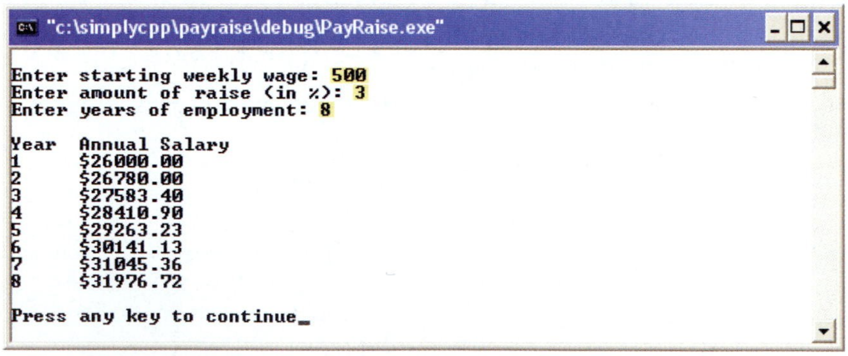

Figure 8.22 **Pay Raise** application output.

a) *Copying the template to your working directory.* Copy the C:\Examples\Tutorial08\Exercises\PayRaise directory to your C:\SimplyCpp directory.

b) *Opening the template source code file.* Open the PayRaise.cpp file in your text editor or IDE.

c) *Defining variables and prompting the user for input.* To store the raise percentage and years of employment that the user inputs, define int variables rate and years, in main after line 12. Also define double variable wage to store the user's annual wage. Then, insert statements that prompt the user for the raise percentage, years of employment and starting weekly wage. Store the values typed at the keyboard in the rate, years and wage variables, respectively. To find the annual wage, multiply the new wage by 52 (the number of weeks per year) and store the result in wage.

d) ***Displaying a table header and formatting output.*** Use the `left` and `setw` stream manipulators to display a table header as shown in Fig. 8.22. The first column should be six characters wide. Then use the `fixed` and `setprecision` stream manipulators to format floating-point values with two positions to the left of the decimal point.

e) ***Writing a for statement header.*** Insert a `for` statement. Before the first semicolon in the `for` statement header, define and initialize the variable `counter` to 1. Before the second semicolon, enter a loop-continuation condition that will cause the `for` statement to loop until `counter` has reached the number of years entered. After the second semicolon, enter the increment of `counter` so that the `for` statement executes once for each number of years.

f) ***Calculating the pay raise.*** In the body of the `for` statement, display the value of `counter` in the first column and the value of `wage` in the second column. Then calculate the new weekly wage for the following year, and store the resulting value in the `wage` variable. To do this, add 1 to the percentage increase (be sure to divide the percentage by `100.0`) and multiply the result by the current value in `wage`.

g) ***Save, compile and run the application.*** Input a raise percentage and a number of years for the wage increase. View the results to ensure that the correct years are displayed and that the future wage results are correct.

h) ***Close the Command Prompt window.***

TUTORIAL

Objectives

In this tutorial, you will learn to:
- Use the `switch` multiple-selection statement to choose among many alternative actions.
- Use `case` labels to identify the alternative actions in `switch` statements.
- Understand the `short` and `long` data types to represent small and large integers.

Outline

Income Tax Calculator Application

Introducing the `switch` Multiple-Selection Statement

In Tutorial 4, you learned that the `if` control statement is used either to choose or ignore a single block of statements, so it is called a single-selection statement. You also learned that the `if...else` control statement is used to choose between two blocks of statements based on a condition, so `if...else` is called a double-selection statement. In this tutorial, you will learn the `switch` **multiple-selection statement**, which is used to choose among many blocks of statements.

9.1 Test-Driving the Income Tax Calculator Application

In this tutorial, you will use the `switch` multiple-selection statement to construct an **Income Tax Calculator** application. This application must meet the following requirements:

Application Requirements

An accounting firm wants an application that estimates the amount of Federal income tax that a client must pay, depending upon that client's annual salary. The application should use the following income ranges and corresponding tax rates:

> *Under $25,000 = 15% income tax*
> *$25,000–74,999 = 25% income tax*
> *$75,000–149,999 = 28% income tax*
> *$150,000–299,999 = 33% income tax*
> *$300,000 and over = 35% income tax*

Your application should display an error message if the user enters an annual salary that is less than or equal to zero. (Note: The actual U.S. Federal income tax rates vary based on many factors. For more information, see the information in IRS Form 1040-ES, which is located at www.irs.gov/pub/irs-pdf/f1040e03.pdf. In Exercise 9.12, you will create an application that calculates a closer approximation of an individual's Federal income tax.)

You begin by test-driving the application. Then, you will learn the additional C++ capabilities you will need to create your own version of this application.

Test-Driving the Income Tax Calculator Application

1. **Locating the completed application.** Open the **Command Prompt** window by selecting **Start > All Programs > Accessories > Command Prompt.** Change to your completed **Income Tax Calculator** application directory by typing `cd C:\Examples\Tutorial09\CompletedApplication\Income-TaxCalculator`.

2. **Running the Income Tax Calculator application.** Type `IncomeTaxCalculator` to run the application (Fig. 9.1).

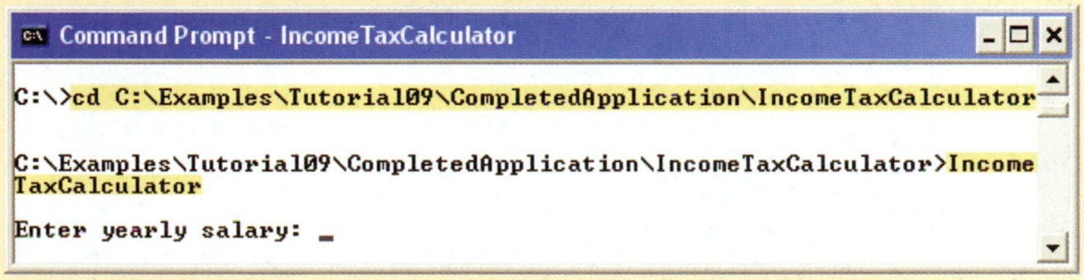

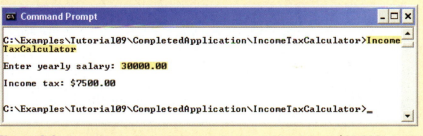

Figure 9.1 Income Tax Calculator application prompting the user for a yearly salary.

3. **Entering a yearly salary.** Type the value `30000.00` at the **Enter yearly salary:** prompt. Notice that 25% of the specified salary, $7500.00, is displayed as the income tax amount a client must pay (Fig. 9.2).

```
Command Prompt                                              _ □ ×
C:\Examples\Tutorial09\CompletedApplication\IncomeTaxCalculator>Income
TaxCalculator
Enter yearly salary: 30000.00
Income tax: $7500.00

C:\Examples\Tutorial09\CompletedApplication\IncomeTaxCalculator>_
```

Figure 9.2 Income Tax Calculator application output for a $30,000 yearly salary.

4. **Entering a different yearly salary.** Run the application again. This time, type the value `100000.00` at the **Enter yearly salary:** prompt. Notice that 28% of the specified salary, $28000.00, is displayed (Fig. 9.3).

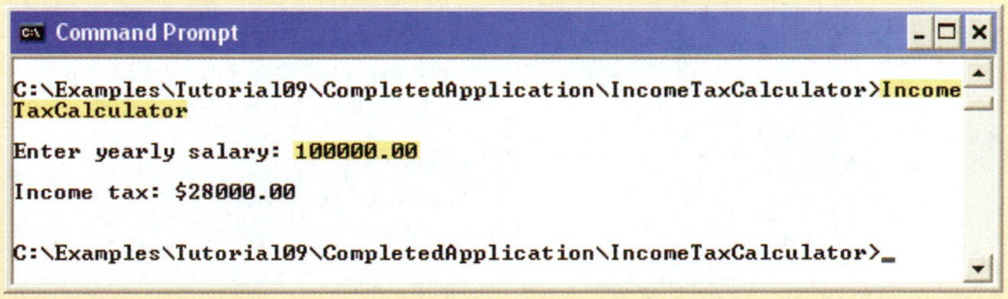

```
Command Prompt                                              _ □ ×
C:\Examples\Tutorial09\CompletedApplication\IncomeTaxCalculator>Income
TaxCalculator
Enter yearly salary: 100000.00
Income tax: $28000.00

C:\Examples\Tutorial09\CompletedApplication\IncomeTaxCalculator>_
```

Figure 9.3 Income Tax Calculator application output for a $100,000 yearly salary.

5. **Close the Command Prompt.**

9.2 Introducing the `switch` Multiple-Selection Statement

In this section, you will learn how to use the **switch** multiple-selection statement. For comparison purposes, first consider a nested if...else statement that performs multiple selections and displays a text message based on a student's grade:

```cpp
if ( grade == 'A' )
{
    cout << "Excellent!";
}
else if ( grade == 'B' )
{
    cout << "Very good!";
}
else if ( grade == 'C' )
{
    cout << "Good.";
}
else if ( grade == 'D' )
{
    cout << "Poor.";
}
else if ( grade == 'F' )
{
    cout << "Failure.";
}
else
{
    cout << "Invalid grade.";
}
```

This statement is used to produce an appropriate output when selecting among multiple values of `grade`. By using the `switch` statement, you simplify every instance like

```cpp
if ( grade == 'A' )
```

to one like

```cpp
case 'A':
```

In this example, `grade` is of the `char` type. The following `switch` multiple-selection statement performs the same function as the preceding `if...else` statement:

```cpp
switch ( grade )
{
    case 'A':
        cout << "Excellent!";
        break;

    case 'B':
        cout << "Very good!";
        break;

    case 'C':
        cout << "Good.";
        break;

    case 'D':
        cout << "Poor.";
        break;

    case 'F':
        cout << "Failure.";
        break;

    default:
        cout << "Invalid grade.";
}
```

Good Programming Practice

Placing a blank line before and after each `case` in a `switch` statement improves readability.

The `switch` statement begins with the `switch` keyword, followed by a **controlling expression** inside parentheses and a left brace, and terminates with a right brace. The preceding `switch` contains five **case labels** (such as `case: 'A'`), each of which consists of the `case` keyword followed by a constant expression and a colon. The **constant expression** can be a character literal, such as `'A'` (which is a `char`) or an integer literal, such as 707 or -11, but cannot be a floating-point literal, such as 9.9. The constant expression also can be a variable that contains a character or integer constant (that is, a `const` variable). The preceding `switch` statement also contains the optional **default** case, which will execute if the controlling expression's value does not match any of the other `cases`. Although a `switch` statement can have any number of `case` labels, it can have at most one `default` case, and no two `cases` can specify the same constant expression.

Only values of types `char`, **short** (an abbreviation for **short int**), `int` and **long** (an abbreviation for **long int**), or values that can be converted to these types, can be tested in a `switch` statement. These are called integral data types because each represents integer values. The minimum range of values for `short` integers is –32,768 to 32,767. The minimum range of values for `long` integers is –2,147,483,648 to 2,147,483,647. On most of today's desktop systems, the `short` and `long` data types store the minimum range of values. On more powerful (64-bit) systems, these data types each might store a larger range of values.

Figure 9.4 shows the UML activity diagram for the preceding `switch` multiple-selection statement. The first guard condition to be evaluated is `grade == 'A'`. If this condition is `true`, the text `"Excellent!"` is displayed, and the **break** statement at the end of the `case` transfers program control to the first statement after the `switch` statement. If the condition is `false` (that is, the other guard condition, `grade != 'A'`, is `true`), the statement continues by testing the next condition, `grade == 'B'`. If that condition is `true`, the text `"Very good!"` is displayed, and the `break` statement at the end of the `case` transfers program control to the first statement after the `switch` statement. If the condition is `false` (that is, the other guard condition, `grade != 'B'`, is `true`), the statement continues to test the next condition. This process continues until a matching `case` is found or until the final guard condition, `grade != 'F'`, evaluates to `true`. If the latter occurs, the `default` case's body is executed, and the text `"Invalid grade."` is displayed. The application then continues with the first statement after the `switch` statement. If the controlling expression's value does not match any of the cases and there is no `default` case, no statements in the `switch` will execute.

When the controlling expression's value matches a `case` and that `case`'s statements do not end with a `break` statement, program control will continue ("fall through") with the statements in the next `case`. This will occur until either a `break` statement is encountered or until the end of the `switch` statement is reached. Note that the UML activity diagram of Fig. 9.4 represents a `switch` statement that includes a `break` statement in every `case`.

Portability Tip

Because the range of values stored by certain data types varies between systems, applications that work on one type of system might not work on another

Good Programming Practice

Indenting the statements in the body of a `case` improves readability.

Common Programming Error

Specifying two or more `cases` with the same constant expression is a syntax error.

Common Programming Error

For most common applications of the `switch` statement, omitting the `break` statement in a `case` is a logic error. For some applications it could yield the desired behavior

SELF-REVIEW

Error-Prevention Tip

A `default` case in a `switch` statement can be used to handle improper values.

1. `switch` is a _____-selection statement.
   a) single
   b) double
   c) multiple
   d) None of the above.

2. When does the `default` case execute?
   a) Every time a `switch` statement executes.
   b) When several `cases` match the controlling expression.
   c) When no `cases` match the controlling expression.
   d) None of the above.

Answers: 1) c. 2) c.

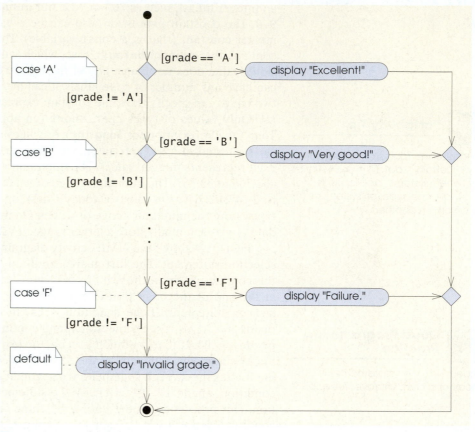

Figure 9.4 `switch` multiple-selection statement UML activity diagram.

9.3 Constructing the Income Tax Calculator Application

The **Income Tax Calculator** application prompts the user for the client's yearly salary and calculates the Federal income tax. The pseudocode in Fig. 9.5 describes the basic operation of the **Income Tax Calculator** application.

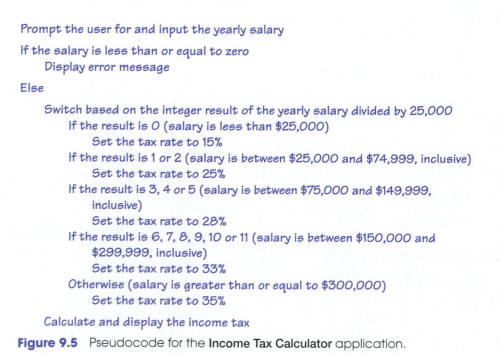

Prompt the user for and input the yearly salary

If the salary is less than or equal to zero
    Display error message

Else

      Switch based on the integer result of the yearly salary divided by 25,000
        If the result is 0 (salary is less than $25,000)
          Set the tax rate to 15%
        If the result is 1 or 2 (salary is between $25,000 and $74,999, inclusive)
          Set the tax rate to 25%
        If the result is 3, 4 or 5 (salary is between $75,000 and $149,999,
          inclusive)
          Set the tax rate to 28%
        If the result is 6, 7, 8, 9, 10 or 11 (salary is between $150,000 and
          $299,999, inclusive)
          Set the tax rate to 33%
        Otherwise (salary is greater than or equal to $300,000)
          Set the tax rate to 35%

      Calculate and display the income tax

Figure 9.5 Pseudocode for the **Income Tax Calculator** application.

Now that you have test-driven the **Income Tax Calculator** application and studied its pseudocode representation, you will build the application. First, you will prompt the user for and store the yearly salary. Later in this tutorial, you will use a `switch` statement to determine the tax rate.

Defining Variables and Inputting the Yearly Salary

1. ***Copying the template to your working directory.*** Copy the `C:\Examples\ Tutorial09\TemplateApplication\IncomeTaxCalculator` directory to your `C:\SimplyCpp` directory.

2. ***Opening the Income Tax Calculator application's template source code file.*** Open the template file `IncomeTaxCalculator.cpp` in your text editor or IDE.

3. ***Defining variables.*** Insert lines 12–14 of Fig. 9.6. Line 13 defines `double` variable `taxRate`, which will contain the tax rate that will be determined using a `switch` statement. Line 14 defines `double` variable `salary`, which will contain the user's yearly salary.

Defining variables to store user input

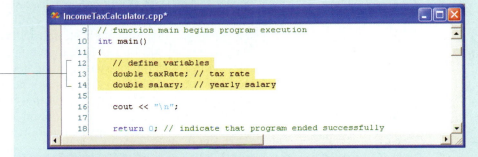

```
 9   // function main begins program execution
10   int main()
11   {
12       // define variables
13       double taxRate; // tax rate
14       double salary;  // yearly salary
15
16       cout << "\n";
17
18       return 0; // indicate that program ended successfully
```

Figure 9.6   Defining variables to contain the tax rate and the yearly salary.

4. ***Prompting the user for and inputting the yearly salary.*** Insert lines 16–18 of Fig. 9.7. Line 17 prompts the user for the yearly salary, and line 18 inputs into `salary` the value that the user entered.

Prompting the user for and inputting the yearly salary

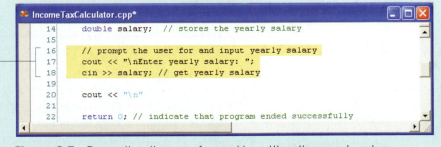
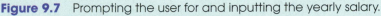

```
14       double salary;  // stores the yearly salary
15
16       // prompt the user for and input yearly salary
17       cout << "\nEnter yearly salary: ";
18       cin >> salary; // get yearly salary
19
20       cout << "\n"
21
22       return 0; // indicate that program ended successfully
```

Figure 9.7   Prompting the user for and inputting the yearly salary.

5. ***Save the application.***

Now that you have written the code to store the yearly salary, you will code a `switch` statement that determines the user's tax rate based on the yearly salary input.

Adding a switch Statement to the Application

1. ***Adding an `if...else` statement.*** Insert lines 20–28 of Fig. 9.8 into `main`. Line 21 begins an `if` statement that determines whether the user entered a salary greater than `0.0`. If not, the `else` part of the `if...else` statement (lines 25–28) executes. In this case, the user has entered an invalid salary, so an error message is displayed (line 27). Otherwise, the user has entered a valid salary. In this case, the body of the `if` statement executes. In the following steps, you will add code that calculates the income tax for a valid salary.

(cont.)

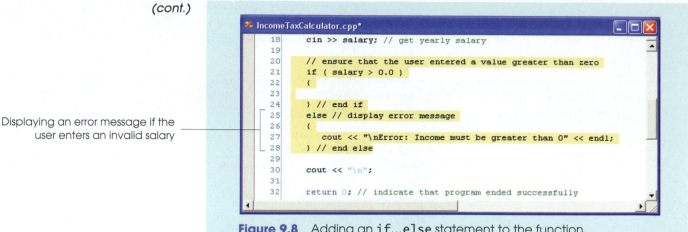

Displaying an error message if the user enters an invalid salary

```
18    cin >> salary; // get yearly salary
19
20    // ensure that the user entered a value greater than zero
21    if ( salary > 0.0 )
22    {
23
24    } // end if
25    else // display error message
26    {
27       cout << "\nError: Income must be greater than 0" << endl;
28    } // end else
29
30    cout << "\n";
31
32    return 0; // indicate that program ended successfully
```

Figure 9.8 Adding an `if...else` statement to the function.

2. ***Adding a switch statement.*** Insert lines 23–27 of Fig. 9.10 to `main`. Line 24 begins the `switch` statement, which contains the controlling expression `static_cast< int > ( salary ) / 25000`. This expression produces an integer value that the application will use to determine the user's tax bracket. If the controlling expression contained `salary / 25000`, the compiler would generate a syntax error because the controlling expression would produce a `double` value (due to the `double` value in the numerator). Therefore, the `static_cast` operator is used to create a copy of the `salary` variable that is truncated to contain an `int` value. This causes the controlling expression to perform integer division and produce an `int` value.

Beginning of the `switch` statement

```
21    if ( salary > 0.0 )
22    {
23       // determine appropriate tax rate based on yearly salary
24       switch ( static_cast< int > ( salary ) / 25000 )
25       {
26
27       } // end switch
28
29    } // end if
```

Figure 9.9 Adding a `switch` statement to the function.

Remember that the controlling expression (the value of `static_cast< int > ( salary ) / 25000`) is compared sequentially with each `case`. If a matching `case` is found, the statements following that `case` execute until reaching the `break` statement that causes program control to continue at the first statement after the right brace that ends the `switch` statement. If the `switch` statement contains a `default` case and the controlling expression does not match any other case, the statement(s) of the `default` case will execute. If there are no matches and the `switch` does not contain a `default` case, the body of the `switch` is skipped and the application continues with the next statement after the `switch`. Line 27 contains a right brace, which terminates the `switch` statement.

3. ***Adding a case to the switch statement.*** Insert lines 26–28 of Fig. 9.10 in the `switch` statement. If the user entered a value less than `25000.00` at the **Enter yearly salary: prompt**, then the `switch` statement's controlling expression, `static_cast< int > ( salary ) / 25000`, is less than 1. Because integer division truncates the result (instead of rounding it), the controlling expression will be 0. This means that the application will execute lines 27–28, because the `case` label in line 26 matches the controlling expression.

(cont.)

Line 27 assigns the value 0.15 to taxRate, the variable containing the tax rate. When the application executes the break statement in line 28, the next statement to execute becomes the first statement after the switch statement's right brace.

Sets the tax rate to 15% if salary is less than 25000

```
IncomeTaxCalculator.cpp*
23        // determine appropriate tax rate based on yearly salary
24        switch ( static_cast< int > ( salary ) / 25000 )
25        {
26           case 0: // yearly salary under $25,000
27              taxRate = 0.15; // 15% tax rate
28              break;
29
30        } // end switch
```

Figure 9.10   Adding a case label to the switch statement.

4. *Specifying the remaining cases.* Add lines 30–48 of Fig. 9.11 to the body of the switch statement. The case labels in lines 30 and 31 determine whether the value of static_cast< int > (salary) / 25000 is equal to 1 or 2, respectively. If the user enters a salary between the values 25000.00 and 74999.00, the statements between the case labels and the next break statement (line 33) execute. In this case, line 32 executes, setting taxRate to 0.25 (25%).

Sets the tax rate to 25% if salary is between 25000 and 74999

Multiple case labels result in the same taxRate (28%)

Multiple case labels result in the same taxRate (33%)

```
IncomeTaxCalculator.cpp*
28              break;
29
30           case 1: // yearly salary in range $25,000-49,999
31           case 2: // yearly salary in range $50,000-74,999
32              taxRate = 0.25; // 25% tax rate
33              break;
34
35           case 3: // yearly salary in range $75,000-99,999
36           case 4: // yearly salary in range $100,000-124,999
37           case 5: // yearly salary in range $125,000-149,999
38              taxRate = 0.28; // 28% tax rate
39              break;
40
41           case 6:  // yearly salary in range $150,000-174,999
42           case 7:  // yearly salary in range $175,000-199,999
43           case 8:  // yearly salary in range $200,000-224,999
44           case 9:  // yearly salary in range $225,000-249,999
45           case 10: // yearly salary in range $250,000-274,999
46           case 11: // yearly salary in range $275,000-299,999
47              taxRate = 0.33; // 33% tax rate
48              break;
49
50        } // end switch
```

Figure 9.11   Finishing the switch statement.

Lines 35–37 specify three case labels. This means that lines 38–39 will be performed if any of these three case labels match the controlling expression. For this example, if the value in salary is between 75000.00 and 149999.00, inclusive, the code in lines 38–39 will execute, assigning 0.28 (28%) to taxRate. Similarly, lines 41–46 specify six case labels. Lines 47–48 will be performed if any of these six case labels match the controlling expression. Therefore, if the value in salary is between 150000.00 and 299999.00, inclusive, the application will assign the value 0.33 (33%) to taxRate.

(cont.)

Good Programming Practice

Always place the `default` case at the end of a `switch` statement's body.

5. *Adding a default case to the switch statement.* Add lines 50–51 of Fig. 9.12 to the `switch` statement. These lines contain the optional `default` case, which is executed if the controlling expression does not match any cases. When the `default` case appears at the end of the `switch` statement's body, you do not need to add the `break` statement. In this case, the `default` case sets `taxRate` to `0.35` (35%). This statement is executed when `salary` contains a value greater than or equal to `300000.00`.

default case at the end of the `switch` statement

```
48              break;
49
50          default: // yearly salary $300,000 or higher
51              taxRate = 0.35; // 35% tax rate
52
53      } // end switch
```

Figure 9.12 Adding a `default` case to the `switch` statement.

6. *Calculating and displaying the income tax.* Insert lines 55–59 of Fig. 9.13 after the `switch` statement. Line 55 calculates the total income tax by assigning the product of `salary` and `taxRate` to `incomeTax`. Lines 58–59 display the total income tax, using the `fixed` and `setprecision` stream manipulators to format floating-point values with two positions to the left of the decimal point.

Calculating the income tax

Displaying the income tax

```
53          } // end switch
54
55          double incomeTax = salary * taxRate; // calculate taxes
56
57          // display income tax
58          cout << "\nIncome tax: $" << fixed << setprecision( 2 )
59              << incomeTax << endl;
60      } // end if
```

Figure 9.13 Calculating and displaying the income tax.

7. *Save, compile and run the application.* Figure 9.14 shows completed application outputs. Enter salaries in several different tax brackets to ensure that the application's output is correct.

```
"c:\SimplyCpp\IncomeTaxCalculator\Debug\IncomeTaxCalculator.exe"

Enter yearly salary: 45678.90
Income tax: $11419.73
Press any key to continue
```

```
"c:\SimplyCpp\IncomeTaxCalculator\Debug\IncomeTaxCalculator.exe"

Enter yearly salary: 123456.78
Income tax: $34567.90
Press any key to continue_
```

Figure 9.14 Completed **Income Tax Calculator** application.

Figure 9.15 displays the code for the completed **Income Tax Calculator** application. The lines of code you added, viewed or modified in this tutorial are highlighted.

```cpp
1   // Tutorial 9: IncomeTaxCalculator.cpp
2   // Calculates a person's Federal income tax
3   // depending on that person's salary.
4   #include <iostream> // required to perform C++ stream I/O
5   #include <iomanip>  // required for parameterized stream manipulators
6
7   using namespace std; // for accessing C++ Standard Library members
8
9   // function main begins program execution
10  int main()
11  {
12     // define variables
13     double taxRate; // tax rate
14     double salary;  // yearly salary
15
16     // prompt user for and input yearly salary
17     cout << "\nEnter yearly salary: ";
18     cin >> salary; // get yearly salary
19
20     // ensure that the user entered a value greater than zero
21     if ( salary > 0 )
22     {
23        // determine appropriate tax rate based on yearly salary
24        switch ( static_cast< int > ( salary ) / 25000 )
25        {
26           case 0: // yearly salary under $25,000
27              taxRate = 0.15; // 15% tax rate
28              break;
29
30           case 1: // yearly salary in range $25,000-49,999
31           case 2: // yearly salary in range $50,000-74,999
32              taxRate = 0.25; // 25% tax rate
33              break;
34
35           case 3: // yearly salary in range $75,000-99,999
36           case 4: // yearly salary in range $100,000-124,999
37           case 5: // yearly salary in range $125,000-149,999
38              taxRate = 0.28; // 28% tax rate
39              break;
40
41           case 6:  // yearly salary in range $150,000-174,999
42           case 7:  // yearly salary in range $175,000-199,999
43           case 8:  // yearly salary in range $200,000-224,999
44           case 9:  // yearly salary in range $225,000-249,999
45           case 10: // yearly salary in range $250,000-274,999
46           case 11: // yearly salary in range $275,000-299,999
47              taxRate = 0.33; // 33% tax rate
48              break;
49
50           default: // yearly salary $300,000 or higher
51              taxRate = 0.35; // 35% tax rate
52
53        } // end switch
54
```

Define variables to store user input — *(lines 13–14)*

Prompt the user for and input the yearly salary — *(lines 17–18)*

Beginning of the `switch` statement — *(line 24)*

Sets the tax rate to 15% if `salary` is less than 25000 — *(line 27)*

Sets the tax rate to 25% if `salary` is between 25000 and 74999 — *(lines 31–32)*

Sets the tax rate to 28% if `salary` is between 75000 and 149999 — *(line 37)*

Sets the tax rate to 33% if `salary` is between 150000 and 299999 — *(line 44)*

`default` case at the end of the `switch` statement — *(line 50)*

Figure 9.15   **Income Tax Calculator** application code. (Part 1 of 2.)

Calculate the income tax

```
55        double incomeTax = salary * taxRate; // calculate taxes
56
57        // display income tax
58        cout << "\nIncome tax: $" << fixed << setprecision( 2 )
59           << incomeTax << endl;
60     } // end if
61     else // display error message
62     {
63        cout << "\nError: Income must be greater than 0" << endl;
64     } // end else
65
66     cout << "\n";
67
68     return 0; // indicate that program ended successfully
69
70  } // end function main
```

Display the income tax

Display an error message if annual salary is not greater than zero

Figure 9.15   **Income Tax Calculator** application code. (Part 2 of 2.)

SELF-REVIEW

1. Only values of the _____ type or values that can be converted to this type can be tested in a `switch` statement.

    a) `short`   b) `int`

    c) `long`   d) All of the above.

2. A _____ always causes program control to proceed with the first statement after the `switch`.

    a) semicolon   b) `stop` keyword

    c) `break` statement   d) colon

Answers: 1) d. 2) c.

9.4 Wrap-Up

In this tutorial, you learned how to use the `switch` multiple-selection statement and discovered its similarities to nested `if...else` statements. You studied pseudocode and a UML activity diagram that illustrates the flow of control in a `switch` statement.

You then applied what you learned to create your **Income Tax Calculator** application. You used a `switch` statement to determine the income tax rate according to the salary that the user entered. You also defined several `case`s and included an optional `default` case, which executes when the salary does not match any of the provided `case` labels. You also learned that `break` statements are used to end cases. If a `break` statement is omitted for a `case`, execution will "fall through" to the next `case`.

In the next tutorial, you will learn how to construct applications from small, manageable pieces of reusable code called functions. You have actually been working with existing functions all along, but now you will learn how to write your own functions—these are often called programmer-defined functions. You will use functions to enhance the **Wage Calculator** application you created earlier in the book.

SKILLS SUMMARY   **Coding a `switch` statement**

■ Use the `switch` keyword, followed by a controlling expression.

■ For each `case`, use the `case` keyword, followed by an expression to compare with the controlling expression.

■ For each `case`, define the statements that execute if the `case`'s expression matches the controlling expression.

- Use a break statement to end each case label. If the break statement is omitted, execution "falls through" to the next case label.

- Use the default case, followed by statements to execute if the controlling expression does not match any of the provided cases.

KEY TERMS

break statement—The statement that typically appears at the end of each case. This statement immediately terminates the switch statement, and program control continues with the next statement after the closing right brace of the switch.

case label—The label that precedes the statements that will execute if the switch's controlling expression matches the expression in the case label.

constant expression—An expression whose value cannot be changed. A case label consists of the case keyword, followed by a constant expression, followed by a colon. This constant expression must be a character literal or an integer literal.

controlling expression—The expression in a switch statement whose value is compared sequentially with each case until either a match occurs, the default case is executed or the closing right brace is reached.

default case—The optional case whose statements execute if the switch's controlling expression does not match any of the cases' values.

long—An integral data type having a minimum range of values of –2,147,483,648 to 2,147,483,647.

multiple-selection statement—A statement, such as a switch statement, that selects one of many actions (or sequences of actions).

short—An integral data type having a minimum range of values of –32,768 to 32,767.

switch statement—The multiple-selection statement that selects one of many actions (or sequences of actions), depending on the value of the controlling expression.

MULTIPLE-CHOICE QUESTIONS

9.1 The _____ signifies the end of a switch statement.

    a) end keyword   b) } character

    c) break keyword   d) default keyword

9.2 _____ is not an integer type.

    a) short   b) long

    c) float   d) Both b and c.

9.3 _____ is a valid case label.

    a) case: 'A'   b) case: "A"

    c) case 'A':   d) case: 1

9.4 Which of the following is a syntax error?

    a) Having duplicate case labels in the same switch statement.   b) Beginning and ending a switch statement body with braces.

    c) Placing a case label after the default label in a switch statement.   d) Failing to end a case with the break statement.

9.5 If the controlling expression in the switch statement is not equal to any of the case labels and there is no default case, _____.

    a) an error occurs   b) an infinite loop occurs

    c) the program continues execution with the next statement after the switch   d) the first case's statements are executed

9.6 _____ separates the case label from the code that will execute if the case label matches the controlling expression.

    a) A colon   b) An underscore

    c) The break keyword   d) A semicolon

9.7 The controlling expression in a `switch` statement cannot be of type _____.
a) `double`
b) `int`
c) `short`
d) `char`

9.8 The correct syntax for a `default` case is _____.
a) `default case`
b) `default`
c) `default case:`
d) `default:`

9.9 The expression in parentheses following the `switch` keyword is called a _____.
a) guard condition
b) controlling expression
c) selection expression
d) case expression

9.10 If you expect your application to process integers greater than 32767 or less than −32768, you should use a controlling expression of the _____ type.
a) `short`
b) `int`
c) `double`
d) `long`

Answers: 9.1) b. 9.2) c. 9.3) c. 9.4) a. 9.5) c. 9.6) a. 9.7) a. 9.8) d. 9.9) b. 9.10) d.

EXERCISES

9.11 *(Sales Commission Calculator Application)* Develop an application that calculates a salesperson's commission from the number of items sold (Fig. 9.16). Assume that all items have a fixed price of $100 per unit. Use a `switch` statement to implement the following sales commission schedule:

Fewer than 10 items sold = 1% commission
Between 10 and 39 items sold = 2% commission
Between 40 and 99 items sold = 3% commission
More than 99 items sold = 4% commission

Note that the rate determined by the application applies to all sales.

Figure 9.16 Sales Commission Calculator application output.

a) *Copying the template to your working directory.* Copy the C:\Examples\ Tutorial09\Exercises\SalesCommissionCalculator directory to your C:\SimplyCpp directory.

b) *Opening the template source code file.* Open the SalesCommissionCalculator.cpp file in your text editor or IDE. In the template, lines 13–15 define variables to contain values you will use to calculate the commission. Line 13 defines int variable items, which will contain the number of items sold. Line 14 defines double constant DOLLARS_PER_UNIT to represent the cost for each item sold. Line 15 defines int variable commission, which will contain the percent commission earned, according to the number of items sold. Lines 18–19 prompt the user for and input the number of items sold. Line 22 formats cout so that it displays floating-point values, such as the gross sales and the salesperson's earnings, with two positions to the left of the decimal point.

c) *Calculate the gross sales.* After line 22, insert a statement that multiplies the number of items that the salesperson has sold (items) by the cost per item (DOLLARS_PER_UNIT), and assigns the result to double variable sales.

d) *Determine the salesperson's commission percentage.* After the statement in *Step c*, insert a switch statement to determine the salesperson's commission percentage from the number of items sold. In this switch statement, assign the commission percentage as a whole number to the commission variable. For example, if the commission percentage is 2%, assign 2 to commission. The controlling expression should be items / 10. Because this is integer arithmetic, any number of items in the range 0–9 will result in 0, any number of items in the range 10–19 will result in 1, etc. Inside the switch statement, provide cases that enable the switch to test for values in the ranges specified by the problem statement.

e) *Calculate the decimal value of commission percentage.* After the switch statement, insert a statement that divides commission by 100.0 and assigns the result to double variable commissionRate.

f) *Calculate the salesperson's earnings.* After the statement you inserted in *Step e*, insert a statement that multiplies the salesperson's sales (calculated in *Step c*) by commissionRate, then assign the result to double variable earnings.

g) *Display the gross sales, the commission percentage and the salesperson's earnings.* After the statement in *Step f*, add three statements that display the values of the sales, commission and earnings variables. To align the displayed values, left justify the descriptive text for each value in a field of width 16 characters. Make sure to display blank lines where appropriate for readability.

h) *Save, compile and run the application.* Test your application to ensure that it runs correctly. Enter different numbers at the **Enter number of items sold:** prompt.

i) *Close the Command Prompt window.*

9.12 *(Enhanced Income Tax Calculator Application)* Modify the **Income Tax Calculator** that you built in this tutorial so that it calculates the user's graduated income tax. Under a graduated income tax, only the portion of a user's salary that falls within a bracket is taxed at the rate for that bracket. For example, using the tax rates presented at the beginning of this tutorial, a user entering a yearly salary of $88,000 would be taxed as follows:

$24,999 × 15% income tax (portion of salary under $25,000)
+ $50,000 × 25% income tax (portion of salary between $25,000 and $74,999)
+ $13,001 × 28% income tax (portion of salary between $75,000 and $149,999)
= $3,749.85 + $12,500.00 + $3,640.28
= $19890.13 total income tax

Assume all salaries are input as integers that are greater than or equal to 0. Your application should operate as shown in Fig. 9.17. [*Note:* The actual U.S. Federal income tax rates are graduated, but vary based on many factors. For more information, see the information in IRS Form 1040-ES, which is located at www.irs.gov/pub/irs-pdf/f1040e03.pdf.]

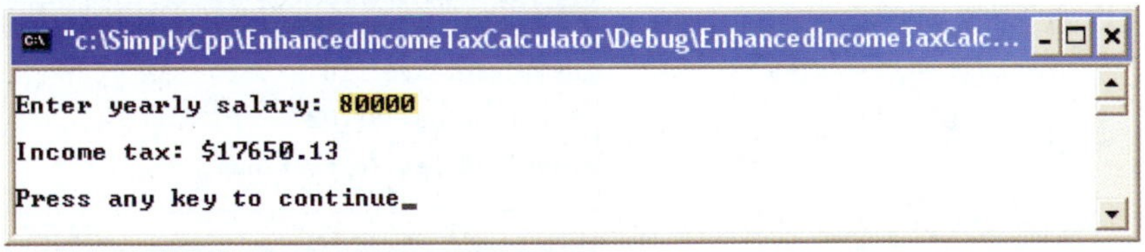

Figure 9.17   Enhanced **Income Tax Calculator** output.

a) *Copying the template to your working directory.* Copy the C:\Examples\ Tutorial09\Exercises\EnhancedIncomeTaxCalculator directory to your C:\SimplyCpp directory.

b) *Opening the template source code file.* Open the IncomeTaxCalculator.cpp file in your text editor or IDE.

c) *Relocating a variable definition.* Remove line 47 of Fig. 9.15 from the template application source code. Then define double variable incomeTax after line 14.

d) *Modifying the switch statement.* If the controlling expression evaluates to 0, the user has entered a salary less than $25,000. Modify line 24 of Fig. 9.15 so that it assigns the product of salary and 0.15 (15%) to incomeTax. If the controlling expression evaluates to 1 or 2, the user has entered a salary between $25,000 and $74,999. In this case, the application should tax the first $24,999 at a 15% rate and the remaining salary at a 25% rate. Modify line 28 of Fig. 9.15 so that it assigns the product of 24999 and 0.15 (15%) to incomeTax. To calculate the remaining tax, add a statement that multiplies the expression salary - 24999 by 0.25 (25%). Use the addition assignment operator to add and store the result into incomeTax.

e) ***Modifying the remaining cases.*** Modify lines 33, 39 and 43 of Fig. 9.15 to calculate the graduated income tax for higher salaries. Replace line 33 of Fig. 9.15 with statements that calculate the appropriate tax on the first $74,999. To calculate the remaining tax, add a statement that multiplies the expression `salary – 74999` by `0.28` (28%). Use the addition assignment operator to add the result to `incomeTax` and store the result in `incomeTax`. Similarly, replace line 39 of Fig. 9.15 with statements that calculate the appropriate tax on the first $149,999. To calculate the remaining tax, add a statement that multiplies the expression `salary – 149999` by `0.33` (33%). Use the addition assignment operator to add the result to `incomeTax` and store the result in `incomeTax`. Finally, replace line 43 of Fig. 9.15 with statements that calculate the appropriate tax on the first $299,999. To calculate the remaining tax, add a statement that multiplies the expression `salary – 299999` by `0.35` (35%). Use the addition assignment operator to add the result to `incomeTax` and store the result in `incomeTax`.

f) ***Save, compile and run the application.*** Test your application to ensure that it runs correctly. Enter different yearly salaries and calculate the income tax.

g) ***Close the Command Prompt window.***

9.13 *(Ticket Price Application)* Many attractions, such as movie theaters, museums and amusement parks, charge different rates for admission according to the customer's age. Develop an application that displays a ticket price according to the age that the user enters (Fig. 9.18). Assume that the user will enter an age greater than zero. Use a `switch` statement to implement the following ticket price schedule:

Under age 10 = $3.50
Between age 10 and 19 = $5.00
Between age 20 and 64 = $7.50
Age 65 or older = $4.50

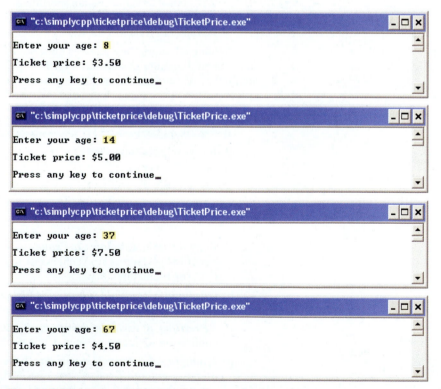

Figure 9.18 **Ticket Price** application output.

a) ***Copying the template to your working directory.*** Copy the `C:\Examples\Tutorial09\Exercises\TicketPrice` directory to your `C:\SimplyCpp` directory.

b) ***Opening the template source code file.*** Open the `TicketPrice.cpp` file in your text editor or IDE.

c) *Defining a variable and retrieving user input.* After line 10, define int variable age, which will contain the user's age. Then prompt the user for and input the user's age into variable age.

d) *Determine the ticket price.* After the statement in *Step c*, insert a switch statement to determine the ticket price according to the user's age. In this switch statement, the controlling expression should be age / 5. Because this is integer arithmetic, any age in the range 0–4 will result in 0, any age in the range 5–10 will result in 1, etc. Inside the switch statement, provide cases that enable the switch to test for values in the ranges specified by the problem statement. Use a single statement for each age range to display the ticket price for that range. Make sure to display blank lines where appropriate for readability.

e) *Save, compile and run the application.* Test your application to ensure that it runs correctly. Enter different ages at the **Enter your age:** prompt.

f) *Close the Command Prompt window.*

What does this code do? ▶

9.14 What is output by the following code? Discuss the output for grade values of 'A', 'B', 'C', 'D', 'F' and an invalid grade.

```cpp
1   // Exercise 9.14: WDTCD.cpp
2   // What does this code do?
3   #include <iostream> // required to perform C++ stream I/O
4
5   using namespace std; // for accessing C++ Standard Library members
6
7   // function main begins program execution
8   int main()
9   {
10      // define variables
11      char grade;
12
13      cout << "\nEnter grade: ";
14      cin >> grade;
15
16      switch ( grade )
17      {
18         case 'A':
19            cout << "\nExcellent!" << endl;
20
21         case 'B':
22            cout << "\nVery good!" << endl;
23
24         case 'C':
25            cout << "\nGood." << endl;
26
27         case 'D':
28            cout << "\nPoor." << endl;
29
30         case 'F':
31            cout << "\nFailure." << endl;
32
33         default:
34            cout << "\nInvalid grade." << endl;
35      } // end switch
36
37      cout << "\n";
38
39      return 0; // indicate that program ended successfully
40
41   } // end function main
```

What's wrong with this code? ▶

9.15 This `switch` statement should determine whether an `int` is even or odd. Find the error(s) in the following code:

```cpp
1   // Exercise 9.15: WWWTC.cpp
2   // This application displays the string "Even Integer" if the
3   // value is even, and "Odd Integer" if the value is odd.
4   #include <iostream> // required to perform C++ stream I/O
5
6   using namespace std; // for accessing C++ Standard Library members
7
8   // function main begins program execution
9   int main()
10  {
11     // define variables
12     int value;
13
14     // prompt the user for and input value
15     cout << "\nPlease enter value: ";
16     cin >> value; // get value
17
18     switch ( value % 2 )
19     {
20        case 0:
21           cout << "\nOdd Integer" << endl;
22           break;
23
24        case 1:
25           cout << "\nEven Integer" << endl;
26           break;
27     } // end switch
28
29     cout << "\n";
30
31     return 0; // indicate that the program ended successfully
32
33  } // end function main
```

Using the Debugger ▶

9.16 (*Discount Calculator Application*) The **Discount Calculator** application determines the discount the user will receive based on how much money the user spends. A 15% discount is received for purchases of $150 or more, a 10% discount is received for purchases between $100–149 and a 5% discount is received for purchases between $50–99. Purchases less than $50 do not receive a discount. While testing your application, you notice that the application is not calculating the discount properly for some values. Use the debugger to find and fix the logic error(s) in the application. Figure 9.19 displays the correct output for values in each range.

a) *Copying the template to your working directory.* Copy the `C:\Examples\Tutorial09\Exercises\Debugger\DiscountCalculator` directory to your `C:\SimplyCpp` directory.

b) *Opening the Command Prompt window and changing directories.* Open the **Command Prompt** window by selecting **Start > All Programs > Accessories > Command Prompt**. Change to your working directory by typing `cd C:\SimplyCpp\DiscountCalculator`.

c) *Compile the application for debugging and run the application.* To test your application, enter the amounts shown in Fig. 9.19. When you enter the value 75 (or any other value in the range 50–99), notice that the application incorrectly indicates a discount of 15%.

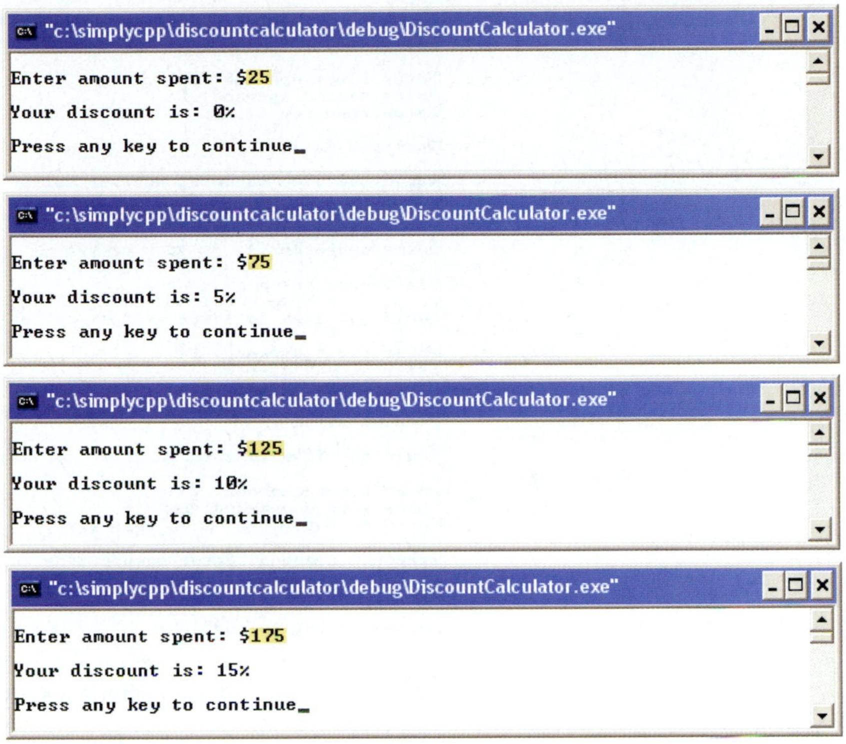

Figure 9.19 Correct output for the **Discount Calculator** application.

d) *Finding and correcting the error(s).* Run the application in the debugger. Use the debugging skills learned in previous tutorials to determine where the application's logic errors exist. Set breakpoints at the break statement in each case (lines 24 and 28) and at line 36 (the first statement after the switch). Use the debugger to inspect the value of the discountRate variable each time the application enters break mode. Resume program execution after inspecting the value of discountRate at each breakpoint. When you find the logic error, modify the application's switch statement so that the proper discount rate is chosen.

e) *Save, compile and run the application.* Test your application by entering the amounts shown in Fig. 9.19 and make sure the resulting discounts are correct.

f) *Close the Command Prompt window.*

Programming Challenge ▶   **9.17** *(Enhanced Arithmetic Calculator Application)* Enhance the application that you created in Exercise 7.17 so that users can enter any valid single-character C++ arithmetic operator (Fig. 9.20). Users should enter each number at an input prompt, then enter the operand at a third input prompt. The application should then display the result of the desired calculation and display a prompt asking the user whether the application should continue. If the user enters either an uppercase or lowercase "y," the application should prompt the user for the next calculation. If the user enters either an uppercase or lowercase "n," the application should exit.

a) *Copying the template to your working directory.* Copy the C:\Examples\ Tutorial09\Exercises\EnhancedArithmeticCalculator directory to your C:\SimplyCpp directory. Then copy the file C:\SimplyCpp\ArithmeticCalcula-tor\ArithmeticCalculator.cpp to your C:\SimplyCpp\EnhancedArithmetic-Calculator directory. If you have not completed Exercise 7.17, follow the steps in Exercise 7.17 before copying the file.

b) *Opening the source code file.* Open the ArirthmeticCalcualtor.cpp file in your text editor or IDE.

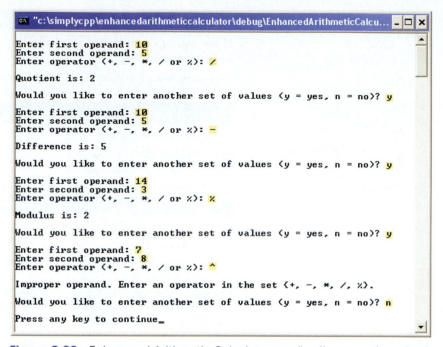

Figure 9.20 Enhanced **Arithmetic Calculator** application sample output.

c) *Replacing the nested if...else statements with a switch statement.* The application you created in Exercise 7.17 contained nested `if...else` statements to perform a calculation and display the result according to the value of the character that the user entered at the **Enter operator:** prompt. The controlling expression for the `switch` statement should contain the value of this character, `char` variable `operation`. Provide `case` labels for operators +, –, *, / and %. Include a `default` case that displays an error message if none of the five operators was entered.

d) *Modifying the Enter operator: prompt.* Modify the **Enter operator:** prompt so that it displays the updated list of operators that the user can enter. Make sure to display blank lines where appropriate for readability.

e) *Save, compile and run the completed application.* Test the application to ensure that it runs correctly. Use several different inputs, and make sure each result is correct.

f) *Close the* Command Prompt *window.*

g) *(Optional) Preventing division by zero and performing traditional division.* Add code to prevent the application from dividing by zero. Also, use the `static_cast` operator on the numerator in the division calculation to prevent the application from performing integer division and thereby truncating the result.

Enhancing the Wage Calculator Application

Introducing Functions

Objectives

In this tutorial, you will learn to:

- Construct applications modularly from pieces called functions—simplifying your application's design, implementation and maintenance.
- Save time by working with "built-in" functions.
- Create your own functions to perform custom tasks.
- Control execution using debugger commands to locate logic errors.

Outline

Most software applications that solve real-world problems are much larger than the applications presented in the first few tutorials of this text. Experience has shown that the best way to develop and maintain a large application is to construct it from smaller, more manageable pieces. This is known as the **divide-and-conquer technique**. These manageable pieces include program blocks, known as **functions**, that simplify the design, implementation and maintenance of large applications. In this tutorial, you will learn how to use several predefined functions from the C++ Standard Library to perform common tasks, such as finding the square root of a number or the maximum of two numbers. You also will learn how to create your own functions.

10.1 Test-Driving the Enhanced Wage Calculator Application

In this tutorial, you will use functions to enhance the **Wage Calculator** application that you created in Tutorial 4. This enhanced application must meet the following requirements:

Application Requirements

Recall the problem statement from Tutorial 4:

A payroll company calculates the gross earnings per week of employees. Employees' weekly salaries are based on the number of hours they work and their hourly wages. Create an application that accepts this information and calculates the employee's total (gross) earnings. The application assumes a standard work week of 40 hours. The wages for 40 or fewer hours are calculated by multiplying the employee's hourly salary by the number of hours worked. Any time worked over 40 hours in a week is considered "overtime" and earns time and a half. Salary for time and a half is calculated by multiplying the employee's hourly wage by 1.5 and multiplying the result of that calculation by the number of overtime hours worked. The total overtime earned is added to the user's gross earnings for the regular 40 hours of work to calculate the total earnings for that week.

*Modify the **Wage Calculator** application from Tutorial 4 to organize its code better by using a function to calculate and return the user's pay.*

The completed application has the same functionality as the application in Tutorial 4, but places all the code involved in the payroll calculation into a function called `calculatePay`. You begin by test-driving the completed application. Then, you will learn the additional C++ capabilities you will need to create your own version of this application by writing your first programmer-defined function.

Test-Driving the Enhanced Wage Calculator Application

1. *Locating the completed application.* Open the **Command Prompt** by selecting **Start > All Programs > Accessories > Command Prompt**. Change to your completed **Wage Calculator** application directory by typing `cd C:\Examples\Tutorial10\CompletedApplication\WageCalculator2`.

2. *Running the Wage Calculator application.* Type `WageCalculator` in the **Command Prompt** window to run the application (Fig. 10.1). The application prompts the user to enter an hourly wage and the number of hours worked in a week. Once these values are entered, the gross earnings for the week are displayed.

3. *Entering the employee's hourly wage and weekly hours.* Enter 10 at the **Enter hourly wage:** prompt and enter 45 at the **Enter hours worked this week:** prompt.

4. *Calculating wages earned.* After you enter the values, the result (`$475.00`) is displayed (Fig. 10.1).

```
C:\Examples\Tutorial10\CompletedApplication\WageCalculator2>WageCalcul
ator

Enter hourly wage: 10
Enter hours worked this week: 45

Gross wages: $475.00


C:\Examples\Tutorial10\CompletedApplication\WageCalculator2>_
```

Figure 10.1 Wage Calculator output.

5. *Close the Command Prompt window.*

10.2 C++ Standard Library Functions and Classes

The key to creating large applications is to break the applications into smaller pieces. In C++, these pieces consist primarily of functions and classes. Programmers typically combine **programmer-defined** functions and classes with pre-existing code available in the C++ Standard Library. Using pre-existing code saves time, effort and money. This concept of **code reuse** increases efficiency for application developers. Figure 10.2 explains and demonstrates several pre-existing C++ functions.

You have already used several pre-existing functions and classes from the C++ Standard Library. For example, the `pow` function that you used to calculate interest on a deposit in Tutorial 8 is part of the math library (`<cmath>`). You have also used objects from pre-existing C++ classes, such as `cin` and `cout` to perform stream I/O and `strings` to store text. Without these libraries, you would need to code these capabilities yourself—a task that would include many lines of code and programming techniques that have not been introduced yet. The pre-existing functions and classes are also thoroughly tested to eliminate bugs, and they are designed to maximize efficiency. You will learn to use other pre-existing classes and functions later in this book.

The C++ Standard Library cannot provide every conceivable function and class that you might need to build all your applications, so C++ allows you to create your own functions and classes to meet the unique requirements of your applications. In

Library	Function	Description	Example
algorithm	max(x, y)	Returns the larger value of x and y	max(2.3, 12.7) returns 12.7 max(-2.3, -12.7) returns -2.3
algorithm	min(x, y)	Returns the smaller value of x and y	min(2.3, 12.7) returns 2.3 min(-2.3, -12.7) returns -12.7
cmath	sqrt(x)	Returns the square root of x	sqrt(9.0) returns 3.0 sqrt(2.0) returns 1.41421356237
string	getline(x)	Stores a line of user input in string x	getline(x); retrieves a line of text that the user entered cout << x << endl; displays the string stored in variable x, which corresponds to the line of text that the user entered

Figure 10.2   Some predefined C++ functions.

the next section, you will learn about function definitions. Later in this tutorial, you will create your own functions. In Tutorial 15, you will create your own classes.

SELF-REVIEW

1. Which of the following function calls returns the value 10?

    a) min(9.0, 10.0)   b) sqrt(100.0)

    c) max(10.0, 11.0)   d) min(10.0, 9.0)

2. Programmers normally use _____.

    a) programmer-defined functions   b) pre-existing functions

    c) both programmer-defined and pre-existing functions

    d) neither programmer-defined nor pre-existing functions

Answers: 1) b. 2) c.

10.3 Function Definitions

The applications presented earlier in this book have called C++ Standard Library functions (such as pow) to help accomplish their tasks. You will now learn how to write your own functions. Before you create the enhanced **Wage Calculator** application, you will learn how to create functions in the context of two small applications. The first uses the Pythagorean Theorem to calculate the length of the hypotenuse of a right triangle. The second application determines the maximum of three numbers.

Let us begin by reviewing the Pythagorean Theorem. A right triangle (which is a triangle with a 90-degree angle) always satisfies the following relationship—the sum of the squares of the two smaller sides of the triangle equals the square of the largest side of the triangle, called the hypotenuse. In this application, the two smaller sides are called side A and side B and their lengths are used to calculate the length of the hypotenuse.

Creating the Hypotenuse Calculator Application

1. **Copying the template application to your working directory.** Copy the `C:\Examples\Tutorial10\TemplateApplication\Hypotenuse-Calculator` directory to your `C:\SimplyCpp` directory.

2. **Opening the Hypotenuse Calculator application's template source code file.** Open the template file `HypotenuseCalculator.cpp.` in your text editor or IDE.

3. **Examining the template code.** Examine the code provided in the template (Fig. 10.3). We have provided an incomplete `main` function (lines 10–32). This function defines two local variables (lines 14–15). The `sideA` and `sideB` variables contain the lengths of sides A and B as `double` values. Lines 25–28 contain an `if` statement. Because real lengths must be larger than zero, the `if` statement's body displays an error message if a negative value (or zero) is input as the length of side A or side B.

Lengths for sides A and B ⎯

Error message displays if negative value (or zero) is entered ⎯

```
9
10    // function main begins program execution
11    int main()
12    {
13       // define variables
14       double sideA; // stores length of side A
15       double sideB; // stores length of side B
16
17       // prompt user for and input side lengths
18       cout << "\nEnter length of side A: ";
19       cin >> sideA; // get side A
20
21       cout << "Enter length of side B: ";
22       cin >> sideB; // get side B
23
24       // display an error message if the user enters invalid input
25       if ( sideA <= 0 || sideB <= 0 )
26       {
27          cout << "You must enter positive nonzero numbers.\n" << endl;
28       } // end if
29
30       return 0; // indicate that program ended successfully
31
32    } // end function main
33
```

Figure 10.3 **Hypotenuse Calculator** template code.

4. **Creating an empty function.** Add lines 10–14 of Fig. 10.4 before `main`. Notice the comment in line 14—this comment identifies the function being terminated.

Function header ⎯

A right brace marks the end of a function definition ⎯

```
6     #include <cmath>      // require to access function sqrt
7
8     using namespace std; // for accessing C++ Standard Library members
9
10    // return the square of side
11    double square( double side )
12    {
13
14    } // end function square
15
16    // function main begins program execution
```

Figure 10.4 Defining the `square` function.

(cont.)

5. ***Understanding the function.*** The function begins at line 11 (Fig. 10.4) with the `double` keyword, followed by a **function name** (in this case, `square`). The function name can be any valid identifier. The function name is followed by a set of parentheses containing a variable declaration. The type name before `square` (in this case `double`) is known as the **return type**. Functions can return either a single piece of information or no information to the caller. If a function returns no information, its return type is declared with the **void** keyword.

The declaration within the parentheses is known as the **parameter list**, where variables (called **parameters**) are declared. Although this application's parameter list contains only one declaration, a parameter list can contain multiple declarations separated by commas. The parameter list declares each parameter's type and name. Parameter variables are used in the function body. Parameters allow functions to receive data that is required to perform the function's tasks.

The first line of a function (including the return type, the function name and the parameter list) is called the **function header**. The function header for the `square` function declares one parameter variable, `side`, to be of the `double` type and sets the return type of `square` as `double`.

Any definitions and statements that appear between the braces in lines 12 and 14 of Fig. 10.4 form the **function body**. The function body contains code that performs actions, generally by manipulating the parameters from the parameter list. In the next step, you will add a statement to the body of the `square` function. The function header, the braces and the body statements collectively make up the **function definition**.

6. ***Adding code to the body of a function.*** You want your function to square the value it receives in the `side` parameter and return that result to the function's caller. Add line 13 of Fig. 10.5 to `square`'s body.

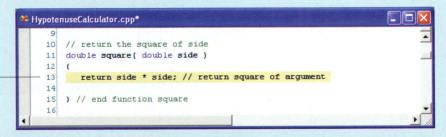

return statement sends a value back to the function's caller

Figure 10.5 Coding the `square` function.

Line 13 uses the multiplication (*) operator to calculate the square of `side`—the parameter of this function. Line 13 also uses a **return statement** to return this value. This statement begins with the `return` keyword, followed by an expression. The `return` statement returns the result of the expression following the `return` keyword—in this case, `side * side`—and terminates execution of the function. This value is returned to the point at which the function was called so that the returned value may be used by the function's caller. You will write the code to call the `square` function in the next box.

7. ***Save, compile and run the completed application.*** Figure 10.6 shows the result of running the updated application. Enter lengths for sides A and B. Notice that the length of the hypotenuse is not displayed. You will add the functionality to calculate and display the length of the hypotenuse in the next box.

Good Programming Practice
Choosing meaningful function names and parameter names makes applications more readable.

Software Design Tip
To promote reusability, each function should perform a single, well-defined task.

Good Programming Practice
Function names should begin with a lowercase letter. Each subsequent word in the name should begin with an uppercase letter.

Good Programming Practice
Placing a blank line between function definitions enhances application readability.

(cont.)

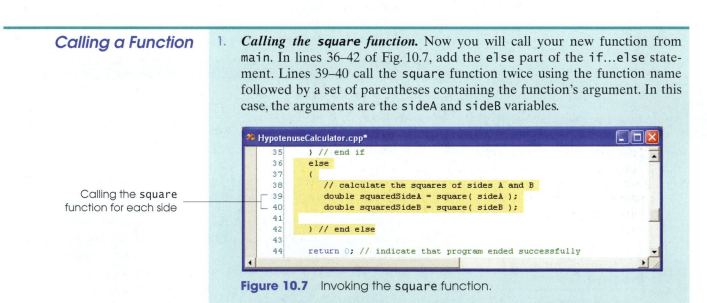

Figure 10.6   Hypotenuse Calculator application updated.

8. *Close the Command Prompt window.*

A function is **invoked** (or **called**—that is, made to perform its designated task) by a **function call**. The function call specifies the function name and provides data (**arguments**) that the **callee** (the function being called) receives as parameter values and uses to do its job. When the called function completes its task, it returns control to point at which the function was called in the **caller** (the calling function). For example, you have typically called the pow function as follows:

```
result = pow( base, exponent );
```

where pow is the name of the function and the base and exponent variables are the arguments passed to this function. The function uses these values to perform its defined task (returning the value of base raised to the exponent power).

Now you will insert code into your application to call your new square function. You will see the benefits of code reuse by calling the function several times, rather than repeatedly having to rewrite code containing the body of the function.

Calling a Function

1. *Calling the square function.* Now you will call your new function from main. In lines 36–42 of Fig. 10.7, add the else part of the if...else statement. Lines 39–40 call the square function twice using the function name followed by a set of parentheses containing the function's argument. In this case, the arguments are the sideA and sideB variables.

Calling the square function for each side

```
35      } // end if
36      else
37      {
38          // calculate the squares of sides A and B
39          double squaredSideA = square( sideA );
40          double squaredSideB = square( sideB );
41
42      } // end else
43
44      return 0; // indicate that program ended successfully
```

Figure 10.7   Invoking the square function.

When program control reaches line 39 of Fig. 10.7, the application calls the square function. At this point, the application stores a copy of argument sideA's value (for this example, let's assume the value of sideA is 3.0) in the square function's side parameter. Then program control transfers to the square function, and the statements of the square function are executed.

(cont.)

When the `return` statement in `square` is reached, the value of the expression `side * side` (in this case, `3.0` times `3.0`, or `9.0`) is calculated and returned to the point in line 39 (of Fig. 10.7) where the `square` function was called, completing the called function's execution. Program control will also be transferred to this point and the application will continue by assigning the return value of `square` (9.0) to the `squaredSideA` variable. These same actions will occur again when program control reaches the second call to `square` in line 40. With this call, the value passed to `square` is the value of the `sideB` variable (for this example, let's assume the value of `sideB` is 4.0) and the value returned (the square of `sideB`, or 16.0) is assigned to the `squaredSideB` variable.

2. ***Calling a pre-existing function of the C++ Standard Library.*** Add lines 42–55 of Fig. 10.8 to the `else` part of the `if...else` statement in your application. Line 44 adds the square of side A and the square of side B and assigns the result to the `squaredHypotenuse` variable. Line 48 then calls the **`sqrt`** function from the math library, which was made accessible by including the `<cmath>` header file in line 6 of Fig. 10.4. Note that you must include the appropriate header file (in this case, `<cmath>`) to access C++ Standard Library functions. The `sqrt` function will calculate the square root of the square of the hypotenuse to find the length of the hypotenuse. Line 51 uses the `fixed` and `setprecision` stream manipulators to ensure that only two decimal digits are displayed for the hypotenuse. The formatted output is then displayed in lines 54–55.

Calling `cmath` function `sqrt`

Formatting and displaying the length of the hypotenuse

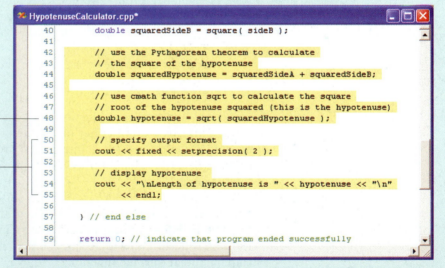

```
    HypotenuseCalculator.cpp*
40        double squaredSideB = square( sideB );
41
42        // use the Pythagorean theorem to calculate
43        // the square of the hypotenuse
44        double squaredHypotenuse = squaredSideA + squaredSideB;
45
46        // use cmath function sqrt to calculate the square
47        // root of the hypotenuse squared (this is the hypotenuse)
48        double hypotenuse = sqrt( squaredHypotenuse );
49
50        // specify output format
51        cout << fixed << setprecision( 2 );
52
53        // display hypotenuse
54        cout << "\nLength of hypotenuse is " << hypotenuse << "\n"
55           << endl;
56
57     } // end else
58
59     return 0; // indicate that program ended successfully
```

Figure 10.8 Completing the `main` function.

3. ***Save, compile and run the application.*** Figure 10.9 shows the completed application running. Enter lengths for sides A and B. The length of the hypotenuse will be displayed. Notice that for sides A and B of lengths `3.0` and `4.0`, the hypotenuse has a length of exactly `5.00`. Test your application using a right triangle where the lengths of sides A and B are `5.0` and `12.0` (with a resulting hypotenuse of `13.00`) and a right triangle where the lengths of sides A and B are `1.5` and `2.0` (with a resulting hypotenuse of `2.50`).

Error-Prevention Tip

Small functions are easier to test, debug and understand than large ones.

(cont.)

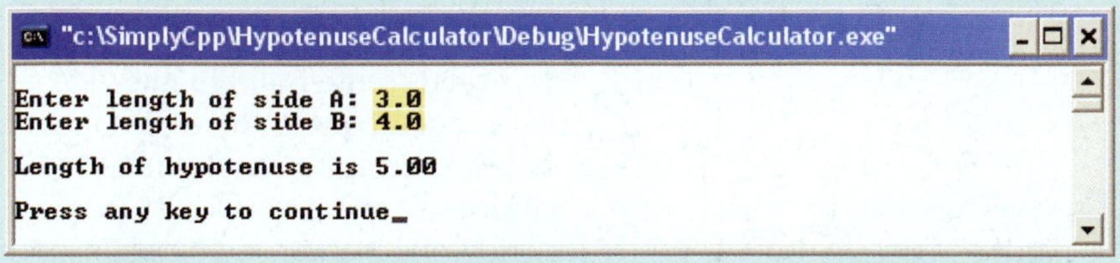

```
c:\SimplyCpp\HypotenuseCalculator\Debug\HypotenuseCalculator.exe"

Enter length of side A: 3.0
Enter length of side B: 4.0

Length of hypotenuse is 5.00

Press any key to continue_
```

Figure 10.9 Output from the completed **Hypotenuse Calculator** application.

4. *Close the Command Prompt window.*

You have now successfully created your first programmer-defined function. You have also tested this function (by running the application) to confirm that it works correctly. This function can now be used in any C++ application where you wish to calculate the square of a `double`. All you need to do is include the function definition in your application. This is an example of code reuse, which helps programmers create applications faster.

As demonstrated in the **Hypotenuse Calculator** application, the syntax used to call a function follows the format

> *name(argument list)*

where the **argument list** is a comma-separated list of the arguments sent to the function. The number, order and type of arguments must agree with the parameters in the function's parameter list. If a function's parameter list is empty (that is, the function name is followed by an empty pair of parentheses), it requires no arguments.

As you saw in the previous example, the statement

> `return` *expression*;

can occur anywhere in a function body and returns the value of *expression* to the caller. Functions return either one value or no value. When a `return` statement is executed, control returns immediately to the point at which that function was called, where the value returned can be used. [*Note:* An expression can contain calls to other functions.]

Note that C++ requires a function's name, the type for each of its parameters and return type to precede any statement that calls that function. Thus, the `square` function definition appeared before `main` in your source code file. In the next tutorial, you will learn how to declare a function so that its definition can appear after a statement that calls the function.

SELF-REVIEW

1. A function is invoked by a(n) _____.

   a) callee   b) caller

   c) argument   d) parameter

2. The _____ statement in a function sends a value back to the calling function.

   a) `return`   b) `back`

   c) `end`   d) `value`

Answers: 1) b. 2) a.

10.4 Completing the `Maximum` Application

You will now create another function. This function, which is part of the **Maximum** application that you will complete, returns the largest of three numbers input by the user.

Creating a Function That Returns the Largest of Three Numbers

1. **Copying the template application to your working directory.** Copy the `C:\Examples\Tutorial10\TemplateApplication\Maximum` directory to your `C:\SimplyCpp` directory.

2. **Opening the Maximum application's template source code file.** Open the template file `Maximum.cpp` in your text editor or IDE.

3. **Coding the main function.** Add lines 11–29 of Fig. 10.10 to `main`. Lines 12–14 define the `double` variables `first`, `second` and `third` to store the first, second and third values entered by the user, respectively. Lines 17–24 prompt the user for three values and input each value into the appropriate variable. Line 27 calls the `determineMaximum` function and passes to it as arguments the three values the user has input in response to the prompts. The `determineMaximum` function has not yet been defined, so this function call will result in a syntax error if you try to compile the code. You will define the `determineMaximum` function in the next step.

Common Programming Error

Calling a function that does not exist or misspelling the function name in a function call is a syntax error.

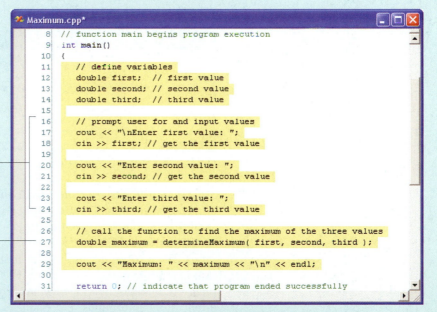

Inputting three values

Calling the `determineMaximum` function

```
 8    // function main begins program execution
 9    int main()
10    {
11       // define variables
12       double first;  // first value
13       double second; // second value
14       double third;  // third value
15
16       // prompt user for and input values
17       cout << "\nEnter first value: ";
18       cin >> first; // get the first value
19
20       cout << "Enter second value: ";
21       cin >> second; // get the second value
22
23       cout << "Enter third value: ";
24       cin >> third; // get the third value
25
26       // call the function to find the maximum of the three values
27       double maximum = determineMaximum( first, second, third );
28
29       cout << "Maximum: " << maximum << "\n" << endl;
30
31       return 0; // indicate that program ended successfully
```

Figure 10.10 Invoking the `determineMaximum` function.

4. **Creating the determineMaximum function.** Add lines 8–12 of Fig. 10.11 before `main`. Line 8 defines the return type of the `determineMaximum` function as `double`. The parameter list (line 9) specifies that the values of the three arguments passed to the `determineMaximum` function will be stored in the `one`, `two` and `three` parameters, all of which are variables of the `double` type.

(cont.)

The empty `determineMaximum` function

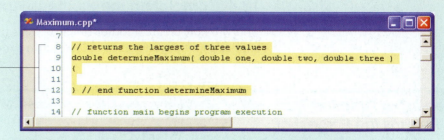

Figure 10.11 Defining the `determineMaximum` function.

5. *Adding functionality to the determineMaximum function.* Add lines 11–14 of Fig. 10.12 to the body of `determineMaximum`. Line 11 creates the `temporary` variable to contain the maximum of the first two numbers passed to this function. This maximum is determined by using the **max** function. This function takes two `double`s and returns the larger value. The value returned by the `max` function is assigned to the `temporary` variable. Line 12 then compares that value to the `determineMaximum` function's third parameter, `three`. The maximum determined in this line, `maximumValue`, is the maximum of the three values. The `return` statement terminates execution of the function and returns the value of the `maximumValue` variable to the calling function. The result is returned to the point (line 27 of Fig. 10.10) where the `determineMaximum` function was called.

Calling **max** twice to determine the maximum of three values

Returning the maximum of all three values

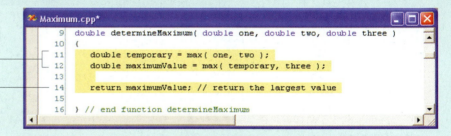

Figure 10.12 `max` returns the larger of its two arguments.

6. *Save, compile and run the application.* Figure 10.13 shows the completed application running. Test the application by entering the values 2, 34 and 5 at the input prompts. Notice that the largest value, 34, is displayed. You should now enter several sets of values. Use at least one set of values in which you input the maximum value at the first prompt. Similarly, use a set of values that places the maximum value at the second prompt and a set of values that places the maximum value at the third prompt. Notice that in each case, the application determines and displays the correct maximum value, whether you input `int` or `double` values.

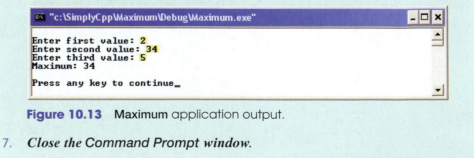

Figure 10.13 **Maximum** application output.

7. *Close the Command Prompt window.*

You have now completed the **Maximum** application. Notice that you can easily modify this application to take and return `int` data. To do this, you will need to store user input in `int` variables. You will also need to modify the header of the `determineMaximum` function to take three `int`s and return an `int`. In the body of the `determineMaximum` function, store the return values of the calls to the `max` function in `int` variables. Finally, make sure that the returned value of the `determineMaximum` function is stored in an `int` variable.

SELF-REVIEW

1. The _____ C++ Standard Library function returns the larger of its two `double` arguments.

   a) `max`   b) `maximum`

   c) `larger`   d) `greater`

2. The _____ is sent to a function when it is called.

   a) return value   b) return type

   c) parameter list   d) argument list

Answers: 1) a. 2) d.

10.5 Using Functions in the Wage Calculator Application

The `main` function in the original version of the **Wage Calculator** application (Tutorial 4) calculated an employee's wages and displayed the result. Next, you will write the `calculatePay` function to calculate the wages. When the user inputs data, `main` will call `calculatePay`. By placing some of the application's functionality in a function, you will successfully divide the **Wage Calculator** application into smaller, more manageable pieces. Using the divide-and-conquer technique provides several advantages. You can now more easily isolate errors in your application making it easier to debug. For instance, if the final application does not correctly calculate the user's pay, you know that the problem probably lies within either the `calculatePay` function or the call to the `calculatePay` function. It is not likely that you'll need to look at the other statements in the application, as they are not related to the calculation of the user's pay. Another advantage is reusability. You will create a function that can be called several times, if you should wish to modify the application to calculate several sets of wages. All you need to do is call the `calculatePay` function each time with the correct arguments.

Software Design Tip

Use functions to increase the clarity and organization of your applications. This not only helps others understand your applications, but it also helps you develop, test and debug them.

Creating a Function within the Wage Calculator Application

1. *Copying the template to your working directory.* Copy the `C:\Examples\Tutorial10\TemplateApplication\WageCalculator2` directory to your `C:\SimplyCpp` directory.

2. *Opening the Wage Calculator application's template file.* Open the template file `WageCalculator.cpp` in your text editor or IDE.

(cont.)

3. **Coding the main function.** Add lines 13–32 of Fig. 10.14 to main. Lines 14–15 define the variables hourlyWage and hoursWorked. Lines 18–19 and lines 22–23 display input prompts, retrieve user input and assign values to the hourlyWage and hoursWorked variables, respectively. Line 26 calls the calculatePay function, which you will define shortly. This function takes two arguments—the hours worked and the hourly wage. Notice that the function's arguments in this example are variables. Arguments also can be constants (such as const variable HOUR_LIMIT) or expressions (such as commission + bonus).

4. **Creating a function.** Add the calculatePay function to your application (lines 10–34 of Fig. 10.15) before main. Note that the function header and function call must agree with regard to the number, type and order of the parameters.

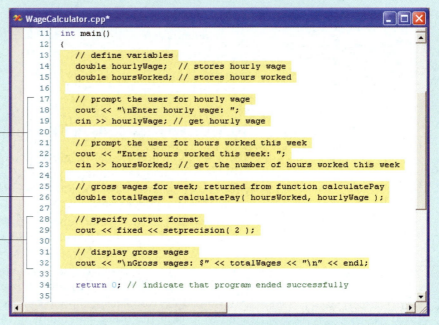

Inputting wage and hours worked

Calling the calculatePay function

Formatting and displaying the total wage

Figure 10.14 main calls the calculatePay function.

The calculatePay function receives the argument values and stores them in the parameters hours and wages. Lines 20–30 define an if...else statement that determines the employee's pay based on the amount of hours worked. The condition for this statement (line 20) determines whether hours is less than or equal to the HOUR_LIMIT constant. If it is, then the employee's earnings without overtime are calculated. Otherwise, the employee's earnings including overtime are calculated.

When the return statement in line 32 is executed, control is returned to the calling function, main (line 26 in Fig. 10.14), where the result then is stored in the totalWages variable. In line 32 of Fig. 10.14, the result is displayed in currency format

5. **Save, compile and run the application.** Figure 10.16 shows the completed application running. Enter 10 at the **Enter hourly wage:** prompt and enter 45 at the **Enter hours worked this week:** prompt to test the application. The result ($475.00) is displayed.

6. **Close the Command Prompt window.**.

Common Programming Error

Defining a variable in the function's body with the same name as a parameter in the function header is a syntax error.

(cont.)

Function header

Calculating gross wages based
on the number of hours worked

Returning the wages for the week

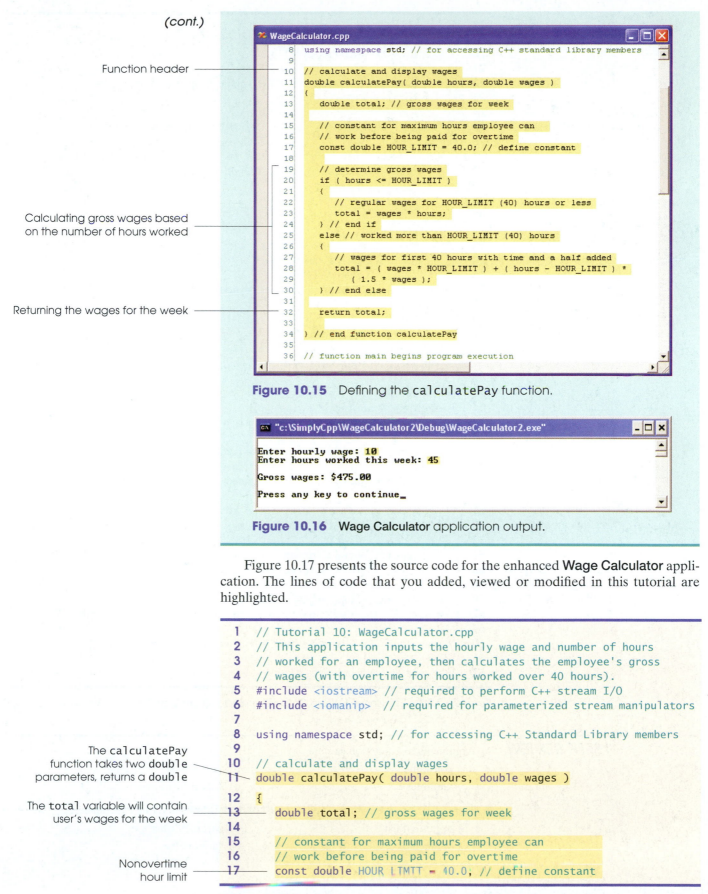

```cpp
  8    using namespace std; // for accessing C++ standard library members
  9
 10    // calculate and display wages
 11    double calculatePay( double hours, double wages )
 12    {
 13        double total; // gross wages for week
 14
 15        // constant for maximum hours employee can
 16        // work before being paid for overtime
 17        const double HOUR_LIMIT = 40.0; // define constant
 18
 19        // determine gross wages
 20        if ( hours <= HOUR_LIMIT )
 21        {
 22            // regular wages for HOUR_LIMIT (40) hours or less
 23            total = wages * hours;
 24        } // end if
 25        else // worked more than HOUR_LIMIT (40) hours
 26        {
 27            // wages for first 40 hours with time and a half added
 28            total = ( wages * HOUR_LIMIT ) + ( hours - HOUR_LIMIT ) *
 29                ( 1.5 * wages );
 30        } // end else
 31
 32        return total;
 33
 34    } // end function calculatePay
 35
 36    // function main begins program execution
```

Figure 10.15 Defining the `calculatePay` function.

```
"c:\SimplyCpp\WageCalculator2\Debug\WageCalculator2.exe"

Enter hourly wage: 10
Enter hours worked this week: 45

Gross wages: $475.00

Press any key to continue_
```

Figure 10.16 **Wage Calculator** application output.

Figure 10.17 presents the source code for the enhanced **Wage Calculator** application. The lines of code that you added, viewed or modified in this tutorial are highlighted.

The `calculatePay` function takes two **double** parameters, returns a **double**

The **total** variable will contain user's wages for the week

Nonovertime hour limit

```cpp
 1    // Tutorial 10: WageCalculator.cpp
 2    // This application inputs the hourly wage and number of hours
 3    // worked for an employee, then calculates the employee's gross
 4    // wages (with overtime for hours worked over 40 hours).
 5    #include <iostream> // required to perform C++ stream I/O
 6    #include <iomanip>  // required for parameterized stream manipulators
 7
 8    using namespace std; // for accessing C++ Standard Library members
 9
10    // calculate and display wages
11    double calculatePay( double hours, double wages )
12    {
13        double total; // gross wages for week
14
15        // constant for maximum hours employee can
16        // work before being paid for overtime
17        const double HOUR_LIMIT = 40.0; // define constant
```

Figure 10.17 Enhanced **Wage Calculator** code. (Part 1 of 2.)

```
18
19        // determine gross wages
20        if ( hours <= HOUR_LIMIT )
21        {
22           // regular wages for HOUR_LIMIT (40) hours or less
23           total = wages * hours;
24        } // end if
25        else // worked more than HOUR_LIMIT (40) hours
26        {
27           // wages for first 40 hours with time and a half added
28           total = ( wages * HOUR_LIMIT ) + ( hours - HOUR_LIMIT ) *
29              ( 1.5 * wages );
30        } // end else
31
32        return total;
33
34     } // end function calculatePay
35
36     // function main begins program execution
37     int main()
38     {
39        // define variables
40        double hourlyWage;  // stores hourly wage
41        double hoursWorked; // stores hours worked
42
43        // prompt user for hourly wage
44        cout << "\nEnter hourly wage: ";
45        cin >> hourlyWage; // get hourly wage
46
47        // prompt user for hours worked this week
48        cout << "Enter hours worked this week: ";
49        cin >> hoursWorked; // get number of hours worked this week
50
51        // gross wages for week; returned from function calculatePay
52        double totalWages = calculatePay( hoursWorked, hourlyWage );
53
54        // specify output format
55        cout << fixed << setprecision( 2 );
56
57        // display gross wages
58        cout << "\nGross wages: $" << totalWages << "\n" << endl;
59
60        return 0; // indicate that program ended successfully
61
62     } // end function main
```

Labels (left margin):
- Calculate wages based on the number of hours worked → lines 19–30
- Return total to calling function → line 32
- Closing brace ends function body → line 34
- Prompt for user inputs → lines 43–49
- Call the calculatePay function → line 52
- Format and display value returned from the calculatePay function → lines 54–58

Figure 10.17 Enhanced **Wage Calculator** code. (Part 2 of 2.)

SELF-REVIEW
1. Arguments to a function can be _____.

   a) constants   b) expressions

   c) variables   d) All of the above.

2. The _____ is a comma-separated list of declarations in a function header.

   a) argument list   b) parameter list

   c) value list   d) variable list

Answers: 1) d. 2) b.

10.6 Using the Debugger: Controlling Execution Using the Step Into, Step Over, Step Out and Continue Commands

In earlier tutorials, you learned how to debug your applications by setting breakpoints and either examining or setting values at those breakpoints. In this section, you will learn how to walk through the application line by line using the debugger to find and fix errors. This can help you verify that a function's code is executing correctly. The commands you will learn in this section allow you to walk through the execution of a function line by line, execute all the statements of a function at once, execute only the remaining statements of a function (if you have already executed some statements within the function) and continue execution until the next breakpoint (or until the application terminates). [*Note:* This section provides instructions for debugging in Microsoft Visual C++ .NET. Instructions for using other popular debuggers are located in the appendices and at www.deitel.com.]

Using the Debugger: Controlling Execution Using the Step Into, Step Over, Step Out and Continue Commands

Setting a breakpoint

1. ***Opening the application***. Open the completed **Wage Calculator** application if it is not already open.

2. ***Setting a breakpoint***. Set a breakpoint at line 52 by clicking in the margin indicator bar (Fig. 10.18).

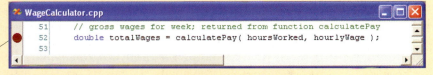

```
51    // gross wages for week; returned from function calculatePay
52    double totalWages = calculatePay( hoursWorked, hourlyWage );
53
```

Figure 10.18 Setting a breakpoint in the **Wage Calculator** application.

3. ***Starting the debugger***. Select **Debug > Start**. The WageCalculator2 application executes. Enter the value 7.50 at the **Enter hours worked this week:** prompt and enter 35 in the **Enter weekly hours:** prompt.

4. ***Using the Step Into command***. The **Step Into command** executes the next statement (the yellow highlighted line) in the application (Fig. 10.19). If the next statement is to execute a function call and you select **Step Into**, control is transferred to the called function. The **Step Into** command allows you to enter a function and confirm the function's execution by individually executing each statement inside the function. Select **Debug > Step Into** to enter the calculatePay function (Fig. 10.20). Note that the debugger does not pause at line 13 of Fig. 10.20. This occurs because variable definitions that do not contain assignments are not executable statements.

Next statement to execute is a function call

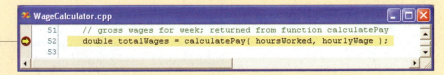

```
51    // gross wages for week; returned from function calculatePay
52    double totalWages = calculatePay( hoursWorked, hourlyWage );
53
```

Figure 10.19 Reaching a breakpoint in the **Wage Calculator** application.

5. ***Using the Step Over command***. Select **Debug > Step Over** to execute the current statement (line 17 in Fig. 10.20) and transfer control to line 20 (Fig. 10.21). The **Step Over command** behaves like the **Step Into** command when the next statement to execute does not contain a function call. You will see how the **Step Over** command differs from the **Step Into** command in *Step 11*.

(cont.)

Definitions (without assignments) are not considered executable statements

Next statement to execute

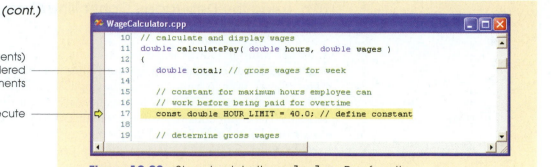

Figure 10.20 Stepping into the `calculatePay` function.

Control is transferred to the `if...else` statement

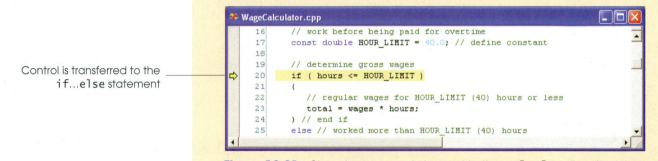

Figure 10.21 Stepping over a statement in the `calculatePay` function.

6. *Using the Step Out command.* Select **Debug > Step Out** to execute the remaining statements in the function and return control to line 52 (Fig. 10.19), which contains the function call. Often, in lengthy functions, you will want to look at a few key lines of code, then continue debugging the caller's code. The **Step Out command** is useful for such situations, where you do not want to continue stepping through the entire function line by line.

7. *Setting a breakpoint.* Set a breakpoint at the `return` statement of `main` at line 60 of Fig. 10.22. You will make use of this breakpoint in the next step.

Setting second breakpoint

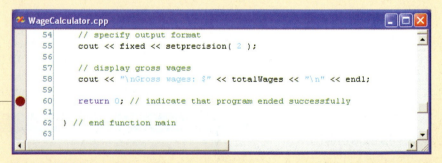

Figure 10.22 Setting a second breakpoint in the enhanced **Wage Calculator** application.

8. *Using the Continue command.* The **Continue command** will execute any statements between the next executable statement and the next breakpoint or the end of `main`, whichever comes first. Notice that there are two executable statements (lines 55 and 58 of Fig. 10.17) before the breakpoint that was set in the previous step. Select **Debug > Continue**. The next executable statement is now line 60 (Fig. 10.23). This feature saves time when you do not want to step line by line through many lines of code to reach the next breakpoint.

(cont.)

9. ***Stopping the debugger.*** Select **Debug > Stop Debugging** to end the debugging session.

10. ***Starting the debugger.*** Before we can demonstrate the next debugger feature, you must start the debugger again. Start the debugger, as you did in *Step 3*, and enter as input the same values. The debugger pauses execution at line 52.

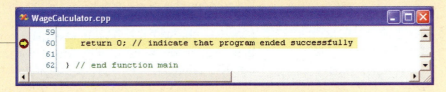

Next executable statement —

Figure 10.23 Using the debugger's **Continue** command.

11. ***Using the Step Over command.*** Select **Debug > Step Over**. Recall that this command behaves like the **Step Into** command when the next statement to execute does not contain a function call. If the next statement to execute contains a function call, the called function executes in its entirety (without pausing execution at any statement inside the function), and the yellow arrow advances to the next executable line (after the function call) in the current function. In this case, the debugger executes line 52, located in `main` (Fig. 10.24). Line 52 calls the `calculatePay` function and assigns the result to `double` variable `totalWages`. The debugger then pauses execution at line 55, the next executable line in the current function, `main`.

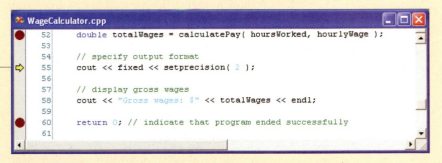

The `calculatePay` function is executed without stepping into it when the **Step Over** command is selected

Figure 10.24 Using the debugger's **Step Over** command.

12. ***Stopping the debugger.*** Select **Debug > Stop Debugging** to end the debugging session.

13. ***Close the Visual Studio .NET IDE.***

SELF-REVIEW

1. During debugging, the _____ command executes the remaining statements in the current function and returns program control to the place where the function was called.

   a) **Step Into**   b) **Step Out**
   c) **Step Over**   d) **Step End**

2. The _____ command behaves like the **Step Into** command when the next statement to execute does not contain a function call.

   a) **Step Next**   b) **Step Out**
   c) **Step Over**   d) **Continue**

Answers: 1) b. 2) c.

10.7 Wrap-Up

In this tutorial, you learned about functions and how they can be used to better organize an application. You learned about the concept of code reuse, where time and effort can be saved by reusing pre-existing code. You used pre-existing functions from the C++ Standard Library and created your own functions.

You also learned the syntax for defining and invoking functions. You examined the components of a function, including the function header, the parameter list, the body and the `return` statement. You learned the order in which execution occurs—from the line where a function is called (invoked) to the function definition, and then back to the point of invocation. You created three programmer-defined functions—`square`, `determineMaximum` and `calculatePay`.

You used debugger commands (including **Step Into**, **Step Out** and **Step Over** and **Continue**) to determine whether a function is executing correctly. The **Step Into** command allows you to enter a function and confirm the function's execution by individually executing each statement inside the function. The **Step Out** command allows you to save time by executing (without pausing) until the current function returns control to its caller. The **Step Over** command allows you to execute a function in its entirety without pausing until the statement following the function call. The **Continue** command executes any statements between the next executable statement and the next breakpoint or the end of `main`, whichever comes first.

In the next tutorial, you will learn more about functions in C++. You will see how C++ treats identifiers that are defined inside and outside of functions, a concept called scope. In this tutorial, you wrote functions that appeared before the corresponding function calls in your source code. In the next tutorial, you will learn how to define functions that can appear anywhere in your application's source code.

SKILLS SUMMARY

Invoking (Calling) a Function

- Specify the function name, followed by a pair of parentheses that contain a comma-separated list of the arguments being passed to the function.
- Ensure that the arguments passed match the function definition's parameters in number, type and order.

Defining a Function

- Give the function a meaningful name, usually a verb that describes what the function does.
- Place the return type before the function name; use `void` if the function doesn't return a value.
- Specify a parameter list declaring each parameter's name and type.
- Add braces to enclose the function body.
- Add code to the function body (within the braces) to perform a specific task.
- Return a value (if one is required) with the `return` statement.

Returning a Value from a Function

- Use the `return` keyword, followed by the variable, constant or expression to be returned.

KEY TERMS

argument—Data that a function call sends to the called function. That data is passed to the corresponding parameter in the called function's header.

argument list—A comma-separated list of the arguments sent to a function. The number, order and type of arguments must agree with the parameters in the function's parameter list.

callee—The function being called.

caller—The function that calls another function. It is also known as the calling function.

calling a function—An action that causes a function to perform its designated task. It is also called invoking a function.

code reuse—Using pre-existing code to save time, effort and money; reusing carefully developed code can result in better programs than if you write all the code yourself.

Continue debugger command—The debugger command used to execute until the next breakpoint is reached or until `main` terminates, whichever comes first.

divide-and-conquer technique—The technique of constructing large applications from small, manageable pieces to make development and maintenance of those applications easier.

invoking a function—Calling a function.

function—A group of statements that performs a task. Functions are used to divide an application into smaller, more manageable pieces that can be called from multiple places within an application.

function body—The braces, definitions and statements that appear after the function header. The function body contains statements that perform actions, generally by manipulating the parameters from the parameter list.

function call—Invoking a function, by specifying the function name and providing data (arguments) that the callee (the function being called) requires to perform its task.

function definition—The function header followed by the function body.

function header—The beginning portion of a function (including the return type, the function name and the parameter list).

function name—The identifier for a function, which when combined with the argument list, distinguishes one function from another. The function name follows the return type, can be any valid identifier and is used to call the function.

max (in the `algorithm` C++ library)—A function that returns the maximum of two `double` argument values.

parameter—A variable declared in a function's parameter list. Values passed as arguments to a function are copied to that function's corresponding parameters and can be used within the function body.

parameter list—A comma-separated list in a function header in which the function declares each parameter.

programmer-defined function—A function created by a programmer to meet the unique needs of a particular application.

return statement—The statement that returns a value from a function. A `return` statement begins with the keyword `return`, followed by an expression, which is evaluated to determine the value to return.

return type—Type of the result returned from a function to its caller.

sqrt (in the `cmath` C++ library)—A function that returns as a `double` the square root of the `double` argument value.

Step Into debugger command—The debugger command used to execute the next statement in an application. The **Step Into** command steps into function calls, allowing the programmer to execute the called function's statements line by line.

Step Out debugger command—The debugger command used to execute the remaining statements in the current function and transfer control to the location where the function was called.

Step Over debugger command—The debugger command used to execute the next statement in an application. The **Step Over** command executes function calls in their entirety.

void keyword—A return type that specifies that the function does not return any information.

C++ LIBRARY REFERENCE

`cmath` This library provides functions that perform common arithmetic calculations.

■ *Functions*

   pow—This function performs exponentiation. The first argument specifies the value that will be raised to a power, and the second argument specifies the power to which the first argument will be raised.

   sqrt—This function returns the square root of a numeric argument.

algorithm This library provides functions that implement common algorithms, such as searching and sorting.

■ *Functions*

`max`—This function returns the larger of two numeric arguments.

`min`—This function returns the smaller of two numeric arguments.

MULTIPLE-CHOICE
QUESTIONS

10.1 A function definition is made up of _____.

a) a function header
b) a function body
c) a function name
d) All of the above.

10.2 The technique of developing large applications from small, manageable pieces is known as _____.

a) divide and conquer
b) counter-controlled repetition
c) debugging
d) code reuse

10.3 Variables in the parentheses after the function name in a function call are known as _____.

a) statements
b) parameters
c) arguments
d) declarations

10.4 What occurs after a function call?

a) Control is given to the called function. After the function is run, the application continues execution at the point where the function was called.
b) Control is given to the called function. After the function is run, the application continues execution with the statement after the called function's definition.
c) The statement before the function call is executed.
d) The application terminates.

10.5 How many values can a `return` statement return to a caller?

a) zero
b) one
c) any number
d) Both a and b.

10.6 Which of the following must be true when making a function call?

a) The number of arguments in the function call must match the number of parameters in the function header.
b) The argument types must be compatible with their corresponding parameter types.
c) Both a and b.
d) None of the above.

10.7 Which of the following statements correctly returns `int` variable `value` from a function?

a) `return value();`
b) `return int value;`
c) `value return;`
d) `return value;`

10.8 The _____ debugger command executes the next statement in the application. If the next statement to execute is a function call, the debugger waits at the first executable statement of the called function.

a) **Step Out**
b) **Step Into**
c) **Step Over**
d) **Continue**

10.9 The first part of a function definition (including the return type, function name and the parameter list) is known as the function _____.

a) body
b) title
c) caller
d) header

10.10 The _____ function from the `cmath` library calculates the square root of the double value passed as an argument.

a) `squareRoot`
b) `root`
c) `sqrt`
d) `square`

EXERCISES   **10.11** (*Temperature Converter Application*) Write an application that performs two types of temperature conversions: degrees Fahrenheit to degrees Celsius and degrees Celsius to degrees Fahrenheit. Your output should look like Fig. 10.25.

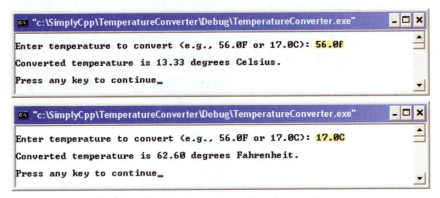

Figure 10.25 Temperature Converter application output.

a) *Copying the template to your working directory.* Copy the C:\Examples\Tutorial10\Exercises\TemperatureConverter directory to your C:\SimplyCpp directory.

b) *Opening the template file.* Open the **Temperature Converter** application source code file in your text editor or IDE.

c) *Adding a function to your application to convert from Celsius to Fahrenheit.* In line 9, add a comment indicating that the function will convert the temperature from Celsius to Fahrenheit. In line 10, add the function header for this function. The function will be called convertToFahrenheit. This function returns a value of the double type and takes an argument of the double type. Name the double parameter degree. In line 11, add a left brace to begin the body of the function. In line 12, add a return statement that performs the conversion calculation. To do this, follow the return keyword with the following expression:

```
( 9.0 / 5.0 ) * degree + 32.0;
```

In line 14, add the right brace to end the body of the function. Follow the brace with a comment indicating the end of this function.

d) *Adding a function to your application to convert the temperature from Fahrenheit to Celsius.* In line 16, add a comment indicating that the function will convert the temperature from Fahrenheit to Celsius. In line 17, add the function header for this function. The function will be called convertToCelsius. This function returns a value of the double type and takes an argument of the double type. Name the double parameter degree. In line 18, add a left brace to begin the body of the function. In line 19, add a return statement that performs the conversion calculation. To do this, follow the return keyword with the following expression:

```
( 5.0 / 9.0 ) * ( degree - 32.0 );
```

In line 21, add the right brace to end the body of the function. Follow the brace with a comment indicating the end of this function.

e) *Invoking the convertToCelsius function.* You will now invoke the convertToCelsius function and input the result in the convertedTemperature variable, to be displayed using cout. In line 38, replace 0.00 with a call to function convertToCelsius. Pass variable temperature to the convertToCelsius function. The temperature variable contains the degrees entered by the user (line 33).

f) *Invoking the convertToFahrenheit function.* You will now invoke the convertToFahrenheit function and input the result in the convertedTemperature variable, to be displayed via cout. In line 43, replace 0.00 with a call to the convertToFahrenheit function. Pass the temperature variable to the convertToFahrenheit function. Again, the temperature variable contains the degrees entered by user (line 33).

g) *Save, compile and run the completed application.* Test the application by entering different degree values followed by uppercase and lowercase "f"s and "c"s. View the output to ensure that the input is being converted correctly.

h) *Close the Command Prompt window.*

10.12 *(Display Square Application)* Write an application that displays a solid square composed of a character input by the user (Fig. 10.26). The user also should input the size of a side of the square.

```
"c:\SimplyCpp\DisplaySquare\Debug\DisplaySquare.exe"                      - □ ×

Enter square size: 6
Enter fill character: #

######
######
######
######
######
######

Press any key to continue_
```

```
"c:\SimplyCpp\DisplaySquare\Debug\DisplaySquare.exe"                      - □ ×

Enter square size: 4
Enter fill character: *

****
****
****
****

Press any key to continue_
```

Figure 10.26 Display Square application output.

a) *Copying the template to your working directory.* Copy the C:\Examples\Tutorial10\Exercises\DisplaySquare directory to your C:\SimplyCpp directory.

b) *Opening the template file.* Open the **Display Square** application source code file in your text editor or IDE.

c) *Adding a function to your application that displays a square of characters.* In line 8, add a comment indicating that the function will display a square. In line 9, add the function header for this function. The function will be called displaySquare. This function contains two parameters—the first, of the int type, should be called size, and the second, of the char type, should be called character. This function does not return a value, but simply performs a task (displaying a square). For such functions, the return type is specified as void. In line 10, add a left brace to begin the body of the function. In line 11, add the right brace to end the body of the function. Follow the brace with a comment indicating the end of this function. You will add code to this function in the next step.

d) *Adding functionality to the displaySquare function.* Copy (but do not remove) the code from lines 29–43. Paste this code into lines 11–25. This code contains the functionality needed to display the square. Now that this code has been placed in its own function, you will need to replace the variable names with the parameter names of this function. In lines 14 and 17, replace squareSize with size. In line 19, replace fillCharacter with character.

e) *Invoking the displaySquare function.* Now that you have placed the logic for displaying a square within the displaySquare function, you can replace the original functionality with a call to the displaySquare function. Replace lines 44–58 with a call to the displaySquare function and pass to this function the size of the square and the fill character as entered by the user. The data entered by the user has been input into variables for you in lines 38 and 42.

f) *Save, compile and run the application.* Test your application by entering various values for the size and fill character of the square. For each set of input, ensure that the square displayed is of the correct size and made up of the correct character.

g) *Close the Command Prompt window.*

10.13 (*Miles Per Gallon Application*) Drivers often want to know how many miles per gallon their cars get so they can estimate gasoline costs. Develop an application that allows the user to input the number of miles driven and the number of gallons used for a tank of gas and computes the miles per gallon (Fig. 10.27).

Figure 10.27   Miles Per Gallon application output.

a) *Copying the template to your working directory.* Copy the `C:\Examples\Tutorial10\Exercises\MilesPerGallon` directory to your `C:\SimplyCpp` directory.

b) *Opening the template file.* Open the **Miles Per Gallon** application source code file in your text editor or IDE.

c) *Adding a function to calculate miles per gallon.* In line 8, add a comment indicating that the function will calculate the amount of miles per gallon. In line 9, add the function header for this function. The function will be called `milesPerGallon`. This function returns a value of the `double` type and takes two arguments of the `double` type. Name the first `double` parameter `milesDriven` and the second `double` parameter `gallonsUsed`. In line 10, add a left brace to begin the body of the function. In line 11, add a `return` statement that performs the calculation. To do this, follow the `return` keyword with the following expression:

```
milesDriven / gallonsUsed;
```

In line 13, add the right brace to end the body of the function. Follow the brace with a comment indicating the end of this function.

d) *Invoking the `milesPerGallon` function.* Lines 31–32 display the value `0.00`. You will now call the `milesPerGallon` function to display the proper miles per gallon, based on the user's input. In line 32, replace `0.00` with a call to the `milesPerGallon` function. Use the variables created in lines 19–20 to pass to this function the miles driven and gallons used, as specified by the user.

e) *Save, compile and run the completed application.* Test your application by entering various values for the number of miles driven and gallons used. For each set of input, verify that the output is correct.

f) *Close the Command Prompt window.*

What does this code do? ▶ **10.14** What does the following code do? Assume the user enters the value 70 at the first input prompt and 80 at the second input prompt. What value is returned from the `mystery` function call? What if the user enters the values 15 and 50 at the first and second input prompts, respectively?

```
 1   // Exercise 10.14: WDTCD.cpp
 2   // What does this code do?
 3   #include <iostream> // required to perform C++ stream I/O
 4   #include <iomanip>  // required for parameterized stream manipulators
 5
 6   using namespace std; // for accessing C++ Standard Library members
 7
 8   int mystery( int number1, int number2 )
 9   {
10      int x;
11      int y;
12
```

```
13        x = number1 + number2;
14        y = x / 2;
15
16        if ( y <= 60 )
17        {
18           return x;
19        } // end if
20        else
21        {
22           return y;
23
24        } // end else
25
26     } // end function mystery
27
28     // function main begins program execution
29     int main()
30     {
31        // declare variables
32        int first;    // first integer
33        int second;   // second integer
34
35        // prompt the user for and input two numbers
36        cout << "\nEnter first number: ";
37        cin >> first;
38
39        cout << "Enter second number: ";
40        cin >> second;
41
42        int result = mystery( first, second );
43
44        cout << "\nResult is: " << result << "\n" << endl;
45
46        return 0; // indicate that program ended successfully
47
48     } // end function main
```

What's wrong with this code? ▶   **10.15** Find the error(s) in the following code, which should take an int value as an argument and return the value of that argument multiplied by 2.5. The value returned should be a double.

```
1     // Exercise 10.15: WWWTC.cpp
2     // Application takes a number from user and displays the number
3     // multiplied by 2.5
4     #include <iostream> // required to perform C++ stream I/O
5
6     using namespace std; // for accessing C++ Standard Library members
7
8     int timesTwo( number )
9     {
10        double result;
11
12        result = number * 2.5;
13
14     } // end function timesTwo
15
```

```
16   // function main begins program execution
17   int main()
18   {
19      int value; // stores value from user
20
21      // prompt the user for an int
22      cout << "\nEnter number: ";
23      cin >> value; // store the value in value
24
25      double result = timesTwo( value );
26
27      cout << "\nNumber * 2.5: " << result << "\n" << endl;
28
29      return 0; // indicate program ended correctly
30
31   } // end function main
```

Using the Debugger ▶   **10.16** (*Gas Pump Application*) The **Gas Pump** application (Fig. 10.28) calculates the cost of gas at a local gas station. This gas station charges $1.61 per gallon for **Regular** grade gas, $1.67 per gallon for **Special** grade gas and $1.77 per gallon for **Super+** grade gas. The user enters the number of gallons to purchase and selects the desired grade from a text-based menu. The application calls a function to compute the total cost from the number of gallons entered and the selected grade. The application provided contains a logic error. In this exercise, you will find and fix the error.

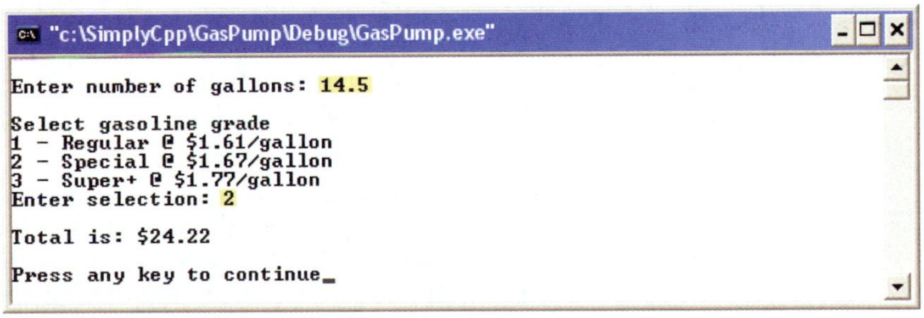

Figure 10.28 **Gas Pump** application running correctly.

a) *Copying the template to your working directory.* Copy the directory C:\Examples\Tutorial10\Exercises\Debugging\GasPump to your C:\SimplyCpp directory.

b) *Opening the template file.* Open the **Gas Pump** application source code file in your text editor or IDE.

c) *Compiling the application for debugging.* If you are not using Visual Studio, make sure to specify the compiler option that includes debugging information.

d) *Running the application.* Run the **Gas Pump** application by typing GasPump at the command line after switching to the application's directory. Enter 14.5 as the starting amount and select the second option from the menu of gasoline choices by entering 2. Notice that the output is incorrect (the correct output is displayed in Fig. 10.28).

e) *Starting the debugger.* Add a breakpoint at the beginning of main. Then start the debugger in Visual Studio .NET by selecting **Debug > Start**.

f) *Finding and correcting the error(s).* Use the **Step Into**, **Step Over** and **Step Out** commands as necessary to walk through the different statements of this function and any functions called from main. You specifically want to walk through the portion of the totalSale function where the user selects the second gasoline option by entering 2 at the second input prompt. Once you have found the error, modify the application so that it displays the correct output.

g) *Save, compile and run the completed application.* Test the application using several different inputs and make sure the resulting output for each set of inputs is correct.

h) *Close the Command Prompt window.*

Programming Challenge ▶

10.17 *(Prime Numbers Application)* An int greater than 1 is said to be prime if it is divisible by only 1 and itself. For example, 2, 3, 5 and 7 are prime numbers, but 4, 6, 8 and 9 are not. Write an application that takes two numbers (representing a lower bound and an upper bound) and determines all of the prime numbers within the specified bounds, inclusive. The application should display an error message if the lower bound is less than zero, the upper bound is less than zero or the upper bound is less than the lower bound. Your application should appear as in Fig. 10.29.

```
"c:\SimplyCpp\PrimeNumbers\Debug\PrimeNumbers.exe"          - □ ×

Enter lower bound: 2
Enter upper bound: 200

2
3
5
7
11
13
```

```
"c:\SimplyCpp\PrimeNumbers\Debug\PrimeNumbers.exe"          - □ ×
173
179
181
191
193
197
199

Press any key to continue_
```

Figure 10.29 Prime Numbers application output.

a) *Copying the template to your working directory.* Copy the C:\Examples\Tutorial10\Exercises\PrimeNumbers directory to your C:\SimplyCpp directory.

b) *Opening the template file.* Open the **Prime Numbers** application source code file in your text editor or IDE.

c) *Adding a function to determine whether a number is prime.* In line 8, add a comment indicating that the function will determine whether a number is a prime number. In line 9, add the function header for this function. The function will be called isPrime. This function returns a value of the bool type and takes an argument of the int type. Name the parameter testValue. In line 10, add a left brace to begin the body of the function. In line 11, add the right brace to end the body of the function. Follow the brace with a comment indicating the end of this function. You will add functionality to this function in the next step.

d) *Converting the argument to a double.* In *Step f*, you will use the sqrt function to find the square root of the testValue argument. Because the sqrt function is not defined for int arguments, you must convert testValue to a double. In line 11, add a comment explaining that you will convert an int to a double. In line 12, add a statement defining double variable number and assign the value of testValue to that variable.

e) *Dealing with the number 1.* The number 1 is not a prime number. In line 14, add a comment stating that 1 is not a valid prime number. In line 15, add an if statement to test whether the value of the variable number is equal to 1. In line 16, start the if statement with a left brace. In line 17, return the boolean value false, indicating that 1 is not a prime number. In line 18, end the if statement with a right brace.

f) *Adding functionality to the isPrime function.* The algorithm to determine whether a number is prime is as follows: Find the square root of the number in question. Loop through the integers from 2 to the square root value. For each iteration of the loop, use the remainder operator, specifying the number in question as the left operand and the current value of the loop counter as the right operand. If any of these operations result in a remainder of 0, the number is not prime. If the loop finishes all iterations and none of the remainder operations have resulted in a remainder of 0, the number is prime. You will now implement this algorithm. In lines 20–21, define double variable limit and assign to this variable the square root of number. In lines 23–

31, define a for loop that iterates from 2 to the largest integer not greater than limit and increments the counter by 1 with each iteration. In the body of the for loop, define an if statement that executes when the remainder of testValue divided by the counter value is 0. In the body of the if statement, use a return statement to return false from the function. Use comments and proper spacing so that the for statement runs from lines 23–31. In line 33, use a return statement to return true from the function.

g) *Invoking the isPrime function.* Lines 70–78 loop from the lower bound to the upper bound, displaying every value using cout in line 75. You will now modify this code so that only the prime numbers are displayed. In line 73, replace true with a call to the isPrime function. Pass to this function the current value in the for loop.

h) *Save, compile and run the completed application.* Test your application by entering various lower and upper bounds. For each set of input, verify the output to ensure that it is correct.

i) *Close the Command Prompt window.*

11

Objectives

In this tutorial, you will learn to:
- Create variables that can be used in all the application's functions.
- Use argument coercion to implicitly convert the value of an argument to a function.
- Use function prototypes to validate your function calls.

Outline

Fundraiser Application

Introducing Scope and Function Prototypes

In this tutorial, you will learn more about global variables and learn more about local variables. You will learn that the difference between a local variable and a global variable is the scope of the variable—the parts of the application that can access the variable. Also, you will learn how the C++ compiler handles conversions between values of different primitive types. Finally, you will learn how the compiler uses function prototypes to reduce logic errors by validating your function calls.

11.1 Test-Driving the Fundraiser Application

You have been asked to create a **Fundraiser** application that determines how much donated money is available to a charity after operating expenses are taken into consideration. This application must meet the following requirements:

Application Requirements

An organization is hosting a fundraiser to collect donations for a charity. A portion of each donation is used to cover the operating expenses of the fundraising organization, and the rest of the donation goes to the charity. Create an application that allows the organization to keep track of the total amount of money raised. The application should deduct 17% of each donation for operating expenses, while the remaining 83% is given to the charity. The application should display the amount of each donation after the 17% in operating expenses are deducted; it also should display the total amount raised for the charity (that is, the total amount donated less all operating costs) for all donations up to that point.

After the user inputs the amount of a donation at the keyboard, the application calculates the net amount the charity receives from that donation after operating expenses have been deducted. In addition, the total amount of money raised for the charity is updated and displayed. You begin by test-driving the completed application. Then, you will learn the additional C++ techniques you will need to create your own version of this application.

Test-Driving the Fundraiser Application

1. ***Locating the completed application.*** Open the **Command Prompt** window by selecting **Start > All Programs > Accessories > Command Prompt**. Change to your completed **Fundraiser** application directory by typing cd C:\Examples\Tutorial11\CompletedApplication\Fundraiser.

2. ***Running the application.*** Type Fundraiser in the **Command Prompt** window to run the application (Fig. 11.1).

```
C:\>cd C:\Examples\Tutorial11\CompletedApplication\Fundraiser

C:\Examples\Tutorial11\CompletedApplication\Fundraiser>Fundraiser
Enter donation amount (0 or less to exit): _
```

Figure 11.1   Running the completed **Fundraiser** application.

3. ***Entering a donation.*** Enter 10 at the **Enter donation amount (0 or less to exit):** prompt. The application calculates the amount of the donation after the operating expenses have been deducted and displays the result ($8.30) after the descriptive text, **After expenses:**. Because this is the first donation entered, the amount is displayed after the descriptive text, **Total raised:**, as well (Fig. 11.2).

```
C:\Examples\Tutorial11\CompletedApplication\Fundraiser>Fundraiser

Enter donation amount (0 or less to exit): 10
After expenses: $8.30
Total raised:   $8.30

Enter donation amount (0 or less to exit): _
```

Figure 11.2   **Fundraiser** application with first donation entered.

4. ***Entering additional donations.*** Enter a $20 donation and notice that the total raised increases (Fig. 11.3).

Total of all donations (minus expenses)

```
C:\Examples\Tutorial11\CompletedApplication\Fundraiser>Fundraiser

Enter donation amount (0 or less to exit): 10
After expenses: $8.30
Total raised:   $8.30

Enter donation amount (0 or less to exit): 20
After expenses: $16.60
Total raised:   $24.90

Enter donation amount (0 or less to exit): _
```

Figure 11.3   Making further donations.

5. ***Exiting the running application.*** Exit the application by entering 0 at the **Enter donation amount (0 or less to exit):** prompt.

6. ***Close the Command Prompt window.***

11.2 Constructing the Fundraiser Application

Now you will create the **Fundraiser** application to enable a user to keep track of the total amount of money raised for charity. First you need to analyze the application. The pseudocode in Fig. 11.4 describes the basic operation of the **Fundraiser** application.

Initialize the total amount raised for charity to zero
Prompt the user for and input a donation value

While the user enters a value greater than zero
    Calculate and display the current donation after expenses
    Update and display the total amount raised for the charity
    Prompt the user for and store the next donation value

Figure 11.4 Pseudocode for the **Fundraiser** application.

Now that you have test-driven the **Fundraiser** application and studied its pseudocode representation, you're ready to begin programming. First, you will define the variables needed in the application. In this discussion, you will learn a new concept—**scope**. Each variable has a scope, which is the portion of an application in which the variable can be accessed. Some variables can be accessed throughout an application, while others can be referenced only from limited portions of an application (such as within a single function). You will now add code to your application to illustrate variables with various scopes.

Examining Scope with the Fundraiser Application

1. *Copying the template to your working directory.* Copy the `C:\Examples\Tutorial11\TemplateApplication\Fundraiser` directory to your `C:\SimplyCpp` directory.

2. *Opening the Fundraiser application's template source code file.* Open the template source code file `Fundraiser.cpp` in your text editor or IDE.

3. *Placing definitions in the code file.* Add lines 9–10 of Fig. 11.5. In this application, you need a variable that stores the total amount of money (after expenses) raised for the charity.

   The `totalNetDonations` variable stores the total amount of money the charity receives. This variable is created and initialized when the application first executes, and retains its value while the application is running (that is, the variable is not recreated and reinitialized each time a function is invoked). The `totalNetDonations` variable is an example of a **global variable**—it is defined inside a source code file, but outside any function definitions of that file. A global variable has **file scope**, which is from the point at which the variable definition appears to the end of the file. Because `totalNetDonations` is defined before any functions in the `Fundraiser.cpp` file, every function will have access to that variable and will be able to read and modify its value.

Defining a global variable ————

```
 7   using namespace std; // for accessing C++ standard library members
 8
 9   // global variable stores total raised for charity
10   double totalNetDonations = 0.00;
11
12   // function main begins program execution
13   int main()
```

Figure 11.5 Defining a global variable in the application.

We use a global variable in this application to demonstrate file scope. Because a global variable has file scope, functions that should not use the variable can read and modify its value, thus violating the principle of least privilege. This can lead to subtle logic errors and makes software difficult to maintain. In general, global variables should be avoided in your applications. If you must use a global variable, declare it as a constant to prevent a function from erroneously modifying its value.

(cont.)

4. ***Defining local variables in main.*** Add lines 15–22 of Fig. 11.6 to main. The grossDonation variable (line 15) stores the donation amount, which is an integer. Lines 18–19 prompt the user for and input the net donation. Line 22 formats floating-point numbers with two positions to the left of the decimal point for output.

Variables, such as grossDonation, that are defined in the body of a function are known as **local variables**. Local variables have **block scope**, which is from the point at which the variable definition appears in the block to the end of that block (denoted with a right brace, }). For example, the scope of grossDonation is from the line of its definition in the function (line 15) to the closing right brace of the function definition (line 27).

Definition of a local variable is the beginning of the variable's scope

Right brace ends the scope of a local variable

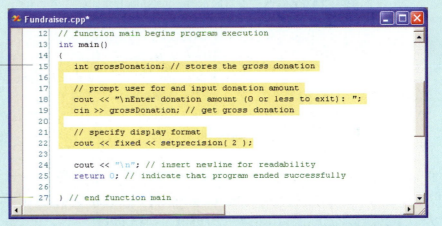

Figure 11.6 Defining a local variable in the **Fundraiser** application.

Local variables cannot be referenced outside the block in which they are defined. If a local variable has the same name as a global variable, the global variable is **hidden** in that block. Any expression containing the variable name will use the local variable's value and not the global variable's value. The global variable's value is not destroyed, though—it can still be accessed outside that block.

Error-Prevention Tip

Hidden variable names can sometimes lead to subtle logic errors. Use unique names for all variables, regardless of scope, to prevent accidental by hiding a global variable.

5. ***Calculating the net donation.*** Add lines 24–29 of Fig. 11.7 to main. The body of the while repetition statement in lines 24–29 repeats until the user enters a sentinel value. The condition of the while statement (line 24) indicates that the loop will terminate when the user enters a donation value that is less than or equal to zero. Later in this tutorial, you will add code to display the net donation and total net donations, then prompt the user for the next donation.

Definition of netDonation is the beginning of the variable's scope

Right brace ends netDonation's scope

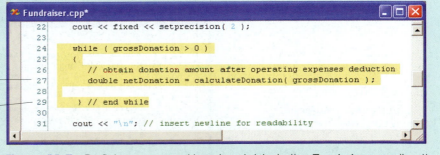

Figure 11.7 Defining a second local variable in the **Fundraiser** application.

(cont.)(

The `netDonation` local variable (line 27) stores the donation amount after the operating expenses have been deducted. Line 27 invokes the `calculateDonation` function with the amount of the donation (`grossDonation`). The result of this function—the net amount that goes to charity after the deduction for operation expenses—is assigned to the `netDonation` variable. The scope of `netDonation` is from the line of its definition in the function (line 27) to the closing right brace of the `while` statement (line 29).

6. ***Save the application.***

11.3 Function Prototypes

One of the most important features of C++ is the function prototype. A **function prototype** tells the compiler the name of a function, the type of data returned by that function, the number of parameters that function expects to receive, the types of those parameters and the order in which the parameters of those types are expected. The compiler uses function prototypes to validate function calls and reports as a syntax error any function call inconsistent with its corresponding function prototype.

The header files we include in C++ programs contain function prototypes (and other information), which enable the compiler to ensure that a program uses functions correctly. In the following box, you will declare a function prototype. As you will see, this will allow you to define a function even after the function is first invoked in your source code file.

Examining Function Prototypes with the Fundraiser Application

1. ***Examining the `calculateDonation` function.*** The template application provides the `calculateDonation` function (lines 36–44 of Fig. 11.8). The function header (line 37) declares a parameter (`donatedAmount`). Function parameters have block scope.

Value of `donatedAmount` implicitly converted to `double`

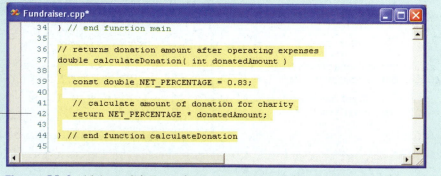

Figure 11.8 Value of `donatedAmount` converted to `double` to perform the calculation.

(cont.)

Line 39 defines the NET_PERCENTAGE constant, which is the net donation percentage (0.83 for 83%). This constant is a local variable and cannot be accessed outside the calculateDonation function. The net donation (the amount that goes to the charity) is calculated by multiplying the NET_PERCENTAGE constant by the donation amount. The result is returned in line 42 to the caller.

The expression in the return statement in line 42 consists of an int value (donatedAmount) multiplied by a double value (NET_PERCENTAGE). Recall that C++ knows how to evaluate only arithmetic expressions in which all of the operands' types are identical. To ensure that the operands are of the same type, C++ implicitly converts the value of donatedAmount (with the int type) to the double type, then the application performs the calculation. The donatedAmount variable is not actually changed; rather, a temporary copy of its value is converted to a double to perform the calculation. In the next section, you will learn the implicit conversion rules among the standard primitive types.

2. ***Inserting a function prototype.*** Notice that the calculateDonation function is defined after main, and that line 27 of main (Fig. 11.7) invokes calculateDonation. To prevent a syntax error from occurring at compile time, insert line 12 of Fig. 11.9.

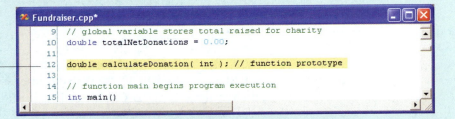

```
 9   // global variable stores total raised for charity
10   double totalNetDonations = 0.00;
11
12   double calculateDonation( int ); // function prototype
13
14   // function main begins program execution
15   int main()
```

Figure 11.9   Declaring a function prototype for the calculateDonation function.

Line 12 is a function prototype. The data type int in parentheses informs the compiler that the calculateDonation function expects an integer value from the caller. Note that prototypes can contain parameter names, but we do not include them in this book. The double data type to the left of the function name calculateDonation informs the compiler that calculateDonation returns a double result to the caller. The compiler refers to the function prototype to check that calls to calculateDonation contain the correct number and types of arguments and that the arguments are in the correct order. In addition, the compiler uses the prototype to ensure that the data type returned by the function can be used correctly in the expression that called the function.

If the arguments passed to a function do not match the types specified in the function's prototype, the compiler attempts to convert the arguments to the types specified in the prototype. Section 7.3 discusses the rules for these conversions. The function prototype is not required if the definition of the function appears before the function's first use in the application. In such a case, the function header also acts as the function prototype.

Note that writing a function prototype is referred to as **declaring a function**, because the function's name, parameters and return type are declared. Writing a function body is called **defining a function**, because the statements in the body of the function define what the function does when called.

3. ***Save the application.***

Error-Prevention Tip

Omitting a function prototype when a function is not defined before it is first invoked is a syntax error.

Error-Prevention Tip

Omitting the semicolon at the end of a function prototype is a syntax error.

The portion of a function prototype that includes the name of the function and the types of its arguments is called the **function signature**, or simply the **signature**. The function signature does not include the function return type. Thus, the signature for the `calculateDonation` function is

```
calculateDonation( int )
```

When compiling a function definition, it is an error if the return type and signature in the function prototype and the function definition disagree. For example, in Fig. 11.9, if the function prototype had been written

```
void calculateDonation( int );
```

the compiler would report an error, because the `void` return type in the function prototype would differ from the `double` return type in the function header.

Another important feature of function prototypes is **argument coercion**— forcing arguments to the appropriate types specified by the parameter declarations. For example, consider a prototype for the square function that you defined in Tutorial 10

```
double square( double );
```

You can call the `square` function with an integer argument even though the function prototype specifies a `double` argument and the function still works correctly. The statement

```
cout << square( 4 );
```

correctly evaluates `square( 4 )` and prints the value 16. The function prototype causes the compiler to convert the integer argument 4 to the `double` value 4.0 before the value is passed to `square`.

In general, copies of argument values that do not correspond precisely to the parameter types in the function prototype are converted to the proper type before the function is called. In the next box, you will display the net donation amount and the total donation amount by applying what you know about the rules the C++ compiler follows when performing such conversions.

Finishing the Fundraiser Application

1. **Displaying the donation amount after the operating expenses are deducted.** Add lines 31–32 of Fig. 11.10 to the `while` statement in `main`. The donation amount after expenses is formatted with two positions to the left of the decimal point (line 22 of Fig. 11.6) and displayed after the descriptive text, **After expenses:**.

Displaying the donation amount after expenses are deducted

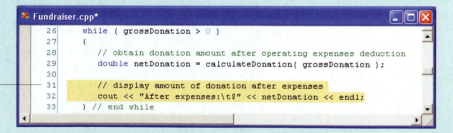

```
Fundraiser.cpp*
26      while ( grossDonation > 0 )
27      {
28          // obtain donation amount after operating expenses deduction
29          double netDonation = calculateDonation( grossDonation );
30
31          // display amount of donation after expenses
32          cout << "After expenses:\t$" << netDonation << endl;
33      } // end while
```

Figure 11.10 Displaying the donation amount after operating expenses are deducted.

2. **Updating and displaying the total donation.** Add lines 34–38 of Fig. 11.11 to the body of the `while` statement. Line 35 updates the global variable `totalNetDonations`. which stores the total amount given to the charity after the operating expenses have been deducted. Line 38 displays the total amount raised for charity.

(cont.)   Local variables, such as `netDonation` (line 27 of Fig. 11.7), are defined in a block and go out of scope at the end of that block. This means that local variables cannot retain their value between function calls or between successive iterations of a repetition statement containing that block. Global variables, however, maintain their value because their scope is from the point at which the definition appears to the end of the file. The `totalNetDonations` variable is a global variable, so it can be used to store the total of the donations over repeated iterations of the `while` statement.

Updating the global variable ——————

Displaying the total amount raised for charity ——————

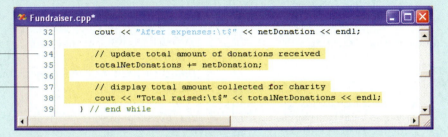

```
Fundraiser.cpp*
32        cout << "After expenses:\t$" << netDonation << endl;
33
34        // update total amount of donations received
35        totalNetDonations += netDonation;
36
37        // display total amount collected for charity
38        cout << "Total raised:\t$" << totalNetDonations << endl;
39     } // end while
```

Figure 11.11   Updating and displaying the total amount raised for charity.

3. ***Prompting the user for and inputting the next donation.*** Add lines 40–42 of Fig. 11.12 to the body of the `while` statement. Lines 41–42 prompt the user for and input the next donation value. After executing line 42, the application evaluates the loop-continuation condition in line 26 to determine whether to continue looping.

Prompting the user for and inputting the next donation ——————

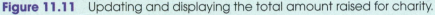

```
Fundraiser.cpp*
38        cout << "Total raised:\t$" << totalNetDonations << endl;
39
40        // prompt user for and input next donation amount
41        cout << "\nEnter donation amount (0 or less to exit): ";
42        cin >> grossDonation; // get gross donation
43     } // end while
44
45     cout << "\n"; // insert newline for readability
```

Figure 11.12   Prompting the user for the next donation.

4. ***Save, compile and run the application.*** Figure 11.13 shows the completed application running. Enter several donation values to the test the application. When done, enter 0 to exit the application.

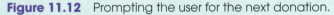

```
"c:\SimplyCpp\Fundraiser\Debug\FundRaiser.exe"

Enter donation amount (0 or less to exit): 10
After expenses: $8.30
Total raised:   $8.30

Enter donation amount (0 or less to exit): _
```

Figure 11.13   Running the completed application.

5. ***Close the Command Prompt window.***

Figure 11.14 presents the source code for the **Fundraiser** application. The lines of code that you added, viewed or modified in this tutorial are highlighted.

Define a global variable

Declare a function prototype

Definition of a local variable is the beginning of the variable's scope

Definition of `netDonation` is the beginning of the variable's scope

Display the donation amount after expenses are deducted

Update global variable

Right brace ends `netDonation`'s scope

Right brace ends the scope of the local variables

Value of `donatedAmount` implicitly converted to `double`

```cpp
1   // Tutorial 11: Fundraiser.cpp
2   // Calculates the amount of a donation after expenses and then
3   // totals repeated donations.
4   #include <iostream> // required to perform C++ stream I/O
5   #include <iomanip>  // required for parameterized stream manipulators
6
7   using namespace std; // for accessing C++ Standard Library members
8
9   // global variable stores total raised for charity
10  double totalNetDonations = 0.00;
11
12  double calculateDonation( int ); // function prototype
13
14  // function main begins program execution
15  int main()
16  {
17      int grossDonation; // stores the gross donation
18
19      // prompt user for and input donation amount
20      cout << "\nEnter donation amount (0 or less to exit): ";
21      cin >> grossDonation; // get gross donation
22
23      // specify display format
24      cout << fixed << setprecision( 2 );
25
26      while ( grossDonation > 0 )
27      {
28          // obtain donation amount after operating expenses deduction
29          double netDonation = calculateDonation( grossDonation );
30
31          // display amount of donation after expenses
32          cout << "After expenses:\t$" << netDonation << endl;
33
34          // update total amount of donations received
35          totalNetDonations += netDonation;
36
37          // display total amount collected for charity
38          cout << "Total raised:\t$" << totalNetDonations << endl;
39
40          // prompt user for and input next donation amount
41          cout << "\nEnter donation amount (0 or less to exit): ";
42          cin >> grossDonation; // get gross donation
43      } // end while
44
45      cout << "\n"; // insert newline for readability
46      return 0; // indicate that program ended successfully
47
48  } // end function main
49
50  // returns donation amount after operating expenses
51  double calculateDonation( int donatedAmount )
52  {
53      const double NET_PERCENTAGE = 0.83;
54
55      // calculate amount of donation for charity
56      return NET_PERCENTAGE * donatedAmount;
57
58  } // end function calculateDonation
```

Figure 11.14 **Fundraiser** application code.

You have learned the rules governing when a variable is in or out of scope. You will now learn what happens when you try to access a local variable that is not in scope.

Accessing a Variable That Is Out of Scope

1. **Attempting to access a local variable that is out of scope.** Now you will learn the limits of local variables. In line 56 of Fig. 11.15, temporarily replace `donatedAmount` in the multiplication operation with `grossDonation`. Variable `grossDonation` is a local variable defined in line 17 of Fig. 11.14 in `main`. This variable is only in scope within `main`. Attempting to access it inside the `calculateDonation` function (line 55 of Fig. 11.15) causes a compilation error.

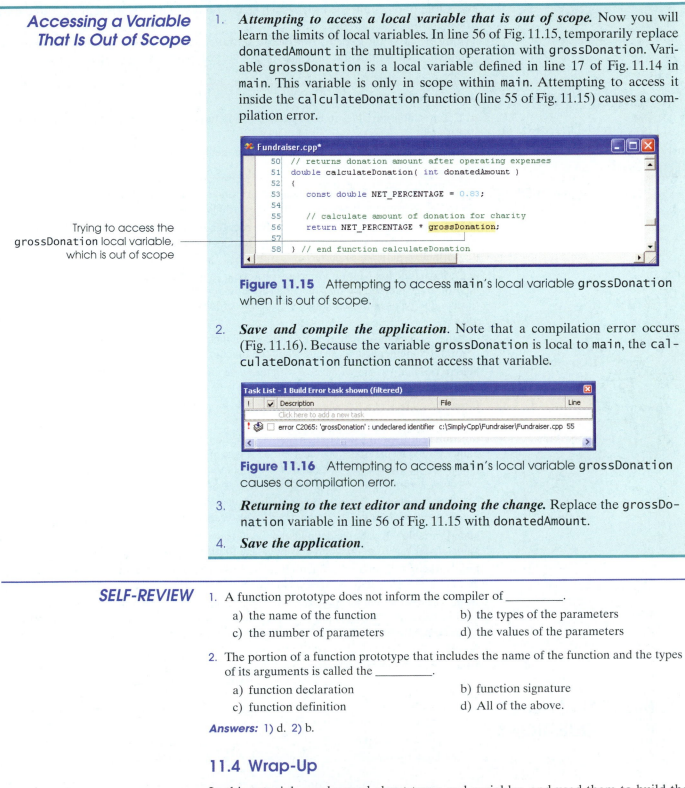

Trying to access the
`grossDonation` local variable,
which is out of scope

Figure 11.15 Attempting to access `main`'s local variable `grossDonation` when it is out of scope.

2. **Save and compile the application.** Note that a compilation error occurs (Fig. 11.16). Because the variable `grossDonation` is local to `main`, the `calculateDonation` function cannot access that variable.

Figure 11.16 Attempting to access `main`'s local variable `grossDonation` causes a compilation error.

3. **Returning to the text editor and undoing the change.** Replace the `grossDonation` variable in line 56 of Fig. 11.15 with `donatedAmount`.

4. **Save the application.**

SELF-REVIEW

1. A function prototype does not inform the compiler of _____.
   a) the name of the function   b) the types of the parameters
   c) the number of parameters   d) the values of the parameters

2. The portion of a function prototype that includes the name of the function and the types of its arguments is called the _____.
   a) function declaration   b) function signature
   c) function definition   d) All of the above.

Answers: 1) d. 2) b.

11.4 Wrap-Up

In this tutorial, you learned about types and variables, and used them to build the **Fundraiser** application. You learned that the scope of a global variable in a file is from the point at which the definition appears to the end of the file. When a global variable is placed at the beginning of a file, it is accessible to all functions in the file in which it is defined. You defined a global variable in the `Fundraiser.cpp` file. You learned that the scope of a local variable is from the point at which the definition appears to the end of the block containing the definition. Local variables are accessible only within the block (such as the body of an `if` statement or a function) in which they are defined.

In the next tutorial, you will learn about random number generation, and you will create an application that simulates the dice game called Craps.

SKILLS SUMMARY

Understanding Scope

- Create global variables to be accessible to any functions in the same file defined after the variable.
- Create local variables to be accessed only in the block in which they are defined.

KEY TERMS

argument coercion—A feature of function prototypes that forces the arguments in a function call to the appropriate types specified by the parameter declarations.

block scope—The scope for a local variable or a function parameter. Block scope is from the variable's definition (or declaration) to the terminating right brace (}) of the block in which the variable is defined (or declared).

declaring a function—Using a function prototype to tell the compiler name of a function, the type of data returned by that function, the number of parameters that function expects to receive, the types of those parameters and the order in which the parameters of those types are expected.

defining a function—Creating a function, which includes a function header followed by a left brace, the statements that execute when the function is called and a right brace.

hidden variable—A global variable with the same name as a local variable is hidden while the local variable is in scope. Hidden variables can lead to logic errors.

file scope—The scope for a global variable. File scope is from the variable's definition to the end of the file.

function prototype—A declaration that tells the compiler the name of a function, the type of data returned by that function, the number of parameters that function expects to receive, the types of those parameters and the order in which the parameters of those types are expected. The compiler uses function prototypes to validate function calls.

function signature—The portion of a function prototype that includes the name of the function and the types of its arguments. It is also called the signature.

global variable—A variable defined in a file outside any functions in that file. The scope of a global variable is from the point at which its definition appears to the end of file.

local variable—A variable defined inside a block. The scope of a local variable is from the point at which the definition appears in the block to the end of that block.

scope—The portion of an application in which an identifier (such as a variable name) can be referenced. Some identifiers can be referenced throughout an application, while others can be referenced only from limited portions of an application (such as within a single function or block).

signature—See function signature.

MULTIPLE-CHOICE QUESTIONS

11.1 A global variable with the same name as a local variable is known as a(n) _____ while the local variable has scope.

a) constant variable
b) implicit variable
c) hidden variable
d) file variable

11.2 A _____ has block scope.

a) function parameter
b) global variable
c) local variable
d) Both a and c.

11.3 A variable defined inside a file, but outside a function, is called a(n) _____.

a) local variable   b) hidden variable

c) global variable   d) constant variable

11.4 _____ happens when a function argument is promoted to the type of the function's corresponding parameter.

a) Argument coercion   b) Explicit conversion

c) Assignment   d) None of the above.

11.5 Accessing a local variable outside the block in which the local variable is defined causes a _____.

a) logic error   b) compile-time error

c) runtime error   d) None of the above.

11.6 A function signature does not include _____.

a) the number of parameters   b) the parameter type(s)

c) the function name   d) the return type

11.7 A function prototype must _____.

a) name its parameters   b) end with a semicolon

c) define the body of the function   d) appear before `main`

11.8 Global variables _____.

a) are defined inside a file   b) are defined outside a function

c) cannot be accessed by any function in the same file

d) Both a and b.

11.9 Writing the body of a function is called _____.

a) declaring the function   b) creating the function signature

c) defining the function   d) prototyping the function

11.10 A local variable's scope ends _____.

a) at the end of the file that contains it   b) at the end of the function that contains it

c) at the beginning of the next function.   d) None of the above.

EXERCISES

11.11 (*Sphere Volume Application*) Create an application that calculates the volume of a sphere according to the radius that the user enters (Fig. 11.17). The formula for determining the volume, V, of a sphere with a radius, r, is

$$V = \frac{4}{3}\pi r^3$$

The application should use a global constant variable to store the value of π, which is approximately 3.14159. Your application's `main` function should calculate the volume using a function named `sphereVolume`, which accepts a single integer parameter and returns a `double`. Declare a function prototype before `main` so that you can define the `sphereVolume` function after it is first called.

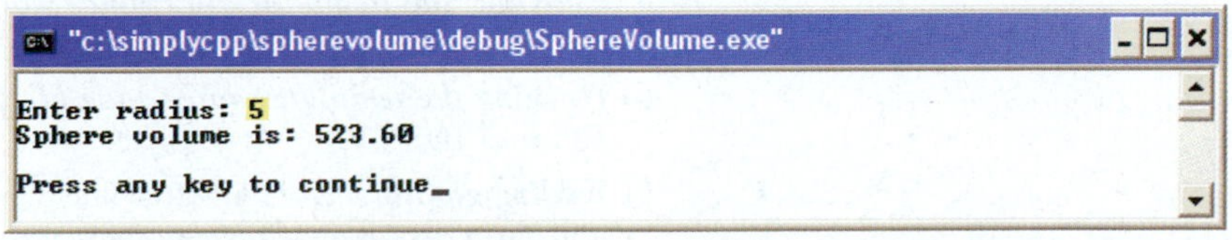

Figure 11.17 Sphere Volume application output.

a) *Copying the template to your working directory.* Copy the C:\Examples\Tutorial11\Exercises\SphereVolume directory to your C:\SimplyCpp directory.

b) *Opening the template source code file.* Open the SphereVolume.cpp file in your text editor or IDE.

c) *Defining a global variable.* Insert a blank line after line 8. In line 10, define the PI global constant variable of the double type and initialize its value to 3.14159.

d) *Declaring a function prototype.* Insert a blank line after line 10. In line 12, declare a function prototype for the sphereVolume function in line 12. The function should return a double and accept a single double parameter.

e) *Adding code to the main function.* In main, define int variable radius. Then use cout and cin to prompt the user for and input the sphere's radius into the radius variable. After inputting the radius, use the fixed and setprecision stream manipulators to format cout's output so that floating-point values are displayed with two digits of precision to the right of the decimal point. Finally, use the sphereVolume function to calculate the sphere's volume and display the result.

f) *Coding the sphereVolume function.* After main, define the sphereVolume function. The function should declare double parameter sphereRadius. Use the pow function to calculate the cube of the radius and use the constant you defined in *Step c* to approximate the value of π.

g) *Save, compile and run the completed application.* Test the application to ensure that it runs correctly by inputting several different integer radii.

h) *Close the Command Prompt window.*

11.12 (*Quiz Average Application*) Develop an application that computes a student's average quiz score for all quiz scores entered. The application's output should appear as in Fig. 11.18. Place the user input in an int and assign that value to a double. [*Note:* Implicit conversion occurs when you assign an int value to a double.] Use global variables to keep track of the sum of all the quiz scores entered and the number of quiz scores entered. Each time a score is submitted, your application should recalculate the average.

```
"c:\simplycpp\quizaverage\debug\QuizAverage.exe"

Enter score (-1 to exit): 97
Number taken: 1
Average score: 97.00

Enter score (-1 to exit): 86
Number taken: 2
Average score: 91.50

Enter score (-1 to exit): 91
Number taken: 3
Average score: 91.33

Enter score (-1 to exit): 74
Number taken: 4
Average score: 87.00

Enter score (-1 to exit): 88
Number taken: 5
Average score: 87.20

Enter score (-1 to exit): 90
Number taken: 6
Average score: 87.67

Enter score (-1 to exit): -1

Press any key to continue_
```

Figure 11.18 Quiz Average application output.

a) *Copying the template to your working directory.* Copy the C:\Examples\ Tutorial11\Exercises\QuizAverage directory to your C:\SimplyCpp directory.

b) *Opening the template source code file.* Open the QuizAverage.cpp file in your text editor or IDE.

c) *Adding global variables.* After line 8, add two global variables. The int global variable quizzesTaken will keep track of the number of quiz scores entered. The double global variable totalScore will keep track of the sum of all the quiz scores entered. These two variables will be used to calculate the class average. Add a comment before you define the global variables.

d) *Adding code to the main function.* The code required in *Steps e–m* should be placed in main, which should begin in line 14.

e) ***Defining variables to store user input.*** Define `int` variable `input` to store the grade that the user enters at the keyboard. Then define `double` variable `score` that will be used to implicitly convert the value of `input` to a `double`.

f) ***Obtaining user input.*** Use `cout` and `cin` to the prompt the user for and input the quiz score into `int` variable `input`. Indicate that the user should enter the value `-1` to end input.

g) ***Defining a while repetition statement and converting the grade to a double.*** Add a `while` repetition statement that repeats while the value that the user enters at the keyboard is greater than or equal to zero. In the body of the `while` statement, assign the value of `input` to `score` to implicitly convert the value to a `double`.

h) ***Updating the number of quiz scores entered.*** Add code to the body of the `while` statement to increment the number of quiz scores entered.

i) ***Updating the sum of all the quiz scores entered.*** Add code to the body of the `while` statement that will add the current quiz score to the current total of all the quiz scores entered.

j) ***Calculating the average score.*** Add code to the body of the `while` statement to divide the sum of all the quiz scores by the number of quiz scores entered to calculate the average score. Notice that the number of quiz scores is an `int`, but will be implicitly converted to a `double` for the division calculation.

k) ***Displaying the number of quizzes taken.*** Display the number of quizzes taken.

l) ***Displaying the average score.*** Display the average quiz grade with two digits of precision.

m) ***Prompting the user for the next score.*** Before the closing brace of the `while` statement, prompt the user for and input the next quiz grade.

n) ***Save, compile and run the application.*** Test the application to ensure that it runs correctly by submitting a number of quiz scores. Check that the average is calculated.

o) ***Close the Command Prompt window.***

11.13 (*Parking Garage Application*) A parking garage charges a $2.00 minimum fee to park for up to three hours. The garage charges an additional $0.50 per hour for each hour *or part thereof* in excess of three hours. The maximum charge for any given 24-hour period is $10.00. Assume that no car parks for longer than 24 hours at a time. Create an application that calculates and displays the parking charges for each of three customers who parked their cars in this garage yesterday. The user should enter the hours parked for each customer. Your application should display the charge for each car that is entered. After the user signals the end of the input by entering the sentinel value, 0, the application should display the total hours and charges for the session (Fig. 11.19). The application should use the `calculate-Charges` function to determine the charge for each customer.

```
 "c:\simplycpp\parkinggarage\debug\ParkingGarage.exe"                    _ □ ×

Enter the hours parked for a car (0 to end): 2.3
Charge: $2.00

Enter the hours parked for a car (0 to end): 5.75
Charge: $3.50

Enter the hours parked for a car (0 to end): 24
Charge: $10.00

Enter the hours parked for a car (0 to end): 0

Total hours:    32.0
Total charges:  $15.50

Press any key to continue_
```

Figure 11.19 Parking Garage application output.

a) ***Copying the template to your working directory.*** Copy the `C:\Examples\Tutorial11\Exercises\ParkingGarage` directory to your `C:\SimplyCpp` directory.

b) ***Opening the template source code file.*** Open the `ParkingGarage.cpp` file in your text editor or IDE. Note that the functionality for `main` is included in the template source code file.

c) ***Adding a function prototype.*** Before `main`, declare the `calculateCharges` function, which should return a `double` and accept a single `double` argument.

d) ***Calling the `calculateCharges` function.*** Modify the statement in line 31 to call the `calculateCharges` function with the `hour` argument. Assign the result to the `charge` variable.

e) ***Coding the `calculateCharges` function.*** After `main`, define the `calculateCharges` function, which returns a `double` and accepts `double` parameter `hours`. In the body of the `calculateCharges` function, return the value 2 if `hours` is less than 3. Note that the application will implicitly convert these `int` values to `double`s when evaluating the `if` condition and when executing the `return` statement. Insert an `else if` statement that executes if `hours` is greater than 3 and less than 19. Recall that the charge for this range of hours is $2 plus $0.50 per hour for each hour or part thereof in excess of three hours. Thus, when `hours` is 19, the charge is $2 (for the first three hours) plus $0.50 per hour for 16 hours, which is $8, for a total of $10. Because the maximum charged for any 24-hour period is $10, the function should not calculate the total using $0.50 per hour if `hours` is greater than or equal to 19. In the body of the `else if` part, use the `<cmath>` standard library function `ceil` (short for "ceiling") to calculate the charge. The `ceil` function rounds its argument to the smallest integer not less than its argument. For example, `ceil( 6.2 )` is 7. Finally, add an `else` part to your nested `if...else` statement that returns the value 10 if the car has been parked between 19 and 24 hours.

f) ***Save, compile and run the application.*** Test your application to ensure that it runs correctly by entering several different values for hours parked. Check that the proper charge is calculated and that the application displays the total hours and total charges at the end of input.

g) ***Close the Command Prompt window.***

What does this code do? ▶ **11.14** What message is displayed when the following code is executed?

```
1   // Exercise 11.14: WDTCD.cpp
2   // What message is displayed when the following code executes?
3   #include <iostream> // required to perform C++ stream I/O
4
5   using namespace std; // for accessing C++ Standard Library members
6
7   // Global Variable
8   int intValue2 = 5;
9
10  // function mystery
11  int mystery( int );
12
13  // function main begins program execution
14  int main( )
15  {
16     int intValue1 = 10;
17     int intValue2 = 3;
18     int result = mystery( intValue1 );
19
20     // display output
21     cout << "\nMystery message: " << result << endl << endl;
22
23     return 0; // indicate that the program ended correctly
24
25  } // end function main
26
27  int mystery( int inputValue )
28  {
29     return inputValue * intValue2;
30
31  } // end function mystery
```

What's wrong with this code? ▶   **11.15** Find the error(s) in the following code (the function should assign the value 14 to the result variable).

```
1   // Exercise 11.15: WWWTC.cpp
2   // This function assigns 14 to variable result
3   #include <iostream> // required to perform C++ stream I/O
4   #include <string>   // required to create and manipulate strings
5
6   using namespace std; // for accessing C++ Standard Library members
7
8   // function sum prototype
9   void sum();
10
11  // function main begins program execution
12  int main()
13  {
14     sum();
15
16     return 0; // indicate that the program ended correctly
17
18  } // end main
19
20  void sum()
21  {
22     // define variables
23     string number4 = "4";
24     int number10 = 10;
25
26     int result = number4 + number10;
27
28     // display result
29     cout << "\n" << result << endl << endl;
30
31  } // end function sum
```

Programming Challenge ▶   **11.16** (*Decryption Application*) An organization wants to use encryption to protect classified information from eavesdroppers. The organization has developed an algorithm that encodes a string of characters into a series of integers between 0 and 94, inclusive. You have been asked to develop an application that decrypts this series of integers into its corresponding string of characters. The user should enter each integer of the encrypted message one at a time. After each integer is entered, the application should convert (that is, decrypt) the integer to its corresponding character, after which the application should display the string of characters that have already been decrypted. If the user enters a value that is less than zero or greater than 94, the application should terminate input. When the user enters the numbers 39, 79, 79, 68, 0, 55, 79, 82, 75, 1 in order, your application should appear as in Fig. 11.20.

    a) *Copying the template to your working directory.* Copy the C:\Examples\Tutorial11\Exercises\Decryption directory to your C:\SimplyCpp directory.

    b) *Opening the template file.* Open the Decryption.cpp file in your text editor or IDE.

    c) *Adding a global variable.* Before main, add a definition for a string named message, which will hold the decrypted message. Initialize message to the empty string. Use one line for a comment.

    d) *Declaring a function prototype.* After the variable you defined in *Step c*, declare a function prototype for the decryptLetter function, which accepts an int parameter and does not return a value.

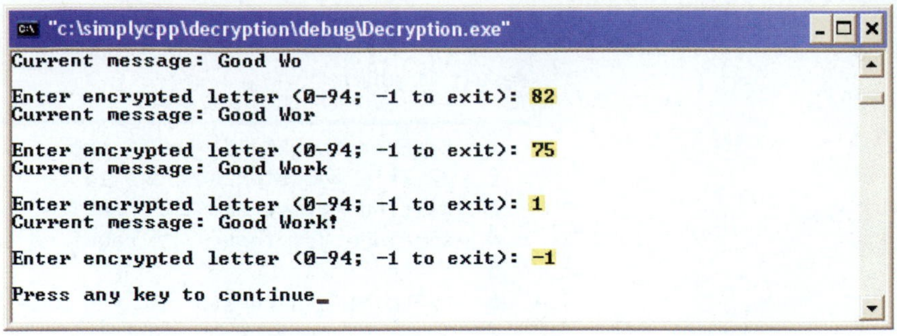

Figure 11.20 **Decryption** application displays a message (only the last four inputs are displayed).

e) *Defining a local variable, prompting the user for and storing the encrypted letter.* Add code in `main` to define `int` variable named `input`, then prompt the user for and store the encrypted letter in that variable.

f) *Testing the user input.* Insert a `while` repetition statement that executes while the user input is in the range 0 to 94. This ensures that input terminates when the user enters a sentinel value.

g) *Decrypting the input.* Inside the `while` statement, call the `decryptLetter` function with `input` as its argument. This function, which you will define in *Step i*, will decrypt the letter and append the character to `string message`.

h) *Displaying output and prompting the user for the next input.* Inside the `while` statement, add code to display the `string message`. Before the closing brace of the `while` statement, add code to prompt the user for and store the next encrypted letter.

i) *Decrypting the input.* After `main`, define the `decryptLetter` function, which accepts `int` parameter `encryptedLetter`. Letters should be decrypted by first adding 32 to the `int`. This value should then be converted to a `char` type. [*Note:* You can implicitly convert an `int` to a `char` by assigning the value of an `int` to a `char` variable.] This calculation results in the number 1 decrypting to the character `'!'` and the number 33 decrypting to the character `'A'`. To append the decrypted character to `message`, use the `+=` operator. For example, `message += 'A'` appends the character `'A'` to the end of `message`.

j) *Save, compile and run the application.* Test your application to ensure that it runs correctly by entering the number 39. The letter `'G'` should be displayed. Now, input the following numbers 79, 79, 68, 0, 55, 79, 82, 75, 1. If your application has been programmed correctly, the application should now display the message Good Work!.

k) *Close the Command Prompt window.*

Craps Game Application

Introducing Random Number Generation and Enumerations

Objectives

In this tutorial, you will learn to:
- Use simulation techniques that employ random-number generation.
- Use the **rand** math library function to generate random numbers.
- Use enumerations to enhance code readability.

Outline

You will now study a popular type of application involving simulation and game playing. In this tutorial, you will develop a **Craps Game** application. There is something in the air of a gambling casino that invigorates people—from the high rollers at the plush mahogany-and-felt Craps tables to the quarter-poppers at the one-armed bandits. It is the element of chance—the possibility that luck will convert a pocketful of money into a mountain of wealth. Unfortunately, that rarely happens because the odds, of course, favor the casinos.

The element of chance can be introduced into computer applications using random numbers. This tutorial's **Craps Game** application introduces random-number generation and the **enum** keyword. It also uses important concepts that you learned earlier in this book, including functions, function prototypes and the switch multiple-selection statement.

12.1 Test-Driving the Craps Game Application

One of the most popular games of chance is a dice game known as "Craps," played in casinos throughout the world. In this tutorial, you will create an application that simulates this popular casino game. This application must meet the following requirements:

Application Requirements

Create an application that simulates playing a simplified version of the dice game "Craps." In this game, a player rolls two dice. Each die has six faces. Each face contains 1, 2, 3, 4, 5 or 6 spots. After the dice have come to rest, the sum of the spots on the two top faces is calculated. If the sum is 7 or 11 on the first throw the player wins. If the sum is 2, 3 or 12 on the first throw (called "craps"), the player loses (the "house" wins). If the sum is 4, 5, 6, 8, 9 or 10 on the first throw, that sum becomes the player's "point." To win, a player must continue rolling the dice until the player rolls the point value. The player loses by rolling a 7 before rolling the point.

You begin by test-driving the completed application. Then, you will learn the additional C++ capabilities you will need to create your own version of this application.

Test-Driving the Craps Game Application

1. *Locating the completed application.* Open the **Command Prompt** window by selecting **Start > All Programs > Accessories > Command Prompt**. Change to your completed **Craps Game** application directory by typing cd C:\Examples\Tutorial12\CompletedApplication\CrapsGame.

2. *Running the Craps Game application.* Type CrapsGame in the **Command Prompt** window to run the application (Fig. 12.1). The application displays the result of the first roll of the dice.

```
cx  Command Prompt - CrapsGame                              - □ ×
C:\>cd C:\Examples\Tutorial12\CompletedApplication\CrapsGame
C:\Examples\Tutorial12\CompletedApplication\CrapsGame>CrapsGame
Player rolled 2 + 3 = 5
Point is 5
Press Enter to continue..._
```

Figure 12.1 Example of an initial appearance of **Craps Game** application.

3. *Continuing the game.* There are three possible outcomes at this point. The player wins by rolling a 7 or an 11 (Fig. 12.2). The player loses by rolling a 2, 3 or 12 (Fig. 12.3). Otherwise, the roll becomes the player's point (4, 5, 6, 8, 9 or 10) for the rest of the game (Fig. 12.4).

```
cx  Command Prompt                                          - □ ×
C:\>cd C:\Examples\Tutorial12\CompletedApplication\CrapsGame
C:\Examples\Tutorial12\CompletedApplication\CrapsGame>CrapsGame
Player rolled 6 + 5 = 11
Player wins

C:\Examples\Tutorial12\CompletedApplication\CrapsGame>_
```

Figure 12.2 Player winning on the first roll by rolling an 11.

```
cx  Command Prompt                                          - □ ×
C:\Examples\Tutorial12\CompletedApplication\CrapsGame>CrapsGame
Player rolled 2 + 1 = 3
Player loses

C:\Examples\Tutorial12\CompletedApplication\CrapsGame>_
```

Figure 12.3 Player losing on the first roll by rolling a 3.

```
cx  Command Prompt - CrapsGame                              - □ ×
C:\Examples\Tutorial12\CompletedApplication\CrapsGame>CrapsGame
Player rolled 4 + 2 = 6
Point is 6
Press Enter to continue...
```

Figure 12.4 Player's first roll setting the point value that the player must match to win (before rolling a 7).

(cont.)

4. ***Continuing the game.*** If the player does not win or lose on the first roll, the application displays **Press enter to continue...**, as in Fig. 12.4. Press *Enter* repeatedly until either you win by matching your point value (Fig. 12.5) or you lose by rolling a 7 (Fig. 12.6).

```
Command Prompt                                              _ □ ×

Press Enter to continue...

Player rolled 4 + 2 = 6
Player wins

C:\Examples\Tutorial12\CompletedApplication\CrapsGame>_
```

Figure 12.5   Player winning the game by matching the point value before rolling a 7.

```
Command Prompt                                              _ □ ×

Press Enter to continue...

Player rolled 6 + 1 = 7
Player loses

C:\Examples\Tutorial12\CompletedApplication\CrapsGame>_
```

Figure 12.6   Player losing by rolling a 7 before matching the point value.

5. ***Close the Command Prompt window.***

12.2 Random Number Generation

Now you will learn how to use the rand standard library function (defined in the <cstdlib> header file) to introduce the element of chance into your applications. The **<cstdlib> standard library header file** contains function prototypes for the conversion of numbers to text and text to numbers, the generation of random numbers and other utility functions. Consider the following statement:

```
int randomNumber = rand();
```

The **rand function** generates an unsigned integer between 0 and **RAND_MAX** (a symbolic constant defined in the <cstdlib> header file). The value of RAND_MAX must be at least 32,767—the maximum positive value for a two-byte (16-bit) signed integer. If rand truly produces integers at random, every number between 0 and RAND_MAX has an equal chance (or probability) of being chosen each time rand is called.

The range of values produced by rand often is different from the range needed in a particular application. For example, an application that simulates coin tossing requires only the random integers 0 for "heads" and 1 for "tails." An application that simulates the rolling of a six-sided die requires only the random integers from 1 to 6. Similarly, an application that randomly predicts the next type of spaceship (out of four possibilities) that flies across the horizon in a video game requires only the random integers from 1 to 4.

By using the modulus operator on the result of the rand function as follows

```
value = 1 + rand() % 6;
```

you can produce random integers in the range from 1 to 6. This new range corresponds nicely with the roll of a six-sided die, for example. Figure 12.7 shows examples of the ranges of random numbers returned by expressions containing calls to the rand function.

It is important to note that, by default, an application that uses the rand function will produce exactly the same sequence of values each time the application

Expression	Resulting range
rand()	0 to RAND_MAX [0 to at least 32,767]
rand() % 30	0 to 29
10 + rand() % 10	10 to 19

Figure 12.7 rand function call expressions with ranges of random numbers produced.

runs. How can these be random numbers? Ironically, this repeatability is an important characteristic of the rand function. When debugging a simulation program, this repeatability is essential for proving that corrections to the program work properly.

If the rand function is to produce truly random values, then every unsigned int value must have an equal chance (or probability) of being chosen when rand is called. The rand function comes close to achieving this goal. Calling the rand function repeatedly actually generates **pseudorandom numbers**—a sequence of numbers that appears to be random. However, the sequence repeats itself each time the application executes. Once an application has been thoroughly debugged, it can be modified to produce a different sequence of random numbers for each execution. This is called **randomizing** and is accomplished with the srand standard library function. The **srand function** takes an unsigned integer argument and **seeds** the rand function, an operation that causes the function to produce a different sequence of random numbers each time the application executes.

If we wish to randomize without the need for entering a seed each time, we may use a statement like

```
srand( time( 0 ) );
```

This causes the computer to read its clock to obtain the value for the seed. The **time** function, when called with the argument 0 (as written in the preceding statement), returns the current "calendar time" in seconds. "Calendar time" is determined by calculating the number of seconds that have passed since midnight on January 1, 1970 (using UTC—Universal Time, also called Greenwich Mean Time). The value returned by time is converted to an unsigned integer and used as the seed to the random number generator. Because the computer's clock will almost always contain a different value each time the user runs the application, the rand function's seed, and thus the series of numbers that the rand function generates, will be different. The function prototype for time is in the **<ctime> Standard Library header file**, which provides access to data types and functions for storing and manipulating the time and date.

SELF-REVIEW

1. The statement _____ returns an integer in the range 8–300.
   a) 7 + rand() % 293;   b) 8 + rand() % 292;
   c) 8 + rand() % 293;   d) None of the above.

2. The statement _____ returns an integer in the range 15–35.
   a) 10 + rand() % 26;   b) 15 + rand() % 21;
   c) 10 + rand() % 25;   d) 15 + rand() % 35;

Answers: 1) c. 2) b.

12.3 Using an enum in the Craps Game Application

The pseudocode in Fig. 12.8 describes the basic operation of the **Craps Game** application.

Roll the two dice using random numbers
Calculate and display the sum of the two dice

Switch based on the sum of the two dice:

    Case where the sum is 7 or 11
        Display the winning message

    Case where the sum is 2, 3 or 12
        Display the losing message

    Default case
        Set the value of the point to the sum of the dice and display the value

While the player has not won or lost
    Roll the two dice using random numbers
    Calculate and display the sum of the two dice

    If the player rolled the point
        Display the winning message

    If the player rolls a 7
        Display the losing message

Figure 12.8 Pseudocode for the **Craps Game** application.

Now that you have test-driven the **Craps Game** application and studied its pseudocode representation, you will use code to generate random numbers for the **Craps Game** application.

Including the `<cstdlib>` and `<ctime>` Standard Library Header Files

1. ***Copying the template to your working directory.*** Copy the `C:\Examples\Tutorial12\TemplateApplication\CrapsGame` directory to your `C:\SimplyCpp` directory.

2. ***Opening the Craps Game application's template source code file.*** Open the template file `CrapsGame.cpp` in your text editor or IDE.

3. ***Including the `<cstdlib>` and `<ctime>` header files.*** Add lines 5–8 of Fig. 12.9 into your code. Line 5 includes the `<ctime>` Standard Library, which allows your application to access the `time` function. You will use this function to seed the `rand` function. Line 8 includes the `<cstdlib>` Standard Library, which allows your application to use the `rand` and `srand` functions to generate random numbers.

Including the `<ctime>` standard library header file
Including the `<cstdlib>` standard library header file

```
 4    #include <string>    // required to access string functions
 5    #include <ctime>     // contains prototype for function time
 6
 7    // contains function prototypes for srand and rand
 8    #include <cstdlib>
 9
10    using namespace std; // for accessing C++ standard library members
```

Figure 12.9 Including the `<cstdlib>` and `<ctime>` Standard Library header files so that the application can produce random numbers.

4. ***Save the application***.

Notice that the numbers 2, 3, 7, 11 and 12 have special meanings during a game of Craps. It would be helpful to create these constants and assign them meaningful names for use in your application. As you learned in Tutorial 4, C++ allows you to create a constant with the `const` keyword. You will now create constants whose identifiers describe significant dice combinations in Craps (SNAKE_EYES, TREY, CRAPS, LUCKY_SEVEN, YO_LEVEN and BOX_CARS). You will use these constants to enhance the readability of your code and ensure that numbers are consistent throughout your application.

Declaring a Function Prototype and Defining Constants

1. **Declaring a function prototype.** Because each execution of the application may require several rolls of the dice, you will define a function named `roll-Dice` that generates random numbers to simulate rolling two dice. Add line 12 of Fig. 12.10 to your application. This function returns an `int` containing the sum of the two dice and does not take any arguments (which is indicated by declaring the argument type `void`).

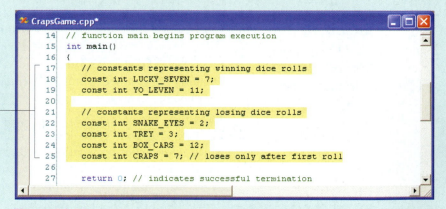

Declaring the `rollDice` function prototype

```
10  using namespace std; // for accessing C++ standard library members
11
12  int rollDice( void ); // function prototype
13
14  // function main begins program execution
15  int main()
```

Figure 12.10   Declaring the `rollDice` function prototype.

2. **Defining constants.** Add lines 17–25 of Fig. 12.11 to your application. Recall that constant definitions contain the `const` keyword before the type of the variable. Notice that you can assign the same value to multiple constants, as in lines 18 and 25—in this case, because 7 has a different meaning on the first roll than on subsequent rolls.

Defining constants

```
14  // function main begins program execution
15  int main()
16  {
17     // constants representing winning dice rolls
18     const int LUCKY_SEVEN = 7;
19     const int YO_LEVEN = 11;
20
21     // constants representing losing dice rolls
22     const int SNAKE_EYES = 2;
23     const int TREY = 3;
24     const int BOX_CARS = 12;
25     const int CRAPS = 7; // loses only after first roll
26
27     return 0; // indicates successful termination
```

Figure 12.11   Defining constants in the **Craps Game** application.

3. **Defining variables.** Add lines 27–29 of Fig. 12.12 below the constant definitions to define three variables. The game of Craps requires that you store the user's point, once established on the first roll, for the duration of the game. Therefore, the `myPoint` variable (line 28) is defined as an `int` to store the sum of the dice on the first roll. Line 27 defines `int` variable `sum` to store the sum of the dice after each subsequent roll. Recall from the application's test drive that the user is prompted to press *Enter* after each roll of the dice. Because you will use `cin` to cause the application to wait for the user to press *Enter*, you must define a variable to store any text extracted from the input stream. Line 29 defines `string` variable `input` to contain any input that is removed from the input stream when the user presses *Enter*.

4. **Save the application**.

(cont.)

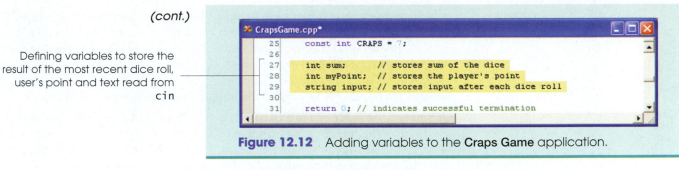

Figure 12.12 Adding variables to the **Craps Game** application.

Defining variables to store the result of the most recent dice roll, user's point and text read from `cin`

In the **Craps Game** application, there are three outcomes to each roll of the dice: win, lose and continue. When determining the course of action to take, a simple `bool` variable, which can be one of only two values (`true` or `false`), is insufficient. In this case, it would be helpful to create a group of related constants and assign them meaningful names for use in your application. C++ allows you to accomplish this by using an **enumeration**. In the following box, you will learn how to create an enumeration that will consist of constant identifiers that describe each result of rolling the dice (CONTINUE, WON, LOST). By providing descriptive identifiers for a group of related constants, enumerations enhance program readability and ensure that numbers are consistent throughout the application.

Good Programming Practice

Use enumerations to group related constants and enhance code readability.

Adding an Enumeration

1. **Declaring an enumeration.** Add lines 27–28 of Fig. 12.13. Line 28 declares an enumeration. An enumeration, introduced by the **enum keyword** and followed by a **type name** (in this case, `Status`), is a set of integer constants represented by identifiers. The values of these **enumeration constants** start at 0, unless specified otherwise, and increment by 1. In this enumeration, the CONTINUE constant has the value 0, WON has the value 1 and LOST has the value 2. The identifiers in an `enum` must be unique, but separate enumeration constants can have the same integer value.

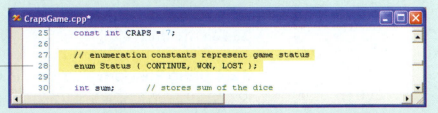

Figure 12.13 Using the `enum` keyword to declare an enumeration.

Declaring an enumeration

Common Programming Error

After an enumeration constant has been defined, attempting to assign another value to it is a syntax error.

Good Programming Practice

Capitalize the first letter of an identifier used as a user-defined type name.

An enumeration creates a **user-defined type** (also called a **programmer-defined type**) that can be used to store only values that you specify. You have used many of C++'s built-in data types, such as `bool`, `int` and `char`, each of which can be assigned a limited range of values. For example, the `bool` type can be assigned only the values `true` or `false`. Similarly, variables of the user-defined `Status` type can be assigned only one of the three values declared in the enumeration.

Another popular enumeration is

```
enum Months { JAN = 1, FEB, MAR, APR, MAY, JUN, JUL, AUG,
    SEP, OCT, NOV, DEC };
```

(cont.)

which creates user-defined type `Months` with enumeration constants representing the months of the year. The first value in the preceding enumeration is explicitly set to 1, and the remaining values increment from 1, resulting in the values 1 through 12. Any enumeration constant can be assigned an integer value in the enumeration definition, and subsequent enumeration constants each have a value 1 higher than the preceding constant in the list.

2. ***Defining a variable of the Status type.*** Add line 34 of Fig. 12.14. The application uses the `gameStatus` variable to keep track of whether the user has won, lost or needs to roll the dice again. The `gameStatus` variable is defined to be of the `Status` type, which you defined in the preceding step.

Defining a variable of type Status

```
CrapsGame.cpp*
32      string input; // stores input after each dice roll
33
34      Status gameStatus; // can contain CONTINUE, WON or LOST
35
36      return 0; // indicates successful termination
```

Figure 12.14   Defining a variable to store values declared in the `Status` enumeration.

3. ***Save the application.***

SELF-REVIEW

1. Use the _____ keyword to define enumerations.
   a) `const`   b) `enum`
   c) `enumeration`   d) `type`

2. The _____ Standard Library header file defines the function prototype for the `rand` function.
   a) `<ctime>`   b) `<rand>`
   c) `<crand>`   d) `<cstdlib>`

Answers: 1) b. 2) d.

12.4 Using Random Numbers in the Craps Game Application

Now you will add code that uses the constants, variables and enumeration that you declared or defined to play the game of Craps. You begin by inserting the code that will execute immediately after the user runs the application.

Coding the main Function

1. ***Seeding the rand function.*** Begin coding the functionality of your application by adding lines 36–37 of Fig. 12.15. Line 37 seeds the `rand` function by calling the `srand` function. Recall that the function call `time( 0 )` returns the current "calendar time," in seconds. Because your computer's current time will almost certainly be different each time you run the application, this technique ensures that the application will generate random dice value combinations for each new game.

2. ***Calling the rollDice function.*** Line 39 of Fig. 12.16 assigns the value returned by rolling the dice to `int` variable `sum` (defined in line 30). This is accomplished by calling the `rollDice` function, which you will define later in this tutorial. The `rollDice` function "rolls" the two dice, displays the value of each die and returns the sum of the dice values.

(cont.)

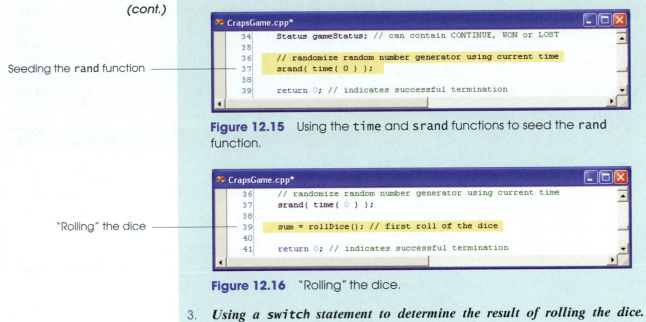

Seeding the **rand** function

Figure 12.15 Using the `time` and `srand` functions to seed the `rand` function.

"Rolling" the dice

Figure 12.16 "Rolling" the dice.

3. ***Using a switch statement to determine the result of rolling the dice.***
Recall that if the user rolls 7 or 11 on the first roll, the user wins, and if the user rolls 2, 3 or 12 on the first roll, the user loses. To enable your application to handle the cases in which the user wins or loses on the first roll, add lines 41–57 of Fig. 12.17 to `main` beneath the code you added in the previous step.

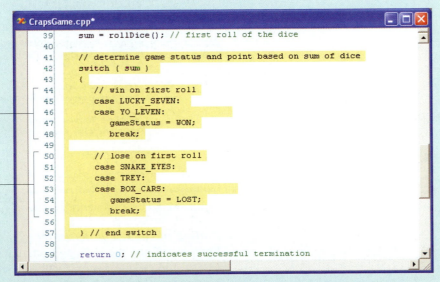

Winning on the first roll

Losing on the first roll

Figure 12.17 `switch` statement in `main`.

The first `case` (lines 45–48) executes for first-roll values of 7 or 11, using the LUCKY_SEVEN and YO_LEVEN constant values. Recall that several case labels can be specified to execute the same statements. If the sum of the dice is 7 (LUCKY_SEVEN) or 11 (YO_LEVEN), the code in line 47 sets the value of gameStatus to the WON enumeration constant. If the sum of the dice is 2 (SNAKE_EYES), 3 (TREY) or 12 (BOX_CARS), the code in line 54 executes and sets the value of gameStatus to the LOST enumeration constant. Later in this box, you will add code that displays a winning or losing message depending on the value of gameStatus. Line 57 ends the `switch` statement.

(cont.)

Common Programming Error

Assigning the integer equivalent of an enumeration constant to a variable of the enumeration type is a syntax error.

4. **Using the `default` case to continue the game.** Add lines 57–62 of Fig. 12.18. If the user did not roll a 2, 3, 7, 11 or 12, then the sum of the dice becomes the point and the user must roll again. Line 59 in the `default` case's body sets the value of the `gameStatus` variable to the enumeration constant `CONTINUE`, indicating that the application must roll the dice again. Line 60 sets `myPoint` variable to the sum of the die values. Next, line 61 displays the value of the point.

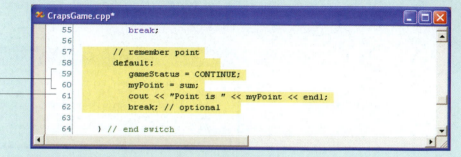

User must match the point ———
Displaying the point ———

```
55          break;
56
57      // remember point
58      default:
59          gameStatus = CONTINUE;
60          myPoint = sum;
61          cout << "Point is " << myPoint << endl;
62          break; // optional
63
64  } // end switch
```

Figure 12.18 `default` case in `main`.

5. **Continuing the game.** Add lines 66–72 of Fig. 12.19. The `while` statement in lines 67–72 uses a sentinel value (defined by the `CONTINUE` enumeration constant) to repeat until the user wins or loses. If the user did not win or lose on the previous roll of the dice, lines 69–70 execute, prompting the user to press *Enter*. The `getline` function (line 70) removes from the input stream any characters that the user may have entered before pressing *Enter*. Those characters, which are stored in `string` variable `input`, will not be used in your application.

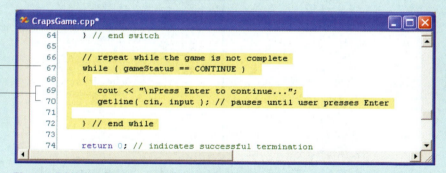

Repeat while the user has neither won nor lost ———
Prompt the user to press *Enter* ———

```
64      } // end switch
65
66      // repeat while the game is not complete
67      while ( gameStatus == CONTINUE )
68      {
69          cout << "\nPress Enter to continue...";
70          getline( cin, input ); // pauses until user presses Enter
71
72      } // end while
73
74      return 0; // indicates successful termination
```

Figure 12.19 Continuing the Craps game.

6. **Rolling the dice and determining the output of the roll.** The user presses *Enter* to roll the dice hoping to match the point before rolling a 7. Add lines 72–82 of Fig. 12.20. Line 72 calls the `rollDice` function to roll the dice and display the result, and assigns the sum of the dice to the `sum` variable.

If the roll matches the point, the user wins and the game ends. However, if the user rolls a 7 (CRAPS), the user loses and the game ends.

The `if` statement (line 75–78) determines whether the sum of the dice in the current roll matches the point. If the sum and point match, the application indicates that the user has won by changing the value of `gameStatus` to the `WON` enumeration constant. This causes the loop-continuation condition in line 67 to evaluate to `false`, and the application continues with the next statement after the `while` statement.

(cont.)

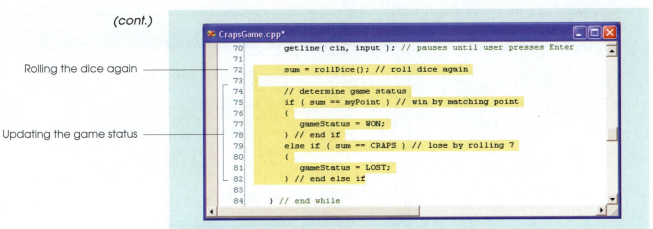

Rolling the dice again ————

Updating the game status ————

```
70        getline( cin, input ); // pauses until user presses Enter
71
72        sum = rollDice(); // roll dice again
73
74        // determine game status
75        if ( sum == myPoint ) // win by matching point
76        {
77           gameStatus = WON;
78        } // end if
79        else if ( sum == CRAPS ) // lose by rolling 7
80        {
81           gameStatus = LOST;
82        } // end else if
83
84     } // end while
```

Figure 12.20   Rolling the dice and determining the outcome of a roll.

The `else` (line 79) contains an `if` (lines 79–82) that determines whether the sum of the dice in the current roll is 7 (CRAPS). If so, the application indicates that the user has lost by changing the value of `gameStatus` to the LOST enumeration constant. This causes the loop-continuation condition in line 67 to evaluate to `false`, and the application continues with the next statement after the `while` statement. If the user neither matches the point nor rolls a 7, then the value of `gameStatus` remains the same (CONTINUE), the loop-continuation condition in line 67 evaluates to `true` and the user is prompted to press *Enter* to roll again.

7. ***Displaying the outcome of the game.*** Add lines 86–94 of Fig. 12.21. The `if` part (lines 87–90) of the `if...else` statement displays the message "Player wins" if gameStatus is WON. Otherwise, the `else` part (lines 91–94) of the `if...else` statement executes, displaying the message "Player loses."

Displaying the outcome of the game ————

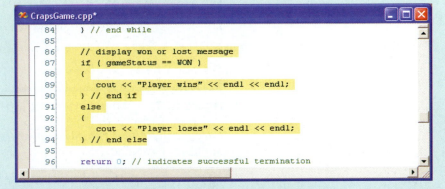

```
84     } // end while
85
86     // display won or lost message
87     if ( gameStatus == WON )
88     {
89        cout << "Player wins" << endl << endl;
90     } // end if
91     else
92     {
93        cout << "Player loses" << endl << endl;
94     } // end else
95
96     return 0; // indicates successful termination
```

Figure 12.21   Displaying the outcome of the game.

8. ***Save the application.***

Next, you will add code that will simulate rolling the dice and display the dice values.

Using Random Numbers to Simulate Rolling Dice

1. ***Using the rand function to simulate dice rolling.*** To begin the `rollDice` function definition, add lines 100–111 of Fig. 12.22 after `main`.

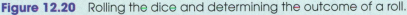

Using Random Numbers to Simulate Rolling Dice

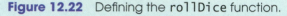

Defining local variables to store die values

Getting two random numbers and storing their sum

```
 98   } // end function main
 99
100   // roll dice, calculate sum and display results
101   int rollDice( void )
102   {
103       int die1;    // stores the value of the first die
104       int die2;    // stores the value of the second die
105       int diceSum; // stores the sum of the dice values
106
107       die1 = 1 + rand() % 6; // pick random die1 value
108       die2 = 1 + rand() % 6; // pick random die2 value
109       diceSum = die1 + die2; // sum die1 and die2
110
111   } // end function rollDice
112
```

Figure 12.22 Defining the rollDice function.

Lines 103–105 define int variables die1, die2 and diceSum to store the value of the first die rolled, the second die rolled and the sum of the dice, respectively. Lines 107–108 set the values of die1 and die2 to random integers between 1 and 6, inclusive, using the expression 1 + rand() % 6. Remember that the value of the expression rand() % 6 is a non-negative integer in the range 0–5. Line 109 stores the sum of the two die values in the diceSum variable.

2. ***Displaying the dice values and returning their sum.*** Add lines 111–115 of Fig. 12.23. Lines 112–113 display the value of each die and the sum of both. Line 115 returns the value of diceSum to the function's caller.

Displaying the sum of the dice

Returning the sum of the dice

```
109       diceSum = die1 + die2; // sum die1 and die2
110
111       // display the results of this roll
112       cout << "\nPlayer rolled " << die1 << " + " << die2
113           << " = " << diceSum << endl;
114
115       return diceSum; // return the sum of the dice
116
117   } // end function rollDice
```

Figure 12.23 Completing the rollDice function definition.

3. ***Save, compile and run the application***. Figure 12.24 shows the completed application running.

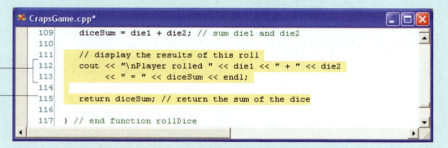

```
Player rolled 2 + 6 = 8
Point is 8

Press Enter to continue...

Player rolled 5 + 3 = 8
Player wins

Press any key to continue_
```

Figure 12.24 Sample output from the completed **Craps Game** application.

4. ***Close the Command Prompt window***.

Figure 12.25 presents the source code for the **Craps Game** application. The lines of code that you added, viewed or modified in this tutorial are highlighted.

Include the `<ctime>` standard library header file

Include the `<cstdlib>` standard library header file

Declare the `rollDice` function prototype

Define constants

Declare an enumeration

Define a variable of the `Status` type

Seed the `rand` function

"Roll" the dice

Win on the first roll

Lose on the first roll

```cpp
1   // Tutorial 12: CrapsGame.cpp
2   // This application plays a simple craps game.
3   #include <iostream> // required to perform C++ stream I/O
4   #include <string>    // required to access string functions
5   #include <ctime>      // contains prototype for function time
6
7   // contains function prototypes for srand and rand
8   #include <cstdlib>
9
10  using namespace std; // for accessing C++ Standard Library members
11
12  int rollDice( void ); // function prototype
13
14  // function main begins program execution
15  int main()
16  {
17     // constants representing winning dice rolls
18     const int LUCKY_SEVEN = 7;
19     const int YO_LEVEN = 11;
20
21     // constants representing losing dice rolls
22     const int SNAKE_EYES = 2;
23     const int TREY = 3;
24     const int BOX_CARS = 12;
25     const int CRAPS = 7; // loses only after first roll
26
27     // enumeration constants represent game status
28     enum Status { CONTINUE, WON, LOST };
29
30     int sum;       // stores sum of the dice
31     int myPoint;   // stores the player's point
32     string input;  // stores input after each dice roll
33
34     Status gameStatus; // can contain CONTINUE, WON or LOST
35
36     // randomize random number generator using current time
37     srand( time( 0 ) );
38
39     sum = rollDice(); // first roll of the dice
40
41     // determine game status and point based on sum of dice
42     switch ( sum )
43     {
44        // win on first roll
45        case LUCKY_SEVEN:
46        case YO_LEVEN:
47           gameStatus = WON;
48           break;
49
50        // lose on first roll
51        case SNAKE_EYES:
52        case TREY:
53        case BOX_CARS:
54           gameStatus = LOST;
55           break;
56
```

Figure 12.25 **Craps Game** application code listing. (Part 1 of 3.)

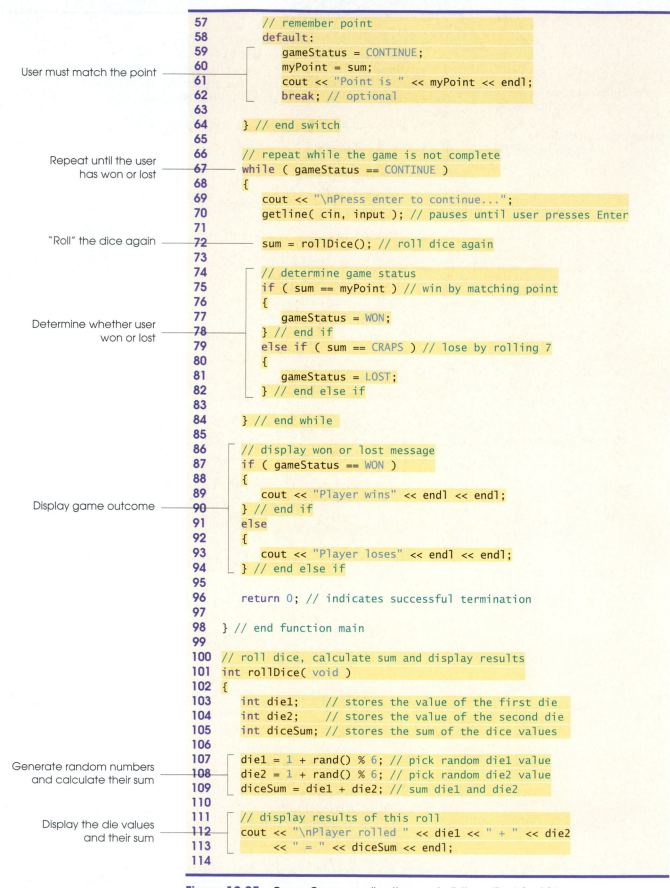

```
57              // remember point
58              default:
59                 gameStatus = CONTINUE;
60                 myPoint = sum;
61                 cout << "Point is " << myPoint << endl;
62                 break; // optional
63
64         } // end switch
65
66         // repeat while the game is not complete
67         while ( gameStatus == CONTINUE )
68         {
69             cout << "\nPress enter to continue...";
70             getline( cin, input ); // pauses until user presses Enter
71
72             sum = rollDice(); // roll dice again
73
74             // determine game status
75             if ( sum == myPoint ) // win by matching point
76             {
77                 gameStatus = WON;
78             } // end if
79             else if ( sum == CRAPS ) // lose by rolling 7
80             {
81                 gameStatus = LOST;
82             } // end else if
83
84         } // end while
85
86         // display won or lost message
87         if ( gameStatus == WON )
88         {
89             cout << "Player wins" << endl << endl;
90         } // end if
91         else
92         {
93             cout << "Player loses" << endl << endl;
94         } // end else if
95
96         return 0; // indicates successful termination
97
98     } // end function main
99
100    // roll dice, calculate sum and display results
101    int rollDice( void )
102    {
103        int die1;    // stores the value of the first die
104        int die2;    // stores the value of the second die
105        int diceSum; // stores the sum of the dice values
106
107        die1 = 1 + rand() % 6; // pick random die1 value
108        die2 = 1 + rand() % 6; // pick random die2 value
109        diceSum = die1 + die2; // sum die1 and die2
110
111        // display results of this roll
112        cout << "\nPlayer rolled " << die1 << " + " << die2
113            << " = " << diceSum << endl;
114
```

Labels (left margin):
- User must match the point — lines 59–62
- Repeat until the user has won or lost — line 67
- "Roll" the dice again — line 72
- Determine whether user won or lost — lines 74–82
- Display game outcome — lines 86–94
- Generate random numbers and calculate their sum — lines 107–109
- Display the die values and their sum — lines 111–113

Figure 12.25 **Craps Game** application code listing. (Part 2 of 3.)

```
115        return diceSum; // return the sum of dice
116
117 } // end function rollDice
```

Figure 12.25 **Craps Game** application code listing. (Part 3 of 3.)

In your **Craps Game** application, you used the `srand( time( 0 ) )` function call to produce a different seed value for the `rand` function each time the application runs. This enabled your application to produce a different sequence of random numbers for each game of Craps. In the next box, you will learn what happens when you do not explicitly set the seed value for the `rand` function.

Running the Craps Game **1.** ***Removing randomization.*** To prevent the application from randomizing the
Application Without   the `rand` function, modify line 37 of your code as shown in Fig. 12.26. Add-
Randomizing   ing the slashes changes line 37 into a comment, ensuring that the `srand` func-
                                  tion call is not executed when the application runs.

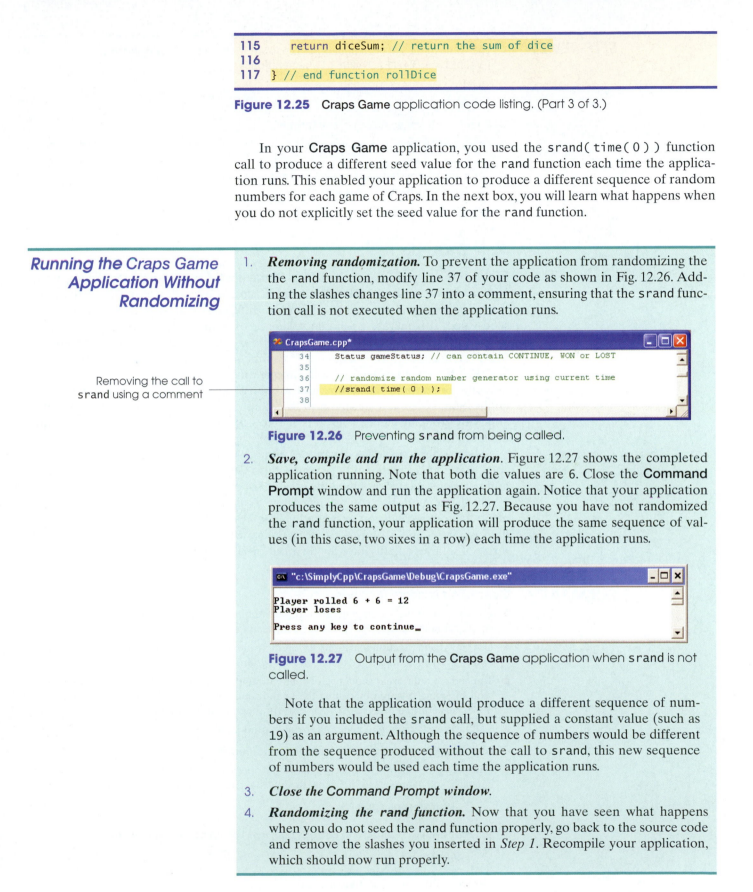

Removing the call to
`srand` using a comment

Figure 12.26 Preventing `srand` from being called.

2. ***Save, compile and run the application.*** Figure 12.27 shows the completed application running. Note that both die values are 6. Close the **Command Prompt** window and run the application again. Notice that your application produces the same output as Fig. 12.27. Because you have not randomized the `rand` function, your application will produce the same sequence of values (in this case, two sixes in a row) each time the application runs.

Figure 12.27 Output from the **Craps Game** application when `srand` is not called.

Note that the application would produce a different sequence of numbers if you included the `srand` call, but supplied a constant value (such as 19) as an argument. Although the sequence of numbers would be different from the sequence produced without the call to `srand`, this new sequence of numbers would be used each time the application runs.

3. ***Close the Command Prompt window.***

4. ***Randomizing the rand function.*** Now that you have seen what happens when you do not seed the `rand` function properly, go back to the source code and remove the slashes you inserted in *Step 1*. Recompile your application, which should now run properly.

1. The value of the VALUE2 enumeration constant in the enum mysteryValues
   { VALUE1 = 4, VALUE2, VALUE3 } enumeration is _____.
   a) 1
   b) 2
   c) 4
   d) 5

2. If you do not randomize the rand function, _____.
   a) a compilation error occurs
   b) rand returns the same value each time it is called while an application executes
   c) rand returns the same sequence of values each time the application runs
   d) None of the above.

Answers: 1) d. 2) c.

12.5 Wrap-Up

In this tutorial, you created the **Craps Game** application to simulate playing a simplified version of the popular dice game Craps. You learned about the rand function and how it can be used to generate a different sequence of numbers for each seed value. To generate a random sequence of numbers for your application, you used the srand function to specify the seed for the rand function. You learned that the current time, returned from the time function, can be used to generate a different seed for your application each time it runs. You then learned how to use the modulus operator to customize the range of random values generated by your application. Later, you learned how to create enumerations to improve code readability by grouping named constants and how to create a user-defined type using the enum keyword.

Using your knowledge of random number generation and functions, you wrote code that added functionality to your **Craps Game** application. You used random-number generation to simulate the element of chance.

In the next tutorial, you will learn how to use arrays, which allow you to use one name to store a collection of related values. You will apply your knowledge of random numbers and arrays to create a **Salary Survey** application that calculates a series of salaries and displays the distribution of salaries.

SKILLS SUMMARY

Generating Random Numbers

- Use the rand function to generate random numbers (but in the same sequence each time you execute the program). This is good for testing and debugging.
- Use the srand function to cause a different sequence of random numbers to be generated (with rand) each time you execute your program.
- To produce a different sequence of random numbers each time the application executes, seed the rand function by calling the srand function. The argument to srand should be the value returned by time(0), the current time on your computer.
- Call the rand function to generate the next random number.

Generating Random Numbers within a Specified Range

- Call the rand function and use the modulus operator to specify a range of random numbers and add a number to this value to shift the range. For example, the expression

    rand() % *maxValue*

generates values from zero to one less than *maxValue*, and the expression

    shiftValue + rand() % *maxValue*

generates values from *shiftValue* to one less than *shiftValue* + *maxValue*.

Declaring Enumerations

■ Begin an enumeration with the enum keyword, followed by the name of the enumeration, then use a comma-separated list of descriptive names between braces, and set each one to the value that you want it to represent.

KEY TERMS

<cstdlib> Standard Library header file—A header file that enables access to functions for conversion of numbers to text and text to numbers, generation of random numbers and other utility functions.

<ctime> Standard Library header file—A header file that enables access to functions and types for manipulating and storing the time and date.

enum keyword—The keyword that begins an enumeration.

enumeration—A user-defined type containing a group of related, named constants.

enumeration constant—A named constant representing a possible value for an enumeration type.

programmer-defined type—See user-defined type.

pseudorandom numbers—A sequence of values produced by a complex mathematical calculation that simulates random-number generation. Note that the calculation will produce the same sequence of numbers for a given seed value.

rand function—A function that generates an int value selected from 0 to RAND_MAX, when called with no arguments. An application that uses the rand function will generate the same sequence of values if the seed value does not change each time the application runs.

RAND_MAX constant—The largest possible value that the rand function will return. The value must be at least 32,767—the maximum positive value for a two-byte (16-bit) integer.

randomizing—Conditioning an application to produce a different sequence of random numbers for each execution.

srand function—A function that sets the seed for the rand function to the value passed as its argument. When the argument is the value returned by the time(0) function call (that is, the current time), srand will cause rand to produce a different sequence of random values each time the application executes.

seed—The value that the application uses to begin calculating random numbers. If an application uses the same seed each time it executes, the application will produce the same sequence of "random" values. By supplying the current time (which changes each time the application runs) as the argument to srand, your application will produce a different sequence of random values each time it runs.

time function—A function in the ctime library that returns the current "calendar time" in seconds elapsed since January 1, 1970. This function is useful for seeding srand so that it produces a different sequence of random numbers each time you execute a program.

type name—A name that identifies a type. Built-in type names include bool, int and double. An example of a user-defined type name is the identifier following the enum keyword.

user-defined type—A named collection of one or more values, each of which is also named. For example, an enumeration is a named collection of constant integer values, and each member value is named. A user-defined type can contain multiple values of different built-in data types.

C++ LIBRARY REFERENCE

cstdlib This header file provides access to functions that convert numbers to text and text to numbers, generate random numbers and perform other utility capabilities.

■ *Functions*

rand—This function generates an int value selected from 0 to RAND_MAX.

srand—This function seeds the rand function, which determines the sequence of numbers that the application will generate. The srand function typically is used with an argument of time(0) to ensure that an application generates a different sequence of random numbers each time it is run.

ctime This header file provides access to functions and types for manipulating and storing the time and date.

■ *Function*

time—This function returns the current time, in seconds. The time is determined by calculating the number of seconds that have passed since midnight on January 1, 1970 (using UTC—Universal Time, also called Greenwich Mean Time).

MULTIPLE-CHOICE QUESTIONS

12.1 The rand function can generate random numbers of the _____ type.
  a) int
  b) string
  c) double
  d) Both a and c.

12.2 A(n) _____ is a group of related, named constants.
  a) namespace
  b) variable
  c) enumeration
  d) None of the above.

12.3 The maximum value that the rand function will return is specified by the _____ constant.
  a) MAX_RAND
  b) MAX_VALUE
  c) VALUE_MAX
  d) RAND_MAX

12.4 The rand function can be called using _____.
  a) one argument
  b) no arguments
  c) two arguments
  d) Both a and b.

12.5 The statement _____ assigns to value a random number in the range 5 to 20.
  a) value = 4 + rand(16);
  b) value = rand(21);
  c) value = 5 + rand() % 15;
  d) value = 5 + rand() % 16;

12.6 The time(0) function call returns _____.
  a) the current time, in milliseconds
  b) the current time, in seconds
  c) a time value of zero
  d) a pseudorandom number

12.7 The <ctime> standard library header file provides access to functions that _____.
  a) generate positive random numbers
  b) seed random numbers
  c) manipulate date and time information
  d) All of the above.

12.8 The srand function _____.
  a) returns a pseudorandom number
  b) accepts one integer argument
  c) is defined in the <cstdlib> header file
  d) Both b and c.

12.9 Which of the following statements contains a syntax error?
  a) enum Example { VALUE1 = 2, VALUE2 = 1, VALUE3 = 2, VALUE4 = 10 }
  b) enum Example { VALUE1 = 2, VALUE2 = 1, VALUE1 = 3, VALUE4 = 10 }
  c) enum Example { VALUE1 = 2, VALUE2, VALUE3, VALUE4 }
  d) None of the above.

12.10 The values of an enumeration's constants _____.
  a) must be declared in ascending order
  b) must begin with the value zero
  c) can be reassigned after the enumeration is declared
  d) None of the above.

EXERCISES

12.11 (*Guess the Number Application*) Develop an application that generates a random number and prompts the user to guess the number using seven or fewer guesses (Fig. 12.28). When the user runs the application, it chooses a number in the range 1 to 100 at random. The user enters guesses at the **Enter guess:** prompt. If the guess is correct, the game ends. If the guess is not correct, the application should indicate if the guess is higher or lower than the correct number. If the user has not guessed the number correctly after seven guesses, the application should indicate that the user has no remaining guesses and display the value of the number.

```
"c:\SimplyCpp\GuessNumber\Debug\GuessNumber.exe"

I'm thinking of a number from 1 to 100.
Can you guess what it is in seven or fewer tries?

Enter guess: 50

Too high...

Enter guess: 25

Too high...

Enter guess: 13

Too low...

Enter guess: 20

Correct!

Press any key to continue_
```

```
"c:\SimplyCpp\GuessNumber\Debug\GuessNumber.exe"

I'm thinking of a number from 1 to 100.
Can you guess what it is in seven or fewer tries?

Enter guess: 1

Too low...

Enter guess: 2

Too low...

Enter guess: 3

Too low...

Enter guess: 4

Too low...

Enter guess: 5

Too low...

Enter guess: 6

Too low...

Enter guess: 7

Too low...

You've run out of guesses!
The number was: 22

Press any key to continue_
```

Figure 12.28 Guess the Number application output.

a) *Copying the template to your working directory.* Copy the C:\Examples\Tutorial12\Exercises\GuessNumber directory to your C:\SimplyCpp directory.

b) *Opening the template source code file.* Open the GuessNumber.cpp file in your text editor or IDE.

c) *Including the <ctime> and <cstdlib> Standard Library header files.* In lines 4–7, include the <ctime> and <cstdlib> standard library header files so that your application can seed and use the rand function.

d) *Defining and initializing variables.* In lines 14–16 of main, define int variables guess and number to store the user's guess and the randomly generated number, respectively. The number variable should store a randomly generated number in the range 1 to 100 created using the rand function. In line 17, define int variable tries and initialize its value to 7. This variable stores the number of remaining guesses for the user. In lines 19–20, include a comment and a statement that randomizes the rand function using the time function and the srand function.

e) *Displaying the initial message.* In lines 22–25, display the application's initial message, which indicates the range of values that the application has used to select its random value and the number of guesses that the application allows.

f) *Inserting a do...while statement.* Add a do...while statement starting in line 21 that repeats until the user's guess matches the randomly generated number or until the value of tries is less than 1. In the body of the do...while statement, add code that prompts the user for and inputs a number into guess, then compares that value to the randomly generated number in number. If the user's guess is lower than the correct answer, display Too low.... If the user's guess is higher than the correct answer, display Too high.... If the guess is correct, display Correct! and terminate the game. Before the closing brace of the do...while loop, decrement the value of tries to indicate that a guess has been used.

g) *Displaying the random value.* After the do...while loop, insert an if statement that determines whether guess is not equal to number. If this condition is true, the application has exited the loop because the user ran out of guesses. In the body of the if statement, insert code to display a message indicating the user has run out of guesses. Then display the value of the random number, contained in number.

h) *Save, compile and run the application.* Test your application to ensure that it runs correctly by playing the game until you guess the correct number.

i) *Close the Command Prompt window.*

12.12 (*Dice Simulator Application*) Develop an application that simulates rolling two six-sided dice. Your application should prompt the user to enter the number of times that the application should "roll" the dice. When the user presses *Enter*, the application should display the result of "rolling" the dice using random numbers. It should also display the number of times each face has appeared. Your application output should appear similar to Fig. 12.29. This application will help you see if dice rolling on your computer is really random. If it is, the number of 1s, 2s, 3s, 4s, 5s and 6s you roll should be about the same, at least for a large number of rolls.

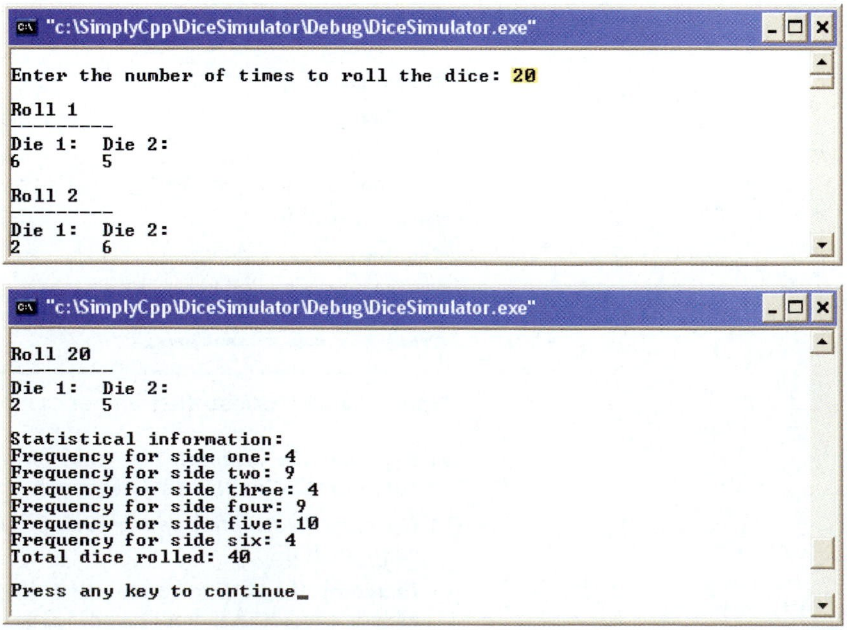

Figure 12.29 **Dice Simulator** application output.

a) *Copying the template to your working directory.* Copy the C:\Examples\ Tutorial12\Exercises\DiceSimulator directory to your C:\SimplyCpp directory.

b) *Opening the template source code file.* Open the DiceSimulator.cpp file in your text editor or IDE.

c) *Completing the main function.* Modify line 37 so that the application seeds the rand function with a different value each time the application runs. Then modify line 46 of main to call the rollDie function and assign the value returned by that function to die1. Similarly, call rollDie and assign its result to die2.

d) *Rolling the dice.* After main, starting in line 72, create a function named rollDie that returns an int and contains no parameters. The function should create a new random integer from 1 to 6 using the rand function and assign that value to the face variable. The function should then call the setFrequency function, passing to it the face variable as an argument, to display the number of times each face has occurred. Finally, the function should return the value stored in face.

e) *Displaying the frequency.* After the rollDie function, create a function named set-Frequency that takes an int representing a die roll as its argument and does not return a value. The function should use a switch statement with the int parameter as the control variable. Use the constants defined by the Faces enumeration as the values in the case labels. Each case should update the number of times its corresponding face has appeared. Before the function terminates, it should increment the total number of dice rolls.

f) *Save, compile and run the application.* Test your application to ensure that it runs correctly by entering 20 at the **Enter the number of times to roll the dice:** prompt. This will cause the application to roll the dice 20 times (that is, roll 40 dice). Make sure that the total number of rolls adds up to 40.

g) *Close the Command Prompt window.*

12.13 (*Lottery Number Picker Application*) A lottery commission offers four different lottery games to play: Three-number, Four-number, Five-number and Five-number + 1 lotteries. Each game has independent numbers. Develop an application that randomly picks numbers for all four games and displays the generated numbers (Fig. 12.30). The games are played as follows:

- Three-number lotteries require players to choose three numbers in the range 0–9.

- Four-number lotteries require players to choose four numbers, in the range 0–9.

- Five-number lotteries require players to choose five numbers in the range 1–39.

- Five-number + 1 lotteries require players to choose five numbers in the range 1–49 and an additional number in the range 1–42.

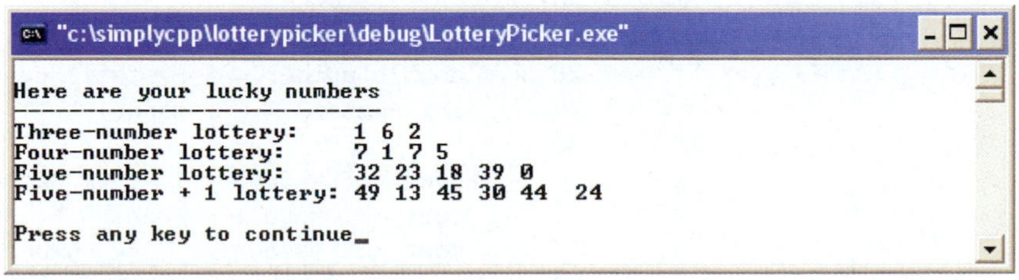

Figure 12.30 Lottery Picker application output.

a) *Copying the template to your working directory.* Copy the C:\Examples\ Tutorial12\Exercises\LotteryPicker directory to your C:\SimplyCpp directory.

b) *Opening the template source code file.* Open the LotteryPicker.cpp file in your text editor or IDE.

c) *Drawing numbers for the games.* Add code to `main` to call the `generate` function and display the generated numbers for all four games. The `generate` function, which you will code in the next step, takes two arguments. The first argument is the smallest number that the function should generate, and the second argument is the largest number that the function should generate. Some lotteries allow repetition of numbers. To make this application simple, allow repetition of numbers for all the lotteries.

d) *Generating random numbers.* After `main`, create a `generate` function that will take two `int`s representing the low and high end of a range of random numbers and return an `int` containing a generated random number in that range.

e) *Save, compile and run the application.* Test your application to ensure that it runs correctly by running it several times to ensure that the resulting lottery numbers are within the bounds given in the rules above.

f) *Close the* Command Prompt *window.*

What does this code do? ▶

12.14 What is the result of the following code?

```cpp
1   // Exercise 12.14: WDTCD.cpp
2   // what does this code do?
3   #include <iostream> // required to perform C++ stream I/O
4   #include <ctime>    // contains prototype for function time
5
6   // contains function prototypes for functions srand and rand
7   #include <cstdlib>
8
9   using namespace std; // for accessing C++ Standard Library members
10
11  // function prototype
12  void pickRandomNumbers();
13
14  // function main begins program execution
15  int main()
16  {
17     pickRandomNumbers();
18
19     return 0; // indicate that program ended correctly
20
21  } // end function main
22
23  void pickRandomNumbers()
24  {
25     srand( time( 0 ) );
26
27     int number1 = rand();
28     double number = 5 * static_cast< double >( rand() ) / RAND_MAX;
29     int number2 = 1 + rand() % 11;
30
31     cout << "\nNumber 1: " << number1 << endl;
32     cout << "Double number: " << number << endl;
33     cout << "Number 2: " << number2 << endl << endl;
34
35  } // end function pickRandomNumbers
```

What's wrong with this code? ▶

12.15 This `randomDouble` function should assign a random `double` number (in the range 0.0 to less than 50.0) to `double number` and display it. The number that is generated should be different each time the function executes. Find the error(s) in the following code.

```cpp
1   // Exercise 12.15: WWWTC.cpp
2   // This program outputs a different random double number
3   // every time that it is run.
4   #include <iostream> // required to perform C++ stream I/O
5   #include <ctime>    // contains prototype for function time
6
7   // contains function prototypes for functions srand and rand
8   #include <cstdlib>
9
10  using namespace std; // for accessing C++ Standard Library members
11
12  // function prototype
13  void randomDouble();
14
15  // function main begins program execution
16  int main()
17  {
18     // call randomDouble
19     randomDouble();
20
21     return 0; // indicate that the program ended correctly
22
23  } // end function main
24
25  // get a random double
26  void randomDouble()
27  {
28     double number;
29
30     number = static_cast< double >( rand() ) / RAND_MAX;
31     cout << "\nRandom double: " << number << endl << endl;
32
33  } // end function randomDouble
```

Programming Challenge ▶

12.16 (*Multiplication Teacher Application*) Develop an application that helps children learn multiplication (Fig. 12.31). Use random-number generation to produce two positive one-digit integers that display in a question, such as "How much is 6 times 7?" The student should type the answer at the keyboard. If the answer is correct, then the application randomly displays one of three messages: "Very Good!", "Excellent!" or "Great Job!" and displays the next question. If the student is wrong, the application displays the prompt "No. Please try again (-1 to end):". If the user enters the value -1, the application should exit.

a) *Copying the template to your working directory.* Copy the C:\Examples\Tutorial12\Exercises\MultiplicationTeacher directory to your C:\SimplyCpp directory.

b) *Opening the template source code file.* Open the MultiplicationTeacher.cpp file in your text editor or IDE.

c) *Completing the main function.* After line 24 in main, insert a while statement that repeats until the user's response is -1. In the body of the while statement, insert a statement that displays the multiplication problem to the user by calling the generateQuestion function, which you will define in *Step d*. Assign the value returned by generateQuestion to the correctAnswer variable. Use cin to input the user's response into userAnswer. Then insert a nested while statement that repeats while the user's answer does not match the answer returned by generateQuestion *and* the user's answer is no -1. The body of this nested while statement should indicate that the user entered an incorrect response and prompt the user to try again. After the nested while statement, but before the end of the outer while statement, insert an if statement that calls the generateOutput function only if the user entered the correct response. You will define the generateOutput function in *Step e*.

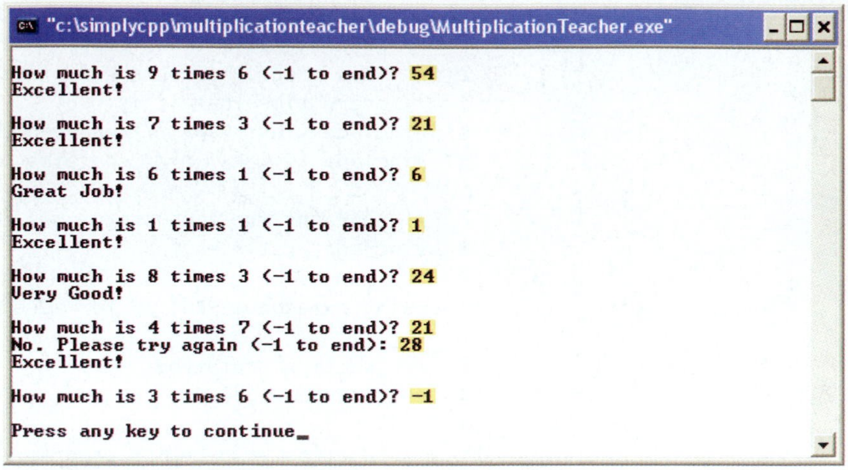

Figure 12.31 Multiplication Teacher application output.

d) *Generating the questions.* Define a function named `generateQuestion` in your application to generate and display each new question. The function should return the product of the two random numbers that it generates.

e) *Displaying a random message.* Add a function named `generateOutput` that displays a random message congratulating the student when the answer is correct.

f) *Save, compile and run the application.* Test your application to ensure that it runs correctly by answering the questions. Make sure that if you continue answering questions, you will see all four possible result messages.

g) *Close the application.* Enter -1 to exit the application.

h) *Close the Command Prompt window.*

Objectives

In this tutorial, you will learn to:

- Create and initialize arrays to store groups of related values.
- Store information in an array.
- Access individual elements of an array.

Outline

Salary Survey Application

Introducing One-Dimensional Arrays

This tutorial introduces basic concepts and features of data structures. **Data structures** group together and organize related data. **Arrays** are data structures that consist of data items of the same type (called **elements**). Each element is referenced by its **index** (**position number** starting from 0—also called **subscript**) within the array. You will learn how to create arrays and how to access the information that they contain.

13.1 Test-Driving the Salary Survey Application

You will now create an application that calculates commission-based salaries and determines how many salaries fall within various ranges. Your application will use an array to store the number of salaries that appear in each salary range. This application must meet the following requirements:

Application Requirements

A company pays its sales staff on a commission basis. Each member of the sales staff receives $200 per week, plus 9% of their gross sales for that week. For example, a salesperson who grosses $5000 in sales in a week receives $200 plus 9% of $5000, a total of $650. Write an application (using an array) to determine how many of the sales staff earned salaries in each of the following ranges (assuming that each person's salary is truncated to an integer amount): $200–299, $300–399, $400–499, $500–599, $600–699, $700–799, $800–899, $900–999 and over $999.

You begin by test-driving the completed application. Then, you will learn the additional C++ capabilities you will need to create your own version of this application.

Test-Driving the Salary Survey Application

1. **Locating the completed application.** Open the **Command Prompt** window by selecting **Start > All Programs > Accessories > Command Prompt**. Change to your completed **Salary Survey** application directory by typing cd C:\Examples\Tutorial13\CompletedApplication\SalarySurvey.

2. **Running the Salary Survey application.** Type SalarySurvey in the **Command Prompt** window to run the application (Fig. 13.1). The application prompts you to enter a sales figure (or –1 to end).

```
Command Prompt - SalarySurvey                                    _ □ ×

C:\>cd C:\Examples\Tutorial13\CompletedApplication\SalarySurvey

C:\Examples\Tutorial13\CompletedApplication\SalarySurvey>SalarySurvey

Enter sales (-1 to end): _
```

Figure 13.1 Running the completed **Salary Survey** application.

3. **Entering a sales figure.** Enter the value 2450.25 at the **Enter sales (-1 to end):** prompt (Fig. 13.2). Notice that the application displays the salary corresponding to this sales figure ($420.52). The application then prompts you to enter the next sales figure.

```
Command Prompt - SalarySurvey                                    _ □ ×

C:\>cd C:\Examples\Tutorial13\CompletedApplication\SalarySurvey

C:\Examples\Tutorial13\CompletedApplication\SalarySurvey>SalarySurvey

Enter sales (-1 to end): 2450.25
Total salary: $420.52

Enter sales (-1 to end): _
```

Displaying the total salary

Figure 13.2 **Salary Survey** application displaying a salary and prompting for the next sales figure.

4. **Entering additional sales figures and viewing the resulting salaries.** Enter the values 7500.50, 456.78, 2600.00; 12759.00 and 3700.45. Note that the corresponding salaries are all greater than $200, which is the base salary for each salesperson (Fig. 13.3).

```
Command Prompt - SalarySurvey                                    _ □ ×

C:\Examples\Tutorial13\CompletedApplication\SalarySurvey>SalarySurvey

Enter sales (-1 to end): 2450.25
Total salary: $420.52

Enter sales (-1 to end): 7500.50
Total salary: $875.04

Enter sales (-1 to end): 456.78
Total salary: $241.11

Enter sales (-1 to end): 2600.00
Total salary: $434.00

Enter sales (-1 to end): 12759.00
Total salary: $1348.31

Enter sales (-1 to end): 3700.45
Total salary: $533.04

Enter sales (-1 to end): _
```

Figure 13.3 Entering several sales figures in the **Salary Survey** application.

5. **Displaying the distribution of salaries and exiting the application.** Enter the value –1 to end input. Before exiting, the application displays a table containing the distribution of salaries within the ranges stated in the application requirements (Fig. 13.4).

(cont.)

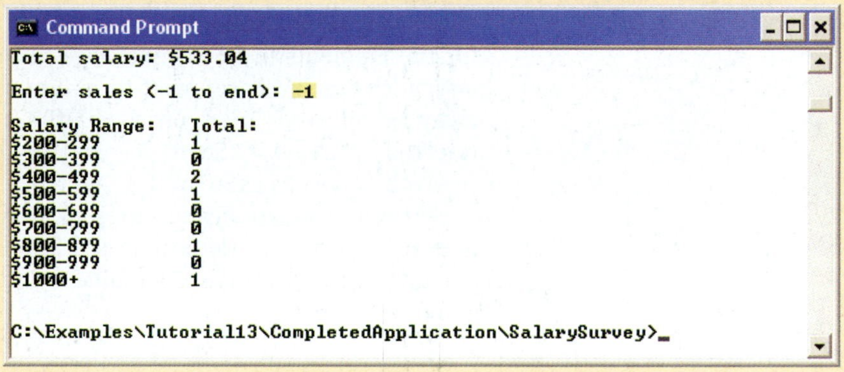

Figure 13.4   Displaying the distribution of salaries.

6. **Close the Command Prompt window.**

13.2 Introducing Arrays

An array is a group of variables (elements) that all have the same data type. Array names follow the same conventions that apply to other identifiers. To refer to a particular variable in an array, you specify the name of the array and the index (position number) of the variable, which is an integer that indicates a specific location within an array. Position numbers begin at 0 (zero) and range as high as one less than the number of elements in the array.

Figure 13.5 depicts an `int` array named `unitsSold` that might be used in a bookstore sales application. This array contains 13 elements. Each element represents the net number of "units sold" of a particular book in a given month at a bookstore. If the bookstore wishes to track sales on a monthly basis, using the month numbers would be a convenient way to access the array elements. For example, `unitsSold[ 1 ]` is the net sales of that book for January (month 1), `unitsSold[ 2 ]` is the net sales for February (month 2), etc. In this example, we simply ignore the first element of the array (at index 0), because there is no month zero.

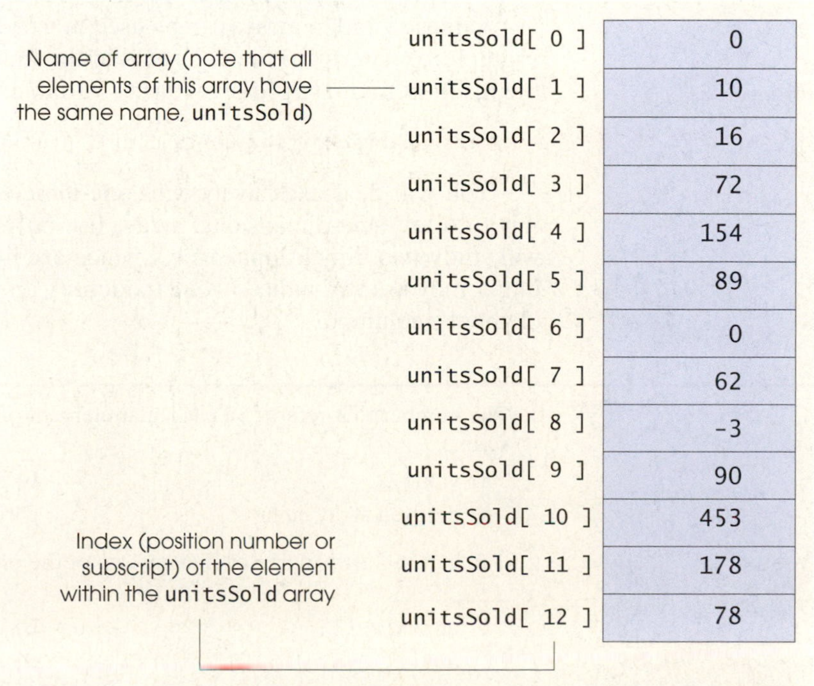

Figure 13.5   Array `unitsSold`, consisting of 13 elements.

Each array element is referred to by providing the array name, followed by the index (position number or subscript) of the element in brackets— []. The indices for the elements in an array always begin with 0. Thus, the **zeroth element** of the unitsSold array is referred to as unitsSold[0], element 1 of the unitsSold array is referred to as unitsSold[1], element 6 of the unitsSold array is referred to as unitsSold[6] and so on. Element *i* of the unitsSold array is referred to as unitsSold[i]. An index must be a constant integer or an integer expression. If an application uses an integer expression as an index, the expression is evaluated first to determine the index. For example, if the value1 variable is equal to 5, and the value2 variable is equal to 6, then the statement

```
unitsSold[ value1 + value2 ] += 2;
```

adds 2 to array element unitsSold[11] to get a value of 180. Note that an **indexed array name** (the array name, followed by an index enclosed in brackets) references a variable in the array and can be used on the left side of an assignment statement to place a new value into an array element.

Note that if the array index contained an invalid value, such as 13, the application would attempt to add 2 to unitsSold[13]. This would be outside the bounds of the array. *C++ has no array bounds checking to prevent the computer from referring to an element that does not exist.* Thus, an executing program can "walk off" either end of an array without warning. You should ensure that all array references remain within the bounds of the array.

Let's examine the unitsSold array in Fig. 13.5 more closely. The name of the array is unitsSold. The 13 elements of the array are referred to as unitsSold[0] through unitsSold[12]. The value of unitsSold[1] is 10, the value of unitsSold[2] is 16, the value of unitsSold[3] is 72, the value of unitsSold[7] is 62 and the value of unitsSold[11] is 178. A positive value for an element in this array indicates that more books were bought than were returned. A negative value for an element in this array indicates that more books were returned than were bought. A value of zero indicates that the number of books sold was equal to the number of books returned.

The brackets used to enclose the subscript of an array are actually an operator in C++. Brackets have the same level of precedence as parentheses.

Values stored in arrays can be used in various calculations and applications. For example, to determine the units sold in the first three months of the year and store the result in the firstQuarterUnits variable, you would write

```
firstQuarterUnits = unitsSold[ 1 ] + unitsSold[ 2 ] + unitsSold[ 3 ];
```

You will deal exclusively with **one-dimensional** arrays, such as unitsSold, in this tutorial. One-dimensional arrays use only one index. In the next tutorial, you will study two-dimensional arrays, which are like tables consisting of rows and columns; they use two indices—one to identify an element's row and one to identify an element's column.

Common Programming Error

Attempting to access elements in the array by using an index outside the array bounds is a logic error, not a syntax error. The (usually serious) effects of referencing elements outside the array bounds are system dependent. Often this results in changes to the value of an unrelated variable or a fatal error that terminates program execution.

SELF-REVIEW

1. The number that refers to a particular element of an array is called its _____ (or subscript).

   a) value   b) size
   c) indexed array name   d) index

2. The indexed array name of element two of the one-dimensional units array is _____.

   a) units[2]   b) units(2)
   c) units[0, 2]   d) units{ 2 }

Answers: 1) d. 2) a.

13.3 Declaring and Initializing Arrays

To declare an array, you provide the array's type and name. The following statement declares the array in Fig. 13.5:

```
int unitsSold[ 13 ];
```

The brackets that follow the array name indicate that `unitsSold` is an array. Arrays can be defined to contain any type. Every element of the array is a variable of the defined type. For example, every element of an `int` array is an `int` variable. The preceding array declaration will cause the application to reserve 13 adjacent `int`-sized slots in memory.

When an array is created as in the preceding statement, the elements in the array are not automatically initialized by the compiler. As a result, any attempt to read a value from an array element that has not been explicitly initialized will result in an indeterminate value. This can lead to subtle or fatal logic errors.

One way to create and initialize an array (`salesPerDay`) is with a statement such as

```
int salesPerDay[] = { 0, 2, 3, 6, 1, 4, 5, 6 };
```

where the comma-separated list enclosed in the braces— { and } —is called an **array initializer** and specifies the initial values of the elements in the array. The preceding statement defines and creates an array called `salesPerDay` containing eight `int`s. C++ determines the array's size from the number of elements in the initializer (in this case, eight).

If the array size and an initializer list are specified in an array declaration, the number of initializers must be less than or equal to the array size. The array declaration

```
int salesPerDay[ 5 ] = { 32, 27, 64, 18, 95, 14 };
```

causes a syntax error, because there are six initializers and only five array elements. If there are fewer initializers than elements in the array, the remaining array elements are initialized to zero. For example, all the elements of the `unitsSold` array in Fig. 13.5 could have been initialized to zero with the declaration

```
int salesPerDay[ 13 ] = { 0 };
```

The declaration explicitly initializes the first element to zero and implicitly initializes the remaining twelve elements to zero, because there are fewer initializers than elements in the array.

Now, you will define and initialize an array, and access the array's elements as you develop code that will total the values in the array.

Error-Prevention Tip

Always initialize elements in an array before accessing them.

Computing the Sum of an Array's Elements

1. ***Copying the template to your working directory.*** Copy the C:\Examples\ Tutorial13\TemplateApplication\SumArray directory to your C:\SimplyCpp directory. In the next several steps, you will program this application to define an array containing the integers 1–10, add these values and display the total.

2. ***Opening the Sum Array application's template source code file.*** Open the template file SumArray.cpp in your text editor or IDE.

(cont.)

3. ***Combining the declaration and creation of an array.*** Add lines 10–15 of Fig. 13.6 to main. Line 11 defines int constant ARRAY_SIZE and initializes its value to 10. Line 14 combines the definition and creation of an array into one statement. Note that it is not necessary to declare the array size (in this case, ARRAY_SIZE) inside the square brackets in line 14 because the array definition uses an initializer list. Line 15 defines and initializes the total variable, which will store the sum of array's elements.

Creating and initializing an array of ints

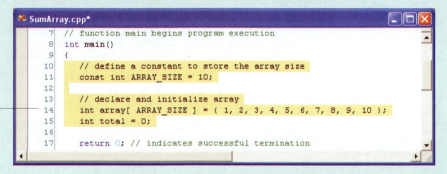

Figure 13.6 Defining and initializing an array in main.

Defining the size of an array as a constant variable (such as ARRAY_SIZE) instead of a literal constant (such as 10) makes programs clearer and easier to modify. This technique eliminates so-called **magic numbers**. For example, repeatedly mentioning the size 10 in array-processing code for a 10-element array gives the number 10 an artificial significance and can unfortunately confuse the reader when the application includes other 10s that have nothing to do with the array size. If you need to modify your program to work with a different size of array, you simply change one line of code—the definition of the ARRAY_SIZE constant—and recompile.

4. ***Calculating the sum.*** Add lines 17–21 of Fig. 13.7 to the function. The for header (line 18) uses the ARRAY_SIZE constant in the loop-continuation condition to iterate through the elements of array. Line 20 retrieves each element's value (one at a time) and adds it to total.

Retrieving the value of each element and adding it to the total, one at a time

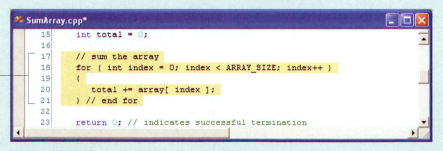

Figure 13.7 Summing the values of an array's elements.

Let's look more closely at this for statement. The first time this statement iterates, index contains the value 0, so line 20 adds the value of array[0] (which is 1) to total. The value of total was set to 0 in line 15, so the new value of total is 0 + 1, or 1. At the end of the first iteration, the value of index is incremented to 1. Line 20 adds the value of array[1] (which is 2) to total. The value of total contains 1 from the last iteration, so the new value of total is 1 + 2, or 3. The statement continues iterating, adding each value in array to total. The last iteration occurs when index contains the value 9. The value of array[9] (which is 10) will be added to total (total at this point will contain the value 55, as you will see shortly). At the end of this iteration, the value of index is incremented and now contains the value 10.

(cont.)

The loop-continuation condition is checked. Because 10 is not less than ARRAY_SIZE (which is also 10), the loop terminates and the application continues with the first statement after the loop.

5. ***Displaying the sum.*** Add lines 23–24 of Fig. 13.8 to the function. Line 24 displays the sum of the values of the array's elements.

```
 SumArray.cpp*
   21        } // end for
   22
   23        // display result
   24        cout << "\nSum of elements is: " << total << endl << endl;
   25
   26        return 0; // indicates successful termination
```

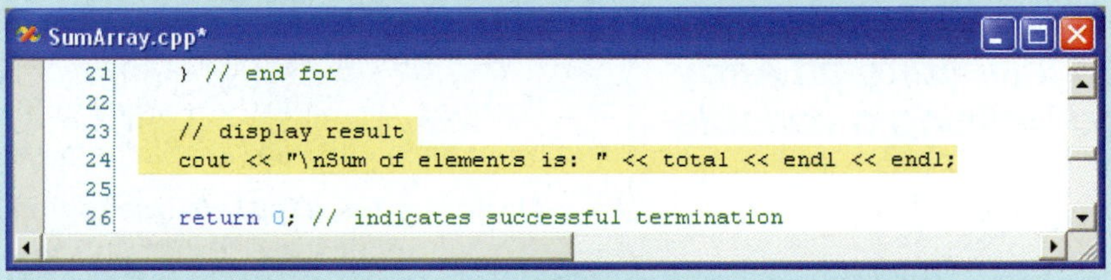

Figure 13.8 Displaying the sum of the values of an array's elements.

6. ***Save, compile and run the application.*** Figure 13.9 shows the completed application's output. Now the total value of the array elements (55) is displayed when you run the application.

Total value of array elements —————

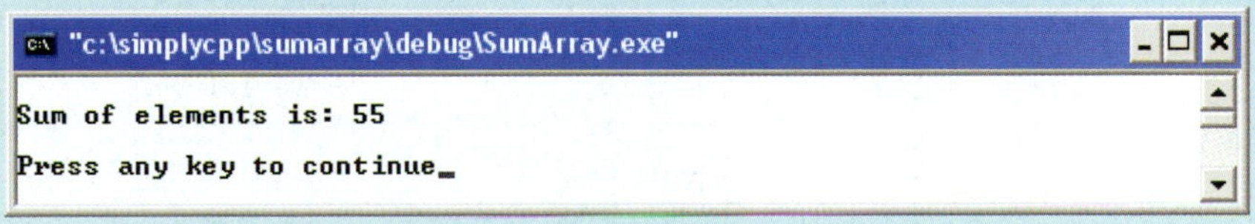

```
 "c:\simplycpp\sumarray\debug\SumArray.exe"
Sum of elements is: 55

Press any key to continue_
```

Figure 13.9 Completed **Sum Array** application output.

7. ***Close the Command Prompt window.***

SELF-REVIEW   1. Which of the following statements does not contain a syntax error?

   a) `int hours[ 5 ] = { 8, 8, 7.5, 8, 8.5 };`
   b) `int scores[ 4 ] = { 85, 92, 91, 88, 76 };`
   c) `int sales[ 7 ] = { 400, 300, 125 };`
   d) `char months[] = { "January", "February", "March" };`

   2. An array's length is _____.

   a) one more than the array's last index   b) one less than the array's last index
   c) the same as the array's last index   d) None of the above.

   Answers: 1) c. 2) a.

13.4 Constructing the Salary Survey Application

Now you will build your **Salary Survey** application by using an array of integers that stores the number of salaries that fall in each range of salaries. The following pseudocode describes the basic operation of the **Salary Survey** application.

> Prompt the user for the first sales figure
>
> While the sales figure is greater than or equal to zero
>   Calculate the salary based on commission
>   Increment the number of salaries within that range
>   Prompt the user for the next sales figure
> Display the distribution of salaries

Figure 13.10 Pseudocode for the **Salary Survey** application.

Now that you have test-driven the **Salary Survey** application and studied its pseudocode representation, you will initialize the variables used in the **Salary Survey** application. In particular, your application requires a `double` variable and a one-dimensional `int` array.

Declaring a Function Prototype, Declaring and Initializing an Array and Defining a Variable

1. ***Copying the template to your working directory.*** Copy the `C:\Examples\Tutorial13\TemplateApplication\SalarySurvey` directory to your `C:\SimplyCpp` directory.

2. ***Opening the Salary Survey application's template source code file.*** Open the template file `SalarySurvey.cpp` in your text editor or IDE.

3. ***Declaring the `displayTotals` function prototype.*** Add line 10 of Fig. 13.11 to your application. Your application will use the `displayTotals` function to display the distribution of salaries before exiting. The `displayTotals` function will accept an `int` array as an argument and will not return a value.

Declaring the `displayTotals` function prototype

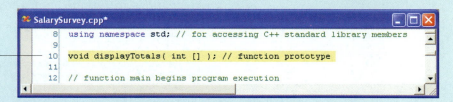

Figure 13.11 Declaring a function prototype for `displayTotals`.

Note the strange appearance of the function prototype for `display-Totals`

    void displayTotals(int []);

This prototype could have been written

    void displayTotals(int anyArrayName[]);

but as you learned in Tutorial 11, C++ compilers ignore variable names in prototypes. Remember, the prototype tells the compiler the number of arguments and the types of each argument (in the order in which the arguments are expected to appear).

4. ***Defining a `double` and creating an array of `int`s.*** Add lines 15–17 of Fig. 13.12. Line 16 defines and initializes `double` variable `sales`, into which will be input the value that the user enters at the **Enter sales (-1 to end):** prompt. Your application will use an array to keep track of the number of salaries corresponding to each range of salaries. Line 17 declares an array of `int`s named `resultArray` that contains 11 elements, then initializes their values to 0 using a single value to explicitly initialize the first element and implicitly initialize the remaining elements.

Defining and initializing `double` variable `sales`
Declaring `int` array `resultArray` and initializing its elements to 0

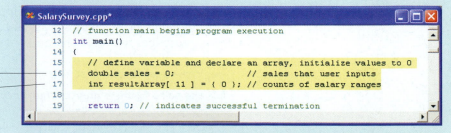

Figure 13.12 Defining a variable to store sales and creating an array of `int`s.

5. ***Save the application.***

Now you will add code to the **Salary Survey** application to prompt the user for and input a salesperson's total sales, then calculate the salary. You will also add code to update the count of the salaries in each salary range before prompting the user for the next salesperson's total sales.

Calculating a Salesperson's Salary

1. ***Prompting the user for and inputting a salesperson's sales.*** Add lines 19–21 of Fig. 13.13. Line 20 prompts the user for a salesperson's sales, and line 21 inputs the value into `double` variable `sales`.

Prompting the user for and inputting a salesperson's total sales

SalarySurvey.cpp*

```
17    int resultArray[ 11 ] = { 0 }; // counts of salary ranges
18
19    // prompt user for and input sales
20    cout << "\nEnter sales (-1 to end): ";
21    cin >> sales; // get sales
22
23    return 0; // indicates successful termination
```

Figure 13.13 Retrieving user input.

2. ***Formatting floating-point values.*** Add lines 23–24 of Fig. 13.14 to display the salary using two digits of precision.

Formatting floating-point values

SalarySurvey.cpp*

```
21    cin >> sales; // get sales
22
23    // display floating-point values as currency
24    cout << fixed << setprecision( 2 );
25
26    return 0; // indicates successful termination
```

Figure 13.14 Using the `fixed` and `setprecision` stream manipulators to display the salary.

3. ***Using a `while` repetition statement to process user input.*** The **Salary Survey** application should process user input and prompt the user for the next salary until the user enters the sentinel value (`-1`). Insert lines 26–30 of Fig. 13.15. This `while` statement repeats until the user enters the value `-1` (or any value less than zero, as all are invalid).

`while` statement will process user input and prompt the user for the next salary

SalarySurvey.cpp*

```
24    cout << fixed << setprecision( 2 );
25
26    // repeat until user enters sentinel value
27    while ( sales >= 0 )
28    {
29
30    } // end while
31
32    return 0; // indicates successful termination
```

Figure 13.15 `while` statement repeats until user enters an invalid value.

4. ***Calculating the salary and determining the corresponding index in the `resultArray` array.*** Insert lines 29–31 of Fig. 13.16 to the body of the `while` statement. Line 30 defines `double` variable `salary` and assigns it the salesperson's salary, which is calculated by adding 200 (the weekly base salary) to 9% of the total sales (the salesperson's commission).

(cont.)

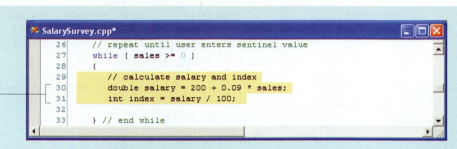

Calculating the salary and its corresponding index in `resultArray`

Figure 13.16 Calculating salary.

Once you have calculated the salary, you must update `resultArray` to accurately reflect the number of salaries in each salary range. For example, if the user's salary were $450, you would increment `resultArray[ 4 ]` to indicate that one more salary in the range $400 to $499 has been entered. Notice that the index of the array element (in this case, 4) is the hundreds digit of the salary. Line 31 of Fig. 13.16 divides `salary` by 100 to store the hundreds digit of `salary` as the ones digit of `index`.

5. ***Compiling the application.*** When you compile the application, the compiler issues a warning, which typically is a message indicating that a line of code might cause a logic error when executed. Unlike a syntax error, a warning does not prevent your application from compiling. (Warnings do not indicate that your application violates the grammatical rules of C++.) In this case, the warning indicates that a `double` value will be converted to an `int` value in line 31, resulting in a possible loss of data (Fig. 13.17). [*Note:* The C++ standard does not specify the warnings or error messages that a compiler issues. As a result, the warning issued by your compiler may differ from the one in Fig. 13.17. In Visual Studio .NET, you may need to select **View > Other Windows > Task List** to view the warning.]

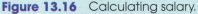

Warning due to possible loss of data

Figure 13.17 Warning issued by the compiler when assigning a `double` value to an `int` variable.

When your application attempts to divide salary (a `double`) by 100 (an `int`) in line 31 of Fig. 13.16, 100 is promoted to a `double` and the application performs floating-point division, as discussed in Tutorial 7. The result of that operation is a floating-point value, which is assigned to `int` variable `index`. In this case, the application must implicitly convert the floating-point result to an `int` before assigning it to `index`. Because data might be lost when the result is truncated, the compiler warns you that your application may lose data.

In this application, you are concerned with only the hundreds place of `salary`, so you can safely ignore the fractional part of `salary / 100`. Thus, the implicit conversion that produced the warning does not lead to a logic error. It is important to note that a compiler warning does not imply that a logic error will occur, only that one might occur. Because warnings do not always indicate logic errors, some programmers find warnings to be a nuisance.

(cont.)

However, compiler warnings should always be treated with caution. For example, a payroll application may use the floating-point result of salary / 100 to calculate dollars and cents. If this result were truncated, your application would lose the cents portion of each amount, which could lead to significant financial errors over time. Thus, it is a good programming practice to remove compiler warnings from your application whenever possible.

 **Error-Prevention Tip**

To help prevent logic errors, remove all compiler warnings from your applications.

6. ***Removing the compiler warning.*** Modify line 31 of your application as shown in Fig. 13.18. To remove the compiler warning, you must explicitly convert the result of salary / 100 to an int, using the static_cast operator.

Explicitly converting the result to an int to prevent a warning

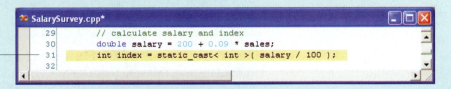

```
29          // calculate salary and index
30          double salary = 200 + 0.09 * sales;
31          int index = static_cast< int >( salary / 100 );
32
```

Figure 13.18 Explicitly converting the floating-point result to an int to prevent the compiler warning.

7. ***Updating the resultArray array.*** Insert lines 33–41 of Fig. 13.19 to the body of the while statement. This if...else statement increments the element of resultArray corresponding to the salary calculated in line 30. If the salary is greater than $1000, resultArray[10] should be incremented. The condition in line 34 determines whether index is greater than or equal to 10 (corresponding to salaries greater than or equal to $1000). If the condition evaluates to true, line 36 executes, incrementing resultArray[10]. Otherwise, line 40 executes, incrementing the value of resultArray[index]. For example, if index contains 4 (corresponding to a salary between $400 and $499), line 40 increments the value of resultArray[4].

Incrementing the appropriate element of resultArray

```
31          int index = static_cast< int >( salary ) / 100;
32
33          // update statistics
34          if ( index >= 10 )
35          {
36             resultArray[ 10 ]++;
37          } // end if
38          else
39          {
40             resultArray[ index ]++;
41          } // end else
42
43       } // end while
```

Figure 13.19 Updating the count of salaries in resultArray.

8. ***Displaying the salary and prompting the user for the next sales figure.*** Insert lines 43–48 of Fig. 13.20 to the body of the while statement. Line 44 displays the salesperson's salary, formatted with two positions to the left of the decimal point due to the statement in line 24. Lines 47–48 prompt the user for and input the next salesperson's total sales.

9. ***Save the application.***

(cont.)

Prompting user for next sales value ⎯⎯⎯

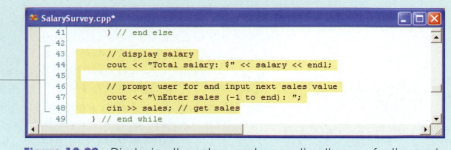

Figure 13.20 Displaying the salary and prompting the user for the next sales figure.

After the user enters the sentinel value (-1) to end input, the application should display the number of salaries in each salary range and exit. In the following box, you will insert a call to displayTotals, then define the displayTotals function. You will also learn how C++ passes an array to a function and how this differs from passing values such as individual ints.

Calling and Defining the displayTotals Function

1. **Calling the displayTotals function to display the number of salaries in each salary range.** Add lines 51–52 of Fig. 13.21 after the while statement. Line 52 passes the resultArray array to the displayTotals function, which you will define in the next step.

Using pass-by-reference when passing resultArray to displayTotal ⎯⎯⎯

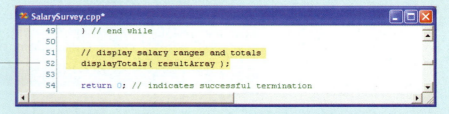

Figure 13.21 Passing resultArray by reference to the displayTotals function.

So far, whenever you have passed an argument to a function, you have used pass-by-value—a copy of the argument's value has been passed to the function. In contrast, line 52 uses **pass-by-reference**. When an argument is passed by reference, no copy of the argument is made—rather, the called function is given access directly to the argument in the caller. The original data in the caller can be modified by the called function. In C++, arrays are always passed by reference, while arguments of primitive types are, by default, passed by value. Because the array is passed by reference, the function can access the original array elements in the caller's memory.

2. **Creating the displayTotals function.** Add lines 58–62 of Fig. 13.22 after main. Line 59 declares the printArray parameter, which you will use to access the values in the argument to this function (in this case, resultArray in line 52).

3. **Defining local variables and displaying a table header.** Add lines 61–66 of Fig. 13.23 to the displayTotals function. Lines 62–63 define int variables lowerBound and upperBound, which you will use in the next step to store the lower bound and upper bound for each salary range. Line 66 displays a header for the table that will display the number of salaries in each salary range. This statement uses a newline (\n) to separate the table header from the input prompts and a tab (\t) to separate the two columns of the table.

(cont.)

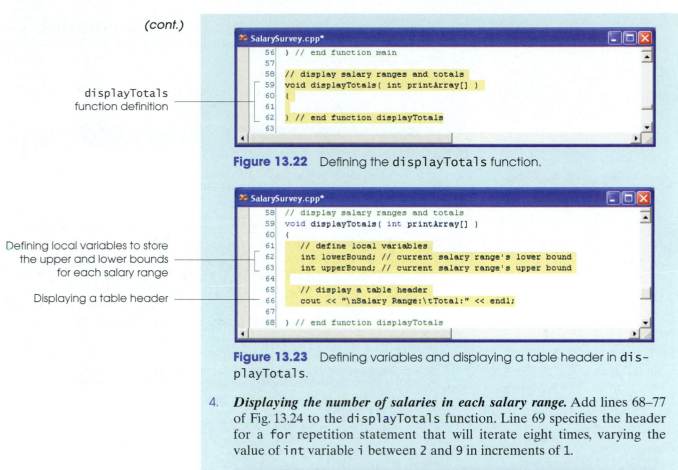

Figure 13.22   Defining the displayTotals function.

displayTotals function definition

Figure 13.23   Defining variables and displaying a table header in dis-playTotals.

Defining local variables to store the upper and lower bounds for each salary range

Displaying a table header

4. ***Displaying the number of salaries in each salary range.*** Add lines 68–77 of Fig. 13.24 to the displayTotals function. Line 69 specifies the header for a for repetition statement that will iterate eight times, varying the value of int variable i between 2 and 9 in increments of 1.

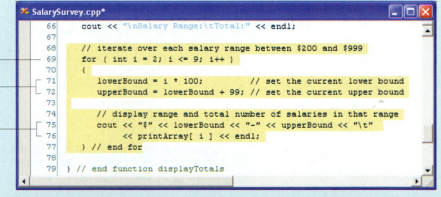

for statement varies i from 2 to 9

Assigning the upper and lower bounds for the current iteration

Displaying the salary range and number of salaries in that range

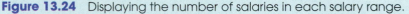

Figure 13.24   Displaying the number of salaries in each salary range.

Note that each iteration of this for statement uses i as the index of printArray (line 76). For example, when i equals 3, printArray[i] is printArray[3], which contains the number of salaries in the range $300–399. Notice that the lower bound for this iteration is i * 100 (in this case, 3 * 100, or 300). The upper bound is simply the lower bound plus 99 (in this case, 300 + 99, or 399). Accordingly, lines 71–72 assign the result of the expression i * 100 to the lower bound (stored in the lowerBound variable) and assign the result of lowerBound + 99 to the upperBound variable, which stores the upper bound for this iteration. Line 75 displays the salary range corresponding to each iteration of the for loop in the first column of the table. Line 76 displays the number of salaries in that range (contained in printArray[i]) in the second column of the table.

(cont.)

5. ***Displaying the number of salaries in the $1000+ salary range.*** There is no upper bound for the $1000+ salary range, so the `for` statement that you created in the preceding step could not display the number of salaries in that range. Insert lines 79–80 of Fig. 13.25. Line 80 displays the salary range ($1000+) in the first column, then displays the number of salaries in that range (`printArray[ 10 ]`).

Displaying the total for the final salary range

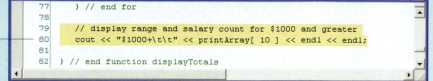

```
77        } // end for
78
79        // display range and salary count for $1000 and greater
80        cout << "$1000+\t\t" << printArray[ 10 ] << endl << endl;
81
82   } // end function displayTotals
```

Figure 13.25   Display the range and salary count for $1000 and greater.

6. ***Save, compile and run the application.*** Test your application by entering sales figures that produce salaries in several different salary ranges (Fig. 13.26). Ensure that each salary that the application calculates is correct. After entering several sales figures, enter –1 to end input and ensure that the proper number of salaries is displayed for each range (Fig. 13.27).

```
"c:\SimplyCpp\SalarySurvey\Debug\SalarySurvey.exe"

Enter sales (-1 to end): 500.00
Total salary: $245.00

Enter sales (-1 to end): 1238.50
Total salary: $311.46

Enter sales (-1 to end): 3456.78
Total salary: $511.11

Enter sales (-1 to end): 9900.00
Total salary: $1091.00

Enter sales (-1 to end): 7634.25
Total salary: $887.08

Enter sales (-1 to end): 5545.90
Total salary: $699.13

Enter sales (-1 to end): 4900.00
Total salary: $641.00
```

Figure 13.26   Sample input and output for the **Salary Survey** application.

```
"c:\SimplyCpp\SalarySurvey\Debug\SalarySurvey.exe"

Enter sales (-1 to end): -1

Salary Range:     Total:
$200-299          1
$300-399          1
$400-499          0
$500-599          1
$600-699          2
$700-799          0
$800-899          1
$900-999          0
$1000+            1

Press any key to continue_
```

Figure 13.27   Total of salaries in each range displayed upon exiting.

7. ***Close the Command Prompt window.***

Figure 13.28 presents the source code for the **Salary Survey** application. The lines of code that you added, viewed or modified in this tutorial are highlighted.

Declare the displayTotals function

Define and initialize double sales

Declare int array resultArray and initialize its elements to 0

while statement processes user input and prompts for the next salary

Calculate the salary and its corresponding index in resultArray

Increment the appropriate element of resultArray

Use pass-by-reference when passing resultArray to displayTotals

```cpp
1   // Tutorial 13: SalarySurvey.cpp
2   // Application that takes information about employee salaries and
3   // uses an array to keep track of the number of employees in each
4   // salary range.
5   #include <iostream> // required to perform C++ stream I/O
6   #include <iomanip>  // required for parameterized stream manipulators
7
8   using namespace std; // for accessing C++ Standard Library members
9
10  void displayTotals( int [] ); // function prototype
11
12  // function main begins program execution
13  int main()
14  {
15      // define variable and declare an array, initialize values to 0
16      double sales = 0;             // sales that user inputs
17      int resultArray[ 11 ] = { 0 }; // count of salary ranges
18
19      // prompt user for and input sales
20      cout << "\nEnter sales (-1 to end): ";
21      cin >> sales; // get sales
22
23      // display floating-point values as currency
24      cout << fixed << setprecision( 2 );
25
26      // repeat until user enters sentinel value
27      while ( sales >= 0 )
28      {
29          // calculate salary and index
30          double salary = 200 + 0.09 * sales;
31          int index = static_cast< int >( salary / 100 );
32
33          // update statistics
34          if ( index >= 10 )
35          {
36              resultArray[ 10 ]++;
37          } // end if
38          else
39          {
40              resultArray[ index ]++;
41          } // end else
42
43          // display salary
44          cout << "Total salary: $" << salary << endl;
45
46          // prompt user for and input next sales value
47          cout << "\nEnter sales (-1 to end): ";
48          cin >> sales; // get sales
49      } // end while
50
51      // display salary ranges and totals
52      displayTotals( resultArray );
53
54      return 0; // indicates successful termination
55
```

Figure 13.28   Salary Survey code. (Part 1 of 2.)

```
56    } // end function main
57
58    // display salary ranges and totals
59    void displayTotals( int printArray[] )
60    {
61        // define local variables
62        int lowerBound; // current salary range's lower bound
63        int upperBound; // current salary range's upper bound
64
65        // display a table header
66        cout << "\nSalary Range:\tTotal:" << endl;
67
68        // iterate over each salary range between $200 and $999
69        for ( int i = 2; i <= 9; i++ )
70        {
71            lowerBound = i * 100;            // set the current lower bound
72            upperBound = lowerBound + 99; // set the current upper bound
73
74            // display range and total number of salaries in that range
75            cout << "$" << lowerBound << "-" << upperBound << "\t"
76                << printArray[ i ] << endl;
77        } // end for
78
79        // display range and salary count for $1000 and greater
80        cout << "$1000+\t\t" << printArray[ 10 ] << endl << endl;
81
82    } // end function displayTotals
```

Define local variables to store the upper and lower bounds for each salary range

Display a table header

for header varies i from 2 to 9

Assign the lower and upper bounds for the current iteration

Display the salary range and number of salaries in that range

Display the count for the final salary range

Figure 13.28 **Salary Survey** code. (Part 2 of 2.)

SELF-REVIEW

1. By default, _____ are passed to functions by reference.
   a) ints
   b) arrays
   c) doubles
   d) primitive data types

2. When an array is declared as a parameter in a function prototype, the array's _____ must be specified.
   a) name
   b) size
   c) type
   d) All of the above.

Answers: 1) b. 2) c.

13.5 Wrap-Up

In this tutorial, you learned about data structures called arrays, which contain elements of the same type. You then learned how to create and initialize one-dimensional arrays. You used an index to access the data of an array and learned that the first index of an array is 0. You created a simple application called **Sum Array** that calculated the sum of the `int` values stored in an array.

In the **Salary Survey** application, you created a one-dimensional array of counters. and you used integer variables to access elements of the array. You learned the difference between passing data to a function by value and by reference. You learned that arrays are passed to functions by reference; array arguments in the caller can be modified from the called function.

In the next tutorial, you will learn how to create two-dimensional arrays, consisting of rows and columns of data. You will use them to create the **Student Grades** application.

SKILLS SUMMARY

Declaring and Initializing an Array

■ Declare the array using the format:

> *arrayType arrayName*[*arraySize*];

where *arrayName* is the reference name of the array, *arrayType* is the type of data that will be stored in the array and *arraySize* is an integer literal (such as 0 or 7) or integer expression representing the size of the array. The largest valid array index for an array is *arraySize* – 1. For example, the statement

> `int intArray[ 10 ];`

declares an array, `intArray`, consisting of 10 `int`s.

■ Use a repetition statement to initialize an array after it has been declared. When an array is created in this way, the elements in the array contain indeterminate values that should not be used until after they have been initialized.

■ Declare an array and initialize it with the expression:

> *arrayType arrayName*[] = { *arrayInitializerList* };

where *arrayInitializerList* is a comma-separated list of the constant values that will initialize the elements of the array. For example, the statement

> `int gradesArray[]= { 85, 99, 100, 65, 70, 81, 77, 93, 89, 59 };`

declares an array, `gradesArray`, consisting of 10 `int`s and initializes the values of its elements to the constants in the initializer list, in order. In this case, the zeroth element is assigned 85, element one is assigned 99, and so on.

Referring to Element *n* of an Array

■ Use index *n*. For example, to access element 3, use index 3; to access element 0, use index 0.

■ Enclose the index in square brackets after the array name. For example, to access element three of `intArray`, use the expression `intArray[ 3 ]`.

KEY TERMS

array—A data structure containing elements of the same type. Elements of an array are accessed by specifying an integer index in the range 0 to one less than the number of elements in the array.

array initializer—A comma-separated list of constant expressions enclosed in braces—{ and }—which is used to initialize the elements in an array. When there are fewer initializers than elements in the array, C++ explicitly initializes the elements corresponding to values in the initializer list and implicitly initializes the remaining elements to zero. When there is no initializer list, the elements in the array are not initialized.

data structure—An entry that groups and organizes related data.

element—An item in an array.

index—An array element's position number, also called a subscript. An index either must be zero, a positive integer, or an expression that evaluates to zero or a positive integer. If an application uses an expression as an index, the expression is evaluated first to determine the index.

indexed array name—The array name followed by an index enclosed in square brackets. The indexed array name can be used on the left side of an assignment statement to place a new value into the array element. The indexed array name can be used in the right side of an assignment to retrieve the value of that array element.

magic number—A number (such as the size of an array) that repeatedly appears in an application. A magic number takes on an artificial significance and can unfortunately confuse the reader when, for example, the application includes other instances of that number that have nothing to do with the size of the array.

one-dimensional array—An array that uses only one index.

pass-by-reference—A technique that allows a called function to access directly the argument in the caller. The original data in the caller can be modified by the called function. In C++, arrays are always passed by reference, while arguments of primitive types are, by default, passed by value. Because the array is passed by reference, the function can access the original array elements in the caller's memory.

position number—An alternate name for an array index. A value that indicates a specific position within an array. Position numbers begin at 0 (zero).

subscript—Another name for the term index or position number.

zeroth element—The first element in an array.

MULTIPLE-CHOICE QUESTIONS

13.1 Arrays can be defined to hold values of _____.

a) the `double` type
b) the `int` type
c) the `string` type
d) any type

13.2 The elements of an array are related by the fact that they have the same name and _____.

a) constant value
b) subscript
c) type
d) value

13.3 The _____ expression increments `intArray` array element 5.

a) `intArray[ 5 ]++;`
b) `intArray[ +5 ];`
c) `intArray[ 5++ ];`
d) `intArray[ ++5 ];`

13.4 The first element in every array is the _____.

a) subscript
b) zeroth element
c) length of the array
d) smallest value in the array

13.5 Arrays _____.

a) are classes
b) always have one dimension
c) keep data in sorted order at all times
d) None of the above.

13.6 To create an array initializer to specify the initial values of the elements in the array, use the _____ symbols.

a) `[` and `]`
b) `<` and `>`
c) `(` and `)`
d) `{` and `}`

13.7 Which of the following array declarations contains a syntax error?

a) `int array[ 7 ] = { 0 };`
b) `int array[] = { 2, 3, 4 };`
c) `int array[ 2 ] = { 18, 4, 56 };`
d) `int array[ 4 ] = { 7, 89, 34, 0 };`

13.8 The C++ compiler determines whether the array index _____.

a) contains an integer literal or expression
b) is greater than zero
c) is less than the number of elements in the array
d) All of the above.

13.9 When an argument is passed to a function and a copy of the argument's value has been passed to the function, this is known as _____.

a) pass-by-call
b) pass-by-value
c) pass-by-reference
d) pass-by-function

13.10 When an array is created without an initializer, each element in the array _____.

a) is initialized to 0
b) is initialized to 1
c) contains in indeterminate value
d) None of the above. Accessing an array element before initializing it is a syntax error.

EXERCISES

13.11 *(Airline Reservation Application)* A small airline has just purchased a computer for its new automated reservations system. You have been asked to program the new system. You are to write an application to assign seats on each flight of the airline's only plane (capacity: 10 seats).

Your application should display a menu of alternatives indicating the values 1 for first class and 2 for economy (Fig. 13.29). If the user types 1, your application should assign a seat in the first class section (seats 1–5). If the user types 2, your application should assign a seat in the economy section (seats 6–10). Your application should display a message indicating the user's seat number and whether it is in the first class or economy section of the plane (Fig. 13.29).

Use a single-subscripted array to represent the seating chart of the plane. Initialize all the elements of the array to 0 to indicate that all seats are empty. As each seat is assigned, set the corresponding element of the array to 1 to indicate that the seat is no longer available.

Your application should, of course, never assign a seat that has already been assigned. When the first class section is full, your application should ask the user if it is acceptable to be placed in the economy section (and vice versa). If yes, then make the appropriate seat assignment. If no, then display the message. "Next flight leaves in 3 hours."

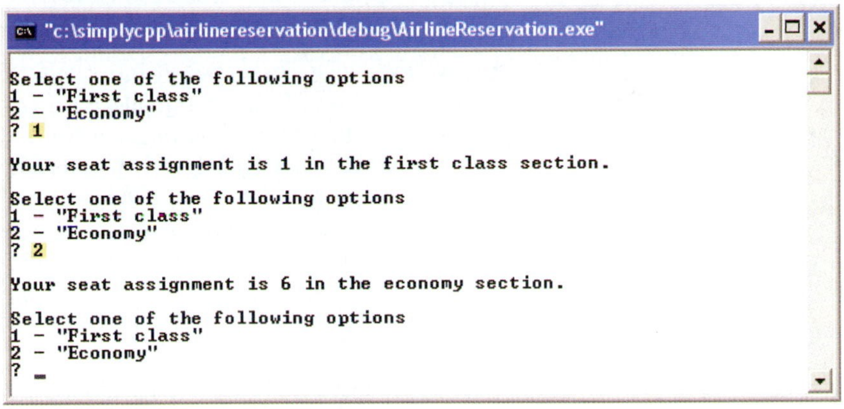

Figure 13.29 Airline Reservation application output.

a) *Copying the template to your working directory.* Copy the C:\Examples\ Tutorial13\Exercises\AirlineReservation directory to your C:\SimplyCpp directory.

b) *Opening the template source code file.* Open the AirlineReservation.cpp file in your text editor or IDE. Notice that most of main has been defined for you. In this exercise, you will add code to create and manipulate the array that determines whether a seat is available.

c) *Defining variables and creating an array.* After line 13, add a statement that defines the int constant SEATS that stores the size of the array that you will use to represent seats on the plane. Because seat numbers start at 1 and end at 10, you will create an array containing 11 elements and ignore the element at the index 0. As a result, you should initialize SEATS to 11. In line 15, add a statement that declares a bool array plane containing the number of elements in SEATS. Initialize its each element to false (recall that false is stored as 0 inside the computer). Finally, in lines 16–18, declare int variables people, economy and firstClass to store the number of reserved seats, the next unreserved economy seat number and the next unreserved first class seat number, respectively. Initialize people to 0, economy to 6 and firstClass to 1.

d) *Updating variables when the user selects first class.* When the body of the if statement beginning in line 34 executes, the user has selected a first class seat and a first class seat is available. To assign the seat, you must indicate that the seat is taken, then increment the variables that store the number of total reserved seats and the number of the next available seat in first class. After the comment in line 39, insert a statement that sets the element of the plane array at the index of firstClass to true to indicate that the seat is taken. Use the postincrement operator on firstClass to increment the value of firstClass after the plane array is updated. Then increment the value of people.

e) *Updating variables when the user selects first class, but no seats are available.* If first class is full, the user is asked whether a seat in economy class is acceptable. If the user enters a "y" (for yes), an economy seat should be reserved. Find the portion of the code that executes in this case and add code that assigns the seat using the same technique as in *Step d* except that you must replace firstClass with economy.

f) *Updating variables when the user selects economy class.* If the user enters 2 at the seat selection menu and an economy seat is available, the application should reserve the seat by updating its array and corresponding variables. Find the portion of the code that executes in this case and add code that assigns the seat using the same technique as in *Step e.*

g) *Updating variables when the user selects economy class, but no seats are available.* If economy class is full, the user is asked whether a seat in first class is acceptable. If the user enters a "y" (for yes), a first class seat should be reserved. Find the portion of the code that executes in this case and add code that assigns the seat using the same technique as in *Step d.*

h) *Save, compile and run the application.* Run the application several times, each time reserving seats in a different order to ensure that the application responds properly when either first class, economy class or both classes are full.

i) *Close the Command Prompt window.*

13.12 (*Enhanced Dice Simulator Application*) The application you created in Exercise 12.12 used global variables to store the frequency with which each die face appeared. In this exercise you will modify the application to use an array to eliminate global variables. Recall the original problem statement:

> *Your application should prompt the user to press* Enter *before each roll of the dice. When the user presses* Enter, *the application should display the result of "rolling" the dice using random numbers. It should also display the number of times each face has appeared. This application will help you see if dice rolling on your computer is really random. If it is, the number of 1s, 2s, 3s, 4s, 5s and 6s you roll should be about the same, at least for a large number of rolls.*

Your application output should appear as in Fig. 13.30.

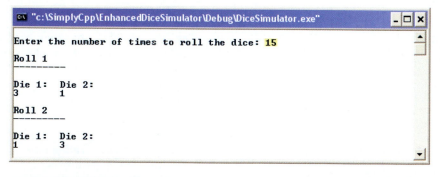

Figure 13.30 Dice Simulator output.

a) ***Copying the template to your working directory.*** Copy the `C:\Examples\ Tutorial13\Exercises\EnhancedDiceSimulator` directory to your `C:\SimplyCpp` directory. Then copy the file `C:\SimplyCpp\DiceSimulator\DiceSimulator.cpp` to your `C:\SimplyCpp\EnhancedDiceSimulator` directory. If you have not completed Exercise 12.12, follow the steps in Exercise 12.12 before copying the file.

b) ***Opening the template source code file.*** Open the `DiceSimulator.cpp` file in your text editor or IDE.

c) ***Removing global variables.*** Remove all global variables from your application, including the constant definitions.

d) ***Modifying the function prototypes.*** Modify the `rollDie` function prototype to declare a function that accepts a single `int` array argument. Then modify the `setFrequency` function prototype to declare a function that accepts an `int` argument and an `int` array argument, in that order.

e) ***Creating a local variable storing an array in `main`.*** Your array will contain seven elements. You will use the first element to store the total number of dice rolls. The elements at indices 1–6 will store the number of times the die face's value is the same as each element's index. For example, if the die face's value is 3, the element at index 3 will be incremented. Define `int` constant `SIZE` and initialize its value to 7. Then, create `int` array `frequency` containing `SIZE` elements and initialize each element's value to 0.

f) ***Passing the array to `rollDie`.*** Modify each call to `rollDie` so that `main` passes the `frequency` array as the argument.

g) ***Completing modifications to `main`.*** Modify the output statements that display statistical information so that they use the values contained in the array. For example, the `frequency1` variable should be replaced with `frequency[ 1 ]`. Similarly, `frequency2` should be replaced with `frequency[ 2 ]`. Be sure to replace `total` with `frequency[ 0 ]`.

h) ***Modifying the `rollDie` function definition.*** Modify the `rollDie` header to specify an `int` array parameter named `frequencyArray`. Then modify the call to `setFrequency` so that it passes to the function the `face` and `frequencyArray` variables, in that order.

i) ***Modifying the `setFrequency` function definition.*** Modify the `setFrequency` header to specify `int` parameter `face` and `int` array parameter `frequencyArray`. Then remove all statements in the body of the function. To update the frequency and the total number of die rolls, you need only write two statements. Recall that the value of the die face serves as the index of the array element that should be updated when that die face appears. Thus, to update the frequency for any value of face, you should insert the expression `frequencyArray[ face ]++`. Each time the `setFrequency` function is called, you should also increment the total using the expression `frequencyArray[ 0 ]++`.

j) ***Save, compile and run the application.*** Test your application to ensure that it runs correctly by pressing *Enter* 30 times (to roll 60 dice). Make sure that the total number of rolls adds up to 60.

k) ***Close the Command Prompt window.***

13.13 (*Cafeteria Survey Application*) Twenty students were asked to rate, on a scale of 1 to 10, the quality of the food in the student cafeteria, with 1 being "awful" and 10 being "excellent." Your application should present the user with a menu of options. Place the 20 responses in an `int` array and determine the frequency of each rating. Display the frequencies as a histogram. Recall that a histogram (also known as a bar chart) is a chart where numeric values are displayed as bars. In such a chart, longer bars represent larger numeric values. One simple way to display numeric data graphically is with a histogram that shows each numeric value as a bar of asterisks (*). Figure 13.31 demonstrates the completed application.

```
"c:\simplycpp\cafeteriasurvey\debug\CafeteriaSurvey.exe"                    _ □ ×

Rate cafeteria food (scale of 1 to 10): 1
Rate cafeteria food (scale of 1 to 10): 12
Error: Specify a number within the valid range.
Rate cafeteria food (scale of 1 to 10): 10
Rate cafeteria food (scale of 1 to 10): _
```

```
"c:\simplycpp\cafeteriasurvey\debug\CafeteriaSurvey.exe"                    _ □ ×

Rate cafeteria food (scale of 1 to 10): 4
Rating  Frequency:
1         *
2         **
3         *
4         *
5         **
6         *****
7         ***
8         **
9         *
10        **

Press any key to continue_
```

Figure 13.31 Cafeteria Survey application output.

a) *Copying the template to your working directory.* Copy the C:\Examples\ Tutorial13\Exercises\CafeteriaSurvey directory to your C:\SimplyCpp directory.

b) *Opening the template source code file.* Open the CafeteriaSurvey.cpp file in your text editor or IDE. Notice that some of main has been coded for you.

c) *Creating an array of the possible ratings.* After line 13, define int constant SIZE an initialize its value to 11. On the next line, define int array responses containing SIZE elements and initialize its values to 0.

d) *Displaying an error message when user input is out of range.* In line 26, replace the condition of the if part of the if...else statement with an expression that evaluates to true if the value that the user enters at the keyboard (contained in input) is not a valid rating.

e) *Completing the else part of the if...else statement.* The body of the else part of the if...else statement executes when the user enters a valid rating. In lines 34–35, increment responseCounter to indicate that another valid response has been entered. Then increment the element of the responses array at the index corresponding to the value of input. For example, if the user enters the value 3, the application should increment responses[3].

f) *Displaying the histogram.* You will now display the results in the form of a histogram. Line 44 begins a for statement. This statement loops once for each rating, displaying the rating in line 46 (followed by a tab character) and a newline character in line 48. You will add the number of stars that will be displayed to the right of each rating. In line 49, add the header of a for statement that loops from 1 until the number of votes for the current rating (stored in responses). Use line 48 for a comment describing the statement. In line 50, add the left brace to begin the for statement's body. In line 51, add an asterisk to the output. Because this for statement will loop the same number of times as there are votes for the current rating, the proper number of asterisks will be displayed. In line 53, add the right brace to end the for statement's body. Follow the brace with a comment indicating the end of the for statement.

g) *Save, compile and run the application.* Test the application to ensure that it runs correctly. Enter 20 different ratings by typing values at the menu's prompt. After 20 ratings have been entered, check that the application displays the proper number of asterisks for each rating.

h) *Close the Command Prompt window.*

What does this code do? ▶ **13.14** The mystery function uses the numbers array to modify the elements in the `mysteryArray` array. What does `mysteryArray` contain at the end of the function?

```cpp
1   // Exercise 13.14: WDTCD.cpp
2   // What does this code do?
3   #include <iostream> // required to perform C++ stream I/O
4
5   using namespace std; // for accessing C++ Standard Library members
6
7   // function prototypes
8   void mystery();
9
10  // function main begins program execution
11  int main()
12  {
13     mystery();
14
15     cout << "\n"; // insert newline for readability
16     return 0; // indicate that program terminated correctly
17
18  } // end function main
19
20  void mystery()
21  {
22     const int ARRAY_SIZE = 5;
23     int numbers[] = { 0, 1, 2, 3, 4 };
24     int mysteryArray[ ARRAY_SIZE ];
25
26     for ( int i = ARRAY_SIZE; i > 0; i-- )
27     {
28        mysteryArray[ ARRAY_SIZE - i ] = numbers[ i - 1 ];
29     } // end for
30
31     for ( int i = 0; i < ARRAY_SIZE; i++ )
32     {
33        cout << "\nmysteryArray[" << i << "] = " << mysteryArray[i]
34           << endl;
35     } // end for
36
37  } // end function mystery
```

What's wrong with this code? ▶ **13.15** The following code uses a `for` loop to sum the elements of an array. Find the error(s) in the following code:

```cpp
1   // Exercise 13.15: WWWTC.cpp
2   // The following code uses a for loop to sum
3   //  the elements of an array, and then display the sum.
4   #include <iostream> // required to perform C++ stream I/O
5
6   using namespace std; // for accessing C++ Standard Library members
7
8   // function prototypes
9   void sumArray();
10
```

```
// function main begins program execution
int main()
{
   sumArray();

   return 0; // indicate that program terminated correctly

} // end function main

// sum an array of integers
void sumArray()
{
   const int ARRAY_SIZE = 8;
   int numbers[] = { 1, 2, 3, 4, 5, 6, 7, 8 };

   for ( int counter = 0; counter <= ARRAY_SIZE; counter++ )
   {
      int sum += numbers[ counter ];
   } // end for

   cout << "\nSum = " << sum << endl << endl;

} // end function sumArray
```

Programming Challenge ▶

13.16 (***Mean, Median and Mode Application***) Computers are commonly used to compile and analyze the results of surveys and opinion polls. Write an application that will input a series of 10 numeric survey responses (in the range 1–5) and display the mean, median and mode of those values. The mean is the arithmetic average of the 11 values, the median is middle value and the mode is the number that appears most frequently. This application should look like Fig. 13.32.

```
"c:\simplycpp\meanmedianmode\debug\MeanMedianMode.exe"

Enter survey response (1-5): 4
Enter survey response (1-5): 3
Enter survey response (1-5): 5
Enter survey response (1-5): 2
Enter survey response (1-5): 3
Enter survey response (1-5): 4
Enter survey response (1-5): 2
Enter survey response (1-5): 3
Enter survey response (1-5): 1
Enter survey response (1-5): 2
Enter survey response (1-5): 2
Mean: 2.9
Median: 3
Mode: 2

Press any key to continue_
```

Figure 13.32 Mean, Median and Mode application.

a) ***Copying the template to your working directory.*** Copy the `C:\Examples\Tutorial13\Exercises\MeanMedianMode` directory to your `C:\SimplyCpp` directory.

b) ***Opening the template source code file.*** Open the `MeanMedianMode.cpp` file in your text editor or IDE. Notice that the template source code file contains function prototypes, an incomplete `main` function and the complete `sortArray` function definition.

c) *Defining variables and constants, and declaring arrays to contain the user's responses and the frequency of each response.* After line 19, define int constants MAX_RESPONSES and MAX_VALUE to store the maximum number of responses that your application will accept and the maximum value for each survey response, respectively. Initialize MAX_RESPONSES to 10 and MAX_VALUE to 5. Then declare int arrays responses and frequency. The responses array will store each survey response in a separate element; the frequency array will store the number of times each response value has been entered. Because you will not use the zeroth element of either array, declare responses to be of size MAX_RESPONSES + 1 and declare frequency to be of size MAX_VALUE + 1. Finally, define int variable response to store the response that the user enters at the keyboard, and define int variable responseCounter to store the number of responses that have been entered. Initialize the value of responseCounter to 1.

d) *Updating variables and array elements after each user response is entered.* main contains a single while statement. This statement contains an if...else statement that determines whether the user entered an invalid value. If the value is valid, the else part of the if...else statement executes. This part should place a copy of the user's response (contained in the response variable) in the responses array. Use the responseCounter variable as an index into the array. The application should then increment the element of the frequency array corresponding to the value of the user's response. Finally, the application should increment responseCounter.

e) *Calculating and displaying the mean, median and mode.* Immediately after main's while statement, insert code that calls the displayMean, displayMedian and displayMode functions. You will define these functions in the following steps. The first argument to the displayMean and displayMedian functions should be the responses array. The second argument must specify the size of the array. The displayMode function call must pass the frequency array as its first argument and the size of that array as the second argument.

f) *Calculating and displaying the mean.* After the sortArray function definition, define the displayMean function. Declare double variable sum to store the sum of all responses. Then, use a repetition statement to add each value in the array to sum. Display the average value of this sum.

g) *Calculating and displaying the median.* In this step, you will define the displayMedian function. In a list of values, the median value is the value that appears in the middle of a sorted (that is, ordered) list of those values. Thus, to obtain the median, you first must sort the array so that the values of elements appear in order (such as smallest to largest). Pass the responseArray array to the sortArray function that has been provided in the template code. The sortArray function uses a simple technique (often called "bubble sort") to sort its parameter (unsortedArray) in ascending order. When the call to sortArray returns, responseArray will be sorted. Thus, to find the median value, insert a statement that accesses the responseArray element that is halfway between the first and last element (excluding the zeroth element). Display this median value before exiting the function.

h) *Calculating and displaying the mode.* In a list of values, the mode is the value that appears most often. Thus, your displayMode function should determine which element of the array passed as an argument (in this application, the frequency array) has the largest value. For simplicity, assume that the survey contains only one mode. Define int variable mostFrequent and initialize its value to 0. The mostFrequent variable will store the index of the element of the array with the highest value. Use a repetition statement to iterate over each element of the frequencyArray array. In the body of the repetition statement, you should determine whether the current element is greater than the element of frequencyArray specified by mostFrequent. If so, the application should assign the index of the current element to mostFrequent. After the repetition statement terminates, display the mode, which is now stored in mostFrequent.

i) *Save, compile and run the application.* Test the application to ensure that it runs correctly. Enter several sets of values answers to make sure that the correct mean, median and mode are displayed.

j) *Close the Command Prompt window.*

14 TUTORIAL

Objectives

In this tutorial, you will learn to:

- Differentiate between one-dimensional and two-dimensional arrays.
- Declare and manipulate two-dimensional arrays.
- Understand applications of two-dimensional arrays.
- Use the `right` stream manipulator to right justify output in a field.

Outline

Student Grades Application

Introducing Two-Dimensional Arrays and References

In this tutorial, you will learn about two-dimensional arrays, which, like one-dimensional arrays, store multiple values of the same type. However, two-dimensional arrays allow you to store multiple rows of values of the same type. Also, you will learn a new stream I/O feature: the `right` stream manipulator, which right justifies text in a field.

14.1 Test-Driving the Student Grades Application

In this tutorial, you will implement the **Student Grades** application by using a two-dimensional array. This application must meet the following requirements:

> ### Application Requirements
>
> *A teacher issues three tests to a class of 10 students. The grades on these tests are integers in the range 0 to 100. The teacher has asked you to develop an application to keep track of each student's grades and average, the average grade for each test and the average of the class as a whole. The application should allow a user to input three test grades for each student, then compute each student's average and the class average. If the user enters an invalid grade, the application should issue an error message and prompt the user to input the grade again.*

The student's average is equal to the sum of the student's three grades divided by three. The average grade for each test is equal to the sum of each student's grade on that test divided by the number of students in the class (10 in this case). The class average is equal to the sum of all of the students' grades divided by the total number of grades. You begin by test-driving the completed application. Then, you will learn the additional C++ techniques you will need to create your own version of this application.

Test-Driving the Student Grades Application

1. *Locating the completed application.* Open the **Command Prompt** window by selecting **Start > All Programs > Accessories > Command Prompt**. Change to your completed **Student Grades** application directory by typing cd C:\Examples\Tutorial14\CompletedApplication\StudentGrades.

2. *Running the Student Grades application.* Type StudentGrades in the **Command Prompt** window to run the application (Fig. 14.1). The application prompts you for the first student's grade on the first test.

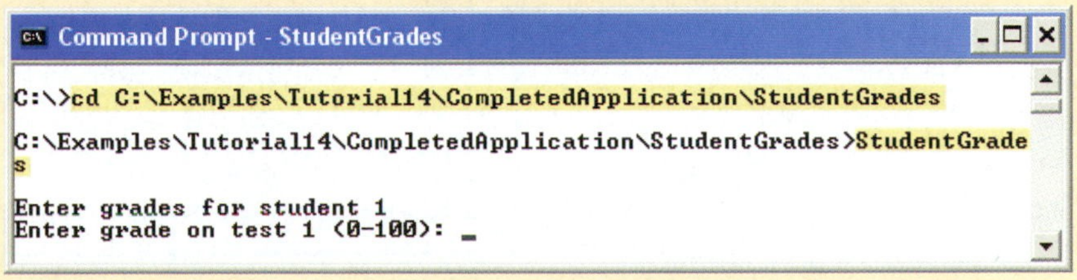

Figure 14.1   Running the completed **Student Grades** application.

3. *Entering grades for the first student.* Type 94, 98 and 51 at the prompts for first student's first, second and third grade, respectively (Fig. 14.2).

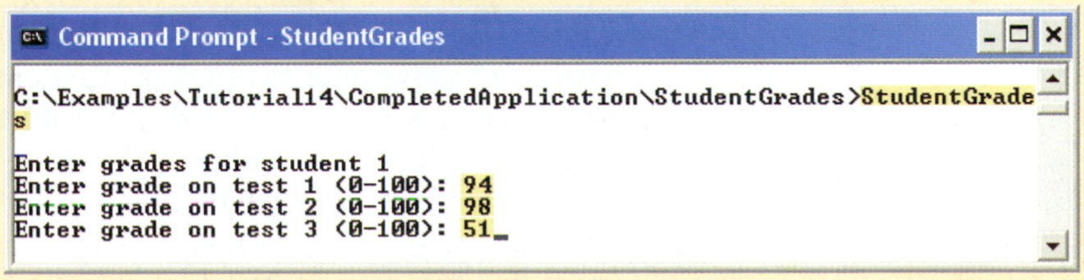

Figure 14.2   Inputting grades into the **Student Grades** application.

4. *Entering an invalid grade.* After you enter three grades for the first student, the application prompts you for the second student's grade on the first test. Enter the value 150 (an invalid grade). Notice that the application displays an error message and prompts you to enter the grade again (Fig. 14.3). Enter 61 at the **Enter grade on test 1 (0-100):** prompt.

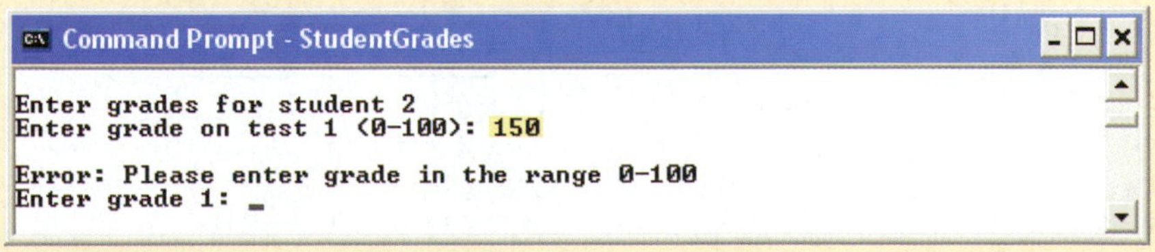

Figure 14.3   Error message displayed after inputting invalid grade.

5. *Entering grades for the remaining students.* Enter additional grades for the remaining nine students. The values that were used in this examples are displayed in the table in Fig. 14.4. Notice that after you enter the last grade, the application displays each student's test grades and average grade, the average grade for each test and the class average (Fig. 14.4).

6. *Close the Command Prompt window.*

(cont.)

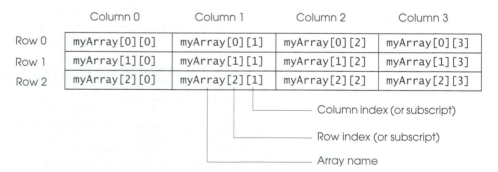

Figure 14.4 Displaying test grades and averages.

14.2 Two-Dimensional Arrays

So far, you have studied one-dimensional arrays, which contain one sequence of values and require one index. In this section, you will learn about **two-dimensional arrays**, which require two indices to identify particular elements. Two-dimensional arrays are often used to represent **tables** of values, which consist of information arranged in **rows** and **columns**. Each row is the same size and therefore has the same number of columns. To identify a particular table element, you must specify its two indices—by convention, the first identifies the element's row and the second identifies the element's column. Figure 14.5 illustrates a two-dimensional array, myArray, containing three rows and four columns. A two-dimensional array with *m* rows and *n* columns is called an ***m*-by-*n* array**; therefore, the array in Fig. 14.5 is a 3-by-4 array.

Figure 14.5 Two-dimensional array with three rows and four columns.

Every element in the myArray array is identified in Fig. 14.5 by an element name of the form myArray[i][j], where myArray is the name of the array and i and j are the indices that uniquely identify the row and column of each element in the myArray array. Notice that the first row number and the first column number in a two-dimensional array are always zero. The elements in row zero each have a first index of 0, and the elements in the last column each have a second index of 3.

Initializing Two-Dimensional Arrays

Two-dimensional arrays are initialized in definitions similarly to one-dimensional arrays. For example, a two-dimensional array, numbers, with three rows and two columns, can be defined and initialized with

```
int numbers[ 3 ][ 2 ];
numbers[ 0 ][ 0 ] = 1;
numbers[ 0 ][ 1 ] = 2;
numbers[ 1 ][ 0 ] = 3;
numbers[ 1 ][ 1 ] = 4;
numbers[ 2 ][ 0 ] = 5;
numbers[ 2 ][ 1 ] = 6;
```

Notice that the integers used to specify the number of rows and columns when the array is created (in this case, 3 and 2) always indicate *exactly* the number of elements in the row or column. The indices in a row or column vary from zero to one less than the number of elements in that row or column. Figure 14.6 illustrates the contents of numbers after its values have been initialized.

	Column 0	Column 1
Row 0	1	2
Row 1	3	4
Row 2	5	6

Figure 14.6   Two-dimensional **numbers** array after initialization.

The preceding definition and initialization statements can be written in a single statement, using an array initializer, as follows:

```
int numbers[ 3 ][ 2 ] = { { 1, 2 }, { 3, 4 }, { 5, 6 } };
```

The values are grouped by row in braces, with 1 and 2 initializing numbers[0][0] and numbers[0][1], respectively, 3 and 4 initializing numbers[1][0] and numbers[1][1], respectively, and 5 and 6 initializing numbers[2][0] and numbers[2][1], respectively. If there are not enough initializers for a given row, the remaining elements of that row are initialized to 0. To initialize every element of numbers to 0, use the statement

```
int numbers[ 3 ][ 2 ] = { 0 };
```

Passing Two-Dimensional Arrays to Functions

In Tutorial 13, you learned that when you declare a one-dimensional array as a parameter to a function, you can leave the array brackets empty in the function's parameter list. For example, the function prototype for a function that accepts a one-dimensional array as a parameter can be declared using the statement

```
void process1DArray( int [] );
```

The number of rows in an array (specified by the first index of a two-dimensional array) is not required either, but the number of columns (specified by the second index) is required. For example, the following prototype declares a function that accepts a two-dimensional array, where the number of columns is specified by int constant SIZE:

```
void process2DArray( int [][ SIZE ] );
```

The compiler uses this size to determine the locations (in memory) of elements in the two-dimensional array parameter. All array elements are stored consecutively in memory. In a two-dimensional array, the first row is stored in memory, followed by the second row. In a two-dimensional array, each row is a one-dimensional array. To locate an element in a particular row, the function must know exactly how many elements are in each row, so it can skip the proper number of memory locations when accessing an array element. Thus, when accessing `numbers[1][2]`, the function knows to skip row zero's three elements in memory to get to row one. Then, the function accesses element two of that row.

1. Arrays that use two indices are referred to as _____ arrays.
   a) single-subscripted
   b) two-dimensional
   c) square
   d) one-dimensional

2. _____ creates an int array of two rows and five columns.
   a) `int[ 2 ][ 5 ];`
   b) `int intArray[ 5 ][ 2 ];`
   c) `int intArray[ 2 ][ 5 ];`
   d) `int[ 1 ][ 4 ];`

Answers: 1) b. 2) c.

14.3 Inserting Code into the Student Grades Application

Your **Student Grades** application will use arrays to store the students' test grades. The application will also display each test grade for each student, each student's average test grade, the average grade for each test and the class average. The pseudocode in Fig. 14.7 describes the basic operation of the **Student Grades** application.

> For each student in the class
>   Prompt the user for and input three test grades
>
>   While the user enters an invalid grade
>   Prompt the user for and input the grade again
>
> Display a table header
>
> For each student
>   Display each student's test grades and average grade
>
> For each test
>   Display the average grade on the test
>
> Display the class average

Figure 14.7 Pseudocode for the **Student Grades** application.

Now that you have test-driven the **Student Grades** application and studied its pseudocode representation, you will build your **Student Grades** application. In the following box, you will declare function prototypes for functions that declare two-dimensional arrays as parameters, then add code to `main`.

Coding the main Function

1. **Copying the template to your working directory.** Copy the `C:\Examples\Tutorial14\TemplateApplication\StudentGrades` directory to your `C:\SimplyCpp` directory.

2. **Opening the Student Grades application template file.** Open the template file `StudentGrades.cpp` in your text editor or IDE.

3. **Defining constants.** Add lines 10–12 of Fig. 14.8 to your code. Line 11 defines int constant TESTS, which contains the number of tests, 3, that each student has taken. Line 12 defines int constant STUDENTS, which contains the number of students, 10, in the class.

(cont.)

Defining constants representing the number of students and tests

```
StudentGrades.cpp*
 8  using namespace std; // for accessing C++ standard library members
 9
10  // define constants
11  const int TESTS = 3; // number of tests per student
12  const int STUDENTS = 10; // maximum students stored
13
14  // function main begins program execution
```

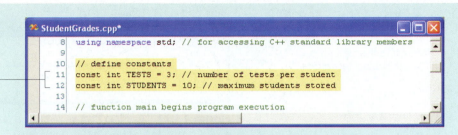

Figure 14.8 Defining constant variables.

4. ***Declaring function prototypes.*** Add lines 14–16 of Fig. 14.9 to your code. Line 15 declares the `getStudentGrades` function, which accepts a two-dimensional `int` array. Note that the two-dimensional array specifies a row size (i.e., the number of columns per row) of `TESTS`, which you initialized to 3 in line 11. As you will see later in this tutorial, each row of the two-dimensional array will contain three grades for a particular student. Line 16 declares the `displayGrades` function, which specifies a two-dimensional `int` array parameter. Again, the two-dimensional array specifies the row size of `TESTS`.

Declaring function prototypes that specify two-dimensional array parameters

```
StudentGrades.cpp*
12  const int STUDENTS = 10; // maximum students stored
13
14  // function prototypes
15  void getStudentGrades( int [][ TESTS ] );
16  void displayGrades( int [][ TESTS ] );
17
18  // function main begins program execution
```

Figure 14.9 Declaring function prototypes.

5. ***Defining and initializing variables.*** Add lines 21–22 of Fig. 14.10 to `main`. Line 22 declares the two-dimensional `studentGrades` array, which will store three grades for each student. This array contains `STUDENTS` rows and `TESTS` columns, so `studentGrades` is a 10-by-3 array. The elements of this array are initialized to zero.

Declaring a two-dimensional array

```
StudentGrades.cpp*
18  // function main begins program execution
19  int main()
20  {
21     // define two-dimensional array to store student grades
22     int studentGrades[ STUDENTS ][ TESTS ] = { 0 };
23
24     return 0; // indicates successful termination
```

Figure 14.10 Defining and initializing a two-dimensional array.

6. ***Prompting the user for and inputting student grades.*** Add line 24 of Fig. 14.11 to `main`. This line calls the `getStudentGrades` function, which you will define later in this tutorial. The `getStudentGrades` function, which prompts the user for and inputs the class's test grades, accepts a two-dimensional `int` array argument (in this case, `studentGrades`). Because arrays are passed by reference, when `getStudentGrades` modifies the values of the array received as its parameter, the values in the `studentGrades` array (declared in line 22) are modified.

(cont.)

Prompting the user for and
inputting test grades

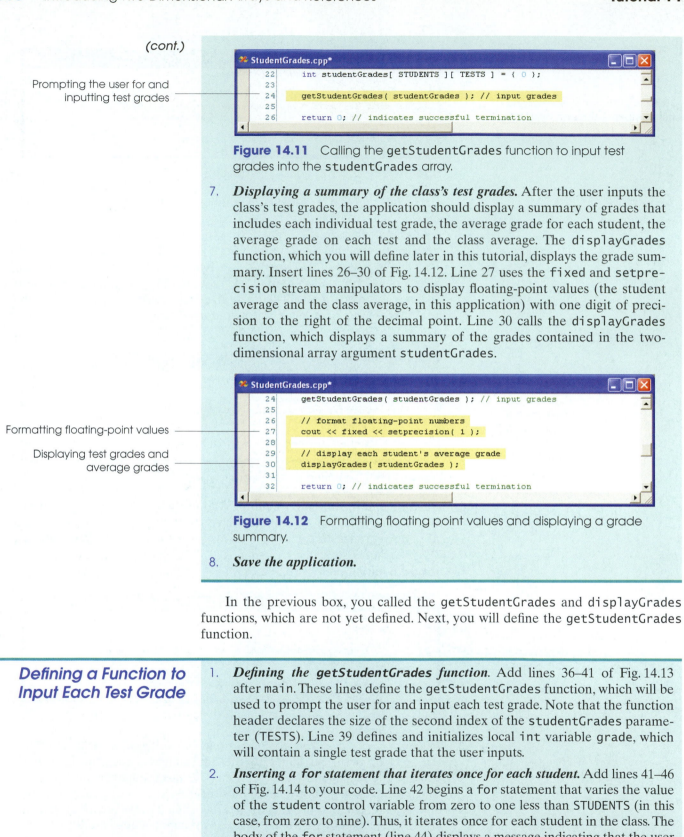

Figure 14.11 Calling the getStudentGrades function to input test grades into the studentGrades array.

7. ***Displaying a summary of the class's test grades.*** After the user inputs the class's test grades, the application should display a summary of grades that includes each individual test grade, the average grade for each student, the average grade on each test and the class average. The displayGrades function, which you will define later in this tutorial, displays the grade summary. Insert lines 26–30 of Fig. 14.12. Line 27 uses the fixed and setprecision stream manipulators to display floating-point values (the student average and the class average, in this application) with one digit of precision to the right of the decimal point. Line 30 calls the displayGrades function, which displays a summary of the grades contained in the two-dimensional array argument studentGrades.

Formatting floating-point values

Displaying test grades and
average grades

Figure 14.12 Formatting floating point values and displaying a grade summary.

8. ***Save the application.***

In the previous box, you called the getStudentGrades and displayGrades functions, which are not yet defined. Next, you will define the getStudentGrades function.

Defining a Function to Input Each Test Grade

1. ***Defining the getStudentGrades function.*** Add lines 36–41 of Fig. 14.13 after main. These lines define the getStudentGrades function, which will be used to prompt the user for and input each test grade. Note that the function header declares the size of the second index of the studentGrades parameter (TESTS). Line 39 defines and initializes local int variable grade, which will contain a single test grade that the user inputs.

2. ***Inserting a for statement that iterates once for each student.*** Add lines 41–46 of Fig. 14.14 to your code. Line 42 begins a for statement that varies the value of the student control variable from zero to one less than STUDENTS (in this case, from zero to nine). Thus, it iterates once for each student in the class. The body of the for statement (line 44) displays a message indicating that the user should enter grades for the current student. For example, when student contains 0, line 44 displays the message "Enter grades for student 1." In the next step, you will add a for statement that iterates once for each test, enabling your application to input three test grades for each student.

(cont.)

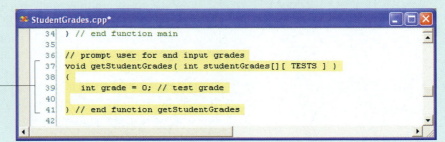

Defining the getStudentGrades function

```
34    } // end function main
35
36    // prompt user for and input grades
37    void getStudentGrades( int studentGrades[][ TESTS ] )
38    {
39        int grade = 0; // test grade
40
41    } // end function getStudentGrades
42
```

Figure 14.13   Defining the getStudentGrades function.

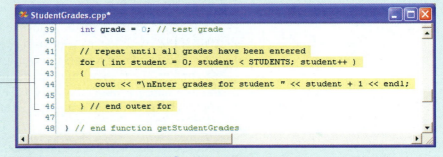

Iterating once for each student

```
39        int grade = 0; // test grade
40
41        // repeat until all grades have been entered
42        for ( int student = 0; student < STUDENTS; student++ )
43        {
44            cout << "\nEnter grades for student " << student + 1 << endl;
45
46        } // end outer for
47
48    } // end function getStudentGrades
```

Figure 14.14   Declaring a for statement.

3.   ***Inputting each grade for a particular student.*** Add lines 46–54 of Fig. 14.15 to the getStudentGrades function. Line 47 begins a for statement that varies the test control variable from zero to one less than TESTS (in this case, from zero to two). As a result, the for statement iterates once for each test. This for statement is called a **nested loop** because it is enclosed (nested) inside another control statement (the for statement from the previous step). Nested loops are particularly useful for processing two-dimensional arrays. This for statement steps through each test for one student in the studentGrades array.

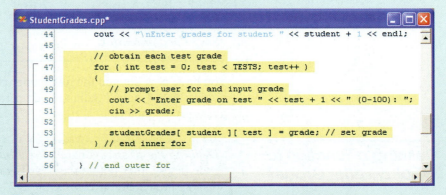

Prompting user for and inputting each of the student's three grades

```
44            cout << "\nEnter grades for student " << student + 1 << endl;
45
46            // obtain each test grade
47            for ( int test = 0; test < TESTS; test++ )
48            {
49                // prompt user for and input grade
50                cout << "Enter grade on test " << test + 1 << " (0-100): ";
51                cin >> grade;
52
53                studentGrades[ student ][ test ] = grade; // set grade
54            } // end inner for
55
56        } // end outer for
```

Figure 14.15   Using a nested loop to input each test grade.

Lines 50–51 prompt the user for and input a single test grade into the grade variable. The value that the user inputs is then assigned to the element of studentGrades located at row student and column test. For example, the first student's first test grade is stored at studentGrades[0][0] because the values of student and test are both zero when the body of the inner for statement executes for the first time. The first student's second and third test grades are stored at studentGrades[0][1] and studentGrades[0][2], respectively.

(cont.)

After the third grade is entered, the inner `for` loop terminates and program execution continues at line 56 of Fig. 14.15. At this point, the outer `for` loop completes one iteration, the control variable, `student`, is incremented and program execution continues at line 44, which displays a message prompting the user to enter grades for the second student. When the nested `for` statement executes again, the application prompts the user for and inputs the second student's first grade into `studentGrades[ 1 ][ 0 ]`. The inner and outer `for` loops repeat until `studentGrades` contains values for three test grades for every student.

4. ***Validating user input.*** To ensure that the user enters only valid grades, the application must ensure that each test grade is in the range 0–100. Add lines 53–62 of Fig. 14.16 to your code. Line 54 begins a `while` loop that determines whether the value in `grade` is invalid (that is, less than zero or greater than 100). If this condition evaluates to `true`, the application displays an error message (line 56), then prompts the user for a valid test grade and inputs the value into `grade`. The loop continues until the user enters a valid grade. Note that if the user enters a valid grade in line 51, the body of the `while` loop is skipped and the value of `grade` is stored in `studentGrades[ student ][ test ]`.

Ensuring that the user enters a valid test grade

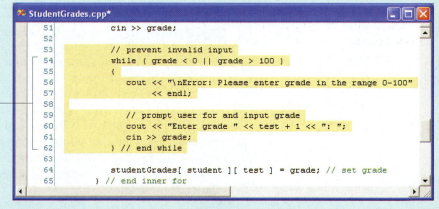

```
51        cin >> grade;
52
53        // prevent invalid input
54        while ( grade < 0 || grade > 100 )
55        {
56           cout << "\nError: Please enter grade in the range 0-100"
57              << endl;
58
59           // prompt user for and input grade
60           cout << "Enter grade " << test + 1 << ": ";
61           cin >> grade;
62        } // end while
63
64        studentGrades[ student ][ test ] = grade; // set grade
65     } // end inner for
```

Figure 14.16 `while` loop repeats until the user enters a valid grade.

5. ***Save the application.***

You have now defined the `getStudentGrades` function to input each student's test grades. Now you will define the `displayGrades` function to output the grades and averages for the class.

Defining a Function to Display Letter Grades

1. ***Defining the `displayGrades` function.*** Add lines 71–78 of Fig. 14.17 to your code. These lines define the `displayGrades` function, which will be used to display grades and averages. Lines 74–76 define and initialize three `double` variables, `studentTotal`, `testTotal`, and `classTotal`, which will contain the sum of each student's test grades, the sum of the students' grades on a particular test and the sum of all test grades for the class, respectively. You will use these values to calculate each student's average grade, the average grade on each test and the class average.

(cont.)

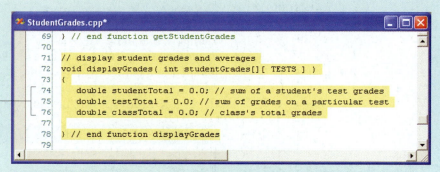

Defining local variables

StudentGrades.cpp*

```
69 } // end function getStudentGrades
70
71 // display student grades and averages
72 void displayGrades( int studentGrades[][ TESTS ] )
73 {
74    double studentTotal = 0.0; // sum of a student's test grades
75    double testTotal = 0.0; // sum of grades on a particular test
76    double classTotal = 0.0; // class's total grades
77
78 } // end function displayGrades
79
```

Figure 14.17 Defining local variables in the `displayGrades` function.

2. ***Displaying a header for the class's grades.*** Lines 78–85 display descriptive text and a header for the table of grades and averages that your application will produce. Line 82 inserts the `right` stream manipulator into `cout`. The **`right` stream manipulator** right justifies output within a field. This causes all grades to be right aligned within their respective fields. Note that `cout` continues to right justify output in fields until the `left` stream manipulator is inserted into the stream.

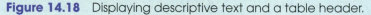

Displaying a table header

StudentGrades.cpp*

```
76    double classTotal = 0.0; // class's total grades
77
78    // display a header
79    cout << "\nGrade summary" << endl;
80    cout << "-------------" << endl;
81    cout << left << setw( 14 ) << "Student number"
82       << right << setw( 8 ) << right << "Test 1"
83       << setw( 8 ) << "Test 2"
84       << setw( 8 ) << "Test 3"
85       << setw( 9 ) << "Average" << endl;
86
87 } // end function displayGrades
```

Figure 14.18 Displaying descriptive text and a table header.

3. ***Creating a loop to iterate once for each student.*** Add lines 87–93 of Fig. 14.19 to your code. Line 88 starts a `for` statement that iterates once for each student in the class. Line 91 displays a number corresponding to each student (1 for the first student, 2 for the second student, and so on), left justified inside a field of width 14.

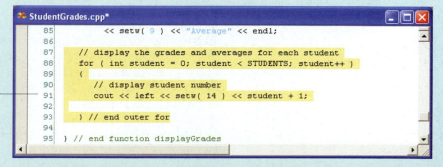

Displaying a number corresponding to each student

StudentGrades.cpp*

```
85       << setw( 9 ) << "Average" << endl;
86
87    // display the grades and averages for each student
88    for ( int student = 0; student < STUDENTS; student++ )
89    {
90       // display student number
91       cout << left << setw( 14 ) << student + 1;
92
93    } // end outer for
94
95 } // end function displayGrades
```

Figure 14.19 Displaying a number corresponding to each student.

(cont.)

4. ***Outputting the student's grades.*** Add lines 93–102 of Fig. 14.20 inside the for statement from the previous step. This nested loop steps through each element in a single row of the studentGrades array, displaying each test grade for a particular student. Line 97 formats each grade so that it is right justified in a field of width 8. Lines 100–101 add each grade to the student-Total and classTotal variables, which you will use to calculate the student's average grade and the class average.

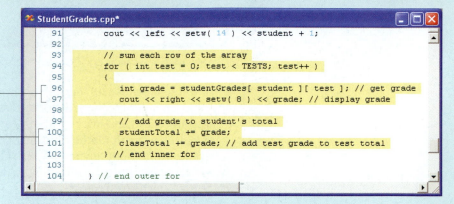

Displaying a test grade, right justified in a field of width 8

Add the test grade to the student's total and the class's total

Figure 14.20 Outputting the student's grades and adding each grade to the total grades.

5. ***Displaying the student's average.*** Add lines 104–107 of Fig. 14.21 to your code. Line 105 calculates and displays the student's average. Note that after the inner for loop terminates, studentTotal will contain the sum of a particular student's test grades. Dividing studentTotal by TESTS (the number of tests) yields the student's average grade. Line 107 resets the value in studentTotal to 0.0. This ensures that the sum of the test grades for the next student begins at 0.0.

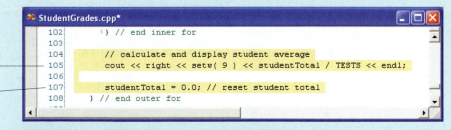

Calculating and displaying the student's average

Resetting the student average

Figure 14.21 Calculating and displaying the student's average grade.

6. ***Displaying the average grade on each test.*** After displaying the test grades and average for each student, you should display the average grade for each test in the final row of your table. To calculate the average grade, you must find the sum of the grades in each column and divide that value by the number of rows in the array, which is specified by STUDENTS. Add lines 110–126 of Fig. 14.22 to your code. Line 111 displays descriptive text indicating that the row contains the average grade for each test.

Line 114 begins a for loop that varies the value of test from zero to one less than TESTS, and line 117 begins a nested for loop that varies student from zero to one less than STUDENTS. Notice that the order of the for loops is reversed compared to the ones you added earlier in this box. This causes line 119 to sum all of the grades for a particular test in the testTotal variable. To calculate the average grade for the test, divide testTotal by the number of students, STUDENTS (line 123). Line 125 resets the value of testTotal to ensure that the sum of the grades for the next test begins at 0.0.

(cont.)

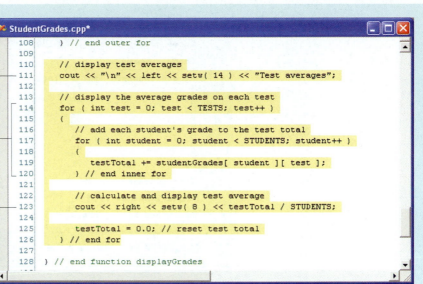

Displaying descriptive text for the row

Summing each column of the table to find the total grade for each test

Calculating and displaying the average grade for each test

Figure 14.22 Calculating and displaying the average grade for each test.

7. ***Calculating and displaying the class average.*** In line 101 of Fig. 14.20, you used `classTotal` to store the sum of each grade in the class. To calculate the average grade for the class, you must divide the sum of all test grades by the total number of test grades, STUDENTS * TESTS. Add lines 128–132 of Fig. 14.23 to your code. Lines 131–132 calculate and display the class average.

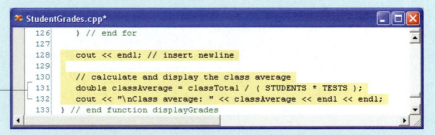

Calculating and displaying the class average

Figure 14.23 Calculating and displaying the class average.

8. ***Save, compile and run the application.*** Figure 14.24 shows the updated application running. Enter three grades for each student. Ensure that your application displays the correct test grades, student average grades, test average grades and class average.

9. ***Close the Command Prompt window.***

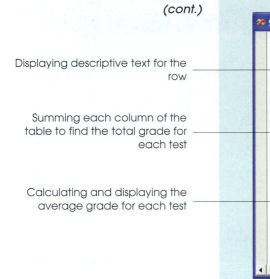

Figure 14.24 Running the completed application.(Part 1 of 2)

(cont.)

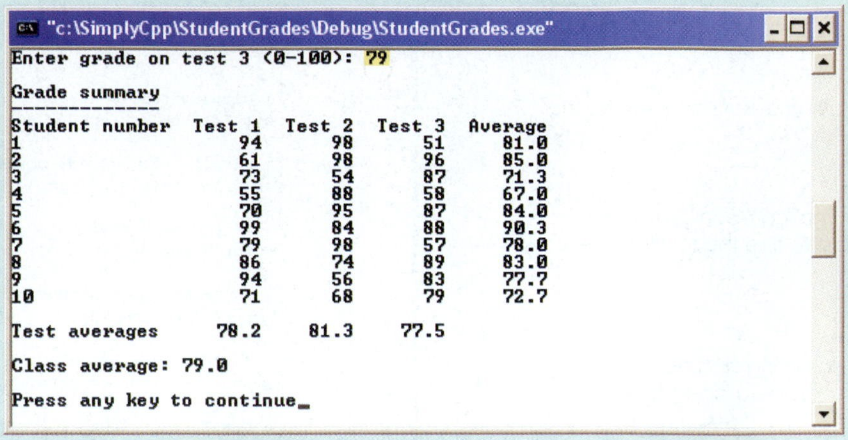

Figure 14.24 Running the completed application. (Part 2 of 2)

Figure 14.25 presents the source code for the **Student Grades** application. The lines of code that you added, viewed or modified in this tutorial are highlighted.

```
1    // Tutorial 14: StudentGrades.cpp
2    // This application computes each student's grade average and
3    // the class average for ten students.
4    #include <iostream> // required to perform C++ stream I/O
5    #include <iomanip>  // required for parameterized stream manipulators
6    #include <string>   // required to access string functions
7
8    using namespace std; // for accessing C++ standard library members
9
10   // define constants
11   const int TESTS = 3; // number of tests per student
12   const int STUDENTS = 10; // maximum students stored
13
14   // function prototypes
15   void getStudentGrades( int [][ TESTS ] );
16   void displayGrades( int [][ TESTS ] );
17
18   // function main begins program execution
19   int main()
20   {
21      // define two-dimensional array to store student grades
22      int studentGrades[ STUDENTS ][ TESTS ] = { 0 };
23
24      getStudentGrades( studentGrades ); // input grades
25
26      // format floating-point numbers
27      cout << fixed << setprecision( 1 );
28
29      // display each student's average grade
30      displayGrades( studentGrades );
31
32      return 0; // indicates successful termination
33
34   } // end function main
35
```

Define constants to represent the number of students and tests — lines 11–12

Declare function prototypes that specify two-dimensional array parameters — lines 15–16

Declare a two-dimensional array — line 22

Prompt the user for and input test grades — line 24

Format floating-point values — line 27

Display test grades and average grades — line 30

Figure 14.25 **Student Grades** code. (Part 1 of 3.)

Iterate once for each student

Prompt user for and
input each of the
student's grades

Ensure that the user enters
a valid test grade

Define local variables

Display a number corresponding
to each student

```cpp
36   // prompt user for and input grades
37   void getStudentGrades( int studentGrades[][ TESTS ] )
38   {
39      int grade = 0; // test grade
40
41      // repeat until all grades have been entered
42      for ( int student = 0; student < STUDENTS; student++ )
43      {
44         cout << "\nEnter grades for student " << student + 1 << endl;
45
46         // obtain each test grade
47         for ( int test = 0; test < TESTS; test++ )
48         {
49            // prompt user for and input grade
50            cout << "Enter grade on test " << test + 1 << " (0-100): ";
51            cin >> grade;
52
53            // prevent invalid input
54            while ( grade < 0 || grade > 100 )
55            {
56               cout << "\nError: Please enter grade in the range 0-100"
57                  << endl;
58
59               // prompt user for and input grade
60               cout << "Enter grade " << test + 1 << ": ";
61               cin >> grade;
62            } // end while
63
64            studentGrades[ student ][ test ] = grade; // set grade
65         } // end inner for
66
67      } // end outer for
68
69   } // end function getStudentGrades
70
71   // display student grades and averages
72   void displayGrades( int studentGrades[][ TESTS ] )
73   {
74      double studentTotal = 0.0; // sum of a student's test grades
75      double testTotal = 0.0; // sum of grades on a particular test
76      double classTotal = 0.0; // class's total grades
77
78      // display a header
79      cout << "\nGrade summary" << endl;
80      cout << "-------------" << endl;
81      cout << left << setw( 14 ) << "Student number"
82         << right << setw( 8 ) << right << "Test 1"
83         << setw( 8 ) << "Test 2"
84         << setw( 8 ) << "Test 3"
85         << setw( 9 ) << "Average" << endl;
86
87      // display the grades and averages for each student
88      for ( int student = 0; student < STUDENTS; student++ )
89      {
90         // display student number
91         cout << left << setw( 14 ) << student + 1;
92
```

Figure 14.25 **Student Grades** code. (Part 2 of 3.)

Display a test grade, right justified in a field of width 8

Add the test grade to the student's total and the class's total

Calculate and display the student's average

Reset the student average

Display descriptive text for the row

Sum each column of the table to find the total grade for each test

Calculate and display the average grade for each test

Calculate and display the class average

```cpp
93          // sum each row of the array
94          for ( int test = 0; test < TESTS; test++ )
95          {
96              int grade = studentGrades[ student ][ test ]; // get grade
97              cout << right << setw( 8 ) << grade; // display grade
98
99              // add grade to student's total
100             studentTotal += grade;
101             classTotal += grade; // add test grade to test total
102         } // end inner for
103
104         // calculate and display student average
105         cout << right << setw( 9 ) << studentTotal / TESTS << endl;
106
107         studentTotal = 0.0; // reset student total
108     } // end outer for
109
110     // display test averages
111     cout << "\n" << left << setw( 14 ) << "Test averages";
112
113     // display the average grades on each test
114     for ( int test = 0; test < TESTS; test++ )
115     {
116         // add each student's grade to the test total
117         for ( int student = 0; student < STUDENTS; student++ )
118         {
119             testTotal += studentGrades[ student ][ test ];
120         } // end inner for
121
122         // calculate and display test average
123         cout << right << setw( 8 ) << testTotal / STUDENTS;
124
125         testTotal = 0.0; // reset test total
126     } // end for
127
128     cout << endl; // insert newline
129
130     // calculate and display the class average
131     double classAverage = classTotal / ( STUDENTS * TESTS );
132     cout << "\nClass average: " << classAverage << endl << endl;
133 } // end function displayGrades
```

Figure 14.25 **Student Grades** code. (Part 3 of 3.)

SELF-REVIEW

1. When the right stream manipulator is inserted in cout, output displayed in a field is right justified _____.

   a) once   b) until the application terminates

   c) until a left stream manipulator is   d) either b or c.
   inserted in cout

2. Programmers commonly use _____ to process each element in two-dimensional array.

   a) nested loops   b) switch statements

   c) sentinel-controlled repetition d) infinite loops

Answers: 1.) d. 2.) a.

14.4 Wrap-Up

In this tutorial, you learned how to use two-dimensional arrays, which are often used to represent tables of values, consisting of information arranged in rows and columns. You learned how to declare and initialize two-dimensional arrays. In the **Student Grades** application, you used a two-dimensional array to store a table of student test grades. You identified a particular table element by specifying the first index (the element's row) and the second index (the element's column). You learned that to declare a two-dimensional array parameter for a function, you must specify the number of columns of the array. You then created nested loops in your functions to process data contained in a two-dimensional array. Finally, you learned how to use the `right` stream manipulator to right justify output in fields.

You have been using objects from classes all along, such as `cout` and `cin`. In the next tutorial, you will learn how to create your own classes to generate objects for use in your applications.

SKILLS SUMMARY

Using Two-Dimensional Arrays

- Define a two-dimensional array to create a table of values (each row will contain the same number of columns). For example, use the code

  ```
  int numbers[ 3 ][ 2 ];
  ```

  to define an array with three rows and two columns.

- When passing a two-dimensional array to a function, specify the number of columns in the second subscript. For example, use the code

  ```
  void processTwoDimensionalArray( int [][ 2 ] );
  ```

  to declare a function prototype for a function that accepts a two-dimensional array containing two columns.

Right Justifying Output in a Field

- Use the `right` stream manipulator before any value that is to be output right-justified in a field.

KEY TERMS

column—In referring to an element of a two-dimensional array, the second index specifies the column.

m-by-n array—A two-dimensional array with *m* rows and *n* columns.

nested loop—A loop (such as a `for` statement) which is enclosed in another control statement.

right stream manipulator—A nonparameterized stream manipulator that causes output to be right justified in a field created by stream manipulator `setw`. Values output in fields continue to be right justified from the point at which `right` is inserted into the output stream until `left` is inserted into the output stream or the application exits.

row—In referring to an element of a two-dimensional array, the first index specifies the row.

table—A two-dimensional array used to contain information arranged in rows and columns.

two-dimensional array—An array requiring two indices to locate an element. These arrays are often used to represent tables of information with values arranged in rows and columns.

C++ LIBRARY REFERENCE

iostream This header file declares basic services required for all stream-I/O operations.

- *Objects*

  `cin`—This object reads characters entered at the keyboard. Text is sent to the application when the user presses *Enter* and can be placed in a variable using the stream extraction operator, `>>`.

  `cout`—This object displays text on the screen. Text can be displayed using the stream insertion operator, `<<`.

■ *Stream manipulators*

`endl`—This object places a newline into the output stream and flushes the stream's buffer so that all text stored in the output stream object is displayed immediately.

`fixed`—This stream manipulator specifies that floating-point numbers should be printed using fixed-point notation (as opposed to scientific notation).

`left`—This object causes values to be left justified in a field. The stream into which `left` is inserted remains left justified until the application terminates or until the stream's justification is changed, whichever comes first.

`right`—This object causes values to be right justified in a field. The stream into which `right` is inserted remains right justified until the application terminates or until the stream's justification is changed, whichever comes first.

MULTIPLE-CHOICE QUESTIONS

14.1 In a function prototype, the _____ of a two-dimensional array must be specified.

- a) name
- b) value
- c) number of columns
- d) number of rows

14.2 The expression `int myArray[ 3 ][ 4 ] = { 0 }` initializes _____ of `myArray` to zero.

- a) only the first element
- b) every element
- c) only the first row
- d) only the first column

14.3 In an *m*-by-*n* array, the *m* stands for _____.

- a) the number of columns in the array
- b) the total number of array elements
- c) the number of rows in the array
- d) the number of elements in each row

14.4 The statement _____ defines the two-dimensional `int` array `myArray` of three columns and five rows.

- a) `int myArray[ 5 ][ 3 ];`
- b) `int myArray[ 4 ][ 2 ];`
- c) `int myArray[ 3 ][ 5 ];`
- d) `int myArray[ 2 ][ 4 ];`

14.5 The _____ stream manipulator right justifies all text that is output by `cout`.

- a) `right`
- b) `setright`
- c) `rightalign`
- d) None of the above.

14.6 Which of the following statements about two-dimensional arrays is true?

- a) The array elements are stored consecutively in memory.
- b) Each element in the two-dimensional array can be of a different type.
- c) Each element's value is initialized to 0 by default.
- d) Both a and c.

14.7 If an array is declared using `int myArray[ 3 ][ 2 ] = { { 2, 4, 6 }, { 1, 3, 5 } };`, the expression `myArray[ 2 ][ 1 ]` will return the value _____.

- a) 5
- b) 4
- c) 3
- d) 0

14.8 Two-dimensional arrays are often used to represent _____.

- a) a pie chart
- b) distances
- c) lines
- d) tables

14.9 A _____ is a loop contained within another control statement.

- a) recursive loop
- b) nested loop
- c) multiple-selection loop
- d) indented loop

14.10 _____ is a correct statement for creating a two-dimensional integer array, myArray, with 5 rows and 5 columns.

    a) `int myArray[][] = int [ 5 ][ 5 ];`
    b) `int myArray( 5, 5 );`
    c) `int myArray[ 5, 5 ];`
    d) `int myArray[ 5 ][ 5 ];`

EXERCISES

14.11 *(Food Survey Application)* To improve its lunch menu, a cafeteria wants to determine how the students rate each food item. The cafeteria requires an application that surveys the student's opinion of various food items, rating each item as "like" or "dislike." The application should use a two-dimensional array to hold counters for each category in the survey. The application will prompt the user to select a food item and rate it, then display the total ratings for each food item (Fig. 14.26).

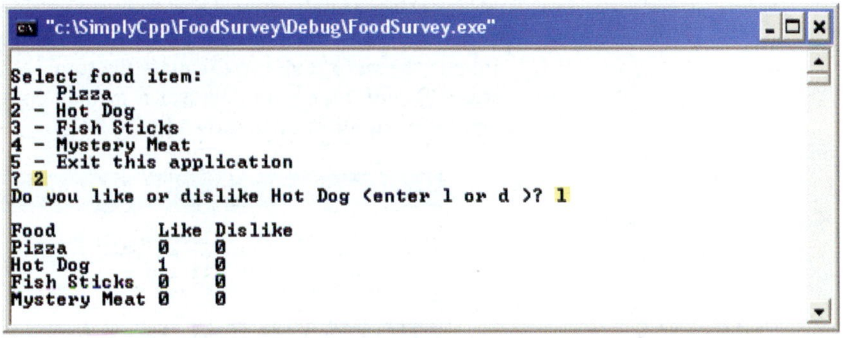

Figure 14.26 Food Survey application.

    a) *Copying the template to your working directory.* Copy the `C:\Examples\Tutorial14\Exercises\FoodSurvey` directory to your `C:\SimplyCpp` directory.

    b) *Opening the template source code file.* Open the `FoodSurvey.cpp` file in your text editor or IDE.

    c) *Declaring a function prototype.* In line 11, insert a function prototype that declares the `displayArray` function, which accepts a two-dimensional `int` array (to contain the food ratings), a constant `string` array (to contain the food names) and an `int` (to contain the number of elements in row). The two-dimensional `int` array will have two columns.

    d) *Defining a two-dimensional `int` array.* In line 20, insert code to define a two-dimensional `int` array named `display`, with 5 rows and 2 columns. Use `int` constant `ARRAY_SIZE` to declare the number of rows. Initialize each element's value to 0.

    e) *Determining which counter to increment.* After the comment in line 53, insert an `if` statement that checks the value contained in `input`, which stores the food rating that the user enters at the keyboard. If the user enters an uppercase or lowercase "l" (for like), increment the counter in column 0 in the `display` array. Also assign the value `true` to `validResponse` to indicate that the user entered a valid rating. Insert an `else` containing a nested `if` that determines whether the user entered an uppercase or lowercase "d" (for dislike). The body of the `else` part should increment the counter in row `menuChoice` and column 1 of the `display` array and assign the value `true` to `validResponse`. Then add an `else` that will execute if the user did not enter a valid rating. The body of the `else` part should display an error message.

    f) *Using a for loop to display the data.* After line 107 in the `displayArray` function, insert a `for` statement that will loop through each row in the `foodChoices` array (1–4). In the body of the loop, display the `string` for the appropriate food. The counter variable of the `for` statement is used as the index of the foodChoices array. Display the `string` left justified in a field of width 13.

g) *Displaying the contents of the display array.* Use a nested for statement to display the contents of your display array after each food item. Use the counter of your first for statement as the first index (row) of display and the counter of your nested for statement as the second index (column) of display. Display each cell of the array left justified in a field of width 5. After the closing brace of the nested for loop, insert a newline using the endl stream manipulator.

h) *Save, compile and run the application.* Test your application to ensure that it runs correctly. Select a food item and rate it. Check to make sure all strings and numbers in the table of ratings are correct. Add several other selections to the **Food Survey** and make sure that the numbers are correct.

i) *Close the application.* Exit your running application by typing 5 at the menu's prompt.

j) *Close the Command Prompt window.*

14.12 *(Sales Report Application)* A clothing manufacturer has asked you to create an application that will calculate that manufacturer's total sales in a week. Sales values should be input separately for each clothing item, but the amount of sales for all five weekdays should be input at once. The application should calculate the total amount of sales for each item in the week and also calculate the total sales for the manufacturer for all the items in the week. Because the manufacturer is a small company, it will produce at most 10 items in any week. The application is shown in Fig. 14.27.

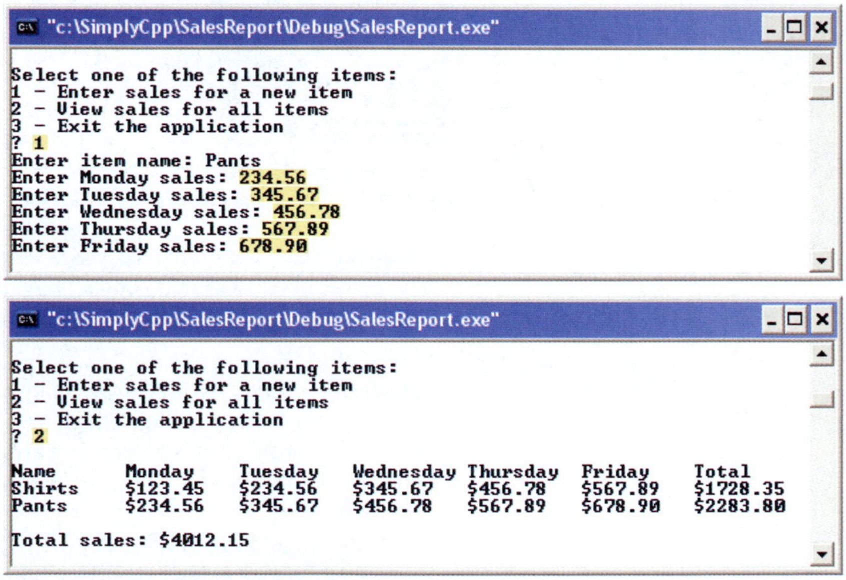

Figure 14.27 **Sales Report** application sample output.

a) *Copying the template to your working directory.* Copy the C:\Examples\Tutorial14\Exercises\SalesReport directory to your C:\SimplyCpp directory.

b) *Opening the template source code file.* Open the SalesReport.cpp file in your text editor or IDE.

c) *Inputting data from the user.* Add code starting after line 48 to input the data from the user. Prompt the user for the name of the item and input the value that the user types at the keyboard into the itemNames array, indexed with itemCount (which stores the number of items added). Then, prompt the user for and input the sales for each day of the week. The values that user enters must be assigned to the two-dimensional dailyItems array. The first index to this array should be itemCount, and the second will range from 0 to 4, for Monday to Friday. Finally, increment the itemCount variable to record that another item's sales data has been added.

d) *Iterating over all the items added.* Inside the `displaySales` function, after `sales-Total` variable has been defined, add code to begin a `for` statement. This `for` statement should iterate from `0` to `itemCount-1`. Define the `item` variable as the `for` statement's counter.

e) *Displaying the item's name.* Insert code in this `for` statement to display the item's name in a field of width 10. Remember that the items' names are stored in `string` array `itemNames`.

f) *Iterating over the days in the week.* Add code to initialize the `weekTotal` variable to 0. This variable keeps track of the total sales for each item over the course of the week. Add code to start a nested `for` statement. This `for` statement will iterate from 0 to the number of days in a week (stored in the `DAYS_PER_WEEK` constant, which is defined in the template) minus one.

g) *Appending daily sales and summing sales for the week.* Add code in this `for` statement to display the daily sales. These sales are stored in the `dailyItems` array. This array must be accessed with the current item and the day of the week. The output is in currency form, so precede each of the values with a dollar sign (`cout` is set to display floating-point values with two positions to the left of the decimal point in line 30). Display the value in a field of width 9. [*Note*: Although the table header uses fields of width 10, the values are displayed in a smaller field due to the dollar sign character that precedes each sales value.]

h) *Calculating weekly sales.* Insert code to add the amount of the daily sales to the `weekTotal` variable. This variable stores the weekly sales for each item. Add a right brace to end the `for` statement started in *Step f*.

i) *Calculating total sales and outputting weekly sales.* Insert code to add the weekly sales to the `salesTotal` variable. This variable keeps track of the total sales for all the items for the week. Add code to display the weekly sales. The weekly sales are also stored as a currency amount, so precede the value with a dollar sign. Also, place this value in a field of width 6 (so that it fits on the same line as the other values) and insert the `endl` stream manipulator to move to the next line. Insert a right brace to end the `for` statement started in *Step d*.

j) *Save, compile and run the application.* Test the application to ensure that it runs correctly. Enter sales figures for several items into your application and calculate and display the correct values.

k) *Closing the application.* Exit your running application by entering 3 at the menu selection prompt.

l) *Close the* Command Prompt *window.*

14.13 *(Profit Report Application)* The clothing manufacturer was so impressed with the **Sales Report** application you created for them (Exercise 14.12), they want you to create a **Profit Report** application as well. This application will be similar to the **Sales Report** application, but it will allow the user to input information as gains (such as the money earned from sales) or losses (such as the money spent on wages). Gains should be displayed as positive values, and losses should be displayed as negative values. You application should provide a menu to allow the user to select whether a certain item is a gain or a loss (Fig. 14.28).

a) *Copying the template to your working directory.* Copy the `C:\Examples\Tutorial14\Exercises\ProfitReport` directory to your `C:\SimplyCpp` directory. Then copy the file `C:\SimplyCpp\DiceSimulator\SalesReport` to your `C:\SimplyCpp\ProfitReport` directory. If you have not completed Exercise 14.12, follow the steps in Exercise 14.12 before copying the file.

b) *Opening the template file.* Rename the `SalesReport.cpp` file to `ProfitReport.cpp`. Then open the `ProfitReport.cpp` file in your text editor or IDE.

c) *Adding a new option to the menu and updating constant values.* Modify the `displayMenu` function so that it displays the menu of options shown in Fig. 14.28. In `main`, modify the values of `EXIT_VALUE` and `DISPLAY_VALUE` appropriately. Then modify the input prompts to change the word "sales" to "value."

```
c:\SimplyCpp\ProfitReport\Debug\ProfitReport.exe

Select one of the following items:
1 - Enter new gain values
2 - Enter new loss values
3 - View profit for all items
4 - Exit the application
? 1

Enter item name: Sales
Enter Monday value: 234.56
Enter Tuesday value: 345.67
Enter Wednesday value: 456.78
Enter Thursday value: 567.89
Enter Friday value: 678.90
```

```
c:\SimplyCpp\ProfitReport\Debug\ProfitReport.exe

Select one of the following items:
1 - Enter new gain values
2 - Enter new loss values
3 - View profit for all items
4 - Exit the application
? 3

Name     Monday    Tuesday   Wednesday Thursday  Friday    Total
Sales    $234.56   $345.56   $456.78   $567.89   $678.90   $2283.69
Wages    -$225.25  -$215.10  -$250.45  -$205.50  -$220.45  -$1116.75

Total profit: $1166.94
```

Figure 14.28 Profit Report application.

d) *Iterating over the days in the week for losses.* If the user selects the value 2 (for "**Enter a new loss**") from the menu, the application should add input values to the array as negative values. In main, before the statement that increments itemCount, add an if statement containing a condition that evaluates to true if the user entered 2 at the menu selection prompt. In the body of the if statement, add code to start a for statement. This for statement will iterate from 0 to the number of days in a week (stored in the DAYS_PER_WEEK constant, which is defined in the template). The body of the for statement should assign to each element in the dailyItems array (in the row specified by itemCount) the opposite of the value stored in that element.

e) *Modifying the displaySales function.* Each time a negative value is displayed, the application should prefix a minus sign (-) before the dollar sign. Add code to the displaySales function to test whether each display value is positive or negative. If the value is positive, the output statement should remain unchanged from Exercise 14.12. Otherwise, the output statement should prefix the dollar sign with a minus sign, reduce the width of the output field by 1, and display the value as a positive number. Also, if the total value of all profits and losses is negative, the application should display the descriptive text, "Total loss: $" before displaying the value of salesTotal.

f) *Save, compile and run the application.* Test your application to ensure that it runs correctly by entering profit and loss figures for several items. Then, calculate and display the correct values.

g) *Closing the application.* Exit your running application by entering 4 at the menu selection prompt.

h) *Close the Command Prompt window.*

What does this code do? ▶

14.14 What does the profit array contain after the mystery function executes? The getStockPrices function modifies a two-dimensional array such that its column zero contains stock prices from the beginning of the day and column one contains the stock prices at the end of the day, for each day of the month.

```
1   // Exercise 14.14: WDTCD.cpp
2   // What does this code do?
3   #include <iostream>  // required to perform C++ stream I/O
4   #include <ctime>     // contains prototype for function time
5   #include <iomanip>   // required for parameterized stream manipulators
```

```cpp
6
7    // contains function prototypes for functions srand and rand
8    #include <cstdlib>
9
10   using namespace std; // for accessing C++ standard library members
11
12   // function prototypes
13   void getStockPrices( double[][ 31 ] );
14   void mystery( double[] );
15
16   // function main begins program execution
17   int main()
18   {
19      // define variables
20      double profit[ 31 ];
21
22      // randomize random number generator using current time
23      srand( time( 0 ) );
24
25      mystery( profit );
26
27      return 0; // indicate that the program terminated correctly
28
29   } // end function main
30
31   // determine what this function does
32   void mystery( double result[] )
33   {
34      double prices[ 2 ][ 31 ];
35
36      getStockPrices( prices );
37
38      cout << "\n" <<left << setw( 4 ) << "Day";
39      cout<< "Price Change" << endl;
40
41      for ( int i = 0; i <= 30; i++ )
42      {
43         result[ i ] = prices[ 0 ][ i ] - prices[ 1 ][ i ];
44
45         cout << fixed << setprecision( 2 );
46         cout << setw( 4 ) << i + 1 << "$" << result[ i ] << endl;
47      } // end for
48
49      cout << "\n";
50   } // end function mystery
51
52   // generate random stock prices
53   void getStockPrices( double price[][ 31 ] )
54   {
55      for( int i = 0; i <= 30; i++ )
56      {
57         for( int j = 0; j <= 1; j++ )
58         {
59            // promote value returned by rand from int to double
60            price[ j ][ i ] = 10 + ( ( rand() % 4000 ) / 100.0 );
61         } // end inner for
62
63      } // end outer for
64
65   } // end function getStockPrices
```

What's wrong with this code? ▶

14.15 Find the error(s) in the following code. The `setArray` function should create a two-dimensional array and initialize all its values to 1.

```
1   // Exercise 14.15: WWWTC.cpp
2   // This application assigns 1 to each element of a two-dimensional
3   // array.
4   #include <iostream> // required to perform C++ stream I/O
5
6   using namespace std; // for accessing C++ standard library members
7
8   // function prototype
9   void setArray();
10
11  // function main begins program execution
12  int main()
13  {
14     setArray();
15
16     cout << "\n"; // insert newline for readability
17
18     return 0; // indicate that the program terminated successfully
19
20  } // end function main
21
22  void setArray()
23  {
24     int array[ 4 ][ 4 ];
25
26     cout << "\n";
27
28     // assign 1 to all cell values
29     for ( int i = 0; i < 4; i++ )
30     {
31        array[ i ][ j ] = 1;
32
33        cout << "array[" << i << "][" << j << "] = "
34           << array[ i ][ j ] << endl;
35
36     } // end for
37
38     cout << "\n"; // insert newline for readability
39  } // end function setArray
```

Programming Challenge ▶

14.16 (*Enhanced Lottery Picker Application*) In Tutorial 12, your **Lottery Picker** application selected numbers for four different types of lotteries. In this exercise, you enhance the **Lottery Picker** to select four different sets of number for the five-number lottery and to prevent duplicate numbers from being selected (Fig. 14.29). Recall that the lottery is played as follows: Five-number lotteries require players to choose five numbers in the range 0–39.

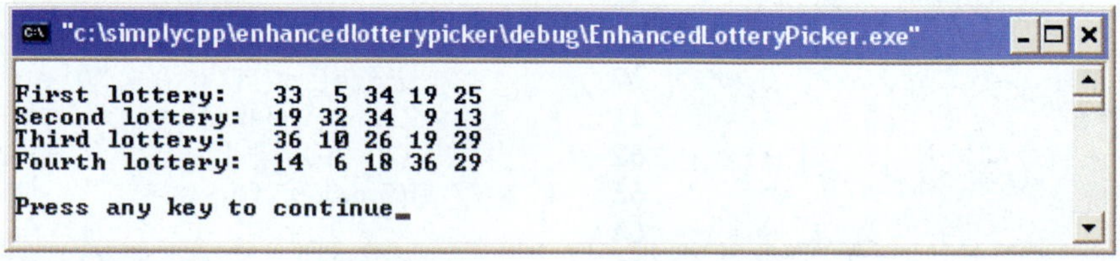

Figure 14.29 Enhanced **Lottery Picker** application.

a) *Copying the template to your work directory.* Copy the `C:\Examples\Tutorial14\Exercises\EnhancedLotteryPicker` directory to your `C:\SimplyCpp` directory.

b) *Opening the template source code file.* Open the `LotteryPicker.cpp` file in your text editor or IDE.

c) *Iterating over the four lotteries.* Add code in line 33 to begin a `for` statement in your application that will execute four times—once for each lottery. Use variable `lottery` as the `for` statement's counter.

d) *Initialize the `bool` array.* To generate unique numbers in each lottery, you will use two-dimensional `bool` array `uniqueNumber` (defined for you in the template). When a number has been selected for a lottery, the value of that variable in the array (indexed by the lottery and the number selected) will be `true`. First, you must initialize the value for the lottery's numbers to `false`. Add a nested `for` statement to set the 40 values in the array for this lottery to `false`. You will need to use `lottery` and the counter in this `for` statement to index the array. Add a right brace to end this inner `for` statement. After initializing the `bool` array, display descriptive text for the lottery numbers that you will generate. Use `lottery` as the index into the `names` array (provided for you in the template) to generate the output. For example, the first iteration of the loop should display the text, "`First lottery:`" followed by a tab.

e) *Iterating over the five numbers selected.* Five unique numbers will need to be selected for each lottery. Add code to begin another `for` statement that will iterate five times. Each time this `for` statement executes, a single, unique lottery number will be generated.

f) *Generating a unique lottery number.* Add a do...while statement inside this `for` statement. The body of this do...while statement should use the `generate` function (defined for you in the template) and pass it the arguments 0 and 39 to return a random number between 0 and 39, inclusive. This value should be assigned to the `selection` variable (also defined for you in the template). The loop continuation condition should test whether the number stored in `selection` has been used for this lottery. This is done using the `uniqueNumber` array indexed with `lottery` and `selection`.

g) *Updating the value in `uniqueNumber`.* Add code to set the value in `uniqueNumber` represented by the selected number (indexed with `lottery` and `selection`) to `true`. This number will not be selected again for this lottery.

h) *Displaying the number.* Insert code to display the value in a field of width 3. Add a right brace to end the inner `for` statement (*Step e*). Then use the `endl` stream manipulator to continue output on the next line. Finally, add another right brace to end the outer `for` statement (*Step c*).

i) *Save, compile and run the completed application.* Test your application to ensure that it runs correctly. Check that all numbers in each five-number lottery are unique. Run the application several times to confirm.

j) *Close the Command Prompt window.*

15

T U T O R I A L

Objectives

In this tutorial, you will learn to:
- Define your own classes.
- Create and use objects of your own classes.
- Control access to data members.
- Use the `public` and `private` keywords.
- Define your own *get* and *set* functions.
- Use the `setfill` stream manipulator to set the fill character for fields.

Outline

Digital Clock Application

Building Your Own Classes and Objects

In earlier tutorials, you used the following application-development methodology: You analyzed a typical problem that required an application to be built and determined what functions and objects from the C++ Standard Library were needed to implement the application. You then used appropriate functions and objects from the library and created any additional functions to complete the application.

Although you have not worked with classes directly, you have used them in each of your applications. When you use `cin` and `cout` to perform I/O, you are using objects (also known as **instances**) of a class that can be accessed by including the `<iostream>` standard library header file. When you create and use an object of a class in an application, your application is known as a **client** of that class.

In this tutorial, you will learn to create and use your own classes (also known as **programmer-defined classes**). Creating your own classes is a key part of object-oriented programming (OOP); hopefully, your classes can be reused by many applications. In the world of C++ programming, applications are created by using a combination of C++ Standard Library classes and functions and user-defined classes and functions. You have already created several functions in this book. Now you will learn to create the classes that contain these functions.

15.1 Test-Driving the Digital Clock Application

You will create a digital clock simulator where the user will enter the current time and the application will update the time every second. To handle the time data, you will create a class called `Time` that will store the number of hours, minutes and seconds (which your **Digital Clock** application will use to keep track of the current time). The class will also provide *get* and *set* functions, which clients of this class can use to access and change the current time, respectively. This application must meet the following requirements:

326

Application Requirements

An electronics company is considering building digital clocks. The company has asked you to develop an application that simulates a digital clock. The clock will update the time once per second. When the clock is first turned on, it should prompt the user to set the current time. The user should be able to enter a number of hours no less than 1 and no greater than 12, a number of minutes no greater than 59 and a number of seconds no greater than 59. Invalid hours entries will be set to 12, invalid minutes entries to 00 and invalid seconds entries to 00. To speed application development, the company has asked for a simplified simulation that displays a time in the range 12:00:00–11:59:59, but does not indicate whether the current time is AM or PM.

You begin by test-driving the completed application. Then, you will learn the additional C++ techniques you will need to create your own version of this application.

Test-Driving the Digital Clock Application

1. *Locating the completed application.* Open the **Command Prompt** window by selecting **Start > All Programs > Accessories > Command Prompt**. Change to the completed **Digital Clock** application directory by typing cd `C:\Examples\Tutorial15\CompletedApplication\DigitalClock`.

2. *Running the Digital Clock application.* Type `DigitalClock` in the **Command Prompt** window to run the application (Fig. 15.1). The application prompts you to enter the current hour.

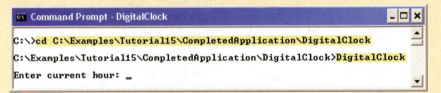

Figure 15.1 **Enter current hour:** prompt displayed when your application is executed.

3. *Entering a time.* Type the current hour at the **Enter current hour:** prompt, the current minute at the **Enter current minute:** prompt and the current second at the **Enter current second:** prompt. In Fig. 15.2, we have entered a current time of `4:41:59`. Note that the number of hours must be less than 12 (this clock displays standard time); otherwise, an invalid hour will be set to 12. Also, the number of minutes and seconds must each be 59 or less. If the user enters an invalid number of minutes or seconds (such as 89), the invalid amount will be set to 0.

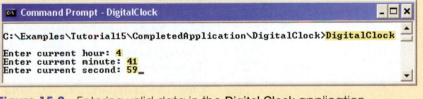

Figure 15.2 Entering valid data in the **Digital Clock** application.

(cont.)

4. ***Watching the clock tick.*** After you enter the current second, the application displays the current time (Fig. 15.3), updating it once per second. At the end of each minute (that is, the clock's second value is 59), the next clock tick correctly increments the minute and sets the second to 0. For example, the next value displayed after 4:41:59 is 4:42:00 (Fig. 15.4). Press and hold *Ctrl* while pressing *C* to exit the application.

```
ᴄ⁏ "c:\Examples\Tutorial15\CompletedApplication\DigitalClock\Debug\DigitalCloc...  _ □ ×
Enter current hour: 4
Enter current minute: 41
Enter current second: 48
04:41:48
```

Figure 15.3 Initial time displayed.

```
ᴄ⁏ Command Prompt - DigitalClock                                              _ □ ×
Enter current hour: 4
Enter current minute: 41
Enter current second: 59

04:42:00
```

Figure 15.4 **Digital Clock** advances the minute and resets the seconds to 0 when the seconds reach 60.

5. ***Entering invalid data.*** Run the application again. Type 11 at the **Enter current hour:** prompt, 72 at the **Enter current minute:** prompt and 20 at the **Enter current second:** prompt (Fig. 15.5). This input is invalid because the number of minutes, 72, is larger than the maximum allowed value, 59, so the number of minutes is set to zero when time is set. Notice in Fig. 15.6 that the number of minutes has been reset to 00, though the number of hours and seconds have been left unchanged.

```
ᴄ⁏ Command Prompt - DigitalClock                                              _ □ ×
Enter current hour: 11
Enter current minute: 72
Enter current second: 20_
```

Figure 15.5 **Digital Clock** application with invalid input.

```
ᴄ⁏ Command Prompt - DigitalClock                                              _ □ ×
Enter current hour: 11
Enter current minute: 72
Enter current second: 20

11:00:20
```

Figure 15.6 **Digital Clock** application after invalid input has been entered.

6. ***Closing the running application.*** Press and hold *Ctrl* while pressing *C* to exit the application.

7. ***Close the* Command Prompt** *window.*

15.2 Designing the Digital Clock Application

The **Digital Clock** application contains a class (called `Time`) whose objects store the current time in hours, minutes and seconds. Other examples of objects that you have used in your applications are the `cin`, `cout`, and `string` objects, which are created from classes defined in the C++ Standard Library. You will create the `Time` class before you finish the program for the **Digital Clock**. The pseudocode in Fig. 15.7 describes the actions that the Time class performs.

> When the time object is created:
> 　　Set the number of hours to 12
> 　　Set the number of minutes and number of seconds to 0
>
> When setting the number of hours:
> 　　If the number of hours is greater than 0 and less than 13
> 　　　set the number of hours to the specified value
> 　　else
> 　　　set the number of hours to 12
>
> When setting the number of minutes:
> 　　If the number of minutes is greater than or equal to 0 and less than 60
> 　　　set the number of minutes to the specified value
> 　　else
> 　　　set the number of minutes to 0
>
> When setting the number of seconds:
> 　　If the number of seconds is greater than or equal to 0 and less than 60
> 　　　set the number of seconds to the specified value
> 　　else
> 　　　set the number of seconds to 0
>
> When the time object is incremented:
> 　　Increment the number of seconds
>
> 　　If the number of seconds is 60
> 　　　set the number of seconds to 0
> 　　　Increment the number of minutes
>
> 　　　If the number of minutes is 60
> 　　　　set the number of minutes to 0
> 　　　　Increment the number of hours
>
> 　　　　If the number of hours is 13
> 　　　　　set the number of hours to 1

Figure 15.7　Pseudocode for the Time class.

When an object of the Time class is created, the number of hours will be initialized to 12 and the number of minutes and number of seconds will both be initialized to 0. Invalid data for the number of hours, minutes or seconds will cause the values to be set to their initial values (12, 0 and 0, respectively). The pseudocode in Fig. 15.8 describes the basic operation of your **Digital Clock** application.

> Prompt the user to enter the current hour, minute and second
> Set the current time to the time that the user entered
>
> While the application is running
>
> 　If one second has passed
> 　　Increment and display the time

Figure 15.8　Pseudocode for the **Digital Clock** application.

In the next section, you will learn how to define a class. Later in this tutorial, you will learn how to add this class to your application. Your Time class will be used to create objects that contain the time in hours, minutes and seconds.

A class can contain data and functions. The variables that store a class's data are called **data members**, and the functions contained in a class are called **member functions**. Thus, classes enable you to create objects that contain **attributes** (the data members) and **behaviors** or **operations** (represented as member functions). For example, a Time object's attributes include the current hour, minute and second, and its operations include setting and incrementing the current time.

1. A class's data members correspond to the _____ for the corresponding object.

    a) attributes   b) behaviors

    c) operations   d) Both a and b.

2. An object's behavior is represented by the corresponding class's _____.

    a) attributes   b) data members

    c) member functions   d) None of the above.

Answers: 1) a. 2) c.

15.3 Separating Interface from Implementation

One of the fundamental principles of good software design is to separate a class's interface from its implementation. A class's **interface** consists of member function prototypes, which name the behaviors of the class and for each provide return types and a list of the parameter types. The **implementation** consists of the code that executes when a member function is invoked. The separation of interface from implementation can be found in everyday life. For example, a car's interface, which includes a steering wheel, gas pedal and brake pedal, supports operations such as turning left, turning right, acceleration and deceleration. The car's internal components that implement these operations, such as the engine, transmission and the exhaust system, are separated from the steering wheel and pedals. As a result, you can drive just about any car effectively without knowing the details of how engines, transmissions and exhaust systems work. Further, if car manufacturers change these details in a new model, you will still be able to drive these cars effectively because you know how to turn the steering wheel and press the gas and brake pedals.

This separation can simplify programming because interfaces change less frequently than implementations. For example, in Exercise 15.12, you will be asked to modify your Time class to display whether the current time is AM or PM. When an implementation changes, any code that relies on that implementation must change accordingly. For example, you will implement the enhanced Time class by increasing the range of possible hour values from 12 to 24 hours. Although you will modify the Time class's member function definitions to implement this change, you will not modify the function prototypes, so the class's interface will not change. Because the interface will not change, the source code for clients of the class will not need to be modified to accommodate the change.

By convention, you should place each class declaration in a separate header file (.h) to form the class's public interface. Any client that wants to use the class must include the header file, which provides the client code with the function prototypes it needs to be able to call the class's member functions. Place the definitions of the class member functions in a source file (.cpp) to form the implementation of the class.

Before you write the code that provides the functionality for your Time class, you will create a header file for the class. You will also learn how to define a class and control access to its members.

Creating a Class Definition

1. *Copying the template to your working directory.* Copy the `C:\Examples\Tutorial15\TemplateApplication\DigitalClock` directory to your `C:\SimplyCpp` directory.

(cont.)

2. ***Opening the Time class template source code header file.*** Open the template file `Time.h` in your text editor or IDE. The files `Time.h` and `Time.cpp` contain the interface and implementation of the `Time` class, respectively. The file `DigitalClock.cpp` contains your application's `main` function. All of these files are need to build the **Digital Clock** application. In general, you should place related source code files in the same directory, as we have done for you.

3. ***Adding the Time header file to your project.*** If you are using Visual Studio .NET, you should add the `Time` header file to your project. In the **Solution Explorer**, right click the **Header Files** folder (Fig. 15.9), then select **Add > Add Existing Item...**. In the **Add Existing Item** dialog that appears, double click the `Time.h` file (Fig. 15.10). `Time.h` should now appear in the **Header Files** folder (Fig. 15.11). [*Note:* If you are not using Visual Studio .NET, skip this step.]

Header Files folder (selected) —————

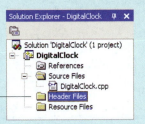

Figure 15.9 **Header Files** folder in the **Solution Explorer** window.

`Time.h` file (selected) —————

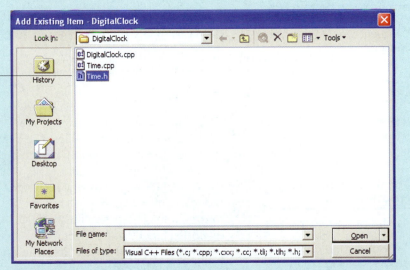
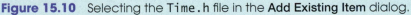

Figure 15.10 Selecting the `Time.h` file in the **Add Existing Item** dialog.

`Time.h` file in **Header Files** folder —————

Figure 15.11 **Header Files** folder containing `Time.h`.

(cont.)

4. ***Viewing the template code.*** Look at lines 1–14 of Fig. 15.12. Lines 1–3 are comments that indicate the name, purpose and location of the member function definitions for your class file. Line 10, which begins the `Time` class definition, contains the `class` keyword, followed by the name of the class (in this case, `Time`). The **class** keyword indicates that what follows is a class definition. The left and right braces (lines 11 and 12) indicate the beginning and end of the **class's body**, respectively. Each class definition terminates with a semicolon (line 12). Functions and variables defined in the body of a class are said to be **members** of that class.

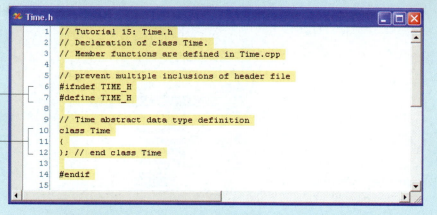

Preventing multiple inclusions of the same header file

Empty class definition

Figure 15.12   Empty class definition.

In Fig. 15.12, note that the class definition is enclosed in the following preprocessor code (lines 6–7 and 14):

```
#ifndef TIME_H
#define TIME_H
    ...
#endif
```

When you build larger applications, other definitions and declarations will also be placed in header files. The preceding preprocessor directives prevent the code between **#ifndef** (which means "if not defined") and **#endif** from being included if the name TIME_H has been defined. If the header has not been included previously in a file, the name TIME_H is defined by the **#define** directive and the header file statements are included. If the header has been included previously, TIME_H is defined already and the header file is not included again. Attempts to include a header file multiple times (inadvertently) typically occur in large applications with many header files that may themselves include other header files. [*Note:* The convention we use for the symbolic constant name in the preprocessor directives is simply the header file name with the underscore character replacing the period.]

5. ***Declaring your class's member functions.*** Insert lines 12–25 of Fig. 15.13 inside the body of the `Time` class. Lines 13–25 contain function prototypes The `public:` label (line 12) is called a **member-access specifier**. Any data member or member function declared after **public** member-access specifier (and before the next member-access specifier) is available to code outside the class by using a `Time` object followed by the member-access operator (`.`). For example, the expression `cin.ignore()` uses the member-access operator to access `cin`'s `public` member function `ignore`. In the following section, we will discuss the meaning and purpose of each of the functions declared in lines 13–25.

Good Programming Practice

By convention, always begin a class name with a capital letter and start each subsequent word in the class name with a capital letter.

Error-Prevention Tip

All class definitions must end with a semicolon (;).

Good Programming Practice

Add comments at the beginning of programmer-defined classes to increase readability. The comments should indicate the name of the file that contains the class and the purpose of the class being defined.

(cont.)

```
 9   // Time abstract data type definition
10   class Time
11   {
12   public:
13       Time();               // constructor
14       void displayTime();   // displays the formatted time
15       void tick();          // increments the time by one second
16
17       // get functions
18       int getHour();    // gets the current hour
19       int getMinute();  // gets the current minute
20       int getSecond();  // gets the current second
21
22       // set functions
23       void setHour( int );   // sets the hour
24       void setMinute( int ); // sets the minute
25       void setSecond( int ); // sets the second
26
27   }; // end class Time
```

Declaring Time's member functions using the `public` member-access specifier

Figure 15.13 Time's member functions.

6. ***Defining your class's data members.*** Add lines 27–30 of Fig. 15.14 to the Time class definition. Lines 28–30 define three `int` data members—`hour`, `minute` and `second`. The Time class will store a time value containing hours, minutes and seconds—the value for hours is stored in `hour`, the value for minutes is stored in `minute` and the value for seconds is stored in `second`. Note the use of the `private` member-access specifier in line 27. Any data member or member function declared after the **private** member-access specifier (and before the next member-access specifier) is accessible only to. member functions of the class. As a result, these members cannot be accessed or modified using the member-access operator. Thus, member-access specifiers enable you to control how the data members and member functions are accessed by users (clients) of your class.

Software Design Tip

Define all data members of a class as `private`. When necessary, provide `public` functions to get and set the values of `private` data members.

```
25       void setSecond( int ); // sets the second
26
27   private:
28       int hour;   // stores the hour (range: 1 - 12)
29       int minute; // stores the minute (range: 0 - 59)
30       int second; // stores the second (range: 0 - 59)
31
32   }; // end class Time
```

Defining Time's data members using keyword `private`

Figure 15.14 Time's data members.

Attempting to access a class's `private` members from outside the class definition is a compilation error. The classes of the C++ Standard Library also include many `private` variables and functions that provide functionality for you, but that you cannot use directly in your own applications. Normally, data members are defined as `private`, whereas functions are defined as `public`. Classes can also have nonpublic member functions, which are declared after the `private` member-access specifier (and before the next member-access specifier).

Common Programming Error

Attempting to access a `private` class member from outside that class is a syntax error.

7. ***Save the application.***

Member-access specifiers are always followed by a colon (:) and can appear multiple times and in any order in a class definition. For the remainder of the text, when we refer to the `public` and `private` member-access specifiers in our discussions of applications, we will omit the colons, as we did in this sentence. In the next section, you will add functionality to your class by defining your application's member functions.

---

1. The _____ keyword begins a class definition.

    a) `define`   b) `new`

    c) `class`   d) None of the above.

2. A class definition must include a pair of _____.

    a) square brackets   b) braces

    c) commas   d) parentheses

Answers: 1) c. 2) b.

15.4 Initializing Objects: Constructors

The class definition in your `Time.h` header file contains prototypes for nine member functions after the `public` member-access specifier. These are the `public` member functions of the class and form its interface. Clients of the class will use these functions to manipulate the class's `private` data.

Once you define a class and declare its member functions, you must define the member functions. If you define your class's member functions outside the class definition, you must precede each member function name with the class name and the **binary scope resolution operator** (`::`)—in this case, `Time::`. This "ties" the member name to the class name to uniquely identify the functions of a particular class. For example, the function header

```
Time::setTime( int hourValue, int minuteValue, int secondValue )
```

begins the definition for the `setTime` function, which is a member of the `Time` class.

Even though a member function declared in a class definition may be defined outside that class definition (and "tied" to the class using the binary scope resolution operator), that member function is still within that class's scope. This means that the function can be accessed only by other members of the class or through an object of the class, a reference to an object of the class or a pointer to an object of the class. (We discuss pointers in Tutorial 16.) In the following box, you will begin defining the `Time` class's functions.

Common Programming Error

When defining a class's member functions outside that class, omitting the class name and binary scope resolution operator on the function name is an error.

Defining a Constructor

1. *Opening the Time class template source code file.* Open the template file `Time.cpp` in your text editor or IDE. Recall that the `Time.cpp` file contains the `Time` class's implementation.

2. *Adding the Time source file to your project.* If you are using Visual Studio .NET, you should add the `Time.cpp` source code file to your project. In the **Solution Explorer**, right click the **Source Files** folder, then select **Add > Add Existing Item...**. In the **Add Existing Item** dialog that appears, double click the `Time.cpp` file. `Time.cpp` should now appear in the **Source Files** folder.

3. *Including the class definition.* Add lines 6–7 of Fig. 15.15 to the `Time.cpp` file. These lines include the header file that defines the `Time` class.

(cont.)

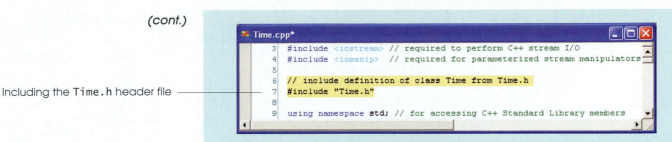

Figure 15.15 Including the `Time` class header file.

Including the `Time.h` header file

Note the name of the header file is enclosed in quotes (`""`) rather than angle brackets (`<>`). Normally, programmer-defined header files are placed in the same directory as the files that contain the class implementations. When the preprocessor encounters a header file name in quotes, it assumes that the header file is in the same directory as the file in which the `#include` directive appears. If the preprocessor cannot find the header file in the current directory, it searches for the header file in the same location as the header files of the C++ Standard Library. When the preprocessor encounters a header file name in angle brackets, it simply assumes that the header is part of the C++ Standard Library and does not look in the local directory.

In `Time.cpp`, the compiler uses the information in `Time.h` to ensure that the member function headers are defined correctly and that the member functions use the class's data correctly. For example, the compiler ensures that each member-function implementation matches its corresponding prototype in the header file. The header file also gives the compiler the information it needs to determine the size of a `Time` object and the locations of its data members.

4. ***Adding a constructor to a class.*** Add lines 11–16 of Fig. 15.16 to the `Time.cpp` file. These lines define a constructor for the `Time` class. A **constructor** is used to initialize data members. The constructor must have the same name as the class that contains it. The definition of a constructor is similar to a function, but unlike a function, a constructor cannot specify a return type (not even `void`). Note that you must use the binary scope resolution operator (`::`) in the constructor's definition (line 13) because you are defining the constructor outside of the class definition. This enables the compiler to tie the constructor to the `Time` class.

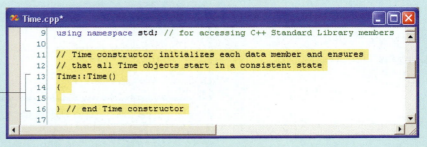

Empty constructor

Figure 15.16 Defining an empty constructor.

Notice that the constructor's name (`Time`) is the same as the class's name. A client of the class invokes the constructor each time it **instantiates** (creates) an object of that class. This enables the author of the class to precisely control the creation and initialization of all objects of the class. Statements within a constructor usually initialize data members. You will add the body statements of this constructor in the following steps.

(cont.)

The constructor in Fig. 15.16 does not accept any arguments, but constructors can accept any number of arguments. Any constructor arguments must be specified in the parameter declarations for the constructor's prototype and the constructor's definition.

Constructors cannot specify a return type. This is an important difference between constructors and functions. Note that the data members of a class cannot be initialized where they are declared in the class body. These data members should be initialized by the class's constructor, or they can be assigned values by *set* functions (such as setSecond in line 25 of Fig. 15.13). We will discuss *set* functions in the next section.

5. ***Initializing variables in a constructor.*** Add lines 15–18 of Fig. 15.17 to the constructor. These lines initialize Time's data members to the earliest possible time (12:00:00). A Time object (such as lunchTime) can now be created with the statement

    ```
    Time lunchTime;
    ```

    which will also cause the constructor to execute and set the time to 12:00:00.

Error-Prevention Tip

Providing a constructor to ensure that every object is initialized with meaningful values can help eliminate logic errors.

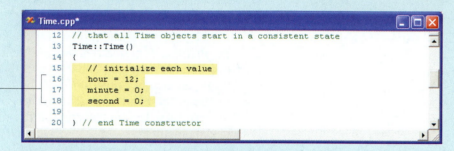

Constructor initializes data members

Figure 15.17 Constructor initializing data members.

6. ***Save the application.***

7. ***Opening the Digital Clock application's template file.*** Open the template file DigitalClock.cpp in your text editor or IDE.

8. ***Including the Time.h header file.*** Before you can use Time objects in your **Digital Clock** application, you must include the Time.h header file. Add lines 7–8 of Fig. 15.18 to your application.

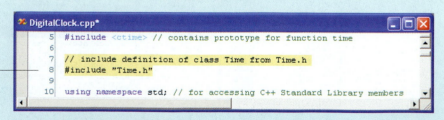

Including the Time.h header file

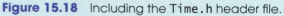

Figure 15.18 Including the Time.h header file.

In DigitalClock.cpp, the compiler uses the information in Time.h to ensure that the client code (that is, main) creates and manipulates the Time object correctly. For example, to access a Time class object, the compiler must know the functions that the Time class supports. Also, to create a Time class object, the compiler must know its size. Note that only an object's data is in the object—the member functions are stored elsewhere. By including Time.h in line 8, we give the compiler access to the information it needs (Fig. 15.14, lines 28–30) to determine the size of a Time class object.

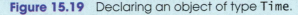

(cont.)

9. ***Creating a Time object.*** After including your Time class header file, you can define your own objects of the Time type. Add line 18 of Fig. 15.19 to your application. When line 18 executes, a Time object is instantiated and the Time constructor is called to initialize its data members so that it stores the time 12:00:00.

Declaring an object of the Time class

```
🔆 DigitalClock.cpp*
17      int second; // store the current second
18      Time localTime;  // instantiate object localTime of class Time
19
20      return 0;
```

Figure 15.19 Declaring an object of type Time.

Notice the use of the class name, Time, as a type. Just as you can create many variables from a primitive type, such as int, you can create many objects from a class. You can also create your own classes as needed. C++ is known as an **extensible language** because the language can be "extended" with new classes.

10. ***Save the application.***

SELF-REVIEW

1. A(n) _____ language is one that can be "extended" with new classes.
   a) data
   b) extensible
   c) typeable
   d) extended

2. Data members can be initialized _____.
   a) when they are defined
   b) by a *set* function
   c) in a constructor
   d) Both b and c.

Answers: 1) b. 2) d.

15.5 *Get* and *Set* Functions

Clients of a class usually want to manipulate that class's data members. For example, assume a class (Person) that stores information about a person, including age information (stored in int data member age). Clients who create an object of the Person class could want to modify age—perhaps incorrectly, by assigning it a negative value. Classes often provide *get* and *set* **functions** to allow clients to access and modify data members in a correct and safe way. *Get* functions (sometimes called **accessors**) typically retrieve a value from an object. *Set* functions (sometimes called **mutators**) typically modify data in an object.

The *get* function allows clients to get (that is, obtain the value of) a data member. For example, the Time class defines a *get* function, getMinute, that returns the value of the class's minute data member. (Note that you can define a *get* function to perform other operations before returning a value.) Assuming that timeObject is an object of the Time type, when the code

```
minuteValue = timeObject.getMinute();
```

executes, the getMinute function executes and returns the value of timeObject's minute data member, which is then assigned to minuteValue.

The *set* function allows clients to set (that is, assign a value to) a data member. For example, the Time class also contains a *set* function, setMinute, that modifies the value of the minute data member. When the code

```
timeObject.setMinute( 35 );
```

Good Programming Practice

While it is not required, it is a good idea to include the words *get* and *set* in the names of *get* and *set* functions.

executes, the setMinute function assigns a new value (in this case 35) to the data member minute. A *set* function could—and should—carefully scrutinize attempts to modify the variable's value. This ensures that the new value is appropriate for that data item. Maintaining an object's data in this manner is known as keeping the data in a **consistent state**. The setMinute function keeps the minute variable in a consistent state by assigning a valid value to minute even if invalid data is passed to the *set* function. Users can specify an amount of minutes only in the range 0 to 59. Values not in this range will be discarded by the *set* function, and minute will be assigned the value 0.

In many of your applications, you have written code that prompts the user to input a new value when the user enters an invalid value. Many C++ applications that use objects, however, do not (or cannot) display a prompt. For example, many microwaves enable the user to set the current time using a keypad, but cannot display a prompt indicating the user entered an invalid time. If the user enters an invalid time (such as 3:68 PM), it is appropriate for the microwave to set the clock to a default valid time (such as 3:00 PM) instead of setting the clock to an invalid time. Similarly, the Time class can prevent errors by ensuring that Time objects always store valid times, regardless of the values specified by clients of the class.

When discussing an object, it is important to distinguish between consistent and correct data. For example, if the user creates a Time object to represent the current time, 7:59:00, and accidentally enters the time 7:69:00, the Time object will discard the invalid minute value (69) and minute will be assigned the value 0. Because the resulting Time object (which stores the time 7:00:00) contains a valid time, it is in a consistent state. However, because the current time is actually 7:59:00, the object's data is incorrect. Thus, an object containing data in a consistent state does not always contain correct data.

In this tutorial, you will learn how to create your own *get* and *set* functions to help clients of a class read and modify the class's private data members. You will create six functions—getHour, setHour, getMinute, setMinute, getSecond and setSecond—for your Time class. By keeping the data private and only allowing access via carefully coded public member functions, you protect the integrity of the class's data.

Defining the Functions of Class *Time*

1. ***Defining a* get *function for hour.*** Add lines 22–27 of Fig. 15.20 to the Time.cpp file. Line 22 begins with the return type (int), which indicates that the function should return an int. After specifying the return type, the function definition includes the class name and the binary scope resolution operator (::), followed by the function name (getHour) and its parameter list. Because you are defining this member function outside of its class definition, you must use the binary scope resolution operator to tie the getHour function definition to the Time class. The parameter list is normally empty for a *get* function. When the getHour function is called, it should return the value of hour, so it uses the return keyword, followed by the hour identifier (line 25).

Returning a value from a *get* function

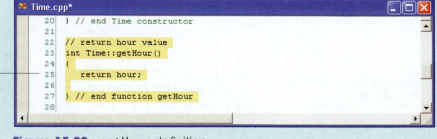

```
20   } // end Time constructor
21
22   // return hour value
23   int Time::getHour()
24   {
25      return hour;
26
27   } // end function getHour
28
```

Figure 15.20 getHour definition.

(cont.)

2. ***Defining a* set *function for hour.*** Add lines 29–43 of Fig. 15.21 to the Time.cpp file. This function should set the value of hour to the int argument the function receives in the hourvalue parameter, but first, it should test that the argument is valid. The setHour function should accept a value greater than 0 and less than 13, a condition that is tested in line 34. If the argument (hourValue) is valid, it will be assigned to hour in line 36. Otherwise, the value 12 will be assigned to hour in line 40. This keeps the value of hour in a consistent state.

Validating data ────

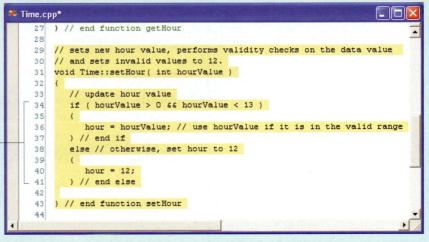

```
27  } // end function getHour
28
29  // sets new hour value, performs validity checks on the data value
30  // and sets invalid values to 12.
31  void Time::setHour( int hourValue )
32  {
33     // update hour value
34     if ( hourValue > 0 && hourValue < 13 )
35     {
36        hour = hourValue; // use hourValue if it is in the valid range
37     } // end if
38     else // otherwise, set hour to 12
39     {
40        hour = 12;
41     } // end else
42
43  } // end function setHour
44
```

Figure 15.21   setHour definition to check validity of data.

3. ***Defining a* get *function for minute.*** Add lines 45–50 of Fig. 15.22 to the Time.cpp file. The getMinute function should return the value of minute just as the getHour function returned the value of hour in *Step 1*.

Returning the minute value ────

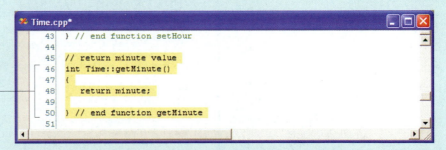

```
43  } // end function setHour
44
45  // return minute value
46  int Time::getMinute()
47  {
48     return minute;
49
50  } // end function getMinute
51
```

Figure 15.22   getMinute definition.

4. ***Defining a* set *function for minute.*** Add lines 52–66 of Fig. 15.23 to the Time.cpp file. Notice that the *set* and *get* functions for minute are similar to the *set* and *get* functions for hour, except that the minute variable is being accessed, as opposed to the hour variable, and the upper limit for the value of minute is 60.

5. ***Defining a* get *function for second.*** Add lines 68–73 of Fig. 15.24 to your application. The getSecond function should return the value of second just as the getMinute function returned the value of minute in *Step 3*.

6. ***Defining a* set *function for second.*** Add lines 75–89 of Fig. 15.25 to the Time.cpp file. Notice that the *set* and *get* functions for second are similar to the *set* and *get* functions for minute and hour, except that the second variable is being accessed, as opposed to the minute or hour variable.

(cont.)

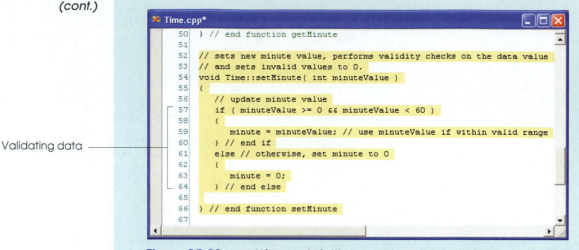

```
50    } // end function getMinute
51
52    // sets new minute value, performs validity checks on the data value
53    // and sets invalid values to 0.
54    void Time::setMinute( int minuteValue )
55    {
56       // update minute value
57       if ( minuteValue >= 0 && minuteValue < 60 )
58       {
59          minute = minuteValue; // use minuteValue if within valid range
60       } // end if
61       else // otherwise, set minute to 0
62       {
63          minute = 0;
64       } // end else
65
66    } // end function setMinute
67
```

Validating data

Figure 15.23 `setMinute` definition used to validate data.

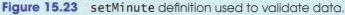

```
66    } // end function setMinute
67
68    // return second value
69    int Time::getSecond()
70    {
71       return second;
72
73    } // end function getSecond
74
```

Returning the **second** value

Figure 15.24 `getSecond` definition.

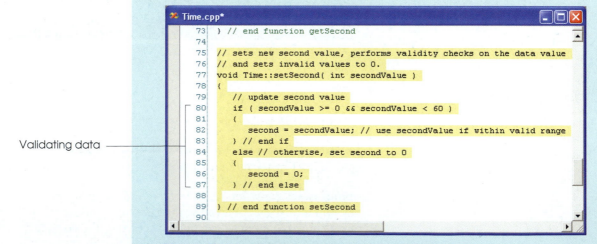

```
73    } // end function getSecond
74
75    // sets new second value, performs validity checks on the data value
76    // and sets invalid values to 0.
77    void Time::setSecond( int secondValue )
78    {
79       // update second value
80       if ( secondValue >= 0 && secondValue < 60 )
81       {
82          second = secondValue; // use secondValue if within valid range
83       } // end if
84       else // otherwise, set second to 0
85       {
86          second = 0;
87       } // end else
88
89    } // end function setSecond
90
```

Validating data

Figure 15.25 `setSecond` definition to validate data.

7. ***Adding the `displayTime` function.*** Add lines 91–98 of Fig. 15.26 to the `Time.cpp` file. When the `displayTime` message is sent to a `Time` object, it displays the time stored by that object. The time must be displayed in the format *hh*:*mm*:*ss*, where *hh* is a two-digit hour (such as 11 or 07), *mm* is a two-digit minute and *ss* is a two digit second.

(cont.)

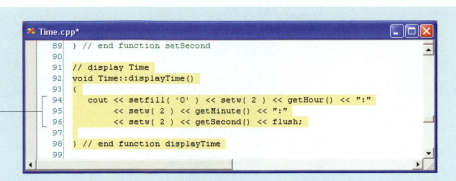

Figure 15.26 `displayTime` definition.

Setting the fill character to 0 for displaying the time in *hh:mm:ss* format

You have used `setw` to output values in fields throughout this book. When the field is wider than the value placed in the field, any field positions that do not contain the value's characters are filled with whitespace characters. The **setfill** parameterized stream manipulator (line 94), declared in the `<iomanip>` header file, specifies a **fill character**, which is a character that will appear in unoccupied positions in a field. If the specified value occupies the entire field, no fill characters are displayed. For example, line 94 specifies a fill character of 0 and a field of width 2. If the value returned by `getHour` is less than 10, then the value will occupy the rightmost position (recall that values are right justified inside fields by default). In this case, the remaining unoccupied position is filled with the fill character, 0. If the value returned by `getHour` is greater than or equal to 10, then the value will occupy both positions in the field, so no fill character will be inserted.

The fill character specified in a call to `setfill` will remain the fill character until the next call to `setfill` or until the application terminates, whichever comes first. The default fill character is the space character. Thus, to reset the default character, use `setfill( ' ' )`.

Note that line 96 contains the **flush** stream manipulator, which causes the contents of the stream output buffer to appear on the screen immediately. Because the current time is displayed on the same line each time it is updated, omitting the `flush` stream manipulator prevents the time from displaying on some systems.

8. *Using set functions.* Modify lines 16–18 of Fig. 15.17 (as shown in Fig. 15.27) to call the correct *set* functions instead of storing values in `hour`, `minute` and `second` directly. Now that you have defined *set* functions, you should reuse the code in these *set* functions to initialize data members in the class constructor to ensure that only valid data will be assigned to `hour`, `minute` and `second`.

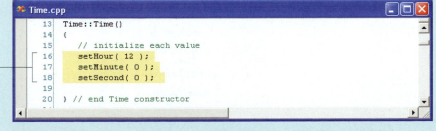

Assigning data by calling the `setHour`, `setMinute` and `setSecond` functions

Figure 15.27 Constructor using *set* functions to initialize variables.

(cont.)   9. ***Defining the tick function.*** Add lines 100–119 of Fig. 15.28 to the `Time.cpp` file. The `tick` function will increment the `Time` object by one second. The `main` function in `DigitalClock.cpp` will call the `tick` function once per second to mimic an actual digital clock. The argument to `setSecond` in line 104 adds one to the current value of `second`, then takes the modulus of the result. If the value of `second + 1` is less than 60, that value is assigned to `second`. If the value is 60, the expression evaluates to 0, which is then assigned to `second` by `setSecond`. If the value of `second` is zero (line 107), the number of minutes is incremented by one (line 109). The expression in line 109 ensures that the new `minute` value is between 0 and 59, inclusive. If the value of `minute` becomes zero (line 112), the value of `hour` is incremented by one (line 114). The expression in line 114 ensures that the argument to `setHour` is in the range 1–12.

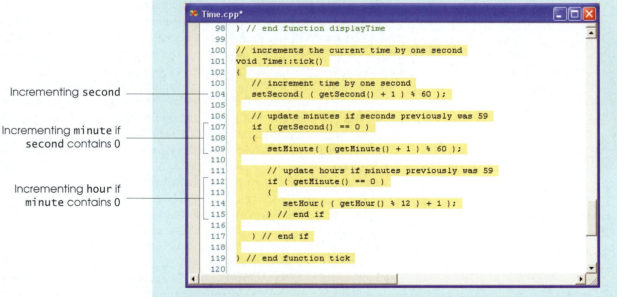

```
 98    } // end function displayTime
 99
100    // increments the current time by one second
101    void Time::tick()
102    {
103        // increment time by one second
104        setSecond( ( getSecond() + 1 ) % 60 );
105
106        // update minutes if seconds previously was 59
107        if ( getSecond() == 0 )
108        {
109            setMinute( ( getMinute() + 1 ) % 60 );
110
111            // update hours if minutes previously was 59
112            if ( getMinute() == 0 )
113            {
114                setHour( ( getHour() % 12 ) + 1 );
115            } // end if
116
117        } // end if
118
119    } // end function tick
120
```

Incrementing `second` — line 104
Incrementing `minute` if `second` contains 0 — lines 107–109
Incrementing `hour` if `minute` contains 0 — lines 112–115

Figure 15.28   Incrementing the time in the `tick` function.

10. ***Save and compile the class.*** To compile the `Time` class, compile the `Time.cpp` file. (Note that the `Time.cpp` file includes the `Time.h` file, which contains the `Time` class definition.) In Visual Studio .NET, this is accomplished by right clicking `Time.cpp` in the **Solution Explorer** window, then selecting **Compile**. If your application does not compile correctly, fix the errors in your code before proceeding to the next section.

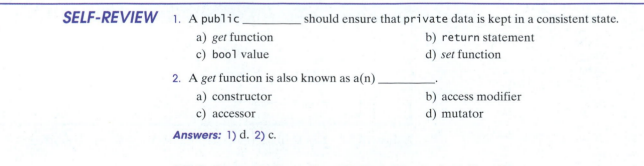

SELF-REVIEW   1. A public _____ should ensure that `private` data is kept in a consistent state.

a) *get* function   b) `return` statement

c) `bool` value   d) *set* function

2. A *get* function is also known as a(n) _____.

a) constructor   b) access modifier

c) accessor   d) mutator

Answers: 1) d. 2) c.

15.6 Completing the Digital Clock Application

Although you have completed your `Time` class, you cannot use the class until you create an object of the class and invoke its member functions. In this section, you will create an object of the Time class to maintain the current time in your application. To update your Time object's current time once per second, you will use members of the <ctime> standard library to access your system's clock.

Completing the *Digital Clock Application*

1. ***Defining a variable to store the correct time according to your system's clock.*** Insert line 19 as shown in Figure 15.29 in the DigitalClock.cpp file. Line 19 defines a variable, currentTime, of the time_t type. An instance of the **time_t** type (declared in the <ctime> header file) stores the value returned by the time standard library function, which you learned about in Tutorial 12. Recall that the time function returns the current "calendar time" in seconds. In *Step 3* and *Step 4* you will learn how to use the value of currentTime so that your application calls localTime's tick function once per second. (Recall that you created the localTime object in Fig. 15.19).

Creating a variable of type time_t

```
 18        Time localTime; // instantiate object localTime of class Time
 19        time_t currentTime; // store duration of program execution
 20
 21        return 0; // indicate that program ended successfully
```

Figure 15.29 Defining a variable of type time_t.

2. ***Prompting the user for and setting localTime.*** Insert lines 21–39 of Fig. 15.30 to main. Lines 22–23 prompt the user for and input the current hour into the hour variable. Line 25 uses the setHour function of the Time class to set localTime's starting hour. Similarly, lines 27–30 prompt the user for and input the current minute into the minute variable, then use the setMinute function of the Time class to set localTime's starting minute. Lines 32–35 prompt the user for and input the current second into the second variable, then use the setSecond function of the Time class to set localTime's starting second. Finally, line 39 calls the displayTime function of the Time class. Recall that this function displays the current time in *hh:mm:ss* format.

Prompting user for and inputting the current hour, minute and second, then using the Time class's *set* functions to set the current time

Displaying the current time

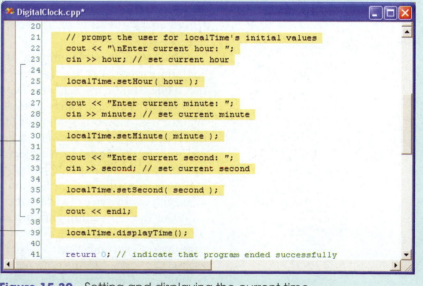

```
 20
 21        // prompt the user for localTime's initial values
 22        cout << "\nEnter current hour: ";
 23        cin >> hour; // set current hour
 24
 25        localTime.setHour( hour );
 26
 27        cout << "Enter current minute: ";
 28        cin >> minute; // set current minute
 29
 30        localTime.setMinute( minute );
 31
 32        cout << "Enter current second: ";
 33        cin >> second; // set current second
 34
 35        localTime.setSecond( second );
 36
 37        cout << endl;
 38
 39        localTime.displayTime();
 40
 41        return 0; // indicate that program ended successfully
```

Figure 15.30 Setting and displaying the current time.

(cont.)

3. ***Setting the `time_t` value.*** Add lines 41–45 of Fig. 15.31 to `main`. Line 42 begins a loop that will iterate indefinitely. Notice that the condition of the `while` statement is `true`, so the loop will repeat until the user closes the application. You will add code to the body of this infinite loop to update the `localTime` object's value once per second. Line 44 calls the `time` function (accessible by including the `<ctime>` header file) and stores the returned `time_t` value in `currentTime`.

Using the `time` function to store the current time, in seconds

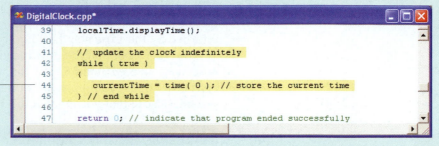

Figure 15.31   Determining the current time.

4. ***Incrementing the Time object once every second.*** To update the `localTime` object's time once per second, your application must use your computer's clock to wait for one second before calling `localTime`'s `tick` function. Add lines 46–51 of Fig. 15.32 to `main`. Line 47 contains a `while` loop that repeats for one second, then terminates so that your application can call the `tick` function in line 49.

Updating and displaying `localTime`'s time once per second

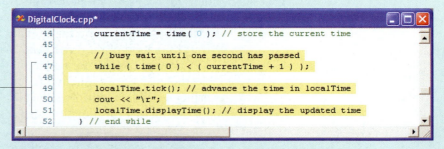
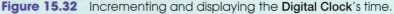

Figure 15.32   Incrementing and displaying the **Digital Clock**'s time.

Let's examine the condition of the `while` statement. The left operand contains a `time( 0 )` function call, which returns the current time each time the `while` statement repeats. The right operand contains the expression `(currentTime + 1)`, which adds one second to the value in `currentTime`. When `time( 0 )` equals `currentTime + 1`, one second will have passed since line 44 executed, and the `while` loop will terminate so that the application can update the `localTime` object. Notice that the `while` statement is followed by a semicolon, indicating that the body of loop contains no statements. As a result, the application will repeatedly test the condition in line 47 until it evaluates to `false`, a technique known as **busy waiting**.

When the loop-continuation condition in line 47 evaluates to `false`, line 49 executes, calling `localTime`'s `tick` function to increment the current time by one second. Line 50 inserts a carriage return (represented by the escape sequence `\r`) into the output stream, which moves the cursor to the beginning of the current line. Finally, line 51 displays the updated time—overwriting the time that was previously displayed on that line. After displaying the current time, the outer `while` loop repeats and program control transfers to line 44.

(cont.)   5. ***Save, compile and run the application.*** This application requires you to compile multiple source code files. In Visual Studio .NET, selecting **Build > Build Solution** will compile all of your application's source code files. The appendices contain instructions for compiling multiple source code files using other compilers. Figure 15.33 shows the completed application running. Notice that your application performs as it did in the test-drive.

```
c:\ "c:\SimplyCpp\DigitalClock\Debug\DigitalClock.exe"          - □ ×
Enter current hour: 10
Enter current minute: 10
Enter current second: 56

10:11:02_
```

Figure 15.33   Running the **Digital Clock** application.

6. ***Close the application.*** Close the running application by pressing and holding *Ctrl* while pressing *C*.

7. ***Close the* Command Prompt *window.***

SELF-REVIEW   1. Use the _____ function call to retrieve the current calendar time, in seconds.

   a) `clock()`   b) `time( 0 )`
   c) `clock( 0 )`   d) `time()`

2. When a `while` statement's header is terminated by a semicolon, it _____.

   a) executes once   b) is a syntax error
   c) does not contain statements in its body   d) creates an infinite loop

Answers: 1) b. 2) c.

15.7 Passing Arguments to a Constructor

When an object is created in a client of a class, values are often specified for that object. For example, a client of a class might want to specify the hour, minute and second of a `Time` object when it is created. In the following box, you will modify your `Time` class and **Digital Clock** application so that clients can specify initial `Time` data member values when a `Time` object is created.

Overloading the Constructor

1. ***Opening the application.*** If `Time.h` is closed, open it in your text editor or IDE.

2. ***Including a prototype that overloads the constructor.*** Modify lines 13–14 of your `Time.h` file as shown in Fig. 15.34. When a constructor specifies no parameter (as in line 13), it is called a **default constructor**. However, you can also create a constructor that specifies a parameter list. Line 14 specifies a `Time` constructor that accepts three `int` arguments, which the constructor definition will use to initialize `hour`, `minute` and `second`.

Time constructor specifies three `int` parameters ⎯⎯⎯⎯

```
Time.h                                                    □ □ ×
12    public:
13        Time();              // default constructor
14        Time( int, int, int ); // three-argument constructor
15        void displayTime();    // displays the formatted time
```

Figure 15.34   Declaring a `Time` constructor prototype that specifies parameters.

(cont.)

Notice that lines 13 and 14 specify two functions with the same name. C++ has a capability called **function overloading** that allows you to create several functions with the same name but different numbers or types of arguments. For example, you can create multiple constructors with different numbers and types of parameters. When the compiler encounters a call to an overloaded function, the compiler uses the numbers and types of arguments in the function call to determine the corresponding overloaded function that should execute.

3. ***Defining the three-argument overloaded constructor.*** If `Time.cpp` is closed, open it in your text editor or IDE. Insert lines 22–31 of Fig. 15.35 after the `Time` default constructor definition. Line 24 specifies three `int` parameters, `hourValue`, `minuteValue` and `secondValue`. Lines 27–29 use the `Time` class's *set* functions to initialize the values of `hour`, `minute` and `second` to the values passed to the constructor by the `hourValue`, `minuteValue` and `secondValue` parameters, respectively. [*Note:* We have updated the comment in line 20 to reflect that the constructor that terminates in line 20 is the default constructor.]

Using the constructor's parameters to set the hour, minute and second

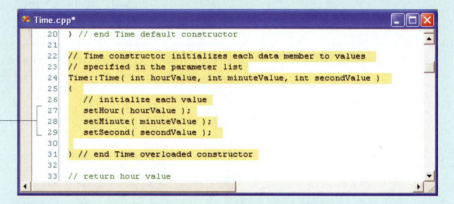

```
20    } // end Time default constructor
21
22    // Time constructor initializes each data member to values
23    // specified in the parameter list
24    Time::Time( int hourValue, int minuteValue, int secondValue )
25    {
26       // initialize each value
27       setHour( hourValue );
28       setMinute( minuteValue );
29       setSecond( secondValue );
30
31    } // end Time overloaded constructor
32
33    // return hour value
```

Figure 15.35 Defining the overloaded `Time` constructor.

4. ***Modifying the Digital Clock application.*** If `DigitalClock.cpp` is closed, open it in your text editor or IDE. Replace lines 18–35 of your application with lines 18–31 of Fig. 15.36. Any arguments that you wish to pass to a constructor must be passed when the object is instantiated. This is accomplished by placing an argument list enclosed in parentheses after the object name. For example, the statement in line 31 creates a `Time` object named `localTime` and passes to the `Time` constructor the `hour`, `minute` and `second` arguments. These arguments are received by the overloaded `Time` constructor (line 24, Fig. 15.35) as the `hourValue`, `minuteValue` and `secondValue` parameters, respectively.

If you are using Visual Studio .NET, you might have noticed text appear in a yellow box (Fig. 15.37). This feature, called ***Intellisense***, is designed to reduce syntax errors by displaying the prototype for the constructor you are calling. In Fig. 15.37, *Intellisense* correctly identifies the function you are typing as a call to the overloaded constructor. By clicking the up or down arrows in the yellow box, you can view other prototypes. In this case, the only other prototype is the default constructor.

5. ***Save, compile and run the application.*** Notice that your application performs as it did in the test-drive. [*Note:* Appendix A contains instructions for compiling multiple source-code files using GCC.]

(cont.)

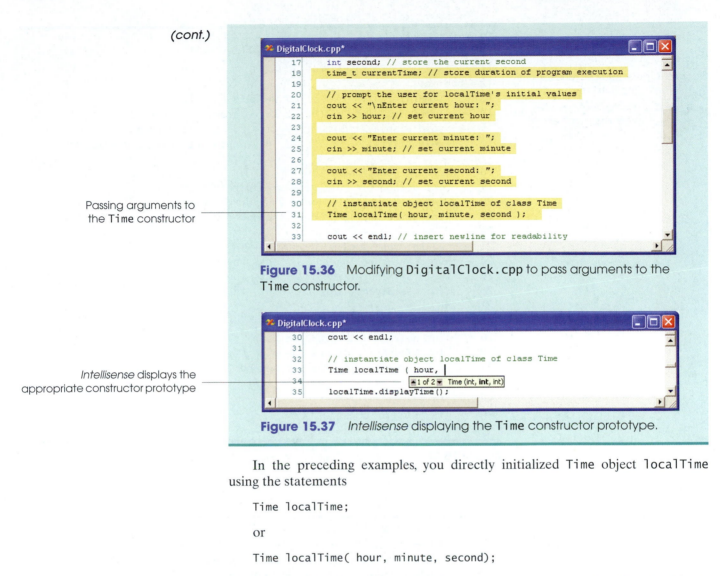

Passing arguments to
the `Time` constructor

Figure 15.36   Modifying `DigitalClock.cpp` to pass arguments to the
`Time` constructor.

Intellisense displays the
appropriate constructor prototype

Figure 15.37   *Intellisense* displaying the `Time` constructor prototype.

In the preceding examples, you directly initialized `Time` object `localTime`
using the statements

```
Time localTime;
```

or

```
Time localTime( hour, minute, second);
```

You can also initialize objects using the assignment operator and calling the object's
constructor. For example, the right side of the assignment expression in the statement

```
localTime = Time( hour, minute, second );
```

creates a `Time` object initialized with the values `hour`, `minute` and `second`. The
assignment operator then copies the data members from the object created on the
right side of the operator to the `localTime` object on the left side of the expression.

Figures 15.38, 15.39 and 15.40 present the source code for the **Digital Clock**
application. The lines of code that you added, viewed or modified in this tutorial are
highlighted.

```
1    // Tutorial 15: Time.h
2    // Declaration of class Time.
3    // Member functions are defined in Time.cpp
4
5    // prevent multiple inclusions of header file
6    #ifndef TIME_H
7    #define TIME_H
8
```

Prevent multiple inclusions of the
same header file

Figure 15.38   Completed `Time` class header file. (Part 1 of 2.)

```
 9   // Time abstract data type definition
10   class Time
11   {
12   public:
13       Time();                // default constructor
14       Time( int, int, int ); // three-argument constructor
15       void displayTime();    // displays the formatted time
16       void tick();           // increments the time by one second
17
18       // get functions
19       int getHour();   // gets the current hour
20       int getMinute(); // gets the current minute
21       int getSecond(); // gets the current second
22
23       // set functions
24       void setHour( int );   // sets the hour
25       void setMinute( int ); // sets the minute
26       void setSecond( int ); // sets the second
27
28   private:
29       int hour;   // stores the hour (range: 1 - 12)
30       int minute; // stores the minute (range: 0 - 59)
31       int second; // stores the second (range: 0 - 59)
32
33   }; // end class Time
34
35   #endif
```

Declare Time's member functions using the **public** keyword
Time constructor that specifies three **int** parameters
Define Time's data members using the **private** keyword

Figure 15.38 Completed **Time** class header file. (Part 2 of 2.)

```
 1   // Tutorial 15: Time.cpp
 2   // Member-function definitions for class Time.
 3   #include <iostream> // required to perform C++ stream I/O
 4   #include <iomanip>  // required for parameterized stream manipulators
 5
 6   // include definition of class Time from Time.h
 7   #include "Time.h"
 8
 9   using namespace std; // for accessing C++ Standard Library members
10
11   // Time constructor initializes each data member and ensures
12   // that all Time objects start in a consistent state
13   Time::Time()
14   {
15       // initialize each value
16       setHour( 12 );
17       setMinute( 0 );
18       setSecond( 0 );
19
20   } // end Time default constructor
21
22   // Time constructor initializes each data member to values
23   // specified in the parameter list
24   Time::Time( int hourValue, int minuteValue, int secondValue )
25   {
```

Include the **Time.h** header file
Constructor initializes data members

Figure 15.39 Completed class **Time** source code. (Part 1 of 3.)

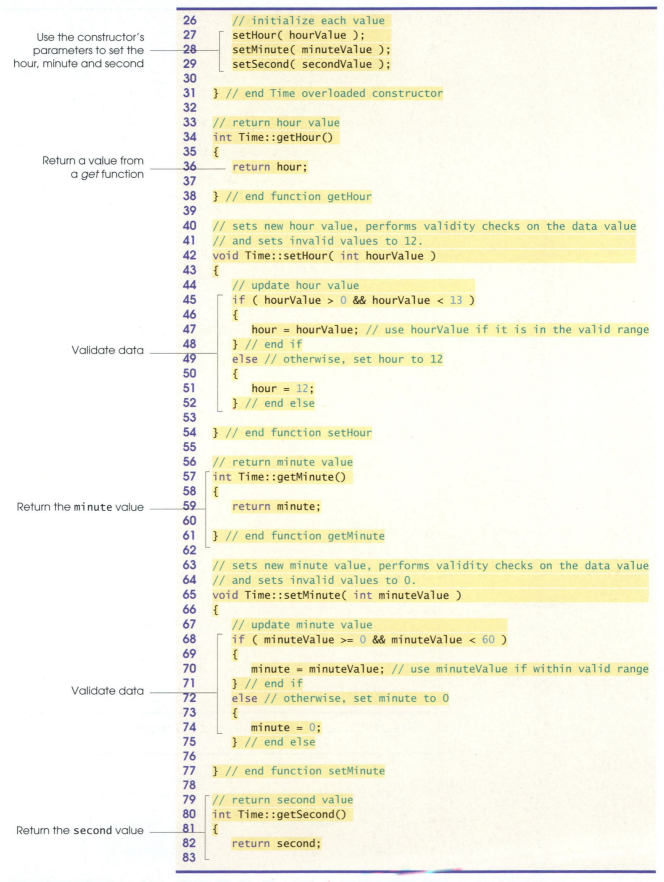

```
26        // initialize each value
27        setHour( hourValue );
28        setMinute( minuteValue );
29        setSecond( secondValue );
30
31    } // end Time overloaded constructor
32
33    // return hour value
34    int Time::getHour()
35    {
36        return hour;
37
38    } // end function getHour
39
40    // sets new hour value, performs validity checks on the data value
41    // and sets invalid values to 12.
42    void Time::setHour( int hourValue )
43    {
44        // update hour value
45        if ( hourValue > 0 && hourValue < 13 )
46        {
47            hour = hourValue; // use hourValue if it is in the valid range
48        } // end if
49        else // otherwise, set hour to 12
50        {
51            hour = 12;
52        } // end else
53
54    } // end function setHour
55
56    // return minute value
57    int Time::getMinute()
58    {
59        return minute;
60
61    } // end function getMinute
62
63    // sets new minute value, performs validity checks on the data value
64    // and sets invalid values to 0.
65    void Time::setMinute( int minuteValue )
66    {
67        // update minute value
68        if ( minuteValue >= 0 && minuteValue < 60 )
69        {
70            minute = minuteValue; // use minuteValue if within valid range
71        } // end if
72        else // otherwise, set minute to 0
73        {
74            minute = 0;
75        } // end else
76
77    } // end function setMinute
78
79    // return second value
80    int Time::getSecond()
81    {
82        return second;
83
```

Use the constructor's parameters to set the hour, minute and second

Return a value from a *get* function

Validate data

Return the **minute** value

Validate data

Return the **second** value

Figure 15.39 Completed class Time source code. (Part 2 of 3.)

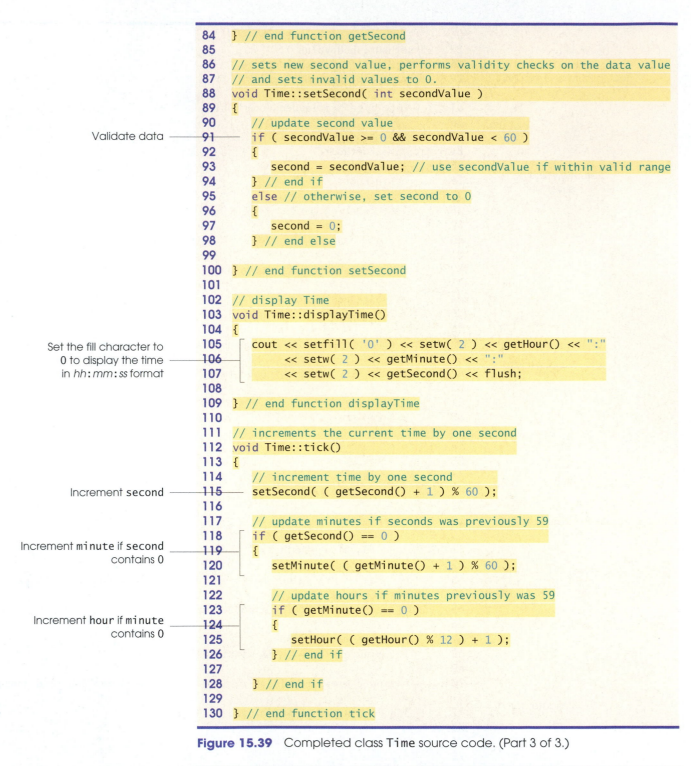

```
84    } // end function getSecond
85
86    // sets new second value, performs validity checks on the data value
87    // and sets invalid values to 0.
88    void Time::setSecond( int secondValue )
89    {
90        // update second value
91        if ( secondValue >= 0 && secondValue < 60 )
92        {
93            second = secondValue; // use secondValue if within valid range
94        } // end if
95        else // otherwise, set second to 0
96        {
97            second = 0;
98        } // end else
99
100   } // end function setSecond
101
102   // display Time
103   void Time::displayTime()
104   {
105       cout << setfill( '0' ) << setw( 2 ) << getHour() << ":"
106           << setw( 2 ) << getMinute() << ":"
107           << setw( 2 ) << getSecond() << flush;
108
109   } // end function displayTime
110
111   // increments the current time by one second
112   void Time::tick()
113   {
114       // increment time by one second
115       setSecond( ( getSecond() + 1 ) % 60 );
116
117       // update minutes if seconds was previously 59
118       if ( getSecond() == 0 )
119       {
120           setMinute( ( getMinute() + 1 ) % 60 );
121
122           // update hours if minutes previously was 59
123           if ( getMinute() == 0 )
124           {
125               setHour( ( getHour() % 12 ) + 1 );
126           } // end if
127
128       } // end if
129
130   } // end function tick
```

Validate data — line 91

Set the fill character to 0 to display the time in *hh*:*mm*:*ss* format — lines 105-107

Increment second — line 115

Increment minute if second contains 0 — line 119

Increment hour if minute contains 0 — line 124

Figure 15.39   Completed class **Time** source code. (Part 3 of 3.)

```
1    // Tutorial 15: DigitalClock.cpp
2    // Simulates the operation of a digital clock.
3    // NOTE: This file must be compiled with Time.cpp.
4    #include <iostream> // required to perform C++ stream I/O
5    #include <ctime> // contains prototype for function time
6
7    // include definition of class Time from Time.h
8    #include "Time.h"
```

Including the Time.h header file — line 8

Figure 15.40   Completed **Digital Clock** source code. (Part 1 of 2.)

```
9
10   using namespace std; // for accessing C++ Standard Library members
11
12   int main()
13   {
14      // define variables
15      int hour;    // store the current hour
16      int minute;  // store the current minute
17      int second;  // store the current second
18      time_t currentTime; // store time program has been running
19
20      // prompt the user for localTime's initial values
21      cout << "Enter current hour: ";
22      cin >> hour;
23
24      cout << "Enter current minute: ";
25      cin >> minute; // set current minute
26
27      cout << "Enter current second: ";
28      cin >> second; // set current second
29
30      // instantiate object localTime of class Time
31      Time localTime( hour, minute, second );
32
33      cout << endl;
34
35      localTime.displayTime();
36
37      // update the clock indefinitely
38      while ( true )
39      {
40         currentTime = time( 0 ); // store the current time
41
42         // busy wait until one second has passed
43         while ( time( 0 ) < ( currentTime + 1 ) );
44
45         localTime.tick(); // advance the time in localTime
46         cout << "\r";
47         localTime.displayTime(); // display the updated time
48      } // end while
49
50      return 0; // indicate that program ended successfully
51
52   } // end function main
```

Labels in left margin:
- Create a variable of type `time_t` (line 18)
- Prompt user for and input current hour, minute and second (line 21)
- Passing arguments to the `Time` constructor (line 31)
- Display the time (line 35)
- Use the `time` function to find the current time (line 40)
- Update and display `localTime`'s time once per second (line 45)

Figure 15.40 Completed **Digital Clock** source code. (Part 2 of 2.)

SELF-REVIEW

1. A constructor that specifies no arguments is called the _____.

   a) empty constructor   b) default constructor

   c) overloaded constructor   d) *set* constructor

2. A function is overloaded if several functions have the same _____ but different _____.

   a) name, number of parameters   b) name, types of parameters

   c) parameter types and number of parameters, names

   d) Both a and b.

Answers: 1) b. 2) d.

15.8 Using the Debugger: The Autos Window

Now you will enhance your knowledge of the debugger by studying the **Autos** window. The **Autos window** allows you to view the values stored in an object's data members. In this section, you will learn how to view the contents of the Time object localTime's data members to verify that your application is executing correctly. [*Note:* This section provides instructions for debugging in Microsoft Visual C++ .NET. Instructions for using other popular debuggers are located in the appendices and www.deitel.com.]

**Using the Debugger:
Using the Autos Window**

1. *Opening the application*. Open the completed DigitalClock.cpp file if it is not already open.

2. *Setting breakpoints*. Set breakpoints at lines 31 and 45 by clicking in the margin indicator bar (Fig. 15.41). This allows you to suspend execution before and after certain properties have been modified, ensuring that data is being modified properly.

```
🔆 DigitalClock.cpp                                            _ □ ✕
    30        // instantiate object localTime of class Time
●   31        Time localTime( hour, minute, second );
    32
    33        cout << endl; // insert newline for readability
    34
    35        localTime.displayTime();
    36
    37        // update the clock indefinitely
    38        while ( true )
    39        {
    40            currentTime = time( 0 ); // store the current time
    41
    42            // busy wait until one second has passed
    43            while ( time( 0 ) < ( currentTime + 1 ) );
    44
●   45            localTime.tick(); // advance the time in localTime
    46            cout << "\r";
```

Setting breakpoints

Figure 15.41 Setting breakpoints in the **Digital Clock** application.

3. *Starting the debugger*. Start the debugger by selecting **Debug > Start**.

4. *Entering data*. At the application's input prompts, enter the values corresponding to the time 3:50:59.

5. *Using the Autos window*. When execution halts at the breakpoint at line 31, open the **Autos** window (Fig. 15.42) by selecting **Debug > Windows > Autos**. The **Autos** window allows you to view the contents of the variables used in the last statement that was executed. This allows you to verify that the previous statement executed correctly. The **Autos** window also lists the values in the next statement to be executed. Notice that the **Autos** window lists the hour, minute, second and localTime variables, their values and their types. Viewing the values stored in an object lets you verify that your application is manipulating these variables correctly.

Autos window displaying name and values of several recently used variables

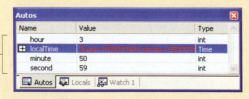

Figure 15.42 **Autos** window displaying the state of several local variables.

(cont.)

Click the plus box next to `localTime` in the **Name** column of the **Autos** window (Fig. 15.41). This allows you to view each of `localTime`'s data member values individually (Fig. 15.43). Notice that `localTime` members `hour`, `minute` and `second` contain large negative values. These values, which may be different each time the application executes, are the `localTime` data members' uninitialized values. These unpredictable (and often undesirable) values demonstrate why it is important to initialize all C++ variables before use.

localTime data members' values ⎯⎯⎯⎯

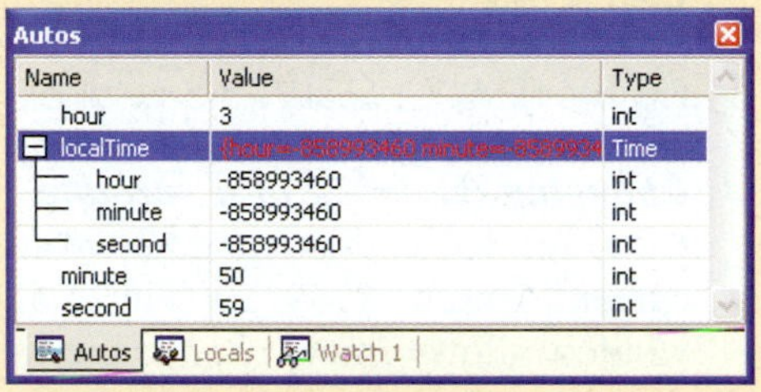

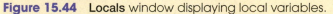

Figure 15.43 **Autos** window displaying the state of `localTime`.

6. *Opening the Locals window.* Open the **Locals** window (Fig. 15.44) by selecting **Debug > Windows > Locals** while the debugger is running. The **Locals** window, which you first used in Section 4.10, allows you to view the state of the variables in the current scope. Recall that the scope of a variable's identifier is the portion of an application in which that identifier can be referenced.

Local variables ⎯⎯⎯⎯

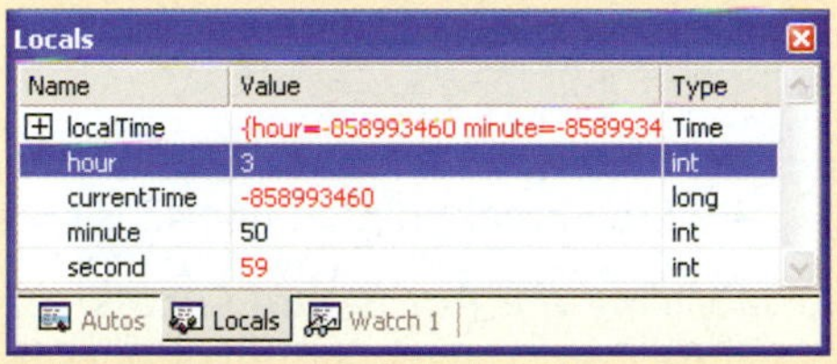

Figure 15.44 **Locals** window displaying local variables.

The **Locals** window lists all the variables that are in the scope of `main`. The `currentTime` local variable, which has not been initialized yet, is displayed in the **Locals** window, but not the **Autos** window. C++ represents the `time_t` data type with `long`s, so `currentTime` is defined as `long`. Notice that the values for `hour`, `minute`, `second` and `localTime` are the same as they were in the **Autos** window. Again, clicking the plus box next to `localTime` will show all of the members of `localTime`, their current values and their types.

7. *Continuing program execution.* Select **Debug > Continue**, and view the values of the `localTime`'s members in both the **Autos** and **Locals** windows. View the **Autos** window. Notice that the variables listed have now changed (Fig. 15.45). This happened because execution is now at a new statement that uses new variables. Also, notice that the value for `localTime`'s seconds, minutes and hours have been changed. View the **Locals** window. Notice that the **Locals** window still lets you view `main`'s local variables. Also, notice that `currentTime` has been initialized (Fig. 15.46).

localTime data members' values have been initialized ⎯⎯⎯⎯

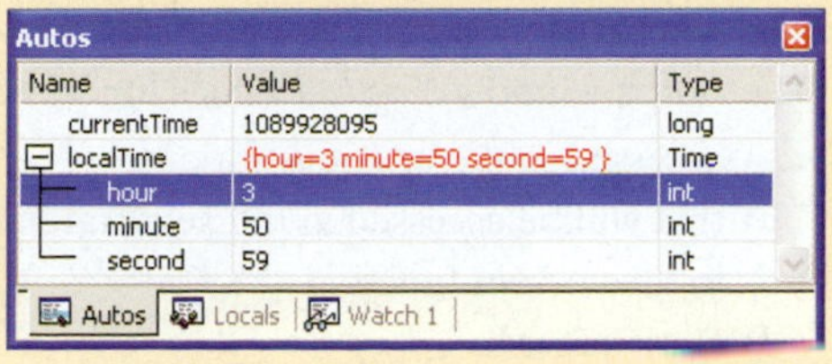

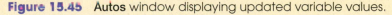

Figure 15.45 **Autos** window displaying updated variable values.

(cont.)

currentTime's value
has changed

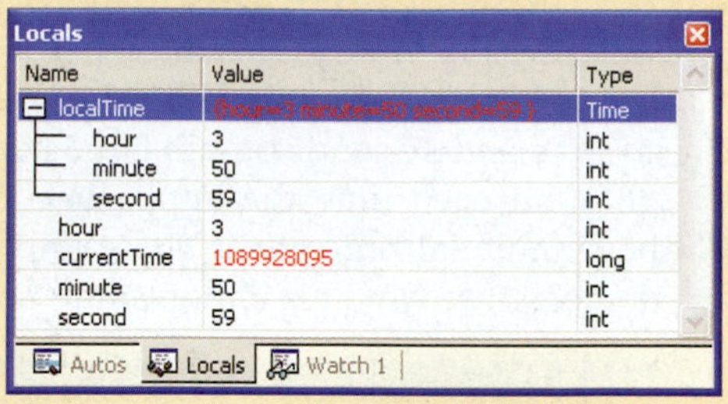

Figure 15.46   **Locals** window displaying changed variable values in red.

8. ***Changing the value of a variable.*** In the **Autos** window, double click the value for localTime member minute. Type 59 and press *Enter* to set the current time to 3:59:59 (Fig. 15.47). Like the **Locals** window, the **Autos** window allows you to change the values of variables to verify that program execution is correct at certain points without having to run the program again for each value.

Value changed by user

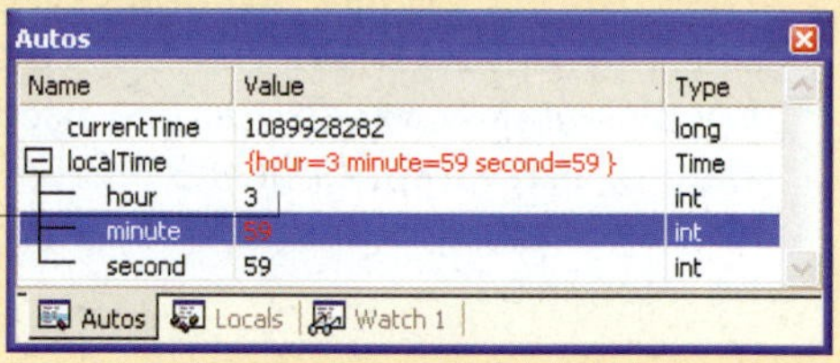

Figure 15.47   Changing the value of a variable in the **Autos** window.

9. ***Continuing execution.*** Select **Debug > Continue**. Execution continues until the breakpoint at line 42 is reached again.

10. ***Viewing the Autos and Locals window.*** View the **Autos** and **Locals** windows. Notice that all of the values listed in the **Autos** window have changed, so they are shown in red (Fig. 15.48).

Modified variable values
displayed in red

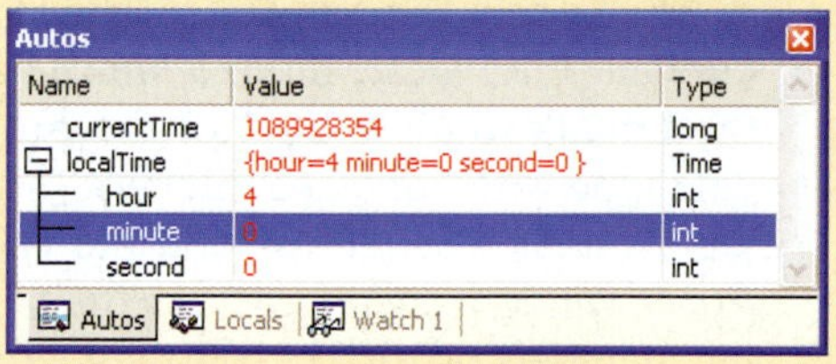

Figure 15.48   Updated variables listed in the **Autos** window.

11. ***Stopping the debugger.*** Select **Debug > Stop Debugging** to end the debugging session.

12. ***Closing the IDE.*** Close Visual Studio .NET by clicking its close box.

In this section, you learned how to use the **Autos** and **Watch** windows to view that state of an object and verify that your application is executing correctly.

SELF-REVIEW   1. The **Autos** window displays values for all variables _____.

a) accessed in the previous statement

b) that will be accessed in the next statement to execute

c) in the current function

d) Both a and b.

2. When a variable's value is changed, it becomes _____ in the **Autos** and **Locals** windows.

   a) red

   b) italic

   c) blue

   d) bold

Answers: 1) d. 2) a.

15.9 Wrap-Up

In this tutorial, you learned how to create your own classes—also known as programmer-defined classes—to provide functionality not available in the C++ class library. In the world of C++ programming, applications are created by using a combination of C++ Standard Library classes and functions and programmer-defined classes and functions.

You created a digital clock simulator using a programmer-defined class called Time. You added constructors, data members and three pairs of *get* and *set* functions to the Time class. You defined your constructor to initialize the class's data members, then you overloaded the constructor with a second version that accepts arguments. For each data member, you defined *get* and *set* functions that allow the class's data members to be safely accessed and modified. You then applied what you have already learned about using classes and functions to create a Time object. You used the functions of the Time class and the <ctime> standard library to access and display the time once per second, starting with the time that the user specified as the digital clock's initial time. You concluded the tutorial by learning how to use the debugger's **Autos** and **Locals** windows to view the state of an object and verify that your application is executing correctly.

In the next tutorial, you will learn about pointers. Pointers enable applications to pass arguments by reference and to create and manipulate dynamic data structures (that is, data structures that can grow and shrink as an application executes). You will use pointers to build an application that creates a shopping list.

SKILLS SUMMARY

Defining a Class

- Use the class keyword, followed by the name of the class.
- Add data members and member functions to the class's body.
- In each member function definition that occurs outside the class definition, prefix the function name with the class name, followed by the binary scope resolution operator (::). For example, if the member function name is setValue and the class name is Time, the function header should appear as

      void Time::setValue(*parameterList*)

  where *parameterList* specifies setValue's parameters.

Defining *get* and *set* Functions

- Define public *get* and *set* functions to access and modify private data members, respectively.
- In the *get* function, provide code to return the value of a data member.
- In the *set* function, provide code to validate the argument and modify the data member.

Defining a Constructor

- Use the name of the class, followed by a set of parentheses enclosing any parameters for the constructor.
- Add code to the constructor to initialize the object's data.

Controlling Access to Members

- Use the public member-access specifier, followed by a colon, to identify members that can be accessed by clients of the class.
- Use the private member-access specifier, followed by a colon, to identify members that can be accessed only by other members of the class.

KEY TERMS

Autos window—A feature of the Microsoft Visual C++ .NET debugger and other popular debuggers that allows you to view the values stored in an object's data members.

accessor—A function that retrieves the value of a data member; a *get* function.

attribute—A characteristic of an object that corresponds to a data member.

behavior—A characteristic of an object that corresponds to a member function.

binary scope resolution operator (::)—The operator that ties a member to a particular class. When a member function is defined outside its class's definition, the name of the function must be preceded by the name of the class followed by the binary scope resolution operator.

busy waiting—This occurs when an application repeatedly tests a condition that will allow it to proceed eventually.

class keyword—The keyword that indicates that what follows is a class definition.

class's body—Code that is included in the { and } of a class definition.

client—When you create and use an object of a class in a function, you and the function are known as clients of that class.

consistent state—A description of an object whose data members contain values that are valid. Classes typically provide *get* and *set* functions to ensure that objects of the class remain in a consistent state.

constructor—A function of a class that initializes the class's variables and has the same name as the class that contains it. A constructor cannot have a return type.

data member—A variable defined within the body of a class.

default constructor—A constructor that accepts no arguments.

#define preprocessor directive—A preprocessor directive that defines the name that appears immediately after the directive.

#endif preprocessor directive—A preprocessor directive that specifies the end of a block of code that begins with the #ifndef directive.

extensible language—A language that can be "extended" with new classes.

fill character—A character that will appear in unoccupied positions in a field.

flush stream manipulator—A stream manipulator that flushes the output buffer so that output is displayed on the screen immediately.

***get* function**—A function used to retrieve the value of a data member.

#ifndef preprocessor directive—A preprocessor directive that specifies the start of a block of code that is passed to the compiler only if the name directly following the directive has not been defined. The specified block of code ends when the #endif preprocessor directive is encountered. Pairs of #ifndef and #endif directives are often used to prevent the same header file from being included multiple times.

implementation—The code that provides the functionality for a particular task.

instance of a class—This is also known as an object of the class.

instantiate an object—Create an object of a class.

***Intellisense* feature**—A Visual Studio .NET feature that aids the programmer during development by providing windows listing available functions and pop-up descriptions of those functions.

interface—The names of a class's variables and functions that are available to clients of that class.

member-access specifier—A keyword, such as public or private, that can be used as part of a label that determines whether a class's members are accessible to non-member functions.

members of a class—Functions and variables defined within the body of a class.

member function—A function declared within the scope of a class.

mutator—A function that alters the value of a data member; a *set* function.

operation—A property of an object that corresponds to a member function.

private member-access specifier—A member-access specifier that specifies that a class's data members or functions are accessible only to members of that class.

programmer-defined class—A class that a programmer defines, as opposed to a class predefined in the C++ Standard Library.

public member-access specifier—A member-access specifier that specifies that a class's data members or member functions can be accessed by clients of the class.

set **function**—A function that sets the value of a data member and validates the value to ensure that it is appropriate for the variable that is being set to keep the object in a consistent state.

setfill parameterized stream manipulator—A stream manipulator that sets the character that is displayed in unused positions in a field.

time_t type (in the ctime C++ library)—A type designed to contain a number of seconds. time_t values are typically represented by longs because the value returned by the time function can be larger than an int on some systems.

C++ LIBRARY REFERENCE

ctime This library header provides function prototypes and types for manipulating the time and date.

- *Function*

  time—This function returns the current time, in seconds. The time is determined by calculating the number of seconds that have passed since midnight on January 1, 1970 (using UTC—Universal Time, also called Greenwich Mean Time).

- *Type*

  time_t—This type can be used to create variables that store a number of seconds. time_t values are typically represented by longs because the value returned by the time function can be larger than an int on some systems.

---

iomanip This library header is used to format stream input and output.

- *Stream manipulators*

  setfill—This stream manipulator specifies the character that fills unoccupied positions in a field.

  setprecision—This stream manipulator specifies that numeric values should be printed using the specified number of digits to the right of the decimal point. The argument to setprecision determines the number of digits that are displayed to the right of the decimal point when a floating-point value is printed.

---

iostream This header file declares basic services required for all stream-I/O operations.

- *Objects*

  cin—This object reads characters entered at the keyboard. Text is sent to the application when the user presses *Enter* and can be placed in a variable using the stream extraction operator, >>.

  cout—This object displays text on the screen. Text can be displayed using the stream insertion operator, <<.

- *Stream manipulators*

  endl—This object places a newline into the output stream and flushes the stream's buffer so that all text stored in the output stream object is displayed immediately.

  fixed—This stream manipulator specifies that floating-point numbers should be printed using fixed-point notation (as opposed to scientific notation).

  flush—This stream manipulator flushes the output buffer so that output is displayed on the screen immediately.

  left—This object causes values to be left justified in a field. The stream into which left is inserted remains left justified until the application terminates or until the stream's justification is changed, whichever comes first.

  right—This object causes values to be right justified in a field. The stream into which right is inserted remains right justified until the application terminates or until the stream's justification is changed, whichever comes first.

MULTIPLE-CHOICE QUESTIONS

15.1 A good name for a function that would set the value of data member number while ensuring its validity is _____.

a) number   b) set

c) setNumber   d) setValid

15.2 The _____ keyword(s) begin(s) a class definition.

a) new class   b) define class

c) define   d) class

15.3 The binary scope resolution operator (::) _____.

a) determines whether clients of a class can access a member

b) ties a class member to its corresponding class

c) must be used when a member function is defined outside the scope of its class

d) Both b and c.

15.4 The _____ stream manipulator specifies the character that is displayed in unoccupied positions of a field.

a) fieldfill   b) fill

c) setchar   d) setfill

15.5 A client of a class uses a _____ to retrieve the value of an object's data member.

a) *get* function   b) public label

c) constructor   d) *set* function

15.6 A private data member cannot be initialized _____.

a) when defined   b) directly by a client of its class

c) in a constructor   d) Both a and b.

15.7 An important difference between constructors and member functions is that _____.

a) constructors cannot specify a return type

b) constructors cannot specify any parameters

c) constructors must appear before member functions in a class definition

d) constructors can assign values to data members

15.8 A class can yield many _____, just as a primitive type can yield many variables.

a) names   b) objects

c) values   d) types

15.9 *Set* functions enable you to _____.

a) provide data validation   b) modify data

c) provide access to private data members

d) All of the above.

15.10 Data members defined private are not directly accessible _____.

a) outside the class   b) by member functions of the class

c) by the constructor of the class   d) inside the same class

EXERCISES

15.11 (*Triangle Creator Application*) Create an application that allows the user to enter the lengths for the three sides of a triangle as integers. Your application should then determine whether the triangle is a right triangle (two sides of the triangle form a 90-degree angle), an equilateral triangle (all sides of equal length) or neither (Fig. 15.49). You must create a class to represent a triangle object and define main.

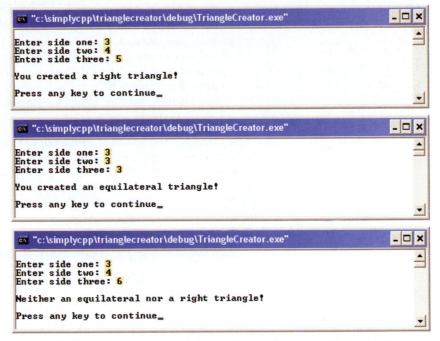

Figure 15.49 **Triangle Creator** application with all possible outputs.

a) *Copying the template to your working directory.* Copy the `C:\Examples\Tutorial15\Exercises\TriangleCreator` directory to your `C:\SimplyCpp` directory.

b) *Opening the template files.* Open the `TriangleCreator.cpp`, `Triangle.h` and `Triangle.cpp` files in your text editor.

c) *Defining variables.* View the `Triangle.h` file and, starting at line 9, define three double variables (`side1`, `side2`, `side3`) to hold the length of each side. The variables should all be defined `private` so that only the functions of this class can access them.

d) *Defining the necessary* **get** *and* **set** *functions.* In the `Triangle.h` file, before the data member definitions, declare `public` member functions. Start by declaring a prototype for a constructor that will take the lengths of the three sides of a triangle as arguments. In the `Triangle.cpp` file, define your constructor so that it sets data members by using the corresponding *set* functions. Following the constructor, create three pairs of *get* and *set* function prototypes in the `Triangle.h` file, then create corresponding definitions in the `Triangle.cpp` file that enable clients to access and modify the lengths of the three sides. If the client passes a negative value to a *set* function, that side should be assigned the value zero. Use this tutorial's `Time` class as your guide in creating the *get* and *set* functions.

e) *Adding additional features.* Following the *get* and *set* functions, create function prototypes in the `Triangle.h` file for `isRightTriangle` and `isEquilateral`, then create corresponding definitions in the `Triangle.cpp` file. These functions are similar to *get* functions except that they return `bool` values. The `isRightTriangle` function returns whether or not the sides form a right triangle using the Pythagorean theorem. This theorem states that in a right triangle, the sum of the squares of the two shorter sides of the triangle equals the square of the longest side of the triangle. Make sure that your function's return value is not affected by the order of sides, as any of the three sides could be the largest. The `isEquilateral` function returns whether or not the sides form an equilateral triangle— a triangle where all the sides are equal in length.

f) *Adding code to the* **main** *function.* Now that you have created your `Triangle` class, you can use it to create objects in your application. Switch to the `TriangleCreator.cpp` file. In `main`, define three new doubles starting in line 13 to store the three lengths that the user enters at input prompts. Use those values to create a new `Triangle` object.

g) *Displaying the result.* Use an if...else statement to determine if the triangle is a right triangle, an equilateral triangle or neither. Display the result.

h) *Save, compile and run the application.* Test your application to ensure that it runs correctly by entering sides all of length 3. Check that the displayed message indicates your triangle is equilateral. Then, make sure that inputs of 3, 4 and 5 indicate a right triangle and inputs of 3, 4 and 6 indicate neither. Finally, try inputting sides of 4, 5 and 3 and the message should indicate that your triangle is a right triangle.

i) *Close the Command Prompt window.*

15.12 (*Modified Digital Clock Application*) Modify the tutorial's **Digital Clock** application to display time as AM or PM. Allow the user to enter an hour value between 0 and 23, inclusive (Fig. 15.50). An hour value of 0 represents the 12:00 AM hour (midnight), and an hour value of 23 represents the 11:00 PM hour. Make sure that your constructor and *set* functions use the time 00:00:00 as the default time when the client does not specify a time or the client specifies an invalid time.

```
"c:\simplycpp\modifieddigitalclock\debug\DigitalClock.exe"

Enter current hour: 11
Enter current minute: 59
Enter current second: 56

11:59:56 AM
```

10 seconds later:

```
"c:\simplycpp\modifieddigitalclock\debug\DigitalClock.exe"

Enter current hour: 11
Enter current minute: 59
Enter current second: 56

12:00:06 PM
```

Figure 15.50 Modified **Digital Clock** application output.

a) *Copying the template to your working directory.* Copy the C:\Examples\Tutorial15\Exercises\ModifiedDigitalClock directory to your C:\SimplyCpp directory.

b) *Opening the template file.* Open the Time.cpp file in your text editor or IDE. Because you used object-oriented programming and separated your interface from your implementation, you need modify only the Time.cpp file to effect the required change.

c) *Modifying the default constructor.* Modify the default constructor to assign time values corresponding to 12:00:00 AM.

d) *Modifying the setHour function.* Modify the setHour function to accept values of 0–23 as valid hour values. If an invalid hour value is entered, the function should assign the default value to hour.

e) *Modifying the getHour function.* Change the return statement of the getHour function to return a value between 1 and 12. [*Hint:* If hour % 12 is 0, you should return 12, otherwise, you should return the value of hour % 12.]

f) *Modifying the displayTime function.* At the end of the displayTime function, add an if...else statement that will display "AM" if hour is less than 12 and "PM" otherwise. Remove the flush stream manipulator from line 114 and insert the flush stream manipulator just before the end of the statements in lines 118 and 122.

g) *Modifying the tick function.* In the tick function, modify the nested if statement to ensure that the hour is incremented to the appropriate value between 0 and 23.

h) *Save, compile and run the application.* Test your application to ensure that it runs correctly by entering different initial times. The clock should handle invalid data correctly, and should update the time appropriately when switching from an AM value to a PM value and vice versa.

i) *Close the application.* Close the running application by pressing and holding *Ctrl* while pressing *C*.

j) *Close the Command Prompt window.*

15.13 (*Account Information Application*) A bank wants you to create an application that will allow its tellers to view client information. The interface is created for you (Fig. 15.51); you need to implement the Client class which stores the data. Once your application is complete, the bank manager should be able to enter an account number to view the corresponding client's information. The information is stored in four arrays containing first names, last names, account numbers and account balances. When the user enters the sentinel value, -1, the application should exit.

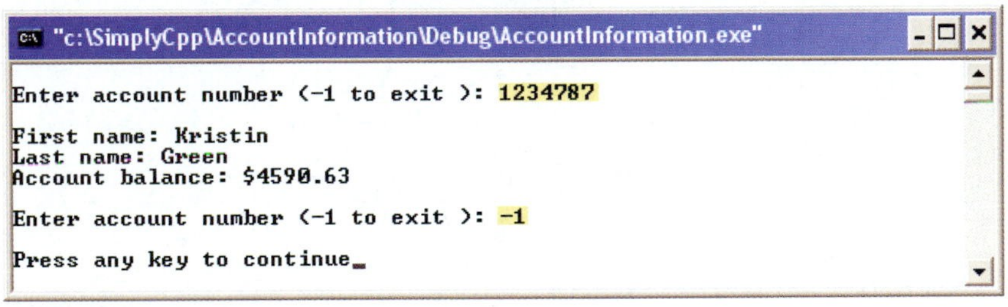

Figure 15.51 Account Information application output.

a) *Copying the template to your working directory.* Copy the C:\Examples\ Tutorial15\Exercises\AccountInformation directory to your C:\SimplyCpp directory.

b) *Opening the template files.* Open the AccountInformation.cpp and Client.cpp files in your text editor or IDE.

c) *Determining variables for the class.* Examine the code from AccountInformation.cpp, including all the *get* function calls that the Client object uses to retrieve information. These function calls can be found in the displayInformation function, beginning in line 69.

d) *Creating the Client header file.* Switch to your Client.h file. Define four private data members, firstName, lastName, account and balance, beginning in line 15, to represent an account number, a balance amount, a first name and a last name. Then declare function prototypes for the default constructor and a constructor that takes two strings, one int and one double argument, as well as the necessary *get* and *set* functions. You will define these functions in the next step.

e) *Creating the Client source code file.* Switch to your Client.cpp file. Define the default constructor to use the *set* functions to assign 0 to the account number and balance amount, and the empty string to the first name and the last name. Then define the constructor that takes arguments and assign the corresponding parameters to the appropriate data members using the *set* functions.

f) *Defining the* get *and* set *functions.* Each data member should have a corresponding *get* and *set* function. Use this tutorial's Time class as your guide in defining the *get* and *set* functions.

g) *Adding more information.* Now switch to your AccountInformation.cpp file. In the initializeAccountRecords function (beginning in line 47), add one more account. Include name, account number and balance. To add an account, insert an additional comma and a number or string value into each of the four array definitions starting in line 50.

h) *Save, compile and run the application.* Test your application to ensure that it runs correctly by entering values at the account number prompt to display the corresponding account record. Make sure that each account indexed in the accountRecords array can be displayed. The information stored in accountRecords can be found in four array definitions starting in line 50.

i) *Close the application.* Close the running application by entering -1 at the application's prompt.

j) *Close the Command Prompt window.*

What does this code do? ▶

15.14 What does the following code do? The first code listing contains the header file for the Shape class. The second code listing contains the implementation for the Shape class. Each Shape object represents a closed shape composed of straight lines (such as a triangle, rectangle or pentagon). The third code listing contains main, which calls the mystery function. What is displayed when this application executes?

```cpp
1   // Exercise 15.14: Shape.h
2   // Declaration of class Shape.
3   // Member functions are defined in Shape.cpp
4
5   // prevent multiple inclusions of header file
6   #ifndef SHAPE_H
7   #define SHAPE_H
8
9   class Shape
10  {
11  public:
12     Shape(); // default constructor
13
14     // overload constructor
15     Shape( int );
16
17     // get and set function definition
18     int getSides();
19     void setSides( int );
20
21  private:
22     int sides;
23
24  }; // end class Shape
25
26  #endif
```

```cpp
1   // Exercise 15.4: Shape.cpp
2   // Member-function declarations for class Shape
3   #include "Shape.h"
4
5   // Shape default constructor
6   Shape::Shape()
7   {
8      setSides( 0 );
9
10  } // end constructor
11
12  // Shape constructor, number of sides supplied
13  Shape::Shape( int numSides )
14  {
15     setSides( numSides );
16
17  } // end constructor
18
19  // return sides value
20  int Shape::getSides()
21  {
22     return sides;
23
24  } // end function getSides
```

```
25
26    // set sides value
27    void Shape::setSides( int numSides )
28    {
29       if ( numSides > 2 )
30       {
31          sides = numSides;
32       } // end if
33       else // set invalid input to 0
34       {
35          sides = 0;
36       } // end else
37
38    } // end function setSides
```

```
 1    // Exercise 15.14: WDTCD.cpp
 2    // What does this code do?
 3    #include <string>     // required to access string functions
 4    #include <iostream>   // required to perform C++ stream I/O
 5
 6    // include definition of class Shape from Shape.h
 7    #include "Shape.h"
 8
 9    using namespace std; // for accessing C++ Standard Library members
10
11    // declare function prototypes
12    string mystery( Shape );
13
14    // function main begins program execution
15    int main()
16    {
17       Shape shape1( 3 );
18       Shape shape2( 4 );
19       Shape shape3( 5 );
20
21       cout << "\nShape1 is a: " << mystery( shape1 ) << endl;
22       cout << "Shape2 is a: " << mystery( shape2 ) << endl;
23       cout << "Shape3 is a: " << mystery( shape3 ) << endl << endl;
24
25       return 0; // indicate program ended successfully
26
27    } // end function main
28
29    string mystery( Shape shape )
30    {
31       string shapeText;
32
33       // switch with number of shape's sides
34       switch ( shape.getSides() )
35       {
36          case 3:
37             shapeText = "Triangle";
38             break;
39
40          case 4:
41             shapeText = "Quadrilateral";
42             break;
43
```

```
44          default:
45              shapeText = "Other polygon";
46
47          } // end switch
48
49      return shapeText;
50
51  } // end function mystery
```

What's wrong with this code? ▶

15.15 Find the error(s) in the following code. The application should create a new Shape object with numberSides sides. Assume the Shape class is from Exercise 15.14.

```
1   // Exercise 15.15: WWWTC.cpp
2   // This application sets the number of sides of an instance of Shape
3   // to the number input by the user
4   #include <iostream>  // required to perform C++ stream I/O
5
6   // include definition of class Shape from Shape.h
7   #include "Shape.h"
8
9   using namespace std; // for accessing C++ Standard Library members
10
11  // declare function prototypes
12  void manipulateShape( int );
13
14  // function main begins program execution
15  int main()
16  {
17     int sides;  // holds the number of sides
18
19     // prompt the user for number of sides
20     cout << "\nPlease enter the number of sides: ";
21     cin >> sides;  // store number of sides in sides
22
23     manipulateShape( sides );
24
25     return 0; // indicate that program ended successfully
26
27  } // end function main
28
29  void manipulateShape( int numberSides )
30  {
31     Shape shape( 3 );
32
33     shape.setSides = numberSides;
34
35     cout << "This shape now has: " << shape.getSides()
36         << " sides\n" << endl;
37
38  } // end function manipulateShape
```

Using the Debugger ▶

15.16 (*View Name Application*) The **View Name** application allows the user to enter the user's first and last name. After the user enters the name, the application stores the name in an object, then displays the user's first and last name, last name first. Your application creates an instance of the Name class. This class uses *set* functions to set the first-name and last-name data members. While testing your application, you noticed that the application did not display the correct output. The last name is displayed, but the first name is not. The correct output is shown in Fig. 15.52.

Figure 15.52 View Name application with correct output.

a) *Copying the template to your working directory.* Copy the C:\Examples\ Tutorial15\Exercises\Debugger\ViewName directory to your C:\SimplyCpp directory.

b) *Opening the template file.* Open the ViewName.cpp source code file in your text editor or IDE.

c) *Compiling the application for debugging.* If you are not using Visual Studio .NET, make sure to specify the compiler option that includes debugging information.

d) *Running the application.* Run the **View Name** application. Enter your first and last names at the input prompts. Notice that the output is incorrect.

e) *Start the debugger.*

f) *Using the debugger.* Use the debugger to find the logic error(s) in your application. Use the **Locals** and **Autos** windows to see all the changes to the data members of the Name class. When you have found the logic error, change the code appropriately. The application with the correct output is displayed in Fig. 15.52.

g) *Save, compile and run the application.* Test your application to ensure that it runs correctly by entering various names at the input prompts. The application should display the last name, followed by a comma, space and the first name.

h) *Close the Command Prompt window.*

Programming Challenge ▶   **15.17** (*DVD Inventory Application*) Create an application that allows the user to inventory DVDs. Users input the title of the DVD and bonus materials, and that information is stored in an object. The application's menu is provided for you (Fig. 15.53). You will create a class (DVDInfo) to represent the DVD object and another class (BonusInfo) to represent bonus materials for a DVD object such as the movie's trailer.

a) *Copying the template to your working directory.* Copy the C:\Examples\ Tutorial15\Exercises\DVDInventory directory to your C:\SimplyCpp directory.

b) *Opening the template source code files.* Open the DVDInventory.cpp, DVDInfo.cpp and BonusInfo.cpp files in your text editor or IDE.

c) *Creating the BonusInfo class.* View the BonusInfo class (declared in the Bonus-Info.h file and defined in the BonusInfo.cpp file). Add code to this class so that its objects will each represent one bonus material item on the DVD. Each BonusInfo object should have a name (name) and a length (itemLength). Use this tutorial's Time class as your guide in creating the *get* and *set* functions for the name and length of each bonus material. Have your *set* function set the minutes of an item to zero if it is passed a negative value. You will also need to define a constructor to create an instance of this class.

d) *Creating the DVDInfo class.* Now, view the DVDInfo class (declared in the DVDInfo.h file and defined in the DVDInfo.cpp file). Add code so that this class contains the movie title (movieTitle) and the length of the movie (movieLength). It should also include an array of BonusInfo items (bonusMaterial). Again, use this tutorial's Time class as your guide in creating the *get* and *set* functions for the name, length and bonus materials. The *get* function for the bonusMaterial member should return no value and accept an array of BonusInfo objects as its parameter. You will also need to define a constructor to create an instance of this class.

Figure 15.53 DVD Inventory application output.

e) *Creating the necessary variables.* View the DVDInventory.cpp file. First, create a DVDInfo variable in main. If the user selects 1 at the menu (to enter new DVD information), the application should prompt the user for the DVD information and store the responses in variables. You will need to create local variables to store this information. Then, inside the while statement provided for you in the template source code, add code that prompts the user for and stores input if the user enters 1 at the menu.

f) *Adding bonus material information.* Create an array of BonusInfo objects to store bonus materials. The template source code file for the DVDInfo class defined a constant variable named MAX_BONUS, which stores the maximum number of bonus items per DVD. To initialize your array of BonusInfo objects to contain this number of elements, use the binary scope resolution operator to reference this variable as DVDInfo::MAX_BONUS. Use the variables you defined in *Step f* to create BonusInfo objects to go in this array.

g) *Creating an instance of DVDInfo.* Use the movie title, the length and the array of bonus materials to make your DVDInfo object.

h) *Displaying the output.* If the user selects 2 from the menu, the application should display information stored in the DVDInfo object. Add a nested else if to your if statement that you wrote in *Steps f–h*. Inside this statement, display all of the information stored by the DVDInfo object, as shown in Fig. 15.53.

i) *Save, compile and run the application.* Test your application to ensure that it runs correctly by selecting option 1 from the menu and entering various values for DVD information at the input prompts. Select option 2 from the menu and verify that all information that is displayed is correct.

j) *Closing the application.* Select menu option 3 to exit the application.

k) *Close the Command Prompt window.*

Objectives

In this tutorial, you will learn to:
- Create and initialize pointers.
- Store the address of a variable in a pointer.
- Create a linked list of objects.
- Access class members using a pointer.
- Use dynamic memory management to create and delete objects.

Outline

Shopping List Application

Introducing Pointers, References and Dynamic Data Structures

This tutorial discusses one of the most powerful features of the C++ programming language, the pointer. A **pointer** is the address of an item, such as a data value, in memory. In the real world, you frequently use locations, instead of names, to refer to a person or thing. For example, the postal service uses the address on the envelope to deliver your mail. When you make a phone call, the phone company uses the number that you dialed, not the name of the recipient, to locate the phone that belongs to the recipient.

In Tutorial 13, you learned that arrays are passed by reference. In this tutorial, you will see that pointers enable applications to pass any variable by reference, even primitive data types, such as ints, doubles, etc. This tutorial explains basic pointer concepts and introduces **dynamic data structures**—ones that can grow and shrink as an application executes. When you declare an array, you must specify its fixed size before you compile your application. In this tutorial, you will learn about the linked list dynamic data structure, which you will use to build your **Shopping List** application and which may vary in size.

16.1 Test-Driving the Shopping List Application

You will now create an application that allows a user to create, modify and display a list of shopping items. Your application will use pointers to build a linked list data structure to store the items on the shopping list. Your application must meet the following requirements:

Application Requirements

*A supermarket has noticed that many of its customers bring a paper shopping list containing the names and quantities of items that they need to purchase. The supermarket would like to create an application that enables users to create and maintain a shopping list on a handheld computer that the user can bring to the store. The **Shopping List** application must enable the user to enter the name and quantity of each shopping item. The user must also be able to display the contents of the shopping list.*

367

You begin by test-driving the completed application. Then, you will learn the additional C++ capabilities you will need to create your own version of this application.

1. ***Locating the completed application.*** Open the **Command Prompt** window by selecting **Start > All Programs > Accessories > Command Prompt**. Change to your completed **Shopping List** application directory by typing cd C:\Examples\Tutorial16\CompletedApplication\ShoppingList.

2. ***Running the Shopping List application.*** Type ShoppingList in the **Command Prompt** window to run the application (Fig. 16.1). The application displays its main menu presenting the options to enter a new item, display the shopping list or exit the application.

```
C:\>cd C:\Examples\Tutorial16\CompletedApplication\ShoppingList

C:\Examples\Tutorial16\CompletedApplication\ShoppingList>ShoppingList

Select one of the following options
1 - Enter new item
2 - Display list
3 - Exit the application
Enter selection: _
```

Figure 16.1   Running the completed **Shopping List** application.

3. ***Entering a shopping item.*** To add a new item to your shopping list, enter 1 at the **Enter selection:** prompt. The application then prompts you for the name and quantity for the item (Fig. 16.2). At the **Enter item name:** prompt, enter the text Apples. At the **Enter quantity:** prompt, enter the value 6.

```
Enter selection: 1

Enter item name: Apples
Enter quantity: 6_
```

Figure 16.2   Adding a new item to the shopping list.

4. ***Displaying the list of items.*** After you enter a new item, the application again displays its main menu as in Fig. 16.1. To view the item that you just added to the list, enter 2 at the **Enter selection:** prompt. Notice that the application displays a header ("Shopping List"), then displays the item that you just added. After displaying the list, the application again displays its menu.

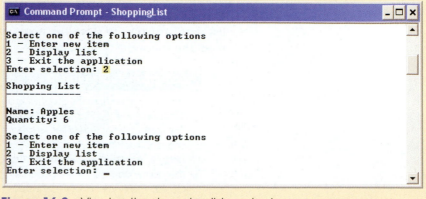

```
Select one of the following options
1 - Enter new item
2 - Display list
3 - Exit the application
Enter selection: 2

Shopping List
-------------

Name: Apples
Quantity: 6

Select one of the following options
1 - Enter new item
2 - Display list
3 - Exit the application
Enter selection: _
```

Figure 16.3   Viewing the shopping list contents.

(cont.)

5. ***Adding more items to the list.*** Repeat *Step 3*, using the text Bags of pret-zels for the item name and the value 2 for the item's quantity. Then repeat *Step 3* once more, using the text Eggs for the item name and the value 12 for the item's quantity (Fig. 16.4).

```
Command Prompt - ShoppingList                               _ □ ×

Select one of the following options
1 - Enter new item
2 - Display list
3 - Exit the application
Enter selection: 1

Enter item name: Bags of pretzels
Enter quantity: 2

Select one of the following options
1 - Enter new item
2 - Display list
3 - Exit the application
Enter selection: 1

Enter item name: Eggs
Enter quantity: 12_
```

Figure 16.4 Adding items to the shopping list.

6. ***Displaying the updated list.*** To view the updated shopping list, enter 2 at the **Enter selection:** prompt (Fig. 16.5). Notice that the names and quantities of the items that you entered are displayed. Note that the items are displayed in reverse order because each new item is added to the top of the shopping list. This is acceptable because a shopping list is typically unordered. Later in the tutorial, you will see why the shopping list is ordered this way.

```
Command Prompt - ShoppingList                               _ □ ×

Enter selection: 2

Shopping List
-------------

Name: Eggs
Quantity: 12

Name: Bags of pretzels
Quantity: 2

Name: Apples
Quantity: 6
```

Figure 16.5 Viewing the updated shopping list contents.

7. ***Closing the running application.*** Close the application by entering 3 at the **Enter selection:** prompt.

8. ***Close the Command Prompt window.***

16.2 Introducing Pointers

Pointer variables contain memory addresses, which are represented internally as non-negative values. Normally, a variable directly contains a specific value. A pointer, on the other hand, contains the address of a variable that contains a specific value. In this sense, a variable name *directly* references a value, and a pointer *indirectly* references a value (Fig. 16.6). Referencing a value through a pointer is often called **indirection**. Note that diagrams typically represent a pointer as an arrow from the pointer variable (which contains a memory address) to the variable it references (located at that address in memory).

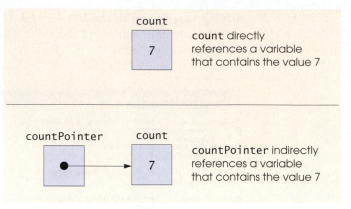

Figure 16.6   Directly and indirectly referencing a variable.

Pointers, like any other variables, must be declared before they can be used. For example, the declaration

```
int *countPointer
```

declares the variable `countPointer` in Fig. 16.6 to be of type `int *` (pronounced "integer pointer" or "a pointer to an `int`") and is read, "`countPointer` is an `int` pointer" or "`countPointer` points to an `int`." When `*` appears in a declaration, it is not an operator; rather, it simply indicates that the variable being declared is a pointer. Pointers can be declared to point to data items of any type.

Pointers should be initialized either when they are declared or in an assignment statement. A pointer may be initialized to 0, NULL or an address. A pointer with the value 0 or NULL points to nothing. Symbolic constant **NULL** is defined in header file `<iostream>` (and in several other standard library header files) to represent the value 0. Initializing a pointer to NULL is equivalent to initializing a pointer to 0, but in C++, 0 is used by convention. When 0 is assigned, it is converted to a pointer of the appropriate type. You cannot assign an integer value other than 0 directly to a pointer variable. In the next section, we will discuss how to assign a variable's address to a pointer.

Error-Prevention Tip

Initialize pointers to prevent pointing to unknown or uninitialized areas of memory.

SELF-REVIEW

1. A variable name _____ a value, whereas a pointer _____ a value.

   a) initializes, does not initialize   b) directly references, indirectly references

   c) declares, defines   d) indirectly references, directly references

2. A pointer can be initialized using _____.

   a) NULL   b) 0

   c) an address   d) All of the above.

Answers: 1) b. 2) d.

16.3 Pointer Operators

The **address operator (&)** is a unary operator that returns the memory address of its operand. For example, assuming the definitions

```
int y = 5;
int *yPointer;
```

the statement

```
yPointer = &y;
```

assigns the address of the variable y to pointer variable `yPointer`. Then variable `yPointer` is said to "point to" y. Now, `yPointer` indirectly references variable y's value. Figure 16.7 shows a schematic representation of memory after the preceding assignment. In the figure, we show the "pointing relationship" by drawing an arrow from the box that represents the pointer yPointer in memory to the box that represents the variable y in memory.

Figure 16.7   Graphical representation of a pointer pointing to a variable in memory.

Figure 16.8 shows another representation of a pointer in memory, assuming that integer variable y is stored at location 600000 and that pointer variable yPointer is stored at location 500000. The operand of the address operator must be something to which a value can be assigned, such as a variable name. The address operator cannot be applied to literal constants, such as in &23, for example.

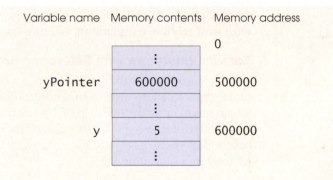

Figure 16.8   Representation of y and yPointer in memory.

The yPointer variable is defined as type int *. In the definition for this variable, the asterisk appeared between a type name (int) and the variable name, so the asterisk became part of the variable's type. When a type name does not precede the asterisk, however, the asterisk is the unary * **operator**, commonly referred to as the **indirection operator** or **dereferencing operator**. This operator, whose operand must be a pointer, returns a synonym (also called an alias or a nickname) for the name of the object to which the operand points. For example, the expression

```
*yPointer
```

returns a synonym for the name y in Fig. 16.7. When an operation is performed on an object's synonym, it is as if the operation were performed directly on the object itself. For example (referring again to Fig. 16.7), the statement

```
cout << *yPointer << endl;
```

displays the value of variable y, namely, 5, just as the statement

```
cout << y << endl;
```

would. Using * in this manner is called **dereferencing a pointer**. Note that a dereferenced pointer may also be used on the left side of an assignment statement, as in

```
*yPointer = 9;
```

which would assign 9 to y in Fig. 16.7. The dereferenced pointer may also be used to receive an input value as in

**Common
Programming Error**

Dereferencing a 0 pointer is normally a fatal execution-time error.

```
cin >> *yPointer;
```

Note in Appendix B that the address operator (&) and the dereferencing operator
(*) are unary operators on the third level of precedence in the chart.

---

1. The _____ operator returns the memory address of its operand.

    a) *   b) &&

    c) &   d) None of the above.

2. The operand of the address operator can be a _____.

    a) variable name   b) constant (like **7**)

    c) dereferenced pointer   d) Both a and c.

Answers: 1) c. 2) d.

16.4 Passing Arguments to Functions by Reference

Tutorial 13 compared and contrasted pass-by-value and pass-by-reference. In this
section, you will learn the two ways to perform pass-by-reference—**pass-by-reference with reference arguments** and **pass-by-reference with pointer arguments**.

Pass-By-Reference with Reference Arguments

As you learned in Tutorial 10, `return` can be used to return one value from a called
function to a caller (or to return control from a called function to a caller without
passing back a value). With pass-by-reference, the caller gives the called function
the ability to access the caller's data directly, and to modify that data if the called
function chooses to do so. The following box demonstrates passing by reference
with reference arguments.

**Passing By Reference
with Reference
Arguments**

1. ***Copying the template to your working directory.*** Copy the `C:\Exam-
ples\Tutorial16\TemplateApplication\PassByReference` directory to
your `C:\SimplyCpp` directory.

2. ***Open the PassByReference.cpp file.*** Open the template file `PassByRef-
erence.cpp` in your text editor or IDE. Notice that `main` contains code that
inputs an integer into local variable `input`.

3. ***Declaring a prototype for a function that uses a reference parameter.*** A **reference parameter** is a synonym for its corresponding argument in a function
call. To indicate that a function parameter is passed by reference, simply follow the parameter's type in the function prototype by an ampersand (&); use
the same convention when listing the parameter's type in the function
header. Insert lines 8–9 of Fig. 16.9 to declare the `incrementAndDisplay`
function, which declares one reference parameter.

Declaring a function that
declares an `int` reference
parameter

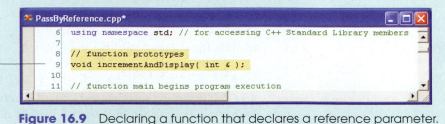

Figure 16.9   Declaring a function that declares a reference parameter.

(cont.)

4. ***Passing a variable by reference using a reference argument.*** To pass a value by reference to a function that declares a reference parameter, simply mention the variable by name in the function call. Insert lines 20–26 of Fig. 16.10 into main. Lines 20–21 display the variable's value before passing it to incrementAndDisplay. Line 23 calls incrementAndDisplay passing input by reference using a reference parameter. Note that the function call looks *exactly* the same as if you were passing the argument input by value. The compiler is able to tell the difference, though, because of the way the parameter is written in the function prototype (line 9 of Fig. 16.9). Lines 25–26 display the variable's value after incrementAndDisplay executes.

Using a variable name to pass-by-reference using a reference argument

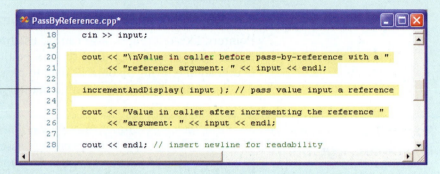

```
18      cin >> input;
19
20      cout << "\nValue in caller before pass-by-reference with a "
21          << "reference argument: " << input << endl;
22
23      incrementAndDisplay( input ); // pass value input a reference
24
25      cout << "Value in caller after incrementing the reference "
26          << "argument: " << input << endl;
27
28      cout << endl; // insert newline for readability
```

Figure 16.10 Passing an argument by reference using a reference argument.

5. ***Defining the incrementAndDisplay function.*** Insert lines 34–41 of Fig. 16.11 after main. The function header (line 35) declares a reference parameter named count. The declaration, int &count, when read from right to left is pronounced "count is a reference to an int." As always, the function prototype and header must agree. Note that the & in the preceding reference parameter declaration is not the address operator, &, which is not preceded by a data-type name.

Incrementing the reference parameter

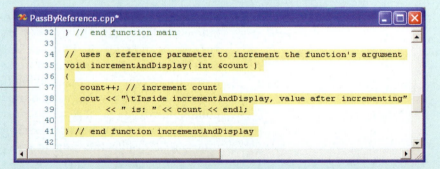

```
32   } // end function main
33
34   // uses a reference parameter to increment the function's argument
35   void incrementAndDisplay( int &count )
36   {
37      count++; // increment count
38      cout << "\tInside incrementAndDisplay, value after incrementing"
39          << " is: " << count << endl;
40
41   } // end function incrementAndDisplay
42
```

Figure 16.11 Defining a function that declares a reference parameter.

Line 37 increments the count parameter and lines 38–39 display its value. Note that mentioning the variable by its parameter name, count, in the body of the called function incrementAndDisplay actually refers to the original variable input in the calling function (line 23 of Fig. 16.10). As a result, the original variable can be modified directly by the called function.

6. ***Save, compile and run the application.*** Figure 16.12 shows the application running. Enter 8 at the **Enter an integer:** prompt. Notice that the expression count++ in the called function increments the value of input in main.

(cont.)

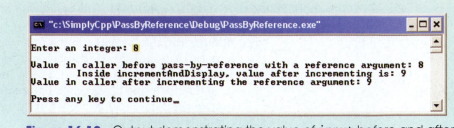

Figure 16.12 Output demonstrating the value of `input` before and after passing a value by reference with a reference argument.

Pass-By-Reference with Pointer Arguments

Pointers, like references, also can be used to modify one or more variables in the caller. They can also be used to pass pointers to large data objects, avoiding the overhead of copying an object's data to pass it by value. The next box demonstrates passing a value by reference with a pointer argument.

**Passing By Reference
with Pointer Arguments**

1. ***Declaring a prototype for a function that uses a pointer argument.*** To indicate that a function parameter is passed by reference using a pointer, simply follow the parameter's type in the function prototype by an asterisk (*); use the same convention when listing the parameter's type in the function header. Insert line 10 of Fig. 16.13 to declare an overloaded `incrementAndDisplay` function that accepts one pointer argument.

Declaring a function that declares an `int` pointer parameter

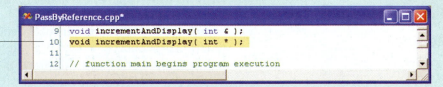

Figure 16.13 Declaring a function that declares a pointer parameter.

2. ***Passing a variable by reference using a pointer argument.*** Insert lines 29–35 of Fig. 16.14 into `main`. Lines 29–30 display `input`'s value before passing it to `incrementAndDisplay`. When calling a function and passing arguments by reference using pointers, the addresses of the arguments are passed. This is normally accomplished by applying the address operator (&) to the name of the variable whose value will be modified (unless that variable is already a pointer, in which case it is simply passed as is). Line 32 calls `incrementAndDisplay`, passing the memory address of `input` using the address operator. Lines 34–35 display the value in the caller after `incrementAndDisplay` executes.

Using the address operator to pass-by-reference using a pointer

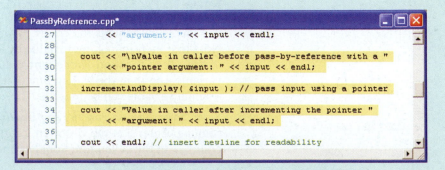

Figure 16.14 Passing a variable by reference using a pointer argument.

(cont.)

3. **Defining an overloaded *incrementAndDisplay* function.** Insert lines 52–59 of Fig. 16.15. The function header (line 53) declares a pointer argument named `countPointer`. The declaration, `int *countPointer`, when read from right to left is pronounced "`countPointer` is a pointer to an `int`."

Dereferencing the pointer and incrementing the result

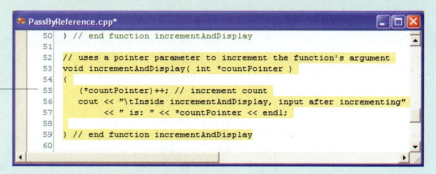

```
50   } // end function incrementAndDisplay
51
52   // uses a pointer parameter to increment the function's argument
53   void incrementAndDisplay( int *countPointer )
54   {
55      (*countPointer)++; // increment count
56      cout << "\tInside incrementAndDisplay, input after incrementing"
57         << " is: " << *countPointer << endl;
58
59   } // end function incrementAndDisplay
60
```

Figure 16.15 Defining a function that declares a pointer argument.

Line 55 dereferences the parameter `countPointer`, then increments the value referenced by `countPointer` (which corresponds to the value of `input` in line 32 of Fig. 16.14). Note that the postincrement operator has higher precedence than the dereferencing operator. As a result, the expression `*countPointer` must be placed in parentheses so that it is evaluated before the result is incremented. If the parentheses were omitted, line 55 would increment the address contained in `countPointer`, causing it to point to the wrong memory location (one address higher than that of `input`); the application would then dereference that memory location and would produce an incorrect result (or a fatal runtime error). Lines 56–57 display the new value of the variable to which `countPointer` points using the dereferencing operator (again, this is the variable `input` in the caller).

Error-Prevention Tip

Not dereferencing a pointer when it is necessary to do so to obtain the value to which the pointer points is an error.

4. **Save, compile and run the application.** Figure 16.16 shows the application running. Enter 8 at the **Enter an integer:** prompt. Notice that the expression `(*countPointer)++` in the overloaded `incrementAndDisplay` function also increments the value of `input` in `main`.

```
"c:\SimplyCpp\PassByReference\Debug\PassByReference.exe"

Enter an integer: 8

Value in caller before pass-by-reference with a reference argument: 8
        Inside incrementAndDisplay, value after incrementing is: 9
Value in caller after incrementing the reference argument: 9

Value in caller before pass-by-reference with a pointer argument: 9
        Inside incrementAndDisplay, input after incrementing is: 10
Value in caller after incrementing the pointer argument: 10

Press any key to continue_
```

Figure 16.16 Output showing `input` before and after passing it by reference using reference and pointer arguments.

In Tutorial 13, you used arrays to pass values by reference, but you did not use the address operator. Arrays are not passed using the address operator, because the name of the array is the starting location in memory of the array—an array name is actually a pointer. For example, if a 10-element array is declared using the statement

```
int arrayName[ 10 ];
```

the name of the array (`arrayName`) is equivalent to the expression `&arrayName[ 0 ]`.

1. Consider the function prototype, `void` myFunction(`int *`). Assume that `intPointer` is a pointer to an `int` value count. Which of the following function calls passes count by reference?

   a) `myFunction( intPointer );`   b) `myFunction( &intPointer );`

   c) `myFunction( *intPointer );`   d) `myFunction( intPointer& );`

2. A function can be called using pass-by-reference if it specifies _____.

   a) a reference parameter   b) a pointer parameter

   c) an array parameter   d) All of the above.

Answers: 1) a. 2) d.

16.5 Designing the Shopping List Application

Now you will build your **Shopping List** application by using pointers and a linked list. The pointers store the addresses of `ShoppingItem` objects in the shopping list. Each `ShoppingItem` object will contain a name and quantity for the item that it represents. Your application will contain a `List` class that manages operations such as adding items to the list and displaying the contents of the list.

Your application will display a menu containing options for adding a new item to the list, displaying the shopping list and exiting the application. The pseudocode in Fig. 16.17 describes the basic operation of the **Shopping List** application.

> Display a menu containing options for adding a new item to the list,
>   displaying the shopping list and exiting the application
> Prompt the user for and input the menu selection
>
> If the user chose to add a new item to the list
>   Prompt the user for and input the name and quantity of the item
>   Create a new ShoppingItem object
>   Add the new ShoppingItem to the linked list of ShoppingItems
> If the user chose to display the shopping list
>
>   For each item in the list
>   Display the item's name and quantity
>
> If the user chose to exit
>   Delete each ShoppingItem and exit the application

Figure 16.17 Pseudocode for the **Shopping List** application.

Now that you have test-driven the **Shopping List** application and studied its pseudocode representation, you will learn how to implement a linked list. You begin by inspecting the `ShoppingItem` class definition.

Viewing the
ShoppingItem Class
Definition

1. *Opening the ShoppingItem class's header file.* Open the template file `ShoppingItem.h` in your text editor or IDE.

2. *Viewing the ShoppingItem class definition.* Lines 11–37 of Fig. 16.18 contain the `ShoppingItem` class definition. The `ShoppingItem` constructor prototype (line 14) demonstrates three different ways to declare function parameters. The first parameter is passed-by-reference using a reference parameter (`string &`), the second parameter is passed-by-value (`int`) and the third parameter is passed-by-reference using a pointer parameter (`ShoppingItem *`).

(cont.)

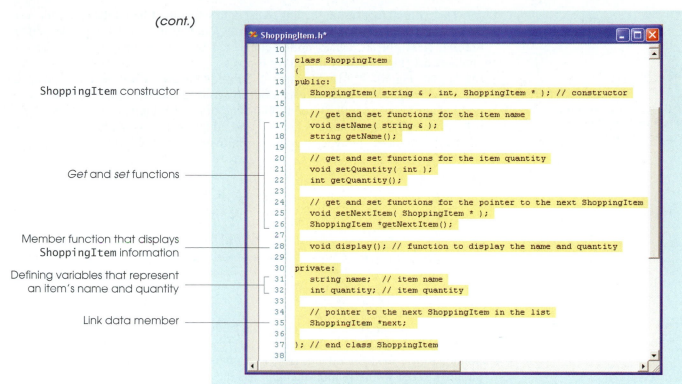

ShoppingItem constructor

Get and *set* functions

Member function that displays ShoppingItem information

Defining variables that represent an item's name and quantity

Link data member

```
10
11   class ShoppingItem
12   {
13   public:
14      ShoppingItem( string & , int, ShoppingItem * ); // constructor
15
16      // get and set functions for the item name
17      void setName( string & );
18      string getName();
19
20      // get and set functions for the item quantity
21      void setQuantity( int );
22      int getQuantity();
23
24      // get and set functions for the pointer to the next ShoppingItem
25      void setNextItem( ShoppingItem * );
26      ShoppingItem *getNextItem();
27
28      void display(); // function to display the name and quantity
29
30   private:
31      string name;  // item name
32      int quantity; // item quantity
33
34      // pointer to the next ShoppingItem in the list
35      ShoppingItem *next;
36
37   }; // end class ShoppingItem
38
```

Figure 16.18   ShoppingItem class definition.

3. ***Examining the private data members and their*** **get** ***and*** **set** ***functions.*** Lines 31–35 of Fig. 16.18 define the ShoppingItem class's private data members. The string variable name (line 31) and the int variable quantity (line 32) represent the name and quantity, respectively, of an item on the shopping list. Notice that line 35 defines the next data member, a pointer to an object of type ShoppingItem (the same type as the current class). When a class contains a pointer member that points to an object of the same class type, it is called a **self-referential class**. The next data member (line 35) is referred to as a **link** because next can be used to "tie" an object of type ShoppingItem to another object of the same type. These links are an important element of dynamic data structures, as you will learn shortly.

Lines 17–26 declare the *get* and *set* functions for each member of the ShoppingItem class. Notice that line 26 specifies a pointer to a ShoppingItem as a return type. This is accomplished by preceding the function name with the class name ShoppingItem and an asterisk. Finally, line 28 declares the display function, which displays a ShoppingItem object's name and quantity.

Self-referential class objects can be linked together to form useful data structures such as lists. Figure 16.19 illustrates two self-referential class objects linked together to form a list. Note that a backslash—representing a null (0) pointer—is placed in the link member of the second self-referential object to indicate that the link does not point to another object. The backslash is only for illustration purposes; it does not correspond to the backslash character in C++. A null pointer normally indicates the end of a data structure.

Self-referential class objects linked together to form a list

Pointer to the first self-referential class object in the list

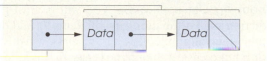

Figure 16.19   Two self-referential class objects linked together.

Error-Prevention Tip

Not setting the link in the last node of a linked data structure to null (0) is a (possibly fatal) logic error.

This tutorial focuses on the linked list data structure. **Linked lists** are collections of data items "lined up in a row." Specifically, a linked list is a collection of self-referential class objects, called **nodes**, connected by pointer links—hence, the term "linked" list (Fig. 16.20). A linked list is accessed using a pointer to the first node of the list (in Fig. 16.20, `firstPointer`). Subsequent nodes are accessed using the link-pointer member stored in each node. By convention, the link pointer in the last node of a list is set to null (0) to mark the end of the list. Data are stored in a linked list dynamically—each node is created and added to the list as necessary. A node can contain data of any type, including primitive data and objects.

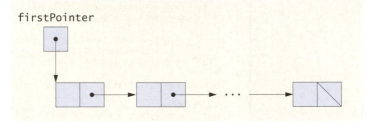

Figure 16.20 Graphical representation of a linked list.

The `ShoppingItem` class represents nodes for a **singly linked list**—the list begins with a pointer to the first `ShoppingItem`, and each `ShoppingItem` contains a pointer to the next `ShoppingItem` "in sequence." This list must terminate with a `ShoppingItem` whose pointer member has the value 0. Because each node contains only pointer to another node in the list (the "next" node), a singly linked list may be traversed in only one direction, from the first item in the list to the last.

Lists of data can be stored in arrays, but linked lists provide several advantages. A linked list is appropriate when the number of data elements to be represented at one time is unpredictable. For example, in the **Shopping List** application, you do not know in advance the number of shopping items that the user will enter. Linked lists are dynamic, so the length of a list can increase or decrease as necessary. The size of a "conventional" C++ array, however, cannot be altered, because the array size is fixed at compile time. "Conventional" arrays can become full when each element of the array is occupied. Linked lists become full only when the system has insufficient memory to create new objects at runtime.

SELF-REVIEW

1. A(n) _____ is accessed using a pointer to the first node of the list. Subsequent nodes are accessed using the link-pointer member stored in each node.

    a) linked list
    b) tree
    c) stack
    d) array

2. Linked lists are more appropriate than arrays when the number of data elements to be represented at one time is unpredictable because _____.

    a) linked lists never become full
    b) the length of a list can change over time
    c) linked lists improve performance
    d) All of the above

Answers: 1) a. 2) b.

16.6 Constructing the Shopping List Application

Now that you have learned about pointers and linked lists, you will add code to the **Shopping List** application. You will begin by modifying your application's `main` function so that the user can add items to, and display the items in, the shopping list. Later, you will implement a `List` class, which you will use to manage your application's linked list of `ShoppingItems`. In the following box, you will define and initialize variables in your application's `main` function.

Defining and Initializing Variables

1. ***Copying the template to your working directory.*** Copy the `C:\Exam-ples\Tutorial16\TemplateApplication\ShoppingList` directory to your `C:\SimplyCpp` directory.

2. ***Opening the Shopping List application's template source code file.*** Open the template file `ShoppingList.cpp` in your text editor or IDE.

3. ***Including the ShoppingItem and List class definitions.*** Add lines 9–10 of Fig. 16.21 to your application. These lines include the `ShoppingItem` and `List` class definitions in the `ShoppingList.cpp` file. You will use objects of class `ShoppingItem` to create new items for the shopping list. You will use the `List` class to manage access to the linked list of `ShoppingItems`.

Including the `ShoppingItem.h` and `List.h` header files

```
 7   using namespace std; // for accessing C++ Standard Library members
 8
 9   #include "ShoppingItem.h" // ShoppingItem class definition
10   #include "List.h" // List class definition
11
12   int displayMenu(); // function prototype
```

Figure 16.21 Including the `ShoppingItem` and `List` class definitions.

4. ***Defining variables to store user input.*** Add lines 17–19 of Fig. 16.22. Your application will display a menu and prompt the user to enter an integer value. The `int` variable `selection`, which is initialized to 0 in line 17, will store the user's menu selection. Each `ShoppingItem` that the user adds to the list will contain a name and quantity, so lines 18–19 define `string` variable `itemName` and `int` variable `itemQuantity` to store those values.

Defining variables to store user input

```
14   // function main begins program execution
15   int main()
16   {
17      int selection = 0; // stores the user's menu selection
18      string itemName; // stores the item name
19      int itemQuantity; // stores the item quantity
20
21      while ( selection != 3 )
```

Figure 16.22 Defining variables to store user input.

5. ***Instantiating a List object.*** Add line 20 of Fig. 16.23, which defines `List` variable `shoppingList`. Your application will use this object to manage the linked list of `ShoppingItems`. Recall that when an object is defined, its default (no-argument) constructor is called. Later in this tutorial, you will add functionality to the `List` class.

Creating a `List` object

```
19      int itemQuantity; // stores the item quantity
20      List shoppingList; // stores a list of shopping items
21
22      while ( selection != 3 )
```

Figure 16.23 Creating a `List` object.

6. ***Save the application.***

Now that you have defined and initialized variables for your `main` function, you will use these variables to add items to, and display a list of items in, the shopping list.

Modifying and Displaying the Shopping List

1. **Prompting the user for and inputting a new item's name and quantity.** Add lines 30–37 of Fig. 16.24 to your application. These lines execute when the user chooses to add a new item to the shopping list. The value that the user enters at the menu's prompt (displayed by the displayMenu function call in line 24) is stored in int variable selection. The selection variable will contain the value 1 if the user chooses to add a new item, so the statements after the case 1: label and before the subsequent break statement will execute.

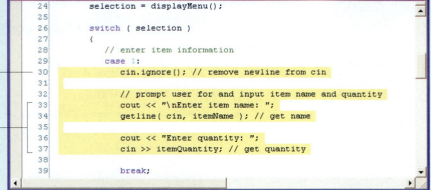

```
24        selection = displayMenu();
25
26        switch ( selection )
27        {
28           // enter item information
29           case 1:
30              cin.ignore(); // remove newline from cin
31
32              // prompt user for and input item name and quantity
33              cout << "\nEnter item name: ";
34              getline( cin, itemName ); // get name
35
36              cout << "Enter quantity: ";
37              cin >> itemQuantity; // get quantity
38
39              break;
```

Removing the newline from the input stream

Prompting the user for and inputting the item's name and quantity

Figure 16.24 Prompting the user for and inputting the item's name and quantity.

Unlike other applications you have built, this application uses the getline function and the stream extraction operator alternately. If the stream extraction operator encounters a newline as the first character in the stream, it removes and ignores the newline. However, if getline encounters a newline as the first character in the stream, the function terminates input and stores an empty string. If the application uses the stream extraction operator to input a value before calling the getline function, the application should remove the newline from the input stream to prevent the getline function from storing an empty string for the item's name. Line 30 calls the **cin.ignore()** function to remove the newline character from cin. This prevents the getline function call (line 34) from reading an empty string, instead of the item's name, into variable itemName. Lines 36–37 prompt the user for and input the item's quantity in variable itemQuantity.

2. **Adding a new item to the list.** Add lines 39–40 of Fig. 16.25. After your application obtains the new item's name and quantity, it should create a ShoppingItem and insert the ShoppingItem into the linked list of ShoppingItems. List member function addItem, which you will define later in this tutorial, accepts as arguments the itemName and itemQuantity for a ShoppingItem object. The addItem function will create and add the corresponding ShoppingItem object to the linked list. Line 40 uses the shoppingList object to invoke the addItem function.

(cont.)

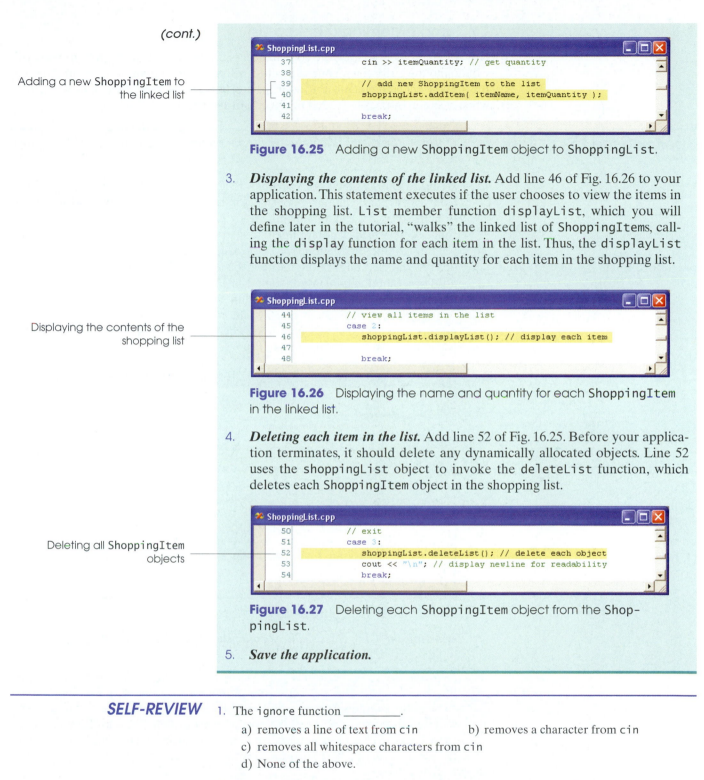

Adding a new `ShoppingItem` to the linked list

```
ShoppingList.cpp
37        cin >> itemQuantity; // get quantity
38
39        // add new ShoppingItem to the list
40        shoppingList.addItem( itemName, itemQuantity );
41
42        break;
```

Figure 16.25   Adding a new `ShoppingItem` object to `ShoppingList`.

3. *Displaying the contents of the linked list.* Add line 46 of Fig. 16.26 to your application. This statement executes if the user chooses to view the items in the shopping list. `List` member function `displayList`, which you will define later in the tutorial, "walks" the linked list of `ShoppingItems`, calling the `display` function for each item in the list. Thus, the `displayList` function displays the name and quantity for each item in the shopping list.

Displaying the contents of the shopping list

```
ShoppingList.cpp
44        // view all items in the list
45        case 2:
46        shoppingList.displayList(); // display each item
47
48        break;
```

Figure 16.26   Displaying the name and quantity for each `ShoppingItem` in the linked list.

4. *Deleting each item in the list.* Add line 52 of Fig. 16.25. Before your application terminates, it should delete any dynamically allocated objects. Line 52 uses the `shoppingList` object to invoke the `deleteList` function, which deletes each `ShoppingItem` object in the shopping list.

Deleting all `ShoppingItem` objects

```
ShoppingList.cpp
50        // exit
51        case 3:
52        shoppingList.deleteList(); // delete each object
53        cout << "\n"; // display newline for readability
54        break;
```

Figure 16.27   Deleting each `ShoppingItem` object from the `ShoppingList`.

5. *Save the application.*

1. The `ignore` function _____.

   a) removes a line of text from `cin`   b) removes a character from `cin`
   c) removes all whitespace characters from `cin`
   d) None of the above.

2. When the stream extraction operator encounters a newline as the first character of input, it _____.

   a) removes and ignores the character
   b) leaves the character in the stream and terminates input
   c) removes the character and terminates input
   d) None of the above.

Answers: 1) b. 2) a.

16.7 Implementing a Linked List

Now that you have written the code to access the linked list of ShoppingItems, you will define the List class. Your List class will maintain a pointer to the first item in the linked list and update the appropriate ShoppingItem object's next pointer when a ShoppingItem is added to the end of the list.

Defining the List Class

1. **Opening the List class's header file.** Open the template file List.h in your text editor or IDE.

2. **Defining the List class.** Add lines 13–26 of Fig. 16.28 to the List.h file. Your List class contains a constructor, one data member, *get* and *set* functions for this data member and three functions that access the linked list. Line 14 specifies a no-argument constructor. Line 26 defines a private pointer to the first ShoppingItem in the list—firstItem. Lines 17–18 declare the *get* and *set* functions for this data member. Line 21 declares the addItem function, which you called in Fig. 16.25 to add a new Shopping-Item to the linked list. Line 22 declares the displayList function, which you called in Fig. 16.26 to display the contents of the linked list. Line 23 declares the deleteList function, which you called in Fig. 16.27 to delete each ShoppingItem in the linked list.

```
List.h*
11   class List
12   {
13   public:
14       List(); // constructor
15
16       // get and set functions for the firstItem pointer
17       void setFirstItem( ShoppingItem * );
18       ShoppingItem *getFirstItem();
19
20       // utility functions
21       void addItem( string, int ); // add an item to front of the list
22       void displayList(); // display each item in the list
23       void deleteList(); // delete each item in the list
24
25   private:
26       ShoppingItem *firstItem; // pointer to the first item in the list
27
28   }; // end class List
```

- List constructor → line 14
- Declaring *set* and *get* functions for the pointer to the first item in the list → lines 17–18
- Declaring functions to manipulate the linked list of ShoppingItems → lines 21–23
- Defining a pointer to the first item in the linked list → line 26

Figure 16.28 List class definition.

3. **Opening the List class's source code file.** Open the template file List.cpp in your text editor or IDE.

4. **Defining the List constructor.** Add lines 12–13 of Fig. 16.29 to the List.cpp file. Line 13 uses the setFirstItem function to initialize the value of the firstItem pointer. Because the linked list is empty initially, the firstItem variable should be a null pointer. By passing the value 0 to this function, you ensure that firstItem is initialized as a null pointer. Note that the definitions for the List class's *get* and *set* functions are provided for you in the template file.

Most calls to member functions you have written required you to precede the function call with a variable name and a dot (as in shoppingList.displayList()). You may have noticed that some function calls do not require a class name or an object name, such as the call to setFirstItem on line 13 of Fig. 16.29.

(cont.)

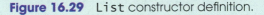

Initializing the `firstItem` variable as a null pointer

```
 9   // List constructor
10   List::List()
11   {
12       // initialize firstItem as a pointer to nothing
13       setFirstItem( 0 );
14
15   } // end constructor
```

Figure 16.29 `List` constructor definition.

The function call in line 13 implicitly invokes `setFirstItem` on the object that is being constructed. Inside a member function, you can explicitly refer to the object of that class on which the function was called with the keyword **this**, also called the **this pointer**. For example, line 13 can be written as

```
this->setFirstItem( 0 );
```

When the compiler encounters function calls like the one in line 13, it automatically adds "`this->`" to the beginning of the function call.

Note the use of the arrow operator (`->`) in the preceding example. The **arrow operator**—which consists of a minus sign (`-`) and a greater than sign (`>`) with no intervening whitespace—accesses a class member using a pointer to an object. The expression `this->setFirstItem()` is equivalent to `(*this).setFirstItem()`, which dereferences the pointer and accesses the member function `setFirstItem` using the dot operator. The parentheses are needed here because the dot operator (`.`) has the same precedence as the pointer dereferencing operator (`*`), but the expression is evaluated from right to left.

5. *Save the application.*

Now that you have defined the `List` class and its constructor, you will add functionality to insert a new `ShoppingItem` at the front of the `List`. When you add a new node to a linked list, you must modify at least one link to ensure that the new node is tied to the existing nodes in the list. Figure 16.30 illustrates how you must modify the `List` to add a new `ShoppingItem` to the front of the `List`. Part a) of the figure shows the `List` (containing three `ShoppingItems`, labeled A, B and C) and the new node (item D) before the operation (for simplicity, we have omitted the item names and quantities). Initially, `firstItem` points to the first node in the list (item A).

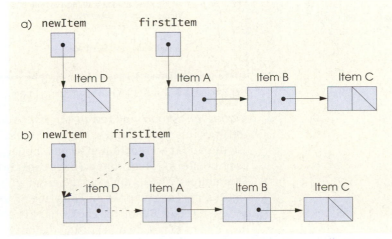

Figure 16.30 Graphical representation of inserting an item at the front of a linked list.

The dotted arrows in part b) illustrate how to add the new ShoppingItem to the front of the List. In this case, your List object must update two pointer values. The ShoppingItem that was previously at the front of the list (item A) now is located "after" the new ShoppingItem (item D) in this list. Because item A appears "next" in the list after item D, item D's link (that is, the next pointer) must point to item A. This modification is represented by the horizontal dotted arrow in Fig. 16.30 (b). Also, the List object's firstItem pointer, which initially pointer to item A, must be updated so that it points to the new ShoppingItem (item D), which is now the first item in the linked list. The dotted arrow from firstItem to item D in Fig. 16.30 (b) represents this operation. In the following box, you will add code to the List class's addItem function that creates a ShoppingItem object and inserts the ShoppingItem at the front of the linked list.

Adding a ShoppingItem to the Linked List

1. ***Dynamically allocating memory for a ShoppingItem.*** Because your application does not specify how many ShoppingItems will be created each time the application runs, the application must be able to obtain more memory at execution time to hold each new ShoppingItem as it is created. This technique is called **dynamic memory allocation**. When dynamically allocated memory is no longer needed by the application, the memory can be released so that it can be reused to allocate other objects in the future.

   Add lines 29–36 of Fig. 16.31 after the getFirstItem function provided in the template. Line 30 declares parameters itemName and quantity, which specify the name and quantity for the new ShoppingItem that should be inserted at the front of the list. Lines 33–34 use the new operator to create an object of type ShoppingItem and assign the object's memory address in the newItem variable. The **new** operator takes as an argument the type of the object being created and returns a pointer to an object of that type. The statement in lines 33–34 dynamically allocates the memory required to store a ShoppingItem object, runs the ShoppingItem constructor to initialize the object and stores a pointer to this memory in newItem. Note that the third argument to the ShoppingItem constructor is 0, indicating that the new ShoppingItem's nextItem member is to be initialized to a null pointer.

 **Error-Prevention Tip**
Assign null (zero) to the link member of a new node. Uninitialized pointers often lead to dangerous runtime errors.

Creating a ShoppingItem using the new operator

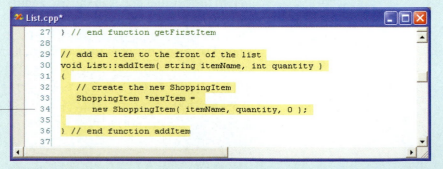

Figure 16.31 Creating a ShoppingItem object in the addItem function.

2. ***Adding an ShoppingItem to the list.*** Add lines 36–38 of Fig. 16.32 to the addItem function. To insert the new ShoppingItem at the front of the linked list, the addItem function first must update the new ShoppingItem's next-Item pointer to point to the ShoppingItem currently at the front of the list. The address of the node at the front of the list is contained in the List object's firstItem pointer. Thus, line 37 uses the setNextItem function to update the new ShoppingItem's nextItem pointer to the value of the List class's firstItem member, using the getFirstItem function.

(cont.)

If the List is empty, then there is no "next" ShoppingItem in the List. In this case, the new ShoppingItem's nextItem pointer should be a null pointer. Thus, the getFirstItem function returns a null pointer when the List is empty.

Updating the new ShoppingItem's nextItem variable and the List's firstItem variable

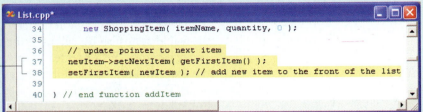

```
34              new ShoppingItem( itemName, quantity, 0 );
35
36         // update pointer to next item
37         newItem->setNextItem( getFirstItem() );
38         setFirstItem( newItem ); // add new item to the front of the list
39
40    } // end function addItem
```

Figure 16.32 Updating pointers when adding an item to the front of a linked list.

After updating the new ShoppingItem's nextItem pointer, the addItem function must update the List object's firstItem pointer so that it points to the new ShoppingItem. Line 38 performs this operation updating the List's firstItem pointer to the value of newItem, which is a pointer to the new ShoppingItem.

3. *Save the application.*

You have now added code that enables your List class to insert a ShoppingItem at the front of the linked list. In the following box, you will add functionality to display the name and quantity for each ShoppingItem in the linked list.

Displaying the Contents of the Linked List

1. ***Defining the*** `displayList` ***function.*** Add lines 42–51 of Fig. 16.33 to your application after the addItem function definition. Line 43 begins the displayList function, which your application uses to display the name and quantity for each ShoppingItem in the list. Line 46 defines currentItem as a pointer to a ShoppingItem object. The value of currentItem is initialized to point to the first ShoppingItem in the linked list, using the getFirstItem function. You will use this pointer to traverse the list of ShoppingItems, calling each ShoppingItem's display function. Lines 49–50 display a header for the list of ShoppingItems that are displayed.

Creating a pointer to the first item in the linked list

Displaying a header

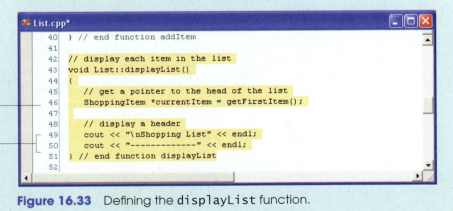

```
40    } // end function addItem
41
42    // display each item in the list
43    void List::displayList()
44    {
45         // get a pointer to the head of the list
46         ShoppingItem *currentItem = getFirstItem();
47
48         // display a header
49         cout << "\nShopping List" << endl;
50         cout << "-------------" << endl;
51    } // end function displayList
52
```

Figure 16.33 Defining the `displayList` function.

(cont.)

2. ***Displaying each ShoppingItem's name and quantity.*** Add lines 52–57 of Fig. 16.34 to the `displayList` function. The `while` statement in line 53 repeats until the end of the list is reached. This occurs when `currentItem` becomes a null (0) pointer. Line 55 calls the current `ShoppingItem`'s `display` function, which displays the `ShoppingItem`'s name and quantity. Line 56 updates the value of `currentItem` so that it points to the next `ShoppingItem` in the list, using the value returned by `currentItem->getNextItem()`. When the value returned by calling `currentItem->getNextItem()` is zero, `currentItem` must be a pointer to the last `ShoppingItem` in the list. In this case the loop-continuation condition evaluates to `false` and the `while` loop terminates. This technique, which accesses each node in the linked list by following link pointers until reaching the end of the list, is called "walking" a linked list.

Displaying the name and quantity for each `ShoppingItem`

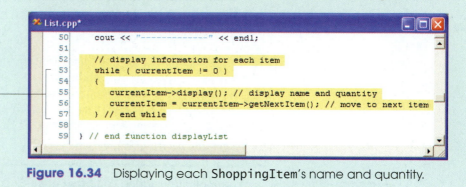

Figure 16.34   Displaying each `ShoppingItem`'s name and quantity.

Error-Prevention Tip

Not releasing dynamically allocated memory when it is no longer needed can cause the system to run out of memory prematurely. This is sometimes called a "memory leak."

Earlier in this section, you learned that creating and maintaining dynamic data structures requires dynamic memory allocation, which enables an application to obtain more memory at execution time to hold new nodes. When that memory is no longer needed by the application, the memory can be released so that it can be reused to allocate other objects in the future. Because available memory must be shared among many applications, it is important to release any dynamically allocated memory that is no longer needed. You will now define the `deleteList` function, which enables clients of your `List` class to release the memory dynamically allocated for `ShoppingItems` by the `addItem` member function.

Completing the List Class

1. ***Defining the deleteList function.*** Add lines 61–73 of Fig. 16.35 after the `displayList` function. Line 65 defines pointer variable `currentItem` and initializes it to the value of the pointer to the first item in the list (returned by member function `getFirstItem`). Lines 68–71 contain an empty `while` statement that repeats while `currentItem` is not a null pointer. Similar to the `while` statement in the `displayList` function, this `while` statement repeats until reaching the end of the list.

2. ***Deleting the current ShoppingItem and moving to the next one.*** Add lines 70–77 of Fig. 16.36 to the `while` statement that you wrote in the preceding step. Line 71 defines temporary variable `nextItem` and initializes its value to the address of the next `ShoppingItem` in the `List`. Lines 72–73 display a message indicating which `ShoppingItem` is being deleted. Line 74 uses the `delete` operator to delete the `ShoppingItem` object to which `currentItem` points. The **delete** operator runs the `ShoppingItem` destructor and deallocates memory allocated with `new`—the memory is returned to the system so that the memory can be reallocated in the future.

(cont.)

Setting `currentItem` so that it points to the first item in the linked list

Repeating until reaching the end of the list

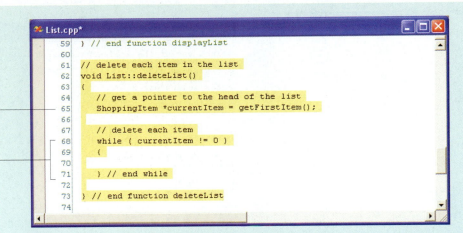

Figure 16.35   Defining the `deleteList` function.

Destructors are functions that execute just before an object's memory is released. C++ provides a default destructor for each object if you do not provide one. You will not define destructors in this book. Note that when line 74 executes, `currentItem` itself is not deleted; rather the object that `currentItem` points to is deleted. If `currentItem` were a null pointer (that is, a 0 pointer), line 74 would have no effect.

Store a temporary copy of a pointer to the next `ShoppingItem`

Delete the `ShoppingItem` to which `currentItem` points

Move to the next item in the `List`

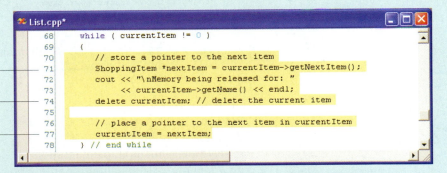

Figure 16.36   Deleting each `ShoppingItem` in the linked list.

Line 77 assigns to `currentItem` the address of the next `ShoppingItem` in the list, contained in `nextItem`. Notice that when `currentItem` is deleted in line 74, the `ShoppingItem`'s memory, including its pointer to the next item in the list, is released so that it may be reallocated as future **new** operators execute. Because line 71 stores a temporary copy of the pointer to the next `ShoppingItem`, however, you can still update the value of `currentItem` in line 77.

3. ***Save, compile and run the application.*** Figure 16.37 shows the completed application running. Add several items to the shopping list, then display the shopping list. After you've tested your application, exit the application by entering 3 at the **Enter selection:** prompt. Notice that the application displays the name of each item as it is deleted (Fig. 16.38).

4. ***Close the Command Prompt window.***

(cont.)

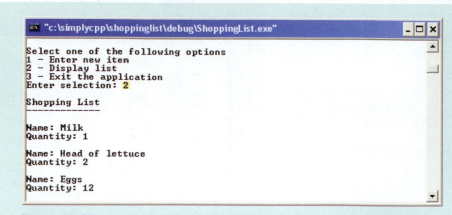

Figure 16.37 **Shopping List** application after entering several items.

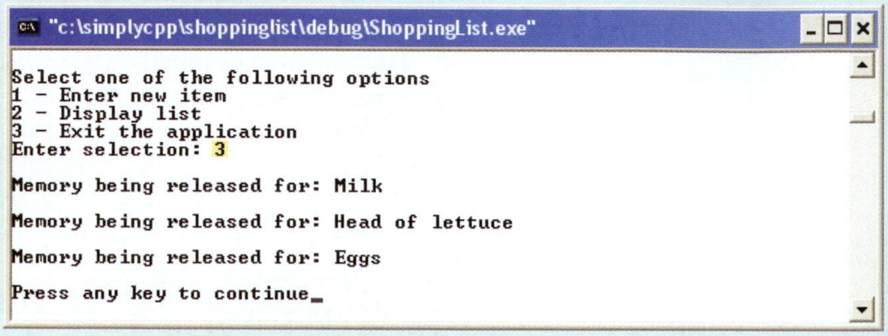

Figure 16.38 Terminating the **Shopping List** application.

Figure 16.39 presents the List class header file and Fig. 16.40 presents its implementation file. Figure 16.41 presents the ShoppingItem class header file and Fig. 16.42 presents its implementation file. Finally, Fig. 16.43 presents the code file containing the main function for your **Shopping List** application. The lines of code that you added, viewed or modified in this tutorial are highlighted.

```
1   // Tutorial 16: List.h
2   // List class stores pointers to the first item in
3   // the linked list and manages the linked list.
4   #ifndef LIST_H
5   #define LIST_H
6
7   #include "ShoppingItem.h" // ShoppingItem class definition
8
9   using namespace std; // for accessing C++ Standard Library members
10
11  class List {
12
13  public:
14      List(); // constructor
15
16      // get and set functions for the firstItem pointer
17      void setFirstItem( ShoppingItem * );
18      ShoppingItem *getFirstItem();
19
```

List constructor → 14

Get function for the pointer to the first item in the list → 17, 18

Figure 16.39 List class header file. (Part 1 of 2.)

Declaring functions to manipulate
the linked list of ShoppingItems

```
20      // utility functions
21      void addItem( string, int ); // add an item to front of the list
22      void displayList(); // display each item in the list
23      void deleteList(); // delete each item in the list
24
25   private:
26      ShoppingItem *firstItem; // pointer to the first item in the list
27
28   }; // end class List
29
30   #endif // LIST_H
```

Pointer to the first
item in the linked list

Figure 16.39 List class header file. (Part 2 of 2.)

```
1    // Tutorial 16: List.cpp
2    // Class List member-function definitions.
3    #include <iostream> // required to perform C++-style stream I/O
4
5    using namespace std; // for accessing C++ Standard Library members
6
7    #include "List.h"  // List class definition
8
9    // List constructor
10   List::List()
11   {
12      // initialize firstItem and lastItem as pointers to nothing
13      setFirstItem( 0 );
14
15   } // end constructor
16
17   // set the pointer for the first item in the list
18   void List::setFirstItem( ShoppingItem *newFirstItem )
19   {
20      firstItem = newFirstItem;
21   } // end function setFirstItem
22
23   // return a pointer to the first item in the list
24   ShoppingItem *List::getFirstItem()
25   {
26      return firstItem;
27   } // end function getFirstItem
28
29   // add an item to the front of the list
30   void List::addItem( string itemName, int quantity )
31   {
32      // create the new ShoppingItem
33      ShoppingItem *nextItem =
34         new ShoppingItem( itemName, quantity, 0 );
35
36      // update pointer to the next item
37      newItem->setNextItem( getFirstItem() );
38      setFirstItem( newItem ); // add new item to the front of the list
39
40   } // end function addItem
41
42   // display each item in the list
43   void List::displayList()
44   {
```

Initialize the firstItem
as a null pointer

Update the firstItem to point
to the new ShoppingItem

Update the appropriate
pointers to add the new
item to the list

Figure 16.40 List class implementation. (Part 1 of 2.)

Create a pointer to the first item in the linked list

```
45         // get a pointer to the head of the list
46         ShoppingItem *currentItem = getFirstItem();
47
48         // display a header
49         cout << "\nShopping List" << endl;
50         cout << "-------------" << endl;
51
52         // display information for each item
53         while ( currentItem != 0 )
54         {
55            currentItem->display(); // display name and quantity
56            currentItem = currentItem->getNextItem(); // move to next item
57         } // end while
58
59      } // end function displayList
60
61      // delete each item in the list
62      void List::deleteList()
63      {
64         // get a pointer to the head of the list
65         ShoppingItem *currentItem = getFirstItem();
66
67         // delete each item
68         while ( currentItem != 0 )
69         {
70            // store a pointer to the next item
71            ShoppingItem *nextItem = currentItem->getNextItem();
72            cout << "\nMemory being released for: "
73               << currentItem->getName() << endl;
74            delete currentItem; // delete the current item
75
76            // place a pointer to the next item in currentItem
77            currentItem = nextItem;
78         } // end while
79
80      } // end function deleteList
```

Display a header — lines 49-50

Display the name and quantity for each ShoppingItem — lines 55-57

Create a pointer to the first item in the linked list

Delete each ShoppingItem in the linked list — lines 71-77

Figure 16.40   List class implementation. (Part 2 of 2.)

```
1      // Tutorial 16: ShoppingItem.h
2      // ShoppingItem class stores item name, quantity and a pointer to
3      // the next item in the list.
4      #ifndef SHOPPINGITEM_H
5      #define SHOPPINGITEM_H
6
7      #include <string>    // required to access string functions
8
9      using namespace std; // for accessing C++ Standard Library members
10
11     class ShoppingItem {
12
13     public:
14        ShoppingItem( string & , int, ShoppingItem * ); // constructor
15
16        // get and set functions for the item name
17        void setName( string & );
18        string getName();
19
```

ShoppingItem constructor — line 14

Figure 16.41   ShoppingItem class header file. (Part 1 of 2.)

Get and set functions

Member function that displays
ShoppingItem information

Defining variables that represent
an item's name and quantity

Link data member

```
20      // get and set functions for the item quantity
21      void setQuantity( int );
22      int getQuantity();
23
24      // get and set functions for the pointer to the next ShoppingItem
25      void setNextItem( ShoppingItem * );
26      ShoppingItem *getNextItem();
27
28      void display(); // function to display the name and quantity
29
30   private:
31      string name;   // item name
32      int quantity;  // item quantity
33
34      // pointer to the next ShoppingItem in the list
35      ShoppingItem *next;
36
37   }; // end class ShoppingItem
38
39   #endif // SHOPPINGITEM_H
```

Figure 16.41   ShoppingItem class header file. (Part 2 of 2.)

```
1    // Tutorial 16: ShoppingItem.cpp
2    // Class ShoppingItem member-function definitions.
3    #include <iostream> // required to perform C++-style stream I/O
4    #include "ShoppingItem.h"  // ShoppingItem class definition
5
6    using namespace std; // for accessing C++ Standard Library members
7
8    // constructor
9    ShoppingItem::ShoppingItem( string &itemName, int itemQuantity,
10      ShoppingItem *nextPointer )
11   {
12      // initialize data members
13      setName( itemName ); // set the name
14      setQuantity( itemQuantity ); // set the quantity
15      setNextItem( nextPointer ); // set pointer to the next item
16
17   } // end constructor
18
19   // set the item's name
20   void ShoppingItem::setName( string &itemName )
21   {
22      name = itemName;
23   } // end function setName
24
25   // return a copy of the item's name so that changes made to
26   // the returned value do not affect the object's name member
27   string ShoppingItem::getName()
28   {
29      return name;
30
31   } // end function getName
32
```

Figure 16.42   ShoppingItem class implementation. (Part 1 of 2.)

```
33   // set the quantity for this item
34   void ShoppingItem::setQuantity( int itemQuantity )
35   {
36      if ( itemQuantity < 0 )
37      {
38         quantity = 0;
39      } // end if
40      else
41      {
42         quantity = itemQuantity;
43      } // end else
44
45   } // end function setQuantity
46
47   // return the item's quantity
48   int ShoppingItem::getQuantity()
49   {
50      return quantity;
51
52   } // end function getQuantity
53
54   // set the pointer to the next ShoppingItem in the list
55   void ShoppingItem::setNextItem( ShoppingItem *nextPointer )
56   {
57      next = nextPointer;
58
59   } // end function setNextItem
60
61   // return the pointer to the next item
62   ShoppingItem *ShoppingItem::getNextItem()
63   {
64      return next;
65
66   } // end function getNextItem
67
68   // return the pointer to the next item
69   void ShoppingItem::display()
70   {
71      cout << "\nName: " << getName() << endl;
72      cout << "Quantity: " << getQuantity() << endl;
73
74   } // end function display
```

Figure 16.42 ShoppingItem class implementation. (Part 2 of 2.)

```
1    // Tutorial 16: ShoppingList.cpp
2    // Enables users to add items to, remove items from and view items in
3    // a shopping list.
4    #include <iostream> // required to perform C++-style stream I/O
5    #include <iomanip>  // required for parameterized stream manipulators
6
7    using namespace std; // for accessing C++ Standard Library members
8
9    #include "ShoppingItem.h" // ShoppingItem class definition
10   #include "List.h" // List class definition
11
12   int displayMenu(); // function prototype
```

Include the ShoppingItem.h and List.h header files

Figure 16.43 Shopping List application code. (Part 1 of 3.)

```
13
14    // function main begins program execution
15    int main()
16    {
17        int selection = 0; // stores the user's menu selection
18        string itemName; // stores the item name
19        int itemQuantity; // stores the item quantity
20        List shoppingList; // stores a list of shopping items
21
22        while ( selection != 3 )
23        {
24            selection = displayMenu();
25
26            switch ( selection )
27            {
28                // enter item information
29                case 1:
30                    cin.ignore(); // remove newline from cin
31
32                    // prompt user for and input item name and quantity
33                    cout << "\nEnter item name: ";
34                    getline( cin, itemName ); // get name
35
36                    cout << "Enter quantity: ";
37                    cin >> itemQuantity; // get quantity
38
39                    // add new shopping item to the list
40                    shoppingList.addItem( itemName, itemQuantity )
41
42                    break;
43
44                // view all items in the list
45                case 2:
46                    shoppingList.displayList(); // display each item
47
48                    break;
49
50                // exit
51                case 3:
52                    shoppingList.deleteList(); // delete each object
53                    cout << "\n"; // display newline for readability
54                    break;
55
56                default:
57                    cout << "Error: Enter a valid menu selection";
58
59            } // end switch
60
61        } // end while
62
63        return 0; // indicate that program ended successfully
64
65    } // end function main
66
67    // displays a menu and returns the selected menu option number
68    int displayMenu()
69    {
70        int selection = 0; // stores the menu option number
```

Define variables to store user input → (lines 17–19)

Create a **List** object → (line 20)

Remove the newline from the input stream → (line 30)

Prompt the user for and input the item's name and quantity → (lines 33–37)

Add a new **ShoppingItem** to the linked list → (lines 39–40)

Display the contents of the shopping list → (line 46)

Delete all **ShoppingItem** objects in the linked list → (line 52)

Figure 16.43   Shopping List application code. (Part 2 of 3.)

```
71
72      // display the menu
73      cout << "\nSelect one of the following options" << endl;
74      cout << "1 - Enter new item" << endl;
75      cout << "2 - Display list" << endl;
76      cout << "3 - Exit the application" << endl;
77      cout << "Enter selection: ";
78      cin >> selection;
79
80      return selection; // return the selection
81
82   } // end function displayMenu
```

Figure 16.43 Shopping List application code. (Part 3 of 3.)

SELF-REVIEW

1. The new operator _____.

    a) returns a pointer to the newly created object

    b) takes as its argument the variable name for the object being created

    c) takes as its argument the type of the object being created

    d) Both a and c.

2. Use the _____ operator to access an object's members when the left operand is a pointer to that object.

    a) <-   b) ->

    c) .   d) &

Answers: 1) d. 2) b.

16.8 Wrap-Up

In this tutorial, you learned about pointers, which are variables that store the address in memory of a data item, such as an `int` or an object. You then learned how to initialize pointers and how to access the data item to which a pointer points. After you saw how to create and use pointers in your applications, you learned how to pass values to functions by reference. Variables are passed by reference either using reference parameters or pointer parameters.

You also learned about data structures called linked lists, which are nodes and links that form a series of objects "in sequence." You used a linked list to create a list of shopping items in your **Shopping List** application. After learning the basics of linked lists, you implemented a `List` class that uses pointers to manage the linked list.

While defining the `List` class, you wrote code to insert items into, delete items from and "walk" the linked list of `ShoppingItems`. To insert a new item at the front of the list, you updated the new item's "next" pointer so that it pointed to the first item in the list. Then you updated the list's pointer to the first item so that it pointed to the new item. To "walk" a linked list of items, you examined the value of the pointer to the first item in the list. If the pointer was not null, you used the pointer to access the first item's members. You then used the current item's "next" pointer to access the next item in the list. You repeated this step until reaching the end of the list, at which point the current item's "next" pointer was null. Finally, to delete each item in the list, you walked the list, using the `delete` operator on the pointer to each item.

In the next tutorial, you will learn how to write classes that use a technique called inheritance to "absorb" capabilities defined in other classes. As you will learn, this technique increases software reuse, which typically improves the quality of your application and reduces application development time. You will learn about a related technique called polymorphism that enables you to "program in the general" rather than having to "program in the specific." As you will see, polymorphism makes it easy to write code to process a variety of related objects. You will use inheritance and polymorphism while building your **Payroll** application.

SKILLS SUMMARY

Declaring a Pointer

- Use the format:

    dataType *pointerName;

    where *dataType* * is the pointer type and *pointerName* is the name of the pointer variable.
- Initialize each pointer before using it. If a pointer does not point to an object, you should initialize its value to 0 or NULL to create a null pointer.

Creating a Pointer to an Object

- Use the unary address operator (&) on a variable name to create a pointer to that variable.
- The operand of the address operator must be something to which a value can be assigned.

Dereferencing a Pointer

- Use the indirection operator (*) on a pointer.
- The result of the indirection operator on a pointer is a synonym for the name of the object to which the pointer points.

Passing Information to a Function by Reference Using Reference Arguments

- In the function header (or function prototype), declare each item that should be passed by reference as a reference parameter.
- To specify a reference parameter, place a & symbol after the data type and before the parameter name in the parameter declaration.
- When calling the function, specify the variable name for each reference argument. C++ will create a synonym for each reference argument when the called function executes.

Passing Information to a Function by Reference Using Pointer Arguments

- In the function header (or function prototype), declare each item that should be passed by reference as a pointer.
- To specify a pointer parameter, place a * symbol after the data type and before the parameter name in the parameter declaration.
- When calling the function, specify a pointer for each argument that is passed by reference using a pointer argument. In the function body, your code must dereference the pointer to access the variable to which it points. If the pointer contains the address of an object, you can use the arrow operator (->) to access the object's members. You also can dereference the pointer and use the dot operator to access the object's members.

Creating a Self-Referential Class

- One of your class's data members must be a pointer to an object of the same class. For example, class ShoppingItem is a self-referential class because it specifies a data member that is a pointer to an object of type ShoppingItem.

Creating a Linked List

- Create a pointer to the first node in the linked list.
- Each node must contain a link to the "next" node in the list.
- To access the linked list, the application must maintain a pointer to the first node in the list.

Performing Dynamic Memory Management

- Use the new operator to allocate memory for an object at runtime.
- Use the delete operator to deallocate memory for an object created with new. This memory then becomes available to allocate for future objects.

KEY TERMS

* operator (unary version)—The dereferencing operator, which, when applied to a pointer, returns a synonym for the object to which its pointer operand points.

address operator (&)—A unary operator that returns the memory address of its operand.

arrow operator (->)—An operator that accesses a class member using a pointer to an object.

delete operator—An operator that deallocates memory allocated with the new operator. The delete operator calls the destructor for its operand.

dereferencing a pointer—Using the * operator on a pointer to create a synonym or alias for the variable to which it points.

dereferencing operator—See * operator.

destructor—A function that executes just before an object is removed from the system.

dynamic data structure—A data structure that can grow and shrink at execution time, such as a linked list.

dynamic memory allocation—Technique that allocates memory for objects at run-time (as opposed to compile-time). When that memory is no longer needed by the application, the memory can be released so that it can be allocated to other objects in the future.

ignore function (of the cin object)—A function that removes a single character of input from the input stream.

indirection—The technique of referencing a value through a pointer.

indirection operator—See * operator.

link—In a self-referential class, the data member that is a pointer to an object of the current class. This pointer can be used to "tie" one object of the class to another object of the same class.

linked list—A collection of data items "lined up in a row." Insertions and removals are made anywhere in a linked list. Specifically, a linked list is a series of nodes connected by pointer links.

new operator—An operator that allocates memory dynamically for a new object. The operator takes as an argument the class of the object being created and returns a pointer to an object of that type.

node—A self-referential class object. A linked list is composed of nodes tied together by pointer links.

NULL constant—A symbolic constant that is defined in the <iostream> header file (and in several other standard library header files) to represent the 0 pointer value. C++ programmers prefer to use 0 directly.

pass-by-reference with pointer arguments—A form of pass-by-reference that uses pointer arguments. The caller must pass a pointer of the appropriate type to the function. The function must use the dereferencing operator (*) or arrow operator (->) to access the data or object to which the pointer points.

pass-by-reference with reference arguments—A form of pass-by-reference that uses reference parameters. To pass a reference argument, the caller simply specifies the variable name for the data that should be passed to the function for each reference argument. When the function call executes, each reference parameter becomes a synonym for its corresponding argument in the function call.

pointer—A variable that contains a memory address.

reference parameter—A function parameter that specifies a synonym for the corresponding argument in a call to its function. A reference parameter is declared by placing an ampersand (&) after the type name in the parameter list.

self-referential class—A class that contains a pointer member that points to an object of the same class. A node class for a linked list is an example of a self-referential class.

singly linked list—A list that begins with a pointer to the first node; each node contains a pointer to the next node "in sequence."

this pointer—In a member function, this is an implicitly defined pointer to the object for which the function is called.

C++ LIBRARY REFERENCE

<iostream> This header file declares basic services required for stream-I/O operations.

■ *Function*

cin.ignore()—Removes the next character from the input stream.

■ *Objects*

cin—Reads characters entered at the keyboard. Text is sent to the application when the user presses *Enter* and can be placed in a variable using the stream extraction operator, >>.

cout—Displays text on the screen. Text can be displayed using the stream insertion operator (<<).

■ *Stream manipulators*

endl—This object places a newline into the output stream and flushes the stream's buffer so that all text stored in the output stream object is displayed immediately.

fixed—This stream manipulator specifies that floating-point numbers should be printed using fixed-point notation (as opposed to scientific notation).

flush—This stream manipulator flushes the output buffer so that output is displayed on the screen immediately.

left—This object causes values to be left justified in a field. The stream into which left is inserted remains left justified until the application terminates or until the stream's justification is changed, whichever comes first.

right—This object causes values to be right justified in a field. The stream into which right is inserted remains right justified until the application terminates or until the stream's justification is changed, whichever comes first.

MULTIPLE-CHOICE QUESTIONS

16.1 Assume that intPointer is a pointer to an int value. The expression _____ dereferences intPointer.

a) *intPointer
b) &intPointer
c) intPointer*
d) intPointer&

16.2 The delete operator releases memory allocated to _____.

a) its operand
b) the object to which the operand points
c) the object for which the operand is a synonym
d) its operand and the object to which it points

16.3 The & operator _____.

a) returns an address in memory
b) dereferences a pointer
c) creates a synonym for its operand
d) returns the value referenced by a pointer

16.4 A singly linked list must have _____.

a) a pointer to the first item in the list
b) a link from each node to the next item in the list
c) a pointer to the first and last items in the list
d) Both a and b.

16.5 The prototype _____ declares a function that declares a reference parameter.

a) int passByReference(int *);
b) int passByReference(int &);
c) int passByReference(int);
d) int passByReference(&int);

16.6 A _____ is a dynamic data structure.

a) pointer
b) "conventional" array
c) linked list
d) reference

16.7 Use the _____ operator to access members of an object using a synonym for that object.

a) ->
b) .
c) <-
d) &

16.8 The _____ pointer, in a member function, points to the object for which the function was called.

    a) `next`   b) `NULL`

    c) `this`   d) `me`

16.9 The new operator returns _____.

    a) `true` after creating a new object   b) a reference to the object it creates

    c) a pointer to the object it creates   d) None of the above.

16.10 When used in a linked list, an object of a self-referential class is called a _____.

    a) link   b) list

    c) node   d) pointer

EXERCISES

16.11 (***Enhanced Shopping List Application***) Enhance the **Shopping List** application by storing items in the shopping list in alphabetical order. Figure 16.44 shows the shopping list after several items have been entered.

Figure 16.44 Enhanced **Shopping List** application's output.

a) ***Copying the template to your working directory.*** Copy the directory `C:\Examples\Tutorial16\Exercises\EnhancedShoppingList` to your `C:\SimplyCpp` directory.

b) ***Opening the template source code file.*** Open the `List.cpp` file in your text editor or IDE.

c) ***Modifying the addItem function.*** If the list is empty when a new `ShoppingItem` is added, the application should simply add the `ShoppingItem` to the list. The application does not need to determine alphabetic order because there are no other `ShoppingItems` to which to compare. Therefore, you will need to add an `if...else` statement to the `addItem` function that determines whether firstItem is null (that is, there are currently no items in the list). If `firstItem` is non null, the body of the `if` statement should declare variable `currentItem`, a pointer to a `ShoppingItem`. Initialize `currentItem`'s value to the value of `List` member `firstItem`, using the `getFirstItem` function. You will use the `currentItem` pointer to access the names of `ShoppingItems` in the linked list.

d) ***Determining whether the new ShoppingItem precedes the first ShoppingItem in the list.*** After initializing `currentItem`, insert an `if` statement that determines whether `itemName` precedes (in alphabetic order) the name of the object to which `currentItem` points. [*Note:* If `string1` precedes `string2` in alphabetic order, then the expression `string1 < string2` evaluates to `true`.] If so, the new item should be inserted at the beginning of the linked list. In this case, the `nextItem` pointer for the object to which `newItem` points should point to the same object as does `currentItem` and the `List` object's `firstItem` pointer should point to the same object as does `newItem`.

e) ***Walking the linked list.*** If the new item does not precede the first item in the list, then your application must walk the linked list of `ShoppingItems` until it finds the correct position at which to insert the new `ShoppingItem`. Add an `else` part to the `if` statement you wrote in the previous step. In the body of the else statement, insert a while statement that repeats until the pointer returned by currentItem->getNextItem() is null. This prevents the application from following a null pointer when it reaches the end of the list. In the body of the while statement, insert a statement that assigns to currentItem the value returned by currentItem->getNextItem(). This moves the currentItem pointer to the next ShoppingItem in the list after each iteration.

f) ***Determining whether the new ShoppingItem precedes the next ShoppingItem in the list.*** Before the assignment statement in the preceding step, insert a nested if statement that determines whether itemName precedes currentItem->getNextItem() ->getName(). This determines whether the name of the new item precedes the name of the "next" item (that is, the object to which currentItem->getNextItem() points). If so, the new item should be inserted after the current item (which just before the "next" item). In this case, nextItem pointer for the object to which newItem points should point to the same object as does currentItem->getNextItem() and the nextItem pointer for the object to which currentItem points should point to the same object as does newItem. After updating the link list's pointers, insert a return statement to exit the function.

g) ***Adding the new item to the end of the list.*** If the while statement terminates without executing the return statement that you added in the previous step, then the new item must belong at the end of the list. After the closing brace for the while statement, and before the closing brace for the else part of the if...else statement, insert code to add the item to the end of the list. In this case, currentItem will point to the last object in the list. Update the object to which currentItem points so that its nextItem pointer contains the value of newItem. Then update the List object's lastItem pointer so that it points to the same object as does newItem.

h) ***Adding the new item if the list is empty.*** Follow the if statement of *Step c* with an else statement. This statement executes when the list is currently empty. In this statement, set firstItem to the new item entered. Remove the code in the function that occurs after the else statement. Recall that this code adds the new item to the list, something that you have already taken care of in previous steps.

i) ***Save, compile and run the completed application.*** Test your application to ensure that it runs correctly. Add items named oranges, apples and zucchinis, in that order. Then display the shopping list to confirm that the items have been inserted into the list in the proper order (Fig. 16.44).

j) ***Close the Command Prompt window.***

16.12 (*Bakery Application*) When the number of customers waiting to order baked goods outnumber the number of clerks waiting on those customers, it is difficult for the clerks to determine which customer to serve next. As a result, many bakeries provide some form of ticket dispenser that guarantees that customers are served fairly. For example, a customer is expected to take a numbered ticket upon entering the bakery. The baker then serves customers by calling numbers in ascending order. Because the tickets are dispensed in ascending order, this ensures a first-come-first-served order.

A bakery has decided to replace its ticket dispenser with an application that enables each customer to enter a name upon entering the store. The bakery's clerks can then choose to have the application display the next person in line. Create a prototype for the **Bakery** application that enables users to enter names and allows clerks to view the name of the next customer to serve.

You will use a queue data structure to implement this application. A queue is a special form of linked list in which objects are added to the end of the list and removed from the front. This corresponds to a line of waiting customers at a bakery, where arriving customers must begin waiting at the end of the line and customers are served only from the front of the line. Figure 16.45 demonstrates the completed application.

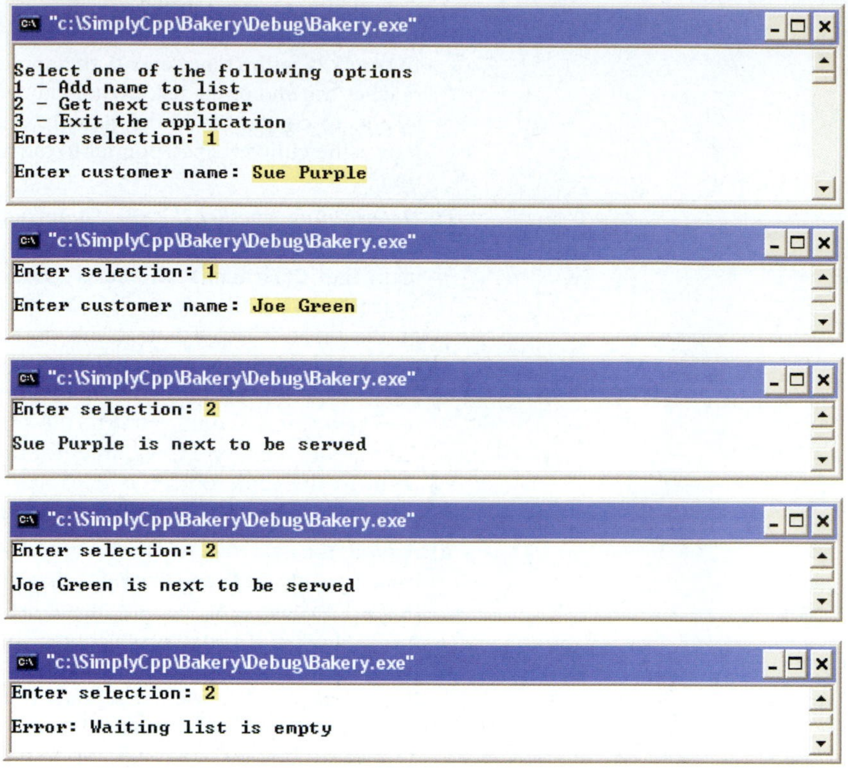

Figure 16.45 **Bakery** application output.

a) *Copying the template to your working directory.* Copy the directory C:\Examples\ Tutorial16\Exercises\Bakery to your C:\SimplyCpp directory.

b) *Opening and viewing the List class's header file.* Open the List.h file in your text editor or IDE. Note that this application's List class is similar to the one for the **Shopping List** application. Other than *get* and *set* functions, this List class supports two operations: adding a customer to the end of the list (addCustomer) and removing a customer from the front of the list (removeCustomer).

c) *Opening and the List class's template source code file.* Open the List.cpp file in your text editor or IDE. The List class's constructor and *get* and *set* functions are defined for you in the template.

d) *Defining the addCustomer function.* After line 41, define the addCustomer function. Name the parameter newCustomer. In the body of the addCustomer function, insert an if...else statement. If this List's lastCustomer pointer is null, then the list is empty. In this case, you should set the firstCustomer pointer to the value of new-Customer, a pointer to the customer being added to the beginning of the waiting list. Otherwise, the list contains waiting customers. In the body of the else part of the if...else statement, modify the Customer object at the end of the list so that its nextCustomer pointer points to the new customer. Regardless of whether the list is empty, the List object's lastCustomer pointer should point to the new customer after the addCustomer function completes. After the if...else statement, insert a statement that copies the value of newCustomer to List member lastCustomer, using the setLastCustomer function.

e) *Defining the removeCustomer function.* After the addCustomer function definition, define that removeCustomer function. Begin by defining currentCustomer, a pointer to a Customer object. Initialize this pointer with the value of the pointer to the first Customer in the List. Then insert an if statement that determines whether currentCustomer is null. If not, the body of the if statement should remove the first customer from the list by setting List member firstCustomer to point to the Customer "after" currentCustomer. If there are no more Customers in the waiting list, you should set to null the pointer to the last Customer in the list. Just before the function's closing brace, insert a statement to return the value of currentCustomer.

f) *Modifying the main function.* Open the Bakery.cpp file in your text editor or IDE. In line 19, create a List object named waitingList, which you will use to maintain your application's queue of waiting customers. In line 20, define nextCustomer, a pointer to a Customer object, and initialize its value to 0.

g) *Adding a Customer to the list.* The displayMenu function, provided in the template file, presents a menu enabling the user to add a name to list, get the next customer from the list or exit the application. The user selects 1 from the menu to add a name to the list. In lines 38–39 of main (after the case 1: label), use the addCustomer List member function to add a new Customer to the list. Use the new operator to create the new Customer, passing customerName as the first argument and 0 as the second argument to the Customer constructor.

h) *Removing a Customer from the list.* The user selects 2 from the application's menu to remove a name from the list. Immediately after the case 2: label, insert a statement that assigns to nextCustomer the value returned by List member function removeCustomer. Then insert an if...else statement that determines whether nextCustomer is a null pointer. If so, the application should display an error message indicating that the waiting list is empty. Otherwise, the application should display a message indicating the name of the customer to be served, then destroy the corresponding Customer object using the delete operator.

i) *Save, compile and run the completed application.* Test your application to ensure that it runs correctly. Add several names to the waiting list. Then get the name of the next customer several times. Check that the application retrieves the names if first-come-first-served order. Also ensure that the correct message is displayed when the waiting list is empty.

j) *Close the Command Prompt window.*

16.13 (*Modified Bakery Application*) A bakery that has been using your **Bakery** application finds that it is helpful to know how many people are waiting to be served. If there is a large number of waiting customers, the manager can temporarily move employees from the back room to the sales counter to assist other customers. Modify the **Bakery** application from Exercise 16.12 so that it allows the user to view the number of waiting customers. Figure 16.46 demonstrates the completed application.

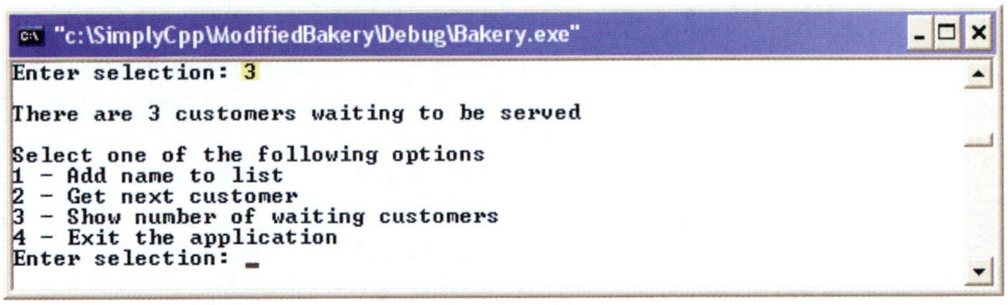

Figure 16.46 Modified **Bakery** application.

a) *Copying the completed application from Exercise 16.12 to your working directory.* Create the directory C:\SimplyCpp\ModifiedBakery. Then copy the contents of directory C:\SimplyCpp\Bakery to your C:\SimplyCpp\ModifiedBakery directory.

b) *Opening the List class header file.* Open the List.h file in your text editor or IDE.

c) *Declaring the length function.* In line 27, declare public member function length. The function returns an int and does not accept any arguments.

d) *Opening the List class source code file.* Open the List.cpp file in your text editor or IDE.

e) *Defining the length function.* After the removeCustomer function definition, define the length function. Begin by defining int variable count and initializing its value to 0. This variable will be used to count the number of customers in the list. Then define currentCustomer as a pointer to a Customer object. Initialize its value to the first customer in the list. After defining variables, add a while statement that repeats while currentCustomer is not a null pointer. The body of the while statement should increment count, then assign to currentCustomer the pointer returned by accessing the nextCustomer pointer for the object to which currentCustomer points. After the closing brace for the while statement, return the value of count.

f) *Opening the Bakery.cpp file.* Open the Bakery.cpp file in your text editor or IDE.

g) *Updating the menu options.* In the displayMenu function, update the menu and its option numbers so that it displays the option to view the number of waiting customers.

h) *Updating the main function.* Because the menu option to exit the application is now 4, you must update line 22 of main so that the while statement terminates when selection contains 4. Inside main's switch statement, modify the case 3: label to a case 4: label. Then insert a case 3: label above the case 4: label. Between the case 3: and case 4: labels, add a statement that displays a message indicating the number of customers currently in the list. Then insert a break statement to exit the switch statement.

i) *Save, compile and run the completed application.* Test your application to ensure that it runs correctly. Add several names to the waiting list, then display the number of customers in the waiting list to ensure that the application works correctly. Then remove several customers from the list and display the number of customers in the list again. Check to make sure that the correct number of customers is displayed in each case.

j) *Close the Command Prompt window.*

What does this code do? ▶

16.14 The mystery function manipulates a List object. Assume that the List class defines an addItem function similar to that of the **Shopping List** application. What does this function do?

```cpp
1   // Exercise 16.14: WDTCD.cpp
2   // What does this code do?
3   #include <iostream> // required to perform C++-style stream I/O
4   #include <iomanip>  // required for parameterized stream manipulators
5
6   using namespace std; // for accessing C++ Standard Library members
7
8   #include "ShoppingItem.h" // ShoppingItem class definition
9   #include "List.h" // List class definition
10
11  // function prototypes
12  int displayMenu();
13  void mystery( List & );
14
15  // function main begins program execution
16  int main()
17  {
18     int selection = 0; // stores the user's menu selection
19     string itemName; // stores the item name
20     int itemQuantity; // stores the item quantity
21     List shoppingList; // stores a list of shopping items
22
23     while ( selection != 3 )
24     {
25        selection = displayMenu();
26
27        switch ( selection )
28        {
29           // enter item information
30           case 1:
31              cin.ignore(); // remove newline from cin
32
```

```
33                        // prompt user for and input item name and quantity
34                        cout << "\nEnter item name: ";
35                        getline( cin, itemName ); // get name
36
37                        cout << "Enter quantity: ";
38                        cin >> itemQuantity; // get quantity
39
40                        // add new item to the shopping list
41                        shoppingList.addItem( itemName, itemQuantity);
42
43                        break;
44
45                    // view all items in the list
46                    case 2:
47                        shoppingList.displayList(); // display each item
48
49                        break;
50
51                    // exit
52                    case 3: // display newline before while loop terminates
53                        mystery( shoppingList );
54                        cout << "\n";
55                        break;
56
57                    default:
58                        cout << "Error: Enter a valid menu selection";
59
60               } // end switch
61
62          } // end while
63
64          shoppingList.deleteList();
65
66          return 0; // indicate that program ended successfully
67
68    } // end function main
69
70    // displays a menu and returns the selected menu option number
71    int displayMenu()
72    {
73          int selection = 0; // stores the menu option number
74
75          // display the menu
76          cout << "\nSelect one of the following options" << endl;
77          cout << "1 - Enter new item" << endl;
78          cout << "2 - Display list" << endl;
79          cout << "3 - Print mystery value" << endl;
80          cout << "Enter selection: ";
81          cin >> selection;
82
83          return selection; // return the selection
84
85    } // end function displayMenu
86
87    void mystery( List &shoppingList )
88    {
89          int counter = 0;
90          ShoppingItem *nextItem = shoppingList.getFirstItem();
91
```

```
92      while ( nextItem != 0 )
93      {
94         counter++;
95         nextItem = nextItem->getNextItem();
96      } // end while
97
98      cout << "Mystery number: " << counter << endl;
99
100 } // end function mystery
```

What's wrong with this code? ▶   **16.15** The following code should use the `List` member function `addItem` to add a pointer to `newItem` to the linked list. Find the error(s) in the following code:

```cpp
1   // Exercise 16.15: WWTC.cpp
2   // Adds one item to a linked list.
3   #include <iostream> // required to perform C++-style stream I/O
4
5   using namespace std; // for accessing C++ Standard Library members
6
7   #include "ShoppingItem.h" // ShoppingItem class definition
8   #include "List.h" // List class definition
9
10  void addItem( string, int );
11
12  // function main begins program execution
13  int main()
14  {
15      int selection = 0; // stores the user's menu selection
16      string itemName; // stores the item name
17      int itemQuantity; // stores the item quantity
18
19      cout << "\nEnter item name: ";
20      cin >> itemName;
21
22      cout << "Enter quantity: ";
23      cin >> itemQuantity;
24
25      addItem( itemName, itemQuantity );
26
27      cout << endl; // insert newline for readability
28
29      return 0; // indicate that program ended successfully
30
31  } // end function main
32
33  void addItem( string name, int quantity )
34  {
35      myList;
36
37      myList.addItem( *name, quantity );
38
39      myList->displayList();
40
41  } // end function addItem
```

Programming Challenge ▶

16.16 (*Modified Shopping List Application*) Modify the **Shopping List** application so that it allows the user to remove an item from the list by specifying the name of the item to remove. If the shopping list contains multiple items with the same name, the application should remove only the first occurrence of that item in the list. Figure 16.47 shows the shopping list before and after an item has been removed.

```
"c:\simplycpp\modifiedshoppinglist\debug\ModifiedShoppingList.exe"

Shopping List
-------------

Name: zucchinis
Quantity: 3

Name: oranges
Quantity: 5

Name: apples
Quantity: 10
```

```
"c:\simplycpp\modifiedshoppinglist\debug\ModifiedShoppingList.exe"

Select one of the following options
1 - Enter new item
2 - Remove an item
3 - Display list
4 - Exit the application
Enter selection: 2

Enter item to be removed: oranges
```

```
"c:\simplycpp\modifiedshoppinglist\debug\ModifiedShoppingList.exe"

Shopping List
-------------

Name: zucchinis
Quantity: 3

Name: apples
Quantity: 10
```

Figure 16.47 Modified **Shopping List** application.

a) *Copying the template to your working directory.* Copy the directory C:\Examples\ Tutorial16\Exercises\ModifiedShoppingList to your C:\SimplyCpp directory.

b) *Modifying the List class's header file.* Open the List.h file in your text editor or IDE. The List constructor, private data members, *get* and *set* functions for those data members and utility functions are provided for you. In line 26, add a declaration for public function removeItem that returns no value and that specifies a single string reference parameter.

c) *Defining the removeItem function.* Open the List.cpp file in your text editor or IDE. Beginning in line 82, define the removeItem function. The string reference parameter should be called itemName. The removeItem function should define a ShoppingItem pointer named currentItem that is initialized to the address of the first ShoppingItem object in the list.

d) *Determining whether the item to be removed is the first item in the list.* After defining currentItem, insert an if statement that executes when itemName matches the name of currentItem. When the first item in the list is removed, the next item in the list will become the first item in the list. Thus, the List object's firstItem pointer should be assigned the address of the next ShoppingItem. The application should delete currentItem using the delete operator. Finally, insert a return statement before terminating the if block. This ensures that exactly one item is removed from the list.

e) *Walking the linked list to find the item to remove.* After the if statement that you wrote in the previous step, insert a while statement that iterates until the last item in the list is reached—that is, when currentItem is a null pointer. The body of the while statement should determine whether the name of the next item in the list is equal to itemName. If so, create a ShoppingItem pointer itemToRemove, and assign it the value of `currentItem->getNextItem()`. Next, determine whether `itemToRemove` is the last item in the list, and if so, set to 0 the value of the `nextItem` pointer for the object to which `currentItem` points, indicating that `currentItem` points to the last item in the list. Otherwise, the item after `itemToRemove` will be the next item after `currentItem`, after removing `itemToRemove`. In this case, use the body of an `else` statement to assign the address of the item after `itemToRemove` to `currentItem`'s `nextItem` pointer. After the `else` statement, delete `itemToRemove` using the `delete` operator. Finally, insert a `return` statement before terminating the `if` block. This ensures that exactly one item is removed from the list.

f) *Displaying an error message.* If the function does not find the specified item, the function will not return to the caller before exiting the `while` loop. In this case, display an error message indicating that the specified item was not found.

g) *Modifying `main`.* Open the `ModifiedShoppingList.cpp` file in your text editor or IDE. After line 20, define `string` variable `itemToRemove` that should store the name of the item to remove from the list. Update the `displayMenu` function and `switch` statement inside `main` to add the option to remove and item from the list (Fig. 16.47). If the user decides to remove an item from the list, the application should prompt for and input the name of the item to be removed into `itemToRemove`. The application then should call the `removeItem` member function, passing to it the `itemToRemove` variable.

h) *Save, compile and run the completed application.* Test your application to ensure that it runs correctly. Remove items from the front, middle and back of the list to test all aspects of the `removeItem` function and ensure that the correct items are removed.

i) *Close the Command Prompt window.*

Objectives

In this tutorial, you will learn to:
- Understand inheritance.
- Form new classes quickly from existing classes using inheritance.
- Use polymorphism to create an application that conveniently processes related objects as though they are the same.

Outline

Payroll Application

Introducing Inheritance and Polymorphism

Inheritance, one of the most useful and important features of object-oriented programming, is a form of software reuse in which a new class is created by absorbing an existing class's data members (attributes) and member functions (behaviors), then embellishing them with new or modified capabilities. Software reusability saves time during application development. It also encourages the reuse of thoroughly debugged high-quality software, which increases the likelihood that a system will be implemented effectively. In this tutorial, you will learn how to create a class by reusing an existing class through inheritance.

Polymorphism is an object-oriented programming concept that enables you to "program in the general" rather than having to "program in the specific." In particular, polymorphism makes it easy to write code to process a variety of related objects. The same function call is made on these objects, and each of the objects will "do the right thing." If, for example, you tell a bird object to move, it will respond by flying; if you tell a fish object to move, it will respond by swimming.

Polymorphic applications handle, in a simple and convenient manner, objects of many classes that belong to the same inheritance hierarchy. These applications focus on the similarities between these classes rather than the differences.

With polymorphism, it is also possible to design and implement systems that are easily extended with new capabilities. New classes can be added with little or no modification to the rest of the application, as long as those classes share the similarities of the classes that the application already processes. These new classes simply "plug right in." After you build a **Payroll** application in this tutorial using inheritance, you will enhance that application using polymorphism.

17.1 Test-Driving the **Payroll** Application

In this tutorial, you will create a **Payroll** application. This application must meet the following requirements:

> **Application Requirements**
>
> *A company pays its employees on a weekly basis. It has three types of employees: salaried employees, who are paid a fixed weekly salary regardless of the number of hours worked; hourly employees, who are paid by the hour and receive overtime pay; and commission employees, who are paid a percentage of their sales. The company wants to implement a C++ application that performs its payroll calculations polymorphically.*

You begin by test-driving the completed application. Then, you will learn the additional C++ capabilities you will need to create your own version of this application.

Test-Driving the *Payroll* **Application**

1. *Locating the completed application.* Open a **Command Prompt** window by selecting **Start > All Programs > Accessories > Command Prompt.** Change to your completed **Payroll** application directory by typing cd C:\Examples\Tutorial17\CompletedApplication\Payroll2.

2. *Running the Payroll application.* Type Payroll in the **Command Prompt** window and press *Enter* to run the application (Fig. 17.1). The application displays a menu that prompts you to enter new employee information, view the payroll for the existing employees or exit the application. Enter 1 at the **Enter selection:** prompt to enter new employee information.

```
Command Prompt - Payroll                                    _ □ ✕

C:\>cd C:\Examples\Tutorial17\CompletedApplication\Payroll2

C:\Examples\Tutorial17\CompletedApplication\Payroll2>Payroll

Select one of the following options
1 - Enter new employee information
2 - View payroll
3 - Exit the application
Enter selection: _
```

Figure 17.1 Running the completed **Payroll** application.

3. *Entering employee information.* At the **Enter employee's first name:** prompt, enter Sue. At the **Enter employee's last name:** prompt, enter Purple. At the **Enter employee's social security number:** prompt, enter the value 111-11-1111. Notice that the **Select the employee type** menu appears (Fig. 17.2). Enter 1 for "**Salaried employee**" at the **Enter selection:** prompt (Fig. 17.3). The application then prompts you for the employee's weekly salary. Enter 750.25 at the **Enter salary:** prompt.

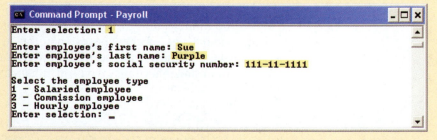

```
Command Prompt - Payroll                                    _ □ ✕
Enter selection: 1

Enter employee's first name: Sue
Enter employee's last name: Purple
Enter employee's social security number: 111-11-1111

Select the employee type
1 - Salaried employee
2 - Commission employee
3 - Hourly employee
Enter selection: _
```

Figure 17.2 Entering employee information in the **Payroll** application.

(cont.)

```
Command Prompt - payroll                              _ □ ×
Select the employee type
1 - Salaried employee
2 - Commission employee
3 - Hourly employee
Enter selection: 1

Enter salary: 750.25_
```

Figure 17.3 Entering salary information in the **Payroll** application.

4. ***Entering information for an hourly employee.*** Enter 1 at the **Enter selec-tion:** prompt to enter another new employee. At the **Enter employee's first name:** prompt, enter Jim. At the **Enter employee's last name:** prompt, enter Orange. At the **Enter employee's social security number:** prompt, enter the value 222-22-2222. Again, the **Select the employee type** menu appears. Enter 3 for "**Hourly employee**" at the **Enter selec-tion:** prompt (Fig. 17.4). The application then prompts you for the employee's hourly wage and hours worked (Fig. 17.4). Enter 14.50 at the **Enter hourly wage:** prompt and 37.5 at the **Enter hours worked:** prompt.

```
Command Prompt - Payroll                              _ □ ×
Enter employee's first name: Jim
Enter employee's last name: Orange
Enter employee's social security number: 222-22-2222

Select the employee type
1 - Salaried employee
2 - Commission employee
3 - Hourly employee
Enter selection: 3

Enter hourly wage: 14.50
Enter hours worked: 37.5_
```

Figure 17.4 Entering a second employee's information into the **Payroll** application.

5. ***Entering information for a commission employee.*** Enter 1 at the **Enter selection:** prompt to enter another new employee. At the **Enter employee's first name:** prompt, enter Alice. At the **Enter employee's last name:** prompt, enter Green. At the **Enter employee's social security number:** prompt, enter the value 333-33-3333. Again, the **Select the employee type** menu appears. Enter 2 for "**Commission employee**" at the **Enter selection:** prompt (Fig. 17.5). The application then prompts you for the employee's sales and commission rate (Fig. 17.5). Enter 915.35 at the **Enter sales:** prompt and 3.5 at the **Enter commission rate (%):** prompt.

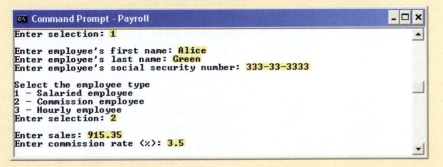

```
Command Prompt - Payroll                              _ □ ×
Enter selection: 1

Enter employee's first name: Alice
Enter employee's last name: Green
Enter employee's social security number: 333-33-3333

Select the employee type
1 - Salaried employee
2 - Commission employee
3 - Hourly employee
Enter selection: 2

Enter sales: 915.35
Enter commission rate (%): 3.5
```

Figure 17.5 Entering a third employee's information into the **Payroll** appli-cation.

(cont.)   6. ***Viewing the payroll.*** Enter 2 at the **Enter selection:** prompt to view the payroll (Fig. 17.6). Notice that the application displays the employee type, name, social security number and total earnings for each employee. The application then displays the total earnings for all employees that have been entered.

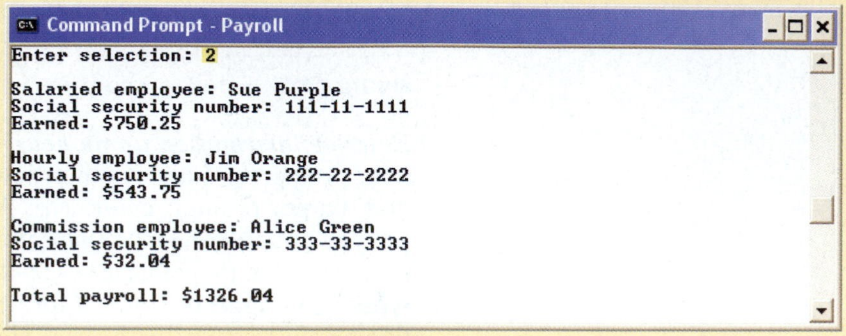

```
Command Prompt - Payroll                                    _ □ ×

Enter selection: 2

Salaried employee: Sue Purple
Social security number: 111-11-1111
Earned: $750.25

Hourly employee: Jim Orange
Social security number: 222-22-2222
Earned: $543.75

Commission employee: Alice Green
Social security number: 333-33-3333
Earned: $32.04

Total payroll: $1326.04
```

Figure 17.6   Displaying the payroll.

7. ***Closing the running application.*** Close your running application by entering 3 at the **Enter selection:** prompt.

8. ***Close the Command Prompt window.***

17.2 Inheritance Overview

Consider an application that a bank uses to maintain information about its clients' accounts. This application might contain a `BankAccount` class specifying data members including a client's name, account number and account balance. However, clients frequently maintain more than one account with the same bank. Such accounts include

- savings accounts, which accrue interest and limit the client to six withdrawals per month

- checking accounts, which do not accrue interest and do not limit the number of withdrawals

- and certificate of deposits (CDs), which accrue interest and can be withdrawn at the maturity date.

When creating a class to represent each account (such as `SavingsAccount`, `CheckingAccount` and `CertificateOfDeposit` classes), rather than completely defining new members (data members and functions), you can designate the new class to inherit the members from an existing class. By **inheriting** from the `BankAccount` class, the `SavingsAccount` class absorbs data members (the client name, account number and account balance) from the `BankAccount` class. The `SavingsAccount` class need only specify additional data members such as the interest rate and monthly withdrawal limit. Similarly, a `CertificateOfDeposit` class that inherits from the `BankAccount` class need only specify data members for an interest rate and a maturity date.

The pre-existing class is called the **base class**, and each new class is called a **derived class**. Once created, each derived class can become a base class for future derived classes. A derived class normally adds its own data members and member functions. Therefore, a derived class is more specialized than its base class and represents a smaller group of objects. Typically, the derived class exhibits the behaviors of its base class and additional behaviors specific to the derived class.

We discuss the relationship between base classes and their derived classes in terms of the *is a* relationship. In an *is a* **relationship**, an object of a derived class also can be treated as an object of its base classes. Often, an object of one class *is an* object of another class as well. For example, in geometry, a rectangle is a quadrilateral (as are squares, parallelograms and trapezoids). Thus, in C++, the `Rectangle` class can be said to inherit from the `Quadrilateral` class. In this context, the `Quadrilateral` class is a base class, and the `Rectangle` class is a derived class. A rectangle is a specific type of quadrilateral, but it is incorrect to claim that every quadrilateral *is a* rectangle—the quadrilateral could be a parallelogram, a trapezoid or some other shape. Figure 17.7 lists several simple examples of base classes and derived classes.

Base Class	Derived Classes
Student	GraduateStudent, UndergraduateStudent
Shape	Circle, Triangle, Rectangle
Loan	CarLoan, HomeImprovementLoan, MortgageLoan
Employee	Faculty, Staff
BankAccount	CheckingAccount, SavingsAccount

Figure 17.7   Inheritance examples.

Because every derived-class object *is an* object of its base class, and because one base class can have many derived classes, the set of objects represented by a base class typically is larger than the set of objects represented by any of its derived classes. For example, the base class `Vehicle` represents all vehicles, including cars, trucks, boats, airplanes and bicycles. By contrast, the `Car` derived class represents a smaller, more specific subset of all vehicles.

The **class hierarchy** defines the inheritance relationships among classes. For example, Fig. 17.8 illustrates a simple class hierarchy containing a `Student` base class and two derived classes, `GraduateStudent` and `UndergraduateStudent`. Each derived class is located at a lower level of the inheritance hierarchy than its base class. A **direct base class** is the base class from which the derived class explicitly inherits. A derived class is located in the inheritance hierarchy one level below its direct base class. An **indirect base class** is inherited by a derived class that is located two or more levels down the class hierarchy.

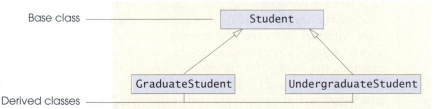

Figure 17.8   Inheritance hierarchy for university students.

Inheritance relationships form tree-like hierarchical structures (Fig. 17.9). A base class exists in a hierarchical relationship with its derived classes. Although classes can exist independently, when they participate in inheritance relationships, they become affiliated with other classes. A class becomes either a base class, supplying data members and functions to other classes, or a derived class, inheriting data members and functions from other classes.

Let's develop a more substantial class hierarchy (also called an **inheritance hierarchy**). A university community has thousands of community members (top line, Fig. 17.9), consisting of employees, students and alumni (second line from top, Fig. 17.9). Employees are either faculty members or staff members (third line, Fig. 17.9). Faculty members are either administrators (such as deans and department chairs) or teachers (bottom line of Fig. 17.9). Note that this inheritance hierarchy could contain many other classes. For example, students can be graduate or undergraduate students. Undergraduate students can be freshmen, sophomores, juniors or seniors. Each upward-pointing arrow in the hierarchy represents an *is a* relationship. For instance, as you follow the arrows in this class hierarchy, you can state, "an `Employee` is a `CommunityMember`" and "a `Teacher` is a `Faculty` member." `CommunityMember` is the direct base class of `Employee`, `Student` and `Alumnus`, and is an indirect base class of all the other classes in the diagram. Starting from the bottom of the hierarchy, the reader can follow the arrows and apply the *is a* relationship all the way to the topmost base class. For example, an `Administrator` *is a* `Faculty` member, *is an* `Employee` and *is a* `CommunityMember`.

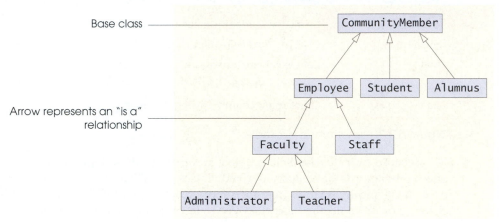

Base class

Arrow represents an "is a" relationship

Figure 17.9   Inheritance hierarchy for university `CommunityMember`s.

Another example of an inheritance hierarchy is the `Shape` hierarchy of Fig. 17.10. To specify that the `TwoDimensionalShape` class is derived from (or inherits from) the `Shape` class, the `TwoDimensionalShape` class could be defined in C++ as follows:

```
class TwoDimensionalShape : public Shape
```

This is an example of `public` inheritance, the most commonly used type of inheritance. With **public inheritance**, all nonprivate base-class members retain their original member access when they become members of the derived class. For example, `public` members of the base class become `public` members of the derived class. Although `private` base-class members are still inherited, the `private` members of a base class are not accessible directly from that class's derived classes. For example, the `Shape` class in Fig. 17.10 might define `private` data member `color`. The `TwoDimensionalShape` and `Circle` classes, for example, will inherit the `color` data member, but cannot change its value using a statement such as

```
color = red;
```

Rather, a derived class can manipulate `private` members of the base class only if the base class provides `public` member functions that access these members, such as *get* and *set* functions (for example, `getColor` and `setColor`).

One problem with inheritance is that a derived class can inherit functions it does not need or should not have. Even when a base-class function is appropriate for a derived class, that derived class often needs to modify that function to perform a specific task. In such cases, the derived class can **redefine** the base-class function with an appropriate implementation—the new function defined in the derived class supersedes the old function defined in the base class. Do not confuse this concept with overloading, which refers to functions with the same name but different parameter lists. Redefined functions have the same name, parameter list and return type. You will redefine a base-class function later in this tutorial.

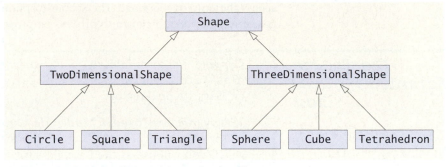

Figure 17.10   Inheritance hierarchy for **Shapes**.

1. A(n) _____ defines the inheritance relationships among a set of related classes.

   a) function redefine   b) class hierarchy

   c) *has a* relationship   d) None of the above.

2. When a base-class function is _____ in a derived class, the new function defined in the derived class supersedes (in the derived class) the corresponding function inherited from the base class.

   a) redefined   b) initialized

   c) overloaded   d) None of the above.

Answers: 1) b. 2) a.

17.3 Creating the Payroll Application

Now that you have been introduced to inheritance, you can begin to develop the **Payroll** application. First, you will use pseudocode to list the actions to be executed and to specify the order of execution. The pseudocode in Fig. 17.11 describes the basic operation of the **Payroll** application.

While the user has not chosen to exit the application
    Prompt the user to enter new employee information, view the payroll or exit

    Switch based on the user selection

        If the user selected to enter new employee information
            Prompt the user for and store the employee information

        If the user selected to view the payroll
            Display each employee's information and wages
            Display the total wages

        If the user selected to exit the application
            Exit the application

        Default case
            Display an error message

Figure 17.11   Pseudocode for the **Payroll** application.

In the following box, you will begin to create the first version of the **Payroll** application, by building the SalariedEmployee class. This class will be a derived class of the existing Employee class that is included in the template application. The Employee class represents an employee, storing a first name, last name and social security number, and provides functionality to display the employee's name and social security number. Your SalariedEmployee class will inherit from the Employee class and add data members and member functions to manipulate and access the employee's wage. The second version of the **Payroll** application will take advantage of polymorphism to process employee information more conveniently.

Creating the SalariedEmployee Class

1. *Copying the template to your working directory.* Copy the `C:\Examples\Tutorial17\TemplateApplication\Payroll` directory to your `C:\SimplyCpp` directory.

2. *Viewing the Employee.h header file.* Open the `Employee.h` file in your text editor or IDE. This header file defines the `Employee` class (lines 10-32), which you will use as the base class for your `SalariedEmployee` class. The `Employee` class in Fig. 17.12 declares a constructor (line 13); public *set* and *get* functions for the employee's first name (lines 15–16), last name (lines 18–19) and social security number (lines 21–22); and a public member function to display information about the employee (line 25). The class contains three private string data members, `firstName`, `lastName` and `socialSecurityNumber` (lines 28–30), to store the employee's first name, last name and social security number, respectively.

```
Employee.h
 8   using namespace std; // for accessing C++ Standard Library members
 9
10   class Employee {
11
12   public:
13      Employee( string &, string &, string & );
14
15      void setFirstName( string & );
16      string getFirstName();
17
18      void setLastName( string & );
19      string getLastName();
20
21      void setSocialSecurityNumber( string & );
22      string getSocialSecurityNumber();
23
24      // member function to be overridden
25      void print(); // display employee information
26
27   private:
28      string firstName;
29      string lastName;
30      string socialSecurityNumber;
31
32   }; // end class Employee
33
34   #endif // EMPLOYEE_H
```

Figure 17.12 `Employee` class definition.

3. *Opening the SalariedEmployee template source code header file.* Open the template file `Salaried.h` in your text editor or IDE.

4. *Including the Employee.h file.* Insert line 6 of Fig. 17.13 into the `Salaried.h` file to include the `Employee.h` header file. Before you create your derived class, `SalariedEmployee`, you must include its base-class definition, located in `Employee.h`.

```
Salaried.h
 4   #define SALARIED_H
 5
 6   #include "Employee.h"   // Employee class definition
 7
 8   #endif // SALARIED_H
```

Including the `Employee.h` header file

Figure 17.13 Including the base-class definition.

(cont.)

5. ***Adding the SalariedEmployee class definition.*** Insert lines 8–22 of Fig. 17.14 into the Salaried.h file. The colon (:) in line 8 of the class definition indicates inheritance. The public keyword indicates the type of inheritance. As a derived class (formed with public inheritance), SalariedEmployee inherits all the members of the Employee class, except for the constructor. Thus, the public services of SalariedEmployee include the SalariedEmployee constructor (lines 11–12), the public member functions inherited from the Employee class, setWeeklySalary and getWeeklySalary member functions (lines 14–15) and the print member function (line 17). Because the derived class uses public inheritance, the SalariedEmployee class inherits the Employee class's firstName, lastName and socialSecurityNumber private data members, but can access them only through the Employee class's public member functions (such as the *get* and *set* functions).

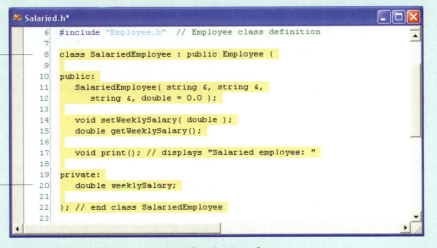

SalariedEmployee inherits from Employee

Creating a data member for the weekly salary

Figure 17.14 Defining class SalariedEmployee.

Note that line 12 declares the SalariedEmployee constructor to include a **default argument**, specifying a default value of 0.0 for the double argument passed to the constructor. When a client of a class calls the constructor without specifying a value for a default argument, the constructor assigns the default value to the argument. For example, if the call to the SalariedEmployee constructor includes only three string arguments, the double value (the fourth argument) will be assigned 0.0.

Notice that the Employee class provides most of the data (such as the employee's first name, last name and social security number) that SalariedEmployee will need. The Employee class, however, has no data member to store wages. Line 20 adds double data member weeklySalary to your new SalariedEmployee class.

6. ***Opening the SalariedEmployee template source code file.*** Open the template file Salaried.cpp in your text editor or IDE.

7. ***Creating the constructor for SalariedEmployee.*** Insert lines 9–17 of Fig. 17.15 into the Salaried.cpp file to define the SalariedEmployee constructor. You need to add a constructor to SalariedEmployee because a derived class does not inherit its base class's constructor. The SalariedEmployee constructor accepts four arguments. The first three arguments are passed to the Employee constructor. The fourth argument specifies the weekly salary for the employee.

(cont.)

The `SalariedEmployee` constructor invokes the `Employee` constructor by using the **base-class initializer syntax** (line 13), which uses a member initializer to pass arguments to the base-class (`Employee`) constructor. **Member initializers**, which are used to initialize a class's data members, appear between a constructor's parameter list and the left brace that begins the constructor's body. The member initializer list is separated from the parameter list with a colon (`:`). To initialize multiple data members, separate each initializer by a comma.

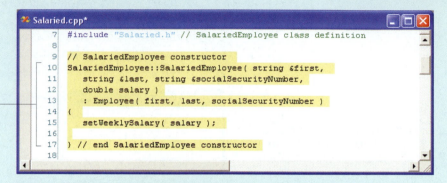

Defining the `SalariedEmployee` class's constructor

Figure 17.15 `SalariedEmployee` constructor definition.

C++ requires a derived-class constructor to call its base-class constructor and initialize the base-class data members that are inherited into the derived class. If the `SalariedEmployee` constructor did not invoke the `Employee` constructor explicitly, the default `Employee` constructor would be invoked implicitly with the default values for its arguments. If the `Employee` class did not provide a default constructor, the compiler would issue a syntax error.

Line 15 passes the constructor's `salary` parameter as an argument to the `SalariedEmployee` class's `setWeeklySalary` member function, which sets the value of `private` data member `weeklySalary`.

8. *Adding the **set** and **get** functions.* Now you will create functions to access the `weeklySalary` data member. Insert lines 19–38 of Fig. 17.16 into the `Salaried.cpp` file to define functions that *set* and *get* the `weeklySalary` data member. Note that lines 22–25 ensure that the `SalariedEmployee` object is in a consistent state by assigning `0.0` to `weeklySalary` if the client specifies a salary that is invalid (that is, less than `0.0`).

9. *Redefining the **print** member function.* Insert lines 40–46 of Fig. 17.17 into the `Salaried.cpp` file. The `print` function is originally defined in the `Employee` base class. These lines redefine the `print` function that is defined in the base class so that the `SalariedEmployee` class's version of the function is called. Redefining `print` enables you to define how to display information for an object of your `SalariedEmployee` class. Line 44 displays a message indicating the type of employee (salaried employee). Line 44 calls the base class's `print` function using the class name (`Employee`), followed by the binary scope resolution operator. Calling the base class's `print` function displays the employee's first name, last name and social security number, which are stored by base-class data members.

10. *Save the application.*

(cont.)

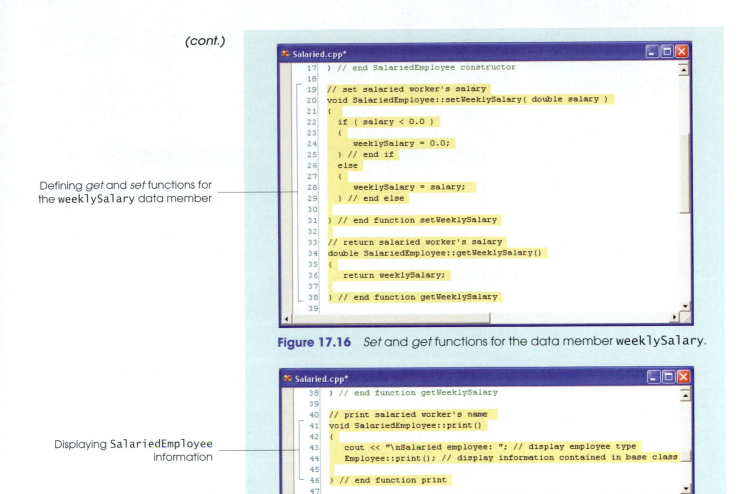

Defining *get* and *set* functions for the `weeklySalary` data member

```
17    } // end SalariedEmployee constructor
18
19    // set salaried worker's salary
20    void SalariedEmployee::setWeeklySalary( double salary )
21    {
22       if ( salary < 0.0 )
23       {
24          weeklySalary = 0.0;
25       } // end if
26       else
27       {
28          weeklySalary = salary;
29       } // end else
30
31    } // end function setWeeklySalary
32
33    // return salaried worker's salary
34    double SalariedEmployee::getWeeklySalary()
35    {
36       return weeklySalary;
37
38    } // end function getWeeklySalary
39
```

Figure 17.16 *Set* and *get* functions for the data member `weeklySalary`.

Displaying `SalariedEmployee` information

```
38    } // end function getWeeklySalary
39
40    // print salaried worker's name
41    void SalariedEmployee::print()
42    {
43       cout << "\nSalaried employee: "; // display employee type
44       Employee::print(); // display information contained in base class
45
46    } // end function print
47
```

Figure 17.17 Redefining the `print` function.

SELF-REVIEW

1. In the class definition, use the _____, followed by an existing class name, to create a derived class of an existing class.

   a) :
   b) ;
   c) ,
   d) ->

2. Given the function header `int calculateSalary( double hours, double wage = 0.0 )`, which of the following calls to this function is a syntax error?

   a) `calculateSalary( 10.5, 10.5 );`
   b) `calculateSalary();`
   c) `calculateSalary( 10.5 );`
   d) None of the above.

Answers: 1) a. 2) b.

17.4 Using a Derived Class in the Payroll Application

Now that you have created the `SalariedEmployee` class, you will complete the first version of your **Payroll** application. You will create an array of `SalariedEmployee` objects and use their member functions to display information about each object.

Creating, Accessing and Deleting SalariedEmployee Objects

1. *Opening the Payroll template source code file.* Open the template file Payroll.cpp in your text editor or IDE.

2. *Including the Salaried.h header file.* Insert line 9 of Fig. 17.18 into Payroll.cpp. This `include` directive enables your application to access the SalariedEmployee class.

Including the `Salaried.h` header file

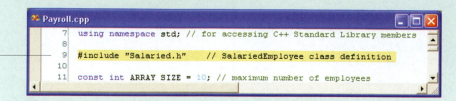

```
 7   using namespace std; // for accessing C++ Standard Library members
 8
 9   #include "Salaried.h"    // SalariedEmployee class definition
10
11   const int ARRAY_SIZE = 10; // maximum number of employees
```

Figure 17.18   Including the `SalariedEmployee` class definition.

3. *Creating an array of pointers to SalariedEmployee objects.* Insert lines 26–27 of Fig. 17.19 into Payroll.cpp. Line 27 creates the employees array, containing pointers to SalariedEmployee objects. The number of elements in the array is specified by ARRAY_SIZE, an `int` constant initialized to 10 (line 11 of Fig. 17.18).

Defining `employees` to store 10 pointers to `SalariedEmployee` objects

```
24   cout << fixed << setprecision( 2 );
25
26      // create an array of SalariedEmployee pointers
27      SalariedEmployee *employees[ ARRAY_SIZE ];
28
29   while ( selection != 3 )
```

Figure 17.19   Creating an array of pointers to `SalariedEmployee` objects.

4. *Examining the createEmployee function.* View lines 77–103 of the Payroll.cpp file, which define the createEmployee function. This function specifies two parameters (line 77)—an array of pointers to SalariedEmployee objects, employees, and the index in the array, index, at which to store a pointer to a new SalariedEmployee object. The array that is passed to the createEmployee function is the same array that you created in line 27. Lines 88–99 prompt the user for and input the employee's first name, last name, social security number and weekly salary in the firstName, lastName, SSN and salary variables, respectively.

5. *Adding a SalariedEmployee to the array.* Insert lines 101–103 of Fig. 17.21 into the createEmployee function in Payroll.cpp. Line 102 uses the new operator to create an object of the SalariedEmployee type and assign a pointer containing the address of this object to an element of the employees array.

6. *Adding code to the displayEmployees function.* Insert lines 116–130 of Fig. 17.22 into the displayEmployees function. The displayEmployees function declares two parameters (line 109), an array of pointers to SalariedEmployee objects, employees, and the number of employees, count, contained in the array. Lines 116–128 define a for statement that iterates over each initialized element of the employees array. Line 120 calls SalariedEmployee member function print to display each employee's information.

(cont.)

Defining variables to
store user input ⎯⎯⎯⎯⎯⎯⎯⎯⎯

Prompting the user for and
inputting an employee's name,
social security number and salary ⎯⎯⎯⎯⎯⎯

```
        Payroll.cpp*                                         _ □ X
    77   int createEmployee( SalariedEmployee *employees[], int index )
    78   {
    79       // define variables
    80       string firstName;  // stores the employee's first name
    81       string lastName;   // stores the employee's last name
    82       string SSN;        // stores the employee's social security number
    83       double salary;     // stores the employee's salary
    84
    85       cin.ignore(); // remove newline
    86
    87       // prompt user for and store generic Employee information
    88       cout << "\nEnter employee's first name: ";
    89       getline( cin, firstName ); // get first name
    90
    91       cout << "Enter employee's last name: ";
    92       getline( cin, lastName ); // get last name
    93
    94       cout << "Enter employee's social security number: ";
    95       getline ( cin, SSN ); // get SSN
    96
    97       // prompt user for and store the salary
    98       cout << "Enter salary: ";
    99       cin >> salary;
   100
   101       return 1; // indicate that employee was created successfully
   102
   103   } // end function createEmployee
```

Figure 17.20 **Payroll** application's `createEmployee` function.

Creating a new
`SalariedEmployee` object ⎯⎯⎯⎯⎯⎯

```
        Payroll.cpp*                                         _ □ X
    99       cin >> salary;
   100
   101       // store pointer to a SalariedEmployee object
   102       employees[ index ] = new SalariedEmployee( firstName,
   103           lastName, SSN, salary );
   104
   105       return 1; // indicate that employee was created successfully
```

Figure 17.21 Creating a new `SalariedEmployee` object.

Line 123 uses the `getWeeklySalary` member function to display each employee's weekly salary. Line 127 adds the salary to `double` variable `total` (defined in line 111), which maintains a running total of all the employee salaries for the company. After the `for` statement terminates, line 130 displays the value of `total`.

7. **Deleting each SalariedEmployee object.** Insert lines 73–77 of Fig. 17.23 into `main` to delete each `SalariedEmployee` object. These lines execute after the user chooses to exit the application. To delete an object that was allocated using the `new` operator, freeing the space for the object, use the `delete` operator.

8. **Save, compile and run the application.** Figure 17.24 shows the application's menu and input prompts for entering an employee's information into the completed **Payroll** application. Figure 17.25 shows the payroll after several employees have been entered. In the next section, you will enhance your **Payroll** application to support multiple employee types.

(cont.)

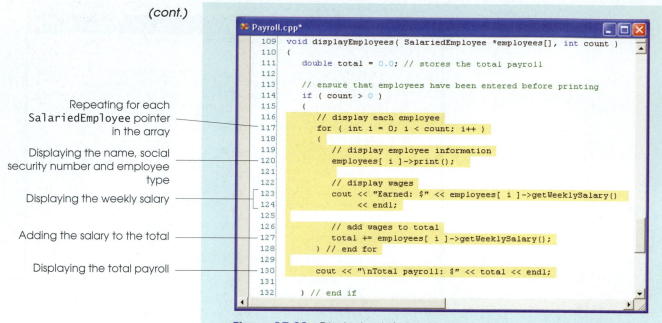

Figure 17.22 Displaying information and wages for each Salaried-Employee.

Repeating for each SalariedEmployee pointer in the array

Displaying the name, social security number and employee type

Displaying the weekly salary

Adding the salary to the total

Displaying the total payroll

```cpp
109  void displayEmployees( SalariedEmployee *employees[], int count )
110  {
111      double total = 0.0; // stores the total payroll
112
113      // ensure that employees have been entered before printing
114      if ( count > 0 )
115      {
116          // display each employee
117          for ( int i = 0; i < count; i++ )
118          {
119              // display employee information
120              employees[ i ]->print();
121
122              // display wages
123              cout << "Earned: $" << employees[ i ]->getWeeklySalary()
124                  << endl;
125
126              // add wages to total
127              total += employees[ i ]->getWeeklySalary();
128          } // end for
129
130          cout << "\nTotal payroll: $" << total << endl;
131
132      } // end if
```

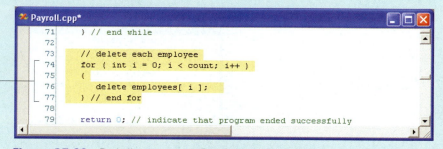

Figure 17.23 Deleting each SalariedEmployee object.

Deleting each SalariedEmployee object

```cpp
71      } // end while
72
73      // delete each employee
74      for ( int i = 0; i < count; i++ )
75      {
76          delete employees[ i ];
77      } // end for
78
79      return 0; // indicate that program ended successfully
```

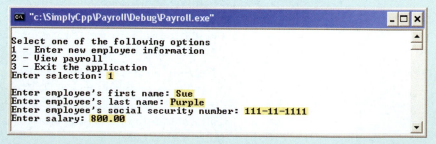

Figure 17.24 Entering information for the **Payroll** application using Sala-riedEmployee.

```
Select one of the following options
1 - Enter new employee information
2 - View payroll
3 - Exit the application
Enter selection: 1

Enter employee's first name: Sue
Enter employee's last name: Purple
Enter employee's social security number: 111-11-1111
Enter salary: 800.00
```

9. *Close the Command Prompt window.*

(cont.)

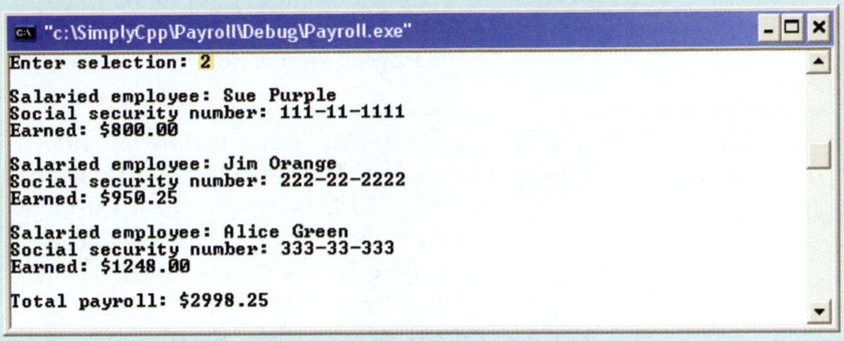

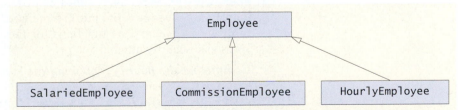

Figure 17.25   Displaying the payroll in the **Payroll** application using Sala-riedEmployee.

SELF-REVIEW

1. When a derived-class function redefines a base-class function, the base-class function can be accessed from the derived class by preceding the base-class function name with the _____ and the _____.

   a) base-class name, colon(:)   b) derived-class name, comma (,)

   c) base-class name, binary scope resolution operator (::)

   d) derived-class name, member-access operator (.)

2. A derived-class function that uses `public` inheritance can access its base class's `private` data members using _____.

   a) the assignment operator   b) the binary scope resolution operator

   c) a `public` *get* or *set* function defined in the base class

   d) a `public` *get* or *set* function defined in the derived class

Answers: 1) c. 2) c.

17.5 Using Multiple Derived Classes in the Payroll Application

You will now enhance your simple payroll system to support a larger Employee inheritance hierarchy. Every Employee will have an earnings function that calculates the employee's weekly pay. These earnings functions vary by employee type—a SalariedEmployee is paid a fixed weekly salary regardless of the number of hours worked. An HourlyEmployee is paid by the hour and receives overtime pay (one and a half times that employee's hourly wage for hours worked in excess of 40 hours). A CommissionEmployee receives a percentage of sales. The UML class diagram of Fig. 17.26 demonstrates the inheritance hierarchy for your **Payroll** application.

```
                        ┌──────────────┐
                        │   Employee   │
                        └──────────────┘
             ┌─────────────────┼─────────────────┐
  ┌────────────────────┐ ┌────────────────────┐ ┌──────────────────┐
  │ SalariedEmployee   │ │ CommissionEmployee │ │  HourlyEmployee  │
  └────────────────────┘ └────────────────────┘ └──────────────────┘
```

Figure 17.26   UML class diagram for the Employee inheritance hierarchy in the **Payroll** application.

In this section, you will modify the **Payroll** application to process multiple employee types using inheritance. You begin by completing the HourlyEmployee class. Then, you will modify the **Payroll** application accordingly. You will see that the application does not produce correct results because the derived classes do not use polymorphism. In the next section, you will learn how to use polymorphism in your **Payroll** application.

Completing the HourlyEmployee Class

1. **Copying the template to your working directory.** Copy the C:\Examples\Tutorial17\TemplateApplication\Payroll2 directory to your C:\SimplyCpp directory. This directory contains header files and implementations for the Employee, SalariedEmployee, CommissionEmployee and HourlyEmployee classes. In this section, you will complete the HourlyEmployee class.

2. **Opening the Employee.h header file.** Open the template file Employee.h in your text editor or IDE. Notice that line 25 of Fig. 17.27 declares the earnings function, which each of Employee's derived classes will redefine. Because the Employee class does not contain information about the earnings for a particular employee type, the earnings function definition (located in lines 71–76 of Employee.cpp) returns the value -1.0 (Fig. 17.28).

Declaring the earnings function ⎯⎯⎯⎯⎯⎯⎯⎯⎯⎯⎯⎯

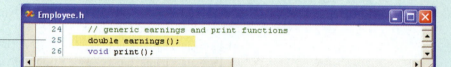

```
Employee.h
24        // generic earnings and print functions
25        double earnings();
26        void print();
```

Figure 17.27   Declaring the earnings function in the Employee class.

Defining the Employee class function earnings ⎯⎯⎯⎯⎯⎯⎯⎯⎯⎯

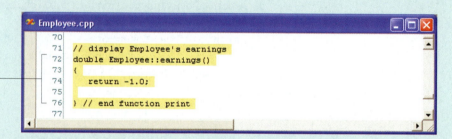

```
Employee.cpp
70
71    // display Employee's earnings
72    double Employee::earnings()
73    {
74        return -1.0;
75
76    } // end function print
77
```

Figure 17.28   earnings function definition for the Employee class.

3. **Viewing the Hourly.h header file.** Open the Hourly.h file in your text editor or IDE. This header file defines the HourlyEmployee class, which is derived from the Employee class (line 8). The HourlyEmployee class in Fig. 17.29 declares a constructor (lines 11–12), public *get* and *set* functions for the employee's hourly wage (lines 14–15) and hours worked (lines 17–18) and public functions that redefine the Employee class's earnings and print functions (lines 20–21). The class also defines two private double data members, wage and hours, to store the employee's hourly wage and hours worked, respectively (lines 24–25). Recall that a derived class such as HourlyEmployee inherits public member functions from it base class—in this case, the *get* and *set* functions for the employee's first name, last name and social security number.

4. **Completing the Hourly.cpp template source code file.** Open the template file Hourly.cpp in your text editor or IDE. Insert lines 63–83 of Fig. 17.30 to redefine the Employee class's earnings and print functions. The earnings function (lines 64–75) calculates the total earnings for the employee, based on the hourly wage and hours worked. If the employee worked for 40 hours or less (lines 66–69), the earnings is simply the product of the hourly wage (wage) and the hours worked (hours). If the employee worked more than 40 hours (lines 70–73), the earnings includes time-and-a-half wages for any hours worked beyond the 40-hour limit.

(cont.)

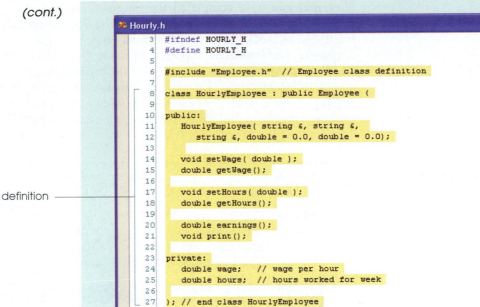

Figure 17.29 HourlyEmployee Class definition.

HourlyEmployee class definition

Lines 78–83 define the HourlyEmployee class's print function, similar to the print function in the SalariedEmployee class. Line 80 displays a message indicating the type of employee (in this case, "Hourly employee"). Line 81 calls the base class's print function using the class name (Employee) followed by the binary scope resolution operator (::). Calling the base class's print function displays the employee's first name, last name and social security number, which are stored by base-class data members.

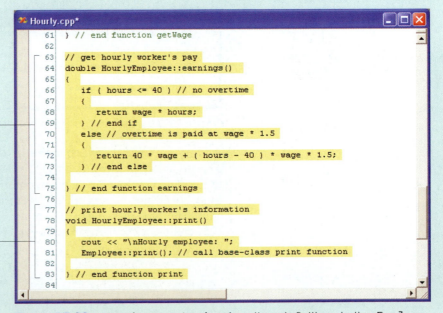

Defining the earnings function in the HourlyEmployee class

Defining the print function in the HourlyEmployee class

Figure 17.30 earnings and print function definitions in the Employee class.

5. *Save the application.*

Now that you have completed the `HourlyEmployee` class, you will modify your **Payroll** application. In the first version of the **Payroll** application, you stored pointers to `SalariedEmployee` objects in an array because there was only one type of employee. Unfortunately, this type of array is insufficient for storing pointers to `HourlyEmployee` objects and `CommissionEmployee` objects, because these objects are of different types. However, due to inheritance, each of these objects *is an* `Employee`. As a result, you can store pointers to the derived classes as pointers to the base class. In the following box, you will modify your **Payroll** application to take advantage of this inheritance feature.

Using Inheritance in the Payroll Application

1. **Opening the Payroll template source code file.** Open the template file `Payroll.cpp` in your text editor or IDE.

2. **Including header files.** Insert lines 11–12 of Fig. 17.31 into `Payroll.cpp`. These `include` directives enable your application to access the `CommissionEmployee` class, which is provided for you in the template files, and the `HourlyEmployee` class, which you just completed.

Including the `Commission.h` and `Hourly.h` header files

```
 9   #include "Employee.h"    // Employee base class definition
10   #include "Salaried.h"    // SalariedEmployee class definition
11   #include "Commission.h"  // CommissionEmployee class definition
12   #include "Hourly.h"      // HourlyEmployee class definition
13
14   const int ARRAY_SIZE = 10;
```

Figure 17.31 Including the `CommissionEmployee` and `HourlyEmployee` class definitions.

3. **Using an array of pointers to Employee objects.** To take advantage of polymorphism, change each declaration of an array of `SalariedEmployee` pointers (lines 17–18, line 30, line 86 and line 167) to an array of `Employee` pointers. Figure 17.32 shows the change made to the array declaration in line 30 of `main`.

`employees` stores ARRAY_SIZE (10) pointers to `Employee` objects

```
27       cout << fixed << setprecision( 2 );
28
29       // create an array of Employees
30       Employee *employees[ ARRAY_SIZE ];
31
32       while ( selection != 3 )
```

Figure 17.32 Creating an array of pointers to `Employee` objects.

4. **Adding a CommissionEmployee to the array.** Notice that the `createEmployee` function, which begins in line 86, has been modified to allow the user to select an employee type when entering employee information (Fig. 17.33). Line 114 begins a `switch` statement that performs actions specific to each employee type, based on the value of `selection`. For example, lines 124–125 create a `SalariedEmployee` object, similar to lines 102–103 of Fig. 17.21.

(cont.)

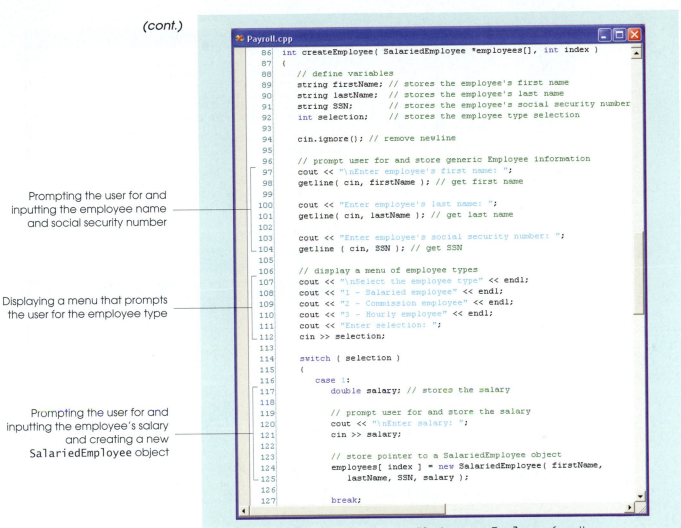

Prompting the user for and inputting the employee name and social security number

Displaying a menu that prompts the user for the employee type

Prompting the user for and inputting the employee's salary and creating a new `SalariedEmployee` object

Figure 17.33 Viewing the modified `createEmployee` function.

Insert lines 140–142 of Fig. 17.34 to the `createEmployee` function. The employee's first name, last name and social security number are stored in the `firstName`, `lastName` and `SSN` variables, respectively. The amount of merchandise in dollars that the commissioned worker sold is contained in the `sales` variable and the commission rate is contained in the `rate` variable. Lines 141–142 use the `new` operator to create an object of the `CommissionEmployee` type and assigns a pointer to that object to an element of the `employees` array. Because `employees` stores pointers to objects of the `Employee` type, and because the `CommissionEmployee` class is derived from `Employee`, the `CommissionEmployee` pointer returned by `new` is implicitly converted to an `Employee` pointer.

5. ***Adding an HourlyEmployee to the array.*** Insert lines 157–159 of Fig. 17.35 to the `createEmployee` function. For this employee, the number of hours worked is contained in `hours` and the hourly wage is contained in `hourlyWage`. Lines 158–159 use the `new` operator to create an object of the `HourlyEmployee` type and assign to an element of the `employees` array a pointer to that object. Similar to the code in lines 141–142 of Fig. 17.34, the `HourlyEmployee` pointer is implicitly converted to an `Employee` pointer. Note that this conversion is allowed because `employees` stores `Employee` pointers and an `HourlyEmployee` *is an* `Employee`.

(cont.)

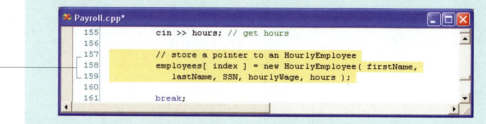

Creating a new `CommissionEmployee` object

Payroll.cpp*

```
      case 2:
         double sales;  // stores the total sales
         double rate; // stores the commission percentage

         // prompt user for and store the total sales and rate
         cout << "\nEnter sales: ";
         cin >> sales; // get total sales

         cout << "Enter commission rate (%): ";
         cin >> rate; // get rate

         // store a pointer to a CommissionEmployee
         employees[ index ] = new CommissionEmployee( firstName,
            lastName, SSN, sales, rate / 100 );

         break;
```

Figure 17.34 Creating a new `CommissionEmployee` object.

Creating a new `HourlyEmployee` object

Payroll.cpp*

```
         cin >> hours; // get hours

         // store a pointer to an HourlyEmployee
         employees[ index ] = new HourlyEmployee( firstName,
            lastName, SSN, hourlyWage, hours );

         break;
```

Figure 17.35 Creating a new `HourlyEmployee` object.

6. ***Modifying the `displayEmployees` function.*** Now that your derived classes use an `earnings` function to calculate and return the amount that each employee has earned, you need to modify the `displayEmployees` function. In lines 189 and 192, replace each `getWeeklySalary` function call with a call to the `earnings` function, as shown in Fig. 17.36. Also modify the comments as shown in lines 188 and 191.

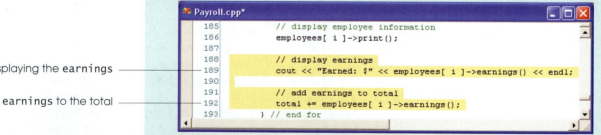

Displaying the `earnings`

Adding the `earnings` to the total

Payroll.cpp*

```
185          // display employee information
186          employees[ i ]->print();
187
188          // display earnings
189          cout << "Earned: $" << employees[ i ]->earnings() << endl;
190
191          // add earnings to total
192          total += employees[ i ]->earnings();
193       } // end for
```

Figure 17.36 Displaying information and wages for each `Employee`.

7. ***Save, compile and run the application.*** Figure 17.37 shows the application output when entering an hourly employee, and Fig. 17.38 shows the application output when entering a salaried employee. Enter similar employee data, then view the payroll. Notice that the application does not display the employee type nor does it display the correct earnings (Fig. 17.39). In fact, based on the output, the application must be using the `Employee` class's `print` and `earnings` functions. Because the `employees` array stores pointers to `Employee` objects, C++ uses the `print` and `earnings` functions defined in the `Employee` class when executing lines 186–192 of Fig. 17.36. This demonstrates that C++ is using the type of a pointer to an object, not the type of the object, to determine which function to call when a derived class redefines a base class function.

(cont.)

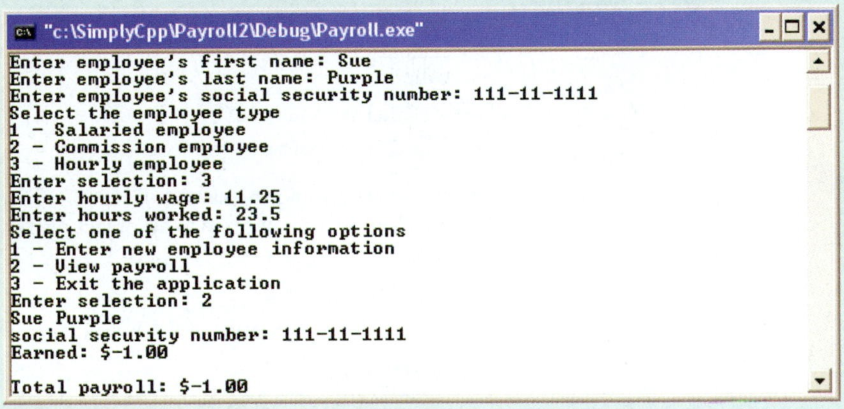

Figure 17.37 Entering hourly employee information in the **Payroll** application.

Entering earnings information for an hourly employee

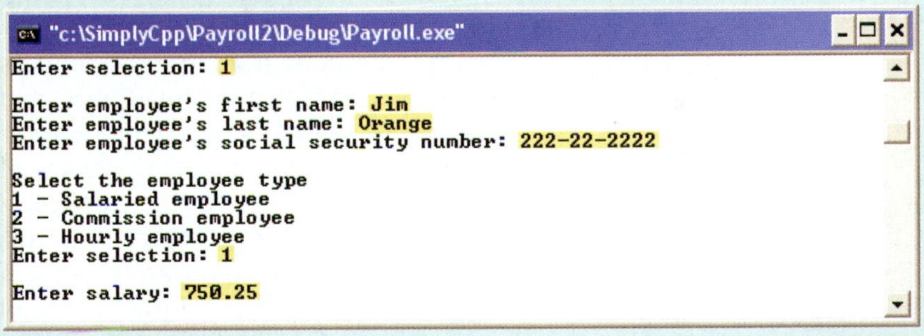

Figure 17.38 Entering salaried employee information in the **Payroll** application.

Entering earnings information for a salaried employee

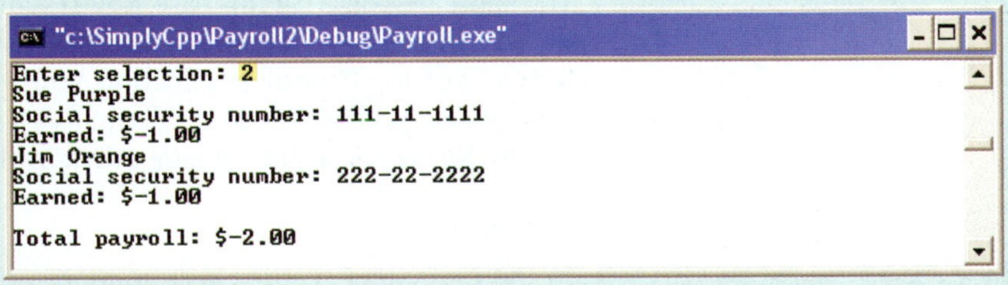

Figure 17.39 **Payroll** application displaying incorrect output.

Application does not display employee type and displays incorrect earnings information

Clearly, you would rather have C++ call the `earnings` and `print` functions defined in the derived class corresponding to each pointer to an Employee object stored in the `employees` array. For example, in Fig. 17.39, the application should use the version of `print` and `earnings` defined in HourlyEmployee. In the next section, you will modify your application so that C++ calls the `print` and `earnings` functions of the derived classes (such as SalariedEmployee, CommissionEmployee and HourlyEmployee) when using a pointer to an object of the base class (in this case, a pointer to an Employee object).

8. *Close the Command Prompt window.*

SELF-REVIEW

1. In this section, when the `earnings` function is called using a variable of the _____ type, the `earnings` function redefined in the `SalariedEmployee` class is called.

   a) `SalariedEmployee`
   b) `Employee *`
   c) `SalariedEmployee *`
   d) Both a and c.

2. In the inheritance hierarchy of Fig. 17.10, a pointer to an object of the _____ type can be assigned to a pointer to an object of the _____ type without causing a syntax error.

   a) `Shape`, `Circle`
   b) `Cube`, `ThreeDimensionalShape`
   c) `Triangle`, `Shape`
   d) Both b and c.

Answers: 1) d. 2) d.

17.6 Polymorphism

You will now continue your study of object-oriented programming by learning about polymorphism with inheritance hierarchies. With polymorphism, the same function call can be used to cause different actions to occur, depending on the type of the object on which the function is invoked.

As an example, suppose you design a video game that manipulates objects of many different types, including objects of the `Bird`, `Fish` and `Snake` classes. Also, imagine that each of these classes inherits from a common base class called `Animal`, which contains the `move` function. Each derived class inherits this function and overrides it with an appropriate implementation. Your video game application would maintain an array of pointers to objects of the various classes. To move the animals, the application would periodically send each object the same message—`move`. Each object responds to this message in a unique way. For example, a `Bird` *flies* across the sky. A `Fish` *swims* through a lake. A `Snake` *slithers* through the grass. The same message (in this case, `move`) sent to a variety of objects would have "many forms" of result—hence the term polymorphism, which means literally "many forms." For the **Payroll** application, you will modify your payroll system so that the same message (in this case, `earnings`) sent to a variety of objects would have "many forms" of result—again, polymorphism.

Virtual Functions

In the preceding section, you pointed a base-class `Employee` pointer at a derived-class `HourlyEmployee` object, then invoked the `print` member function through that pointer. Recall that the type of the pointer determined which class's functionality to invoke. In that case, the `Employee` pointer invoked `Employee` member function `print` on the `Employee`, despite the fact that the pointer was aimed at an `HourlyEmployee` that defined its own customized `print` function. When you use **virtual functions**, the type of the object being pointed to, not the type of the pointer, determines which version of a `virtual` function to invoke. Thus, `virtual` functions enable polymorphism.

First, let's consider why `virtual` functions are useful. Suppose a set of shape classes, such as `Circle`, `Rectangle` and `Square`, are all derived from the `Shape` base class. In object-oriented programming, each of these classes might be endowed with the ability to draw itself using the `draw` function. Although each class has its own `draw` function, the function for each shape is quite different. When drawing a shape, whatever that shape may be, it would be nice to be able to treat all these shapes generically as objects of the `Shape` base class. Then, to draw any shape, we could use a base-class `Shape` pointer to invoke the `draw` function and let the application determine **dynamically** (that is, at run time) which derived-class `draw` function to use, based on the type of the object to which the base-class `Shape` pointer points at any given time.

Good Programming Practice

Even though certain functions are implicitly `virtual` because of a declaration made higher in the class hierarchy, explicitly declare these functions `virtual` at every level of the hierarchy to promote program clarity.

Software Design Tip

Once a function is declared `virtual`, it remains `virtual` all the way down the inheritance hierarchy from that point, even if that function is not explicitly declared `virtual` when a class overrides it.

To enable this kind of behavior, declare `draw` in the base class as a `virtual` function, then **override** the `draw` function in each of the derived classes to draw the appropriate shape. From an implementation perspective, overriding a function is no different than redefining one (which is the approach you have been using until now). An overridden function in a derived class has the same signature as the function it overrides in its base class. If you do not declare the base-class function as `virtual`, you can redefine that function. By contrast, if you declare the base-class function as `virtual`, you can override that function. To declare a `virtual` function, precede the function's prototype with the **virtual keyword** in the base class. For example,

```
virtual void draw();
```

would appear in the `Shape` base class. The preceding prototype declares that the `draw` function is a `virtual` function that takes no arguments and returns nothing.

Abstract Classes

Many of today's computer systems provide a graphical interface containing items such as windows, icons and buttons. These systems typically use a screen manager application that displays each graphic on the screen. Suppose the screen manager uses the `Shape` class hierarchy in Fig. 17.10 to represent objects that it can display on the screen. Recall that the `Shape` class hierarchy contains two derived classes: `TwoDimensionalShape` and `ThreeDimensionalShape`. The next level of the hierarchy contains several specific two-dimensional shapes, such as `Circle`, `Square` or `Triangle` and three-dimensional shapes, such as `Sphere`, `Cube` and `Tetrahedron`. In this example, the purpose of the `Shape` class is to define basic shape attributes (for example, the shape's color). Objects of derived classes, such as `Circle` and `Cube`, inherit these basic attributes.

The screen manager should be able to send a message to a `Shape` telling it to draw itself on the screen. Thus, we might expect the `Shape` class to declare a `draw` member function that each derived class can inherit. Unfortunately, the `Shape` class does not know what to do when its `draw` function is called because it doesn't know *what* shape it is. Thus, you cannot define a `draw` function for the `Shape` class. Classes that are too generic to define real objects are called **abstract classes**; you need to be more specific before you can think of instantiating objects. In Tutorial 15, we discussed the notion of separating a class's interface from its implementation. An abstract class defines an interface without an implementation. Because abstract classes normally are used as base classes in inheritance hierarchies, we refer to such classes as **abstract base classes**. An inheritance hierarchy does not need to contain any abstract classes, but many good object-oriented systems have class hierarchies headed by abstract base classes. In some cases, abstract classes constitute several top levels of the hierarchy.

Classes that can be used to instantiate objects are called **concrete classes**. Such classes must provide implementations of every one of their member functions, defining the "missing pieces" in their abstract base classes. For example, we could derive such concrete classes as `Square`, `Circle` and `Triangle` from a `TwoDimensionalShape` abstract base class. Similarly, we could derive such concrete classes as `Cube`, `Sphere` and `Tetrahedron` from a `ThreeDimensionalShape` abstract base class. Concrete classes provide the specifics that make it reasonable to instantiate objects.

To define an abstract class, you must declare one or more of its `virtual` functions to be "pure." A **pure virtual function** is one with an initializer of = 0 in its declaration, as in

```
virtual void draw() = 0; // pure virtual function
```

Pure `virtual` functions do not provide implementations. Thus, the value 0 in the preceding statement serves as a null pointer, indicating that the `draw` function is

Common Programming Error

Attempting to instantiate an object of an abstract class causes a compilation error.

not defined. Every concrete derived class must override all base-class pure `virtual` functions and provide concrete implementations of those functions. The difference between a `virtual` function and a pure `virtual` function is that a `virtual` function has an implementation and gives the derived class the option of overriding the function, while pure `virtual` function does not provide an implementation and *requires* the derived class to override the function (for that derived class to be concrete). By declaring a pure `virtual draw` function in the Shape class, for example, you require every concrete derived class to provide a `draw` function.

Although we cannot instantiate objects of abstract base classes, we *can* use abstract base classes to declare pointers and references that can refer to objects of any concrete classes derived from these abstract classes. For example, consider the following code, which defines a pointer to a Shape object and points it at an object of a derived class—a `Circle` object

```
Shape *shapePointer = new Circle();
```

The next line of code contains the following statement, which calls the `draw` function

```
shapePointer->draw();
```

Because `draw` is a `virtual` function, C++ uses the type of the object to which `shapePointer` points, `Circle`, to call the `draw` function. The result of the preceding statement is that the `Circle` class's draw function is called. Similarly, if `shapePointer` pointed to a Cube object, the `Cube` object's draw function would be called. Programs typically use such pointers and references to manipulate such derived-class objects polymorphically.

Common Programming Error

Failure to override a pure `virtual` function in a derived class and then attempting to instantiate objects of that derived class is a compilation error.

SELF-REVIEW

1. Use the _____ keyword to enable derived-class functions to override a base-class function.

   a) `void`   b) `virtual`

   c) `new`   d) `override`

2. With _____, the same function call can be used to cause different actions to occur, depending on the type of the object on which the function is invoked.

   a) inheritance   b) dynamic memory management

   c) polymorphism   d) function redefining

   Answers: 1) b. 2) c.

17.7 Completing the Payroll Application

Now that you have learned how to create an abstract class, you will use the `virtual` keyword to enable your application to process Employee objects polymorphically. Because the Employee class does not contain wage information, you will declare the `earnings` function as a pure `virtual` function. As a result, the Employee abstract class will not define the `earnings` function (although any concrete derived classes must define this function). Any class that has one or more pure `virtual` functions is an abstract class.

***Declaring virtual
Functions***

1. ***Opening the Employee header file.*** Open the `Employee.h` file in your text editor or IDE.

2. ***Declaring functions as virtual.*** Modify lines 25–26 of `Employee.h` as shown in Fig. 17.40. Line 25 uses an initializer of = 0 to indicate that the `earnings` function is a pure `virtual` function and therefore not defined by the `Employee` class. Line 26 declares the `print` function as a `virtual` function. Because `print` is not a pure `virtual` function, the `Employee` class must define a `print` function, and derived classes are not required to override that function with their own versions of the `print` function. However, derived classes typically do override virtual functions to provide customized behavior. Add the `virtual` keyword before the `earnings` and `print` member function declarations in the `Salaried.h`, `Hourly.h` and `Commission.h` files. Although these functions are already `virtual` because they were declared `virtual` in the `Employee` base class, it is best to use the `virtual` keyword again in the derived classes to make your code more clear.

Declaring functions as `virtual` so that they can be overridden

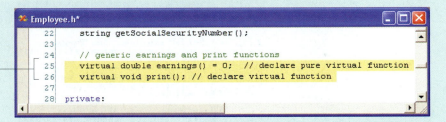

Figure 17.40   Declaring a `virtual` function and a pure `virtual` function in the `Employee` class.

3. ***Removing the Employee class's earnings function definition.*** Because you have defined the `earnings` function as a pure `virtual` function, you should remove the function definition from the `Employee.cpp` file. Open the `Employee.cpp` file and remove lines 71–76. This transforms the `Employee` class into an abstract class.

4. ***Updating the comments in the displayEmployees function.*** Now that the `print` and `earnings` functions operate polymorphically, you should update the comments in lines 185 and 188 in the `displayEmployee` function in the `Payroll.cpp` (Fig. 17.41).

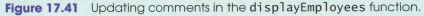

Figure 17.41   Updating comments in the `displayEmployees` function.

5. ***Save, compile and run the application.*** Figure 17.42 shows sample input for the **Payroll** application, and Fig. 17.43 shows the application output for all three employee types. Enter employee data for all three employee types, then view the payroll. Notice that the application correctly displays the employee types and earnings.

(cont.)

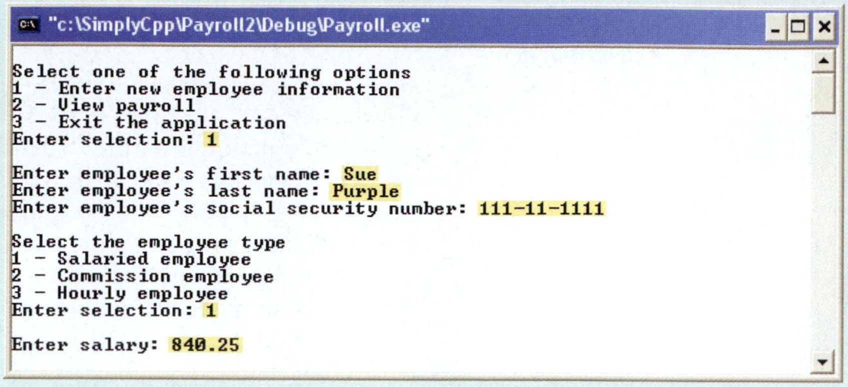

Figure 17.42 Entering employee information in the completed **Payroll** application.

Displaying employee type and correct earnings

Figure 17.43 **Payroll** application using `virtual` functions to access objects polymorphically.

6. *Close the Command Prompt window.*

The source code for the **Payroll** application is listed in Fig. 17.44–Fig. 17.52. The header file for the Employee abstract base class, which includes the print virtual function and the pure virtual earnings function, is listed in Fig. 17.44. Figure 17.45. contains the Employee.cpp file's source code, which provides the implementation for all the Employee class's functions except earnings. The header file for the SalariedEmployee class, which is derived from the Employee class, is listed in Fig. 17.46. Figure 17.47 contains the SalariedEmployee class implementation, which overrides the print and earnings functions inherited from its base class. The header file for the HourlyEmployee class, which also is derived from the Employee class, is listed in Fig. 17.48. Figure 17.49 contains the HourlyEmployee class implementation, which also overrides the print and earnings functions inherited from its base class. The header file for the CommissionEmployee class, which also is derived from the Employee class, is listed in Fig. 17.50. Figure 17.51 contains the CommissionEmployee class implementation, which also overrides the print and earnings functions inherited from its base class. Figure 17.52 lists the code in the file containing the **Payroll** application's main function. The lines of code that you added, viewed or modified in this tutorial are highlighted.

```
1   // Tutorial 17: Employee.h
2   // Employee abstract base class.
3   #ifndef EMPLOYEE_H
4   #define EMPLOYEE_H
5
6   #include <string> // required to access string functions
7
8   using namespace std; // for accessing C++ Standard Library members
9
10  class Employee {
11
12  public:
13     Employee( string &, string &, string & );
14
15     void setFirstName( string & );
16     string getFirstName();
17
18     void setLastName( string & );
19     string getLastName();
20
21     void setSocialSecurityNumber( string & );
22     string getSocialSecurityNumber();
23
24     // generic earnings and print functions
25     virtual double earnings() = 0; // declare pure virtual function
26     virtual void print(); // declare virtual function
27
28  private:
29     string firstName;
30     string lastName;
31     string socialSecurityNumber;
32
33  }; // end class Employee
34
35  #endif // EMPLOYEE_H
```

Declare functions as `virtual` so that they can be processed polymorphically

Figure 17.44   Completed **Employee** class header file.

```
1   // Tutorial 17: Employee.cpp
2   // Abstract-base-class Employee member-function definitions.
3   // Note: No definition is given for the pure virtual function.
4   #include <iostream> // required to perform C++-style stream I/O
5
6   using namespace std; // for accessing C++ Standard Library members
7
8   #include "Employee.h" // Employee class definition
9
10  // constructor
11  Employee::Employee( string &first, string &last,
12     string &SSN )
13     : firstName( first ),
14       lastName( last ),
15       socialSecurityNumber( SSN )
16  {
17     // empty body
18
19  } // end Employee constructor
20
```

Figure 17.45   Completed **Employee** class source code file. (Part 1 of 2.)

```cpp
21   // return first name
22   string Employee::getFirstName()
23   {
24      return firstName;
25
26   } // end function getFirstName
27
28   // return last name
29   string Employee::getLastName()
30   {
31      return lastName;
32
33   } // end function getLastName
34
35   // return social security number
36   string Employee::getSocialSecurityNumber()
37   {
38      return socialSecurityNumber;
39
40   } // end function getSocialSecurityNumber
41
42   // set first name
43   void Employee::setFirstName( string &first )
44   {
45      firstName = first;
46
47   } // end function setFirstName
48
49   // set last name
50   void Employee::setLastName( string &last )
51   {
52      lastName = last;
53
54   } // end function setLastName
55
56   // set social security number
57   void Employee::setSocialSecurityNumber( string &number )
58   {
59      socialSecurityNumber = number;   // should validate
60
61   } // end function setSocialSecurityNumber
62
63   // print Employee's information
64   void Employee::print()
65   {
66      cout << getFirstName() << ' ' << getLastName()
67          << "\nSocial security number: "
68          << getSocialSecurityNumber() << endl;
69
70   } // end function print
```

Figure 17.45 Completed **Employee** class source code file. (Part 2 of 2.)

```cpp
1    // Tutorial 17: Salaried.h
2    // SalariedEmployee class derived from Employee.
3    #ifndef SALARIED_H
4    #define SALARIED_H
5
```

Figure 17.46 Completed **SalariedEmployee** class header file. (Part 1 of 2.)

```
 6   #include "Employee.h" // Employee class definition
 7
 8   class SalariedEmployee : public Employee {
 9
10   public:
11      SalariedEmployee( string &, string &,
12         string &, double = 0.0 );
13
14      void setWeeklySalary( double );
15      double getWeeklySalary();
16
17      // member functions to be overridden
18      virtual double earnings();
19      virtual void print();
20
21   private:
22      double weeklySalary;
23
24   }; // end class SalariedEmployee
25
26   #endif // SALARIED_H
```

Overridden Virtual Functions ── (points to lines 18–19)

Figure 17.46 Completed `SalariedEmployee` class header file. (Part 2 of 2.)

```
 1   // Tutorial 17: Salaried.cpp
 2   // SalariedEmployee class member-function definitions.
 3   #include <iostream> // required to perform C++-style stream I/O
 4
 5   using namespace std; // for accessing C++ Standard Library members
 6
 7   #include "Salaried.h" // SalariedEmployee class definition
 8
 9   // SalariedEmployee constructor
10   SalariedEmployee::SalariedEmployee( string &first,
11      string &last, string &socialSecurityNumber,
12      double salary )
13      : Employee( first, last, socialSecurityNumber )
14   {
15      setWeeklySalary( salary );
16
17   } // end SalariedEmployee constructor
18
19   // set salaried worker's salary
20   void SalariedEmployee::setWeeklySalary( double salary )
21   {
22      // ensure a valid salary
23      if ( salary < 0.0 )
24      {
25         weeklySalary = 0.0;
26      } // end if
27      else
28      {
29         weeklySalary = salary;
30      } // end else
31
32   } // end function setWeeklySalary
33
```

Figure 17.47 Completed `SalariedEmployee` class source code file. (Part 1 of 2.)

```
34    // return salaried worker's salary
35    double SalariedEmployee::getWeeklySalary()
36    {
37       return weeklySalary;
38
39    } // end function getWeeklySalary
40
41    // calculate salaried worker's pay
42    double SalariedEmployee::earnings()
43    {
44       return getWeeklySalary();
45
46    } // end function earnings
47
48    // print salaried worker's name
49    void SalariedEmployee::print()
50    {
51       cout << "\nSalaried employee: "; // display employee type
52       Employee::print(); // call base-class print function
53
54    } // end function print
```

earnings function definition in the SalariedEmployee class — (lines 42–46)

print function definition in the SalariedEmployee class — (lines 49–54)

Figure 17.47 Completed SalariedEmployee class source code file. (Part 2 of 2.)

```
1     // Tutorial 17: Hourly.h
2     // HourlyEmployee class derived from Employee.
3     #ifndef HOURLY_H
4     #define HOURLY_H
5
6     #include "Employee.h"  // Employee class definition
7
8     class HourlyEmployee : public Employee {
9
10    public:
11       HourlyEmployee( string &, string &,
12          string &, double = 0.0, double = 0.0 );
13
14       void setWage( double );
15       double getWage();
16
17       void setHours( double );
18       double getHours();
19
20       // member functions to be overridden
21       virtual double earnings();
22       virtual void print();
23
24    private:
25       double wage;   // wage per hour
26       double hours;  // hours worked for week
27
28    }; // end class HourlyEmployee
29
30    #endif // HOURLY_H
```

Overridden virtual functions — (lines 21–22)

Figure 17.48 Completed HourlyEmployee class header file.

```
1    // Tutorial 17: Hourly.cpp
2    // HourlyEmployee class member-function definitions.
3    #include <iostream> // required to perform C++-style stream I/O
4
5    using namespace std; // for accessing C++ Standard Library members
6
7    #include "Hourly.h" // HourlyEmployee class definition
8
9    // constructor for class HourlyEmployee
10   HourlyEmployee::HourlyEmployee( string &first,
11      string &last, string &socialSecurityNumber,
12      double hourlyWage, double hoursWorked )
13      : Employee( first, last, socialSecurityNumber )
14   {
15      setWage( hourlyWage );
16      setHours( hoursWorked );
17
18   } // end HourlyEmployee constructor
19
20   // set hourly worker's wage
21   void HourlyEmployee::setWage( double wageAmount )
22   {
23      if ( wageAmount < 0 )
24      {
25         wage = 0.0;
26      } // end if
27      else
28      {
29         wage = wageAmount;
30      } // end else
31
32   } // end function setWage
33
34   // set hourly worker's hours worked
35   void HourlyEmployee::setHours( double hoursWorked )
36   {
37      // ensure that hoursWorked is less than hours in one week
38      if ( hoursWorked < 168.0 )
39      {
40         hours = hoursWorked;
41      } // end if
42      else
43      {
44         hours = 0.0;
45      } // end else
46
47   } // end function setHours
48
49   // return hours worked
50   double HourlyEmployee::getHours()
51   {
52      return hours;
53
54   } // end function getHours
55
56   // return wage
57   double HourlyEmployee::getWage()
58   {
```

Figure 17.49   Completed `HourlyEmployee` class source code file. (Part 1 of 2.)

```
59        return wage;
60
61   } // end function getWage
62
63   // get hourly worker's pay
64   double HourlyEmployee::earnings()
65   {
66      if ( hours <= 40 ) // no overtime
67      {
68         return wage * hours;
69      } // end if
70      else // overtime is paid at wage * 1.5
71      {
72         return 40 * wage + ( hours - 40 ) * wage * 1.5;
73      } // end else
74
75   } // end function earnings
76
77   // print hourly worker's information
78   void HourlyEmployee::print()
79   {
80      cout << "\nHourly employee: ";
81      Employee::print(); // call base-class print function
82
83   } // end function print
```

earnings function definition in the HourlyEmployee class

print function definition in the HourlyEmployee class

Figure 17.49   Completed **HourlyEmployee** class source code file. (Part 2 of 2.)

```
1    // Tutorial 17: Commission.h
2    // CommissionEmployee class derived from Employee.
3    #ifndef COMMISSION_H
4    #define COMMISSION_H
5
6    #include "Employee.h"  // Employee class definition
7
8    class CommissionEmployee : public Employee {
9
10   public:
11      CommissionEmployee( string &, string &,
12         string &, double = 0.0, double = 0.0 );
13
14      void setCommissionRate( double );
15      double getCommissionRate();
16
17      void setGrossSales( double );
18      double getGrossSales();
19
20      // member functions to be overridden
21      virtual double earnings();
22      virtual void print();
23
24   private:
25      double grossSales;      // gross weekly sales
26      double commissionRate;  // commission percentage
27
28   }; // end class CommissionEmployee
29
30   #endif  // COMMISSION_H
```

Overridden virtual functions

Figure 17.50   Completed **CommissionEmployee** class header file.

```cpp
1   // Tutorial 17: Commission.cpp
2   // CommissionEmployee class member-function definitions.
3   #include <iostream> // required to perform C++-style stream I/O
4
5   using namespace std; // for accessing C++ Standard Library members
6
7   #include "Commission.h"  // Commission class definition
8
9   // CommissionEmployee constructor
10  CommissionEmployee::CommissionEmployee( string &first,
11     string &last, string &socialSecurityNumber,
12     double grossWeeklySales, double percent )
13     : Employee( first, last, socialSecurityNumber )
14  {
15     setGrossSales( grossWeeklySales );
16     setCommissionRate( percent );
17
18  } // end CommissionEmployee constructor
19
20  // return commission worker's rate
21  double CommissionEmployee::getCommissionRate()
22  {
23      return commissionRate;
24
25  } // end function getCommissionRate
26
27  // return commission worker's gross sales amount
28  double CommissionEmployee::getGrossSales()
29  {
30      return grossSales;
31
32  } // end function getGrossSales
33
34  // set commission worker's weekly base salary
35  void CommissionEmployee::setGrossSales( double sales )
36  {
37     // ensure a valid sales value
38     if ( sales < 0.0 )
39     {
40        grossSales = 0.0;
41     } // end if
42     else
43     {
44        grossSales = sales;
45     } // end else
46
47  } // end function setGrossSales
48
49  // set commission worker's commission
50  void CommissionEmployee::setCommissionRate( double rate )
51  {
52     // ensure a valid commission rate
53     if ( rate > 0.0 && rate < 1.0 )
54     {
55        commissionRate = rate;
56     } // end if
57     else
58     {
```

Figure 17.51 Completed CommissionEmployee class source code file. (Part 1 of 2.)

```
59            commissionRate = 0.0;
60       } // end else
61
62   } // end function setCommissionRate
63
64   // calculate commission worker's earnings
65   double CommissionEmployee::earnings()
66   {
67       return getCommissionRate() * getGrossSales();
68
69   } // end function earnings
70
71   // print commission worker's name
72   void CommissionEmployee::print()
73   {
74       cout << "\nCommission employee: ";
75       Employee::print(); // call base-class print function
76
77   } // end function print
```

earnings function definition in the CommissionEmployee class — (lines 65–69)

print function definition in the CommissionEmployee class — (lines 72–75)

Figure 17.51 Completed CommissionEmployee class source code file. (Part 2 of 2.)

```
1    // Tutorial 17: Payroll.cpp
2    // Stores employee information and calculates payroll for
3    // employees of various types.
4    #include <iostream> // required to perform C++-style stream I/O
5    #include <iomanip>  // required for parameterized stream manipulators
6
7    using namespace std; // for accessing C++ Standard Library members
8
9    #include "Employee.h"    // Employee base class definition
10   #include "Salaried.h"    // SalariedEmployee class definition
11   #include "Commission.h"  // CommissionEmployee class definition
12   #include "Hourly.h"      // HourlyEmployee class definition
13
14   const int ARRAY_SIZE = 10;
15
16   // function prototypes
17   int createEmployee( Employee * [], int );
18   void displayEmployees(  Employee * [], int );
19
20   // function main begins program execution
21   int main()
22   {
23       int count = 0;      // stores the number of employees entered
24       int selection = 0; // stores the user's menu selection
25
26       // format output as currency
27       cout << fixed << setprecision( 2 );
28
29       // create an array of Employee pointers
30       Employee *employees[ ARRAY_SIZE ];
31
32       while ( selection != 3 )
33       {
34           cout << "\nSelect one of the following options" << endl;
35           cout << "1 - Enter new employee information" << endl;
36           cout << "2 - View payroll" << endl;
```

Including header files for classes derived from Employee — (lines 10–12)

Function prototypes declaring parameters using an array of Employee pointers — (lines 17–18)

Array of pointers to Employees that enables the application to process employees polymorphically — (line 30)

Figure 17.52 Completed Payroll application source file. (Part 1 of 4.)

```
37              cout << "3 - Exit the application" << endl;
38              cout << "Enter selection: ";
39              cin >> selection;
40
41              switch ( selection )
42              {
43                 // enter employee information
44                 case 1:
45                    // ensure that there is space in the array
46                    if ( count < ARRAY_SIZE )
47                    {
48                       count += createEmployee( employees, count );
49                    } // end if
50                    else
51                    {
52                       cout << "Error: You cannot enter any more employees."
53                          << endl;
54                    } // end else
55
56                    break;
57
58                 // view payroll
59                 case 2:
60                    displayEmployees( employees, count );
61
62                    break;
63
64                 // exit
65                 case 3:
66
67                    break;
68
69                 default:
70                    cout << "Error: Enter a valid menu selection";
71
72              } // end switch
73
74           } // end while
75
76           // delete each employee
77           for ( int i = 0; i < count; i++ )
78           {
79              delete employees[ i ];
80           } // end for
81
82           return 0; // indicate that program ended successfully
83
84        } // end function main
85
86        int createEmployee( Employee *employees[], int index )
87        {
88           // define variables
89           string firstName; // stores the employee's first name
90           string lastName;  // stores the employee's last name
91           string SSN;       // stores the employee's social security number
92           int selection;    // stores the employee type selection
93
94           cin.ignore(); // remove newline
```

Use **delete** to destroy each object referenced by a pointer in the **employees** array

Figure 17.52 Completed **Payroll** application source file. (Part 2 of 4.)

```
95
96          // prompt user for and store generic Employee information
97          cout << "\nEnter employee's first name: ";
98          getline( cin, firstName ); // get first name
99
100         cout << "Enter employee's last name: ";
101         getline( cin, lastName ); // get last name
102
103         cout << "Enter employee's social security number: ";
104         getline ( cin, SSN ); // get SSN
105
106         // display a menu of employee types
107         cout << "\nSelect the employee type" << endl;
108         cout << "1 - Salaried employee" << endl;
109         cout << "2 - Commission employee" << endl;
110         cout << "3 - Hourly employee" << endl;
111         cout << "Enter selection: ";
112         cin >> selection;
113
114      switch ( selection )
115      {
116         case 1:
117            double salary; // stores the salary
118
119            // prompt user for and store the salary
120            cout << "\nEnter salary: ";
121            cin >> salary;
122
123            // store a pointer to a SalariedEmployee object
124            employees[ index ] = new SalariedEmployee( firstName,
125               lastName, SSN, salary );
126
127            break;
128
129         case 2:
130            double sales;  // stores the total sales
131            double rate; // stores the commission percentage
132
133            // prompt user for and store the total sales and rate
134            cout << "\nEnter sales: ";
135            cin >> sales; // get total sales
136
137            cout << "Enter commission rate (%): ";
138            cin >> rate; // get rate
139
140            // store a pointer to a CommissionEmployee object
141            employees[ index ] = new CommissionEmployee( firstName,
142               lastName, SSN, sales, rate / 100 );
143
144            break;
145
146         case 3:
147            double hourlyWage;  // stores the hourly wage
148            double hours;       // stores the hours worked
149
150            // prompt user for and store the hourly wage and total hours
151            cout << "\nEnter hourly wage: ";
152            cin >> hourlyWage; // get hourly wage
```

Figure 17.52   Completed **Payroll** application source file. (Part 3 of 4.)

```
153
154          cout << "Enter hours worked: ";
155          cin >> hours; // get hours
156
157          // store a pointer to an HourlyEmployee object
158          employees[ index ] = new HourlyEmployee( firstName,
159             lastName, SSN, hourlyWage, hours );
160
161          break;
162
163       default:
164          cout << "Error: You must select a valid employee type."
165             << endl;
166
167          return 0;
168
169    } // end switch
170
171    return 1;
172
173 } // end function createEmployee
174
175 void displayEmployees( Employee *employees[], int count )
176 {
177    double total = 0.0; // stores the total payroll
178
179    // ensure that employees have been entered before printing
180    if ( count > 0 )
181    {
182       // display each employee
183       for ( int i = 0; i < count; i++ )
184       {
185          // display employee information polymorphically
186          employees[ i ]->print();
187
188          // display earnings polymorphically
189          cout << "Earned: $" << employees[ i ]->earnings() << endl;
190
191          // add earnings to total
192          total += employees[ i ]->earnings();
193       } // end for
194
195       cout << "\nTotal payroll: $" << total << endl;
196
197    } // end if
198    else
199    {
200       cout << "Error: You must enter at least one employee first."
201          << endl;
202    } // end else
203
204 } // end function displayEmployees
```

Use **new** to create a new
`HourlyEmployee` object and
store a pointer to it in the
`employees` array

Display each employee's name
and type using polymorphism

Process each object derived from
`Employee` polymorphically; the
overridden **earnings** function
defined by each subclass is called

Add earnings to total

Display total earnings

Figure 17.52 Completed **Payroll** application source file. (Part 4 of 4.)

SELF-REVIEW   1. An abstract class must contain _____.

   a) at least one data member   b) the abstract keyword

   c) at least one pure virtual function   d) All of the above.

2. The _____ keyword enables polymorphism.

a) `abstract`   b) `void`

c) `inherit`   d) `virtual`

Answers: 1) c. 2) d.

17.8 Wrap-Up

In this tutorial, you learned about inheritance and polymorphism. You learned about the relationships among base classes and derived classes within a class hierarchy. You also learned how a derived class can redefine functions provided by a base class.

You then learned how polymorphism enables the same function call to be used to cause different actions to occur, depending on the type of the object on which the function is invoked. You enabled polymorphism in your application by declaring `virtual` functions in a base class and overriding them in derived classes. You also learned that abstract classes are incomplete classes that provide a description for a category of objects, but cannot be used to instantiate objects directly. Only concrete classes, which provide implementations for each of their functions, can be used to instantiate objects directly. You learned how to create an abstract class by declaring at least one of its functions as pure `virtual`, meaning that the class provides no implementation for that function.

You used inheritance and polymorphism in the **Payroll** application. While building the **Payroll** application, you used an inheritance hierarchy consisting of the `Employee` base class and the `SalariedEmployee`, `CommissionEmployee` and `HourlyEmployee` derived classes. You created these classes by inheriting from the `Employee` class and adding earnings information to implement the pure `virtual` `earnings` function declared in the `Employee` class. You also handled objects of the three derived classes polymorphically—by treating them as objects of the `Employee` base class.

In the next tutorial, you will learn how sets of related data are represented in a computer. You will be introduced to the concepts of files and streams, and you will learn how to store data in sequential-access files.

SKILLS SUMMARY   **Accessing Base-Class Functions from a Derived-Class Object**

- Prefix the function name with the class name, followed by the binary scope resolution operator (`::`), such as `Employee::print()`.

Calling a Base-Class Constructor

- Use the base class name, followed by a set of parentheses containing the base-class constructor arguments. In a constructor for a derived class, the base-class initializer appears between the constructor's parameter list and the left brace that begins the constructor's body. For example,

```
SalariedEmployee::SalariedEmployee( string &firstName,
    string &lastName, string &SSN, double weeklySalary ) :
    Employee( firstName, lastName, SSN )
```

declares a `SalariedEmployee` class constructor that calls its base-class constructor, `Employee`.

Creating a Derived Class from an Existing Class

- In the class definition, follow the class name with a colon, the `public` keyword and the name of the direct base class. For example, in this tutorial, the `SalariedEmployee` class is derived from the `Employee` class with the notation

```
class Salaried Employee : public Employee
```

Declaring a `virtual` Function

■ In a class definition, precede the function return type with the `virtual` keyword. For example, the code

```
virtual void print();
```

declares a `virtual` function named `print` that returns no value and accepts no arguments.

Redefining or Overriding a Base-Class Function

■ Use the same function header in the derived class to redefine the base-class function. If the base-class function is declared `virtual`, the function in the derived class will override the base-class function.

Declaring a Pure `virtual` Function

■ In a class definition, precede the function return type with the `virtual` keyword. Between the closing parenthesis for the function's argument list and the semicolon at the end of the statement, insert the code = 0. For example, the code

```
virtual void earnings() = 0;
```

declares a pure `virtual` function named `earnings` that returns no value and accepts no arguments. The class containing a pure `virtual` function is an abstract class and cannot provide an implementation for that function.

Creating an Abstract Class

■ In a class definition, declare at least one pure `virtual` function. Objects cannot be instantiated directly from an abstract class.

Enabling Polymorphism

■ In your class's inheritance hierarchy, declare at least one `virtual` function in a base class. Objects of a derived class are treated polymorphically by overriding a `virtual` function declared in a base class.

KEY TERMS

abstract class—A class that cannot be used to instantiate objects. It is often called an abstract base class because it is usable only as a base class in an inheritance hierarchy. These classes are incomplete; they are missing pieces necessary for instantiation that concrete derived classes must implement. The missing pieces are pure `virtual` functions.

base class—A class that is extended by another class to form a derived class. The derived class inherits from the base class.

base-class initializer syntax—A technique for initializing a base class's `private` data members from a derived-class constructor. A base-class initializer is formed using the base-class name, followed by a set of parentheses containing the base-class constructor arguments. In a constructor for a derived class, the base-class initializer appears between the constructor's parameter list and the left brace that begins the constructor's body. The base-class initializer is separated from the parameter list with a colon. For example,

```
SalariedEmployee::SalariedEmployee( string &firstName,
    string &lastName, string &SSN, double weeklySalary ) :
    Employee( firstName, lastName, SSN )
```

declares a `SalariedEmployee` class constructor that calls its base-class constructor, `Employee`.

class hierarchy—A definition of the inheritance relationships among classes. It is also known as an inheritance hierarchy.

concrete class—A class that can be used to instantiate objects.

derived class—A class that is derived from (inherits from) another class (called a base class).

direct base class—The base class from which the derived class inherits.

indirect base class—A base class that is two or more levels up in the class hierarchy from a derived class.

inheritance—A form of software reuse in which a class absorbs an existing class's data members (attributes) and member functions (behaviors) and extends them with new or modified capabilities.

inheritance hierarchy—The inheritance relationships among classes. It is also known as a class hierarchy.

***is a* relationship**—A relationship in which an object of a derived class also can be treated as an object of its base class.

member initializer—A set of values that is used to initialize a class's data members. Member initializers appear between a member function's parameter list and the left brace that begins the member function's body. For example, in the constructor header

```
SalariedEmployee::SalariedEmployee( string &firstName,
    string &lastName, string &SSN, double weeklySalary ) :
    Employee( firstName, lastName, SSN )
```

the expression `Employee( firstName, lastName, SSN )` calls the base-class constructor, passing the `firstName`, `lastName` and `SSN` arguments to the `SalariedEmployee` constructor.

override—Supersede a base-class `virtual` function with a new implementation defined in the derived class.

polymorphism—A concept that allows you to write applications that handle in a more general manner objects of a wide variety of classes related by inheritance.

pure `virtual` function—A member function that is declared but not defined. A pure `virtual` function uses an initializer of `= 0` (representing a NULL pointer) in its declaration. Any class with a pure `virtual` function is an abstract class. For example, the code

```
virtual void earnings() = 0;
```

declares a pure `virtual` function named `earnings` that returns no value and accepts no arguments.

redefine—Supersede a base-class function that is non-`virtual` with a new implementation defined in the derived class.

virtual function—A function that can be overridden by a derived class. A function is made virtual by preceding its return type with the `virtual` keyword.

virtual keyword—A keyword that declares that a function can be overridden by a derived class. If the function is a pure `virtual` function, it *must* be overridden by a concrete derived class.

MULTIPLE-CHOICE QUESTIONS

17.1 Polymorphism involves using a pointer or reference to an object of a _____ type to invoke functions on base class and derived-class objects.

a) primitive   b) base class
c) derived class   d) None of the above.

17.2 A pure `virtual` function is declared by _____.

a) using an initializer of = 0   b) by setting default arguments of 0
c) preceding the function name with the `virtual` keyword   d) Both a and c.

17.3 A member initializer _____.

a) is separated from a constructor's parameter list with a colon
b) processes objects polymorphically
c) can be used to initialize a class's data members
d) Both a and c.

17.4 If the `Truck` class is derived from the `Vehicle` class, the `Truck` class is called the _____, and the `Vehicle` class is called the _____.

a) base class, derived class   b) derived class, base class
c) base class, direct base class   d) direct base class, base class

17.5 When a derived class overrides its base class's function, _____.

a) the base class's function has the same header as the derived class's function

b) the base class's function is superseded by the derived class's function in the derived class

c) the base-class function is preceded by the virtual keyword in the class definition

d) All of the above.

17.6 Because of polymorphism, using the same _____ can cause different actions to occur depending on the type of the object on which a function is invoked.

a) function return type

b) instance variable

c) local variable

d) function call

17.7 In a(n) _____ relationship, an object of a derived class also can be treated as an object of its base class.

a) "is a"

b) "like a"

c) "has a"

d) None of the above.

17.8 If MyTruck is derived from MyVehicle, _____.

a) a pointer to a MyTruck object can be assigned to a pointer variable of the MyVehicle type

b) a pointer to a MyVehicle object can be assigned to a pointer variable of the MyTruck type

c) pointers to objects of either class cannot be assigned to pointers to objects of the opposite class

d) Both a and b.

17.9 A class hierarchy _____.

a) enables polymorphism

b) contains base classes and derived classes

c) defines the inheritance relationship among classes

d) Both b and c.

17.10 Polymorphism allows you to program _____.

a) "in the concrete"

b) "in the general"

c) "in the specific"

d) "in the virtual"

EXERCISES

17.11 (*Enhanced Payroll Application*) The company that requested the **Payroll** application that you created in this tutorial was so impressed with the final product that they want to use the application to calculate the payroll for an additional category of employees. Modify the **Payroll** application so that it accepts input and displays output for a piece worker. A piece worker is paid a fixed amount of money per item produced. When inputting information for a piece worker, the application should prompt the user for the number of items produced and the amount that the worker is paid per item. When displaying the earnings for a piece worker, the application should display the product of those two values. The completed application should appear as in Fig. 17.53.

a) *Copying the template to your working directory.* Copy the C:\Examples\ Tutorial17\Exercises\EnhancedPayroll directory to your C:\SimplyCpp directory.

b) *Opening the PieceWorker template header file.* Open the template file Piece-Worker.h in your text editor or IDE.

c) *Beginning the PieceWorker class definition.* Beginning in line 8, define the Piece-Worker class, which should be derived from the Employee class. In line 10, include the public: member-access specifier, which will declare your class's member functions as public. In lines 11–12, declare a PieceWorker constructor that accepts three references to strings, followed by an int and a double value. The int and double parameters should have default values of 0.

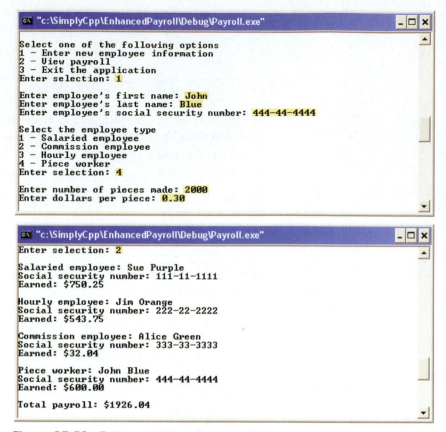

Figure 17.53 Enhanced **Payroll** application.

d) *Completing the PieceWorker class definition.* Your `PieceWorker` class will contain two data members—an `int` to store the number of items produced and a `double` to store the dollars earned per item. After the constructor, declare *get* and *set* functions for these values. The names of the functions should be `getPieces`, `setPieces`, `getValuePerPiece` and `setValuePerPiece`. Also, declare the `earnings` and `print` functions that will override the corresponding functions declared in the `Employee` class. Finally, use the `private:` member-access specifier to define `int` data member `pieces` (which will contain the number of items produced) and `double` data member `valuePerPiece` (which will contain the dollars earned per item produced).

e) *Opening the PieceWorker template source code file.* Open the template file `Piece-Worker.cpp` in your text editor or IDE.

f) *Defining the PieceWorker member functions.* Beginning in line 9, define the `Piece-Worker` member functions. In the constructor, use base-class initializer syntax to initialize the `PieceWorker` class's inherited data members. Then, use the *set* functions that you declared in the header file to set the values of the `PieceWorker` class's data members. After completing the constructor, define the *get* and *set* functions for the class. To ensure that the `PieceWorker` object is in a consistent state, assign 0 to a data member if the value passed to its set functions is less than zero. The `print` function should display the text "Piece worker: " on a new line, then call the `Employee` class's `print` function. Finally, the `earnings` function should return the product of `pieces` and `valuePerPiece`, using the appropriate *get* functions.

g) *Opening the Payroll template source code file.* Open the template file `Payroll.cpp` in your text editor or IDE.

h) *Enabling users to enter piece worker information.* To access the `PieceWorker` class, insert an `include` directive in line 13 to include the `PieceWorker.h` file. Next, modify the menu that begins at line 108 so that it presents the option to enter piece worker information, as shown in Fig. 17.53. If the user enters 4 at the **Enter selection:** prompt, the application should prompt the user for information regarding the piece worker, then create and store a pointer to a `PieceWorker` object. Beginning in line 165, insert a case 4: label, followed by statements that prompt the user for and store the number of items made and the dollars earned per item. Then, insert a statement that uses the new operator to create a new PieceWorker object. The pointer returned by the new operator should be stored in employees[index]. Remember to include a break statement after creating the PieceWorker object.

i) *Save, compile and run the completed application.* Test your application to ensure that it runs correctly by entering piece worker employee information. Then view the payroll to ensure that earnings are calculated and displayed properly.

j) *Close the Command Prompt window.*

17.12 (*Area Calculator Application*) A surveyor must calculate the area contained within plots of land by measuring the length of each border. The surveyor most commonly measures plots of land that are triangles and rectangles. Create an application that accepts the lengths of the sides of a triangle or rectangle, then calculates the area (Fig. 17.54). In this exercise, most of the functionality has been provided for you. You will use polymorphism to declare and override a function that will calculate the area for each shape.

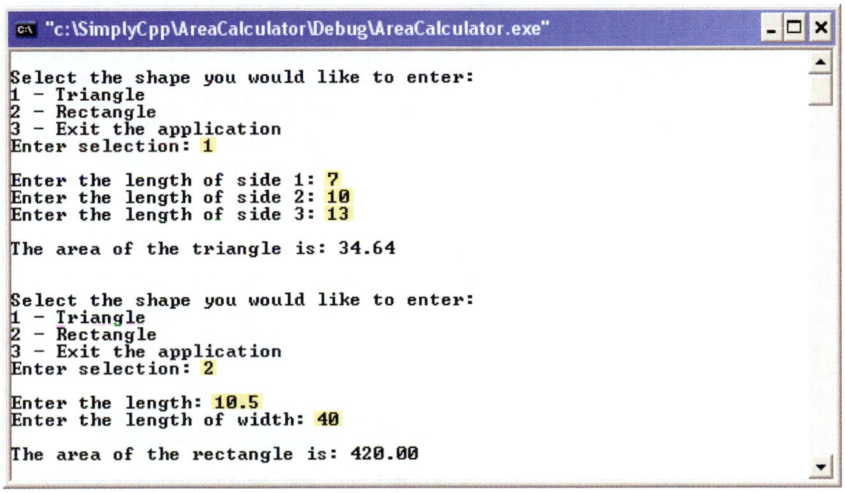

Figure 17.54 Area Calculator application.

a) *Copying the template to your working directory.* Copy the C:\Examples\ Tutorial17\Exercises\AreaCalculator directory to your C:\SimplyCpp directory. The template directory contains header files and source code for the TwoDimensionalShape base class and the Triangle and Rectangle classes, which are derived from TwoDimensionalShape. The directory also contains the AreaCalculator.cpp file, which contains the application's main function.

b) *Opening the TwoDimensionalShape.h template header file.* Open the template header file TwoDimensionalShape.h in your text editor or IDE.

c) *Declaring a pure virtual function.* Starting in line 18, declare a pure virtual function named area that specifies zero parameters and returns a double. In the following steps, you will override this function.

d) *Opening the Triangle.h template header file.* Open the template header file Triangle.h in your text editor or IDE.

e) *Overriding the area function.* Declare a public area function in the Triangle class definition. Then open the template source code file Triangle.cpp. Beginning in line 82, define the area function. Use the class's *get* functions to retrieve the values required by the following triangle area formula

$$A = \sqrt{s(s-x)(s-y)(s-z)},$$

where A is the area, x, y and z are the lengths of the three sides and s is

$$\frac{x+y+z}{2}.$$

f) *Opening the Rectangle.h template header file.* Open the template header file Rectangle.h in your text editor or IDE.

g) *Overriding the area function.* Declare a public area function in the Rectangle class definition. Then, open the template source code file Rectangle.cpp. Beginning in line 60, define the area function. For a rectangle, the area is simply the product of the length and the width. Use the class's *get* functions to retrieve the requisite values.

h) *Calculating the displaying the area.* Open the template source code file AreaCalculator.cpp. Line 21 declares a pointer to a TwoDimensionalShape object named shape. Lines 23–79 prompt the user for and store the selected shape's side lengths in an object from a class that is derived from TwoDimensionalShape. The pointer to this object is stored in shape. If the input is invalid, shape is assigned a null pointer. To complete the application, you must add code that displays the name of the shape and the area, as shown in Fig. 17.54. Just after the switch statement and just before the end of the while statement, insert an if statement that checks shape and displays the name of the shape that the user entered (using the base-class function getName) and the area contained in the shape (using the area function that you overrode) if shape is not null.

i) *Save, compile and run the completed application.* Test your application to ensure that it runs correctly by entering various lengths for the sides of the triangle or rectangle (make sure that no side of a triangle is longer than the sum of the other two sides). Ensure that your application displays the correct shape name and area contained inside the shape.

j) *Close the Command Prompt window.*

17.13 (*Payroll Application with Salary Survey*) The company that requested the **Payroll** application has requested a feature that displays a salary survey (Fig. 17.55). Modify the **Payroll** application so that it allows the user to select a menu option to display a salary survey. Then add the functionality to display the table listing the number of salaries in each salary range.

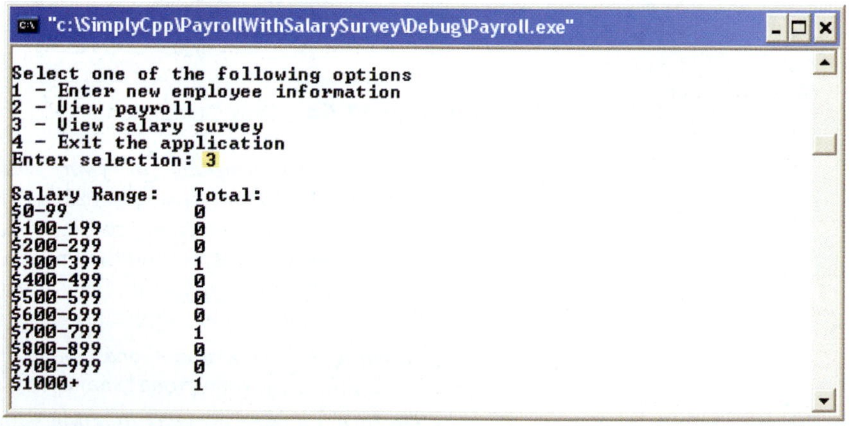

Figure 17.55 **Payroll** application with a salary survey feature.

a) *Copying the template to your working directory.* Copy the C:\Examples\Tutorial17\Exercises\PayrollWithSalarySurvey directory to your C:\SimplyCpp directory.

b) *Opening the Payroll.cpp template source code file.* Open the file Payroll.cpp in your text editor or IDE.

c) *Adding a function prototype.* In line 19, insert a prototype for the displaySurvey function, which should specify an array of pointers to Employee objects and an int as parameters, and return no value.

d) *Modifying the main function.* To enable the salary survey feature, you will need to add another option to the menu that begins in line 35. As a result, the value that the user will enter to exit the application will be 4 instead of 3. Modify line 33 so that the while statement repeats until selection contains 4. Then modify the menu in lines 35–39 so that it appears as shown in Fig. 17.55. In line 67, modify the case 3: label so that it reads case 4:, corresponding to the new value for the exiting the application. Immediately above the case 4: label, insert a case 3: label. After the case 3: label, call displaySurvey, passing to the function employees and count as arguments. Then, insert a break statement.

e) ***Defining the displaySurvey function.*** Beginning in line 215, define the display-Survey function. Assign the name employees to the parameter that is an array of pointers to Employees and assign the name maximumIndex to the int parameter. Then, define local int variables lowerBound and upperBound, which will store the lower bound and upper bound, respectively, for each salary range. Next, define the int array printArray as an array of 11 elements and initialize its values to 0.

f) ***Counting salaries the displaySurvey function.*** After the variable definitions, insert a for statement that initializes the counter variable to zero, increments the counter by one after each iteration and repeats while the counter is less than maximumIndex. You will use this counter as the index into the employees array to access the each employee. Inside the for statement, insert statements that divide the current employee's earnings by 100, then store the result as an int in a variable index, defined inside the for statement. Use an if...else statement to increment the appropriate element of printArray. If index is greater than or equal to 10, increment printArray[10]. Otherwise, increment printArray[index].

g) ***Completing the displaySurvey function.*** After the for statement you wrote in *Step f*, display a table header as shown in Fig. 17.55. Then, insert another for statement that displays the salary range in the first column of a table and the number of salaries in that range in the next column of the table. Display the table using the same techniques that you learned while building the **Salary Survey** application in Tutorial 13.

h) ***Save, compile and run the completed application.*** Test your application to ensure that it runs correctly by entering information for several employees. Ensure that your application displays the correct number of employees in each salary range when you select the View salary survey option.

i) ***Close the Command Prompt window.***

What does this code do? ▶

17.14 Assume that this code uses the source code for your completed **Payroll** application. What does this code do?

```
1   // Exercise 17.14: WDTCD.cpp
2   #include <iostream> // required to perform C++-style stream I/O
3   #include <iomanip>  // required for parameterized stream manipulators
4
5   using namespace std; // for accessing C++ Standard Library members
6
7   #include "Employee.h" // Employee base class definition
8   #include "Hourly.h" // HourlyEmployee class definition
9
10  const int ARRAY_SIZE = 5;
11
12  // function prototype
13  void mystery( string [], string [], string [], double [], double [],
14     const int );
15
16  // function main begins program execution
17  int main()
18  {
19     // define variables
20     string firstNames[ ARRAY_SIZE ]; // first names
21     string lastNames[ ARRAY_SIZE ];  // last names
22     string SSNs[ ARRAY_SIZE ];       // social security numbers
23     double hourlyWages[ ARRAY_SIZE ];    // wages
24     double hours[ ARRAY_SIZE ];      // hours worked
```

```
25
26        // format output as currency
27        cout << fixed << setprecision( 2 );
28
29        // enter employee information
30        for ( int count = 0; count < ARRAY_SIZE; count++ )
31        {
32           // prompt user for and input generic Employee information
33           cout << "\nEnter employee " << count + 1 << "'s first name: ";
34           getline( cin, firstNames[ count ] ); // get first name
35
36           cout << "Enter employee " << count + 1 << "'s last name: ";
37           getline( cin, lastNames[ count ] ); // get last name
38
39           cout << "Enter employee " << count + 1 << "'s SSN: ";
40           getline ( cin, SSNs[ count ] ); // get SSN
41
42           // prompt user for and input the hourly wage and total hours
43           cout << "Enter employee " << count + 1 << "'s hourly wage: ";
44           cin >> hourlyWages[ count ]; // get hourly wage
45
46           cout << "Enter employee " << count + 1 << "'s hours worked: ";
47           cin >> hours[ count ]; // get hours
48
49           cin.ignore(); // remove newline
50
51        } // end for
52
53        mystery( firstNames, lastNames, SSNs, hourlyWages, hours,
54           ARRAY_SIZE );
55
56        cout << endl;
57
58        return 0; // indicate that program ended successfully
59
60     } // end function main
61
62     void mystery( string firstNames[], string lastNames[], string SSNs[],
63        double wages[], double hours[], const int ARRAY_SIZE )
64     {
65        HourlyEmployee *currentEmployee;
66
67        for ( int i = 0; i < ARRAY_SIZE; i++ )
68        {
69           currentEmployee = new HourlyEmployee( firstNames[ i ],
70              lastNames[ i ], SSNs[ i ], wages[ i ], hours[ i ] );
71
72           currentEmployee->print();
73           cout << "Earned: " << currentEmployee->earnings() << endl;
74
75           delete currentEmployee;
76        } // end for
77
78     } // end function mystery
```

What's wrong with this code? ▶   **17.15** Find the error(s) in the following code. Assume that this code file uses the code from your completed **Payroll** application

```cpp
1   // Tutorial 17: Payroll.cpp
2   // Stores employee information and calculates payroll for
3   // employees of various types.
4   #include <iostream> // required to perform C++-style stream I/O
5   #include <iomanip>  // required for parameterized stream manipulators
6
7   using namespace std; // for accessing C++ Standard Library members
8
9   #include "Employee.h" // Employee base class definition
10  #include "Salaried.h" // SalariedEmployee class definition
11
12  // function prototype
13  void createEmployee( string &, string &, string &, double );
14
15  // function main begins program execution
16  int main()
17  {
18     // define variables
19     string firstName; // first name
20     string lastName;  // last name
21     string SSN;       // social security number
22     double salary; // salary
23
24     // format output as currency
25     cout << fixed << setprecision( 2 );
26
27     // prompt user for and input generic Employee information
28     cout << "\nEnter employee's first name: ";
29     getline( cin, firstName ); // get first name
30
31     cout << "Enter employee's last name: ";
32     getline( cin, lastName ); // get last name
33
34     cout << "Enter employee's social security number: ";
35     getline ( cin, SSN ); // get SSN
36
37     // prompt user for and input the salary
38     cout << "Enter salary: ";
39     cin >> salary;
40
41     createEmployee( firstName, lastName, SSN, salary );
42
43     cout << endl << endl;
44
45     return 0; // indicate that program ended successfully
46
47  } // end function main
48
49  // create and display a SalariedEmployee
50  void createEmployee( string &firstName, string &lastName, string
51     &SSN, double salary )
52  {
53     Employee temporary = new Employee( firstName, lastName, SSN );
54
55     SalariedEmployee *salaried = temporary;
56
```

```
57          salaried->setWeeklySalary( salary );
58
59          salaried->print();
60          cout << "Earned: " << salaried->earnings();
61
62    } // end function createEmployee
```

Programming Challenge ▶ **17.16** (*Enhanced Area Calculator Application*) After using the **Area Calculator** application that you built in Exercise 17.12, the surveyor requested that you modify the application to include another common shape—the trapezoid. Enhance the **Area Calculator** application so that it can accept input for the lengths of the sides of a trapezoid and display the area of that trapezoid (Fig. 17.56).

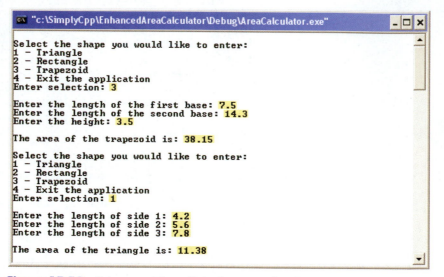

Figure 17.56 Enhanced **Area Calculator** application.

a) *Copying your completed Area Calculator application to your working directory.* Copy the directory C:\Examples\Tutorial17\Exercises\EnhancedAreaCalculator directory to your C:\SimplyCpp directory. Then, copy the files from your completed **Area Calculator** application (Exercise 17.12), located in C:\SimplyCpp\AreaCalculator, to your C:\SimplyCpp\EnhancedAreaCalculator directory.

b) *Opening the Trapezoid.h template header file.* Open the template header file Trapezoid.h in your text editor or IDE.

c) *Defining the Trapezoid class.* Beginning in 8, define the Trapezoid class, which is derived from the TwoDimensionalShape class. The surveyor will specify the length of the trapezoid's two bases and the height of the trapezoid. Declare a constructor that accepts three doubles, with default values of 0.0. Then define three sets of public *get* and *set* functions to retrieve and store the trapezoid's two base lengths and its height. Next, include a function declaration that overrides the area function declared in TwoDimensionalShape.h. Finally, define private double data members base1, base2 and height to store the trapezoid's two base lengths and its height, respectively.

d) *Defining the Trapezoid member function.* Open the template source code file Trapezoid.cpp in your text editor or IDE. Beginning in line 8, define the Trapezoid member functions. In the constructor, use base-class initializer syntax to initialize the Trapezoid class's inherited data member, name. Then use the *set* functions that you declared in the header file to set the values of the Trapezoid class's data members. After completing the constructor, define the *get* and *set* functions for the class. To ensure that the Trapezoid object is in a consistent state, assign 0 to a data member if the value passed to its *set* function is less than zero. The area function should use *get* functions to return the area of the trapezoid, which is given by the formula

$$A = \frac{1}{2}(b_1 + b_2) \cdot h$$

where A is the area, b_1 and b_2 are the base lengths and h is the height of the trapezoid.

e) ***Opening the AreaCalculator template source code file.*** Open the template file AreaCalculator.cpp in your text editor or IDE.

f) ***Enabling users to enter trapezoid information.*** To access the Trapezoid class, insert an include directive in line 9 to include the Trapezoid.h file. Because you will add another option to the menu in lines 26–30, the number corresponding to "Exit the application" will be 4. Modify the while statement in line 24 so that the continuation condition is selection != 4. Next, modify the menu that appears in lines 26–29 so that the it presents the option to enter trapezoid information, as shown in Fig. 17.56. If the user enters 3 at the **Enter selection:** prompt, the application should prompt the user for information regarding the size of trapezoid, then create and store a pointer to a Trapezoid object in the shape variable. Beginning in line 73, insert a case 3: label, followed by statements that prompt the user for and store the lengths of the two trapezoid bases and the height of the trapezoid. Then, insert a statement that uses the new operator to create a new Trapezoid object. The pointer returned by the new operator should be stored in shape. Remember to include a break statement after creating the Trapezoid object.

g) ***Save, compile and run the completed application.*** Test your application to ensure that it runs correctly by entering various lengths for the bases and height of a trapezoid. Ensure that your application displays the correct shape name for the trapezoid and area contained inside the trapezoid.

h) ***Close the Command Prompt window.***

18

Objectives

In this tutorial, you will learn to:
- Create, read from, write to and update files.
- Understand a computer's data hierarchy.
- Become familiar with sequential-access file processing.
- Use the `ifstream` object to read values and text from a sequential-access file.
- Use the `ofstream` object to write values and text to a sequential-access file.
- Use the `exit` function to terminate the application and send an error message to the system.

Outline

Ticket Information Application

Introducing Sequential-Access Files

Y ou have used variables and arrays to store data temporarily—the data is lost when a function or application terminates. When you want to store data for a longer period of time, you use files. A **file** is a collection of data that is given a name, such as `data.txt` or `Welcome.cpp`. Data in files exists even after the application that created the data terminates. Such data is called **persistent data**. Computers store persistent data files on **secondary storage media**, including magnetic disks (such as the hard drive of your computer), optical disks (such as CD-ROMs or DVDs) and magnetic tapes (which are similar to music cassette tapes).

File processing, which includes creating, reading from and writing to files, is an important capability of C++. It enables C++ to support commercial applications that typically process massive amounts of persistent data. In this tutorial, you will learn about **sequential-access files**, which contain information that is read from a file in the same order that it was originally written to the file. You will learn how to create, open and write to a sequential-access file by building the **Write Event** application. This application allows the user to create or open a **text file** (a file containing human-readable characters) and to input the dates, times and descriptions of community events (such as concerts or sporting matches).

You will then learn how to read data from a file by building the **Ticket Information** application. This application displays data from a file created by the **Write Event** application. Along the way, you will get more practice using two-dimensional arrays, which are used in this application to store data read from a file.

18.1 Test-Driving the Write Event and Ticket Information Applications

Many communities and businesses use computer applications to allow their members and customers to view information about upcoming events, such as movies, concerts and sporting contests. The **Write Event** application that you will build in this tutorial writes the community event information to a sequential-access file. The **Write Event** application must meet the following requirements:

> **Application Requirements**
>
> *To create an application that reads event information from a file, you first need to create another application that writes event information to a file. The user should be prompted for the day, time, price, name and description of each event. The user should be able to specify the name of the file that will contain the event information.*

The **Ticket Information** application that you will build displays the data stored in the file generated by the **Write Event** application. The **Ticket Information** application must meet the following requirements:

> **Application Requirements**
>
> *A local town has asked you to write an application that allows its residents to view community events for the current month. Events taking place in the town include concerts, sporting contests and movies. The events have already been written to the file* `calendar.txt` *using the **Write Event** application. When the user selects a date, if there is an event scheduled for that day, the application should display the event information. When displaying event information, the application should display the time, price and a brief description of the event. The application should inform the user when there are no events scheduled for a selected day.*

Your **Ticket Information** application will allow a user to specify a date at an input prompt. For simplicity, the day will be an integer value between 1 and 31 (inclusive). It is assumed that the events are for the current month of the current year, so the user should be interested in only the day of the month. We also assume that the month contains 31 days. This application will open a text file and read its contents to display information about an event scheduled for the selected date. You begin by test-driving the completed applications. Then, you will learn the additional C++ capabilities you will need to create your own version of these applications.

Test-Driving the Ticket Information and Write Event Applications

1. *Locating the completed application.* Open the **Command Prompt** window by selecting **Start > All Programs > Accessories > Command Prompt**. Change to your completed **Ticket Information** application directory by typing cd C:\Examples\Tutorial18\CompletedApplication\TicketInformation.

2. *Running the Ticket Information application.* Type TicketInformation in the **Command Prompt** window to run the application (Fig. 18.1). The application begins by prompting you for an event date.

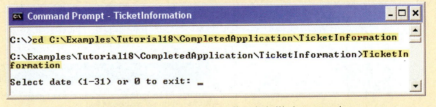

```
Command Prompt - TicketInformation

C:\>cd C:\Examples\Tutorial18\CompletedApplication\TicketInformation

C:\Examples\Tutorial18\CompletedApplication\TicketInformation>TicketIn
formation

Select date (1-31) or 0 to exit: _
```

Figure 18.1   **Ticket Information** application's initial prompt.

3. *Getting event information.* Select the 19th day of the month by entering 19. The application displays an event's information (Fig. 18.2), consisting of the time (a value between **0:00** and **23:59**), price and description of the event, **Film Festival**, for this day.

(cont.)

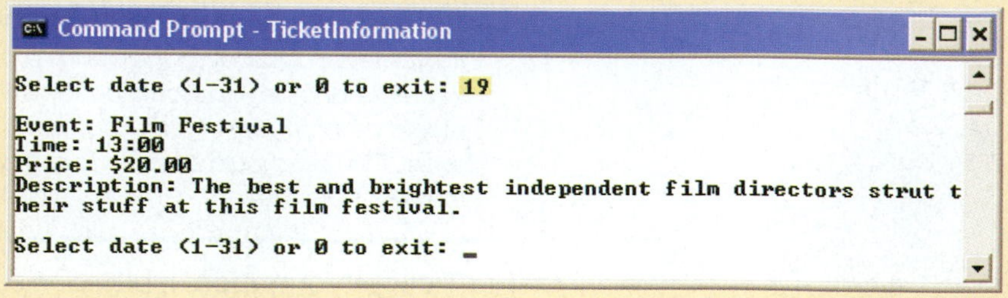

Event information displayed —

Figure 18.2 **Ticket Information** application displaying event information.

4. ***Viewing other events.*** Select other dates (such as the 4th, the 5th and the 28th) and view the results. The 4th should display no events, the 5th should display information about a talent show event and the 28th should display information about a city tour.

5. ***Closing the running application.*** Exit your running application by entering 0 at the **Select date (1-31) or 0 to exit:** prompt. Leave the **Command Prompt** window open.

6. ***Adding events using the Write Event application.*** In the **Command Prompt** window, change to your completed **Write Event** application directory by typing cd C:\Examples\Tutorial18\CompletedApplication\WriteEvent. Type WriteEvent in the **Command Prompt** window to run the application (Fig. 18.3). A file must be opened before event data can be written to it.

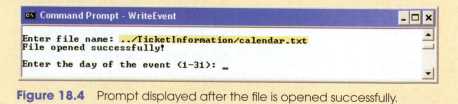

Figure 18.3 **Write Event** application enables user to store event data.

7. ***Opening a file.*** The file used by your **Ticket Information** application is calendar.txt, located in the TicketInformation directory. Before adding events to this file, you need to open it. To open a file from a different directory, you must specify the file's **path name**, which is a string that identifies a file by a series of directories separated by "/" or "\," depending on the operating system. (Windows operating systems use "\" and UNIX-based systems use "/.") For example, the **Write Event** application's path name is C:\Examples\Tutorial18\CompletedApplication\WriteEvent. For the calendar.txt file, enter the path name ../TicketInformation/calendar.txt (Fig. 18.4).

Command Prompt - WriteEvent

```
Enter file name: ../TicketInformation/calendar.txt
File opened successfully!

Enter the day of the event (1-31): _
```

Figure 18.4 Prompt displayed after the file is opened successfully.

(cont.)

The "**..**" **directory** specifies your application's **parent directory**, which is the directory that contains your application's directory. In this case, the **Write Event** application's parent directory is `C:\Examples\Tutorial18\CompletedApplication`. When opening the file, the system will replace "**..**" with `C:\Examples\Tutorial18\CompletedApplication` to form the path name `C:\Examples\Tutorial18\CompletedApplication\TicketInformation\calendar.txt`. After opening the file, the application notifies the user that the file has been opened successfully.

8. ***Entering an event.*** After the application opens the output file, the user is prompted to enter the day, time, price, name and description of an event. Enter information for an event as shown in Fig. 18.5. The data entered is written to the file specified in the previous step (`calendar.txt`).

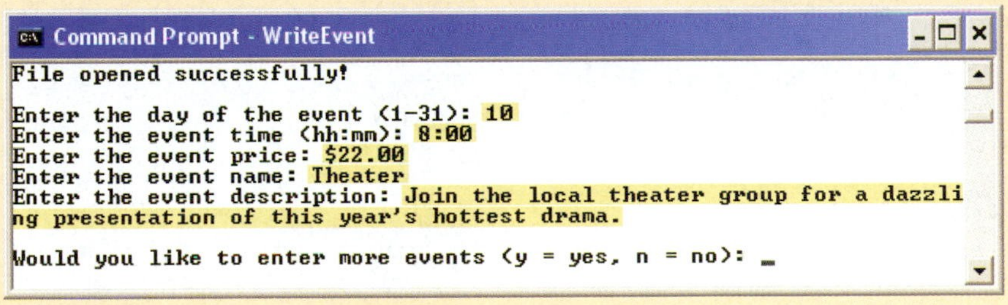

Figure 18.5   Adding an event to `calendar.txt`.

9. ***Entering additional events and closing the file.*** At the **Would you like to enter more events** prompt, enter y (for "yes") to add another event. Then enter another event as shown in Fig. 18.6. Next, enter n (for "no") at the **Would you like to enter more events** prompt to exit the application. The file `calendar.txt` has now been closed.

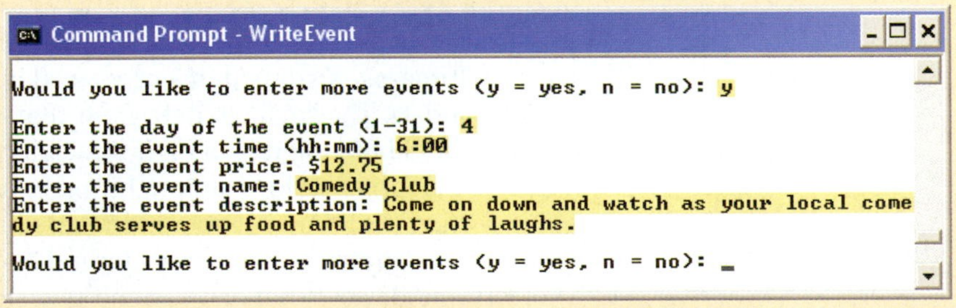

Figure 18.6   Entering another event and closing the file.

10. ***Viewing the new events.*** Change to your completed **Ticket Information** application directory by typing cd `..\TicketInformation`. Type the command `TicketInformation` in the **Command Prompt** window to run the application. You have now added events on the 10th and 4th. Select these days and notice that the events are now displayed. Recall from Fig. 18.2 that the 4th did not have an event.

11. ***Closing the running application.*** Exit your running application by entering 0 at the **Select date (1-31) or 0 to exit:** prompt.

12. ***Close the Command Prompt window.***

18.2 Data Hierarchy

Data items processed by computers form a **data hierarchy** (Fig. 18.7), in which data items become larger and more complex in structure as they progress from bits to characters to fields and, finally, to larger data structures.

Throughout this book, you have been manipulating data in your applications. The data has been in several forms: **decimal digits** (0, 1, 2, 3, 4, 5, 6, 7, 8 and 9), **letters** (A–Z and a–z) and **special symbols** ($, @, %, &, *, (,), -, +, ", :, ?, / and many others). Digits, letters and special symbols are referred to as **characters**. The set of all characters used to write applications and represent data items on a particular computer is called that computer's **character set**.

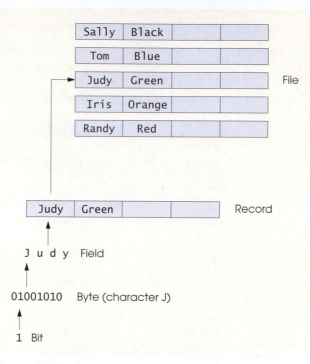

Figure 18.7 Data hierarchy.

Ultimately, all data items processed by a computer are reduced to combinations of 0s and 1s. The smallest data item that computers support is called a **bit**. "Bit" is short for "**binary digit**"—a digit that can be one of two values, 0 or 1. Computer circuitry performs various simple bit manipulations, such as examining the value of a bit, setting the value of a bit and reversing the value of a bit (from 1 to 0 or from 0 to 1). This approach has been adopted because it is simple and economical to build electronic devices that can assume two stable states—one state representing 0 and the other representing 1. It is remarkable that the extensive functions performed by computers involve only the most fundamental manipulations of 0s and 1s.

Every character in a computer's character set is represented as a pattern of 0s and 1s. **Bytes** are composed of 8 bits. Characters map bytes (or groups of bytes) to symbols such as letters, numbers, punctuation and new lines. Many systems use 8-bit characters and thus can have 2^8, or 256, possible characters in their **character sets**. Two of the most popular character sets in use today are **ASCII (American Standard Code for Information Interchange)** and **Unicode**®.

ASCII stores characters as 8-bit bytes and thus can have 256 possible characters in its character set. Due to ASCII's small character size, it does not support international character sets. Unicode is an internationally recognized standard that is popular in Internet and multilingual applications. Its goal is to use a unique number to represent every character in all the world's languages. Unicode provides 8-, 16- and 32-bit representations of its character set. To simplify conversion from ASCII to Unicode characters, the 8-bit representation of Unicode, called UTF–8 (Unicode character set Translation Format–8 bit), corresponds directly to the ASCII character set. HTML files are typically encoded using UTF–8. UTF–16 and UTF–32 each provide larger character sets, enabling applications to store information containing charac-

Tutorial 18　　　　　　　　　　　　　　　　　　Ticket Information Application　**461**

ters from multiple alphabets, such as Greek, Cyrillic, Chinese and a great many others. However, they require larger files to store the same number of characters when compared to UTF–8. For example, the 12-character string "Hello, world" requires 12 bytes of storage using 8-bit characters, 24 bytes using 16-bit characters and 48 bytes using 32-bit characters.

Characters stored by the char data type are bytes. C++ also provides the **wchar_t data type**, which can occupy more than one byte to support larger character sets, such as the Unicode character set. Programming with data in the low-level form of bits is difficult, so programmers create applications and data items with characters, and computers manipulate and process these characters as patterns of bits.

Just as characters are composed of bits, fields are composed of characters (Fig. 18.7). A **field** is a group of characters that conveys some meaning. For example, a field consisting of uppercase and lowercase letters might represent a person's name.

Typically, a **record** (which usually is represented as a class in C++) is a collection of several related fields (called data members in C++). In a payroll system, for example, a record for a particular employee might include the following fields:

1. Employee identification number

2. Name

3. Address

4. Hourly pay rate

5. Number of exemptions claimed

6. Year-to-date earnings

7. Amount of taxes withheld

Thus, a record is a group of related fields. In the preceding example, each field is associated with the same employee.

A file is a group of related records. A company's payroll file normally contains one record for each employee. Hence, a payroll file for a small company might contain only 22 records, whereas a payroll file for a large company might contain 100,000 or more. It is not unusual for a company to have many files, some containing millions, billions or even trillions of characters of information.

To facilitate the retrieval of specific records from a file, at least one field in each record is chosen as a record key. A **record key** identifies a record as belonging to a particular person or entity and distinguishes that record from all other records. Therefore, the record key must be unique. In the payroll record just described, the employee identification number normally would be chosen as the record key because each employee's identification number is different.

There are many ways to organize records in a file. The most common type of organization is called a sequential file, in which records are stored in order by a record key field. In a payroll file, records usually are ordered by employee identification number. The first employee record in the file contains the lowest employee identification number, and subsequent records contain increasingly higher employee identification numbers.

Most businesses use many different files to store data. For example, a company might have payroll files, accounts receivable files (listing money due from clients), accounts payable files (listing money due to suppliers), inventory files (listing facts about all the items handled by the business) and many other types of files. A **database** is a group of related files. A collection of programs designed to create and manage databases is called a **database management system (DBMS)**.

1. The smallest data item a computer can process is called a _____.

    a) database   b) byte

    c) file   d) bit

2. A _____ is a group of related records.

    a) file   b) field

    c) bit   d) byte

Answers: 1) d. 2) a.

18.3 Files and Streams

C++ views files as sequences of bytes or characters called **streams** (Fig. 18.8). Each file ends either with an **end-of-file marker** or at a specific byte number recorded in a system-maintained, administrative data structure. In this tutorial, you will learn how to manipulate files that contain characters. When a file is opened, an object is created, and a stream is associated with the object. Throughout this book, you have used the `cin` and `cout` stream objects. The streams associated with these objects provide communication channels between an application and a device. For example, the `cin` object enables an application to input data from the keyboard, and the `cout` object enables an application to output data to the screen. In this tutorial, you will create streams that enable communication channels between an application and a file.

Figure 18.8 C++'s conceptual view of an *n*-byte file as a stream.

The **`<fstream>`** header file defines classes that you will use to write characters into and read characters from a file. You will be briefly introduced to some of these classes in this section.

You will use objects of the **`ofstream`** and **`ifstream`** classes to open text files for output and input of characters, respectively. These classes allow you to write characters to and read characters from files. Because these objects inherit from classes in the `<iostream>` header file, all member functions, operators and manipulators that you could apply to objects such as `cout` and `cin` can be applied to the `ofstream` and `ifstream` objects.

In the test-drive of the **Write Event** application, you saw the application process information such as strings and numbers. The `ofstream` object, however, can write only strings of characters to a file. For example, when the `ofstream` object writes the string literal `"36"` to a file, it writes two one-byte `char`s, `'3'` and `'6'`. The `int` value 36, however, is represented as a single value containing multiple bytes (typically four bytes). Before the `ofstream` could write this value, it would need to cast it to a `char` data type. According to Appendix D, the result of this conversion is the dollar sign, `$`, not the string literal `"36"`. Fortunately, C++ enables you to output numbers (and many other types) as characters because the stream insertion operator "knows" how to convert C++'s primitive types to characters. Thus, when outputting the `int` value 36 using the stream insertion operator with an `ofstream` object, the string literal `"36"` is written to a file.

Similarly, the `ifstream` object reads input from a file as a string of characters. In the **Ticket Information** application, the `ifstream` object reads one line of text at a time from the file created by the **Write Event** application. C++ enables you to input values read from a file into strings and numbers (and many other types) because the stream extraction operator also "knows" how to convert strings of characters to C++'s primitive types. For example, when an `ifstream` object inputs the value `"36"` from a file into an `int` variable, the stream extraction operator converts the string literal to the `int` value 36.

SELF-REVIEW

1. A(n) _____ object can write strings and numbers to a text file.

   a) `ifstream`   b) `charstream`

   c) `ofstream`   d) `textstream`

2. C++ views a file as a sequential _____ of bytes.

   a) stream   b) loop

   c) string   d) record

Answers: 1) c. 2) a.

18.4 Creating the Write Event Application: Writing to a File

Now you will create the **Write Event** application to enable a user to write community event information to a sequential-access text file. First you need to analyze the application. The following pseudocode describes the basic operation of the **Write Event** application.

> Prompt the user for a file name
> Attempt to open the file
>
> If the file was not opened successfully
>   Display an error message and exit the application
>
> Do
>   Prompt the user for the day, time, price, name and description of the event
>   Add the day of the event and a newline to the file
>   Add the time of the event and a newline to the file
>   Add the price of the event and a newline to the file
>   Add the name of the event and a newline to the file
>   Add a description of the event and a newline to the file
>   Prompt the user whether there are more events to be added
> While the user indicates that there are more events to add

Figure 18.9 Pseudocode for the **Write Event** application.

An important aspect of the **Ticket Information** application is its ability to read data sequentially from a text file. You will need to create the file from which the **Ticket Information** application will read its data. Therefore, before you create this application, you must learn how to write data to a file sequentially.

The **Write Event** application stores in a file the information input by a user. Input prompts are provided for the user to enter the day, time, price, name and description of an event. Data is entered in response to the input prompts and written to a file specified by the user. To open and write to the text file, your application will create an `ofstream` object. The **Write Event** application should enable the user to create a new file or open an existing file—if an existing file is opened, the new events will be added to the end of the file.

Creating an *ofstream* Object, Opening a File

1. **Copying the template to your working directory.** Copy the C:\Examples\Tutorial18\TemplateApplication\WriteEvent directory to your C:\SimplyCpp directory.

2. **Opening the Write Event application's template source code file.** Open the template file WriteEvent.cpp in your text editor or IDE.

3. **Including the *<fstream>* and *<cstdlib>* header files.** Add lines 6–7 of Fig. 18.10 to your code to include the <fstream> and <cstdlib> header files. The <fstream> header file will allow you to access the classes and functions needed to perform file processing with sequential-access files. The <cstdlib> header file will allow you to access the **exit** function, which you will use to exit the application if the file that the user specifies cannot be opened.

Including the <fstream> and <cstdlib> header files —

```
WriteEvent.cpp*
  5   #include <string>   // required to access string functions
  6   #include <fstream>  // required to perform C++ file I/O
  7   #include <cstdlib>  // required for the exit function
  8
  9   using namespace std; // for accessing C++ Standard Library members
```

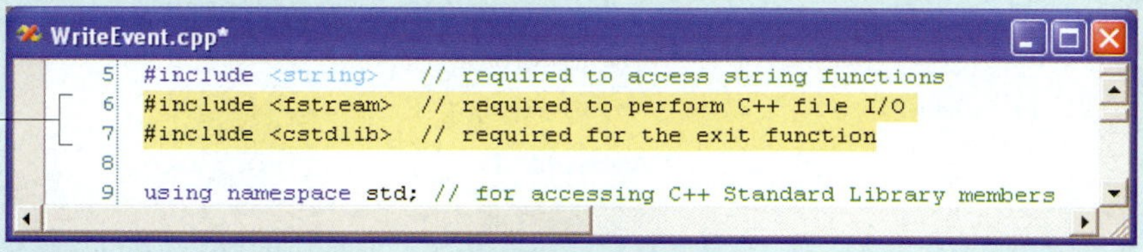

Figure 18.10 Including the <fstream> and <cstdlib> header files in the WriteEvent.cpp file.

4. **Defining variables.** Add lines 14–21 of Fig. 18.11 to main to define variables that your application will use to store user input. The name of the file that will store event information will be stored in string variable fileName. The date, time, price, eventName and description variables will store the event's day, time, price, name and description, respectively, that the user enters. Finally, char variable response will store a character indicating whether the user wishes to enter additional event data.

Defining variables —

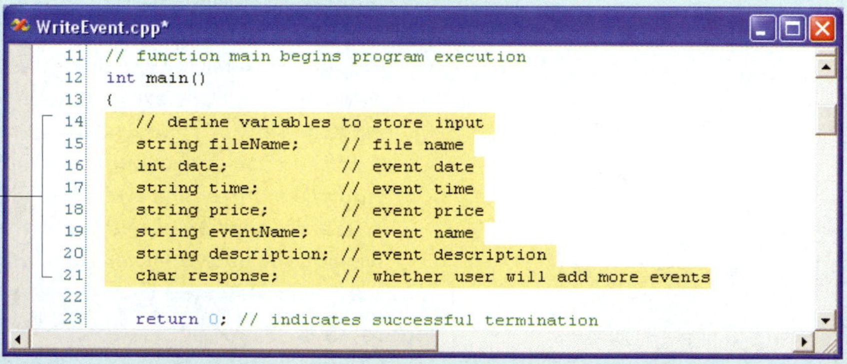

```
WriteEvent.cpp*
 11   // function main begins program execution
 12   int main()
 13   {
 14      // define variables to store input
 15      string fileName;    // file name
 16      int date;           // event date
 17      string time;        // event time
 18      string price;       // event price
 19      string eventName;   // event name
 20      string description; // event description
 21      char response;      // whether user will add more events
 22
 23      return 0; // indicates successful termination
```

Figure 18.11 Defining variables to store the file name, event information and whether the application should input additional event data.

5. **Retrieving the file name.** Add lines 23–25 of Fig. 18.12 to your code. Lines 24–25 prompt the user for and store the file name in string variable file-Name, using the getline function.

(cont.)

Inputting the file name —

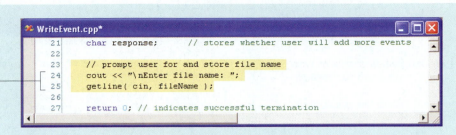

```
WriteEvent.cpp*
21      char response;      // stores whether user will add more events
22
23      // prompt user for and store file name
24      cout << "\nEnter file name: ";
25      getline( cin, fileName );
26
27      return 0; // indicates successful termination
```

Figure 18.12   Retrieving the file name that the user entered.

6. ***Creating an `ofstream` object and opening a file.*** Add lines 27–28 of Fig. 18.13 to your code to create an `ofstream` object, `outputFile`, and pass arguments to its constructor. The first argument to the `ofstream` constructor is an array of characters (`char []` type) specifying the file name. In this case, the argument contains the result of calling `string` member function `c_str` on `fileName`. The `string` class's **`c_str`** member function returns the characters stored in a `string` object as an array of characters. Note that the `ofstream` constructor requires the file name to be specified as an array of characters, not as a `string` object.

Defining an `ofstream` object —

```
WriteEvent.cpp*
25      getline( cin, fileName );
26
27      // ofstream constructor opens file for appending output
28      ofstream outputFile( fileName.c_str(), ios::app );
29
30      return 0; // indicates successful termination
```

Figure 18.13   Defining an `ofstream` object.

The second argument to the `ofstream` constructor is the **file-open mode**, which specifies how data will be added to the file. For an `ofstream` object, the file-open mode can be either **`ios::out`**, to output data to a file, or **`ios::app`**, to append data to the end of a file (without modifying any data already in the file). Existing files opened with the `ios::out` mode are **truncated**—all data in the file is discarded. If the specified file does not yet exist, then `ofstream` creates the file, using that file name.

When line 28 executes, the application creates an `ofstream` object, then attempts to open the specified file using the specified file-open mode. In the next step, you will add code that determines whether the file was successfully opened.

Error-Prevention Tip

Exercise caution when using (`ios::out`) to open an existing file for output, especially when you want to preserve the file's contents, which will be discarded without warning.

7. ***Determining whether the file was opened.*** Add lines 30–38 of Fig. 18.14 to your code. Line 31 determines whether the file specified in the `ofstream` object's constructor was successfully opened. As you learned in Tutorial 5, the logical negation operator (`!`) is designed to enable a programmer to "reverse" the meaning of a `bool` condition. However, `outputFile` is an object of the `ofstream` type, not a `bool` expression. When the logical negation operator is applied to `outputFile`, a function is called that returns `false` if the file associated with the `outputFile` object was opened successfully and `true` otherwise.

(cont.)

Determining whether the file was opened successfully

Exiting the application

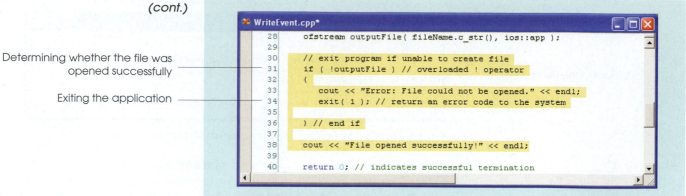

```
28      ofstream outputFile( fileName.c_str(), ios::app );
29
30      // exit program if unable to create file
31      if ( !outputFile ) // overloaded ! operator
32      {
33          cout << "Error: File could not be opened." << endl;
34          exit( 1 ); // return an error code to the system
35
36      } // end if
37
38      cout << "File opened successfully!" << endl;
39
40      return 0; // indicates successful termination
```

Figure 18.14 Exiting the application if the specified file could not be opened.

If the specified file could not be opened, lines 33–34 display an error message and cause the application to exit immediately by calling the `exit` function. An argument of 0 to the `exit` function notifies the operating system that the application exited normally; an argument of 1 indicates that application terminated due to an error. Line 38 displays a message indicating that the file was opened successfully.

8. *Save, compile and run the application.* Type `test.txt` at the **Enter file name:** prompt and press *Enter* (Fig. 18.15). This will create the file `test.txt` and store it in your `WriteEvent` directory.

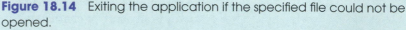

```
"c:\SimplyCpp\WriteEvent\Debug\WriteEvent.exe"

Enter file name: test.txt
File opened successfully!
Press any key to continue_
```

Figure 18.15 Creating a file.

After the application creates the file and opens it, the application exits. Browse to your `WriteEvent` directory. Notice that `test.txt` has been created but does not yet contain any data. You can also open an existing file with the current application, but you will not be able to add data to the file until the next box, where you will learn to write data to a file.

9. *Close the* **Command Prompt** *window.*

Now that the application can open a file, you will learn how to enable the user to input information that will be written to that file. Next, you will add code to `main` that will write data entered by the user into a text file.

Writing Information to a Sequential-Access File

1. *Prompting the user for and inputting the date.* Add lines 40–49 of Fig. 18.16 to `main`. Line 40 begins a do...while statement that repeats until the user indicates that there are no more events to enter (line 49). Lines 44–45 prompt the user for and input the day of the event. Because the application will be using the `getline` function to read the remaining input values, you must use the `ignore` function in line 46 to remove the newline character from `cin`. Otherwise, the next call to the `getline` function will return the empty string.

(cont.)

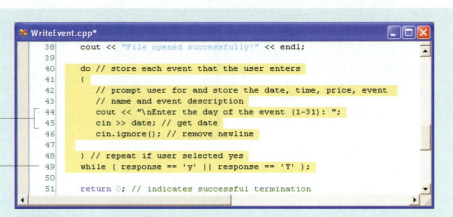

Obtaining the event day

do...while statement repeats until user indicates that there are no more events to enter

Figure 18.16   Prompting the user for and inputting the event date.

2. ***Prompting the user for and inputting the time, price, name and description of the event.*** Add lines 48–58 of Fig. 18.17 to your code to prompt the user for and store the event time, price, name and description. The `getline` function ensures that input does not terminate when whitespace characters such as spaces or tabs are encountered.

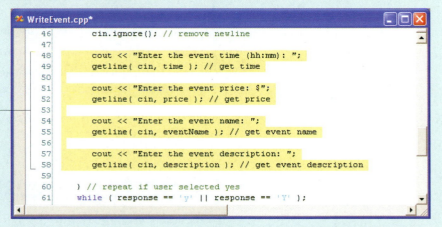

Obtaining the event time, price, name and description

Figure 18.17   Inputting the time, price, event name and event description.

3. ***Writing the date and time of the event to a file.*** When storing event data, you will add each piece of information on a separate line in the file. Add lines 60–62 of Fig. 18.18 to the `do...while` statement. Lines 60–62 write the user input line by line to the file by using multiple stream insertion operators (`<<`) on `ofstream` object `outputFile`. In the first part of line 61, the application writes to the file the day entered by the user, followed by a newline. Recall that the stream insertion operator "knows" how to convert numeric data, such as `int` variable `date`, to characters. These characters are then placed in the `outputFile` file stream object, which writes the characters to the file specified by the `fileName` variable. Line 61 then adds to the file a line that contains time information and a line containing a dollar sign and the price. Line 62 adds the event name and description to the file, each on separate lines.

(cont.)

Appending the event date, time, price, name and description to the file

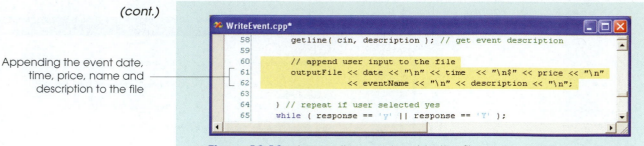

Figure 18.18 Appending user input to the file.

4. *Determining whether the user wants to add more events.* Add lines 64–67 of Fig. 18.19 to your code. Lines 65–66 prompt the user to enter the y character if there are more events to enter and the n character otherwise. Line 67 stores the user input in char variable response. Line 69 causes the application to repeat the loop if the user entered an uppercase or lowercase y. This enables the user to enter several events during a single session.

Determining whether there are more events to enter

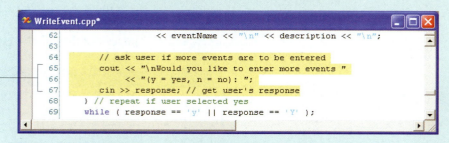

Figure 18.19 Determining if there are more events to enter.

5. *Save, compile and run the application.* At the **Enter file name:** prompt, enter the name test.txt, the file to which the application will write event data. (Fig. 18.20).

```
Enter file name: test.txt
File opened successfully!

Enter the day of the event (1-31): _
```

Figure 18.20 Opening a file for writing.

6. *Inputting event information.* At the **Enter the day of the event (1-31):** prompt, enter 4 to indicate that the event is scheduled for the 4th day of the month. Enter 12:30 at the **Enter the event time (hh:mm):** prompt. Type 12.50 at the **Enter the event price: $** prompt. Enter Arts and Crafts Fair at the **Enter the event name:** prompt. At the **Enter the event description:** prompt, type Take part in creating various types of arts and crafts at this fair (Fig. 18.21). The application will then add this event's information to the test.txt file.

7. *Close the application.*

8. *Close the Command Prompt window.*

(cont.)

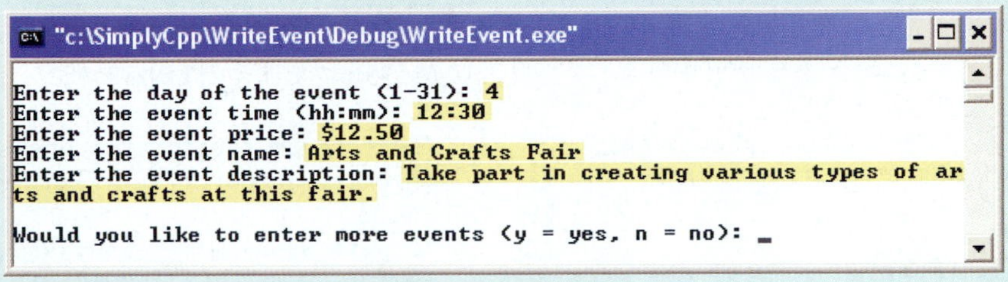

Figure 18.21   Adding the **Arts and Crafts Fair** event to `test.txt`.

9. ***Opening and closing the sequential-access file.*** Open `test.txt` with a text editor. Scroll down towards the bottom of the file. The information you entered in *Step 6* should appear in the file, similar to Fig. 18.22. Normally, information is not stored in this way, with each piece of data on a separate line. Rather, the information for an event would be all on one line, with each piece of information separated by a special character, such as a space or a tab. We have chosen to organize the file as shown in Fig. 18.22 for simplicity—now we can read each piece of information by reading a line from the file, rather than reading all the information at once and splitting the data based on the special characters that separate them. Close the `test.txt` file.

Data written to file ——

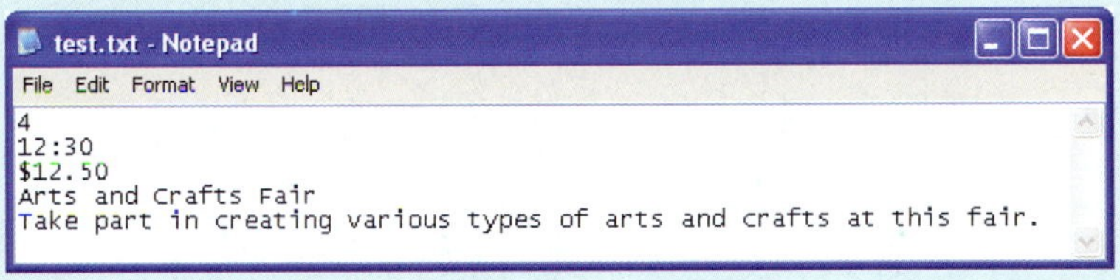

Figure 18.22   Sequential-access file generated by **Write Event** application.

Figure 18.23 presents the source code for the **Write Event** application. The lines of code that you added, viewed or modified in this tutorial are highlighted.

Include the `<fstream>` header file to access files and the `<cstdlib>` header file to use the `exit` function

Define variables ——

Define variables ——

```cpp
1   // Tutorial 18: WriteEvent.cpp
2   // This application writes information about an event on a given
3   // date to a file.
4   #include <iostream> // required to perform C++ stream I/O
5   #include <string>   // required to access string functions
6   #include <fstream>  // required to perform C++ file I/O
7   #include <cstdlib>  // required for the exit function
8
9   using namespace std; // for accessing C++ Standard Library members
10
11  // function main begins program execution
12  int main()
13  {
14     // define variables to store input
15     string fileName;    //  file name
16     int date;           // event date
17     string time;        // event time
18     string price;       // event price
19     string eventName;   // event name
20     string description; // event description
21     char response;      // whether user will add more events
22
```

Figure 18.23   **Write Event** application code. (Part 1 of 2.)

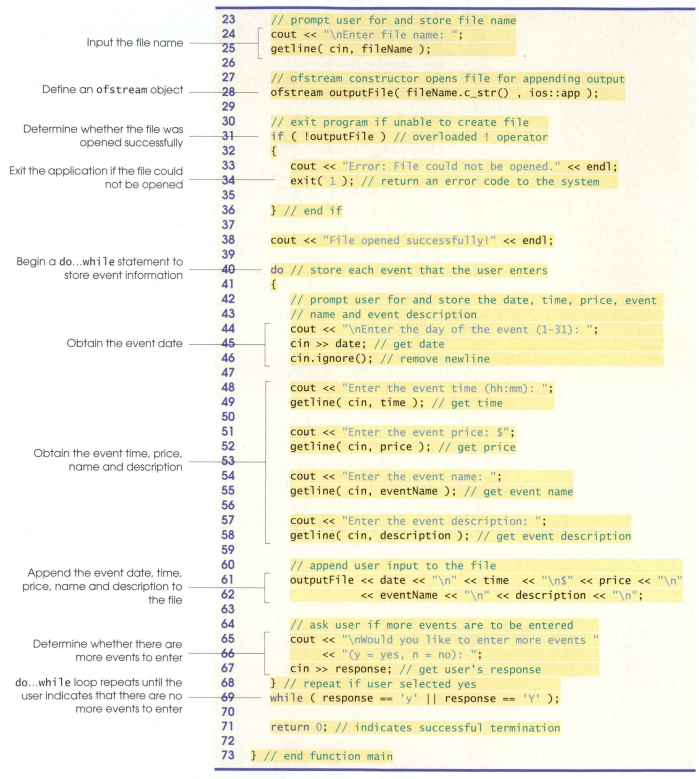

Input the file name

```
23     // prompt user for and store file name
24     cout << "\nEnter file name: ";
25     getline( cin, fileName );
26
```

Define an `ofstream` object

```
27     // ofstream constructor opens file for appending output
28     ofstream outputFile( fileName.c_str() , ios::app );
29
```

Determine whether the file was opened successfully

```
30     // exit program if unable to create file
31     if ( !outputFile ) // overloaded ! operator
32     {
```

Exit the application if the file could not be opened

```
33         cout << "Error: File could not be opened." << endl;
34         exit( 1 ); // return an error code to the system
35
36     } // end if
37
38     cout << "File opened successfully!" << endl;
39
```

Begin a `do...while` statement to store event information

```
40     do // store each event that the user enters
41     {
42         // prompt user for and store the date, time, price, event
43         // name and event description
```

Obtain the event date

```
44         cout << "\nEnter the day of the event (1-31): ";
45         cin >> date; // get date
46         cin.ignore(); // remove newline
47
```

Obtain the event time, price, name and description

```
48         cout << "Enter the event time (hh:mm): ";
49         getline( cin, time ); // get time
50
51         cout << "Enter the event price: $";
52         getline( cin, price ); // get price
53
54         cout << "Enter the event name: ";
55         getline( cin, eventName ); // get event name
56
57         cout << "Enter the event description: ";
58         getline( cin, description ); // get event description
59
```

Append the event date, time, price, name and description to the file

```
60         // append user input to the file
61         outputFile << date << "\n" << time  << "\n$" << price << "\n"
62                 << eventName << "\n" << description << "\n";
63
```

Determine whether there are more events to enter

```
64         // ask user if more events are to be entered
65         cout << "\nWould you like to enter more events "
66             << "(y = yes, n = no): ";
67         cin >> response; // get user's response
68     } // repeat if user selected yes
```

`do...while` loop repeats until the user indicates that there are no more events to enter

```
69     while ( response == 'y' || response == 'Y' );
70
71     return 0; // indicates successful termination
72
73  } // end function main
```

Figure 18.23 **Write Event** application code. (Part 2 of 2.)

SELF-REVIEW   1. The _____ function causes the application to terminate.

    a) `quit`   b) `exit`

    c) `end`   d) `stop`

2. The append file-open mode is specified by _____.

    a) `ios::app`   b) `app::ios`

    c) `append`   d) `ios::append`

Answers: 1) b. 2) a.

18.5 Creating the Ticket Information Application

Now that you have created the **Write Event** application to enable a user to write community event information to a sequential-access text file, you will create the **Ticket Information** application from the test-drive section at the beginning of the tutorial. First, you need to analyze the application. The following pseudocode describes the basic operation of the **Ticket Information** application.

> While the user has not entered the sentinel value to exit the application
>
> > Prompt the user for and store a day of the month
> > Open calendar.txt file to read from
> >
> > While there are events left in the file
> >
> > > If the current event is for the day selected by the user
> > > > Read the event information from the file
> > > > Display the event information
> > >
> > > Read the next event's information
> >
> > If there are no events for the specified day
> > > Display a message indicating that there are no events for that day

Figure 18.24   Pseudocode for the **Ticket Information** application.

For this application, you will create the `displayEvent` function. The `displayEvent` function searches the `calendar.txt` file for an event on the specified day and, if found, displays the event's information. Otherwise, the application displays a message indicating that there are no events for the specified day.

Beginning to Build the Ticket Information Application

1. ***Copying the template to your working directory.*** Copy the `C:\Examples\Tutorial18\TemplateApplication\TicketInformation` directory to your `C:\SimplyCpp` directory.

2. ***Opening the Ticket Information application's template source code file.*** Open the template file `TicketInformation.cpp` in your text editor or IDE. Notice that the template file includes all of the header files that this application requires, and provides an incomplete `main` function and a complete `getDate` function. The `getDate` function contains code that prompts the user for and inputs a day of the month. An empty `displayEvent` function also is provided for you in the template application.

3. ***Calling the displayEvent function.*** Add line 26 of Fig. 18.25 to `main`, which calls the `displayEvent` function when the user enters a nonzero date. The function call passes as the argument `int` variable `date`, which contains the date the user entered. You will define this function in the next box.

4. ***Save the application.***

(cont.)

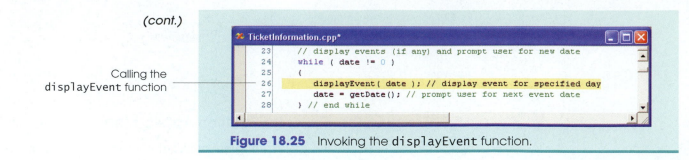

Calling the
`displayEvent` function

Figure 18.25 Invoking the `displayEvent` function.

The `displayEvent` function, which you will define in the next box, determines whether `calendar.txt` contains any events on the date that the user selected. If so, the function displays detailed information for an event on that day. Otherwise, the function displays a message indicating that there are no events on the specified date.

**Adding Code to the
`createEventList`
Function**

1. ***Defining the `displayEvent` function and its local variables.*** Add lines 60–71 of Fig. 18.26 to your code. Line 61 declares the `date` parameter for the `displayEvent` function. Lines 64–67 define `string` variables `time`, `price`, `name` and `description`, which will store information regarding the event. Line 68 defines `string` variable `contents`, which will store a line of text from the `calendar.txt` file. Finally, line 69 defines `int` variable `day`, which will store a day of the month for an event read from the `calendar.txt` file.

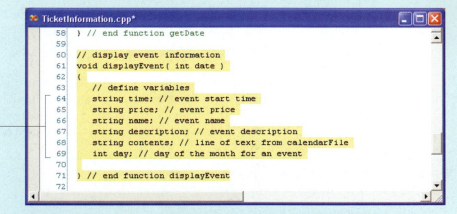

Defining local variables

Figure 18.26 Creating the `createEventList` function definition.

2. ***Opening the `calendar.txt` file for reading.*** Add lines 71–79 of Fig. 18.27 to the `displayEvent` function. Line 72 creates an `ifstream` object named `calendarFile` and passes the string literal `"calendar.txt"` to its constructor. This creates an `ifstream` object that opens the file `calendar.txt` for reading. Because the `calendar.txt` file is located in the same directory as the executable file, no path is required. Note that you do not have to specify an open-file mode for this `ifstream` object because the `ifstream` constructor opens the file for reading by default. Also note that the compiler treats the string `"calendar.txt"` as an array of characters, as required by the `ifstream` constructor.

(cont.)

Creating an `ifstream` object that opens the `calendar.txt` file

Exiting the application if the file could not be opened

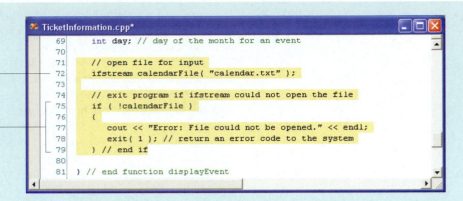

```
69        int day; // day of the month for an event
70
71        // open file for input
72        ifstream calendarFile( "calendar.txt" );
73
74        // exit program if ifstream could not open the file
75        if ( !calendarFile )
76        {
77           cout << "Error: File could not be opened." << endl;
78           exit( 1 ); // return an error code to the system
79        } // end if
80
81     } // end function displayEvent
```

Figure 18.27   Creating an `ifstream` object and opening the `calendar.txt` file for reading.

Lines 75–79 determine whether the file was opened successfully and, if not, cause the application to exit immediately, notifying the operating system that an error occurred.

3. ***Extracting the day from an event in the file.*** Add lines 81–89 of Fig. 18.28 to the `displayEvent` function. Line 82 uses the stream extraction operator to read the first `int` value contained in `calendar.txt` (using `ifstream` object `calendarFile`) and input it into day. This first line contains the day of the first event in the file. If the first event in the file is a talent show on the 12th, the value returned by the first line of the file is 12. Note that the stream extraction operator terminates input when any whitespace character is encountered. Because you will be using `getline` to retrieve additional lines from `calendarFile`, you must use the `ignore` function in line 83 to remove the newline from the file input stream.

Reading the date of the first event

Repeating while there is more data in the file

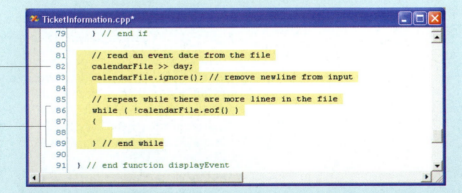

```
79        } // end if
80
81        // read an event date from the file
82        calendarFile >> day;
83        calendarFile.ignore(); // remove newline from input
84
85        // repeat while there are more lines in the file
86        while ( !calendarFile.eof() )
87        {
88
89        } // end while
90
91     } // end function displayEvent
```

Figure 18.28   Reading the first date from the file.

The `while` statement (line 86) begins by determining whether there is more data to read in the file. The **eof** file input stream member function (which stands for "end-of-file") returns `true` if there is no more data in the file and `false` otherwise. In the next step, you will add code that reads data for a single event from the file. Thus, the `while` statement that begins in line 86 causes the application to read each event from the file until the application reaches the end of the file.

(cont.)

4. ***Reading and displaying event information from the sequential-access file.***
Add lines 88–104 of Fig. 18.29 to the `while` statement to read each event's
information sequentially from the file. If the day of the event read from the
file (`day`) and the specified day (`date`) are equal (line 89), then the event
information (time, ticket price, name and description) is read from the file
and is stored in the `time`, `price`, `name` and `description` variables. Recall
that the **Write Event** application writes each piece of data (day, time, price,
event and description) to `calendar.txt` on a separate line, so the event
data can be retrieved using the `getline` function. Lines 97–100 then display
the event information to the user. After successfully finding and displaying
an event for the specified day, the function can return program control to the
caller (line 102).

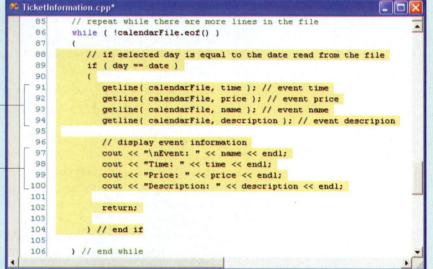

Inputting event information from a file

Displaying event information

```
85        // repeat while there are more lines in the file
86        while ( !calendarFile.eof() )
87        {
88            // if selected day is equal to the date read from the file
89            if ( day == date )
90            {
91                getline( calendarFile, time ); // event time
92                getline( calendarFile, price ); // event price
93                getline( calendarFile, name ); // event name
94                getline( calendarFile, description ); // event descripion
95
96                // display event information
97                cout << "\nEvent: " << name << endl;
98                cout << "Time: " << time << endl;
99                cout << "Price: " << price << endl;
100               cout << "Description: " << description << endl;
101
102               return;
103
104           } // end if
105
106       } // end while
```

Figure 18.29 Sequentially reading event entries from the file.

Notice that each piece of data is read in order—remember that sequential
files contain information that is read in the same order that it was originally
written. Every time a piece of data is read from a file (in this case, using
method `getline`), the file stream references the next piece of data in the
file. Therefore, we must first read the event's time before we can read the
event's price, the event's price must be read before the event's name, and so
on.

5. ***Finding the next date in the sequential-access file.*** Add lines 106–118 and
121 of Fig. 18.30 to your code. If `day` and the selected day (`date`) do not
match, then the `ifstream` object should skip to the next event. Because you
are reading from an sequential-access file, you must use the `ifstream` object
to input a line of text before the application can access the next line of text.
To access the next event in the file, your application must each line of text
corresponding to the current event. This is accomplished using a `for` statement (lines 109–112) that reads into a temporary variable (`contents`) the
next four lines of text. These four lines of text contain the time, ticket price,
name and description for an event that does not occur on the specified day.

(cont.)

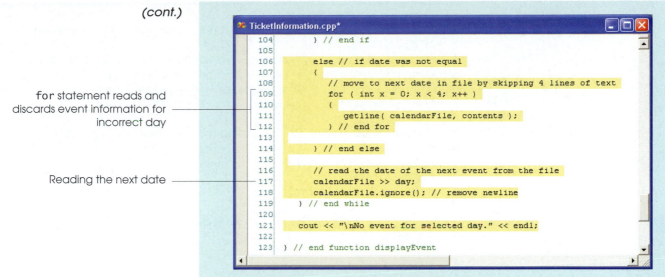

for statement reads and
discards event information for
incorrect day

Reading the next date

```
104        } // end if
105
106        else // if date was not equal
107        {
108            // move to next date in file by skipping 4 lines of text
109            for ( int x = 0; x < 4; x++ )
110            {
111                getline( calendarFile, contents );
112            } // end for
113
114        } // end else
115
116        // read the date of the next event from the file
117        calendarFile >> day;
118        calendarFile.ignore(); // remove newline
119     } // end while
120
121     cout << "\nNo event for selected day." << endl;
122
123  } // end function displayEvent
```

Figure 18.30 Finding the next date in the file.

After the `for` statement terminates, the next `int` value is read from the file (line 117). This value contains the next event's date. In line 118, the `ignore` function removes a newline from the `ifstream` so that the `get-line` function will not return an empty string the next time it is called. Lines 106–118 are executed repeatedly until the end of the file is reached. If the `while` loop terminates without finding a matching date from `calendar.txt`, line 121 executes, displaying a message indicating that there was no event for the specified date.

6. ***Save, compile and run the application.*** Figure 18.31 shows the completed application running. Notice that the event name, times price and description are displayed correctly.

```
Select date (1-31) or 0 to exit: 5

Event: Talent Show
Time: 19:00
Price: $15.00
Description: The best talent in the best venue! Come on down!

Select date (1-31) or 0 to exit: _
```

Figure 18.31 Completed **Ticket Information** application.

7. ***Close the application.*** Exit your running application by entering 0 at the **Select date (1-31) or 0 to exit:** prompt.

8. ***Close the Command Prompt window.***

Figure 18.32 presents the source code for the **Ticket Information** application. The lines of code that you added, viewed or modified in this tutorial are highlighted.

```cpp
 1   // Tutorial 18: TicketInformation.cpp
 2   // This application reads information about events on different
 3   // dates from a file.
 4   #include <iostream> // required to perform C++ stream I/O
 5   #include <fstream>  // required to perform C++ file I/O
 6   #include <string>   // required to access string functions
 7   #include <cstdlib>  // required for the exit function
 8
 9   using namespace std; // for accessing C++ Standard Library members
10
11   // function prototypes
12   int getDate();
13   void displayEvent( int );
14
15   // function main begins program execution
16   int main()
17   {
18      int date; // event day
19
20      // prompt user for and input the day for an event
21      date = getDate();
22
23      // display events (if any) and prompt user for new date
24      while ( date != 0 )
25      {
26         displayEvent( date ); // display event for specified day
27         date = getDate(); // prompt user for next event date
28      } // end while
29
30      cout << "\n"; // insert newline for readability
31
32      return 0; // indicate that program ended successfully
33
34   } // end function main
35
36   // prompt user for and input date, then return the date if valid
37   int getDate()
38   {
39      int date; // user input
40
41      // prompt user for and input the requested date
42      cout << "\nSelect date (1-31) or 0 to exit: ";
43      cin >> date;
44
45      // ensure that the date is valid before proceeding
46      while ( date < 0 || date > 31 )
47      {
48         cout << "\nError: Enter a date between 1 and 31, inclusive\n"
49            << endl;
50
51         // prompt user for and input the requested date
52         cout << "\nSelect date (1-31) or 0 to exit: ";
53         cin >> date;
54      } // end while
55
56      return date; // return the date
57
58   } // end function getDate
```

Call the `displayEvent` function —— (line 26)

Figure 18.32 Ticket Information code. (Part 1 of 3.)

```
59
60     // display event information
61     void displayEvent( int date )
62     {
63         // define variables
64         string time; // event start time
65         string price; // event price
66         string name; // event name
67         string description; // event description
68         string contents; // line of text from calendarFile
69         int day; // day of the month for an event
70
71         // open file for input
72         ifstream calendarFile( "calendar.txt" );
73
74         // exit program if ifstream could not open the file
75         if ( !calendarFile )
76         {
77             cout << "Error: File could not be opened." << endl;
78             exit( 1 ); // return an error code to the system
79         } // end if
80
81         // read an event date from the file
82         calendarFile >> day;
83         calendarFile.ignore(); // remove newline from input
84
85         // repeat while there are more lines in the file
86         while ( !calendarFile.eof() )
87         {
88             // if selected day is equal to the date read from the file
89             if ( day == date )
90             {
91                 getline( calendarFile, time ); // event time
92                 getline( calendarFile, price ); // event price
93                 getline( calendarFile, name ); // event name
94                 getline( calendarFile, description ); // event descripion
95
96                 // display event information
97                 cout << "\nEvent: " << name << endl;
98                 cout << "Time: " << time << endl;
99                 cout << "Price: " << price << endl;
100                cout << "Description: " << description << endl;
101
102                return;
103
104            } // end if
105
106            else // if date was not equal
107            {
108                // move to next date in file by skipping 4 lines of text
109                for ( int x = 0; x < 4; x++ )
110                {
111                    getline( calendarFile, contents );
112                } // end for
113
114            } // end else
115
```

Labels in left margin:
- Define local variables (lines 64–69)
- Create an `ifstream` object that opens the `calendar.txt` file (line 72)
- Exit the application if the file could not be opened (lines 75–79)
- Read the date of the first event (line 82)
- Repeat while there is more data in the file (line 86)
- Input event information (lines 91–94)
- Display event information (lines 97–100)
- `for` statement reads and discards event information for incorrect day (lines 109–112)

Figure 18.32 Ticket Information code. (Part 2 of 3.)

Read the next date

```
116        // read the date of the next event from the file
117        calendarFile >> day;
118        calendarFile.ignore(); // remove newline
119     } // end while
120
121     cout << "\nNo event for selected day." << endl;
122
123  } // end function displayEvent
```

Figure 18.32   Ticket Information code. (Part 3 of 3.)

SELF-REVIEW

1. To open a file for reading, you would use a(n) _____ object.

    a) istream   b) inputStream

    c) ofstream   d) ifstream

2. The _____ function of the ifstream class returns true if the end of the file has been reached.

    a) empty   b) endOfFile

    c) end   d) eof

Answers: 1) d. 2) d.

18.6 Wrap-Up

In this tutorial, you learned how to store and retrieve data in sequential-access files. This type of data is called persistent data because it is maintained after the application that generates the data terminates. Computers store files on secondary storage devices.

Sequential-access files store data items in the order that they are written to the files. These files can be composed of records, which are collections of related fields. Fields are made up of characters, which in C++ are composed of one byte. (C++ also provides the wchar_t type that uses the Unicode character set, which represents each character using two bytes.) Bytes are composed of bits—the smallest data items that computers can support.

You learned that C++ views each file as a sequential stream of bytes. You created a sequential-access file in the **Write Event** application by associating an ofstream object with a specified file name. You used the ofstream object and the stream insertion operator to add information to that file. After creating a file of community events with the **Write Event** application, you developed the **Ticket Information** application, which uses an ifstream object to read information from that file sequentially. The user enters a date and the application extracts event information from a sequential-access file about the event scheduled for that date.

In the next tutorial, you will learn about the functions in the string class that allow you to manipulate strings. These functions will help you build a screen scraper application that can search the text on a Web page for specific information.

SKILLS SUMMARY

Writing to a Sequential-Access File

- Include the <fstream> header file.

- Create an ofstream object that takes two arguments—the name of the file to write to and the file-open mode (ios::app means information will be appended to the file; ios::out means information will be written at the beginning of the file, overwriting any old data).

- Use the stream insertion operator (<<) to write information to the file.

Reading from a Sequential-Access File

- Include the <fstream> header file.

- Create an `ifstream` object that takes as its argument the name of the file to read from.
- Use the stream extraction operator or the `getline` function to read information from the file.
- Use `ifstream` member function `eof` to determine whether the end of the file has been reached.

Exiting the Application When an Error Is Detected

- Include the `<cstdlib>` header file.
- Call the `exit` function with an argument of 1 to notify the operating system that the application terminated due to an error.

KEY TERMS

.. directory—A shortcut to the parent directory.

binary digit—A digit that can assume one of two values (0 or 1).

bit—Short for "binary digit," this is the smallest date item a computer can support.

byte—A piece of data typically composed of eight bits.

character—A digit, letter or special symbol. (Characters in C++ are normally composed of one byte. Characters represented by the `wchar_t` type are composed of multiple bytes.)

character set—The set of all characters used to represent data items on a particular computer. C++ uses the ASCII character set by default.

c_str function (of the `string` class)—A function that returns the text contained in a `string` as an array of characters.

data hierarchy—The collection of data items processed by computers, which become larger and more complex in structure as you progress from bits to characters to fields to files, to databases.

database—A group of related files.

database management system (DBMS)—A collection of programs designed to create and manage databases.

decimal digits—The digits 0, 1, 2, 3, 4, 5, 6, 7, 8 and 9.

end-of-file marker—A special character that marks the end of a file.

eof function (of the `ifstream` class)—A function that returns `true` if its `ifstream` object has reached the end of a file and `false` otherwise.

exit function—A function declared in the `<cstdlib>` header file that causes the application to terminate. An argument of 0 to the function notifies the system that application terminated normally; an argument of 1 indicates that the application terminated due to an error.

field—A group of characters that conveys some meaning. For example, a field consisting of uppercase and lowercase letters might represent a person's name.

file—A file is a collection of bytes. Applications often organize those bytes into records. Files often are used for long-term persistence of data, even after the application that created the data terminates.

file-open mode—The mode that specifies how a file is to be opened. For example, a file-open mode can enable an application to write new data starting at the beginning (`ios::out`) or the end (`ios::app`) of the file, or the file-open mode can enable the application to read data from the file.

file processing—Creating, reading from and writing to files.

`<fstream>` standard library header file—A C++ Standard Library header file that provides access to functions and classes that enable you to perform file stream I/O.

ifstream object—An object that enables an application to input data from a file stream.

ios::app file-open mode—A file-open mode that specifies that data is written to the end of the file.

ios::out file-open mode—A file-open mode that specifies that data is written to the beginning of the file. If the file already contains data, that file is truncated, so the original contents of the file are lost.

letter—An uppercase letter A–Z or a lowercase letter a–z.

ofstream object—An object that enables an application to write output to a file stream.

parent directory—The directory that contains the current directory.

path name—A string that identifies a file by a series of directories separated by "/" or "\".

persistent data—Data that exists even after the application that created the data terminates and even when the computer is turned off.

record—A collection of related fields. A record is usually represented as a class in C++.

record key—A unique field used to identify a record and distinguish that record from all other records.

secondary storage media—Devices such as magnetic disks, optical disks and magnetic tapes on which computers store files.

special symbols—Characters such as $, @, %, &, *, (,), -, +, ", :, ?, /.

sequential-access file—A file that contains data that is read in the order that it was written.

stream—A sequence of bytes. C++ reads from and writes to files using streams.

text file—A file containing human-readable characters.

truncation (of a file)—Discarding all of the data in a file. This occurs when a file is opened with the `ios::out` file-open mode.

Unicode character—A character that can be stored using multiple bytes. The `wchar_t` data type can be used to represent members of the Unicode character set.

Unicode character set—An internationally recognized standard that is popular in Internet and multilingual applications. Its goal is to use a unique number to represent every character in all the world's languages.

wchar_t data type—A data type that stores characters using more than one byte, often to represent characters in the Unicode character set.

C++ LIBRARY REFERENCE

cstdlib This library contains function prototypes for conversion of numbers to text and text to numbers, generation of random numbers and other utility functions.

■ *Function*

`exit`—This function causes the application to terminate. An argument of 0 to the function notifies the system that the application terminated normally; an argument of 1 indicates that the application terminated due to an error.

`rand`—This function generates an `int` value selected from 0 to RAND_MAX.

`srand`—This function seeds the `rand` function, which determines the sequence of numbers that the application will generate. The `srand` function typically is used with an argument of `time( 0 )` to ensure that an application generates a different sequence of random numbers each time it is run.

fstream This header file contains functions and classes that access files.

■ *Constructors*

`ifstream`—This constructor takes a file name as an argument and opens that file for reading. The resulting `ifstream` object can read data from the specified file. The following code demonstrates the use of this constructor.

```
ifstream inputFile( "current.txt" );
```

`ofstream`—This constructor opens the file corresponding to the name specified by the string in the first argument using the file-open mode specified as the second argument. The second argument indicates whether new data should be appended (`ios::app`) to the end of the file or replace the existing data (`ios::out`). If the second argument is not specified, the file is opened in `ios::out` mode. The following code demonstrates the use of this constructor.

```
ofstream currentFile( "current.txt", ios::app );
```

■ *Functions*

eof—This function returns true if the ifstream has reached the end of the file and false otherwise.

---

string This header file declares classes and functions that store and manipulate strings.

■ *Object*

string—This object stores a string of characters.

■ *Functions*

c_str—This function returns an array of characters containing the text stored by a string.

getline—This function places characters from the specified input stream into the specified string object until a newline is reached. For example, the statements

```
string string1;
getline( cin, string1 );
```

cause the application to read from cin an entire line of text and store it in string variable string1.

size—This function returns the number of characters (as an int) in the string on which it is called.

MULTIPLE-CHOICE QUESTIONS

18.1 C++ views files as sequences of bytes or characters called _____.

a) strings
b) classes
c) streams
d) character arrays

18.2 The _____ standard library header file(s) provides access to the classes and functions that you need to use to perform file processing.

a) <fstream>
b) <ifstream> and <ofstream>
c) <iostream>
d) Both a and c.

18.3 A _____ is a group of related files.

a) field
b) database
c) collection
d) byte

18.4 Digits, letters and special symbols are referred to as _____.

a) constants
b) streams
c) strings
d) characters

18.5 Assuming the outputFile is an ofstream object, the expression !outputFile returns true if the file corresponding to outputFile _____.

a) is open in append mode
b) could not be opened
c) has been truncated
d) did not exist before it was opened

18.6 Bytes are typically composed of _____ bits.

a) 4
b) 8
c) 1
d) 2

18.7 An argument of _____ to the exit function indicates that an error occurred.

a) void
b) 0
c) 1
d) -1

18.8 _____ can be used to read data from an ifstream object.

a) getline
b) <<
c) >>
d) Both a and c.

18.9 The _____ directory specifies the parent directory.

a) `..`

b) `.`

c) `/`

d) `C:\`

18.10 _____ is a valid file-open mode.

a) `ios::out`

b) `ios::app`

c) `ios::open`

d) Both a and b.

EXERCISES

18.11 (*Birthday Saver Application*) Create an application that stores people's names and birthdays in a file (Fig. 18.33). The user enters a file name and inputs each person's first name, last name and birthday. The information then is written to the file, as shown in the lower image of Fig. 18.33.

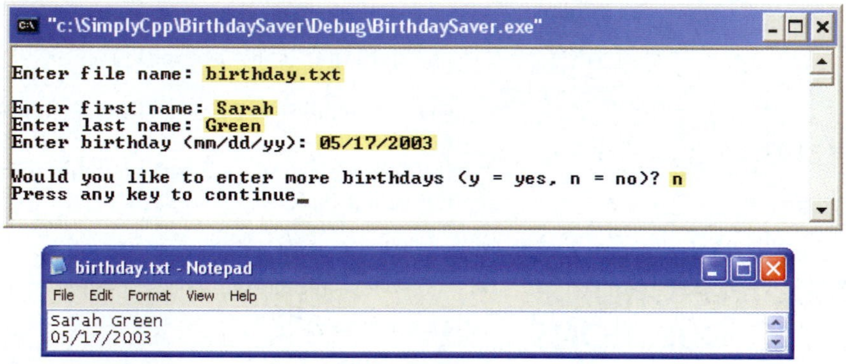

Figure 18.33 **Birthday Saver** application output

a) *Copying the template to your working directory.* Copy the `C:\Examples\Tutorial18\Exercises\BirthdaySaver` directory to your `C:\SimplyCpp` directory.

b) *Opening the template source code file.* Open the `BirthdaySaver.cpp` file in your text editor or IDE.

c) *Defining variables.* In lines 14–19, define `string` variables `fileName`, `firstName`, `lastName` and `birthday` to store the file name, first name, last name and birthday, respectively, that the user enters. Then, define `char` variable `response` to store a value indicating whether the user would like to enter another birthday.

d) *Prompting the user for and inputting a file name.* In lines 21–23, prompt the user for and store a file name in the `fileName` variable. In lines 25–30, use an `if` statement to issue an error message and exit the application if the user entered the empty string for the file name.

e) *Opening the file.* In lines 32–40, open the specified file in append mode using an `ofstream` object named `outputFile`. After creating the `ofstream` object, use an `if` statement to issue an error message and exit the application if the `ofstream` object could not open the file.

f) *Obtaining birthday information.* In lines 42–54, insert a do...while statement that repeats while the response contains an uppercase or lowercase "y" character. In the body of the do...while statement, prompt the user for and input the first name, last name and birthday. Store these values in the `firstName`, `lastName` and `birthday` variables, respectively.

g) *Outputting the birthdays to the file.* After the code you added in the preceding step, but before the end of the do...while statement, insert code that places the first name and last name on a single line of the file, separated by a space. Then output the birthday on a new line. Be sure to add a newline after outputting the birthday.

h) *Determining whether the user wants to enter more birthdays.* Before the end of the body of the do...while statement, prompt the user to enter a character indicating whether there are more birthdays to enter, as shown in Fig. 18.33. Store the value in the `response` variable. Be sure to use the `ignore` function to remove the newline from `cin` before the end of the do...while statement.

i) *Save, compile and run the application.* Test your application to ensure that it runs correctly by entering several names and birthdays into a text file. Then, open the text file in your text editor to make sure it was written properly.

j) *Close the Command Prompt window.*

18.12 (*File Decryption Application*) Create an application that reads encrypted text from a file specified by the user and outputs the text to a different file, as shown in Fig. 18.34. Assume that the contents of the encrypted file have been encrypted using the technique in Exercise 6.13. The decrypted text should be placed in the file `decryptedText.txt`. We have provided the file `encryptedText.txt` for you to test your application (Fig. 18.35).

Figure 18.34   **File Decryption** application output.

Figure 18.35   Contents of `encryptedText.txt`.

a) *Copying the template to your working directory.* Copy the `C:\Examples\Tutorial18\Exercises\FileDecryption` directory to your `C:\SimplyCpp` directory.

b) *Opening the template source code file.* Open the `FileDecryption.cpp` file in your text editor or IDE.

c) *Defining variables.* In lines 14–17, define `string` variables `fileName` and `contents` and `char` variable `currentCharacter`. These variables will store the file name for the encrypted text, the contents of that file and a single character of the encrypted text, respectively.

d) *Prompting the user for and inputting the file name.* Prompt the user for the name of the file that will contain the encrypted text and store that name in the `fileName` variable.

e) *Opening files for reading and writing.* Create an `ifstream` object named `input` that inputs data from the file that the user specified. Then create an `ofstream` object named `output` in the `ios::out` file-open mode that writes to the file named `decryptedText.txt`. Add an `if` statement that causes the application to exit if either file could not be opened.

f) *Reading information from the file.* Use the `getline` function to read a line of text from the file and store the text in the `contents` variable. Then define `int` variable `counter` and initialize its value to one less than the number of characters in `contents`. The number of characters in the `string` is returned by the function call `contents.size()`.

g) *Decrypting the text.* Insert a `while` statement that repeats while the value of `counter` is greater than or equal to zero. To decrypt the text, you will read each character in the `contents`, add 15 to the character value and output the character to the `output` object. To decrypt the message, you must read characters in order from the end of the string to the beginning. Use the expression `contents.at( counter )` to retrieve the character in each iteration of the loop, then decrement `counter` before the end of the body of the loop. After the `while` loop completes, display a message indicating that the file has been decrypted successfully.

h) *Save, compile and run the application.* Test your application to ensure that it runs correctly by decrypting the `encryptedText.txt` file. If your application works correctly, `decryptedText.txt` will contain a special message for you.

i) *Close the Command Prompt window.*

What does this code do? ▶ **18.13** What is the result of the following code when the following code is executed?

```
1   // Exercise 18.13: WDTCD.cpp
2   // What does this code do?
3   #include <iostream> // required to perform C++ stream I/O
4   #include <string>   // required to access string functions
5   #include <fstream>  // required to perform C++ file I/O
6   #include <cstdlib>  // required for the exit function
7
8   using namespace std; // for accessing C++ Standard Library members
9
10  // function main begins program execution
11  int main()
12  {
13     // define variables
14     string file1 = "oldFile.txt";
15     string file2 = "newFile.txt";
16     string line;
17
18     ofstream output( file2.c_str() );
19     ifstream input ( file1.c_str() );
20
21     if ( !output || !input )
22     {
23        cout << "\nError: File could not be opened.\n" << endl;
24        exit( 1 );
25     } // end if
26
27     cout << endl;
28
29     while( !input.eof() )
30     {
31        getline( input, line );
32        output << line << endl;
33        cout << line << endl;
34     } // end while
35
36     return 0; // indicate that program ended successfully
37
38  } // end function main
```

What's wrong with this code? ▶ **18.14** Find the error(s) in the following code, which is supposed to read a line from some-file.txt into string variable contents. The code should then append the string literal "Appended data:", followed by contents, to the end of somefile.txt.

```
1   // Exercise 18.14: WWWTC.cpp
2   // This application takes data from one file and appends
3   // that data to the same file.
4   #include <iostream>  // required to perform C++ stream I/O
5   #include <string>    // required to access string functions
6   #include <fstream>   // required to perform C++ file I/O
7   #include <cstdlib>   // required for the exit function
8
9   using namespace std; // for accessing C++ Standard Library members
10
```

```
11   // function main begins program execution
12   int main()
13   {
14      // define variables
15      string file = "someFile.txt";
16      string contents;
17
18      ifstream input( file, ios::app );
19      ofstream output( file );
20
21      getline( input, contents ); // store input in contents
22
23      cout << "\n" << contents;
24      cout << "\nAppend data:" << endl << contents << endl;
25      output << "\nAppended data:" << endl << contents << endl;
26
27      cout << "\n"; // insert newline for readability
28      return 0; // indicate that program ended successfully
29
30   } // end function main
```

Programming Challenge ▶

18.15 (*Car Reservation Application*) Create an application that allows a user to reserve a car for a specified day (Fig. 18.36). The car reservation company can rent out only four cars per day. Let the application allow the user to specify a certain day. If four cars have already been reserved for that day, indicate to the user that no vehicles are available. Reservations are stored in reservations.txt.

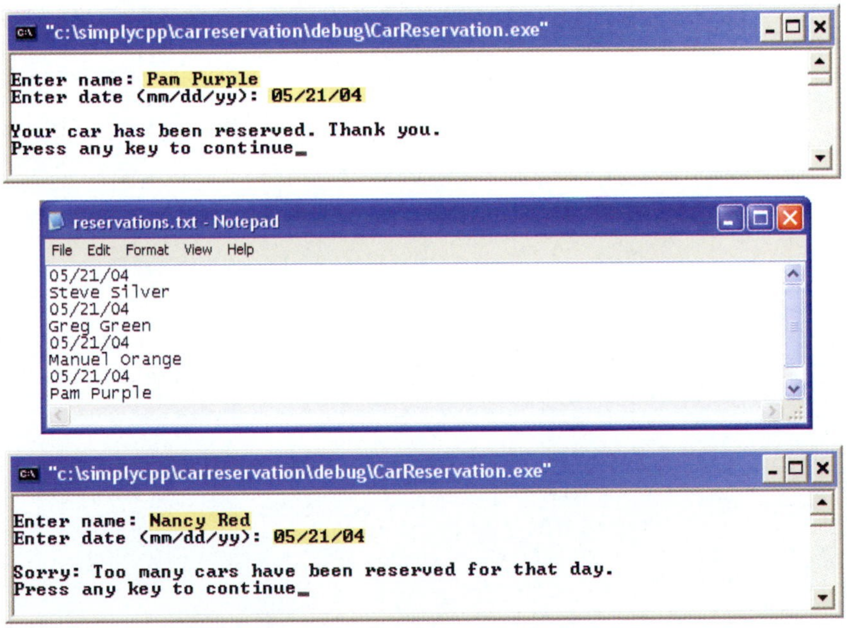

Figure 18.36 Car Reservation application output.

a) *Copying the template to your working directory.* Copy the C:\Examples\ Tutorial18\Exercises\CarReservation directory to your C:\SimplyCpp directory.

b) *Opening the template source code file.* Open the CarReservation.cpp file in your text editor or IDE. Note that the beginning of main has been provided for you.

c) *Opening the reservations.txt file for input.* Beginning in line 30, create an ifstream object named input, which will be used to read from the reservations.txt file. Use an if statement to issue an error message and exit the application if the file could not be opened.

d) *Reading text from the file.* Read a line from the file and input the line into `string` `contents`. Next, add a `while` statement that will read data from the file. Have the `while` statement loop while `input` has not reached the end of the file. Inside the `while` loop, add an `if` statement that executes when the value of `contents` equals the value of `date`. Use the compare member function of the `string` class in the condition of the `if` statement. The expression `string1.compare( string2 )` returns 0 if `string1` and `string2` contain the same text. Within this `if` statement, define an `if...else` statement where the `if` part increments `dateCount` if there are still less than four people reserving a car on that day. The `else` part should display a message informing the user that there are no more cars available for this day and exit the application. After the outer `if` statement, read the next line of the file for the next iteration of the `while` loop. After the `while` loop, close the file by calling the close member function on the `input` object, using the member-access operator (`.`). If you do not close the file, you will be unable to open it for writing in the next step.

e) *Writing to the text file.* If the remainder of the function is reached, there is still room for a reservation on the current day. After the `while` loop, open `reservations.txt` for appending. Use an `if` statement to issue an error message and exit the application if the file could not be opened. Next, write the value of `date` to the file (in its own line), followed by the name contained in `name` (also on its own line). Display a message informing the user that the car has been reserved.

f) *Save, compile and run the application.* Test your application to ensure that it runs correctly by reserving cars on different dates. Also, be sure that you receive an error message when trying to reserve too many cars for one day.

g) *Close the Command Prompt window.*

19

Objectives

In this tutorial, you will learn to:

- Create and manipulate `string` objects.
- Use properties and functions of the `string` class.
- Search for substrings within `strings`.
- Extract substrings from `strings`.
- Replace substrings within `strings`.
- Convert a `string` of numbers to its corresponding numeric value.

Outline

Screen Scraping Application

Introducing *string* Processing

This tutorial introduces C++'s `string` processing capabilities. The techniques presented in this tutorial can be used to create applications that process text. Earlier tutorials introduced the `string` class and several of its functions. In this tutorial, you will learn how to search `strings`, retrieve substrings from `strings` and replace substrings in `strings`. You will create an application that uses these `string` processing capabilities to manipulate a `string` containing HTML (HyperText Markup Language)—a technology used for describing Web content. Extracting desired information from the HTML that composes a Web page is called **screen scraping**. A **screen scraper** is a tool used to extract Web page data, such as weather conditions or stock prices, so that the information can be formatted and manipulated more easily by computer applications. In this tutorial, you will create a simple **Screen Scraping** application.

19.1 Test-Driving the Screen Scraping Application

This application must meet the following requirements:

Application Requirements

An online European auction house wants to expand its business to include bidders from the United States. However, all of the auction house's Web pages currently display their prices in euros, not dollars. The auction house wants to generate separate Web pages for American bidders that will display the prices of auction items in dollars. These new Web pages will be generated by using screen-scraping techniques on the already existing Web pages. You have been asked to build a prototype application that will test the screen-scraping functionality. The application should search a sample string of HTML and extract information about the price of a specified auction item. For testing purposes, a menu should be provided that contains auction items listed in the HTML. The selected item's amount must then be converted to dollars, so the user is prompted to enter the current conversion rate. The application will search and extract the price in euros of the item selected, convert this value to dollars and display the resulting price.

The **Screen Scraping** application searches for the name of a specified auction item in a string of HTML. Users select from a menu the item whose price they want to find. The application then extracts the price of this item in euros, converts it and displays it in dollars. You begin by test-driving the completed application. Then, you will learn the additional C++ capabilities you will need to create your own version of this application.

Test-Driving the Screen Scraping Application

1. *Locating the completed application.* Open the **Command Prompt** window by selecting **Start > All Programs > Accessories > Command Prompt**. Change to your completed **Screen Scraping** application directory by typing `cd C:\Examples\Tutorial19\CompletedApplication\ScreenScraping`.

2. *Running the Screen Scraping application.* Type ScreenScraping in the **Command Prompt** window to run the application (Fig. 19.1). Notice that the HTML string is displayed after the application begins. (You will learn about this text shortly.) The application then displays a menu of items from which the user can select. Figure 19.2 displays the HTML page in Internet Explorer.

HTML source is displayed

Figure 19.1   Running the completed **Screen Scraping** application.

Figure 19.2   Displaying the HTML page in Internet Explorer.

3. *Selecting an item.* The menu contains three items. Enter 2 at the **Enter selection:** prompt as shown in Fig. 19.3. Once you select an item, the **Enter conversion rate:** prompt is displayed.

(cont.)

```
Command Prompt - ScreenScraping
The HTML source is:
<HTML><BODY><TABLE><TR><TD>Antique Rocking Chair</TD><TD>&euro;82.67</
TD></TR><TR><TD>Silver Teapot</TD><TD>&euro;64.55</TD></TR><TR><TD>Gol
d Pocket Watch</TD><TD>&euro;128.83</TD></TR></TABLE></BODY></HTML>

Which item would you like to search for?
1 - Antique Rocking Chair
2 - Silver Teapot
3 - Gold Pocket Watch
4 - Exit the application
Enter selection: 2
Enter conversion rate: _
```

Figure 19.3 Selecting an item from the menu.

4. ***Searching for an item's price.*** The **Enter conversion rate:** prompt is provided for the user to enter the conversion rate. For instance, if the current conversion rate is `1.5` (meaning that `1` euro is equal to `1.5` dollars), the user would enter `1.5` at the **Enter conversion rate:** prompt. Once the user selects an item and enters a conversion rate, the price in euros for that item will be found in the HTML, converted to dollars and displayed.

   Enter a conversion rate of `1.20` at the **Enter conversion rate:** prompt. Conversion rates change constantly, which is why we have provided an input prompt rather than defining a constant conversion rate. Current conversion rates are provided by various Web sites. One such site, known as The Universal Currency Converter®, can be found at `www.xe.com/ucc`. Notice that after you enter the conversion rate, the application displays the price for the selected item in dollars (Fig. 19.4). The application then displays a menu prompting you to select another item or exit the application.

Price located in HTML string (specified in euros)

Extracted price (converted to dollars)

```
Command Prompt - ScreenScraping
The HTML source is:
<HTML><BODY><TABLE><TR><TD>Antique Rocking Chair</TD><TD>&euro;82.67</
TD></TR><TR><TD>Silver Teapot</TD><TD>&euro;64.55</TD></TR><TR><TD>Gol
d Pocket Watch</TD><TD>&euro;128.83</TD></TR></TABLE></BODY></HTML>

Which item would you like to search for?
1 - Antique Rocking Chair
2 - Silver Teapot
3 - Gold Pocket Watch
4 - Exit the application
Enter selection: 2
Enter conversion rate: 1.20

Price is: $77.46
```

Figure 19.4 Searching for the item's price and displaying the price in dollars.

5. ***Close the running application.*** Exit your running application by entering 4 at the **Enter selection:** prompt.

6. ***Close the* Command Prompt *window.***

19.2 Fundamentals of `string`s

Recall from Tutorial 2 that a string is a sequence of characters treated as a single unit. These characters can be uppercase letters, lowercase letters, digits and various special characters, such as +, -, *, /, $, whitespace characters, such as blank lines, spaces and tabs, and others. A string is an object of the `basic_string` class in the `<string>` header file. For simplicity, we will refer to objects of this class simply as `string`s. You write string literals, or string constants (often called **literal `string` objects**), as sequences of characters in double quotation marks:

```
"This is a string!"
```

You've created and used `strings` in previous tutorials. You know that a definition can assign a string literal to a `string` variable. For example, the definition

```
string color = "blue";
```

initializes the `color` `string` with the string literal `"blue"`. Characters of a `string` object can be accessed as if they were elements of an array of `chars`. For example, the statement

```
char firstCharacter = color[ 0 ];
```

Error-Prevention Tip

Accessing an element beyond the size of the `string` using the subscript operator is a logic error.

assigns the character "b" to `firstCharacter`.

Unlike arrays, `strings` always "know" their own size. You can access this size using `string` function **length**, which returns the length of the `string` (that is, the number of characters in the `string`). For example, the function call `color.length()` returns 4 for the `string` `"blue"`. Note that the `string` class also provides the **size** function, which returns the same value as `length`.

Another useful function of the `string` class is **at**, which returns the character located at a specific index in a `string`. The `at` function takes an `int` argument specifying the index and returns the character at that index. An index ranges from 0 to the length of the `string` minus 1. As with arrays, the first element of a `string` is at index 0. For example, the following code

```
if ( string1.at( 0 ) == string2.at( 0 ) )
{
    cout << "The first characters of string1 and string2 are the
same.";
}
```

compares the character at index 0 (that is, the first character) of `string1` with the character at index 0 of `string2` and prints a message if they are equal.

Error-Prevention Tip

Accessing a `string` subscript outside the bounds of the `string` using the `at` function throws an `out_of_range` exception.

The `at` function provides **checked access** (or **range checking**), meaning that going past the end of the `string` causes C++ to generate a special type of error called an **out_of_range exception**. We will discuss exceptions in Tutorial 20. Note that the subscript operator, [], does not provide checked access. This is consistent with its use in arrays.

In Exercise 18.15, you used the **compare** function of the `string` class to determine if two `string` objects contained the same text. For example, the expression

```
string1.compare( string2 )
```

returns 0 if the `strings` are equivalent, a negative number if `string1` precedes `string2` in alphabetical order or a positive number if `string1` follows `string2` in alphabetical order. The `string` class also enables applications to compare two strings using the equality operator, ==, so the statement

```
string1 == string2
```

will evaluate to `true` if the strings are equivalent and `false` otherwise. The <, >, <=, >= and != operators also can be used to compare two `string` objects. You will learn new `string` functions later in this tutorial.

SELF-REVIEW

1. The _____ function of the `string` class returns the number of characters in the string.

   a) `maxChars`   b) `length`
   c) `characterCount`   d) `value`

2. A string can be composed of _____.

   a) digits   b) lowercase letters
   c) special characters   d) All of the above.

Answers: 1) b. 2) d.

19.3 Constructing the Screen Scraping Application

Now you will build your **Screen Scraping** application by using `string` processing to locate and manipulate `string` data. The pseudocode in Fig. 19.5 describes the basic operation of the **Screen Scraping** application.

Store the HTML that contains the items' prices in a string
Display the HTML

While the user wants to search for prices
    Prompt the user for and input the selected item for which to search
    Search the HTML for the item the user selected
    Extract the item's price
    Convert the item's price from euros to dollars
    Display the item's price

Figure 19.5 Pseudocode for the **Screen Scraping** application.

Now that you've analyzed the **Screen Scraping** application's pseudocode, you will learn about the `string` functions that you will use to construct the application.

19.4 Locating Substrings in `strings`

In many applications, it is necessary to search for a character or a group of characters in a `string`. For example, a word-processing application might provide capabilities that allow users to search their documents. The `string` class provides functions that search for specified substrings in a `string`. A **substring** is a sequence of characters that make up part or all of a `string`. For instance, `"lo"` is a substring of the `string "hello"`, as is `"ll"`, `"he"`, `"e"` and many others, including `"hello"` itself. Next, you will use the `find` function to search for substrings in `strings`.

Locating the Selected Item's Price

1. **Copying the template to your working directory.** Copy the `C:\Examples\Tutorial19\TemplateApplication\ScreenScraping` directory to your `C:\SimplyCpp` directory.

2. **Opening the Screen Scraping application's template source code file.** Open the template file `ScreenScraping.cpp` in your text editor or IDE.

3. **Viewing the application's function prototypes.** View lines 12–14 of your application (Fig. 19.6). Notice that the `displayMenu` and `getPrice` functions declare `string` reference parameters by following the type name (`string`) with an ampersand (`&`). By default, `string` arguments are passed by value, meaning that the function manipulates a copy of the `string`. As you will see in the following steps, the caller must access the modified `strings` produced by `displayMenu` and `getPrice`, so the `string` arguments to these functions are passed by reference. This enables the called function to access and modify the `string` reference arguments passed by the caller.

Declaring functions that pass `string` values by reference

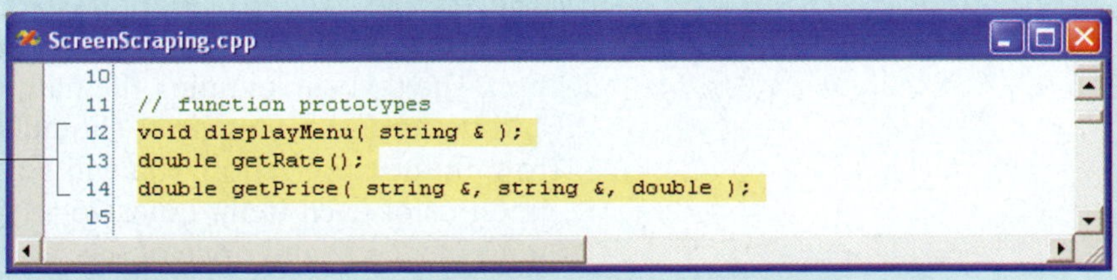

```
10
11   // function prototypes
12   void displayMenu( string & );
13   double getRate();
14   double getPrice( string &, string &, double );
15
```

Figure 19.6 Function prototypes that use pass-by-reference.

(cont.) 4. ***Defining variables and displaying the HTML.*** Add lines 19–32 of Fig. 19.7 to main. Line 20 defines **string** variable **searchText**, which will store the name of the item that the user requests. Lines 23–30 define the **htmlText** variable and assign it several lines of HTML source code. Notice that the string assignment statement begins in line 23 and terminates at the semicolon in line 30. When multiple string literals appear sequentially in an assignment statement, C++ appends each consecutive string literal to the one that appeared before it. This operation often is referred to as **concatenation**. Line 32 displays the HTML source code contained in **string** variable **htmlText**.

Concatenating **strings** ————

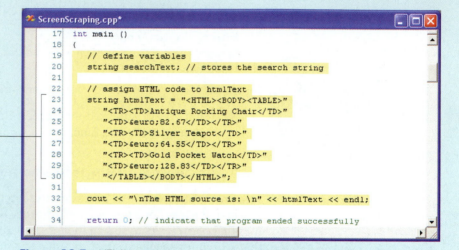

```
17  int main ()
18  {
19     // define variables
20     string searchText; // stores the search string
21
22     // assign HTML code to htmlText
23     string htmlText = "<HTML><BODY><TABLE>"
24        "<TR><TD>Antique Rocking Chair</TD>"
25        "<TD>&euro;82.67</TD></TR>"
26        "<TR><TD>Silver Teapot</TD>"
27        "<TD>&euro;64.55</TD></TR>"
28        "<TR><TD>Gold Pocket Watch</TD>"
29        "<TD>&euro;128.83</TD></TR>"
30        "</TABLE></BODY></HTML>";
31
32     cout << "\nThe HTML source is: \n" << htmlText << endl;
33
34     return 0; // indicate that program ended successfully
```

Figure 19.7   HTML containing the price of the auction items.

You are not expected to understand HTML—in this tutorial, we will briefly describe only the HTML of Fig. 19.7. HTML markup contains text that represents the content of a document and elements that specify a document's structure. HTML documents delimit an element with start and end tags. Line 23 contains start tags for the HTML, BODY and TABLE elements. A start tag consists of an element name enclosed in angle brackets (such as <HTML>). An end tag consists of the element name preceded by a / in angle brackets (such as </HTML>). In this example, lines 23 and 30 define the start and end tags for the HTML, BODY and TABLE elements. The HTML start and end tags indicate the beginning and end of HTML markup, respectively, for the document. The BODY element contains the page's content that the browser displays when the user visits the Web page.

The TABLE element specifies a table consisting of rows (specified by the TR element) and columns (specified by the TD element). Thus, the HTML in lines 24–29 contains the names and prices of three auction items. Lines 24–25 display the portion of HTML that contains the name and price of the first item. The name of the item is specified in line 24 as "Antique Rocking Chair", and the price of this item is specified in line 25 as "€82.67". The **string** "€" is the HTML representation of the euro symbol (€), which appears before every price value in the HTML string in this application. The text surrounding the name and price values specify that each item and its corresponding price should appear in different columns of the same row. In this application, you will be concerned only with the name and price in euros of each item. Lines 26–27 display the portion of HTML that contains the name and price of the second item, and lines 28–29 display the portion of HTML that contains the name and price of the third item.

(cont.)

5. ***Retrieving the specified item name.*** Add lines 34–41 of Fig. 19.8 to `main`. Line 35 calls the `displayMenu` function and passes `string` variable `search-Text` as the argument. Recall that the `displayMenu` function definition's reference parameter forces `searchText` to be passed by reference. The `displayMenu` function, which is provided for you after `main` in lines 49–92, displays a menu of items for which the user can search. The function stores the selected text in `searchText` using its reference parameter. Thus, after the `displayMenu` function completes, `main`'s local `searchText` variable contains the name of the item that the user selected.

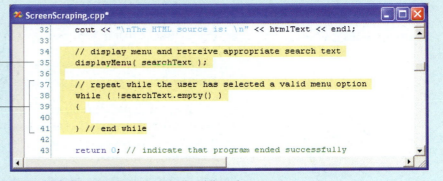

Prompting the user for and inputting an item name (stored in the `searchText` variable)

Repeating until `searchText` contains the empty string

Figure 19.8 Locating the desired item's name.

If the user chooses to exit the application, `displayMenu` will place the empty string in `searchText`. The `while` statement's condition in line 38 calls `string` member function `empty` on `searchText`. The **empty** function returns `true` if the `string` on which it is called contains the empty string. Therefore, if the user chooses to exit the application, the `empty` function returns `true` and the condition in line 38 evaluates to `false`, due to the logical negation operator, `!`. In this case, the application skips the `while` statement and exits at the `return` statement in line 43.

6. ***Determining the price of the item.*** Add lines 40–52 of Fig. 19.9 to the body of the `while` statement. Line 41 calls the `getRate` function, which prompts the user for the conversion rate from euros to dollars and returns the value that the user entered as a `double`. The value returned by the `getRate` function is stored in `double` variable `rate`. Line 45 calls the `getPrice` function, passing it `string` variables `htmlText`, `searchText` and `double` `rate` as parameters. The `getPrice` function, which you will define in the next step, uses the name of the item contained in `searchText` to search for the item's price in the HTML (contained in `htmlText`) and convert the price from euros to dollars. Line 45 stores the converted value in `double` variable `price`. Then, lines 48–49 display `price` in currency format. Finally, line 52 calls the `displayMenu` function to prompt the user to select another item for which to search or exit the application.

7. ***Locating the specified item name.*** Add lines 124–125 of Fig. 19.10 to the `getPrice` function. Line 125 calls `string` function **find** to locate the first occurrence of the specified item name (`searchtext`) in the HTML `string` `htmlText`. You will use two versions of `find` in this application. Line 124 uses the version that takes a single argument—the substring for which to search. The `find` function locates the first occurrence of the specified substring (in this case, the name of the selected item) within `htmlText`. The index at which the substring begins in `htmlText` is returned.

(cont.)

Prompting the user for and inputting the conversion rate

Searching for the price and calculating the converted price

Displaying the price as currency

Prompting the user to select the next item for which to search

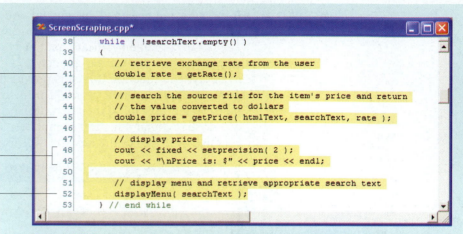

```
ScreenScraping.cpp*
38      while ( !searchText.empty() )
39      {
40          // retrieve exchange rate from the user
41          double rate = getRate();
42
43          // search the source file for the item's price and return
44          // the value converted to dollars
45          double price = getPrice( htmlText, searchText, rate );
46
47          // display price
48          cout << fixed << setprecision( 2 );
49          cout << "\nPrice is: $" << price << endl;
50
51          // display menu and retrieve appropriate search text
52          displayMenu( searchText );
53      } // end while
```

Figure 19.9   Calculating and displaying the price of the item.

The `find` function (and other `string` find-related functions) returns the value **`string::npos`**, a constant value defined in the `string` class, to indicate that a substring or character was not found in the `string`. Line 124 stores the result in `itemLocation`.

Search for the `searchText` in the `string htmlText`

```
ScreenScraping.cpp*
120  // find the price for the selected item
121  double getPrice( string &htmlText, string &searchText,
122                   double conversionRate )
123  {
124      // search for location of item and price
125      int itemLocation = htmlText.find( searchText );
126  } // end function getPrice
```

Figure 19.10   Locating the desired item's name.

8. ***Locating the start of the price.*** Add line 126 of Fig. 19.11 to the `getPrice` function. Line 126 locates the index at which the item's price begins. This line of code uses the version of the `find` function that takes two arguments—the substring for which to search (`"&euro;"`) and the starting index in the `string` at which the search should begin. The first argument to the `find` function must be in the range 0 to the length of the `string`, inclusive. The function does not examine any characters that occur prior to the starting index (specified by `itemLocation`), because you are concerned only with the portion of `htmlText` that includes the price of the selected item. Remember that the first price that follows the specified item name will be the desired price, which will begin with the `"&euro;"` substring. The value returned by `find` contains the index where the price of the current item begins (including the `string "&euro;"`). Because you will be displaying the monetary values as dollars, you do not need the euro symbol; by adding 6 to `priceBegin`, you are excluding the first 6 characters, namely `"&euro;"`. The result is stored in the `priceBegin` variable.

(cont.)

Locating the beginning of the price in `htmlText`

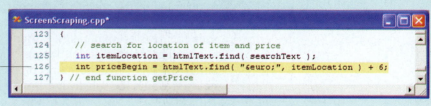

```
ScreenScraping.cpp*
123  {
124      // search for location of item and price
125      int itemLocation = htmlText.find( searchText );
126      int priceBegin = htmlText.find( "&euro;", itemLocation ) + 6;
127  } // end function getPrice
```

Figure 19.11   Locating the desired item's price.

9. ***Locating the end of the price.*** Add line 127 of Fig. 19.12 to the `getPrice` function. Line 127 finds the index at which the desired price ends by passing the `string` `"</TD>"` and the starting index `priceBegin` to the `find` function. Recall that a `</TD>` tag directly follows every price (excluding any spaces) in the HTML string, so the index of the first `</TD>` tag after `priceBegin` marks the end of the current price. The index returned from the `find` function is stored in variable `priceEnd`.

Locating the end of the price in `htmlText`

```
124        // search for location of item and price
125        int itemLocation = htmlText.find( searchText );
126        int priceBegin = htmlText.find( "&euro;", itemLocation ) + 6;
127        int priceEnd = htmlText.find( "</TD>", priceBegin );
128  } // end function getPrice
```

Figure 19.12   Locating the end of the item's price.

10. ***Save the application.*** You have now stored the index where the price of the selected item begins (`priceBegin`) and the index directly after the location where the price of the selected item ends (`priceEnd`). No value is yet returned by the `getPrice` function, so if you compile and run your application then select an item name, no price will be displayed. You will add this functionality later in the tutorial.

Another `string` class function that is similar to the `find` function is the `rfind` function. The **rfind** function locates the last occurrence of the specified substring in a `string`; it performs the search backwards, starting from the end of the `string`. The `rfind` function returns the starting index of the specified substring in the `string`—if the substring does not exist, `string::npos` is returned.

There are two versions of the `rfind` function that search for substrings in a `string`. The first takes a single argument—the substring for which to search. The second takes two arguments—the substring for which to search and the index from which to begin searching backwards for the substring. Figure 19.13 demonstrates searching for substrings using the `find` and `rfind` functions.

Function	Example expression (assume text = "My string is a long string")	Returns
`find`(*string*)	`text.find( "ring" )`	5
`find`(*string, int*)	`text.find( "ring", 10 )`	22
`rfind`(*string*)	`text.rfind( "ring" )`	22
`rfind`(*string, int*)	`text.rfind( "ring", 3 )`	`string::npos`

Figure 19.13   Demonstration of `find` and `rfind` functions.

SELF-REVIEW

1. The _____ function locates the first occurrence of a substring within the `string` on which the function is called.

   a) `find`   b) `firstIndexOf`
   c) `findFirst`   d) `rfind`

2. In the version of the `rfind` function that takes a `string` followed by an `int` as arguments, the second argument passed to the `rfind` function is _____.

   a) the number of characters to search
   b) the starting index from which to start searching forward

c) the length of the substring to locate

d) the starting index from which to start searching backward

Answers: 1) a. 2) d.

19.5 Extracting Substrings from **strings**

You will now learn how to use the substr function to retrieve the price of the selected item from the HTML string. The **substr** function returns a new string object that contains a copy of a specified part of an existing string object.

Retrieving the Desired Item's Price

1. ***Extracting the price.*** Add lines 129–134 of Fig. 19.14 to the getPrice function. Lines 130–131 extract the price from htmlText using the substr function. The first argument (priceBegin), specifies the starting index from which the function copies characters from the original string. Like with the find function, this argument must be in the range 0 to the length of the string, inclusive.

   The second argument (priceEnd - priceBegin) specifies the number of characters to be copied, beginning at the starting index (priceBegin). The priceEnd variable contains the index where the text "</TD>" begins, which is found directly after the price of the current item. The substring returned on line 130 (priceText) contains a copy of the specified characters from the original string. In this case, the substring returned is the item's price (without the euro symbol). For example, if the item selected were the **Antique Rocking Chair**, the string stored in price would be "82.67", as you can see from the data in Fig. 19.1. (This value is found in the HTML's second line of text.)

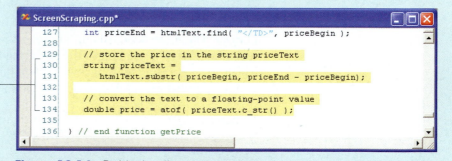

Setting priceText to the htmlText substring, converting priceText to a double and storing it in price

```
127       int priceEnd = htmlText.find( "</TD>", priceBegin );
128
129       // store the price in the string priceText
130       string priceText =
131          htmlText.substr( priceBegin, priceEnd - priceBegin);
132
133       // convert the text to a floating-point value
134       double price = atof( priceText.c_str() );
135
136    } // end function getPrice
```

Figure 19.14 Retrieving the desired price.

The string class provides two versions of the substr function. The other version takes only one int argument. The argument specifies the starting index from which the function copies characters in the original string. The substring returned contains a copy of the characters from the starting index to the end of the string. You will not use this version of the substr function in the **Screen Scraping** application.

Line 134 uses the atof function to convert priceText into a double (stored in the price variable), so that this price may be multiplied by the conversion rate. The **atof** function (which stands for "ASCII to floating-point value"), declared in the <cstdlib> header file, converts an array of ASCII characters to a floating-point value. Because the atof function does not accept string objects as parameters, line 134 calls the c_str function to create an array of characters containing the string's text. If the string cannot be converted (for example, if the first character of the string is a letter), the atof function returns 0.

(cont.)

2. ***Converting from euros to dollars.*** You must now multiply the price extracted from the HTML by the conversion rate entered by the user. Add lines 136–137 of Fig. 19.15 to the `getPrice` function. Line 137 multiplies the `conversionRate` by the `price` and returns the result to the caller.

Converting the price from euros to dollars using the conversion rate entered by the user

```
ScreenScraping.cpp*
134        double price = atof( priceText.c_str() );
135
136        // convert price from euros to dollars
137        return price * conversionRate;
138
139   } // end function getPrice
```

Figure 19.15   Converting prices from euros to dollars.

3. ***Save, compile and run the application.*** Figure 19.16 shows the completed application running. Select an item from the menu and enter a conversion rate to display the price of that item in dollars.

```
"c:\SimplyCpp\ScreenScraping\Debug\ScreenScraping.exe"

Which item would you like to search for?
1 - Antique Rocking Chair
2 - Silver Teapot
3 - Gold Pocket Watch
4 - Exit the application
Enter selection: 3
Enter conversion rate: 1.2

Price is: $154.60
```

Figure 19.16   Running the completed **Screen Scraping** application.

4. ***Closing the application.*** Exit your running application by entering 4 at the **Enter selection:** prompt.

5. ***Close the Command Prompt window.***

SELF-REVIEW

1. The `substr` function _____.
   a) accepts either one or two arguments
   b) returns a new `string` object
   c) creates a `string` object by copying part of an existing `string` object
   d) All of the above

2. When a call is made to the two-argument version of the `substr` function, the second argument specifies _____.
   a) the index from which to begin copying backwards
   b) the length of the substring to copy
   c) the index one beyond the last character to be copied
   d) the last index to be copied

Answers: 1) d. 2) b.

19.6 Other `string` Functions

The `string` class provides several additional functions that allow you to manipulate `string`s. Figure 19.17 lists some of these functions. The first argument to the `replace` function must be in the range 0 to the length of the `string`, inclusive.

Function	Description	Sample Expression (assume text = " My string")
`find_first_of(`*string*`)`	Returns the index of the first occurrence in a string of any character contained in the *string* argument.	`text.find_first_of` `( "aeiouy" );` Returns: 2 (The position of the "y" in "My")
`find_first_not_of` `(`*string*`)`	Returns the index of the first occurrence in a string of any character not contained in the *string* argument.	`text.find_first_not_of` `( " My" );` Returns: 4 (The position of the "s" in "string")
`replace(`*index,* *numberOfCharacters,* *string*`)`	Replaces in a string a number of characters beginning at the specified index with the *string* argument.	`text.replace( 0, 4, "Shoe");` text contains: `"Shoestring"`

Figure 19.17 Description of other `string` functions.

Figure 19.18 presents the source code for the **Screen Scraping** application. The lines of code that you added, viewed or modified in this tutorial are highlighted.

```
1   // Tutorial 19: ScreenScraping.cpp
2   // Search an HTML code string for an item and display its price
3   // converted from euros to American dollars.
4   #include <iostream> // required to perform C++ stream I/O
5   #include <iomanip>  // required for parameterized stream manipulators
6   #include <string>   // required to access string functions
7   #include <cstdlib>  // required for the atof function
8
9   using namespace std; // for accessing C++ Standard Library members
10
11  // function prototypes
12  void displayMenu( string & );
13  double getRate();
14  double getPrice( string &, string &, double );
15
16  // function main begins program execution
17  int main ()
18  {
19     // define variables
20     string searchText; // stores the search string
21
22     // assign HTML code to htmlText
23     string htmlText = "<HTML><BODY><TABLE>";
24        "<TR><TD>Antique Rocking Chair</TD>";
25        "<TD>&euro;82.67</TD></TR>";
26        "<TR><TD>Silver Teapot</TD>";
27        "<TD>&euro;64.55</TD></TR>";
28        "<TR><TD>Gold Pocket Watch</TD>";
29        "<TD>&euro;128.83</TD></TR>";
30        "</TABLE></BODY></HTML>";
31
32     cout << "\nThe HTML source is: \n" << htmlText << endl;
33
```

Declare functions that declare `string` reference parameters —— (lines 12–14)

Concatenate strings —— (line 23)

Figure 19.18 Screen Scraping code. (Part 1 of 3.)

Prompt the user for an item name and input it into the `searchText` variable

Repeat until `searchText` contains the empty string

Prompt the user for and store the conversion rate

Search for the price and calculate the converted price

Display the price as currency

Prompt the user to select the next item for which to search

```
   // display menu and retrieve appropriate search text
   displayMenu( searchText );

   // repeat while the user has selected a valid menu option
   while ( !searchText.empty() )
   {
      // retrieve exchange rate from the user
      double rate = getRate();

      // search the source file for the item's price and return
      // the value converted to dollars
      double price = getPrice( htmlText, searchText, rate );

      // display price
      cout << fixed << setprecision( 2 );
      cout << "\nPrice is: $" << price << endl;

      // display menu and retrieve appropriate search text
      displayMenu( searchText );
   } // end while

   return 0; // indicate that program ended successfully

} // end function main

// prompt the user for a search item and return the appropriate
// search string
void displayMenu( string &searchText )
{
   // define local variable to store user selection from the menu
   int selection = 0;

   while ( selection < 1 || selection > 4 )
   {
      // display the menu
      cout << "\nWhich item would you like to search for?\n";
      cout << "1 - Antique Rocking Chair" << endl;
      cout << "2 - Silver Teapot" << endl;
      cout << "3 - Gold Pocket Watch" << endl;
      cout << "4 - Exit the application" << endl;
      cout << "Enter selection: ";
      cin >> selection; // retrieve the selection

      // assign the appropriate search string to searchText
      switch ( selection )
      {
         case 1:
            searchText = "Antique Rocking Chair";
            break;

         case 2:
            searchText = "Silver Teapot";
            break;

         case 3:
            searchText = "Gold Pocket Watch";
            break;

```

Figure 19.18 Screen Scraping code. (Part 2 of 3.)

```
92              case 4:
93                  searchText = "";
94                  cout << endl;
95                  break;
96
97          default: // if invalid option was selected
98                  searchText = "";
99                  cout << "Error: Please enter a valid selection."
100                     << endl;
101         } // end switch
102
103     } // end while
104
105 } // end function displayMenu
106
107 // get currency conversion rate
108 double getRate()
109 {
110     double rate; // stores the conversion rate
111
112     // prompt the user for and input the conversion rate
113     cout << "Enter conversion rate: ";
114     cin >> rate; // get the rate
115
116     return rate; // return a copy of the rate
117
118 } // end function getRate
119
120 // find the price for the selected item
121 double getPrice( string &htmlText, string &searchText,
122     double conversionRate )
123 {
124     // search for location of item and price
125     int itemLocation = htmlText.find( searchText );
126     int priceBegin = htmlText.find( "&euro;", itemLocation ) + 6;
127     int priceEnd = htmlText.find( "</TD>", priceBegin );
128
129     // store the price in the string priceText
130     string priceText =
131         htmlText.substr( priceBegin, priceEnd - priceBegin);
132
133     // convert the text to a floating-point value
134     double price = atof( priceText.c_str() );
135
136     // convert price from euros to dollars
137     return price * conversionRate;
138
139 } // end function getPrice
```

Search for the `searchText` in the `htmlText` string

Locate the beginning of the price in `htmlText`

Locate the end of the price in `htmlText`

Set `priceText` to the `htmlText` substring, convert `priceText` to a `double` and store it in price

Convert the price from euros to dollars using the conversion rate entered by the user and return the dollar price to the user

Figure 19.18   Screen Scraping code. (Part 3 of 3.)

SELF-REVIEW   1. The _____ function replaces specified characters in a `string` with a specified substring.

    a) `stringReplace`   b) `substring`

    c) `replace`   d) `truncate`

2. The expression `text.find_first_of( "hello" )` returns _____ if the `string` on which the function is called contains the value "Goodbye".

    a) `false`   b) `0`

    c) `1`   d) `2`

Answers: 1) c. 2) c.

19.7 Wrap-Up

In this tutorial, you were introduced to `string` processing, using the functions of the `string` class. You learned how to create and manipulate `string` objects and locate, retrieve and replace substrings in `string`s using functions `find` and `substr`. You applied your knowledge of `string`s to create a simple **Screen Scraping** application which extracted desired information from HTML in a Web page. You also learned about `string` functions `length`, `at`, `compare`, `rfind`, `find_first_of`, `find_first_not_of` and `replace`, which provide additional capabilities to access and manipulate `string` data. Finally, you used the `atof` function to convert a string of characters to its corresponding floating point value.

In the next tutorial, you will learn how to use exception handling—a technique for resolving problems within an application. Using exception handling enables your applications to detect and handle problems without having to end execution. You will enhance your **Car Payment Calculator** application so that it will use exception handling to recognize and react properly to invalid input from the user.

SKILLS SUMMARY

Determining the Size of a `string`

- Use `string` function `length`.

Locating Substrings in `string`s

- Use `string` function `find` to locate the first occurrence of a substring in a `string`. The return value is the index where the first occurrence of the substring begins. If the substring is not found in the `string`, `string::npos` is returned.

- Use `string` function `rfind` to locate the last occurrence of a substring in a `string`. The return value is the index where the last occurrence of the substring begins. If the substring is not found in the `string`, `string::npos` is returned.

Retrieving Substrings from `string`s

- Use `string` function `substr` with one argument to obtain a substring that begins at the specified starting index and contains the remainder of the original `string`.

- Use `string` function `substr` with two arguments to obtain a substring that begins at the specified starting index (the first argument) and contains the specified number of characters (the second argument).

Locating a Character in a `string`

- Use `string` function `find_first_of` to find the first occurrence in a `string` of any character in the `string` argument.

- Use `string` function `find_first_not_of` to find the first occurrence in a `string` of any character not in the `string` argument.

Replacing Characters in a `string`

- Use `string` function `replace` to replace in a `string` a number of characters (the second argument) beginning at the specified index (the first argument) with the specified `string` (argument).

KEY TERMS

at function of the `string` class—A function that returns the character located at a specific index in a `string`.

atof function of the `<cstdlib>` library—A function that converts its argument—an array of ASCII characters that represents a floating-point number—to a `double` value. If the array of characters cannot be converted, the `atof` function returns 0.

checked access—This ensures that an application can access only data made available by a variable. For example, range checking prevents an application from accessing data outside the range of values contained in a variable.

compare function of the `string` class—A function that compares the contents of two `string`s. It returns 0 if the two `string`s are equal. In the expression `string1.compare( string2 )` the `compare` function returns a negative number if `string1` precedes `string2` in alphabetical order or a positive number if `string2` precedes `string1` in alphabetical order.

concatenation of two strings—This occurs when one `string` is appended to another `string`.

empty function of the `string` class—A Function that returns `true` if the `string` does not contain any characters, and returns `false` otherwise.

find function of the `string` class—A function that returns the index of the first occurrence of its `string` argument in a `string`, and returns `string::npos` if the substring is not found.

`find_first_not_of` function of the `string` class—A function that returns the index of the first occurrence in a `string` of any character not in a particular `string` argument, and returns `string::npos` if all of the argument `string`'s characters are contained in the `string`.

`find_first_of` function of the `string` class—A function that returns the index of the first occurrence in a `string` of any character in a particular `string` argument, and returns `string::npos` if none of the argument `string`'s characters are contained in the `string`.

length function of the `string` class—A function that returns the number of characters in a `string`.

literal `string` object—A string constant written as a sequence of characters in double quotation marks (also called a string literal).

`out_of_range` exception—An error that occurs when an application uses the subscript operator to access a `string` element that is not part of the `string`.

range checking—This prevents an application from accessing data outside the range of values contained in a variable. For example, range checking prevents an application from using the subscript operator to access an element that is not part of an array.

replace function of the `string` class—A function that replaces in a `string` a number of characters (the second argument) beginning at the specified index (the first argument) with the specified `string` (third) argument.

rfind function of the `string` class—A function that returns the index of the last occurrence of its `string` argument in a `string`, and returns `string::npos` if the `string` argument is not found.

screen scraping—The process of extracting desired information from the HTML that composes a Web page.

size function of the `string` class—A function that returns the number of characters in a `string`.

`string::npos` constant—A value returned by the `string` find-related functions to indicate that a `string` or character was not found in the `string`.

substring—A sequence of characters that makes up part or all of a `string`.

substr function of the `string` class—A function that returns a new `string` object by copying a specified part of an existing `string` object.

C++ LIBRARY REFERENCE

`cstdlib` This library contains function prototypes for conversion of numbers to text, and text to numbers, generation of random numbers and other utility functions.

■ *Function*

`atof`—This function converts its argument—an array of ASCII characters that represents a floating-point number—to a `double` value. If the an array of characters cannot be converted, the `atof` function returns 0.

`exit`—This function causes the application to terminate. An argument of 0 to the function notifies the system that the application terminated normally; an argument of 1 indicates that the application terminated due to an error.

`rand`—This function generates an `int` value selected from 0 to RAND_MAX.

srand—This function seeds the rand function, which determines the sequence of numbers that the application will generate. The srand function typically is used with an argument of time(0) to ensure that an application generates a different sequence of random numbers each time it is run.

---

string The string class represents a sequence of characters treated as a single unit.

- *Functions*

  at—This function returns the character located at a specific index in a string.

  c_str—This function returns an array of characters containing the text stored by a string.

  compare—This function compares the contents of two strings and returns 0 if the two strings are equal. In the expression string1.compare(string2), the compare function returns a negative number if string1 precedes string2 in alphabetical order or a positive number if string2 precedes string1 in alphabetical order.

  empty—This function returns true if the string does not contain any characters, and returns false otherwise.

  find—This function returns the index of the first occurrence of its string argument in the string, and -1 if the string argument is not found.

  find_first_not_of—This function returns the index of the first occurrence in a string of any character not in its string argument, and returns string::npos if all of the string argument's characters are contained in the string.

  find_first_of—This function returns the index of the first occurrence in a string of any character in the function's string argument, and returns string::npos if none of the string argument's characters are contained in the string.

  getline—This function places characters from the specified input stream into the specified string object until a newline is reached. For example, the statements

  ```
  string string1;
  getline( cin, string1 );
  ```

  cause the application to read from cin an entire line of text and store it in string variable string1.

  length—This function returns the number of characters in a string. Same as size.

  replace—This function replaces in a string a number of characters (the second argument) beginning at the specified index (the first argument) with the specified string (third) argument.

  rfind—This function returns the index of the last occurrence of its string argument in a string. It returns -1 if the string argument is not found.

  size—This function returns the number of characters in a string. Same as length.

  substr—This function creates a new string object by copying part of an existing string object.

- *Constant*

  npos—A value returned by the string find-related functions to indicate that a string or character was not found in the string.

MULTIPLE-CHOICE QUESTIONS

19.1 Extracting desired information from Web pages is called _____.

a) Web crawling   b) screen scraping

c) querying   d) redirection

19.2 If the find function does not find the specified string, it returns _____.

a) false   b) 0

c) -1   d) None of the above.

19.3 The string class allows you to _____ strings.

a) search   b) retrieve characters from

c) determine the number of characters in   d) All of the above.

19.4 _____ is a technology for describing Web content.
- a) The string class
- b) A string literal
- c) HTML
- d) A screen scraper

19.5 The _____ function returns the character located at a specific index in a string.
- a) get
- b) at
- c) getAt
- d) charAt

19.6 The _____ function creates a new string object by copying part of an existing string object.
- a) strCopy
- b) substr
- c) copyStr
- d) copySubstr

19.7 The compare function returns _____ if the two strings are equal.
- a) 1
- b) 0
- c) -1
- d) string::npos

19.8 The version of the find function that takes two arguments does not examine any characters that occur prior to the _____.
- a) second argument
- b) first match
- c) last character of the string
- d) None of the above.

19.9 The _____ function returns the index of the first occurrence in a string of any characters contained in its string argument.
- a) find_first_not_of
- b) rfind
- c) find_first_of
- d) find

19.10 The replace function's parameters specify _____.
- a) the position of the first character to replace in the string
- b) the position of the last character to replace in the string
- c) the replacement substring
- d) Both a and c.

EXERCISES

19.11 (*Enhanced Screen Scraping Application*) When a user enters an invalid number (such as 13x.20 instead of 13.20) at a prompt that expects a numeric type, such as a double, an error occurs that typically prevents your application from continuing. Modify your **Screen Scraper** application so that the application removes any non-numeric characters from the value entered at the **Enter conversion rate:** prompt (Fig. 19.19). Only numeric characters and the decimal point (.) should be allowed in the converted value.

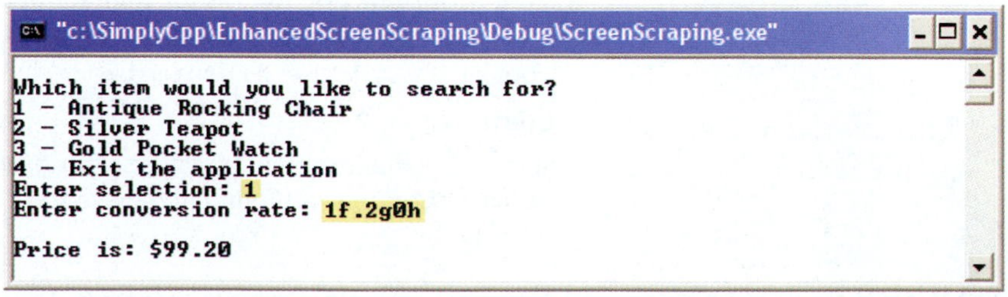

Figure 19.19 Enhanced **Screen Scraping** application output.

a) *Copying the template to your working directory.* Copy the C:\Examples\Tutorial19\Exercises\EnhancedScreenScraping directory to your C:\SimplyCpp directory.

b) *Opening the template source code file.* Open the ScreenScraping.cpp file in your text editor or IDE.

c) *Adding code to the getRate function.* In the getRate function (lines 108–118), define two additional variables—the first should be a string (called response), which will store the value that the user enters at the **Enter conversion rate:** prompt. The second will be an int (called index) used to store the index of an invalid character within the string. Initialize the value of index to 0. Then, modify the getRate function so that the user's response at the **Enter conversion rate:** prompt is stored in the response variable instead of rate.

d) *Finding and removing any invalid characters.* Just before the return statement, insert a statement that uses the find_first_not_of function on response to find the index of any characters that are not a number between 0 and 9 or a decimal point. Then, insert a while statement that repeats while the value of index is not equal to string::npos. Add a statement to the body of the while statement that uses the substr function to create a new string that does not contain the invalid character. This can be accomplished by concatenating the substring that appears to the right of the invalid character to the substring that appears to the left of the invalid character. The new string should be assigned to response. Before the end of the body of the while statement, insert a statement that assigns to index the position of the next occurrence of an invalid character in response.

e) *Converting the result to a double.* Immediately following the while statement you completed in *Step d*, use the atof function and the c_str function to convert response to a double. Store the value returned by the atof function in rate.

f) *Save, compile and run the completed application.* Test your application to ensure that it runs correctly by specifying a conversion rate that contains invalid characters, such as letters. Check that the price calculates correctly.

g) *Closing the application.* Exit your running application by entering 4 at the **Enter selection:** prompt.

h) *Close the Command Prompt window.*

19.12 (*Encryption Application*) Write an application that encrypts a message from the user (Fig. 19.20). The application should be able to encrypt the message using either a substitution cipher or a transposition cipher (both described below). The user should be able to enter the message at a prompt, then select the desired type of encryption from a menu. The encrypted message is then displayed.

In a substitution cipher, every character in the English alphabet is represented by a different character in a substitution string, which we will refer to as the substitution alphabet. Every time a letter occurs in the English sentence, it is replaced by the letter in the corresponding index of the substitution alphabet. As an example of a substitution cipher, let's encrypt the string "code". If the corresponding characters for "c", "o", "d" and "e" in the substitution alphabet are "e", " ", "f" and "g" (respectively), the encrypted string is "e fg".

In a transposition cipher, two strings are created. The first new string contains all the characters at the even indices of the input string. The second new string contains all of the characters at the odd indices. The second string is then appended to the first string with a space between them. For example a transposition cipher for the word "code" would be: "cd oe".

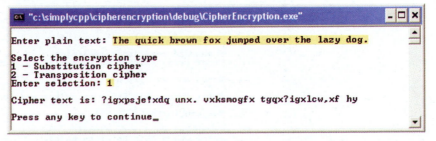

Figure 19.20 Encryption application output.

a) *Copying the template to your working directory.* Copy the C:\Examples\ Tutorial19\Exercises\CipherEncryption directory to your C:\SimplyCpp directory.

b) *Opening the template source code file.* Open the Encryption.cpp file in your text editor or IDE.

c) *Adding code to the `substitutionCipher` function.* In the `substitutionCipher` function (lines 47–60), English and substitution alphabet `string`s have been defined for you as `normalAlphabet` and `cipherAlphabet`, respectively. Other `string`s that you will be using have already been defined for you—`cipher` is an empty `string` you will use to store the encrypted text, and `plain` contains the text entered by the user. After the definition of the `string`s, add an empty `for` statement that loops for each character in `plain`.

d) *Performing the substitution encryption.* Inside the `for` statement you added in *Step c*, create `int` variable `index` and assign to it the index in `normalAlphabet` where the current character in `plain` appears. If `index` is not equal to `string::npos`, retrieve the character in `cipherAlphabet` at the location stored in `index` and append this character to the end of `cipher`. Now the original `string` has been substituted with all the corresponding cipher characters. After the `for` statement, add code to display `cipher`.

e) *Adding code to the `transpositionCipher` function.* Find the `transpositionCipher` function, which immediately follows `substitutionCipher`. The `firstWord` and `lastWord` `string`s have been defined for you in this function, as well as `plainText`, which contains the text entered by the user. After the definition of the `string`s, add an empty `for` statement that loops for each character in `plainText`. This `for` statement will be used to add each proper character to the two words.

f) *Performing the transposition encryption.* Inside the `for` statement you added in *Step e*, add an `if...else` statement whose `if` portion executes when `counter` is an even number. [*Hint*: Recall that when an even number is divided by 2, the remainder is 0.] Within the `if` statement, extract the current character in `plainText` and append it to `firstWord`. Within the `else` statement, extract the current character in `plainText` and append it to `lastWord`. After the `for` statement, add code to display the `firstWord` followed by the `lastWord`, separated by a space.

g) *Save, compile and run the completed application.* Test your application to ensure that it runs correctly by using both ciphers on different texts. Check that you can get the same results as the **Encryption** application shown in Fig. 19.20.

h) *Close the Command Prompt window.*

19.13 (*Anagram Game Application*) Write an **Anagram Game** application that contains an array of preset words. The game should randomly select a word and scramble its letters (Fig. 19.21). The first letter is extracted and placed back in the `string` at a random location. This process is repeated 20 times to ensure that the `string` is sufficiently scrambled. The application displays the scrambled word for the user to guess. If the user guesses correctly, display a congratulatory message and repeat the process with a different word. If the guess is incorrect, display an error message and let the user try again.

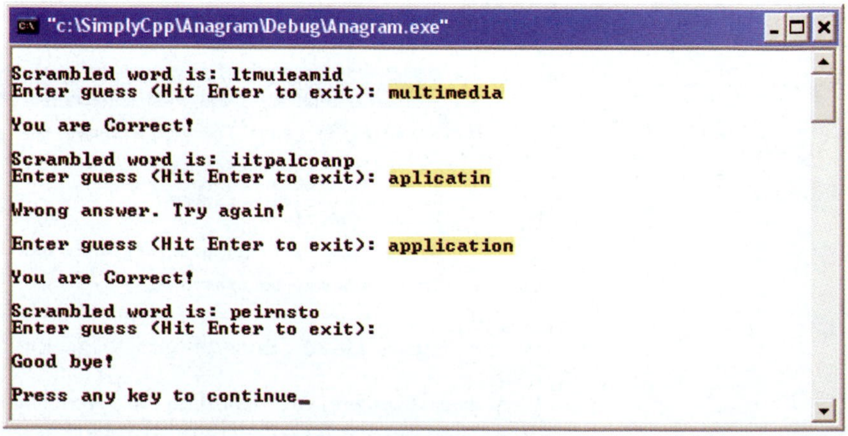

Figure 19.21 Anagram Game application output.

a) *Copying the template to your working directory.* Copy the `C:\Examples\Tutorial19\Exercises\Anagram` directory to your `C:\SimplyCpp` directory.

b) ***Opening the template source code file.*** Open the Anagram.cpp file in your text editor or IDE.

c) ***Adding a for statement to the generateAnagram function.*** The generateAnagram function (lines 65–76) selects a string from a predefined array and scrambles this string for the user. The string to be scrambled is stored in the scrambled variable for you. A random index in this string has been generated for you and stored in the randomIndex variable. In this exercise, you will be completing only the generate-Anagram function—the rest of the application has been provided for you. After the variable definitions inside the generateAnagram function, add an empty for statement that will loop 20 times.

d) ***Generating the scrambled word.*** Inside the for statement you added in *Step c*, define char variable firstCharacter and assign to it the first character in scrambled. Use the substr function to remove the first character from scrambled. Then, create string variables temporary1 and temporary2. In temporary1, store the characters in scrambled from the beginning of the string until randomIndex. In temporary2, store the remaining characters from scrambled. Append the firstCharacter to temporary1, then concatenate temporary1 and temporary2 and store the result in scrambled. You have moved the first character of scrambled to a random location. This process is repeated 20 times to further scramble the string before it is displayed for the user.

e) ***Generating a random index.*** You now need to generate a new randomIndex for the next iteration of the for statement. After concatenating temporary1 and temporary2 in *Step d*, use the rand function (which was seeded for you in the template) to generate a random integer between the values 0 and the last index of scrambled, inclusive. Store the random integer in randomIndex.

f) ***Displaying the anagram.*** After the for statement you completed in *Steps c–e*, display scrambled and return the value of randomNumber, the index of the scrambled word in the ANAGRAM_LIST array, to the caller.

g) ***Save, compile and run the completed application.*** Test your application to ensure that it runs correctly.

h) ***Close the Command Prompt window.***

What does this code do? ▶   **19.14** What strings are stored in array words after the following code executes?

```
1   // Exercise 18.14: WDTCD.cpp
2   // What does this code do?
3   #include <iostream> // required to perform C++ stream I/O
4   #include <string>   // required to access string functions
5   #include <iomanip>  // required for parameterized stream manipulators
6
7   using namespace std; // for accessing C++ Standard Library members
8
9   // function main begins program execution
10  int main()
11  {
12     // define variables
13     string words[] = { "dance", "walk", "talking", "eat" };
14
15     for ( int counter = 0; counter <= 3; counter++ )
16     {
17        if ( words[ counter ].rfind( "e" ) ==
18           words[ counter ].size() - 1 )
19        {
20           words[ counter ] = words[ counter ].substr(
21              0, words[ counter ].length()   1 );
22        } // end if
23
```

```
24          if ( words[ counter ].find( "ing" ) == string::npos )
25          {
26             words[ counter ] += "ing";
27          } // end if
28
29       } // end for
30
31       cout << "\n" << left << setw( 12 ) << "Word Number"
32          << "Word" << endl;
33
34       for ( int counter = 0; counter <= 3; counter++ )
35       {
36          cout << setw( 12 ) << counter + 1 << words[ counter ] << endl;
37       } // end for
38
39       cout << endl; // insert newline for readability
40
41       return 0; // indicate that program ended successfully
42
43    } // end function main
```

What's wrong with this code? ▶   **19.15** This code should remove each space from test. Find the error(s) in the following code.

```
1   // Exercise 19.15: WWWTC.cpp
2   // This application removes each space from test.
3   #include <string>     // required to access string functions
4   #include <iostream>   // required to perform C++ stream I/O
5
6   using namespace std; // for accessing C++ Standard Library members
7
8   // function main begins program execution
9   int main()
10  {
11     string test = "s p a c e s";
12     int index;
13
14     while( test.find( " " ) == string::npos )
15     {
16        index = test.find( " " );
17        test = test.substr( 0, index - 1 ) + test.substr( index );
18     } // end while
19
20     cout << "\n" << test << endl << endl;
21
22     return 0; // indicate that program ended successfully
23
24  } // end function main
```

Programming Challenge ▶   **19.16** (*Pig Latin Application*) Write an application that encodes English language phrases into Pig Latin (Fig. 19.22). Pig Latin is a form of coded language often used for amusement. Use the following algorithm to form the Pig Latin words:

> To form Pig Latin words from an English-language phrase, the translation proceeds one word at a time, as follows: Place the first letter of the English word (if it is a consonant) at the end of the English word and add the letters "ay." If the first letter of the English word is a vowel, place it at the end of the word and add "y." Using this func-

tion, the word "jump" becomes "umpjay," the word "the" becomes "hetay" and the word "ace" becomes "ceay." Blanks between words remain blanks.

Assume the following: The English phrase entered by the user consists of words separated by blanks, there are no punctuation marks and all words have two or more letters. The translateToPigLatin function should translate the sentence into Pig Latin, word by word.

```
c:\  "c:\simplycpp\piglatin\debug\PigLatin.exe"                              - □ ×

Enter a sentence: This sentence is converted to Pig Latin
Pig Latin: histay entencesay siy onvertedcay otay igpay atinlay
Press any key to continue_
```

Figure 19.22 Pig Latin application.

a) *Copying the template to your working directory.* Copy the C:\Examples\ Tutorial19\Exercises\PigLatin directory to your C:\SimplyCpp directory.

b) *Opening the template source code file.* Open the PigLatin.cpp file in your text editor or IDE.

c) *Adding a while statement to the translateToPigLatin function.* In the translateToPigLatin function (lines 37–48), six variables have been provided for you—char variables prefix, strings suffix and word (which you will use shortly to convert each word) and string variable translatedText, which will be used to store the translated sentence. The function also defines unsigned int variables beginWord and endWord, to store the index of the beginning and end of a word, respectively. After the variable definitions, add an empty while statement that will loop while endWord is less than the last position in parameter englishPhrase.

d) *Retrieving the word's first letter.* Inside the while statement you added in *Step c*, retrieve the first letter of the current word and store its lowercase equivalent in prefix. [*Hint*: Use the substr function to retrieve the first letter and assign it to prefix. Then assign to prefix the value returned by calling the tolower function with prefix as the argument. This function, which is provided by the <cctype> library, will return the letter's lowercase equivalent.] If you have reached the end of the phrase, assign to endWord the value returned by englishPhrase.size().

e) *Determining the suffix.* After retrieving the first letter, add an if...else statement whose if statement executes when the letter in prefix is a vowel (that is, when the letter in prefix is equal to one of the following letters: a, e, i, o or u). In the body of the if statement, assign the string "y" to suffix. In the else statement, assign "ay" to suffix.

f) *Translating the current word to Pig Latin.* After the if...else statement, translate the current word to its Pig Latin equivalent as follows: Have the first portion contain all the letters in the original word except for the first letter. Append to this text the value in prefix then the value in suffix. This new word should be stored in word. Then, append the contents of word to translatedText, followed by a space. This line concatenates all the converted Pig Latin words back into a sentence.

g) *Returning the new sentence.* After the while statement, display the contents of translatedText, preceded by descriptive text.

h) *Save, compile and run the completed application.* Test your application to ensure that it runs correctly by translating multiple sentences into Pig Latin and checking that each translates correctly.

i) *Close the Command Prompt window.*

Objectives

In this tutorial, you will learn to:
- Use exception handling to make your programs more robust.
- Understand what exceptions are.
- Use **try** blocks to monitor code that may cause exceptions.
- Use **catch** blocks to handle exceptions.
- Use the **throw** statement to rethrow an exception from a **catch** block.

Outline

Enhanced Car Payment Calculator Application

Introducing Exception Handling

In this tutorial, you will learn about exception handling. An **exception** is an indication of a problem that occurs during an application's execution. The name "exception" comes from the fact that, although a problem can occur, the problem occurs infrequently—if the "rule" is that a statement normally executes correctly, then the "exception to the rule" is that a problem occurs. **Exception handling** enables you to create applications that can resolve (or handle) exceptions as the applications execute. In many cases, handling an exception allows an application to continue executing as if no problem had been encountered.

We begin with a test-drive of the **Enhanced Car Payment Calculator** application, then introduce exception-handling concepts and demonstrate basic exception-handling techniques. You will learn the specifics of exception handling with the **try** and **catch** blocks and the **throw** statement, then use these blocks to handle exceptions raised when the user enters invalid data.

20.1 Test-Driving the Enhanced Car Payment Calculator Application

In this tutorial, you will enhance the **Car Payment Calculator** application from Tutorial 6 by adding exception-handling statements that enable the application to continue executing after the user enters invalid data. This application must meet the following requirements:

Application Requirements

*A bank wishes to prevent users from entering incorrect data on their car loans. Although the application you developed in Tutorial 6 continues running when incorrect data is entered, it will not calculate the result. Modify the **Car Payment Calculator** application to allow the user to enter only an integer at the prompt for the car price. If the user enters anything besides an integer (such as non-numeric data), a message should be displayed instructing the user to enter an integer. The application then should prompt the user to reenter the value for the car price.*

When the user provides valid inputs, the **Enhanced Car Payment Calculator** application calculates monthly payments for car loans when financed for 24, 36, 48 and 60 months. The user inputs the car price, the down payment and the annual interest rate. You begin by test-driving the completed application. Next, you will learn the additional C++ capabilities you will need to create your own version of this application.

Test-Driving the Enhanced Car Payment Calculator Application

1. **Locating the completed application.** Open the **Command Prompt** window by selecting **Start > All Programs > Accessories > Command Prompt**. Change to your completed **Enhanced Car Payment Calculator** application directory by typing cd C:\Examples\Tutorial20\CompletedApplication\EnhancedCarPayment.

2. **Running the Enhanced Car Payment Calculator application.** Type CarPayment in the **Command Prompt** window to run your application (Fig. 20.1).

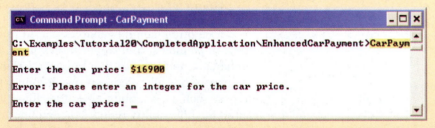

Figure 20.1　Running the completed Enhanced **Car Payment Calculator** application.

3. **Entering non-numeric data at the Enter the car price: prompt.** Enter the value $16900 at the **Enter the car price:** prompt. Although 16900 is a valid integer, the dollar sign ($) that precedes it is not an acceptable character in an integer. Because your application expects numeric characters but encounters a dollar sign, an exception occurs. In this case, the application handles the exception by displaying an error message and prompting the user to reenter the car price (Fig. 20.2).

Figure 20.2　Entering a non-numeric character at the **Enter the car price:** prompt.

4. **Correcting the input.** Enter 16900 at the **Enter the car price:** prompt, 6000 at the **Enter the down payment:** prompt and 7.5 at the **Enter the annual interest rate:** prompt. The application displays the monthly car payments for loans of 24, 36, 48 and 60 months (Fig. 20.3).

5. **Close the Command Prompt window.**

(cont.)

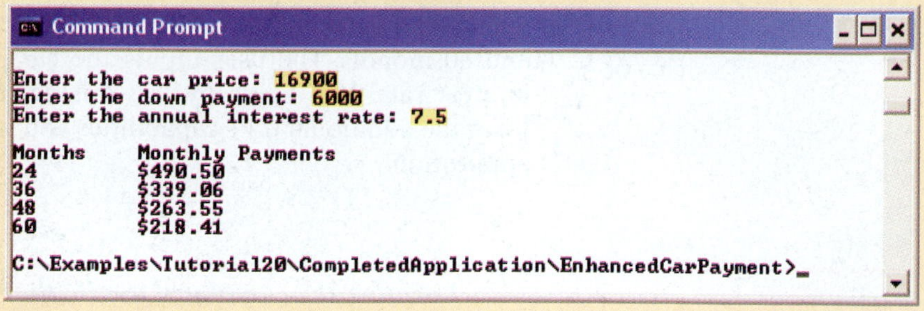

Figure 20.3 Displaying the monthly car payments after input is corrected.

20.2 Introduction to Exception Handling

Programs frequently test conditions that determine how execution should proceed. Consider the pseudocode in Fig. 20.4. You begin by performing a task. Then you test whether the task executed correctly. If not, you perform error processing. Otherwise, you continue with the next task. Although this form of error checking works, intermixing error-handling logic with application logic can make the application difficult to read, modify, maintain and debug—especially in large applications. In fact, if problems occur infrequently, intermixing error-handling and application logic can degrade an application's performance, because the application must explicitly test for errors after each task to determine whether the next task can be performed.

> Perform a task
>
> If the preceding task did not execute correctly
>   Perform error processing
>
> Perform next task
>
> If the preceding task did not execute correctly
>   Perform error processing
>
> ...

Figure 20.4 Pseudocode for performing tasks without exception handling.

Exception handling enables you to remove error-handling code from the code that implements your application's logic, which improves application clarity and enhances modifiability. You can decide to handle only the exceptions you choose—all exceptions, all exceptions of a certain type or all exceptions of a group of related types (such as exception types that share a common base in an inheritance hierarchy). Such flexibility reduces the likelihood that errors will be overlooked, thereby making an application more robust.

A function **throws an exception** if a problem occurs but the function is unable to correct the problem. There is no guarantee that there will be an **exception handler**—code that executes when the application detects an exception—to process the exception. If there is, the application **catches** the exception and executes the code in the exception handler (this is sometimes called "handling" the exception), allowing the application to continue executing correctly. An **uncaught exception**—an exception that does not have an exception handler—causes the application to terminate.

SELF-REVIEW

1. When an exception occurs, the application attempts to execute a(n) _____.

    a) exception   b) default processor

    c) exception handler   d) None of the above.

2. A function will _____ an exception if the function is unable to correct the problem.

　　a) throw　　　　　　　　　　　　　b) catch

　　c) return　　　　　　　　　　　　　d) None of the above.

Answers: 1) c. 2) a.

20.3 Throwing Exceptions in C++

C++ provides the **throw** keyword to enable a function to throw an exception when the function detects that a problem has occurred but is unable to correct the problem. The statement

```
throw throwOperand;
```

causes the application to throw the exception specified by *throwOperand*. Normally, a throw statement specifies one operand. (In the next section, we discuss how to use a throw statement that specifies no operands.)

The operand of a throw can be of any type. For example, when an error occurs, a function might throw an int value, using a statement such as

```
throw 5;
```

where the value 5 indicates the type of error that has occurred. The operand might also be a string literal, as in

```
throw "Error: Invalid input";
```

where the string literal indicates the error that has occurred. You can also throw an object. For example, the statement

```
throw string( "Error: Attempt to divide by zero" );
```

throws a string object containing the text "Error: Attempt to divide by zero." If the operand is an object, we call it an **exception object**. Finally, a throw operand also can assume other values, such as the value of an expression (for example, throw x > 5, which throws the bool value true or false).

Functions in the C++ Standard Library throw exception objects created from classes that are derived from the **exception** class (defined in the <exception> header file), which is the standard C++ base class for exceptions. You can also throw objects of classes that you create and use inheritance (which you learned about in Tutorial 17) to create a family of related exception classes.

For example, consider the DivideByZeroException class, which inherits from the exception class (Fig. 20.5). Line 1 of Fig. 20.5 includes the <exception> header file, which contains the exception class definition. You must include this file because the DivideByZeroException class definition, which begins in line 7, indicates that the DivideByZeroException inherits from the exception class. The DivideByZeroException class's only member is a constructor, defined in lines 12–13, that uses the base-class initializer syntax to call the exception class constructor and contains no statements in its body. Line 13 passes the string literal argument "Attempt to divide by zero" to the exception constructor. We will discuss the purpose of this argument in the next section.

Before an application can throw an exception of a user-defined class, such as a DivideByZeroException object, the application must include the class definition. To throw a DivideByZeroException object, for example, a function should include the statement

```
throw DivideByZeroException();
```

```
1    #include <exception>
2
3    using namespace std;
4
5    // DivideByZeroException objects should be thrown by functions
6    // upon detecting an attempt to divide by zero
7    class DivideByZeroException : public exception
8    {
9    public:
10
11       // constructor specifies default error message
12       DivideByZeroException::DivideByZeroException()
13          : exception( "Attempt to divide by zero" ) {} // empty body
14
15   };   // end class DivideByZeroException
```

Figure 20.5 DivideByZeroException exception class definition.

which instantiates and throws a DivideByZeroException object. In this case, the DivideByZeroException class defined a no-argument constructor, so no arguments are specified in parentheses. If the exception object's class contains a constructor that declares one or more parameters, you can pass a comma-separated list of arguments to the constructor between parentheses in the throw statement. In the next section, we discuss how to handle exceptions that are thrown using the throw statement.

SELF-REVIEW

1. A throw operand can be of the _____ type.
    a) int   b) char[]
    c) string   d) All of the above.

2. A(n) _____ argument can be passed to an exception class constructor.
    a) int   b) string literal
    c) double   d) None of the above.

Answers: 1) d. 2) b.

20.4 Handling Exceptions in C++

This section discusses how C++ applications can catch exceptions. C++ provides try statements to enable exception handling. A **try statement** consists of a **try block** (consisting of the keyword try, followed by braces {}), followed by one or more **catch blocks**. For example, the try statement in Fig. 20.6 contains a try block followed by two catch blocks.

```
try
{
   ...
} // end try block
catch( exceptionType1 &exception1 )
{
   ...
} // end first catch block
catch( exceptionType2 &exception2 )
{
   ...
} // end second catch block
...
```

Figure 20.6 try statement example.

The purpose of the `try` block is to contain statements that might cause exceptions and statements that should not execute if an exception occurs. At least one `catch` block (also called an exception handler) must immediately follow the `try` block. Each `catch` block specifies in parentheses a parameter (known as the **exception parameter**) that identifies the exception type that the exception handler can process. In Fig. 20.6, the first `catch` block catches an exception of type *exceptionType1* and declares an exception parameter named `exception1`. By default, exceptions are passed by value. Because `exception1` is declared as a reference parameter, this exception is passed by reference. The second `catch` block catches an exception of type *exceptionType2* and declares an exception reference parameter named `exception2`.

When a function throws an object, you can use the corresponding `catch` block's exception parameter to access the object's `public` members. For example, in Fig. 20.5, you defined the `DivideByZeroException` class, which passed a string literal to the `exception` base-class constructor. To access this value, the `catch` block should call the **what** member function of base-class `exception`. The following `catch` block handles an exception of type `DivideByZeroException`:

```
catch( DivideByZeroException &error )
{
    cout << "\nError: " << error.what();
}
```

In this case, the `catch` handler's body uses the `error` exception parameter to access the `what` function and display the error message "`Error: Attempt to divide by zero.`"

Now that you have learned how to throw and catch exceptions, you will learn how the flow of program control changes when an exception occurs. If an exception occurs because a `throw` statement executes inside a `try` block, the `try` block terminates immediately. As with any other block of code, when a `try` block terminates, local variables defined in the block go out of scope.

Common Programming Error

Exception classes need not be derived from the `exception` class. Thus, writing `catch( exception &anyException )` is not guaranteed to catch all the exceptions an application could encounter.

Next, the application searches for the first `catch` block (starting with the one immediately following the `try` block) that can process the type of exception that occurred. A match occurs if the types are identical or if the thrown exception's type is a derived class of the exception-parameter type. For example, a `catch` statement specifying an exception-parameter of type `exception` will catch exceptions of type `exception` or exceptions of classes derived from the `exception` class, such as a `DivideByZeroException` object.

A function may contain multiple `catch` blocks that can handle the same exception type, such as a `catch( exception &error )` block that precedes a `catch( DivideByZeroException &error )` block. In this case, if the function throws an `exception` object, only the `catch( exception &error )` block will execute, because C++ executes only the first `catch` block (after the `try` block) that can process the type of exception that has occurred.

When a `catch` block's exception-parameter type matches the type of the thrown exception, the code contained within the matching `catch` handler executes. When a `catch` handler finishes processing, local variables defined within the `catch` handler (including the `catch` parameter) go out of scope. Any remaining `catch` handlers that correspond to the `try` block are ignored, and execution resumes at the first line of code after the last `catch` block.

If no exceptions occur in a `try` block, the `try` block terminates, the application skips the `catch` block(s) and execution resumes with the next statement after the last `catch` block.

If an exception that occurs in a `try` block has no matching `catch` handler in the `try` statement, the application attempts to locate an enclosing `try` block. If it cannot locate an enclosing `try` block in the current function, the application attempts to locate one in the calling function. For example, consider the case in which `main` calls the `calculateQuotient` function, which throws an exception but does not contain a matching `catch` block. In this case, after the application fails to find a matching `catch` block in `calculateQuotient`, it determines whether the call to the `calculateQuotient` function is contained in a `try` block in the calling function, `main`. If so, the application attempts to find a matching `catch` block in `main`. Similarly, if a function throws an exception from a statement that is not in a `try` block in that function, the application attempts to locate an enclosing `try` block in the calling function. If an exception goes uncaught because there is no matching `catch` block, the application terminates.

It is possible that a `catch` block is not able to process the exception or can process the exception only partially. In such cases, the exception handler can defer the handling (or perhaps a portion of it) to another `catch` block. The handler achieves this by **rethrowing the exception** using the `throw` statement with no operand inside a `catch` block:

```
throw; // rethrow the exception
```

When a rethrow occurs, the next enclosing `try` block (if any) detects the rethrown exception, and a matching `catch` block, if there is one, attempts to handle the exception. Again, if an exception goes uncaught, the application terminates.

When you provide exception handling in an application, you might not know in advance every type of exception that must be handled. To catch all the exceptions that may be thrown in a `try` block, use `catch( ... )`. Be aware that one weakness associated with catching exceptions in this manner is that, without a named parameter, there is no way to refer to the exception object inside the exception handler. You can use `catch( ... )` to recover from errors that do not depend on the exception type. For example, to prevent a function from terminating prematurely because it does not contain a matching `catch` block for an exception that is thrown, you might want to include a `catch( ... )` whose body closes any open files, releases dynamically allocated memory or performs any other "housekeeping" operations to prevent loss of data or other problems caused by premature termination. The exception also can be rethrown to alert more specific enclosing `catch` handlers.

SELF-REVIEW

1. When an exception occurs inside a `try` block, _____.
   a) the `try` block terminates immediately   b) local variables go out of scope
   c) the application executes the next statement after the `try` block
   d) Both a and b.

2. An exception handler can rethrow an exception using keyword _____.
   a) `throw`   b) `return`
   c) `try`   d) `rethrow`

Answers: 1) d. 2) a.

20.5 C++ Stream Error States and Exceptions

By default, a stream object (such as `cin`) does not throw an exception when an error occurs. Instead, the stream object alters its **stream state**—a series of bits whose values indicate which stream I/O errors, if any, have occurred. Objects created from classes that are derived from the `ios_base` standard library class (e.g., objects such as `cin` and `cout`), maintain this series of bits. One such bit is the **failbit**, which is set when a format error occurs in the stream. For example, if the application attempts to input an integer and the user types `"$16900"` at the keyboard, `cin` sets its `failbit` when it encounters the `$` (which is not a valid character in an integer).

C++ prevents any stream I/O operations from occurring on a stream object while any of its error bits are set. Thus, to resume stream I/O, your application must detect that error bits have been set, then clear them. Your application can detect that an input error has occurred by calling the `cin` object's **fail** member function, which returns `true` when the `failbit` is set. For example, the code

```
int integerValue;

cout << "Enter value: ";
cin >> integerValue;

if ( cin.fail() ) // cin.fail() returns true if format error occurred
{
    cout << "Error: Non-integer character entered";
} // end if
```

displays an error message if the user enters a non-integer value (such as A, b or $) at the input prompt. After your application detects an error, it can call the `cin` object's **clear** member function to restore a stream's state to "good," so that I/O may proceed on that stream.

When a stream format error occurs, the characters that the user entered at the keyboard remain in the input buffer. To prevent the application from reading these characters again after the `failbit` has been cleared, you should remove them from the input buffer. For example, the code

```
string streamContents;

if ( cin.fail() ) // cin.fail() returns true if format error occurred
{
    cin.clear();
    getline( cin, streamContents );
} // end if
```

determines whether an error has occurred and if so, uses the `clear` function to clear the stream error state and the `getline` function to remove from the input buffer any characters entered at the keyboard before the user pressed *Enter*.

Although stream objects do not throw exceptions by default, you can force a stream object to throw an exception. The **exceptions** function, which the `cin` object inherits from the `ios` class, causes a stream object to throw an exception when the specified stream error bit is set. For example, the code

```
cin.exceptions( ios_base::failbit );
```

causes `cin` to throw an exception of type **ios_base::failure** when its `failbit` is set. The `ios_base::failure` exception is defined in the `ios_base` class (accessible by including the `<iostream>` header file), which is the base class for all C++ stream I/O objects, including `cin` and `cout`. Once you cause `cin` to throw exceptions, you no longer need to test the value of the `failbit` explicitly—an exception will be thrown immediately after the `failbit` is set. In the next section, you will use the `exceptions` function to cause `cin` to throw exceptions when errors occur, and you will use a `try...catch` block to handle such errors.

SELF-REVIEW

1. The _____ function of the `ios` class, when called on a stream object, causes exceptions to be thrown when stream I/O errors occur on that object.

    a) `fail`   b) `exceptions`
    c) `failbit`   d) `failure`

2. If an error occurs during stream processing, the stream's _____ is set.

    a) `failurebit`   b) `errorbit`
    c) `failbit`   d) `clearbit`

Answers: 1) b. 2) c.

20.6 Constructing the Enhanced Car Payment Calculator Application

Now that you have been introduced to exception handling, you will construct your enhanced **Car Payment Calculator** application. You will use exception handling to catch exceptions that occur when the user inputs invalid data at the **Enter the car price:** prompt. In Exercise 20.13, you will add code to handle exceptions that occur if the user inputs invalid data at any of the application's three input prompts. The pseudocode in Fig. 20.7 describes the basic operation of the enhanced **Car Payment Calculator** application:

Do

    Try to prompt the user for and store the car price

    Catch a stream input error
        Reset the input stream state
        Remove all characters from the input buffer
        Display an error message

While a stream input error has occurred

Prompt the user for and store the down payment
Prompt the user for and store the annual interest rate

Calculate and display monthly payments for 2, 3, 4 and 5 years

Figure 20.7 Pseudocode for enhanced **Car Payment Calculator** application.

Now that you've analyzed the enhanced **Car Payment Calculator** application's pseudocode, you will learn how to place exception handling in your code

Handling the `ios_base::failure` Exception

1. ***Copying the template to your working directory.*** Copy the `C:\Examples\Tutorial20\TemplateApplication\EnhancedCarPayment` directory to your `C:\SimplyCpp` directory.

2. ***Opening the template source code file.*** Open the template file `CarPayment.cpp` in your text editor or IDE.

3. ***Studying the code.*** In Fig. 20.8, the statements that read the values from the keyboard (lines 25, 28 and 31) each use the stream-extraction operator to input the value that the user typed into variables of numeric data types. Because the `price` and `downPayment` variables are defined as `int`s, lines 25 and 28 attempt to input `int` values; line 31 attempts to input a `double` value.

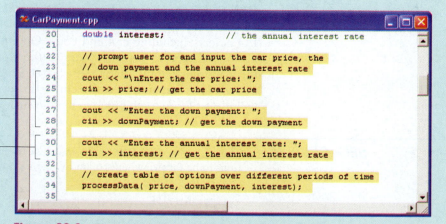

Prompting the user for and inputting two `int`s

Prompting the user for and inputting a `double`

Figure 20.8 Obtaining the user input.

Once the data has been input into two `int`s and a `double`, the `processData` function is called to determine the monthly payments (line 34).

(cont.)   4. ***Including the `<exception>` header file.*** Add line 7 of Fig. 20.9 to your code. The `<exception>` header file enables your application to access members of the `exception` class. Recall that the `ios_base::failure` exception is derived from the `exception` class.

Including the `<exception>` header file

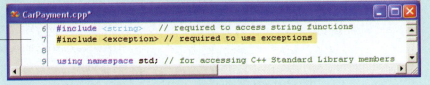

```
6   #include <string>    // required to access string functions
7   #include <exception> // required to use exceptions
8
9   using namespace std; // for accessing C++ Standard Library members
```

Figure 20.9   Including the `<exception>` header file.

5. ***Prompting the user for and inputting an `int` value.*** Add lines 22–30 and 34–38 of Fig. 20.10 to your code. Also, indent the body of the do...while statement (lines 31–32) as shown to improve readability. The application should repeatedly prompt the user to enter a car price until the user enters a valid integer price. Line 22 defines `bool` variable `errorOccurred`, which your application will use to determine whether a stream I/O error has occurred. The value of `errorOccurred` is initialized to `false` to indicate that no error has occurred yet. Line 25 defines `string` variable `invalidInput`, which you will use to store the (invalid) contents of the input buffer when a stream input error occurs. Line 28 begins a do...while statement that executes while `errorOccurred` equals `true` when its value is tested in line 35. Later in this box, you will add code to ensure that the application does not exit the do...while statement until the user has entered a valid car price at the input prompt in lines 31–32.

Variable determines whether an error occurred during input

Beginning a do...while loop

Repeating the loop if an input error occurred

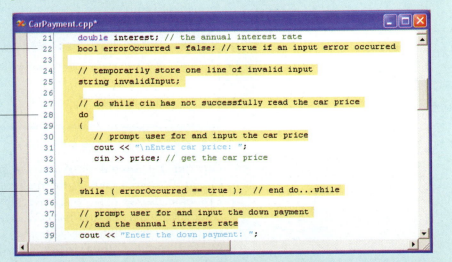

```
21       double interest; // the annual interest rate
22       bool errorOccurred = false; // true if an input error occurred
23
24       // temporarily store one line of invalid input
25       string invalidInput;
26
27       // do while cin has not successfully read the car price
28       do
29       {
30          // prompt user for and input the car price
31          cout << "\nEnter car price: ";
32          cin >> price; // get the car price
33
34       }
35       while ( errorOccurred == true );  // end do...while
36
37       // prompt user for and input the down payment
38       // and the annual interest rate
39       cout << "Enter the down payment: ";
```

Figure 20.10   do...while loop repeats until the user enters a valid value at the first input prompt.

6. ***Adding a try block.*** Add lines 30–34 and lines 40–42 of Fig. 20.11 to your code. Note that the code that prompts the user to enter the car price is now contained in the `try` block. You should indent lines 36–38 for readability after adding the highlighted code in Fig. 20.11. Lines 34 and 38 are included in the `try` block because they might throw an exception. Line 34, which uses the `exceptions` function, causes `cin` to throw an `ios_base::failure` exception whenever its `failbit` is set. If the `failbit` is already set when `exceptions` is called, the `ios_base::failure` exception is thrown immediately. Therefore, the call to `exceptions` should always be placed in a `try` block.

(cont.)

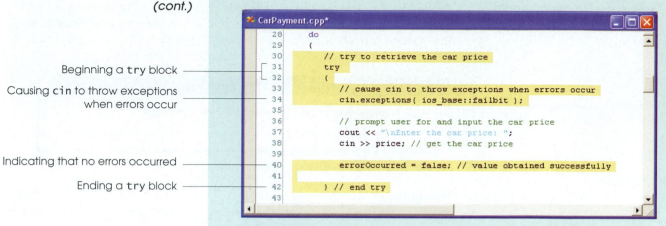

Beginning a `try` block

Causing `cin` to throw exceptions when errors occur

Indicating that no errors occurred

Ending a `try` block

Figure 20.11   Creating a `try` statement containing code that might throw an exception.

Line 40 does not execute if an exception occurs in one of the preceding lines inside the `try` block. If the user has entered a valid value at the input prompt, line 40 sets `errorOccurred` to `false` to indicate that the application should exit the `do...while` loop.

7. *Adding a catch block*. Only one `catch` block is needed following the `try` block in this example because only one type of exception—an `ios_base::failure`—can occur. Add lines 43–46 of Fig. 20.12 to your code. Line 43 specifies that this catch block handles the `ios_base::failure` exception. In this case, the `catch` block specifies an exception parameter named `inputError`.

Adding a `catch` block

Figure 20.12   Adding a `catch` block.

8. *Clearing the stream state and the stream contents*. Add lines 45–48 of Fig. 20.13 to your code. If the body of the `catch` block executes, then the `cin` object's `failbit` is set. Recall that stream I/O operations cannot resume until the `failbit` has been cleared. Line 45 calls the `clear` function to clear the `failbit`. Line 48 inputs the contents of the input buffer into `string` variable `invalidInput`, removing those characters from the buffer. This ensures that the input buffer is empty before the user inputs another value for the car's price—this prevents the application from reading the invalid data again.

Clearing the error state

Removing characters from `cin`

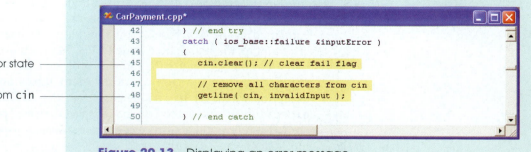

Figure 20.13   Displaying an error message.

(cont.)

9. ***Displaying an error message.*** Add lines 50–53 of Fig. 20.14 to your code. If an `ios_base::failure` exception does occur, you should display an error message and prompt the user to input valid data. Line 50 assigns to error-Occurred the value `true`, indicating that an error has occurred and that the application must prompt the user for another value. Lines 52–53 display an error message indicating that the user must enter an integer value.

Indicating that an error occurred ⎯⎯⎯

Displaying an error message ⎯⎯⎯

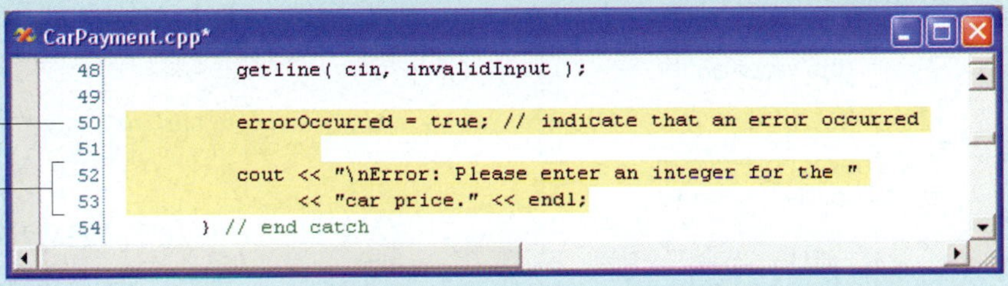

Figure 20.14   Clearing the stream error state and removing the user input from the input buffer.

10. ***Save, compile and run the completed application.*** Figure 20.15 shows the result when the user attempts to enter invalid input. Test your application using the values that you entered in the test drive, using your new version of the application to see that it works properly.

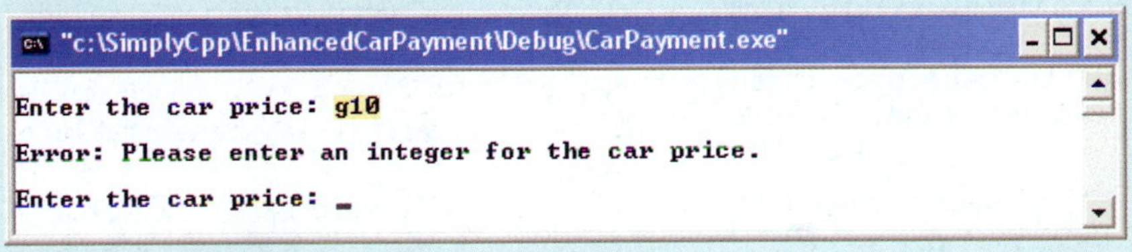

Figure 20.15   Error message displayed when an `ios_base::failure` exception occurs.

11. ***Close the*** Command Prompt ***window.***

Figure 20.16 presents the source code for the Enhanced **Car Payment Calculator** application. The lines of code you added, viewed or modified in this tutorial are highlighted.

Include the `<exception>` header file ⎯⎯⎯

```
1   // Tutorial 20: CarPayment.cpp
2   // Calculate different billing plans for a car loan.
3   #include <iostream> // required to perform C++ stream I/O
4   #include <iomanip> // required for parameterized stream manipulators
5   #include <cmath> // required to use the C++ math library functions
6   #include <string> // required to access string functions
7   #include <exception> // required to use exceptions
8
9   using namespace std; // for accessing C++ Standard Library members
10
11  // function prototypes
12  double calculateMonthlyPayment( double, int, int );
13  void processData( int, int, double );
14
15  // function main begins program execution
16  int main()
17  {
```

Figure 20.16   Enhanced **Car Payment Calculator** application's code. (Part 1 of 3.)

errorOccurred is true if an input error occurred

Stores invalid input from the input buffer

Repeats until a valid car price is entered

Begin a **try** block

Cause **cin** to throw exceptions when errors occur

Prompt the user for and input car price

Indicate that no error occurred

End **try** block, begin **catch** block for **ios_base::failure** exception

Clear the error state

Remove all characters from the input buffer

Indicate that an error occurred

Display an error message

Repeat if an error occurred during input

```cpp
18        // define variables
19        int price; // price of the car
20        int downPayment; // the down payment
21        double interest; // the annual interest rate
22        bool errorOccurred = false; // true if an input error occurred
23
24        // temporarily store one line of invalid input
25        string invalidInput;
26
27        // do while cin has not successfully read the car price
28        do
29        {
30           // try to retrieve the car price
31           try
32           {
33              // cause cin to throw exceptions when errors occur
34              cin.exceptions( ios_base::failbit );
35
36              // prompt user for and input the car price
37              cout << "\nEnter the car price: ";
38              cin >> price; // get the car price
39
40              errorOccurred = false; // values obtained successfully
41
42           } // end try
43           catch ( ios_base::failure &inputError )
44           {
45              cin.clear(); // clear fail flag
46
47              // remove all characters from cin
48              getline( cin, invalidInput );
49
50              errorOccurred = true; // indicate that an error occurred
51
52              cout << "\nError: Please enter an integer for the car "
53                 << " price." << endl;
54           } // end catch
55
56        }
57        while ( errorOccurred == true ); // end do...while
58
59        // prompt user for and input the down payment
60        // and the annual interest rate (no exception handling)
61        cout << "Enter the down payment: ";
62        cin >> downPayment; // get the down payment
63
64        cout << "Enter the annual interest rate: ";
65        cin >> interest; // get the annual interest rate
66
67        // create table of options over different periods of time
68        processData( price, downPayment, interest);
69
70        return 0; // indicate that program ended successfully
71
72     } // end function main
73
```

Figure 20.16 Enhanced **Car Payment Calculator** application's code. (Part 2 of 3.)

```
74   // function calculates payments for each time interval
75   void processData( int price, int downPayment, double interest )
76   {
77      // calculate loan amount and monthly interest
78      int loanAmount = price - downPayment;
79      double monthlyInterest = interest / 1200;
80
81      // set precision for output values
82      cout << fixed << setprecision( 2 );
83
84      // add header to output
85      cout << endl << left << setw( 10 ) << "Months"
86          << "Monthly Payments" << endl;
87
88      // calculate and display payments
89      for ( int years = 2; years <= 5; years++ )
90      {
91         // convert payment period to months
92         int months = 12 * years;
93
94         // get monthlyPayment
95         double monthlyPayment = calculateMonthlyPayment(
96            monthlyInterest, months, loanAmount );
97
98         // insert result into output stream
99         cout << left << setw( 10 ) << months
100             << "$" << monthlyPayment << endl;
101
102     } // end for
103
104  } // end function processData
105
106  // calculate monthlyPayment
107  double calculateMonthlyPayment( double monthlyInterest,
108     int months, int loanAmount )
109  {
110     double base = pow( 1 + monthlyInterest, months );
111
112     return loanAmount * monthlyInterest / ( 1 - ( 1 / base ) );
113
114  } // end function calculateMonthlyPayment
```

Figure 20.16 Enhanced **Car Payment Calculator** application's code. (Part 3 of 3.)

SELF-REVIEW

1. If you are attempting to catch multiple exception types, you may use several _____ blocks after the _____ block.

   a) try, catch   b) catch, try
   c) if, try   d) None of the above.

2. The exception you wish to handle should be declared as a parameter of the _____ block.

   a) try   b) catch
   c) if   d) None of the above.

Answers: 1) b. 2) b.

20.7 Wrap-Up

In this tutorial, you learned some basic exception-handling concepts and how exception handling is used in C++. You learned to use the `try` block and the `catch` block to handle exceptions in your applications. You also learned how to use the `throw` keyword to rethrow an exception that cannot be handled in a `catch` block. You applied your knowledge of exception handling in C++ to enhance your **Car Payment Calculator** application to check for input errors before calculating car loan payments.

Because the `cin` object does not throw exceptions by default, you used the `exceptions` function on the `cin` object to cause it to throw an exception when a stream error occurs. You used a `try` block to enclose the statements that may throw an `ios_base::failure` exception and a `catch` block to handle that exception. Finally, you used the `cin` object's `clear` function and the `getline` function to enable future stream I/O operations to proceed properly.

In the next tutorial, you will learn about C++ templates, which allow you to solve many problems by coding functions and classes "generically." You will learn how to create a function template that specifies actions to perform regardless of the data types of the values supplied as parameters. You also will learn how to use a class template that you can use to create many classes, each of which contains data members of different data types.

SKILLS SUMMARY

Handling an Exception

- Enclose in a `try` block the code that may generate an exception and the code that should not execute if an exception occurs.
- Follow the `try` block with one or more `catch` blocks. Each `catch` block is an exception handler that specifies the type of exception it can handle.

Enabling Exceptions for Stream Objects

- Call the `exceptions` function on a stream object, such as `cin`, specifying the stream error state that should raise an exception.

Clearing a Stream Error State

- Call the `clear` function on the stream object.
- If necessary, call the `getline` function on the stream object to remove from the input buffer the input that caused the error.

KEY TERMS

catch an exception—Execute an exception handler when the application detects an exceptional situation and throws an exception of the type specified by the exception handler.

catch block—Also called an exception handler, this block executes when the corresponding `try` block in the application detects an exceptional situation and throws an exception of the type the `catch` block declares as its exception parameter.

clear function of class ios—Restores a stream's state to "good," so that I/O may proceed on the stream.

exception—An indication of a problem that occurs during an application's execution.

exception class—Represents a type of exceptional situation occurring in a C++ application that should be caught and handled by the application.

exception handler—A `catch` block that executes when the application detects an exceptional situation and throws an exception of a type that matches the handler's exception parameter.

exception handling—A technique that enables you to separate error-handling from your application's logic by treating errors as exceptional situations. A function can throw an exception when an error occurs and provide one or more exception handlers that execute when the matching exception occurs.

<exception> header file—The C++ Standard Library header file containing class definitions and function prototypes that support exception handling.

exception object—An object that is thrown by a `throw` statement.

exception parameter—Identifies the exception type that the exception handler can process.

exceptions function of class `ios`—Causes a stream object to throw an exception when a stream error occurs.

fail function of class `ios_base`—Returns `true` if a stream error has occurred, such as when `failbit` is set. For example, the function call `cin.fail()` returns `true` if the user enters a non-numeric character when the application attempts to input an integer from the standard input stream.

failbit of class `ios_base`—A bit that is set when a format error occurs on a stream. This occurs, for example, if the user enters a non-numeric character when the application attempts to input an integer from the standard input stream.

`ios_base::failure` class—A derived class of `exception` that is used to create an exception object that is thrown when a stream object encounters an error. This can occur if the application encounters non-numeric characters when attempting to input an integer.

rethrow an exception—A `catch` block can use `throw` to defer the exception handling (or perhaps a portion of it) to another `catch` block associated with an enclosing `try` block.

stream state—A series of bits whose values indicate which stream I/O errors, if any, have occurred. For example, the `failbit` is set when the application encounters a stream format error (that is, encounters unexpected characters when inputting a value).

throw statement—A statement that throws an exception, so that it can be processed by an enclosing `try` block. A `throw` statement can specify zero or one operand, which can be of any type.

throw statement in a `catch` block—A statement that rethrows an exception from a `catch` block, so that it can be processed by an enclosing `try` block.

throw an exception—A function throws an exception if the function encounters a problem that it cannot handle.

try block—A block that consists of keyword `try`, followed by braces (`{}`) that contain statements that might cause exceptions and statements that should not execute if an exception occurs. If an exception occurs inside a `try` block, the application executes the corresponding `catch` block, if one exists.

uncaught exception—An exception that does not have an exception handler. Uncaught exceptions terminate application execution.

what function (of the exception class)—The `exception` class member function that typically returns a string describing the error. If the `exception` object was created by passing a string to the `exception` class's constructor, the `what` function typically returns this value.

C++ LIBRARY REFERENCE

exception This header file contains the definition of the base class that represents most exceptions.

- *Class*

   `exception`—A class that represents an exceptional situation occurring in a C++ application that should be caught and handled by the application.

iostream This header file declares basic services required for all stream-I/O operations.

- *Data member*

   `failbit`—A bit that is set when a format error occurs on a stream.

- *Exception*

   `ios_base::failure`—Exception thrown when the error bit specified by the `exceptions` function call is set.

- *Functions*

   `clear`—Restores a stream's state to "good," so that I/O may proceed on the stream.

   `exceptions`—Causes a stream object to throw an exception of type `ios_base::failure` when the specified error occurs.

   `fail`—Returns `true` if an error has occurred, such as when `failbit` is set.

   `ignore`—Removes the next character from the input stream.

■ *Objects*

cin—Reads characters entered at the keyboard. Text is sent to the application when the user presses *Enter* and placed in a variable using the stream extraction operator, >>.

cout—Displays text on the screen. Text is displayed using the stream-insertion operator (<<).

■ *Stream manipulators*

endl—This object places a newline into the output stream and flushes the stream's buffer, so that all the text stored in the output stream buffer is displayed immediately.

fixed—This stream manipulator specifies that floating-point numbers should be printed using fixed-point notation (as opposed to scientific notation).

flush—This stream manipulator flushes the output buffer so that output is displayed on the screen immediately.

left—This stream manipulator causes values to be left justified in a field. The stream into which left is inserted remains left justified until the application terminates or until the stream's justification is changed, whichever comes first.

right—This stream manipulator right justifies output in a field.

MULTIPLE-CHOICE QUESTIONS

20.1 Dealing with exceptional situations as a program executes is called exception _____.

a) detection
b) handling
c) resolution
d) debugging

20.2 A(n) _____ is always followed by at least one catch block.

a) if statement
b) exception block
c) try block
d) None of the above.

20.3 Stream objects throw exceptions of type _____.

a) ios_base::failure
b) ios_base::exception
c) ios_base::fail
d) ios_base::error

20.4 If no exceptions are thrown in a try block, _____.

a) its catch block(s) are skipped
b) all its catch blocks are executed
c) an error occurs
d) the default exception is thrown

20.5 A catch block specifies a(n) _____ that identifies the exception type the handler can process.

a) try block
b) parameter
c) error handler
d) thrower

20.6 A try block can have _____ associated with it.

a) only one catch block
b) zero catch blocks
c) one or more catch blocks
d) None of the above.

20.7 After a stream I/O format error occurs, the application should _____ to enable future input operations.

a) clear the contents of the input buffer
b) clear the failbit
c) delete the cin object
d) Both a and b.

20.8 To cause cin to throw an exception when an input error occurs, call member function _____ with argument _____ .

a) exceptions, ios_base::failbit
b) exception, ios_base::failbit
c) exceptions, ios_base::failure
d) exception, ios_base::failure

20.9 The exception class is defined in the _____ header file.

a) <stdexcept>
b) <exceptions>
c) <iostream>
d) <exception>

20.10 The _____ function, when called on a stream object, resets the object's error state.

a) `reset`   b) `clear`

c) `good`   d) `unset`

EXERCISES

20.11 (*Enhanced Miles Per Gallon Application*) Modify the **Miles Per Gallon** application (Exercise 10.17) so that it uses exception handling to handle the `ios_base::failure` exception generated when inputting `double` values (Fig. 20.17). The original application allowed the user to input the number of miles driven and the number of gallons used for a tank of gas to determine the miles per gallon.

Error message displayed after exception is caught

```
 "c:\simplycpp\enhancedmilespergallon\debug\EnhancedMilesPerGallon.exe"      _ □ ×

Enter miles driven: ninety

Error: Please enter floating-point values.

Enter miles driven: 90
Enter gallons used: 4.5

Miles per gallon: 20.00

Press any key to continue_
```

Figure 20.17   Enhanced **Miles Per Gallon** application output.

a) *Copying the template to your working directory.* Copy the `C:\Examples\Tutorial20\Exercises\EnhancedMilesPerGallon` directory to your `C:\SimplyCpp` directory.

b) *Opening the template source code file.* Open the `MilesPerGallon.cpp` file in your text editor or IDE.

c) *Adding a do...while loop that executes while the user has not entered valid data.* In line 19, define `bool` variable `errorOccurred` and initialize its value to `false`. Then define a `string` variable `invalidInput` that will contain any invalid characters removed from the input buffer when a stream input error occurs. Then enclose lines 24–30 in a do...while statement that repeats while `errorOccurred` is `true`. Add a level of indentation to the contents of the do...while statement.

d) *Adding a try block.* Enclose the contents of the do...while statement in a `try` block. Add a level of indentation to the contents of the `try` block. Immediately after the `try` block's opening brace, insert a statement that causes the `cin` object to throw exceptions. Then insert a statement immediately before the closing brace of the `try` block that sets `errorOccurred` to `false`.

e) *Adding a catch block.* Immediately following the `try` block you added in *Step d*, add a `catch` block to catch an `ios_base::failure` exception. Inside the `catch` block, add code to display an error message, reset the error state in `cin`, clear the contents of the input buffer and set `errorOccurred` to `true`.

f) *Save, compile and run the completed application.* Test your application to ensure that it runs correctly. The error message displayed when your completed **Miles Per Gallon** application throws an exception should look similar to the one shown in Fig. 20.17.

g) *Close the Command Prompt window.*

20.12 (*Enhanced Prime Numbers Application*) Modify the **Prime Numbers** application (Exercise 10.17) so that it uses exception handling to handle errors that occur when inputting `int` values (Fig. 20.18). The original application took two numbers (representing a lower bound and an upper bound) and ascertain all of the prime numbers within the specified bounds, inclusive. An `int` greater than 1 is said to be prime if it is divisible only by 1 and itself. For example, 2, 3, 5 and 7 are prime numbers, but 4, 6, 8 and 9 are not.

Error message displayed after exception is caught

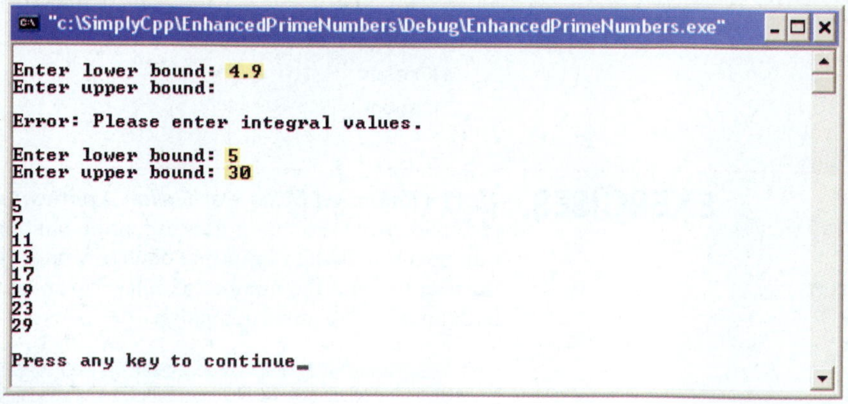

Figure 20.18 Enhanced **Prime Numbers** application output.

a) *Copying the template to your working directory.* Copy the C:\Examples\ Tutorial20\Exercises\EnhancedPrimeNumbers directory to your C:\SimplyCpp directory.

b) *Opening the template source code file.* Open the PrimeNumbers.cpp file in your text editor or IDE.

c) *Adding a do...while loop that executes while the user has not entered valid data.* In line 20, define bool variable errorOccurred and initialize its value to false. Then define a string variable invalidInput that will contain any invalid characters removed from the input buffer when a stream input error occurs. Then enclose lines 25–31 in a do...while statement that repeats while errorOccurred is true. Add a level of indentation to the contents of the do...while statement.

d) *Adding a try block.* Enclose the contents of the do...while statement inside a try block. Add a level of indentation to the contents of the try block. Immediately after the try block's opening brace, insert a statement that causes the cin object to throw exceptions when input errors occur. Then insert a statement immediately before the closing brace of the try block that sets errorOccurred to false.

e) *Adding a catch block.* Immediately following the try block you added in *Step d*, add a catch block to catch an ios_base::failure exception. Inside the catch block, add code to display an error message, reset the error state in cin, clear the contents of the input buffer and set errorOccurred to true.

f) *Save, compile and run the completed application.* Test your application to ensure that it runs correctly The error message displayed when your completed **Prime Numbers** application throws an exception should look similar to the dialog shown in Fig. 20.18.

g) *Close the Command Prompt window.*

20.13 (*Modified Car Payment Calculator Application*) Modify the **Car Payment Calculator** application so that it handles exceptions thrown when the user inputs invalid data in any of its input prompts. The application should ensure that the value inputted as downPayment is an integer and the value inputted as interest is a floating-point number (Fig. 20.19).

a) *Copying the template to your working directory.* Copy the C:\Examples\ Tutorial20\Exercises\ModifiedCarPayment directory to your C:\SimplyCpp directory.

b) *Opening the template source code file.* Open the CarPayment.cpp file in your text editor or IDE.

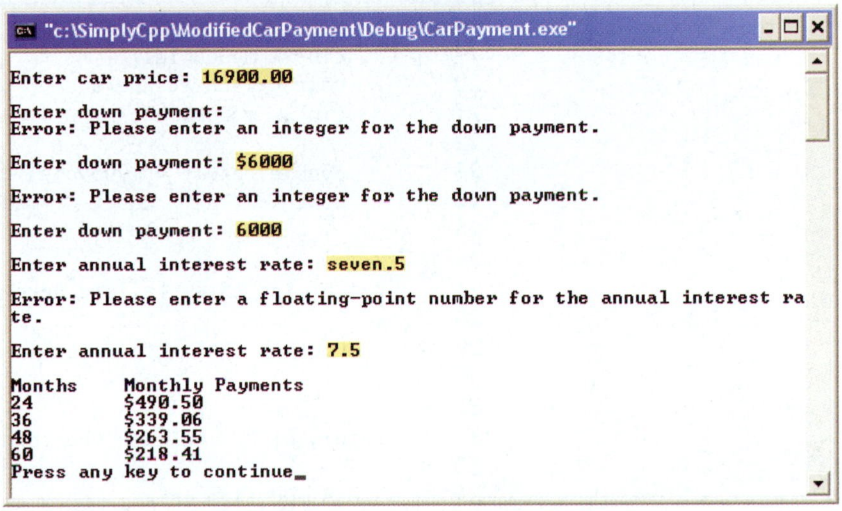

Figure 20.19 Modified **Car Payment Calculator** application.

c) *Adding a do…while loop that repeats until the user enters a valid down payment.* Starting in line 59, add a do…while loop that repeats until the user enters a valid integer for the down payment. This do…while loop should be similar to the one used to prompt the user for and input the car price. Because line 34 in Fig. 20.16 causes cin to throw exceptions, you do not need to call the exceptions function inside this do…while loop.

d) *Adding a do…while loop that executes while the user has not entered valid annual interest rate.* After the do…while loop you added in *Step c*, add a do…while loop that repeats until the user enters a valid floating-point number for the annual interest rate. This do…while loop should be similar to the one used to prompt the user for and input the down payment, except that it should input a floating-point value.

e) *Save, compile and run the completed application.* Test your application to ensure that it runs correctly. The error messages displayed when your completed **Car Payment Calculator** application receives invalid input should match those in Fig. 20.19.

f) *Close the Command Prompt window.*

What does this code do? ▶　　**20.14** What does the following code do?

```
1   // Exercise 20.14: WDTCD.cpp
2   // What does this code do?
3   #include <iostream>  // required to perform C++ stream I/O
4   #include <exception> // required to use exceptions
5
6   using namespace std; // for accessing C++ Standard Library members
7
8   // function main begins program execution
9   int main()
10  {
11     double myDouble1;
12     double myDouble2;
13
14     try
15     {
16        cin.exceptions( ios_base::failbit );
17
```

```
18        cout << "\nEnter the first operand: ";
19        cin >> myDouble1;
20        cout << "Enter the second operand: ";
21        cin >> myDouble2;
22
23        double result = myDouble1 * myDouble2;
24        cout << "The product of the two numbers is: " << result
25           << endl << endl;
26     }
27     catch( ios_base::failure &exception )
28     {
29        cout << "\nPlease enter floating-point numbers.\n\n";
30     }
31
32     return 0; // indicate that program ended successfully
33
34  } // end function main
```

What's wrong with this code? ▶   **20.15** The following code should add integers from two input prompts and display the sum of the two numbers. Find the error(s) in the following code:

```
1   // Exercise 20.15: WWWTC.cpp
2   // This application tries to input two integral numbers
3   // and then displays the result of their sum
4   #include <iostream>  // required to perform C++ stream I/O
5   #include <exception> // required to use exceptions
6
7   using namespace std; // for accessing C++ Standard Library members
8
9   // function main begins program execution
10  int main()
11  {
12     int first;
13     int second;
14
15     try
16     {
17        cout << "\nEnter the first operand: ";
18        cin >> first;
19        cout << "Enter the second operand: ";
20        cin >> second;
21
22        int result = first + second;
23     }
24
25     cout << "The sum is: " << result << endl << endl;
26
27     catch()
28     {
29        cout << "\nPlease enter integral numbers." << endl << endl;
30     }
31
32     return 0; // indicate that program ended successfully
33
34  } // end function main
```

Programming Challenge ▶

20.16 (*Guess the Word Application*) The **Guess the Word** application contains an array of pre-set words. The game should randomly select a word and hide its text by creating a string that replaces each character of the word with an asterisk. The application displays the hidden word for the user to guess. The user can display a character of the hidden word by entering the position of the character. The application then replaces the asterisk with the corresponding letter in the hidden word. If the user guesses correctly, display a congratulatory message and exit. If the guess is incorrect, display an error message and let the user try again. In this exercise, you will be adding exception handling to handle the `ios_base::failure` exception that occurs when the user enters a non-numeric character when an integer is expected, and the `out_of_range` exception that occurs when the user attempts to reveal a character that is not contained in the `string`, such as the sixth character of a five-letter word. (Fig. 20.20).

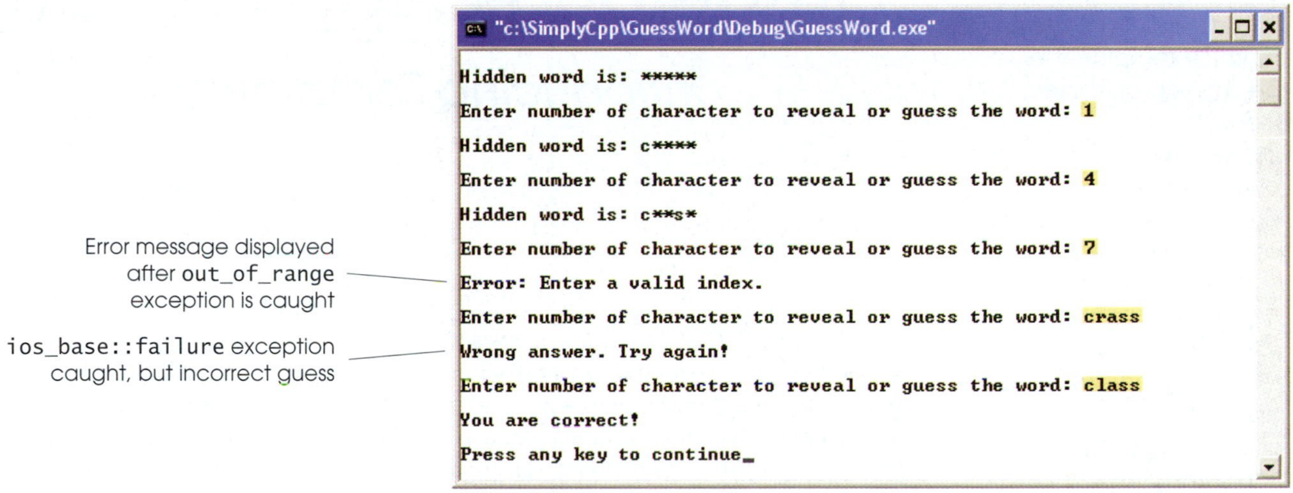

Error message displayed after `out_of_range` exception is caught

`ios_base::failure` exception caught, but incorrect guess

Figure 20.20 **Guess the Word** application.

a) *Copying the template to your working directory.* Copy the C:\Examples\ Tutorial20\Exercises\GuessWord directory to your C:\SimplyCpp directory.

b) *Opening the template source code file.* Open the GuessWord.cpp file in your text editor or IDE.

c) *Adding a try block.* Enclose lines 41–51 inside a `try` block. Add a level of indentation to the contents of the `try` block. Immediately after the `try` block's opening brace, insert a statement that causes the `cin` object to throw exceptions when input errors occur.

d) *Adding a catch block.* Immediately following the `try` block you added in *Step c*, add a `catch` block to catch an `ios_base::failure` exception. If this exception is thrown, then the user did not enter an integer at the input prompt. In this case, your application should interpret the input as an attempt to guess the word. Inside the `catch` block, add code to reset the error state in `cin` so that you can resume stream input operations. Then add code that stores the contents of `cin` in `string` variable `text`. Compare the contents of the text to the hidden word (WORD_LIST[randomNumber]). If the two words are identical, display a congratulatory message and set `correctAnswer` to `true` to indicate that the user guessed the word correctly. Otherwise, display a message indicating that the user guessed incorrectly and should try again.

e) *Adding a second catch block.* Immediately following the `catch` block you added in *Step d*, add another `catch` block to catch an `out_of_range` exception. If this exception is thrown, then the user entered an integer at the input prompt, but the value of the integer did not correspond to a character in the string. In this case, your application should display an error message describing the error.

f) *Save, compile and run the completed application.* Test your application to ensure that it runs correctly. The error message displayed when your completed **Guess the Word** application throws an `out_of_range` exception should be similar to the one in Fig. 20.20.

g) *Close the Command Prompt window.*

21 TUTORIAL

Objectives

In this tutorial, you will learn to:
- Use function templates to create a group of related functions.
- Use class templates to create a group of related classes.
- Understand the concept of generic programming.

Outline

Grade Book Application

Introducing Templates

In Tutorial 10, you learned that when you call a function, the number, order and type of the arguments must agree with the parameters in the function's parameter list. For example, when you wrote a maximum function that returns the largest of the three ints passed to it, the function call must specify three int values. To find the largest of three doubles, you would have to write another, overloaded, maximum function that specifies three double parameters.

In this tutorial, we discuss one of C++'s more powerful features—**templates**. **Function templates** enable you to specify, with a single code segment, an entire range of related (overloaded) functions called **function-template specializations**. For example, you can write a single function template for a maximum function, which returns the largest of the three values passed to it, then have C++ generate separate overloaded functions that will take and return ints, doubles, chars and so on. Function templates allow the function caller to call a function at different points with different argument types. The compiler then generates code for each function-template specialization, saving time for the programmer.

You can also create class templates, which enable you to specify, with a single code segment, an entire range of related classes. For example, in Tutorial 16, you used a List class to represent a linked list of ShoppingItems. Using a List class template, you can represent a linked list of any number of objects, such as a list of students, courses or books.

Note the distinction between templates and template specializations: Function templates and class templates are like stencils out of which we can trace shapes; function-template specializations and class-template specializations are like separate tracings that all have the same shape but could, for example, be drawn in different colors.

21.1 Test-Driving the Grade Book Application

In this section, you will test-drive the **Grade Book** application. This application must meet the following requirements:

Application Requirements

A local college will soon require its professors to record their students' grades using an electronic grade book. You have been asked to build a prototype grade book application that inputs student grades. The application prompts the user for and inputs the number of students in the course and then prompts the user to input each student's grade. After the grades have been entered, the application must display all the students' grades, the highest grade in the class, the lowest grade in the class, and the class average. Some professors prefer to enter grades as floating-point numbers and others prefer integers. Thus, your application must determine which type of grade the user will enter, then process the grades as floating-point or integer values, accordingly.

You begin by test-driving the completed application. Then, you will learn the additional C++ capabilities you will need to create your own version of this application.

Test-Driving the Grade Book Application

1. *Locating the completed application.* Open the **Command Prompt** window by selecting **Start > All Programs > Accessories > Command Prompt**. Change to your completed **Grade Book** application directory by typing cd C:\Examples\Tutorial21\CompletedApplication\GradeBook.

2. *Running the Grade Book application.* Type GradeBook in the **Command Prompt** window to run the application (Fig. 21.1). At the **Enter the number of students:** prompt, enter 10 to specify the size of the class.

```
Command Prompt - GradeBook                          _ □ ×

C:\>cd C:\Examples\Tutorial21\CompletedApplication\GradeBook

C:\Examples\Tutorial21\CompletedApplication\GradeBook>GradeBook

Enter the number of students: 10_
```

Figure 21.1   Running the completed **Grade Book** application.

3. *Entering the primitive type.* At the prompt for the **Select the grade type:** menu (Fig. 21.2), enter 1 to indicate that you would like to input grades as integer values.

```
Command Prompt - GradeBook                          _ □ ×

Enter the number of students: 10

Select the grade type:
1 - Integer
2 - Floating-point
Enter selection: 1_
```

Figure 21.2   Selecting the grade type.

4. *Entering the student's grades.* Enter 10 grades, as shown in Fig. 21.3. Note that if you enter a grade outside the range 0–100, the application displays an error message and prompts you to reenter the student's grade.

(cont.)

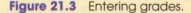

Figure 21.3 Entering grades.

5. *Displaying the class results.* After you enter the last grade, the application displays each student's grade, the class average, the lowest and the highest grade (Fig. 21.4). Each of these is displayed in the grade type you entered in Fig. 21.2, except for the class average, which is always displayed as a floating-point number.

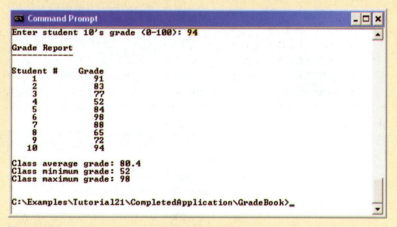

Figure 21.4 Displaying the students' grades and class statistics.

6. *Entering floating-point grades.* Repeat *Step 2*. At the prompt for the **Select the grade type:** menu (Fig. 21.5), enter 2 to indicate that you would like to input grades as floating-point values.

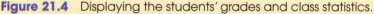

Figure 21.5 Selecting floating-point grades as input.

7. *Entering and displaying the floating-point grades.* Enter the grades as shown in Fig. 21.6. Note that the application outputs all grades as floating-point values (again, the class average is always output as a floating-point value).

8. *Close the Command Prompt window.*

(cont.)

```
Command Prompt                                              - □ ×
Enter selection: 2

Enter student 1's grade (0-100): 93.5
Enter student 2's grade (0-100): 84.6
Enter student 3's grade (0-100): 87.2
Enter student 4's grade (0-100): 76.8
Enter student 5's grade (0-100): 62.5
Enter student 6's grade (0-100): 88.5
Enter student 7's grade (0-100): 95.9
Enter student 8's grade (0-100): 54.7
Enter student 9's grade (0-100): 77.3
Enter student 10's grade (0-100): 89.5

Grade Report
------------

Student #       Grade
    1            93.5
    2            84.6
    3            87.2
    4            76.8
    5            62.5
    6            88.5
    7            95.9
    8            54.7
    9            77.3
   10            89.5

Class average grade: 81.0
Class minimum grade: 54.7
Class maximum grade: 95.9

C:\Examples\Tutorial21\CompletedApplication\GradeBook>_
```

Figure 21.6 Entering floating-point grades and displaying the results.

21.2 Function Templates

Overloaded functions typically perform similar operations. However, the operations may involve different program logic, use different data types or both. For example, consider the overloaded function divideByTwo, which accepts an int or double parameter. The overloaded function containing an int parameter might be defined as follows:

```
double divideByTwo( int value )
{
    return value / 2.0;
} // end function divideByTwo
```

This function simply returns the variable value divided by 2. The overloaded function containing a double parameter might be defined as follows:

```
double divideByTwo( double value )
{
    return value / 2.0;
} // end function divideByTwo
```

When the operations performed by overloaded functions are identical, as in this case, overloading may be performed more compactly and conveniently using function templates. Defining a function as a function template allows the data types for the parameters, the return type and locally defined variables to vary, depending on how the function is called. All function template definitions begin with the **template** keyword followed by a list of **formal type parameters** to the function template enclosed in angle brackets (< and >). Every formal type parameter is preceded by the class keyword. A function template for the divideByTwo function may be written as

```
template< class T >
double divideByTwo( T value )
{
    return value / 2.0;
} // end function template divideByTwo
```

Error-Prevention Tip

Not placing class before each formal type parameter of a function template is a syntax error.

In this example, the divideByTwo function template declares one formal type parameter, T. The formal type parameters are placeholders for variable types that are built in (such as int or double) or user defined. The name of the formal type parameter can be any valid identifier. By convention, we use the name T for the first formal type parameter in a template declaration.

You can use a formal type parameter to specify the types of the parameters to the function, to indicate the return type of the function and to define variables in the body of the function definition. In the preceding example, the formal type parameter specifies the type of the function's parameter, value. When the compiler encounters a call to a function template, C++ uses the argument type(s) to generate a separate function-template specialization to handle the call appropriately. For example, when the compiler encounters the statements

```
double sum = 21.0;
double half = divideByTwo( sum );
```

it determines the argument type in the function call—in this case, sum is a double. Because the corresponding parameter in the function template, value, uses the formal type parameter, T, the compiler generates a function-template specialization by replacing every instance of T with double.

Similarly, when the compiler encounters the statements

```
int sum = 21;
double half = divideByTwo( sum );
```

it determines the argument type in the function call—in this case, sum is an int. Because the corresponding parameter in the function template, value, uses the formal type parameter, T, the compiler generates a function-template specialization by replacing every instance of T with int. Thus, a single function template can generate a whole family of function-template specializations. This technique is called **generic programming** because function templates allow you to write functions without specifying a particular data type.

In the following box, you will create a function template that returns the largest of three values. Calling this function using different argument types will cause the compiler to generate multiple function-template specializations.

Creating a Function Template

1. ***Copying the template application to your working directory.*** Copy the C:\Examples\Tutorial21\TemplateApplication\Max directory to your C:\SimplyCpp directory. [*Note:* Throughout the tutorials, we refer to "template" source code files and "template" applications. These references should not be confused with the template feature of the C++ programming language.]

2. ***Open the Max application's template source code file.*** Open the template file Max.cpp in your text editor or IDE.

3. ***Declaring the maximum function.*** Insert lines 7–9 of Fig. 21.7 into your application. Line 8 uses the template keyword to declare maximum as a function template and specifies a single formal type parameter named T. Recall that the formal type parameter can be any valid identifier. Line 9 declares the return type and all three function parameters using the formal type parameter T.

(cont.)

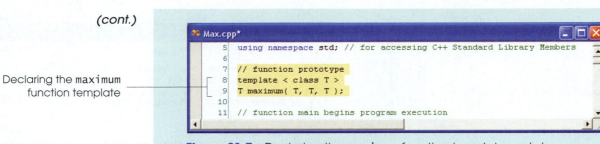

Figure 21.7   Declaring the `maximum` function template prototype.

4. ***Defining variables in main.*** Insert lines 14–20 of Fig. 21.8 into your application. Lines 15–17 define three `int` variables that you will pass as arguments to the `maximum` function template. Lines 18–20 define three `double` variables that you will pass as arguments to the `maximum` function template.

Figure 21.8   Defining variables.

5. ***Prompting the user for and inputting three integer values.*** Add lines 22–30 of Fig. 21.9 to `main` to prompt the user for and input three integer values.

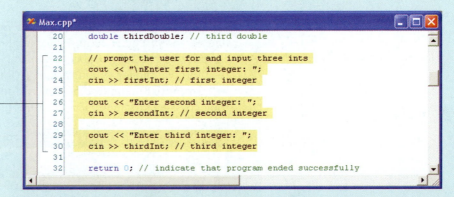

Figure 21.9   Prompting the user for and inputting three integer values.

6. ***Calling the maximum function template using int arguments.*** Insert lines 32–35 of Fig. 21.10 in your application. Note that the call to `maximum` in line 35 specifies three `int` arguments. As a result, the compiler will infer that T (lines 8–9 in Fig. 21.7) is an `int`. The compiler will instantiate a `maximum` function-template specialization that replaces type parameter T with `int`. In this case, the prototype for the function-template specialization will appear as follows:

```cpp
int maximum( int, int, int )
```

(cont.)

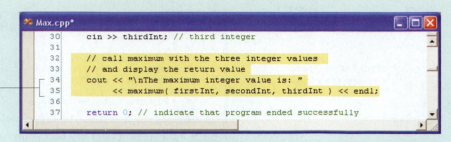

Calculating and displaying the largest of three `int`s

Figure 21.10 Using integer arguments when calling the `maximum` function.

7. *Prompting the user for and inputting floating-point values.* Add lines 37–45 of Fig. 21.11 to `main` to prompt the user for and input three floating-point values.

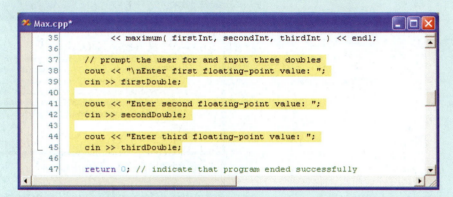

Prompting the user for and inputting three floating-point values

Figure 21.11 Prompting the user for and inputting three floating-point values.

8. *Calling the maximum function template using double arguments.* Insert lines 47–51 of Fig. 21.12 into your application. Lines 49–51 display the largest `double` by calling `maximum`, specifying three `double` arguments. As a result, the compiler will infer that T (lines 8–9 in Fig. 21.7) is a `double` and will instantiate another `maximum` function-template specialization that replaces type parameter T with `double`.

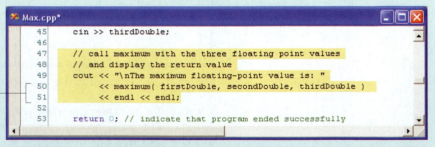

Calculating and displaying the largest of three `double`s

Figure 21.12 Passing `double` arguments to the `maximum` function template.

9. *Defining the maximum function template.* Insert lines 57–62 of Fig. 21.13 into your application. Line 59 uses the `template` keyword to declare the `maximum` function as a function template and specifies a single formal type parameter T. Line 58 uses T to declare `maximum`'s return type and parameter types.

(cont.)

Defining the `maximum` function template

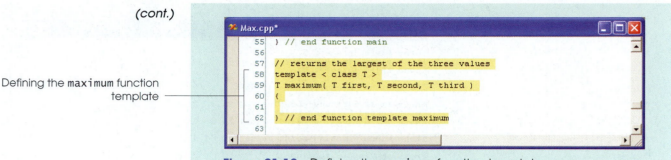

Figure 21.13   Defining the `maximum` function template.

10. ***Determining the largest of three values.*** Insert lines 61–73 of Fig. 21.14 into your application. Line 61 uses the type parameter T to define variable `max` and assign to it the value of `first`. Thus, when a maximum function-template specialization is instantiated, `max`'s type will be the same as the function's parameters. Lines 63–66 use an `if` statement that determines whether `second` is greater than `max`. If so, line 65 assigns to `max` the value of `second`—the largest value the application has encountered so far. Similarly, lines 68–71 use an `if` statement to determine whether `third` is greater than `max`, and if so, assigns to `max` the value of `third`. Finally, line 73 returns the value of `max`, which now contains the largest of the three parameter values, to the caller.

Determining which value is the greatest

Return value of type T

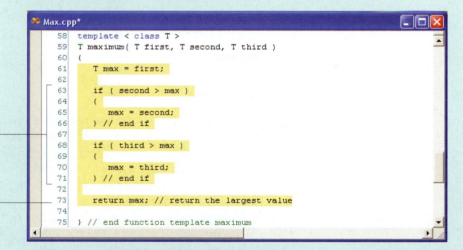

Figure 21.14   Determining the largest value.

The type of the return value for this function depends on the type of the arguments passed into the function. When `maximum` is invoked using `int` arguments, the compiler infers that T is an `int`, so the function returns an `int` value. Similarly, when `maximum` is invoked using `double` arguments, the compiler infers that T is a `double`, so the function returns a `double` value.

11. ***Save, compile and run the application.*** Figure 21.15 shows the completed application's output. Note that you needed to define only one function template even though you invoked the function using different argument types.

(cont.)

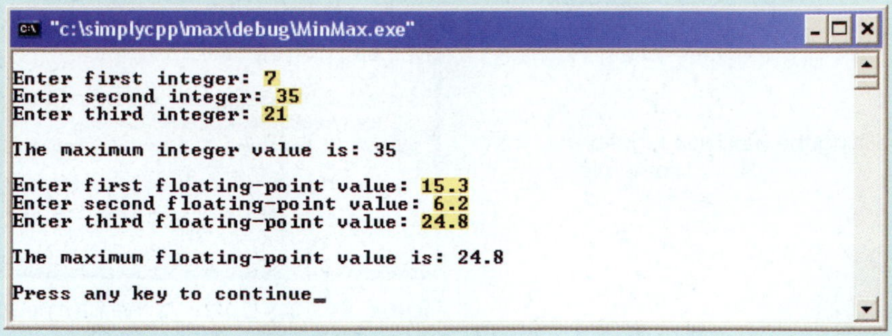

Figure 21.15 Completed **Max** application output.

12. *Close the Command Prompt window.*

SELF-REVIEW

1. The _____ keyword must precede each formal type parameter in a template function.

    a) `template`
                b) `type`

    c) `class`
                d) `array`

2. The compiler uses the _____ in a function call to determine the appropriate function-template specialization.

    a) argument type
                b) return type

    c) argument name
                d) All of the above.

Answers: 1) c. 2) a.

21.3 Class Templates

Like function templates, **class templates** enable you to produce a variety of class-template specializations by writing only one class-template definition. Whenever you need an additional class-template specialization, you use a concise, simple notation, and the compiler writes the source code for the specialization that is required.

For example, consider a `List` class template similar to the class that you used in Tutorial 16 to manage a linked list of `ShoppingItem` objects. This class template could become the basis for creating many different types of `List`s, such as a "`List` of `Employees`," a "`List` of `InvitedGuests`," and a "`List` of `GroceryItems`." Consider the following `List` class definition:

```
template< class T >
class List
{
public:
    List();
    ...
private:
    T *firstItem;
    ...
}; // end class List
```

At first glance, the `List` class-template definition looks like a conventional class definition. However, it is preceded by the header

```
template< class T >
```

to specify a class-template definition with type parameter T that indicates the type of `List` class to be created. Note that you need not specifically use identifier T—you can use any valid identifier. The type of items contained in the `List` is mentioned generically as T in the `List` class header and member function definitions. In the next section, you will learn how to declare and define class template member functions, which must be defined as function templates.

Note that the name of the List class template is List< T >. To instantiate an object of the List class template, you must specify the type for its type parameter T. For example, the statement

```
List< GroceryItem > groceries;
```

instantiates a groceries object from the List class template. The groceries object is of class List< GroceryItem > (pronounced "List of GroceryItems"). The compiler associates type GroceryItem with type parameter T in the template to produce the source code for a List class of type GroceryItem. Class templates are called **parameterized types** because they require one or more type parameters to specify how to customize a generic class template to form a **class-template specialization**. Although you do not see this class-template specialization before compiling your application, it is included in the program and compiled. In the next section, you will create a class template for the application that you test-drove earlier in this tutorial.

SELF-REVIEW

1. To instantiate an object of a class template, you must specify _____.

    a) the class name   b) the type for its type parameter
    c) an object name   d) All of the above.

2. A class template is a _____.

    a) generic class   b) virtual class
    c) parameterized type   d) Both a and c.

Answers: 1) d. 2) d.

21.4 Constructing the Grade Book Application

Now you will build a **Grade Book** application that uses a class template to create objects that store the grades for a class and display statistics for those grades. The source code for this tutorial's template application provides much of the **Grade Book** application's functionality so that you may concentrate on the code that manipulates your GradeBook class template. The pseudocode in Fig. 21.16 describes the basic operation of your **Grade Book** application.

> Prompt the user for and input the course name
> Prompt the user for and input the number of students in the course
> Display a menu prompting the user whether grades will be entered as integer
> values or as floating-point values.
>
> If the user selects integer values
>   Create a GradeBook of ints
>   Prompt the user for and input each student's grade
>   Display the class's grades
>   Display the average, minimum and maximum grade
>
> If user selects floating-point values
>   Create a GradeBook of doubles
>   Prompt the user for and input each student's grade
>   Display the class's grades
>   Display the average, minimum and maximum grades

Figure 21.16   Pseudocode for the **Grade Book** application.

Now that you have learned how to define function templates and class templates, you will build your own class template whose member functions are function templates. In the following box, you will define the GradeBook class template. Later in this tutorial, you will use the class template to instantiate a class template specialization whose member functions will be function-template specializations.

Defining the GradeBook Class Template

1. **Copying the template application to your working directory.** Copy the C:\Examples\Tutorial21\TemplateApplication\GradeBook directory to your C:\SimplyCpp directory.

2. **Opening the GradeBook class template header file.** In the GradeBook directory, you will find the GradeBook.h and GradeBook.cpp files, which contain the GradeBook class template's interface and implementation, respectively. The GradeBookManager.cpp file contains your application's main function. Open the file GradeBook.h in your text editor or IDE.

3. **Viewing the GradeBook class template header file.** Lines 11–12 of Fig. 21.17 use the template and class keywords to declare GradeBook as a class template with one formal type parameter, T. Lines 12–33 contain the GradeBook class template definition. Lines 30–31 define the GradeBook class template's two data members: int variable classSize, which contains the number of students in the class and a pointer to an object of type T, grades, which will point to the zeroth element of an array of grades. (Recall from Tutorial 16 that array names are pointers.) The number of students is not known before the application is compiled, so you will use the new operator to dynamically allocate an array of classSize elements when the constructor runs. The type of elements contained in the array will be specified by the type parameter when the GradeBook class template's client instantiates an object of type GradeBook< T >.

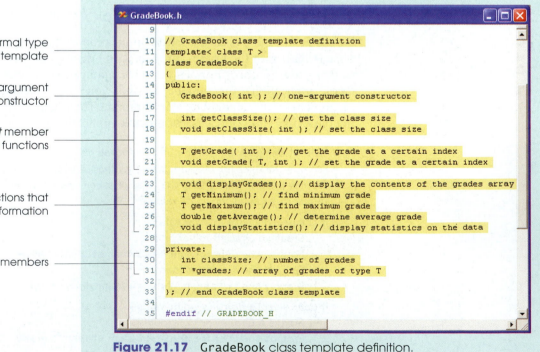

Declaring a formal type parameter for a class template

Declaring the one-argument constructor

Declaring *get* and *set* member functions

Declaring member functions that display statistical information

Defining private data members

```
 9
10  // GradeBook class template definition
11  template< class T >
12  class GradeBook
13  {
14  public:
15      GradeBook( int ); // one-argument constructor
16
17      int getClassSize(); // get the class size
18      void setClassSize( int ); // set the class size
19
20      T getGrade( int ); // get the grade at a certain index
21      void setGrade( T, int ); // set the grade at a certain index
22
23      void displayGrades(); // display the contents of the grades array
24      T getMinimum(); // find minimum grade
25      T getMaximum(); // find maximum grade
26      double getAverage(); // determine average grade
27      void displayStatistics(); // display statistics on the data
28
29  private:
30      int classSize; // number of grades
31      T *grades; // array of grades of type T
32
33  }; // end GradeBook class template
34
35  #endif // GRADEBOOK_H
```

Figure 21.17 GradeBook class template definition.

(cont.)

Lines 15–27 declare GradeBook's member functions. Line 15 declares the one-argument GradeBook constructor. The constructor specifies an int parameter for the number of students in the class. Lines 17–21 declare *get* and *set* functions for the class's private data members. Line 23 declares the displayGrades function, which displays all the grades contained in the grades array. Lines 24–26 declare the getMinimum, getMaximum and getAverage functions, which return the minimum, maximum and average grades, respectively. The getMinimum and getMaximum functions specify a T return type—the type of each grade. The getAverage function specifies a double return type, because the average grade might not be a whole number, even if each grade is an integer. Finally, line 27 declares the displayStatistics function, which displays the minimum, maximum and average grades.

Now that you have defined the GradeBook class template, you will define its member functions.

Implementing the GradeBook Class Template

1. **Opening the GradeBook class template source code file.** Open the template file GradeBook.cpp in your text editor or IDE.

2. **Defining the constructor.** Add lines 14–24 of Fig. 21.18 to the Grade-Book.cpp file to define the GradeBook class template constructor. Note that class-template member function definitions outside the class must begin with the header

   ```
   template< class T >
   ```

   Thus, each definition resembles a conventional function-template definition except that the GradeBook type is always generically listed as type parameter T. Also note that the binary scope resolution operator (::) is always preceded by the class template name (in this case, GradeBook< T >) to tie the member function to the class template.

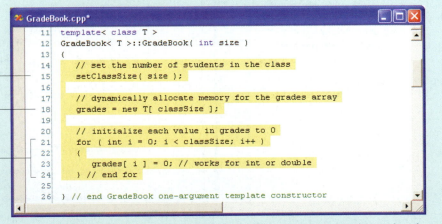

Setting the value of private data member classSize

Dynamically allocating memory for an array of elements of type T containing classSize elements

Initializing all grades to 0

```
11   template< class T >
12   GradeBook< T >::GradeBook( int size )
13   {
14       // set the number of students in the class
15       setClassSize( size );
16
17       // dynamically allocate memory for the grades array
18       grades = new T[ classSize ];
19
20       // initialize each value in grades to 0
21       for ( int i = 0; i < classSize; i++ )
22       {
23           grades[ i ] = 0; // works for int or double
24       } // end for
25
26   } // end GradeBook one-argument template constructor
```

Figure 21.18 Defining the GradeBook class's one-argument constructor.

In the body of the constructor, line 15 calls member function setClassSize, which assigns to private data member classSize the value of size. Line 18 creates an array containing classSize elements, using the new operator to allocate memory dynamically. The new operator returns a pointer to the zeroth element in this array, which is assigned to grades. Lines 21–24 initialize each element in the grades array to 0.

(cont.)   Note that the type of the elements in the `grades` array is T, the formal type parameter specified in lines 11–12. Recall that the compiler replaces the type parameter T with the type specified in the angle brackets when a client of the class calls the constructor. For example, when a client of the class creates a `GradeBook` object using the statement

```
GradeBook< double > myDoubleGradeBook;
```

the compiler generates a class-template specialization containing `double` wherever the identifier T occurs in the class-template and member-function templates.

3. ***Defining the getMinimum function.*** Add lines 71–90 of Fig. 21.19 after the `displayGrades` function, which is provided for you in the `GradeBook.cpp` file. The `getMinimum` function examines each element of the `grades` array and returns the smallest value. Line 75 defines the `lowGrade` variable, which will contain the smallest value encountered as the application examines each element of the `grades` array. Line 75 also initializes `lowGrade` to contain the value of the zeroth element of the `grades` array. Lines 78–86 contain a `for` statement that iterates once for each of the remaining elements in the `grades` array. During each iteration, the `if` statement in line 81 determines whether the current element of the array is smaller than `lowGrade`. If so, the application will update `lowGrade` to contain the value of the current element of the array, `grades[ i ]` (line 83), which is now the smallest grade encountered so far. When the `for` loop terminates, `lowGrade` will contain the smallest grade in the array. Line 88 returns this value to the caller.

Defining `lowGrade` to contain the smallest value encountered so far

Iterating over the remaining elements of `grades`

Updating `lowGrade` if a smaller value is found

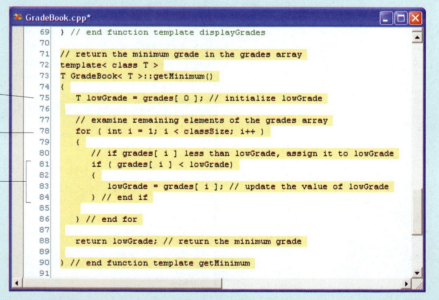

```
69   } // end function template displayGrades
70
71   // return the minimum grade in the grades array
72   template< class T >
73   T GradeBook< T >::getMinimum()
74   {
75       T lowGrade = grades[ 0 ]; // initialize lowGrade
76
77       // examine remaining elements of the grades array
78       for ( int i = 1; i < classSize; i++ )
79       {
80           // if grades[ i ] less than lowGrade, assign it to lowGrade
81           if ( grades[ i ] < lowGrade)
82           {
83               lowGrade = grades[ i ]; // update the value of lowGrade
84           } // end if
85
86       } // end for
87
88       return lowGrade; // return the minimum grade
89
90   } // end function template getMinimum
91
```

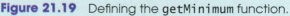

Figure 21.19   Defining the `getMinimum` function.

4. ***Defining the getMaximum function.*** Add lines 92–112 of Fig. 21.20 after the `getMinimum` function. Like the `getMinimum` function, the `getMaximum` function examines each element of the `grades` array and returns the largest value. Line 96 defines the `highGrade` variable, which will contain the largest value encountered as the application examines each element of the `grades` array. Line 96 also initializes `highGrade` to contain the value of the zeroth element of the `grades` array. Lines 99–108 contain a `for` statement that iterates once for each of the remaining elements in the `grades` array. During each iteration, the `if` statement in line 103 determines whether the current element of the array is larger than `highGrade`.

(cont.)(

If so, the application will update `highGrade` to contain the value of the current element of the array, `grades[ i ]` (line 105), which is now the largest grade encountered so far. When the `for` loop terminates, `highGrade` will contain the largest grade in the array. Line 110 returns this value to the caller.

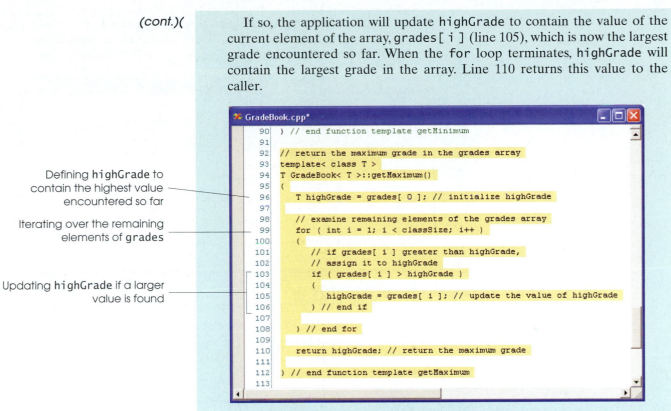

Defining `highGrade` to contain the highest value encountered so far

Iterating over the remaining elements of `grades`

Updating `highGrade` if a larger value is found

Figure 21.20   Defining the `getMaximum` function.

5. ***Defining the getAverage function.*** Add lines 114–128 of Fig. 21.21 to define the `getAverage` function. Line 118 defines the `double` variable `total` and initializes its value to `0.0`. Lines 121–124 contain a `for` statement that sums the students' grades by adding the value of each element of `grades` to `total`. Line 126 divides `total` by `classSize` to calculate the average grade. Because `total` is a `double`, the application uses floating-point division when calculating the average in line 126, regardless of whether the class-template specialization replaces T with `int` or `double`.

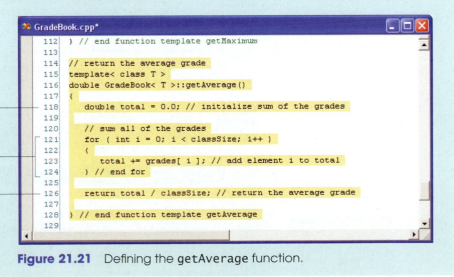

Defining and initializing `double` variable `total`

Summing the values of all the elements in the `grades` array

Dividing `total` by `classSize` to calculate the average grade

Figure 21.21   Defining the `getAverage` function.

(cont.)

6. ***Defining the `displayStatistics` function.*** Add lines 130–141 of Fig. 21.22 to GradeBook.cpp. The `displayStatistics` function outputs the average (line 135), minimum (line 138) and maximum (line 139) grades.

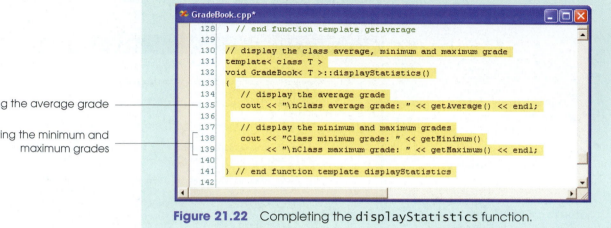

Outputting the average grade

Outputting the minimum and maximum grades

Figure 21.22 Completing the `displayStatistics` function.

In the preceding box, you completed the implementation for the GradeBook class template. In the next box, you will complete the **Grade Book** application by creating GradeBook class-template specializations to instantiate objects containing `int` and `double` grades.

Creating and Using GradeBook Class-Template Specializations

1. ***Opening the GradeBookManager source code file.*** Open the file Grade-BookManager.cpp in your text editor or IDE.

2. ***Including the GradeBook class-template source code files.*** Add lines 8–9 of Fig. 21.23 to GradeBookManager.cpp to include the source code from the GradeBook.h and GradeBook.cpp files. Note that you must include a class template's `.h` and `.cpp` files for your application to compile correctly.

```
 6    #include <iomanip> // required for parameterized stream manipulation
 7
 8    #include "GradeBook.h" // GradeBook class definition
 9    #include "GradeBook.cpp" // GradeBook implementation
10
11    using namespace std; // for accessing C++ Standard Library members
```

Including the GradeBook class `.h` and `.cpp` files

Figure 21.23 Including the GradeBook class definition and implementation.

3. ***Declaring the processGrades function template.*** Add lines 13–15 of Fig. 21.24 before `main` to declare the `processGrades` function template, which specifies a GradeBook< T > object parameter.

```
11    using namespace std; // for accessing C++ Standard Library members
12
13    // function prototype
14    template< class T >
15    void processGrades( GradeBook< T > & );
16
17    // function main begins program execution
```

Declaring the `processGrades` function

Figure 21.24 Declaring the `processGrades` function template.

(cont.)

4. ***Creating a GradeBook< int > object.*** Lines 20–59 of main, which are provided for you in the template file, prompt the user for and input the number of students in the class into variable students. The application then determines whether the user will input integer grades or floating-point grades.

Add lines 60–69 of Fig. 21.25 to main. Line 61 determines whether the user chose to input integer grades by selecting 1 from the application's menu. If so, line 64 instantiates a GradeBook< int > object myIntGradeBook containing the number of students specified by the students variable. This object is declared to be of class GradeBook< int > (pronounced "GradeBook of int"). The compiler associates type int with type parameter T in the class template (line 11 of Fig. 21.17) and produces the source code for a Grade-Book class of type int. Although you don't see this source code, it is included in the program by the compiler and compiled. Line 67 calls the process-Grades function, passing to it the myIntGradeBook object as its argument. You will define the processGrades function later in this box.

Instantiating a GradeBook< int > object

Calling the processGrades function

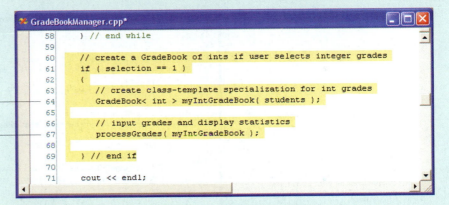

Figure 21.25 Creating an object of class GradeBook< int >.

5. ***Creating an object of type GradeBook< double >.*** Add lines 71–81 of Fig. 21.26 to GradeBookManager.cpp to define the else part of the if...else statement that begins in line 61. The body of the else statement executes if the user chose to input floating-point grades by selecting 2 from the application's menu. In this case, line 76 instantiates a GradeBook< double > object myDoubleGradeBook containing the number of students specified by the students variable. This object is declared to be of class GradeBook< double > (pronounced "GradeBook of double"). The compiler associates type double with type parameter T in the class template (line 11 of Fig. 21.17) and produces the source code for a GradeBook class of type double.

6. ***Defining the processGrades function.*** Add lines 89–121 of Fig. 21.27 after main to define the processGrades function. Line 92 declares the GradeBook< T > parameter myGrades, which was passed as an argument from main in lines 67 and 79 of Fig. 21.25 and Fig. 21.26, respectively. Line 95 defines variable grade using the formal type parameter T to contain a grade that the user inputs. Line 100 begins a for loop that iterates once for each student in the class, prompting the user for and inputting each student's grade (lines 102–104). Lines 107–114 contain a while loop that ensures that the user enters a valid grade. Once the user has entered a valid grade, line 117 uses the setGrade member function of the myGrades object to store the value of grade in the grades[count] member of the myGrades object.

(cont.)

Instantiating a
GradeBook< double > object

Calling the processGrades
function

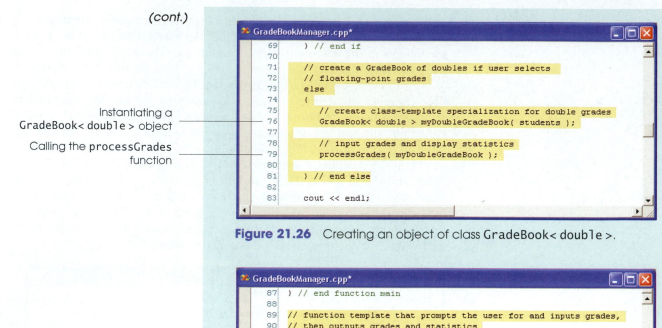

```
69        } // end if
70
71        // create a GradeBook of doubles if user selects
72        // floating-point grades
73        else
74        {
75           // create class-template specialization for double grades
76           GradeBook< double > myDoubleGradeBook( students );
77
78           // input grades and display statistics
79           processGrades( myDoubleGradeBook );
80
81        } // end else
82
83        cout << endl;
```

Figure 21.26 Creating an object of class GradeBook< double >.

Defining the variable
to store a grade

Iterating once for each
student in the class

Prompting the user for and
inputting a grade

Repeating until the user
inputs a valid grade

Storing the grade in
myGradeBook's grades array

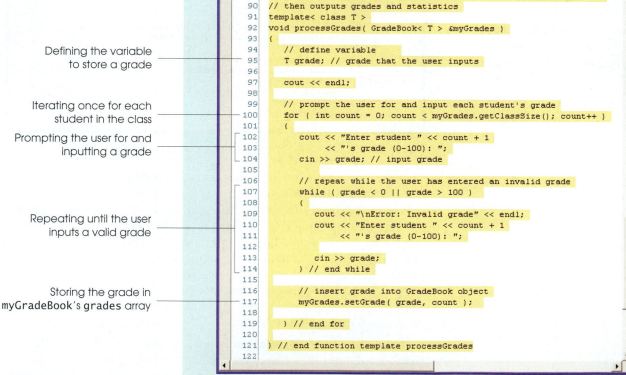

```
87   } // end function main
88
89   // function template that prompts the user for and inputs grades,
90   // then outputs grades and statistics
91   template< class T >
92   void processGrades( GradeBook< T > &myGrades )
93   {
94      // define variable
95      T grade; // grade that the user inputs
96
97      cout << endl;
98
99      // prompt the user for and input each student's grade
100     for ( int count = 0; count < myGrades.getClassSize(); count++ )
101     {
102        cout << "Enter student " << count + 1
103             << "'s grade (0-100): ";
104        cin >> grade; // input grade
105
106        // repeat while the user has entered an invalid grade
107        while ( grade < 0 || grade > 100 )
108        {
109           cout << "\nError: Invalid grade" << endl;
110           cout << "Enter student " << count + 1
111                << "'s grade (0-100): ";
112
113           cin >> grade;
114        } // end while
115
116        // insert grade into GradeBook object
117        myGrades.setGrade( grade, count );
118
119     } // end for
120
121  } // end function template processGrades
122
```

Figure 21.27 Prompting the user for and inputting grades.

(cont.)

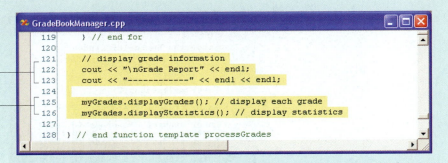

Displaying a grade report header ⎯⎯

Displaying grades and statistics ⎯⎯

Figure 21.28 Displaying grades and statistics in the `processGrades` function template.

7. ***Displaying the GradeBook< T > object's grades and statistics***. Add lines 121–126 of Fig. 21.28 to the `processGrades` function template. Lines 122–123 display a title for the grade report. Line 125 calls the `displayGrades` member function to display the grades that the user entered. Line 126 calls the `displayStatistics` member function, which displays the class's average, minimum and maximum grades.

8. ***Save, compile and run the application***. Figure 21.29 displays the application output when the user selects integer grades. Figure 21.30 displays the application output when the user selects floating-point grades.

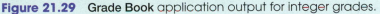

Figure 21.29 **Grade Book** application output for integer grades.

(cont.)

```
"c:\SimplyCpp\GradeBook\Debug\GradeBook.exe"

Enter the number of students: 7

Select the grade type:
1 - Integer
2 - Floating-point
Enter selection: 2

Enter student 1's grade (0-100): 85.8
Enter student 2's grade (0-100): 52.8
Enter student 3's grade (0-100): 97.9
Enter student 4's grade (0-100): 63.8
Enter student 5's grade (0-100): 75.9
Enter student 6's grade (0-100): 84.2
Enter student 7's grade (0-100): 95.7

Grade Report
------------

Student #    Grade
    1         85.8
    2         52.8
    3         97.9
    4         63.8
    5         75.9
    6         84.2
    7         95.7

Class average grade: 79.4
Class minimum grade: 52.8
Class maximum grade: 97.9

Press any key to continue_
```

Figure 21.30 Grade Book application output when entering floating-point grades.

9. ***Close the Command Prompt window.***

Figure 21.31 presents the source code for the `GradeBook` class template header, Fig. 21.32 presents the source code for the `GradeBook` class implementation and Fig. 21.33 contains the source code for the **Grade Book** application's `main` and `processGrades` functions. The lines of code that you added, viewed or modified in this tutorial are highlighted.

Create a class template with one formal type parameter

Declare the one-argument constructor

Declare *get* and *set* member functions

Declare *get* and *set* member function templates

```
// Tutorial 21: GradeBook.h
// GradeBook class template definition.

using namespace std; // for accessing C++ Standard Library members

// prevent multiple inclusions of header file
#ifndef GRADEBOOK_H
#define GRADEBOOK_H

// GradeBook class template definition
template< class T >
class GradeBook
{
public:
   GradeBook( int ); // one-argument constructor

   int getClassSize(); // get the class size
   void setClassSize( int ); // set the class size

   T getGrade( int ); // get the grade at a certain index
   void setGrade( T, int ); // set the grade at a certain index

```

Figure 21.31 `GradeBook` class header file. (Part 1 of 2.)

Declare member function and member function templates that display statistical information

```
23      void displayGrades(); // output the contents of the grades array
24      T getMinimum(); // find minimum grade
25      T getMaximum(); // find maximum grade
26      double getAverage(); // determine average grade
27      void displayStatistics(); // display statistics on the data
28
29   private:
30      int classSize; // number of grades
31      T *grades; // array of grades of type T
32
33   }; // end GradeBook class template
34
35   #endif // GRADEBOOK_H
```

Figure 21.31 GradeBook class header file. (Part 2 of 2.)

```
1    // Tutorial 21: GradeBook.cpp
2    // GradeBook member function templates definitions.
3    #include <iostream> // required to perform C++ stream I/O
4    #include <iomanip> // required for parameterized stream manipulation
5
6    #include "GradeBook.h" // include GradeBook class definition
7
8    using namespace std; // for accessing C++ Standard Library members
9
10   // one-argument constructor
11   template< class T >
12   GradeBook< T >::GradeBook( int size )
13   {
14      // set the number of students in the class
15      setClassSize( size );
16
17      // dynamically allocate memory for the grades array
18      grades = new T[ classSize ];
19
20      // initialize each value in grades to
21      for ( int i = 0; i < classSize; i++ )
22      {
23         grades[ i ] = 0; // works for int or double
24      } // end for
25
26   } // end GradeBook two-argument template constructor
27
28   // return the class size
29   template< class T >
30   int GradeBook< T >::getClassSize()
31   {
32      return classSize;
33   } // end function template getClassSize
34
35   // set the class size
36   template< class T >
37   void GradeBook< T >::setClassSize( int value )
38   {
39      classSize = value;
40   } // end function template setClassSize
41
```

Set the value of private data member classSize

Dynamically allocate memory for an array of type T containing classSize elements

Initialize all grades to 0

Figure 21.32 GradeBook class-template implementation. (Part 1 of 3.)

```
42    // return the grade at a specified index
43    template< class T >
44    T GradeBook< T >::getGrade( int index )
45    {
46        return grades[ index ];
47    } // end function template getGrade
48
49    // set specified element of grades array to specified value
50    template< class T >
51    void GradeBook< T >::setGrade( T value, int index )
52    {
53        grades[ index ] = value;
54    } // end function template setGrade
55
56    // display each element in the grades array
57    template< class T >
58    void GradeBook< T >::displayGrades()
59    {
60        cout << "Student #    Grade" << endl;
61
62        // output each student's grade
63        for ( int student = 0; student < classSize; student++ )
64        {
65            cout << setw( 5 ) << student + 1 << setw( 13 )
66                << grades[ student ] << endl;
67        } // end for
68
69    } // end function template displayGrades
70
71    // return the minimum grade in the grades array
72    template< class T >
73    T GradeBook< T >::getMinimum()
74    {
75        T lowGrade = grades[ 0 ]; // initialize lowGrade
76
77        // examine remaining elements of the grades
78        for ( int i = 1; i < classSize; i++ )
79        {
80            // if grades[ i ] less than lowGrade, assign it to lowGrade
81            if ( grades[ i ] < lowGrade)
82            {
83                lowGrade = grades[ i ]; // update the value of lowGrade
84            } // end if
85
86        } // end for
87
88        return lowGrade; // return the minimum grade
89
90    } // end function template getMinimum
91
92    // return the maximum grade in the grades array
93    template< class T >
94    T GradeBook< T >::getMaximum()
95    {
96        T highGrade = grades[ 0 ]; // initialize highGrade
97
98        // examine remaining elements of the grades array
99        for ( int i = 1; i < classSize; i++ )
100       {
```

Define `lowGrade` to contain the smallest value encountered so far

Iterate over the remaining elements of `grades`

Update `lowGrade` if a smaller value is found

Figure 21.32 GradeBook class-template implementation. (Part 2 of 3.)

```
101        // if grades[ i ] greater than highGrade,
102        // assign it to highGrade
103        if ( grades[ i ] > highGrade )
104        {
105            highGrade = grades[ i ]; // update the value of highGrade
106        } // end if
107
108     } // end for
109
110     return highGrade; // return the maximum grade
111
112 } // end function template getMaximum
113
114 // return the average grade
115 template< class T >
116 double GradeBook< T >::getAverage()
117 {
118     double total = 0.0; // initialize sum of the grades
119
120     // sum all of the grades
121     for ( int i = 0; i < classSize; i++ )
122     {
123         total += grades[ i ]; // add element i to total
124     } // end for
125
126     return total / classSize; // return the average grade
127
128 } // end function template getAverage
129
130 // display the class average, minimum and maximum grade
131 template< class T >
132 void GradeBook< T >::displayStatistics()
133 {
134     // display the average grade
135     cout << "\nClass average grade: " << getAverage() << endl;
136
137     // display the minimum and maximum grades
138     cout << "Class minimum grade: " << getMinimum()
139         << "\nClass maximum grade: " << getMaximum() << endl;
140
141 } // end function template displayStatistics
```

Define highGrade to contain the largest value encountered so far

Update highGrade if a larger value is found

Define and initialize double variable total

Sum the values of all the elements in the grades array

Divide total by classSize to calculate the average grade

Output the average grade

Output the minimum grade

Output the maximum grade

Figure 21.32 GradeBook class-template implementation. (Part 3 of 3.)

```
1  // Tutorial 21: GradeBookManager.cpp
2  // This application stores and processes student grades as ints or
3  // doubles by using templates
4  #include <iostream> // required to perform C++ stream I/O
5  #include <string> // required to access string functions
6  #include <iomanip> // required for parameterized stream manipulation
7
8  #include "GradeBook.h" // GradeBook class definition
9  #include "GradeBook.cpp" // GradeBook implementation
10
11 using namespace std; // for accessing C++ Standard Library members
12
13 // function prototype
14 template< class T >
15 void processGrades( GradeBook< T > & );
```

Include the GradeBook class.h and .cpp files

Declare the processGrades function template

Figure 21.33 Grade Book application source code. (Part 1 of 3.)

```
16
17   // function main begins program execution
18   int main()
19   {
20      // define variables
21      int students; // number of students in the course
22
23      // determines whether grades are stored as ints or doubles
24      int selection; // 1 = ints, 2 = doubles
25
26      // format the output to one digit of precision
27      cout << fixed << setprecision( 1 );
28
29      // prompt the user for and input number of students
30      cout << "\nEnter the number of students: ";
31      cin >> students; // get number of students
32
33      // repeat if the user enters an invalid number of students
34      while ( students <= 0 )
35      {
36         cout << "\nError: Must have a positive number of students";
37         cout << "\nEnter the number of students: ";
38         cin >> students;
39      } // end while
40
41      // prompt user to choose to process grades as ints or doubles
42      cout << "\nSelect the grade type:" << endl;
43      cout << "1 - Integer" << endl;
44      cout << "2 - Floating-point" << endl;
45      cout << "Enter selection: ";
46      cin >> selection;
47
48      // repeat until the user selects a valid option
49      while ( selection != 1 && selection != 2 )
50      {
51         cout << "\nError: Invalid choice" << endl;
52         cout << "\nSelect the grade type:"
53            << endl;
54         cout << "1 - Integer" << endl;
55         cout << "2 - Floating-point" << endl;
56         cout << "Enter selection: ";
57         cin >> selection;
58      } // end while
59
60      // create a GradeBook of ints if user selects integer grades
61      if ( selection == 1 )
62      {
63         // create class-template specialization for int grades
64         GradeBook< int > myIntGradeBook( students );
65
66         // input grades and display statistics
67         processGrades( myIntGradeBook );
68
69      } // end if
70
71      // create a GradeBook of doubles if user selects
72      // floating-point grades
73      else
```

Create a `GradeBook< int >` object ⎯⎯⎯ 64

Call the `processGrades` function ⎯⎯⎯ 67

Figure 21.33   Grade Book application source code. (Part 2 of 3.)

Create a GradeBook< double > object

Call the processGrades function

Iterate once for each student in the class

Prompt the user for and input a grade

Repeat until the user inputs a valid grade

Store the grade in myGrades' grades array

Display grade report title

Display grades and statistics

```cpp
74      {
75          // create class-template specialization for double grades
76          GradeBook< double > myDoubleGradeBook( students );
77
78          // input grades and display statistics
79          processGrades( myDoubleGradeBook );
80
81      } // end else
82
83      cout << endl;
84
85      return 0; // indicates successful termination
86
87  } // end function main
88
89  // function template that prompts the user for and inputs grades,
90  // then outputs grades and statistics
91  template< class T >
92  void processGrades( GradeBook< T > &myGrades )
93  {
94      // define variable
95      T grade; // grade that the user inputs
96
97      cout << endl;
98
99      // prompt the user for and input each student's grade
100     for ( int count = 0; count < myGrades.getClassSize(); count++ )
101     {
102         cout << "Enter student " << count + 1
103             << "'s grade (0-100): ";
104         cin >> grade; // input grade
105
106         // repeat while the user has entered an invalid grade
107         while ( grade < 0 || grade > 100 )
108         {
109             cout << "\nError: Invalid grade" << endl;
110             cout << "Enter student " << count + 1
111                 << "'s grade (0-100): ";
112
113             cin >> grade;
114         } // end while
115
116         // insert grade into GradeBook object
117         myGrades.setGrade( grade, count );
118
119     } // end for
120
121     // display grade information
122     cout << "\nGrade Report" << endl;
123     cout << "------------" << endl << endl;
124
125     myGrades.displayGrades(); // display each grade
126     myGrades.displayStatistics(); // display statistics
127
128 } // end function processGrades
```

Figure 21.33 Grade Book application source code. (Part 3 of 3.)

1. Consider the Shape class template, which specifies one formal type parameter, T. To tie a member function to the class template, precede the binary scope resolution operator with _____.

   a) Shape   b) Shape(T)
   c) Shape< T >   d) Shape[T]

2. Class-template specializations are generated by the _____.
   a) programmer   b) compiler
   c) preprocessor   d) operating system

Answers: 1) c. 2) b.

21.5 Wrap-Up

In this tutorial, you learned how to program generically using templates. You learned that function templates enable you to specify, with a single code segment, an entire range of related (overloaded) functions called function-template specializations. Function templates allow the function caller to call a function using several parameter types. The compiler then generates code for each function-template specialization, saving time for the programmer. You used the `template` keyword followed by a list of formal type parameters enclosed in angle brackets (`<` and `>`) to create a `maximum` function template that found the largest of three values. The `maximum` function could be called using arguments of many different built-in types because you defined the `maximum` function template's parameters using the formal type parameter.

You then learned how to create class templates, which enable you to specify, with a single code segment, an entire range of related classes. Class templates are called parameterized types because they require one or more type parameters to specify how to customize a "generic class" template to form a class-template specialization. Although you do not see this class-template specialization before compiling your application, it is included in the program by the compiler and compiled. In the **Grade Book** application, you created a `GradeBook` class template that you used to create a "GradeBook of `int`" or a "GradeBook of `double`," depending on whether the user chose to enter integer or floating-point grades. You also learned how to write member function templates and how to instantiate objects from class-template specializations.

In the next tutorial, you will learn about operator overloading, a technique that enables you to use C++'s rich set of operators with objects. You will use overloaded stream extractions and stream insertion operators to input phone numbers from the keyboard and display them on the screen, respectively, in the **Phone Book** application.

SKILLS SUMMARY

Declaring a Function Template

■ Insert the keyword `template` followed by the angle brackets and type parameter(s), each preceded by the `class` keyword. Then declare the function normally substituting the type parameter(s) for parameters, local variables and return types as needed. For example, the function prototype

```
template < class T >
T divideByTwo( T );
```

declares a function template named `divideByTwo` that accepts one parameter of type T and returns a value of the same type as the parameter.

Calling a Function Template

■ When the compiler encounters a call to a function template, C++ uses the argument type(s) to generate a separate function-template specialization to handle the call appropriately. For example, when the compiler encounters the statements

```
double sum = 21.0;
double half = divideByTwo( sum );
```

it determines the argument type in the function call—in this case, sum is a double. The corresponding parameter in the function template uses the formal type parameter, T, so the compiler generates a function-template specialization by replacing every instance of T with double.

Declaring a Class Template

■ Insert the keyword template followed by the angle brackets and type parameter(s), each preceded by the class keyword. Then declare the class normally, substituting the type parameter(s) for member function parameters and return types, and data member types, as needed. For example, the GradeBook class template may be defined as follows:

```
template< class T >
class GradeBook
{
public:
    GradeBook();
    T getGrade( int );
    void setGrade( T, int );
    ...
private:
    T *grades;
    ...
}; // end class GradeBook
```

■ When referring to the class template name, use the class name followed by the type parameter(s) in angle brackets. For example, the GradeBook class template's name is Gradebook< T >.

Defining Class Template Member Functions

■ Insert the keyword template followed by the angle brackets and type parameter(s), each preceded by the class keyword specified by the class template. Specify the return type, then tie the member function to the class template by mentioning the class template name followed by the binary scope resolution operator and the function name. Define the rest of the function normally, substituting the type parameter(s) for function parameters, local variables and return types as needed. For example, the following code

```
template < class T >
T GradeBook< T >::getMaximum()
{
    T maxValue;
    ...
    return maxValue;
}
```

is the header for the getMaximum member function of the GradeBook< T > class template, which specifies a return type T, the GradeBook< T >'s class template's type parameter.

Instantiating a Class Template Object

■ To instantiate an object of a class template, you must specify the class template's name, substituting a type for each of its type parameter(s), followed by the object's name. For example, the statement

```
Gradebook< int > myIntGradeBook;
```

instantiates a Gradebook of int named myIntGradeBook. The compiler associates type int with type parameter T in the template and produces the source code for a GradeBook class of type int.

KEY TERMS

class template—A placeholder for a class that is defined using the `template` keyword and that specifies at least one formal type parameter. A class template is defined generically to allow several different class-template specializations to be created from one class template definition.

class-template specialization—A class that the compiler generates and compiles using the corresponding class template. For example, when a client of a class template instantiates an object, the client specifies the type for each of the class template's type parameters. The compiler then associates each specified type with the corresponding type parameter in the class template to produce the source code for the class-template specialization.

formal type parameter—A placeholder for a built-in or user-defined variable type. The type parameter is specified as an identifier, preceded by the `class` keyword, inside angle brackets following the `template` keyword. For example, in the expression `template < class T >`, the formal type parameter is T.

function template—A placeholder for a function that is declared using the `template` keyword and that specifies at least one formal type parameter. A function template is a means for describing a function generically. When the compiler encounters a call to a function template, it creates a function-template specialization, replacing the formal type parameter(s) with the corresponding argument type(s).

function-template specialization—A function that the compiler generates and compiles using the corresponding function template. When the compiler encounters a call to a function template, it creates a function-template specialization, replacing the formal type parameter(s) with the corresponding argument type(s).

generic programming—A technique that uses templates to describe classes and functions generically by describing data types using formal type parameters. Generic programming enables the programmer to specify a family of solutions with a single code segment, thus speeding the program-development process.

parameterized type—A class template, so named because it requires one or more type parameters to specify a class-template specialization.

template—A C++ code unit that enables programmers to specify, with a single code segment, an entire range of related functions or classes.

MULTIPLE-CHOICE QUESTIONS

21.1 Templates are a means to _____.
a) generate code
b) program generically
c) reuse software
d) All of the above.

21.2 Formal type parameters can specify the type _____.
a) returned by a function
b) of a function's local variables
c) of a function's parameters
d) All of the above.

21.3 A formal type parameter is _____.
a) specified inside square brackets
b) named using any valid identifier
c) specified using the `template` keyword
d) Both b and c.

21.4 A class template can specify _____ formal type parameter(s).
a) zero
b) only one
c) no more than two
d) any number of

21.5 The statement _____ instantiates a `GradeBook` of `double` object named `myGradeBook`.
a) `GradeBook< double > myGradeBook;`
b) `GradeBook myGradeBook< double >;`
c) `myGradeBook GradeBook< double >;`
d) `myGradeBook< double > GradeBook;`

21.6 Generic programming improves a program's _____.
a) performance
b) usability
c) code reuse
d) memory efficiency

21.7 Which of the following is a correct class-template member function header for the GradeBook< T > class template?

a) `template< class T >`
   `T GradeBook::getGrade()`

b) `template< T >`
   `T GradeBook::getGrade()`

c) `template< class T >`
   `T GradeBook< T >::getGrade()`

d) `template< T >`
   `T GradeBook< class T >getGrade()`

21.8 It is appropriate to convert a group of overloaded functions to a single function template if the overloaded functions _____.

a) perform identical operations

b) perform similar operations

c) specify the same parameter types

d) specify different numbers of parameters

21.9 The caller of a function template must _____.

a) precede the function call with the template keyword

b) explicitly specify the formal type parameter(s) in angle brackets

c) instantiate a function-template specialization

d) None of the above.

21.10 A formal type parameter must be directly preceded by the keyword _____.

a) `template`

b) `type`

c) `class`

d) `T`

EXERCISES

21.11 (*College Applications Application*) A local high school has asked you to help with its statistical analysis of graduating seniors applying to college. The high school has asked you to create a program that allows the user to enter the standardized test scores and GPAs of its students. The application should use a function template to calculate the averages of the test scores and GPAs (Fig. 21.34).

```
Enter the number of students in the class: 4

Enter student #1's standardized test score (0 - 1600): 1280
Enter student #1's GPA (0.0 - 4.0): 3.7

Enter student #2's standardized test score (0 - 1600): 1720

Error: Please enter a value between 0 and 1600

Enter student #2's standardized test score (0 - 1600): 1600
Enter student #2's GPA (0.0 - 4.0): 4.0

Enter student #3's standardized test score (0 - 1600): 1060
Enter student #3's GPA (0.0 - 4.0): 2.8

Enter student #4's standardized test score (0 - 1600): 1120
Enter student #4's GPA (0.0 - 4.0): 4.3

Error: Please enter a value between 0.0 and 4.0

Enter student #4's GPA (0.0 - 4.0): 3.4

Standardized test class average: 1265
Class GPA average: 3.5

Press any key to continue_
```

Figure 21.34 College Applications application output.

a) *Copying the template to your working directory.* Copy the `C:\Examples\Tutorial21\Exercises\CollegeApplications` directory to your `C:\SimplyCpp` directory.

b) *Opening the template source code file.* Open the `CollegeApplications.cpp` file in your text editor or IDE.

c) *Declaring the calculateAverage function template prototype.* In lines 10–12, declare the `calculateAverage` function-template prototype. The `calculateAverage` function template has one formal type parameter, T, and two function parameters, an array of type T and an `int` containing the size of the array. `calculateAverage` returns a value of type T. Use line 10 for a comment.

d) *Calling the `calculateAverage` function.* After the full-line comment in line 77, insert code to format the output similar to Fig. 21.34. Cascade the stream insertion operator so that the call to `calculateAverage` is in the same `cout` statement as the label for the function call. The first function call should declare the `int` array `tests` and `int` variable `classSize` as arguments, respectively. This will cause the compiler to create a copy of function-template `calculateAverage`, substituting type `int` for the formal type parameter T. Insert a second statement to display the label for the class GPA (Fig. 21.34) and call `calculateAverage`, this time with `GPAs` and `classSize` declared as its arguments, respectively.

e) *Defining function template `calculateAverage`.* After `main`, begin the definition for function-template `calculateAverage` with `values` and `size` the names of the parameters, respectively. `calculateAverage` should initially define T variable `total`, (which will store the sum of the `values` array) and assign it the value of 0. After defining `total`, insert a `for` loop to iterate once for every value of the array `values`, and add them to `total`. Finally, divide `total` by `size` to obtain the average of the `values` array and return the value to the caller.

f) *Save, compile and run the application.* Test your application to ensure that it runs correctly. Enter several different test and GPA values and check that the averages are displayed properly.

g) *Close the Command Prompt window.*

21.12 (*Encryption Template Application*) In this exercise, you will create an **Encryption Template** application that is similar to the **Password Generator** application in Exercise 5.17. This application displays a menu prompting the user to choose whether to encrypt an integer or a string or to exit the application. The application then uses a function template to input the plaintext value and displays the corresponding encrypted value. Figure 21.35 shows the application output when encrypting an `int` and a `string`.

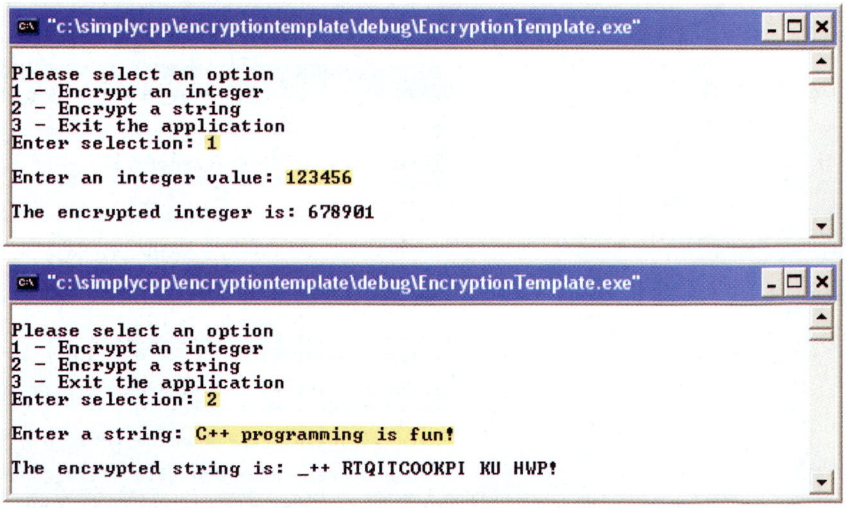

Figure 21.35 Encrypting an `int` and a `string` in the **Encryption Template** application.

a) *Copying the template to your working directory.* Copy the `C:\Examples\Tutorial21\Exercises\EncryptionTemplate` directory to your `C:\SimplyCpp` directory.

b) *Opening the template source code file.* Open the `EncryptionTemplate.cpp` file in your text editor or IDE.

c) *Declaring the encrypt function template.* Starting in line 10, insert the `encrypt` function-template prototype. The function template should specify one formal type parameter, T. The `encrypt` function should declare three parameters of type T. The first parameter specifies the value to be encrypted. The second and third parameters limit the range of values that the `encrypt` function returns by specifying the lower and upper limits for the return value. Use the type parameter T to specify the return value for the encrypt function. In lines 39–41, insert a full-line comment, followed by statements that prompt the user for and input int variable value starting at line 39.

d) *Calling the encrypt function using an int value.* The application encrypts an integer by encrypting each of its decimal digits individually. The application provides the code that extracts each digit into variable singleDigit. In line 50, call the encrypt function template, specifying singleDigit as the first argument. Because the range of values for a single decimal digit is 0–9, specify 0 as the second argument and 9 as the third argument.

e) *Calling the encrypt function using a char value.* The application encrypts a string one character at a time. The for loop in lines 80–83 iterates once for each character in the input string plainText. Call the encrypt function specifying plainText.at(i) as the first argument, where i is the for loop's control variable. To indicate the range for the encrypt function, specify the char literal 'A' as the second argument and 'z' as the third argument.

f) *Defining the encrypt function template.* After main, define the encrypt function template. Declare parameters plainText, min and max to represent the value to encrypt, the minimum encrypted value and the maximum encrypted value. Insert an if statement that determines whether plainText is outside the range specified by min and max. If so, the function should return the unencrypted character. Otherwise, the encrypt function should define variable offset of type T and initialize its value to half of the result of subtracting min from max. To encrypt plainText, add offset to plainText and assign the result to int variable returnValue. Insert an if...else statement that determines whether returnValue is greater than max. If so, the application should "wrap around" the range of valid output values by returning the result of the expression min + (returnValue % (max + 1)). Otherwise, the application should simply return returnValue.

g) *Save, compile and run the completed application.* Test your application to ensure that it runs correctly. Enter several integer and string values and check that they are encrypted correctly.

h) *Close the Command Prompt window.*

What does this code do? ▶   **21.13** What is the result of the following code?

```cpp
1   // Exercise 21.13: WDTCD.cpp
2   // What does this code do?
3   #include <iostream> // required for C++ stream I/O
4
5   using namespace std; // for accessing C++ Standard Library members
6
7   template< class T >
8   T mystery( T, T ); // function template prototype
9
10  // function main begins program execution
11  int main()
12  {
13     // define variables
14     int int1;
15     int int2;
16     double double1;
17     double double2;
18
19     // prompt the user for and input two integers
20     cout << "\nEnter integer 1: ";
21     cin >> int1;
22
23     cout << "Enter integer 2: ";
24     cin >> int2;
25
```

```
26        cout << "\nMystery number is: " << mystery( int1, int2 ) << endl;
27
28        // prompt the user for and input two floating-point values
29        cout << "\nEnter floating-point value 1: ";
30        cin >> double1;
31
32        cout << "Enter floating-point value 2: ";
33        cin >> double2;
34
35        cout << "\nMystery number is: " << mystery( double1, double2 )
36           << endl << endl;
37
38        return 0; // indicate that program ended successfully
39
40    } // end function main
41
42    template< class T >
43    T mystery( T value1, T value2 )
44    {
45       if ( value1 > value2 )
46       {
47          return value2;
48       } // end if
49
50       return value1;
51
52    } // end function template mystery
```

What's wrong with this code? ▶

21.14 This code should prompt the user for and input values into arrays of type double and int. The displayArray function template should display the contents of each array in reverse order. Find the error(s) in the following code.

```
1    // Exercise 21.14: WWWTC.cpp
2    // This application uses a function template to display
3    // several different types of arrays in reverse order.
4    #include <iostream> // required for C++ stream I/O
5
6    using namespace std; // for accessing C++ Standard Library members
7
8    template< class T >
9    void displayArray( T [] ); // function template prototype
10
11   // function main begins program execution
12   int main()
13   {
14      // define variables
15      double doubleArray[ 5 ];
16      int intArray[ 5 ];
17
18      cout << endl;
19
20      // prompt user for and input five floating-point value
21      for ( int i = 0; i < 5; i++ )
22      {
23         cout << "Enter floating point value: ";
24         cin >> doubleArray[ i ];
25      } // end for
26
```

```
27        displayArray( doubleArray ); // display the contents of the array
28
29        // prompt user for and input five integer value
30        for ( int i = 0; i < 5; i++ )
31        {
32           cout << "Enter integer: ";
33           cin >> intArray[ i ];
34        } // end for
35
36        displayArray( intArray ); // display the contents of the array
37
38        return 0; // indicate that program ended successfully
39
40     } // end function main
41
42     // displays the contents of the array
43     template< T >
44     void displayArray( T myArray )
45     {
46        cout << endl;
47
48        // display myArray in reverse order
49        for ( int i = 4; i <= 0; i-- )
50        {
51           cout << "Array[ " << i << " ] = " << myArray[ i ] << endl;
52        } // end for
53
54        cout << endl;
55     } // end function template displayArray
```

Programming Challenge ▶   **21.15** (*Universal Sorter Application*) In this exercise, you will create a **Universal Sorter** application that sorts arrays of multiple data types. The application prompts the user to choose whether to enter char, int, or double values. Then the user is prompted to input the number of items to sort. After the user enters each item, the application must use a function-template specialization to sort the array and display the results. Fig. 21.36, Fig. 21.37 and Fig. 21.38 show the application output for sorting a set of chars, ints and doubles.

Figure 21.36 **Universal Sorter** application output for sorting chars.

```
"c:\simplycpp\universalsorter\debug\UniversalSorter.exe"

Select a data type:
1-char
2-int
3-double
Enter selection: 2

Enter number of items to sort: 6

Enter int #1: 23
Enter int #2: -75
Enter int #3: 268
Enter int #4: 755
Enter int #5: -6
Enter int #6: 4

Sorted array of ints:
 -75 -6 4 23 268 755

Press any key to continue_
```

Figure 21.37 Universal Sorter application output for sorting `int`s.

```
"c:\simplycpp\universalsorter\debug\UniversalSorter.exe"

Select a data type:
1-char
2-int
3-double
Enter selection: 3

Enter number of items to sort: 6

Enter double #1: 12.6
Enter double #2: 43.75
Enter double #3: 43.23
Enter double #4: 67.5
Enter double #5: 12.4
Enter double #6: 23.7

Sorted array of doubles:
 12.4 12.6 23.7 43.23 43.75 67.5

Press any key to continue_
```

Figure 21.38 Universal Sorter application output for sorting `double`s.

a) ***Copying the template to your working directory.*** Copy the `C:\Examples\Tutorial21\Exercises\UniversalSorter` directory to your `C:\SimplyCpp` directory.

b) ***Opening the template source code file.*** Open the `UniversalSorter.cpp` file in your text editor or IDE.

c) ***Declaring the `sortAndPrintArray` function template prototype.*** In lines 9–11, declare the `sortAndPrintArray` function template prototype. The `sortAndPrintArray` function template specifies one formal type parameter, `T`, and two function parameters, an array of type `T` and an `int` containing the size of that array. The `sortAndPrintArray` does not return any values.

d) ***Calling the `sortAndPrintArray` function for `char`s.*** Lines 64–81 execute if the user enters `char` values. In this case, the application stores each value in the `charArray` array, which contains the number of values specified by `size`. After line 79, call the `sortAndPrintArray` function, passing `charArray` and `size` as arguments.

e) ***Calling the `sortAndPrintArray` function for `int`s.*** Lines 83–100 execute if the user enters `int` values. In this case, the application stores each value in the `intArray` array, which contains the number of values specified by `size`. After line 98, call the `sortAndPrintArray` function, passing `intArray` and `size` as arguments.

f) ***Calling the `sortAndPrintArray` function for `double`s.*** Lines 102–119 execute if the user enters `double` values. In this case, the application stores each value in the `doubleArray` array, which contains the number of values specified by `size`. After line 117, call the `sortAndPrintArray` function, passing `doubleArray` and `size` as arguments.

g) ***Defining the `sortAndPrintArray` function.*** After function `main`, add a function header for the `sortAndPrintArray` function so that it matches the prototype you declared in *Step c*. The first parameter should be named `arrayToSort`, and the second parameter should be named `size`. The `sortAndPrintArray` function should call the `sort` function, accessible by including the `<algorithm>` header file. The `sort` function sorts an array of values in ascending order. The first argument is a pointer to the first element of the array, and the second argument is a pointer to the position just after the last element of the array. Recall that the name of an array is a pointer to the first element of the array. To specify a pointer to the position just after the last element of the array, add the number of elements (`size`) to the name of the array. C++ uses this expression to generate a pointer to the last element of the array.

h) *Completing the `sortAndPrintArray` function.* After the array is sorted, the application should display its values. Insert a `for` statement that iterates once for each element in the `arrayToSort` array. The body of the `for` statement should display the value of the current element and a space character. After the loop terminates, the application should display a newline for readability.

i) *Save, compile and run the application.* Test your application using multiple data types to ensure that it runs correctly by outputting a sorted array.

j) *Close the Command Prompt window.*

Objectives

In this tutorial, you will learn to:
- Use overloaded operators.
- Declare operator functions.
- Overload the stream insertion operator to support a user-defined type.
- Overload the stream extraction operator to support a user-defined type

Outline

Phone Book Application

Introducing Operator Overloading

In Tutorial 15, you learned how to build your own classes and to manipulate objects of those classes by sending messages (in the form of member-function calls) to them. Throughout this book, you have used C++ operators to perform many common manipulations on objects, such as input and output using stream objects, and appending text to `string` objects. In this tutorial, you will be introduced to **operator overloading**, a technique that enables you to use C++'s rich set of built-in operators to specify common object manipulations (instead of explicitly calling member functions). For example, the += operator, which the C++ language uses to perform an addition assignment on two numeric values, can perform an entirely different operation when overloaded for use with `strings`, namely concatenation.

Classes in the C++ Standard Library provide implementations for several overloaded operators. For example, the `string` class provides overloaded versions of the == and += operators. The C++ language itself also overloads the + and – operators, which perform differently, depending on their context in integer arithmetic, floating-point arithmetic and pointer arithmetic.

C++ enables the programmer to overload most operators to be sensitive to the context in which they are used—the compiler generates the appropriate code based on the context. Some operators are overloaded frequently, especially the assignment operator and various arithmetic operators such as + and –. The jobs performed by overloaded operators can also be performed by explicit function calls, but operator notation is often clearer and more familiar to programmers. In this tutorial, you will overload the stream insertion and stream extraction operators to read and display phone numbers, as you build your **Phone Book** application.

22.1 Test-Driving the Phone Book Application

In this tutorial, you will create a **Phone Book** application. The application must meet the following requirements:

Application Requirements

A salesperson would like to record client names and phone numbers electronically. Develop an application that enables the user to input a name and a phone number for each client. The phone number should be entered in the form (123) 456-7890 (with the digits, the parentheses, the space and the dash in the indicated places). The user should have the option to display all the names and phone numbers that have been stored in the application.

You begin by test-driving the completed application. Then, you learn the additional C++ capabilities you will need to create your own version of this application.

Test-Driving the Phone Book Application

1. *Locating the completed application.* Open a **Command Prompt** window by selecting **Start > All Programs > Accessories > Command Prompt**. Change to your completed **Phone Book** application directory by typing cd C:\Examples\Tutorial22\CompletedApplication\PhoneBook.

2. *Running the Phone Book application.* Type PhoneBook in the **Command Prompt** window and press *Enter* to run the application (Fig. 22.1). The application prompts you to select from a menu of options.

Figure 22.1   Running the completed **Phone Book** application.

3. *Entering a phone book entry.* Enter 1 at the **Enter selection:** prompt to enter a new phone book entry. The application then prompts you for a name and phone number (Fig. 22.2). Enter James Purple as the name and (001) 555-4567 as the telephone number.

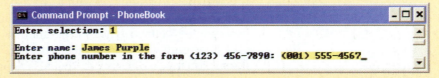

Figure 22.2   Entering a name and phone number in the **Phone Book** application.

4. *Entering a second entry.* After you enter a phone book entry, the application's menu appears again. Enter 1 at the **Enter selection:** prompt to enter another new phone book entry. Enter Sue Orange as the name and (890) 555-1234 as the telephone number (Fig. 22.3).

5. *Viewing the phone book entries.* To view the phone book entries, enter 2 at the **Enter selection:** prompt. Notice that the application correctly displays the names and numbers that you entered in *Steps 3* and *4* (Fig. 22.4).

(cont.)

```
Command Prompt - PhoneBook
Enter selection: 1

Enter name: Sue Orange
Enter phone number in the form (123) 456-7890: (890) 555-1234_
```

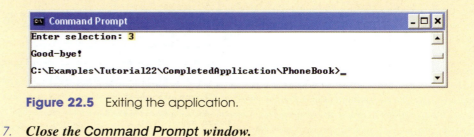

Figure 22.3 Entering a second name and phone number.

```
Command Prompt - PhoneBook
Enter selection: 2


Listing of phone numbers
------------------------
Name: James Purple
Number: (001) 555-4567

Name: Sue Orange
Number: (890) 555-1234
```

Figure 22.4 Displaying phone book entries.

6. ***Closing the running application.*** Enter 3 at the **Enter selection:** prompt to exit the application (Fig. 22.5).

```
Command Prompt
Enter selection: 3

Good-bye!

C:\Examples\Tutorial22\CompletedApplication\PhoneBook>_
```

Figure 22.5 Exiting the application.

7. ***Close the Command Prompt window.***

22.2 Fundamentals of Operator Overloading

Throughout this book, you have used built-in types (such as `int`s and `double`s) and defined new types (such as the `Time` class, the `List` class and the `Employee` class). The built-in types can be used with C++'s rich collection of operators. These operators provide programmers with a concise notation for expressing manipulations of data of built-in types. However, C++ does not define how these operators work with programmer-defined types—programmers must do that themselves. For example, C++ does not know what it means to "add" two `Color` objects or how to determine if two `Employee` objects are "equal." A programmer might want to use operator overloading to "teach" C++ how to use the + operator to blend two `color`s to form a new `color`. A programmer might want to overload the == operator to determine if two `Employee`s have the same job classification—or are similarly qualified for a new position with the company.

C++ allows you to overload operators to work with programmer-defined types as well. Although C++ does not allow new operators to be created, it does allow most existing operators to be overloaded so that, when these operators are used with objects, the operators have meanings appropriate to those objects. This is a powerful feature.

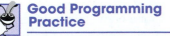

Good Programming Practice

Use operator overloading when it makes a program clearer than if it accomplished the same operations with explicit function calls.

Although operator overloading sounds like an exotic capability, you have implicitly used overloaded operators in earlier tutorials. For example, the addition operator (+) operates quite differently on variables of type `int` and `double`, but nevertheless does work fine with these types and a number of other built-in types because (+) has been overloaded to handle these different possibilities in the C++ language itself.

Operators are overloaded by writing a function definition (with a header and body) as you normally would, except that the function name now becomes the keyword **operator** followed by the symbol for the operator being overloaded. For example, the function `operator+` is used to overload the addition operator (+) and `operator==` is used to overload the equality operator.

To use an operator on class objects, that operator *must* be overloaded—with two exceptions. The assignment operator (=) may be used with two objects of the same class without explicit overloading. The default behavior of the assignment operator is a **memberwise assignment** of the data members of the class—C++ copies the value of each data member of the object in the right operand to the corresponding data members of the object in the left operand. The address operator (&) may also be used with objects of any class without overloading; it simply returns the address of the object in memory.

The point of operator overloading is to provide the ability for programmers to write the same kinds of concise and familiar expressions for programmer-defined types that C++ provides with its rich collection of operators for built-in types. Operator overloading is not automatic, however; you must define operator-overloading functions to perform the desired operations.

Good Programming Practice

Overloaded operators should mimic the functionality of their built-in counterparts—for example, the + operator should be overloaded to perform addition, not subtraction. Avoid excessive or inconsistent use of operator overloading, as this can make a program cryptic and difficult to read.

SELF-REVIEW

1. The function name used for overloading the + operator is _____.
   a) `+operator`   b) `operator+`
   c) `+`   d) `operator(+)`

2. The _____ operator must be overloaded in order to be used with objects of a programmer–defined class.
   a) `-`   b) `==`
   c) `=`   d) Both a and b.

Answers: 1) b. 2) d.

22.3 Restrictions on Operator Overloading

Most of C++'s operators can be overloaded (Fig. 22.6). Figure 22.7 shows the C++ operators that cannot be overloaded. [*Note:* Several operators listed in Fig. 22.6 and Fig. 22.7 are not discussed because they are beyond the scope of this book.] Other restrictions on operator overloading follow the figures.

Operators that can be overloaded							
+	–	*	/	%	^	&	|
~	!	=	<	>	+=	-=	*=
/=	%=	^=	&=	|=	<<	>>	>>=
<<=	==	!=	<=	>=	&&	||	++
--	->*	,	->	[]	()	new	delete
new[]	delete[]						

Figure 22.6 Operators that can be overloaded.

Operators that cannot be overloaded			
.	.*	::	?:

Figure 22.7 Operators that cannot be overloaded.

Common Programming Error

Attempting to overload a non-over-loadable operator is a compilation error.

Common Programming Error

Attempting to create new operators using operator overloading is a compilation error.

Common Programming Error

Attempting to modify how an operator works with objects of built-in types is a compilation error.

Common Programming Error

Assuming that overloading an operator such as + automatically overloads related operators such as +=, or that overloading == automatically overloads a related operator like != can lead to errors. Operators can be overloaded only explicitly; there is no implicit overloading.

- The precedence of an operator cannot be changed by overloading. This can lead to awkward situations if the fixed precedence for an operator that you overload is inappropriate for the operation you want to perform. However, you can always use parentheses to force the order of evaluation of over-loaded operators in an expression.

- The associativity of an operator (i.e., whether the operator is applied right-to-left or left-to-right) cannot be changed by overloading.

- It is not possible to change the number of operands an operator takes: Over-loaded unary operators remain unary operators; overloaded binary opera-tors remain binary operators.

- It is not possible to create new operators; only existing operators can be overloaded. Unfortunately, this prevents you from introducing popular nota-tions like the ** operator used in some other programming languages for exponentiation.

- The meaning of how an operator works on objects of built-in types cannot be changed by operator overloading. The programmer cannot, for example, change the meaning of how + adds two integers.

- Operator overloading works only with objects of programmer-defined types or with a mixture of an object of a programmer-defined type and an object of a built-in type.

- Overloading an assignment operator and an addition operator to allow statements like

      object2 = object2 + object1;

does not imply that the += operator is also overloaded to allow statements such as

      object2 += object1;

Such behavior can be achieved only by explicitly overloading operator += for that class.

SELF-REVIEW

1. An operator can be overloaded when the operands consist of _____.
   a) only built-in data types
   b) only programmer-defined types
   c) a mixture of built-in and programmer-defined types
   d) Both b and c.

2. The _____ operator cannot be overloaded.
   a) &
   b) ::
   c) *
   d) []

Answers: 1) d. 2) b.

22.4 Overloaded Operator Functions

As we discussed earlier in this tutorial, operators are overloaded by defining a func-tion with a special name—the keyword `operator` followed by the symbol for the operator that you are overloading. In this section, you will learn how to define these functions for unary and binary operators.

Overloading Unary Operators

Let's begin by overloading the unary preincrement operator (++) so that it works on objects instantiated from the `Time` class that you defined in Tutorial 15. When the statement

      ++myTime;

executes, the time contained in `myTime`, which is an object of type `Time`, should be incremented by one second. To overload the unary preincrement operator, you must define a function named `operator++`.

An operator function can be defined as a member of a class or as a non-member. If an overloaded unary operator function is defined as a member of a class, the function must specify zero parameters. For example, the overloaded `operator++` function for the `Time` class should be declared in the `Time` class definition as follows:

```
class Time
{
public:
   void operator++();
   ...
};
```

Because the operator function is declared as a member function of the `Time` class, it can access the `Time` class's `private` data members directly to perform the increment operation. It can also use `public` functions to modify the `Time` object's value. The preceding `operator++` function can be defined as follows:

```
void Time::operator++()
{
   tick(); // increment current time by one second
} // end function operator++
```

In this case, when the compiler encounters the expression `++myTime`, it generates the function call `myTime.operator++()`. Because `operator++` is a member of the `Time` class, the `tick` function is called on the `myTime` object, incrementing its time value by one second.

When an overloaded unary operator function is not defined as a member of a class, it must specify one parameter, which the operator function uses to access the operand. For example, the overloaded `operator++` function that is not defined as a member of a class can be declared using the following prototype:

```
void operator++( Time & );
```

Because the operator function is not declared as a member function of the `Time` class, it can access only `public` data members and member functions to modify the `Time` object's value. The preceding `operator++` function can be defined as follows:

```
void operator++( Time &timeReference)
{
   timeReference.tick(); // increment current time by one second
} // end function operator++
```

In this case, when the compiler encounters the expression `++myTime`, it generates the function call `operator++( myTime )`. The body of the function uses the reference parameter `timeReference` to invoke the `tick` member function. Because `timeReference` is a synonym for `myTime`, the `tick` function increments the time contained in `myTime` by one second.

Overloading Binary Operators

Now let's overload a binary operator for the `Time` class. Consider overloading the `+=` operator to work with `Time` objects and `int` values so that the expression

```
myTime += 60;
```

causes the application to add 60 seconds to the time contained in the `myTime` object. If an overloaded binary operator function is defined as a member of a class, the function must specify one parameter that represents the operator's right operand.

For example, the overloaded `operator+=` function that works with `Time` objects and `int` values should be declared in the `Time` class definition as follows:

```
class Time
{
public:
   void operator+=( int );
   ...
};
```

In this case, when the compiler encounters the expression `myTime += 60`, it generates the function call `myTime.operator+=( 60 )`. Note that the left operand (`myTime`) is specified to the left of the member-access operator and that the `operator+=` function specifies the right operand (the `int` value 60) as its argument. The preceding `operator+=` function can be defined as follows

```
void Time::operator+=( int numberOfSeconds )
{
   // increment the current time by numberOfSeconds
   for ( int i = 0; i < numberOfSeconds; i++ )
   {
      tick(); // increment current time by one second
   } // end for

} // end function operator++
```

The body of the function uses a `for` statement to call the `tick` function `numberOf-Seconds` times. Because `operator+=` is a member of the `Time` class, the `tick` function accesses the `myTime` object, incrementing its time value by one second.

When an overloaded binary operator function is not defined as a member of a class, it must specify two parameters, which the operator function uses to access each of the corresponding operands. For example, the overloaded `operator+=` function, which is not defined as a member of a class, can be declared using the following prototype:

```
void operator+=( Time &, int );
```

Because the operator function is not declared as a member function of the `Time` class, it can access only `public` data members and member functions to modify the `Time` object's value. The preceding `operator+=` function can be defined as follows:

```
void operator+=( Time &timeReference, int numberOfSeconds )
{
   // increment the current time by numberOfSeconds
   for ( int i = 0; i < numberOfSeconds; i++ )
   {
      timeReference.tick(); // increment current time by one second
   } // end for

} // end function operator++
```

In this case, when the compiler encounters the expression `myTime += 60`, it generates the function call `operator+=( myTime, 60 )`. The body of the function uses a `for` statement to call the `tick` member function of the `timeReference` reference parameter `numberOfSeconds` times. Because `timeReference` is a synonym for `myTime`, the `tick` function increments the time contained in `myTime` by one second.

SELF-REVIEW

1. The operator function for an overloaded binary operator specifies _____ arguments.

a) zero

b) one

c) two

d) Either b or c.

2. Upon encountering the expression ++myObject, the C++ compiler may generate the function call _____.

    a) myObject.operator++()   b) operator++()

    c) myObject.operator++(myObject)   d) Either a or b.

Answers: 1) d. 2) a.

22.5 Creating the Phone Book Application

Now that you have been introduced to operator overloading, you can begin to develop the **Phone Book** application. The pseudocode in Fig. 22.8 describes the basic operation of the **Phone Book** application.

While the user has not chosen to exit the application:
  Display a menu that presents the option to add a new phone
    book entry, display existing phone book entries or exit the application

  If the user chooses to add a new phone book entry
    Prompt the user for and store the person's name
    Prompt the user for and store the person's phone number

  If the user chooses to view the existing phone book entries

    For each phone book entry
      Display the entry name and phone number

Figure 22.8 Pseudocode for the **Phone Book** application.

To complete the **Phone Book** application, you will need to create a PhoneNumber class that you will use to store and display each entry's phone number. You will overload the stream insertion and stream extraction operators so that you can input and output PhoneNumber values using a concise notation. In the following box, you will use the stream extraction and stream insertion operators with PhoneNumber objects. Later in this tutorial, you will provide the functionality for these overloaded operators.

Using Overloaded Operators

1. ***Copying the template to your working directory.*** Copy the C:\Examples\Tutorial22\TemplateApplication\PhoneBook directory to your C:\SimplyCpp directory. Most of the functionality for this application has been provided for you in the template files. In this tutorial, you will add the functionality to create and use overloaded operators.

2. ***Opening the Phone Book application's template source code file.*** Open the template file PhoneBook.cpp in your text editor or IDE.

3. ***Declaring the overloaded stream insertion operator function.*** Insert lines 9–10 of Fig. 22.9 into the PhoneBook.cpp file. Line 10 declares an overloaded stream insertion operator function, operator<< that can be used with a statement such as

```
cout << myPhoneNumber;
```

where myPhoneNumber is an object of type PhoneNumber. When the compiler encounters the preceding expression and the overloaded operator function prototype in line 10, the compiler converts cout << myPhoneNumber to the function call operator<<(cout, myPhoneNumber). Because cout is an object of type **ostream**, whose class definition is accessible when you include the <iostream> header file, the first parameter in line 10 specifies a reference to an ostream object. The second parameter specifies a reference to a PhoneNumber object because myPhoneNumber is an object of type PhoneNumber.

Software Design Tip

New input/output capabilities for programmer-defined types can be added to C++ without modifying C++'s Standard input/output Library classes. This is another example of the extensibility of the C++ programming language.

(cont.)

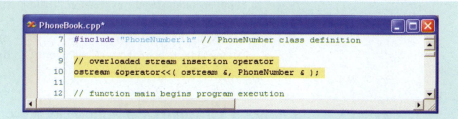

Figure 22.9   Declaring an overloaded stream insertion operator function.

Notice that the return type for the `operator<<` function is a reference to an `ostream` object. Most overloaded stream insertion operator functions return a reference to the output stream object specified as the left operand. This enables you to **chain** multiple stream insertion operators together. For example, when the statement

```
cout << "Hello " << "World";
```

executes, the expression `cout << "Hello "` is evaluated first. After the call to `operator<<( cout, "Hello " )` is completed, the expression `cout << "Hello "` is replaced by the return value, a reference to `cout`. The remaining portion of the expression is then interpreted simply as `cout << "World"`, which is another valid stream insertion expression.

4. ***Declaring the overloaded stream extraction operator function***. Insert lines 12–13 of Fig. 22.10 into the `PhoneBook.cpp` file. Line 13 declares an overloaded stream extraction operator function, `operator>>` that can be used with a statement such as

```
cin >> myPhoneNumber;
```

where `myPhoneNumber` is an object of class `PhoneNumber`. When the compiler encounters the preceding expression and the overloaded operator function prototype in 13 the compiler converts `cin >> myPhoneNumber` to the function call `operator>>( cin, myPhoneNumber )`. Because `cin` is an object of type **istream**, whose class definition is accessible when you include the `<iostream>` header file, the first parameter in line 13 specifies a reference to an `istream` object. The second parameter specifies a reference to a PhoneNumber object. Notice that the return type for the `operator>>` function is a reference to an `istream` object. This enables you to "chain" multiple stream extraction operators together.

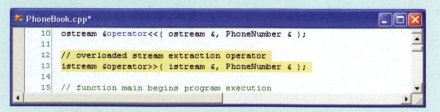

Figure 22.10   Declaring an overloaded stream extraction operator function.

Note that the `operator>>` and `operator<<` functions are declared as non-member functions. These operators must be non-members because the object of class `PhoneNumber` appears in each case as the right operand of the operator. The class operand must appear on the left of the operator to enable us to overload that operator as a member function of that class.

(cont.)

5. ***Declaring arrays to contain names and phone numbers****. Insert lines 23–24 of Fig. 22.11 into the main function. Line 23 declares an array of PhoneNumber objects named numbers. The size of the array is determined by the value of the constant int ARRAY_SIZE, which is set to 10 in line 18. Line 24 declares an array of string objects called names. The element at index *i* of the numbers array stores the telephone number for the *i*th entry in the telephone book; the element at index *i* of the names array stores the person's name for that entry.

Defining arrays of PhoneNumber objects and name strings

```
 22       int selection = 0; // stores the user's menu selection
 23       PhoneNumber numbers[ ARRAY_SIZE ]; // array of PhoneNumber objects
 24       string names[ ARRAY_SIZE ]; // array of phone book entry names
 25
 26       // repeat until the user chooses to exit
```

Figure 22.11 Declaring arrays to store phone book entries.

6. ***Inputting a phone book entry****. If the user chooses to enter a new entry by selecting 1 at the application menu's **Enter selection:** prompt, the statements after the case 1: label and through the next break statement execute. Insert lines 46–58 of Fig. 22.12 into the main function. The body of the if statement that begins in line 44 executes only if there are empty slots in the phone book. Line 46 calls the ignore function to remove the newline character that remained in the input stream after the application reads the user's menu selection. This prevents the getline function in line 50 from reading a blank line instead of reading the name for the phone book entry and inputting the name that the user enters into the next available element in the names array (names[count]). Lines 52–56 prompt the user for and input the phone number for this entry. Notice that the right operand of the stream extraction operator, numbers[count], is a PhoneNumber object. In the next box, you will define the overloaded stream extraction operator function that inputs PhoneNumber data. Line 58 increments the value of count, which contains the index of the next available elements in the names and numbers arrays.

Removing the newline from the input buffer

Prompting the user for and inputting a name

Prompting the user for a phone number and using the overloaded >> operator to input the value

Updating the number of entries

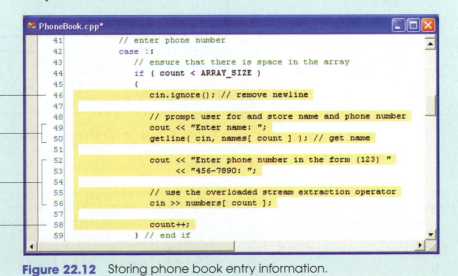

```
 41         // enter phone number
 42         case 1:
 43            // ensure that there is space in the array
 44            if ( count < ARRAY_SIZE )
 45            {
 46               cin.ignore(); // remove newline
 47
 48               // prompt user for and store name and phone number
 49               cout << "Enter name: ";
 50               getline( cin, names[ count ] ); // get name
 51
 52               cout << "Enter phone number in the form (123) "
 53                  << "456-7890: ";
 54
 55               // use the overloaded stream extraction operator
 56               cin >> numbers[ count ];
 57
 58               count++;
 59            } // end if
```

Figure 22.12 Storing phone book entry information.

(cont.)

Note that the statements in lines 49 and 52–53 use the stream insertion operator to output string literals. When C++ encounters these statements, it converts each expression using the stream insertion operator into an `operator<<` function call. The statement in line 49 is converted to

```
cout.operator<<( "Enter name: " );
```

because this overloaded stream insertion operator function is defined as a member of the `ostream` class.

7. ***Displaying each phone book entry.*** If the user chooses to display the phone book's entries by selecting 2 at the application menu's **Enter selection:** prompt, the statements after the `case 2:` label and through the next `break` statement execute. Insert lines 71–83 of Fig. 22.13 into the `main` function. Lines 71–72 display a header for the listing of phone book entries. Lines 75–83 contain a `for` statement that iterates once for each phone book entry that the user has entered. Line 78 displays the entry's name (contained in `names[ i ]`) and line 81 displays the phone number (contained in `numbers[ i ]`). Notice that the right operand for the stream insertion operator in line 81 is a `PhoneNumber` object. In the next box, you will define an overloaded stream insertion operator that displays data contained in a `PhoneNumber` object.

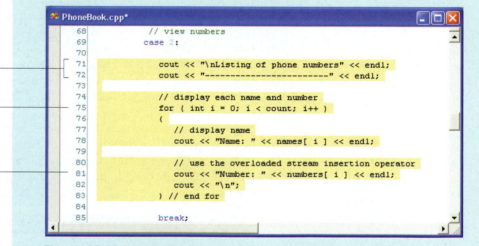

Displaying a header

Beginning a `for` statement to display each entry

Using the overloaded `<<` operator to output a phone number

Figure 22.13 Displaying each phone book entry using overloaded stream insertion operators.

8. ***Save the application.***

Now that you have written code that uses the stream insertion and stream extraction operators with `PhoneNumber` objects, you will need to define the corresponding overloaded operator functions.

Overloading the Stream Insertion and Stream Extraction Operators

1. ***Defining the stream insertion operator function.*** Insert lines 104–111 of Fig. 22.14 below the `main` function. Recall that the `operator<<` function that you declared in line 10 is called when C++ encounters the statement

```
cout << "Number: " << numbers[ i ] << endl;
```

(cont.)

2. **Defining the stream insertion operator function.** Insert lines 104–111 of Fig. 22.14 below the `main` function. Recall that the `operator<<` function that you declared in line 10 is called when C++ encounters the statement

```
cout << "Number: " << numbers[ i ] << endl;
```

in line 81 of Fig. 22.13. When the compiler encounters this statement, the expression `cout << "Number: "` executes first, returning a reference to `cout`. This reference is used to form the expression `cout << numbers[ i ]`, which the compiler converts to the function call

```
operator<<( cout, numbers[ i ] )
```

Because line 105 of Fig. 22.14 declares reference parameters `output` and `number`, `output` becomes a synonym for `cout` and reference parameter `number` becomes a synonym for `numbers[ i ]`.

Outputting phone number by accessing **number** members using *get* functions

Returning a reference to an `ostream` object to enable chaining

```
102  } // end main
103
104  // overloaded stream-insertion operator for PhoneNumber objects
105  ostream &operator<<( ostream &output, PhoneNumber &number )
106  {
107     output << "(" << number.getAreaCode() << ") "
108             << number.getExchange() << "-" << number.getLine();
109
110     return output; // enables cout << a << b << c;
111  } // end function operator<<
112
```

Figure 22.14 Defining the `operator<<` function.

This overloaded `operator<<` function should display the phone number contained in the `PhoneNumber` object in the format (123) 456-7890. Lines 107–108 use the `number` object's *get* functions to access the components of the phone number contained in `number` and insert them into the `ostream` object, `output`, that appeared as the left operand of the stream insertion operator. Note that the `operator<<` function must use the `number` object's `public` *get* functions to access the values of the object's `private` data members because the function is not a member of the `PhoneNumber` class. Before the function terminates, line 110 returns a reference to the output stream object, `output`. Recall that this technique enables you to chain together several stream output operators.

3. **Defining the stream insertion operator function.** Insert lines 113–145 of Fig. 22.15 into the `PhoneBook.cpp` file. Recall that the `operator>>` function is called when C++ encounters the statement

```
cin >> numbers[ count ];
```

in line 56 of Fig. 22.12. Because `operator>>` is a non-member function, C++ generates the function call

```
operator>>( cin, numbers[ count ] )
```

when this statement executes. Line 114 of Fig. 22.15 declares reference parameters `input` and `num`, so `input` becomes a synonym for `cin` and `num` becomes a synonym for `numbers[ count ]`.

(cont.)

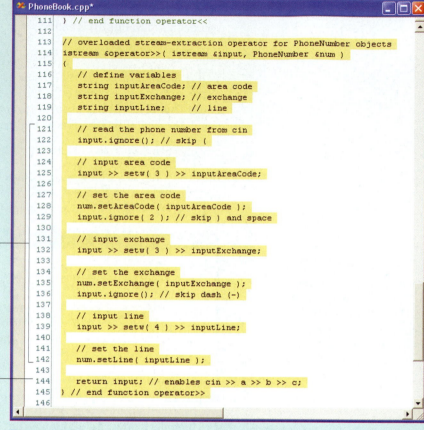

Using `setw` to input numbers and using `ignore` to remove non-numeric characters

Returning a reference to an `istream` object to enable chaining

```
111  } // end function operator<<
112
113  // overloaded stream-extraction operator for PhoneNumber objects
114  istream &operator>>( istream &input, PhoneNumber &num )
115  {
116     // define variables
117     string inputAreaCode; // area code
118     string inputExchange; // exchange
119     string inputLine;     // line
120
121     // read the phone number from cin
122     input.ignore(); // skip (
123
124     // input area code
125     input >> setw( 3 ) >> inputAreaCode;
126
127     // set the area code
128     num.setAreaCode( inputAreaCode );
129     input.ignore( 2 ); // skip ) and space
130
131     // input exchange
132     input >> setw( 3 ) >> inputExchange;
133
134     // set the exchange
135     num.setExchange( inputExchange );
136     input.ignore(); // skip dash (-)
137
138     // input line
139     input >> setw( 4 ) >> inputLine;
140
141     // set the line
142     num.setLine( inputLine );
143
144     return input; // enables cin >> a >> b >> c;
145  } // end function operator>>
146
```

Figure 22.15 Defining the `operator>>` function.

The `PhoneNumber` class defines three data members that store the phone number's area code, exchange and line. To input a phone number into a `PhoneNumber` object, the `operator>>` function must separate a phone number such as (123) 456-7890 into the area code 123, exchange 456 and line 7890. Lines 117–119 define three `string` variables to store the three parts of the phone number extracted from the input stream. You will use the `num` object's *set* functions to assign these values to the `PhoneNumber` object's data members.

The operator function uses the `input` reference parameter, which is a synonym for `cin`, to input as `strings` the three parts of the telephone number. Line 125 inputs the area code into `inputAreaCode`, line 132 inputs the exchange into `inputExchange` and line 139 inputs the line into `inputLine`. Lines 128, 135 and 142 use `num`'s *set* functions to assign the values of `inputAreaCode`, `inputExchange`, and `inputLine` to the `num` object's private `areaCode`, `exchange` and `line` data members, respectively. Again, because the `operator>>` function is not a member of the `PhoneNumber` class, the function must use `public` *set* functions to change the value of `num`'s `private` data members.

(cont.)

Note that lines 125, 132 and 139 use the `setw` stream manipulator to input values from `input`. When used with an `istream` object, the `setw` stream manipulator restricts the number of characters read to its argument. For example, `setw( 3 )` causes three characters to be input from a stream input object. To skip the parentheses, space and dash characters in the phone number that the user entered, lines 122, 129 and 136 call `istream` member function `ignore`, which removes the specified number of characters from the input stream buffer. Line 144 returns `istream` reference `input` (in this application, `cin`) to the caller. This enables you to chain multiple stream extraction operations.

Note that the statements in lines 125, 132 and 139 use the stream extraction operator to input values in `string`s. When C++ encounters these statements, it converts each expression using the stream extraction operator into an `operator>>` function call. The last portion of the statement in line 125 is converted to

```
input.operator>>( inputAreaCode );
```

because this overloaded stream extraction operator function is defined as a member of the `istream` class.

4. ***Save, compile and run the application.*** Figure 22.16 shows the **Phone Book** application running. Test your application by entering several phone numbers, then displaying the entries stored in the application.

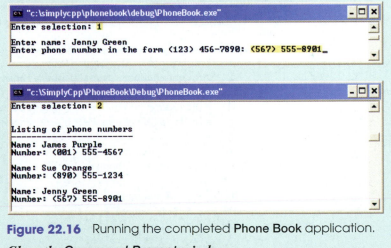

Figure 22.16 Running the completed **Phone Book** application.

5. ***Close the Command Prompt window.***

Figure 22.17 presents the header file for the `PhoneNumber` class; Fig. 22.18 provides the `PhoneNumber` class implementation. Figure 22.19 presents the source code for the `PhoneBook.cpp` file, which contains your application's `main` function. The lines of code that you added, viewed or modified in this tutorial are highlighted.

```
1   // Tutorial 22: PhoneNumber.h
2   // PhoneNumber class definition. Overloads the stream
3   // extraction and insertion operators.
4   #ifndef PHONE_NUMBER_H
5   #define PHONE_NUMBER_H
6
7   #include <string> // required to access string functions
8
```

Figure 22.17 PhoneNumber class header file (`PhoneNumber.h`). (Part 1 of 2.)

```
 9   using namespace std; // for accessing C++ Standard Library members
10
11   // PhoneNumber class definition
12   class PhoneNumber
13   {
14   public:
15      PhoneNumber(); // constructor
16
17      // get and set functions
18      string getAreaCode();
19      void setAreaCode( string );
20
21      string getExchange();
22      void setExchange( string );
23
24      string getLine();
25      void setLine( string );
26
27   private:
28      string areaCode;   // 3-digit area code; aaa of (aaa) eee-1111
29      string exchange;   // 3-digit exchange; eee of (aaa) eee-1111
30      string line;       // 4-digit line; 1111 of (aaa) eee-1111
31   }; // end class PhoneNumber
32
33   #endif // PHONE_NUMBER_H
```

Figure 22.17 PhoneNumber class header file (**PhoneNumber.h**). (Part 2 of 2.)

```
 1   // Tutorial 22: PhoneNumber.cpp
 2   // PhoneNumber class member-function and nonmember-function
 3   // definitions.
 4   #include <iostream> // required to perform C++ stream I/O
 5   #include "PhoneNumber.h" // PhoneNumber class definition
 6
 7   // constructor
 8   PhoneNumber::PhoneNumber()
 9   {
10      setAreaCode( "" );
11      setExchange( "" );
12      setLine( "" );
13   } // end constructor
14
15   // returns the area code
16   string PhoneNumber::getAreaCode()
17   {
18      return areaCode;
19   } // end function getAreaCode
20
21   // sets the area code
22   void PhoneNumber::setAreaCode( string inputAreaCode )
23   {
24      areaCode = inputAreaCode;
25   } // end function setAreaCode
26
27   // returns the exchange
28   string PhoneNumber::getExchange()
29   {
```

Figure 22.18 PhoneNumber class implementation (**PhoneNumber.cpp**). (Part 1 of 2.)

```
30          return exchange;
31      } // end function getExchange
32
33      // sets the exchange
34      void PhoneNumber::setExchange( string inputExchange )
35      {
36          exchange = inputExchange;
37      } // end function setExchange
38
39      // returns the line
40      string PhoneNumber::getLine()
41      {
42          return line;
43      } // end function getLine
44
45      // sets the line
46      void PhoneNumber::setLine( string inputLine )
47      {
48          line = inputLine;
49      } // end function setLine
```

Figure 22.18 PhoneNumber class implementation (PhoneNumber.cpp). (Part 2 of 2.)

```
1       // Tutorial 22: PhoneBook.cpp
2       // Stores and displays phone book entries using
3       // overloaded operators
4       #include <iostream> // required to perform C++ stream I/O
5       #include <string> // required to access string functions
6       #include <iomanip> // required for parameterized stream manipulators
7       #include "PhoneNumber.h" // PhoneNumber class definition
8
9       // overloaded stream insertion operator
10      ostream &operator<<( ostream &, PhoneNumber & );
11
12      // overloaded stream extraction operator
13      istream &operator>>( istream &, PhoneNumber & );
14
15      // function main begins program execution
16      int main()
17      {
18          const int ARRAY_SIZE = 10; // maximum number of phone book entries
19
20          // define variables
21          int count = 0; // stores the number of entries in the phone book
22          int selection = 0; // stores the user's menu selection
23          PhoneNumber numbers[ ARRAY_SIZE ]; // array of PhoneNumber objects
24          string names[ ARRAY_SIZE ]; // array of phone book entry names
25
26          // repeat until the user chooses to exit
27          while ( selection != 3 )
28          {
29              // display menu
30              cout << "\nSelect one of the following options\n" << endl;
31              cout << "1 - Enter new phone number" << endl;
32              cout << "2 - View phone numbers" << endl;
33              cout << "3 - Exit the application" << endl;
```

Declare arrays to store phone numbers and names ⟶ (lines 23–24)

Figure 22.19 Phone Book application code (PhoneBook.cpp). (Part 1 of 3.)

```
34          cout << "Enter selection: ";
35          cin >> selection;
36          cout << endl;
37
38          // determine which option the user selected
39          switch ( selection )
40          {
41             // enter phone number
42             case 1:
43                // ensure that there is space in the array
44                if ( count < ARRAY_SIZE )
45                {
46                   cin.ignore(); // remove newline
47
48                   // prompt user for and store name and phone number
49                   cout << "Enter name: ";
50                   getline( cin, names[ count ] ); // get name
51
52                   cout << "Enter phone number in the form (123) "
53                      << "456-7890: ";
54
55                   // use the overloaded stream extraction operator
56                   cin >> numbers[ count ]; // input phone number
57
58                   count++;
59                } // end if
60                else
61                {
62                   cout << "Error: You cannot enter any more numbers."
63                      << endl;
64                } // end else
65
66                break;
67
68             // view numbers
69             case 2:
70
71                cout << "\nListing of phone numbers" << endl;
72                cout << "------------------------" << endl;
73
74                // display each name and number
75                for ( int i = 0; i < count; i++ )
76                {
77                   // display name
78                   cout << "Name: " << names[ i ] << endl;
79
80                   // use the overloaded stream insertion operator
81                   cout << "Number: " << numbers[ i ] << endl;
82                   cout << "\n";
83                } // end for
84
85                break;
86
87             // exit
88             case 3:
89                cout << "Good-bye!\n" << endl;
90
91                break;
92
```

Annotations (left margin):
- Prompt the user for and input a name → (lines 49–50)
- Prompt the user for and input a phone number, using the overloaded >> operator → (lines 52–56)
- Update the number of entries → (line 58)
- Display a header → (lines 71–72)
- for statement displays each name and phone number that has been entered → (line 75)
- Output the phone numbers using the overloaded << operator → (lines 81–82)

Figure 22.19 Phone Book application code (PhoneBook.cpp). (Part 2 of 3.)

```
 93              default:
 94                 cout << "Error: Enter a valid menu selection";
 95
 96          } // end switch
 97
 98      } // end while
 99
100      return 0; // indicate that program ended successfully
101
102 } // end function main
103
104 // overloaded stream-insertion operator for PhoneNumber objects
105 ostream &operator<<( ostream &output, PhoneNumber &number )
106 {
107      output << "(" << number.getAreaCode() << ") "
108              << number.getExchange() << "-" << number.getLine();
109
110      return output; // enables chaining: cout << a << b << c;
111 } // end function operator<<
112
113 // overloaded stream-extraction operator for PhoneNumber objects
114 istream &operator>>( istream &input, PhoneNumber &num )
115 {
116      // define variables
117      string inputAreaCode; // area code
118      string inputExchange; // exchange
119      string inputLine;     // line
120
121      // read the phone number from cin
122      input.ignore(); // skip (
123
124      // input area code
125      input >> setw( 3 ) >> inputAreaCode;
126
127      // set the area code
128      num.setAreaCode( inputAreaCode );
129      input.ignore( 2 ); // skip ) and space
130
131      // input exchange
132      input >> setw( 3 ) >> inputExchange;
133
134      // set the exchange
135      num.setExchange( inputExchange );
136      input.ignore(); // skip dash (-)
137
138      // input line
139      input >> setw( 4 ) >> inputLine;
140
141      // set the line
142      num.setLine( inputLine );
143
144      return input; // enables chaining: cin >> a >> b >> c;
145 } // end function operator>>
```

Use number's *get* and *set* functions to output the phone number — (lines 107–108)

Enables output chaining — (line 110)

Use setw and ignore to read phone numbers and discard nonnumeric characters — (line 129)

Use setw to read phone numbers — (line 134)

Enables input chaining — (line 144)

Figure 22.19 Phone Book application code (PhoneBook.cpp). (Part 3 of 3.)

SELF-REVIEW

1. The `operator<<` function should return a reference to an object of type _____ to enable chaining multiple stream insertion statements together.

   a) `istream`

   b) `ostream`

   c) `PhoneNumber`

   d) None of the above.

2. Consider the expression `cin >> myEmployee`, where `myEmployee` is of type `Employee`. The `operator>>` function should accept _____.

   a) a single parameter that is a reference to an `istream`

   b) a single parameter that is a reference to an `Employee`

   c) a first parameter that is a reference to an `istream` and a second that is a reference to an `Employee`

   d) a first parameter that is a reference to an `Employee` and a second that is a reference to an `istream`

Answers: 1) b. 2) c.

22.6 Wrap-Up

In this tutorial, you learned about operator overloading. You learned how C++ provides overloaded operators for built-in data types and that the C++ Standard Library overloads operators for certain class types. You also learned several restrictions on operator overloading.

You then learned how to overload unary and binary operators. For a unary operator, the operator function should declare no parameters if it is declared as a member of a class. In this case, the operator function accesses its corresponding operand by accessing class members. If the unary operator function is not a member of a class, it should specify one parameter that corresponds to the operand. In this case, the operator function can access only the operand's public members.

For a binary operator, the operator function should declare one parameter if it is declared as a member of the class. This parameter represents the right operand. To access the left operand's members, simply mention their names in the operator function. If a binary operator function is not declared as a member of a class, it should specify two parameters. The first parameter corresponds to the left operand and the second parameter corresponds to the right operand. In this case, the operator function can access only the operands' public members.

You overloaded the stream insertion and stream extraction operators in the **Phone Book** application. You defined the overloaded stream extraction operator function so that it read a phone number from `cin` and defined the overloaded stream insertion operator so that it displayed a phone number using `cout`. You also learned how to enable chaining with stream insertion and extraction operators. These overloaded operators helped to make your **Phone Book** application's code clearer and more concise.

SKILLS SUMMARY

Naming an Overloaded Operator Function

■ Write a function definition (with a header and body) as you normally would, except that the function name now becomes the keyword `operator` followed by the symbol for the operator being overloaded. For example, the function name `operator+` would be used to overload the addition operator (+).

Declaring an Operator Function For a Unary Operator

■ For a unary operator, the operator function should declare no parameters if it is declared as a member of a class. In this case, the operator function accesses its corresponding operand by accessing class members. If the unary operator function is not a member of a class, it should specify one parameter that corresponds to the operand. In this case, the operator function can access only the operand's `public` members.

Declaring an Operator Function For a Binary Operator

- For a binary operator, the operator function should declare one parameter if it is declared as a member of the class of the object in the left operand. This parameter represents the right operand. To access the left operand's members, simply mention their names in the operator function. If a binary operator function is not declared as a member of a class, it should specify two parameters. The first parameter corresponds to the left operand and the second parameter corresponds to the right operand. In this case, the operator function can access only the operands' public members.

- For the overloaded stream insertion operator function, return a reference to an ostream object to enable chaining (such as cout << a << b << c).

- For the overloaded stream extraction operator function, return a reference to an istream object to enable chaining (such as cin >> a >> b >> c).

KEY TERMS

chaining stream insertion or extraction operators—Occurs when multiple stream insertion (<<) or extraction (>>) operators are used in a single statement.

istream class—The class that is used to create input stream objects, such as cin.

memberwise assignment—Assigns the values of the data members in the object in the right operand of an = operator to the data members of the object in the left operand. This is the default behavior of the = operator.

operator overloading—A technique that allows the programmer to make C++'s operators work with objects (that is, any types that are not built in). To overload an operator, write a function definition (with a header and body) as you normally would, except that the function name now becomes the keyword operator followed by the symbol for the operator being overloaded. For example, the function name operator+ would be used to overload the addition operator (+).

ostream class—The class that is used to create output stream objects, such as cout.

MULTIPLE-CHOICE QUESTIONS

22.1 The _____ operator need not be explicitly overloaded for class objects.

  a) *   b) &

  c) ==   d) !

22.2 The cin object is a member of the _____ class.

  a) ostream   b) iostream

  c) istream   d) inputstream

22.3 Which of the following restrictions on operator overloading is false?

  a) No new operators can be created.

  b) Operators cannot be overloaded for built-in data types.

  c) The & and = operators cannot be overloaded.

  d) Both b and c.

22.4 The name of the overloaded operator function for the unary increment operator is _____.

  a) operator+   b) ++operator

  c) +operator   d) operator++

22.5 The operator>> function should return a reference to a(n) _____ object to enable chaining multiple stream extraction operators together.

  a) istream   b) ostream

  c) string   d) None of the above.

22.6 The _____ operator cannot be overloaded.

  a) .   b) &=

  c) %   d) /=

22.7 If you do not explicitly overload the _____ operator, _____ occurs when you try to use the operator with two programmer-defined objects of the same type as operands.

a) &, a syntax error

b) =, a syntax error

c) =, memberwise assignment

d) &, memberwise assignment

22.8 When used properly operator overloading _____.

a) increases application performance

b) makes applications clearer

c) is implemented by the preprocessor

d) All of the above.

22.9 Which of the following restrictions on operator overloading is false?

a) The associatively of an operator cannot be changed.

b) The precedence of an operator cannot be changed.

c) The number of operands that an operator accepts cannot be changed.

d) None of the above.

22.10 If a binary operator function declares two parameters, the left operand can be accessed _____.

a) using the first parameter

b) using the second parameter

c) by accessing the class's data members directly

d) Both a and c.

EXERCISES

22.11 (*String Demonstration Application*) In this exercise, you will complete an application that demonstrates overloaded operators for the string class provided by the C++ Standard Library. The **String Demonstration** application inputs two strings from the user, then demonstrates the overloaded <<, ==, >, + and [] operators (Fig. 22.20).

```
c:\simplycpp\stringdemonstration\debug\StringDemonstration.exe

Enter a string: book
Enter a second string: phone

First string: book
Second string: phone

"book" precedes "phone" in alphabetic order

"book" + "phone": bookphone
"phone" + "book": phonebook

Character 0 from "book": b
Character 1 from "book": o
Character 2 from "book": o
Character 3 from "book": k

Character 0 from "phone": p
Character 1 from "phone": h
Character 2 from "phone": o
Character 3 from "phone": n
Character 4 from "phone": e

Press any key to continue_
```

Figure 22.20 String Demonstration application output.

a) *Copying the template to your working directory.* Copy the C:\Examples\ Tutorial22\Exercises\StringDemonstration directory to your C:\SimplyCpp directory.

b) *Opening the StringDemonstration.cpp source code template file.* Open the template file StringDemonstration.cpp in your text editor or IDE. Lines 15–20 prompt the user for and input two strings. Lines 23–24 display the two strings.

c) *Using the string comparison operators.* Beginning in line 27, insert code to determine whether string1 is equal to string2, using an if statement and the overloaded equality comparison operator (==). If the two strings are equal, the body of the if statement should execute, displaying a message indicating that the two strings are equal. Otherwise, the application should determine whether string1 is "greater" than string2. Insert an else if statement in line 32. The condition of the else if statement should contain an expression that determines whether string1 is "greater" than string2 using the overloaded greater than operator (>). This operator returns true if its right operand precedes its left operand in alphabetic order. In this case, the application should display a message indicating that string2 precedes string1 in alphabetic order (Fig. 22.20). Otherwise, string1 must be "less than" string2. Insert an else statement that displays a message indicating that string1 precedes string2 in alphabetic order.

d) ***Using the string concatenation operators.*** After the else statement you inserted in the previous step, insert code that uses the overloaded + operator to concatenate the two strings. Recall that the overloaded + operator, when used with two string operands, performs string concatenation. The application should display descriptive text and the result of concatenating string2 to string1 and string1 to string2 (Fig. 22.20).

e) ***Using the string subscript operator.*** After concatenating the strings, display a newline for readability, then insert a for loop into the application. The for loop header should define int variable i and initialize it to 0. This loop should increment i by one after each iteration and continue to loop while i is less than the length of string1. In the body of the for loop, use the overloaded subscript operator ([]), display each character of each string individually. The subscript operator, when used on a string object, accesses the string as an array of characters. For example, the expression string1[0], returns the zeroth character in the string. To display each character of string1 individually, use i as the index for the overloaded subscript operator in the body of the for loop. Finally, display another newline for readability, then, use the same technique to display each character of string2 individually.

f) ***Save, compile and run the completed application.*** Test your application to ensure that it runs correctly by inputting several pairs of strings. Check that the application correctly determines the alphabetic order correctly for the two strings, concatenates the strings and displays each string's characters individually.

g) ***Close the Command Prompt window.***

22.12 (***Modified Payroll Application***) The company for which you wrote the **Payroll** application in Tutorial 17 would like you to modify it to detect duplicate entries when entering employee information. In this exercise, you will modify the **Payroll** application by overloading the == operator for the Employee class to enable the application to determine whether two Employee objects represent the same person. Fig. 22.21 demonstrates the output after the user enters information for the same employee twice in the modified **Payroll** application.

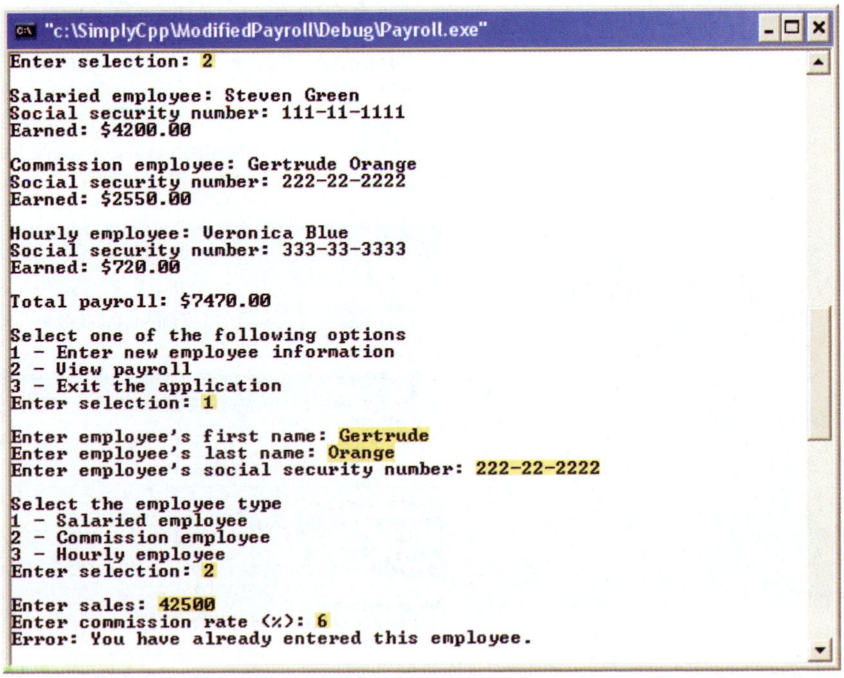

Figure 22.21   Entering a duplicate entry in the modified **Payroll** application.

a) *Copying the template to your working directory.* Copy the C:\Examples\ Tutorial22\Exercises\ModifiedPayroll directory to your C:\SimplyCpp directory.

b) *Overloading the == operator.* Open the template file Payroll.cpp in your text editor or IDE. Insert function prototype for the operator== function in line 19. The operator== function should return a bool value and accept references to two Employee objects as parameters.

c) *Modifying the Payroll source code template.* Define an Employee pointer named newEmployee in line 94. The newEmployee pointer will store the address of the dynamically allocated Employee object. Replace employees[index] with newEmployee in lines 126, 143 and 160. After the switch statement, add a for loop that iterates once for each Employee object in the employees array, using count as the control variable. During each iteration, use the == operator to compare the current Employee object, located at the address contained in employees[count], to the object to which newEmployee points. Because both employees[count] and newEmployee are pointers to Employee objects, you must dereference them using the * operator to ensure that the objects, and not the addresses of the objects, are passed by reference to the operator== function. If the expression evaluates to true, display an error message indicating that this employee has already been entered. Then use the delete operator to release the memory allocated to the object to which newEmployee points and return 0 to indicate that the application did not add another employee to the employees array. After the for loop, assign the Employee object address in newEmployee to employees[index] and return 1.

d) *Defining the operator== function.* Add a function definition for the operator== function after function displayEmployees. Name the first and second Employee object reference parameters person1 and person2, respectively. The body of the operator== function should return a boolean expression that determines whether person1's firstName, lastName and socialSecurityNumber data members contain the same values as person2's corresponding data members. If all three data members match, then the function should return true. Otherwise the function should return false.

e) *Save, compile and run the completed application.* Test your application to ensure that it runs correctly by inputting information for several employees. Then input the same information that you entered for a previous employe and check that the error message is displayed and that the employee does not appear in the payroll twice.

f) *Close the* Command Prompt *window.*

22.13 (*Enhanced Phone Book Application*) In this exercise, you will modify the **Phone Book** application so that it maintains its phone numbers in ascending order (by area code, then exchange, then line). This version of the **Phone Book** application should overload the > operator so that the application can compare two PhoneNumber objects. Figure 22.22 shows the enhanced **Phone Book** application's output.

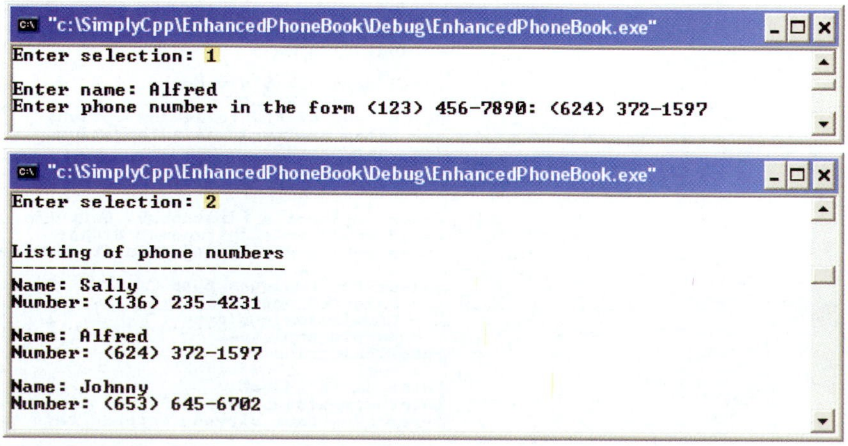

Figure 22.22 Enhanced **Phone Book** application output.

a) *Copying the template to your working directory.* Copy the C:\Examples\ Tutorial22\Exercises\EnhancedPhoneBook directory to your C:\SimplyCpp directory.

b) *Overloading the > operator.* Open the template file PhoneBook.cpp in your text editor or IDE. Insert a comment and a function declaration for the operator> function in lines 15–16. The operator> function should return a bool value and accept two PhoneBook-object reference parameters.

c) *Modifying the PhoneBook source code template file.* In lines 48–49, define a Phone-Number object called number and a string object called name. Change the statements in lines 55 and 61 to input the response into number and name instead of into the numbers and names arrays, respectively.

d) *Determining where in the array to insert the new PhoneNumber.* In this step, you will use a while loop to determine where the new PhoneNumber object should be entered in the numbers array. In line 63, define a control variable i and initialize its value to 0. This variable will contain the index of the element of the array into which the new PhoneNumber object will be inserted. Define a while loop that examines each element of the numbers array until it finds the first PhoneNumber not greater than number or until every occupied element of the array has been examined (when i contains the same value as count) whichever occurs first. Thus, this while loop's continuation condition should determine whether the conditions i < count and number > numbers[i] both evaluate to true. The body of the while loop should increment the value of i. After the while statement terminates, i will contain the index of the array at which the new PhoneNumber should be placed.

e) *Reordering the existing PhoneNumber entries.* If the element of the array specified by i already contains a PhoneNumber object, you will need to move the existing object to the next element of the array, indicating that the existing object is "after" the new object in the array. Similarly, the application must move all PhoneNumbers in elements located at indices greater than i to the next element in the array. Use a for loop that uses a control variable named j iterate once for each of the occupied elements in the numbers array, from numbers[count - 1] to numbers[i]. During each iteration, the application must replace copy the value of numbers[j] to numbers[j + 1] and copy the value of names[j] to names[j + 1]. After the for loop terminates, the application should assign the values of number and name to numbers[i] and names[i], respectively.

f) *Defining the operator> function.* Add a function definition for the operator> function after the operator>> function. Name the PhoneNumber object reference parameters num1 and num2. The body of the operator> function should perform comparison tests on the three string components of a PhoneNumber object: areaCode, exchange and line. First, determine whether num1's areaCode is greater than num2's. If so, return true. Otherwise, determine whether num1's areaCode is less than num2's. If so, return false. Otherwise, the two areaCode data members must contain the same value, so and compare the values of the exchange data members in the same manner. If the values of the two exchange data members are also the same, then you can simply return result of the expression num1.getLine() > num2.getLine().

g) *Save, compile and run the completed application.* Test your application to ensure that it runs correctly by inputting several names and phone numbers. After inputting each phone book entry, display the list of phone numbers and check that the new phone book entry has been inserted at the proper location.

h) *Close the Command Prompt window.*

What does this code do? ▶ **22.14** Assume that the following code uses the source code from the **Payroll** application from Tutorial 17. What occurs when this application executes?

```
1  // Exercise 22.14: WDTCD.cpp
2  #include <iostream> // required to perform C++-style stream I/O
3  #include <iomanip> // required for parameterized stream manipulators
4
```

```cpp
5   #include "Employee.h"      // Employee base class definition
6   #include "Salaried.h"      // SalariedEmployee class definition
7
8   using namespace std; // for accessing C++ Standard Library members
9
10  // function prototype
11  ostream &operator<<( ostream &, Employee * );
12
13  // function main begins program execution
14  int main()
15  {
16     string firstName; // first name
17     string lastName;  // last name
18     string SSN;       // social security number
19     double salary;    // salary
20
21     Employee *myEmployee; // pointer to an Employee object
22
23     // prompt user for and input Employee information
24     cout << "\nEnter employee's first name: ";
25     getline( cin, firstName ); // get first name
26
27     cout << "Enter employee's last name: ";
28     getline( cin, lastName ); // get last name
29
30     cout << "Enter employee's social security number: ";
31     getline ( cin, SSN ); // get social security number
32
33     cout << "Enter salary: ";
34     cin >> salary; // get salary
35
36     myEmployee = new SalariedEmployee( firstName, lastName, SSN,
37        salary ); // create SalariedEmployee object
38
39     // format output as currency
40     cout << fixed << setprecision( 2 );
41
42     cout << myEmployee << endl << endl;
43
44     delete myEmployee; // delete SalariedEmployee object
45
46     return 0; // indicate that program ended successfully
47
48  } // end function main
49
50  // overloaded stream insertion operator
51  ostream &operator<<( ostream &output, Employee *myEmployee )
52  {
53     myEmployee->print();
54     output << "Earned: " << myEmployee->earnings();
55
56     return output;
57
58  } // end function operator<<
```

What's wrong with this code? ▶   **22.15** Find the error(s) in the following code. The operator>> function should be called when C++ encounters an expression such as cin >> number, where number is a PhoneNumber object.

```
1   // Exercise 22.15: WWWTC.cpp
2   // Stores and displays phone book entries using
3   // overloaded operators.
4   #include <iostream> // required to perform C++ stream I/O
5   #include <string>    // required to access string functions
6   #include "PhoneNumber.h" // PhoneNumber class definition
7
8   // function prototype
9   istream &operator>>( istream &, PhoneNumber & );
10
11  // function main begins program execution
12  int main()
13  {
14     PhoneNumber number; // phone number
15
16     cout << "\nEnter phone number in the form (123) 456-7890: ";
17     cin >> number;
18     cout << "\nPhone number is " << number << endl << endl;
19
20     return 0; // indicate that program ended successfully
21
22  } // end main
23
24  ostream &operator>>( istream &input, PhoneNumber &number )
25  {
26     string inputValue; // phone number that the user entered
27
28     getline( input, number ); // input a line of text
29
30     areaCode = inputValue.substr( 1, 3 );
31     exchange = inputValue.substr( 6, 3 );
32     line = inputValue.substr( 10, 4 );
33  } // end function operator>>
```

Programming Challenge ▶

22.16 (*CharArray Comparison Application*) In Exercise 22.11, you used overloaded operators to compare two strings. In this exercise, you will overload comparison operators for the CharArray class, which stores text as an array of chars. You will overload the == and > operators to compare the values of elements in two CharArray objects' char arrays. Fig. 22.23 shows the output of the **CharArray Comparison** application.

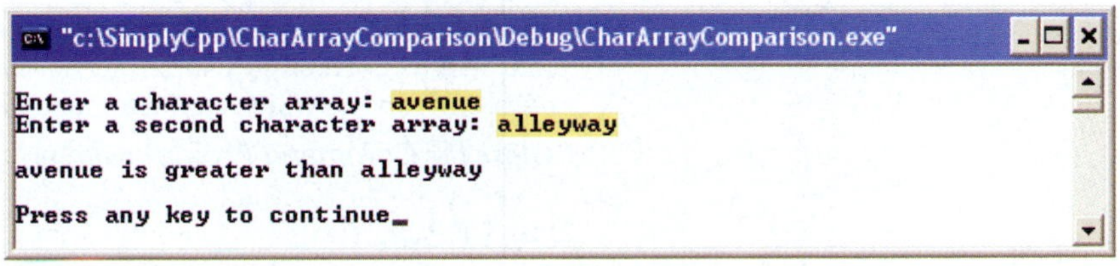

Figure 22.23 CharArray Comparison application output.

a) *Copying the template to your working directory.* Copy the C:\Examples\ Tutorial22\Exercises\CharArrayComparison directory to your C:\SimplyCpp directory. The completed CharArray.h and CharArray.cpp files has been provided for you. The CharArray class defines two data members: a pointer to an array of chars named text and an int named length that contains the number of characters in the char array.

b) *Overloading the == and > operators.* Open the template file CharArrayComparison.cpp in your text editor or IDE. Insert a comment and a function prototype for the operator== function in lines 15–16. The operator== function should return a bool value and specify two CharArray reference parameters. Insert a comment and a function prototype for the operator> function in lines 18–19. The operator> function also returns a bool value and specifies two CharArray reference parameters.

c) ***Defining the operator== function.*** Add a function definition for the operator== function starting in line 93. Name the CharArray reference parameters leftOperand and rightOperand. The operator== function should determine whether the text array for each of the CharArray objects contains the same string of text by comparing each character individually. Add a for loop to iterate once for each element of the char arrays and that terminates when it reaches the end of either array.

d) ***Defining the body of the for loop.*** In the body of the for loop, the application must determine whether the char elements at the ith index of each text array contain the same value. You should access each element using the getChar member function, which takes an integer index position as its argument and returns the char located at the specified position in text. If the two char values are the same, the for loop will advance to the next char element. Otherwise, the operator== function returns false because the CharArray object's text arrays contain different chars. If the for loop terminates without returning false and both CharArray's are the same size (specified by data member length), then the two CharArray objects contain the same text. Thus, use a return statement after the for loop to return the bool value of leftOperand.getLength() == rightOperand.getLength(). This returns true if the lengths of the two CharArrays are the same and false otherwise.

e) ***Defining the operator> function.*** Add a function definition for the operator> function after the operator== function. Name the CharArray parameters leftOperand and rightOperand. The operator> function should determine whether the text contained in the leftOperand's text array is "greater" than that of the rightOperand's text array by comparing each element of the text arrays individually. Use a for loop header similar to the one that you created in *Step d* and name the control variable i. During each iteration, the application should determine whether the value returned by leftOperand.getChar(i) is greater than the value returned by rightOperand.getChar(i). If so, then leftOperand is greater than rightOperand, so the application should return true. Otherwise, determine whether leftOperand.getChar(i) is less than rightOperand.getChar(i). If so, the application should return false.

f) ***Completing the operator> function.*** If neither of the conditions in the preceding steps evaluates to true, then the two char elements are equal and the for loop advances to the next char element. If the for loop terminates, then each element of the two char arrays that were examined is the same. Because the CharArray that containing more characters is greater, insert a statement after the closing brace of the for loop that returns the result of evaluating the expression leftOperand.getLength() > rightOperand.getLength(). This statement returns true if the number of elements in the leftOperand object's text array is larger than that of the rightOperand object's text array, and false otherwise.

g) ***Save, compile and run the completed application.*** Test your application to ensure that it runs correctly by inputting several strings of text. Check that the application correctly reports which character array is greater, or if they are equal.

h) ***Close the Command Prompt window.***

A

Dive Into™ the GNU C++ Tools

T his appendix provides instructions for compiling and debugging C++ applications with the GNU toolset. The GNU C++ Tools are available on most UNIX and UNIX-like systems, such as Linux and Mac OS X. Each section in this appendix corresponds directly to each compiler-specific section in the book.

A.1 Compiling and Running the Completed Welcome Application

In Tutorial 1, you learned that a C++ program's source-code file (a file with the .cpp extension) must be compiled and linked to form an executable image before it can be run. In this section, you will learn how to compile and run the **Welcome** application using the GNU Compiler Collection (GCC) toolset.

[*Note:* Throughout this appendix, we assume your home directory is called

/home/student

Also, all of the sample screen captures show a Linux environment and a *bash* shell. Depending on your particular version of UNIX/Linux/Mac OS X and your default shell, your screen may appear differently. We highlighted user input in the screen captures to distinguish input from output.]

Compiling the Welcome Application

1. *Copying the template to your working directory.* Copy the `/home/student/Examples/Tutorial02/CompletedApplication/Welcome` directory to your `/home/student/SimplyCpp` directory.

2. *Locating the template application.* Open a shell window. Change to your working directory, `Welcome`, by typing `cd /home/student/SimplyCpp/Welcome`, then pressing the *Enter* key. Type `ls`, then press *Enter* to list the contents of the directory (Fig. A.1). Inside this directory should be the `Welcome.cpp`, `Welcome.exe`, `Welcome.sln` and `Welcome.vcproj` files, but no `Welcome` file.

Change directories ———
Display a directory listing ———
No executable file ———

```
Shell Window
~$ cd /home/student/SimplyCpp/Welcome
/home/student/SimplyCpp/Welcome$ ls
Welcome.cpp  Welcome.exe  Welcome.sln  Welcome.vcproj
/home/student/SimplyCpp/Welcome$ _
```

Figure A.1 Compiling the template **Welcome** application.

3. *Compiling the application.* In the shell window, type

```
g++ -o Welcome Welcome.cpp
```

and press *Enter*. The g++ command will compile a C++ source-code file. Notice that the g++ command is followed by three strings of text separated by spaces. The first string (-o) is a command-line option. In general, you specify a command-line option using a hyphen (-), followed by one or more characters. The -o command-line option indicates that you will specify the name of the file that should contain your application's compiled code. The file name is specified by entering a space after the -o command-line option, then typing the name of the file (in this case, Welcome). The third string, Welcome.cpp, specifies the name of the file to compile. Type ls and press *Enter* again to see that the directory now contains the Welcome file (Fig. A.2).

Compile `Welcome.cpp` ———
Display a directory listing ———
Executable file was created ———

```
Shell Window
~$ cd /home/student/SimplyCpp/Welcome
/home/student/SimplyCpp/Welcome$ ls
Welcome.cpp  Welcome.exe  Welcome.sln  Welcome.vcproj
/home/student/SimplyCpp/Welcome$ g++ -o Welcome Welcome.cpp
/home/student/SimplyCpp/Welcome$ ls
Welcome  Welcome.cpp  Welcome.exe  Welcome.sln  Welcome.vcproj
/home/student/SimplyCpp/Welcome$ _
```

Figure A.2 Compiling the template **Welcome** application.

4. Once you have compiled the **Welcome** application, you run the application by typing

```
./Welcome
```

and pressing *Enter*. The ./ specifies that the file to execute is in the current directory, and Welcome specifies the name of that file. The application executes in the same window (Fig. A.3).

5. *Closing the shell window.* Close the shell window by clicking its close button.

(cont.)

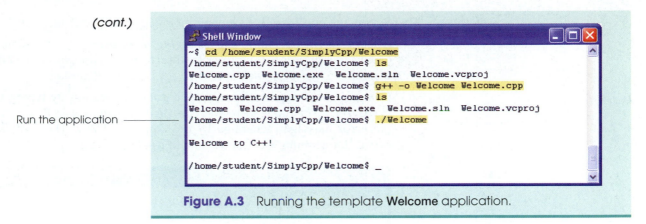

Figure A.3   Running the template **Welcome** application.

A.2 Syntax Errors

In the preceding section, you compiled the **Welcome** application using GCC. If you do not write your code correctly, your application will not compile and errors will be displayed. Even after an application compiles correctly, it may still contain errors. **Debugging** is the process of locating and removing errors in an application. There are two types of errors—syntax errors and logic errors.

   Syntax errors (also called **compilation errors** or **compile-time errors**) occur when code statements violate the grammatical rules of the programming language. Examples of such errors include misspelling a word that is special to C++ and not placing a semicolon at the end of each statement in to your application. An application cannot execute until all of its syntax errors are corrected and the application compiles.

   Logic errors do not prevent your application from compiling successfully, but do cause your application to produce erroneous results when it runs. Most compiler vendors provide software called a **debugger**, which helps locate logic errors in your applications.

*Using the Debugger:
Syntax Errors*

1. ***Copying the template to your working directory.*** Copy the /home/ student/Examples/Tutorial03/CompletedApplication/Inventory directory to your /home/student/SimplyCpp directory.

2. ***Opening the application.*** If the **Welcome** application source code is not currently open, locate the Welcome.cpp file and open it in your text editor or IDE. Figure A.4 shows the code in Microsoft Visual Studio .NET. Your text editor or IDE may display the source code differently.

3. ***Creating your own syntax errors.*** You will now create your own syntax errors, for demonstration purposes. Insert the backslash character (\) before the second double quote in line 10 and capitalize the return keyword in line 12. Figure A.4 shows the two modified (incorrect) lines.

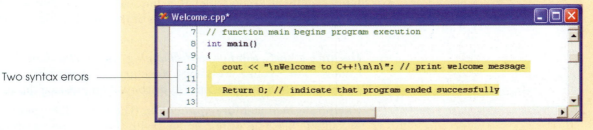

Figure A.4   Introducing two syntax errors into your code.

(cont.)

4. ***Saving the application.*** Save your modified source code file.

5. ***Opening a shell window and changing directories.*** Open a shell window. Change directories to your working directory, `Welcome`, by typing `cd /home/student/SimplyCpp/Welcome`, then pressing the *Enter* key

6. ***Compiling the application.*** Compile your application by typing the command `g++ -o Welcome Welcome.cpp`, then pressing *Enter*. Figure A.5 shows the error messages generated by the compiler. [*Note:* The error messages may differ depending on the version of `g++` that you use.]

Description of the errors including file name and line number

```
Shell Window
~$ cd /home/student/SimplyCpp/Welcome
/home/student/SimplyCpp/Welcome$ ls
Welcome   Welcome.cpp   Welcome.exe   Welcome.sln   Welcome.vcproj
/home/student/SimplyCpp/Welcome$ g++ -o Welcome Welcome.cpp
Welcome.cpp:10:12: missing terminating " character
Welcome.cpp: In function `int main()':
Welcome.cpp:12: error: parse error before numeric constant
/home/student/SimplyCpp/Welcome$ _
```

Figure A.5 Two syntax error messages generated by the compiler.

7. ***Locating the first syntax error.*** Each error that the compiler finds is accompanied by the file name (`Welcome.cpp`), the line number, a description of the error and the function in which the error occurs.

8. ***Fixing the syntax errors.*** Now that the compiler has told you where the syntax errors are located, go back to the source code and correct the two errors you created in *Step 2*. Save the file and return once more to the shell window. Recompile your application, which should now compile correctly.

9. ***Close the shell window.***

A.3 Using the Debugger: Breakpoints

In Section A.2, you learned that there are two types of errors—syntax errors and logic errors—and you learned how to eliminate syntax errors from your code. In this section, you will learn how to use the GNU debugger (`gdb`), which allows you to monitor the execution of your applications to locate and remove logic errors.

The debugger will be one of your most important application development tools. You begin your study of the debugger by learning about **breakpoints**, which are markers that can be set at any executable line of code. When application execution reaches a breakpoint, execution pauses, allowing you to examine the values of variables and ensure that there are no logic errors. For example, you can examine the value of a variable that stores the result of a calculation to ensure that the calculation was performed correctly. Note that setting a breakpoint at a line of code that is not executable (such as a comment) causes the debugger to pause execution at the next executable statement located after that line. You will use breakpoints and various debugger commands to examine the values of the variables defined in `main`.

Using the Debugger Breakpoints and the `run, continue, delete` ***and*** `print` ***Commands***

1. ***Opening a shell window and changing directories.*** Open a shell window. Change to your working directory, `Inventory`, by typing `cd /home/student/SimplyCpp/Inventory`, then pressing the *Enter* key.

2. ***Compiling the Inventory application.*** The GNU debugger works only with executable files that were compiled with the `-g` compiler option, which generates information that is used by the debugger to help you debug your applications. Compile the **Inventory** application with the `-g` command-line option by typing `g++ -g -o Inventory Inventory.cpp`.

(cont.)

3. ***Starting the debugger.*** At the **Command Line**, type gdb Inventory (Fig. A.6). This command will start the GNU debugger and enable you to use the debugger's features. Your GNU debugger configuration information may be different from what is displayed in Fig. A.6.

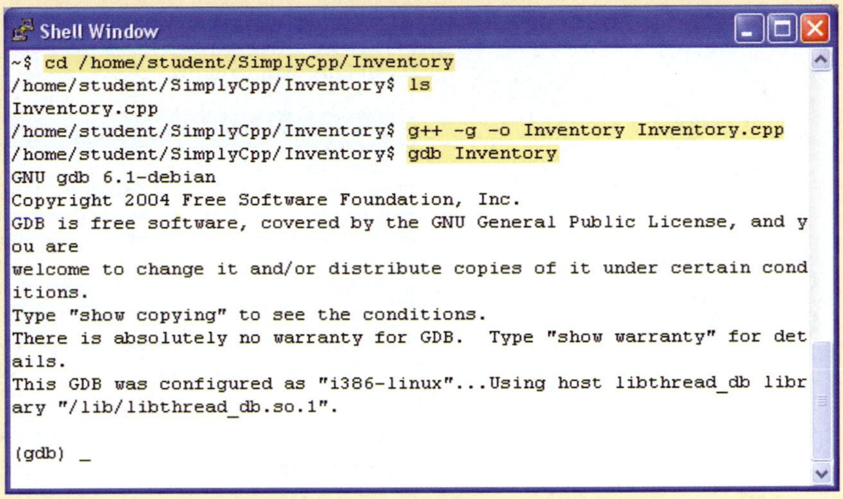

Start the GNU debugger ⎯⎯⎯

```
Shell Window
~$ cd /home/student/SimplyCpp/Inventory
/home/student/SimplyCpp/Inventory$ ls
Inventory.cpp
/home/student/SimplyCpp/Inventory$ g++ -g -o Inventory Inventory.cpp
/home/student/SimplyCpp/Inventory$ gdb Inventory
GNU gdb 6.1-debian
Copyright 2004 Free Software Foundation, Inc.
GDB is free software, covered by the GNU General Public License, and y
ou are
welcome to change it and/or distribute copies of it under certain cond
itions.
Type "show copying" to see the conditions.
There is absolutely no warranty for GDB.  Type "show warranty" for det
ails.
This GDB was configured as "i386-linux"...Using host libthread_db libr
ary "/lib/libthread_db.so.1".

(gdb) _
```

Figure A.6   Starting the GNU debugger.

4. ***Running an application in the debugger.*** Run the **Inventory** application through the debugger by typing **run** (Fig. A.7). When you do not set any breakpoints before running your application in the debugger, the application will run to completion.

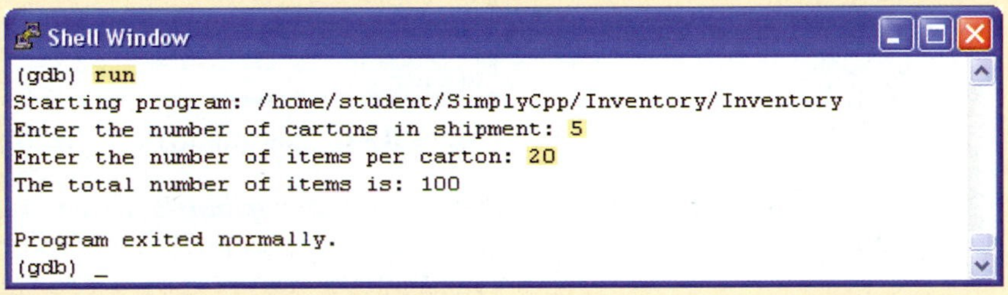

Run the **Inventory** application ⎯⎯⎯

```
Shell Window
(gdb) run
Starting program: /home/student/SimplyCpp/Inventory/Inventory
Enter the number of cartons in shipment: 5
Enter the number of items per carton: 20
The total number of items is: 100

Program exited normally.
(gdb) _
```

Figure A.7   Running the **Inventory** application through the debugger.

5. ***Inserting breakpoints using the GNU debugger.*** You set a breakpoint at a specific line of code in your application. Set a breakpoint at line 25 of your code by typing break 25 (Fig. A.8). You can set as many breakpoints as necessary. Set another breakpoint at line 28 of your code by typing break 28 (Fig. A.8). Each breakpoint is identified by the order in which it was created. The first breakpoint created is known as Breakpoint 1. When the application runs, it suspends execution at any line that contains a breakpoint. The application is said to be in **break mode** when the debugger pauses the application's execution. Breakpoints also can be set after the debugger has started.

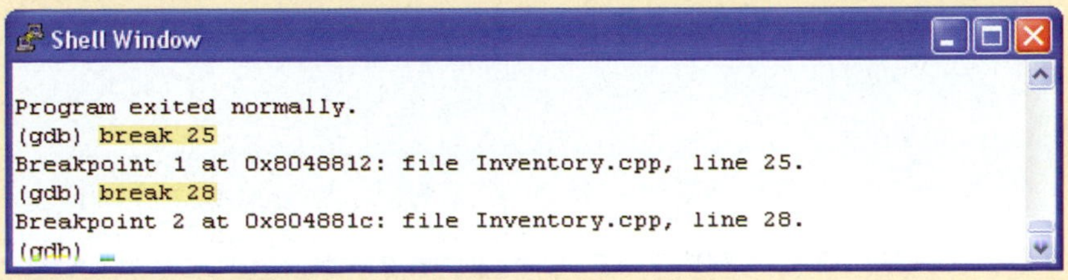

Set a breakpoint at line 25 ⎯⎯⎯
Set a breakpoint at line 28 ⎯⎯⎯

```
Shell Window
Program exited normally.
(gdb) break 25
Breakpoint 1 at 0x8048812: file Inventory.cpp, line 25.
(gdb) break 28
Breakpoint 2 at 0x804881c: file Inventory.cpp, line 28.
(gdb) _
```

Figure A.8   Setting two breakpoints.

(cont.)

6. ***Running the application.*** Type `run` to execute your application and begin the debugging process.

7. ***Beginning the debugging process.*** Enter 10 and 7 at the prompts. The application will pause when execution reaches the breakpoint at line 25 (Fig. A.9). The debugger displays a message indicating that it has reached a breakpoint at line 25 and displays that source code. Note that gdb displays the next statement that will execute.

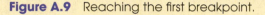

```
Shell Window                                                    _ □ X
(gdb) run
Starting program: /home/student/SimplyCpp/Inventory/Inventory
Enter the number of cartons in shipment: 10
Enter the number of items per carton: 7

Breakpoint 1, main () at Inventory.cpp:25
25              result = cartons * items;
(gdb) _
```

Breakpoint is reached ———
Next line of code to be executed ———

Figure A.9 Reaching the first breakpoint.

8. ***Using the `continue` command to resume execution.*** To resume execution, type **continue**. The application executes until it stops at the next breakpoint at line 28 (Fig. A.10).

```
Shell Window                                                    _ □ X
Breakpoint 1, main () at Inventory.cpp:25
25              result = cartons * items;
(gdb) continue
Continuing.

Breakpoint 2, main () at Inventory.cpp:28
28              cout << "The total number of items is: " << result << endl;
(gdb) _
```

Another breakpoint is reached ———

Figure A.10 Execution reaches the second breakpoint.

9. ***Examining a variable's value.*** Type `print cartons`. The current value stored in the `cartons` variable will be displayed (Fig. A.11). The **print** command allows you to peek inside the computer at the value of one of your variables. This command will help you find and eliminate logic errors in your code. Use the `print` command to output the values stored in the `cartons`, `items` and `result` variables (Fig. A.11).

```
Shell Window                                                    _ □ X
(gdb) print cartons
$1 = 10
(gdb) print items
$2 = 7
(gdb) print result
$3 = 70
(gdb) _
```

Displaying the value in `cartons` ———
Displaying the value in `items` ———
Displaying the value in `result` ———

Figure A.11 Examining three variable values.

(cont.)   10. ***Using convenience variables.*** When the `print` command is used, the result is stored in a convenience variable such as $1. Convenience variables, which are temporary variables, named using a dollar sign followed by an integer, are created by gdb as you print values during your debugging session. A convenience variable can be used in the debugging process to perform arithmetic and evaluate boolean expressions. Type `print $1`. The debugger displays the value of $1, which contains the value of `cartons`. Note that printing the value of $1 creates a new convenience variable—$4.

```
Shell Window                                                    _ □ X
(gdb) print cartons
$1 = 10
(gdb) print items
$2 = 7
(gdb) print result
$3 = 70
(gdb) print $1
$4 = 10
(gdb) _
```

Displaying the value in $1 ——

Figure A.12   Display value of convenience variable.

11. ***Continuing application execution.*** Type `continue` to continue the application's execution. There are no more breakpoints, so the application continues executing and displays the result of its calculation (Fig. A.13).

```
Shell Window                                                    _ □ X
(gdb) continue
Continuing.
The total number of items is: 70

Program exited normally.
(gdb) _
```

Execution resumes ——

Figure A.13   Continue application execution.

12. ***Removing a breakpoint.*** You can display a list of all of the breakpoints in the application by typing `info break` (Fig. A.14). To remove a breakpoint, type **delete**, followed by a space and the number of the breakpoint to remove. Remove the first breakpoint by typing `delete 1`. Remove the second breakpoint (line 28) as well. Now type `info break` to list the remaining breakpoints in the application. The debugger should indicate that no breakpoints are set (Fig. A.14).

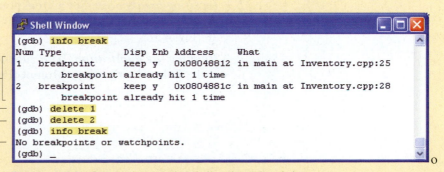

Two breakpoints are set ——
Delete breakpoint at line 25 ——
Delete breakpoint at line 28 ——
Both breakpoints are removed ——

```
Shell Window                                                    _ □ X
(gdb) info break
Num Type           Disp Enb Address    What
1   breakpoint     keep y   0x08048812 in main at Inventory.cpp:25
        breakpoint already hit 1 time
2   breakpoint     keep y   0x0804881c in main at Inventory.cpp:28
        breakpoint already hit 1 time
(gdb) delete 1
(gdb) delete 2
(gdb) info break
No breakpoints or watchpoints.
(gdb) _
```

Figure A.14   Displaying and deleting breakpoints.

13. ***Executing the application without breakpoints.*** Type `run` to execute the application. Enter the values 9 and 4 at the prompts. Because you successfully removed the two breakpoints, the application's output (36) is displayed without gdb entering break mode (Fig. A.15).

(cont.)

```
Shell Window                                          _ □ ✕
(gdb) run
Starting program: /home/student/SimplyCpp/Inventory/Inventory
Enter the number of cartons in shipment: 9
Enter the number of items per carton: 4
The total number of items is: 36

Program exited normally.
(gdb) _
```

Figure A.15 Application executes with no breakpoints set.

14. ***Stopping the debugging session.*** Type `quit` to stop debugging.

15. ***Close the shell window.***

A.4 Using the Debugger: The `print` and `set` commands

GNU includes several debugging features that are accessible from the command-line debugger. As you learned in Section A.3, the `print` command allows you to examine the value of a variable in `gdb`. In this section, you will learn how to use the GNU debugger's `print` command to display the value of more complex expressions. You will also learn how to use the `set` command, which allows the programmer to assign new values to variables.

Using the Debugger: The `print` and `set` commands

1. ***Copying the template to your working directory.*** Copy the `/home/student/Examples/Tutorial04/CompletedApplication/WageCalculator` directory to your `/home/student/SimplyCpp` directory.

2. ***Opening a shell window and changing directories.*** Open a shell window. Change to your working directory, `WageCalculator`, by typing `cd /home/student/SimplyCpp/WageCalculator`, then pressing the *Enter* key.

3. ***Compiling the application for debugging.*** Compile the application with the `-g` command-line option by typing `g++ -g -o WageCalculator WageCalculator.cpp`. This will generate an output file named `WageCalculator`. The GNU debugger works only with executable files compiled with the `-g` compiler option.

4. ***Starting debugging.*** At the **Command Line**, type `gdb WageCalculator`. This command will start the GNU debugger for the `WageCalculator` application.

5. ***Inserting breakpoints.*** Set a breakpoint at line 23 in the source code by typing `break 23`. Set another breakpoint at line 36 of the code by typing `break 36` (Fig. A.16).

6. ***Running the application.*** Type `run` to begin the debugging process. Type 12 at the **Enter Hourly wage:** prompt (Fig. A.17).

(cont.)

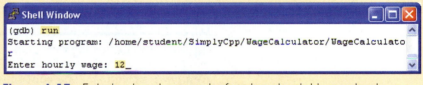

Figure A.16 Setting breakpoints at lines 23 and 36.

```
Shell Window                                                    _ □ X
(gdb) run
Starting program: /home/student/SimplyCpp/WageCalculator/WageCalculato
r
Enter hourly wage: 12_
```

Figure A.17 Entering hourly wage before breakpoint is reached.

7. ***Suspending program execution.*** Press *Enter* so that your application reads the value you just entered. This causes the application to execute until the breakpoint at line 23. When the application reaches line 23, gdb suspends program execution and switches the application into break mode (Fig. A.18). At this point, the hourly wage input by the user (12) has been assigned to the hourlyWage variable, and the statement in line 23 is the next statement that will execute.

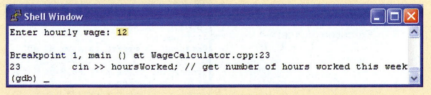

Figure A.18 Application execution suspended when debugger reaches the breakpoint at line 23.

8. ***Examining data.*** Once the application has entered break mode, you can explore the values of your variables using the debugger's print command. At the gdb prompt, type print hourlyWage. The value will be displayed (Fig. A.19). Notice that this value is 12—the value assigned to hourlyWage in line 19.

(cont.)

```
Shell Window                                                          _ □ X
Breakpoint 1, main () at WageCalculator.cpp:23
23            cin >> hoursWorked; // get number of hours worked this week
(gdb) print hourlyWage
$1 = 12
(gdb) _
```

Value of the **hourlyWage** variable

Figure A.19   Examining variable **hourlyWage**.

9. ***Evaluating arithmetic and boolean expressions.*** At the **Command Line**, type print (hourlyWage + 3) * 5. Notice that the print command can evaluate arithmetic expressions. In this case, it returns the value 75 (Fig. A.20). At the gdb prompt, type print hourlyWage == 3. Expressions containing the == symbol are treated as bool expressions. The value returned is false (Fig. A.20), because hourlyWage does not currently contain the value 3.

```
Shell Window                                                          _ □ X
(gdb) print hourlyWage
$1 = 12
(gdb) print ( hourlyWage + 3 ) * 5
$2 = 75
(gdb) print hourlyWage == 3
$3 = false
(gdb) _
```

Evaluating an arithmetic expression

Evaluating a **bool** expression

Figure A.20   Examining the values of expressions.

10. ***Resuming execution.*** Type continue to resume execution (Fig. A.21). The application will continue to execute until the next breakpoint (line 36). Line 23 executes, enabling you to enter a value at the **Enter hours worked this week:** prompt. Enter 40 at the prompt. Line 27 defines the HOUR_LIMIT constant and initializes its value to 40.0. Line 30 declares the wages variable to store the gross wages. The if condition in line 33 evaluates to true, so the if statement's body executes and the application is once again suspended at line 36. Type print hoursWorked (Fig. A.21) to display the value of hoursWorked.

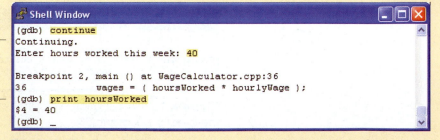

Execution resumes

Display value of the **hoursWorked** variable

```
Shell Window                                                          _ □ X
(gdb) continue
Continuing.
Enter hours worked this week: 40

Breakpoint 2, main () at WageCalculator.cpp:36
36            wages = ( hoursWorked * hourlyWage );
(gdb) print hoursWorked
$4 = 40
(gdb) _
```

Figure A.21   Resuming execution and displaying the value of the variable **hoursWorked**.

11. ***Modifying values.*** Based on the values input by the user (12 and 40), the gross wages output by the **Wage Calculator** application should be $480.00. However, by using the debugger, you can change the values of variables during the application's execution. This can be valuable for experimenting with different values and for locating logic errors in applications. You can use the debugger's **set** command to change the value of a variable. Type set hoursWorked = 10.0. The debugger changes the value of variable hoursWorked. Type print hoursWorked to display its new value (Fig. A.22).

(cont.)

Value modified in the debugger ———

```
Shell Window                                    _ □ X
(gdb) set hoursWorked = 10.0
(gdb) print hoursWorked
$5 = 10
(gdb) _
```

Figure A.22   Modifying values.

12. ***Viewing the application result.*** Type `continue` to continue application execution. The `main` function executes until the `return` statement in line 54 and displays the result. Notice that the result is $120.00 (Fig. A.23). This shows that the previous step changed the value of `hoursWorked` from the user input value (40) to 10.0.

Gross wages result based on altered value of the `hoursWorked` variable ———

```
Shell Window                                    _ □ X
(gdb) continue
Continuing.
Gross wages: $120.00

Program exited normally.
(gdb) _
```

Figure A.23   Output displayed after the debugging process.

13. ***Stopping the debugging session.*** Type `quit` to stop debugging.

14. ***Close the shell window.***

A.5 Using the Debugger: Controlling Execution Using the `step`, `finish` and `next` Commands

In the preceding sections, you learned how to debug your applications by setting breakpoints and either displaying or setting values at those breakpoints. In this section, you will learn how to walk through the application line by line using the debugger to find and fix errors. This can help you verify that a function's code is executing correctly. The commands you will learn in this section allow you to walk through the execution of a function line by line, execute all the statements of a function at once, execute only the remaining statements of a function (if you have already executed some statements within the function) or continue execution until the next breakpoint (or until the application terminates).

Using the Debugger: Controlling Execution Using the `step`, `finish` and `next` Commands

1. ***Copying the template to your working directory.*** Copy the `/home/student/Examples/Tutorial10/CompletedApplication/WageCalculator2` directory to your `/home/student/SimplyCpp` directory.

1. ***Opening a shell window and changing directories.*** Open a shell window. Change to your working directory, `WageCalculator2`, by typing `cd /home/student/SimplyCpp/WageCalculator2`, then pressing the *Enter* key.

2. ***Compiling the application for debugging.*** Compile your application by typing `g++ -g -o WageCalculator WageCalculator.cpp`.

3. ***Starting the debugger.*** Start the debugger by typing `gdb WageCalculator`.

4. ***Setting a breakpoint.*** Type `break 52` to set a breakpoint at line 52 (Fig. A.24).

5. ***Running the application.*** Run the application by typing `run` (Fig. A.25).

(cont.)

Starting the debugger ——————

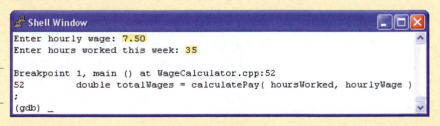

```
Shell Window                                                    [_][□][X]
/home/student/SimplyCpp/WageCalculator2$ g++ -g -o WageCalculator Wage
Calculator.cpp
/home/student/SimplyCpp/WageCalculator2$ gdb WageCalculator
GNU gdb 6.1-debian
Copyright 2004 Free Software Foundation, Inc.
GDB is free software, covered by the GNU General Public License, and y
ou are
welcome to change it and/or distribute copies of it under certain cond
itions.
Type "show copying" to see the conditions.
There is absolutely no warranty for GDB.  Type "show warranty" for det
ails.
This GDB was configured as "i386-linux"...Using host libthread_db libr
ary "/lib/libthread_db.so.1".

(gdb) break 52
Breakpoint 1 at 0x8048938: file WageCalculator.cpp, line 52.
(gdb) _
```

Setting a breakpoint ——————

Figure A.24   Setting a breakpoint in the **Wage Calculator** application.

Running the application ——————

```
Shell Window                                                    [_][□][X]
(gdb) run
Starting program: /home/student/SimplyCpp/WageCalculator2/WageCalculat
or

Enter hourly wage: _
```

Figure A.25   Running the **Wage Calculator** application.

6. ***Reaching the breakpoint.*** Enter the value 7.50 in the **Enter hourly wage:** prompt and enter the value 35 in the **Enter hours worked this week:** prompt. The debugger indicates that the breakpoint has been reached and displays the line of code for you (Fig. A.26). The debugger and application then pause and wait for the next command to be entered in the gdb prompt.

Reaching a breakpoint ——————

```
Shell Window                                                    [_][□][X]
Enter hourly wage: 7.50
Enter hours worked this week: 35

Breakpoint 1, main () at WageCalculator.cpp:52
52              double totalWages = calculatePay( hoursWorked, hourlyWage )
;
(gdb) _
```

Figure A.26   Reaching the breakpoint in the **Wage Calculator** application.

7. ***Using the* step *command.*** The **step** command executes the next statement in the application. If the next statement is to execute a function call and the **step** command is used, control is transferred to the called function. The **step** command allows you to enter a function and confirm the function's execution by executing each statement inside the function individually. As you do, you also can use the **print** and **set** commands to view and modify the variables within the function. You will now use the **step** command to enter the **calculatePay** function by typing **step** (Fig. A.27). The debugger displays the next executable statement—in this case, line 17. Note that the debugger does not pause at line 13. This occurs because variable declarations that do not contain assignments are not considered executable statements. [*Note*: Variable declarations containing assignments are considered executable statements.]

(cont.)

Stepping through an application

Application currently paused at
line 17 in the `calculatePay`
function

```
Shell Window
Breakpoint 1, main () at WageCalculator.cpp:52
52              double totalWages = calculatePay( hoursWorked, hourlyWage )
;
(gdb) step
calculatePay (hours=35, wages=7.5) at WageCalculator.cpp:17
17              const double HOUR_LIMIT = 40.0;
(gdb) _
```

Figure A.27   Stepping into the `calculatePay` function.

8. *Using the `finish` command.* After you have stepped into the `calculate-Pay` method, type **finish**. This command executes the statements in the function and returns control to line 52, which contains the function call (Fig. A.28). In lengthy functions, you often will want to look at a few key lines of code, then continue debugging the caller's code. The `finish` command is useful when you do not want to continue stepping through the entire function line by line.

Execute remaining statements
in the current function

```
Shell Window
calculatePay (hours=35, wages=7.5) at WageCalculator.cpp:17
17              const double HOUR_LIMIT = 40.0;
(gdb) finish
Run till exit from #0  calculatePay (hours=35, wages=7.5)
    at WageCalculator.cpp:17
0x0804894a in main () at WageCalculator.cpp:52
52              double totalWages = calculatePay( hoursWorked, hourlyWage )
;
Value returned is $1 = 262.5
(gdb) _
```

Figure A.28   Stepping out of a function.

9. *Using the `continue` command.* Tell the debugger to continue program execution by typing `continue`. There are no more breakpoints, so the program will run to completion.

10. *Starting the debugger.* Before we can demonstrate the next debugger feature, you must start the debugger again. Start the debugger, as you did in *Step 5*, inputting the same values you entered in *Step 6*. The debugger pauses execution at line 52.

11. *Using the `next` command.* Type **next**. This command behaves like the `step` command, except when the next statement to execute contains a function call. Recall from *Step 7* that the `step` command allows you to enter a function when the next statement to execute is a function call. When using the `next` command, the called function executes in its entirety (without pausing execution at any statement inside the function), and the application advances to the next executable line after the function call (Fig. A.29). In this case, the debugger executes line 52, located in the `main` function. Line 52 calls the `calculatePay` function and assigns the result to `double` variable `totalWages`. The debugger then pauses execution at line 55, the next executable line in the current function, `main`.

(cont.)

Using the **next** command

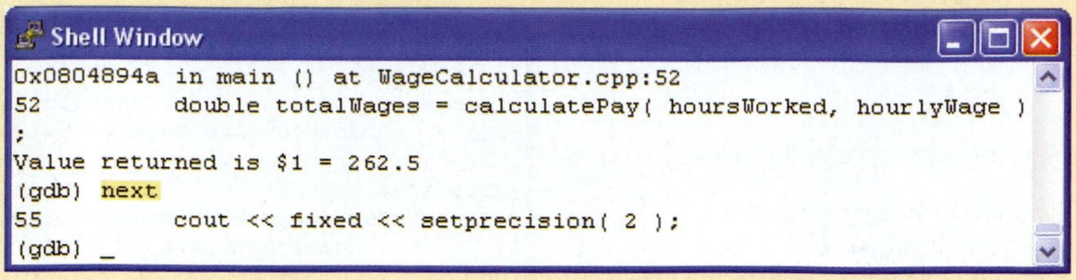

Figure A.29 Stepping over a function call.

12. ***Using the quit command.*** Use the `continue` command to run the application to completion. Then use the `quit` command to terminate the debugger.

13. ***Close the shell window.***

A.6 Compiling and Running the Digital Clock Application

Tutorial 15 introduced classes using the `Time` class in the **Digital Clock** application. Because applications that use classes typically contain multiple source code files, they must be compiled differently from applications containing one source code file. In this section, you will learn how to compile applications containing multiple source code files with GCC. In the next section, you'll learn how to debug such applications with the GNU debugger.

Compiling the Digital Clock Application

1. ***Copying the completed application to your working directory.*** Copy the `/home/student/Examples/Tutorial15/CompletedApplication/DigitalClock` directory to your `/home/student/SimplyCpp` directory.

2. ***Locating the completed application.*** Open a shell window. Change to your working directory, `DigitalClock`, by typing `cd /home/student/SimplyCpp/DigitalClock`, then pressing the *Enter* key. Type `ls`, then press *Enter* to list the contents of the directory (Fig. A.30). Inside this directory should be the `DigitalClock.cpp`, `Time.cpp`, `Time.h`, `DigitalClock.exe`, `DigitalClock.sln` and `DigitalClock.vcproj` files, but no `DigitalClock` file.

Change directories
Display a directory listing
No executable file

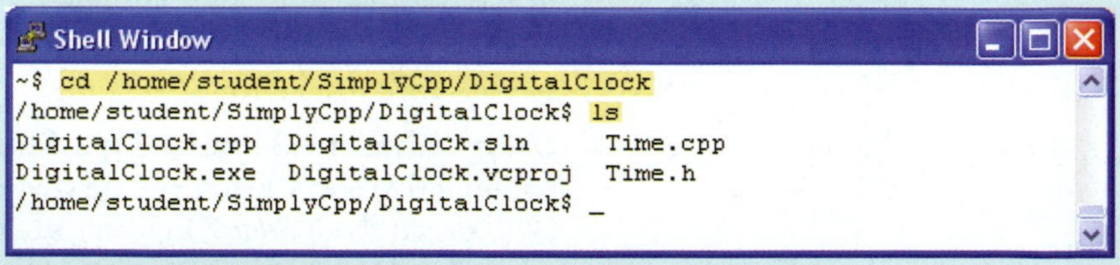

Figure A.30 Locating the **Digital Clock** application.

3. ***Compiling the application.*** In the shell window, type

```
g++ -o DigitalClock DigitalClock.cpp Time.cpp
```

and press *Enter*. The g++ command will create a single executable file named `DigitalClock`. Notice that the name of the main source code file, `DigitalClock.cpp`, is followed by another file name, `Time.cpp`. The `Time.cpp` file contains the source code for the `Time` class. When compiling multiple source code files, list each file name, separated by a space, after the name of the output file. Note that it is not necessary to specify the header file `Time.h` in the compilation command. Header files are included automatically. Type `ls` and press *Enter* again to see that the directory now contains the `DigitalClock` file (Fig. A.31).

(cont.)

Compile `DigitalClock.cpp` and
`Time.cpp`

Display a directory listing

Executable file is created

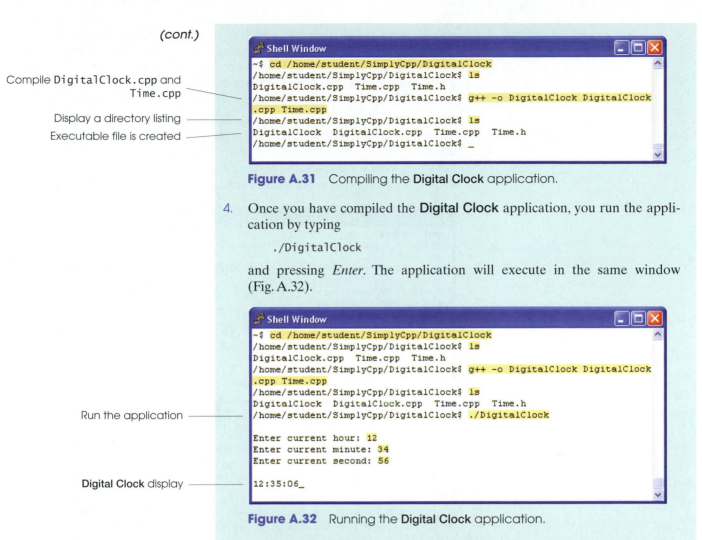

Figure A.31   Compiling the **Digital Clock** application.

4. Once you have compiled the **Digital Clock** application, you run the application by typing

    `./DigitalClock`

and pressing *Enter*. The application will execute in the same window (Fig. A.32).

Run the application

Digital Clock display

Figure A.32   Running the **Digital Clock** application.

5. ***Closing the shell window.*** Close the shell window by clicking its close button.

A.7 Using the Debugger: The watch Command

Now you will enhance your knowledge of the debugger by studying the watch command. The watch command tells the debugger to watch a variable. When that variable changes, the debugger will notify you. In this section, you will learn how to use the watch command to see how the Time object's second variable is modified during the application's execution.

Using the Debugger:
Using the watch
command

1. ***Locating the completed application.*** Open a shell window. Change to your working directory, DigitalClock, by typing cd /home/student/Simply-Cpp/DigitalClock.

2. ***Compiling the application for debugging.*** Compile your application by typing g++ -g -o DigitalClock DigitalClock.cpp Time.cpp. This command compiles both DigitalClock.cpp and Time.cpp. Recall that the -g option compiles the application for use with the debugger.

3. ***Starting the debugger.*** Start the debugger by typing gdb DigitalClock.

(cont.)

4. ***Running the application.*** Set a breakpoint at line 35 by typing break 35. Run the application with the run command. The application will prompt you to enter the current hour, minute and second values. Enter 12 for the hour, 34 for the minutes, and 56 for the seconds. After a Time object is instantiated in line 33, program execution pauses at the breakpoint at line 35.

5. ***Watching a class's instance variable.*** Set a watchpoint on Time's second data member by typing **watch** localTime.second (Fig. A.33). You can set a watch on any variable currently in scope during program execution in the debugger. Whenever the value of a watched variable is about to change, the debugger enters break mode and indicates that the change that will occur.

Setting the watchpoint on
localTime.second

```
Shell Window
(gdb) break 35
Breakpoint 1 at 0x80489ed: file DigitalClock.cpp, line 35.
(gdb) run
Starting program: /home/student/SimplyCpp/DigitalClock/DigitalClock

Enter current hour: 12
Enter current minute: 34
Enter current second: 56


Breakpoint 1, main () at DigitalClock.cpp:35
35          localTime.displayTime();
(gdb) watch localTime.second
Hardware watchpoint 2: localTime.second
(gdb) _
```

Figure A.33   Setting a watchpoint on localTime.second.

6. ***Changing the second data member.*** Type continue to continue program execution. After a one second pause, the while statement in line 43 will terminate, and line 45 will call localTime's tick function. Recall that the tick function adds one to the current value of the second data member and assigns to second the remainder of that value divided by 60. In this case, the value of localTime.second is about to change from 56 to 57, and the debugger indicates this change as shown in Fig. A.34. Note that the value of localTime.second is modified by line 93 of the Time.cpp file, in the setSecond function.

Changing the value of
localTime.second causes the
debugger to enter break mode

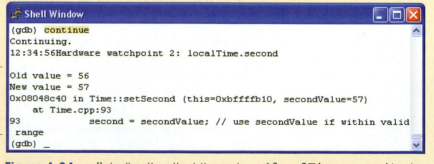
```
Shell Window
(gdb) continue
Continuing.
12:34:56Hardware watchpoint 2: localTime.second

Old value = 56
New value = 57
0x08048c40 in Time::setSecond (this=0xbffffb10, secondValue=57)
    at Time.cpp:93
93              second = secondValue; // use secondValue if within valid
  range
(gdb) _
```

Figure A.34   gdb indicating that the value of localTime.second is about to change.

7. ***Continuing execution.*** Type continue—the application will continue executing. After about a second, the tick function will be called and the application will enter break mode again. The debugger notifies you that the value of localTime.second is about to change again (Fig. A.35).

(cont.)

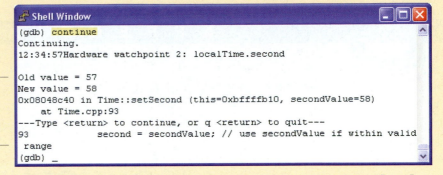

Changing the value of `localTime.second` causes the debugger to enter break mode

Figure A.35 Debugger enters break mode when the value of `local-Time.second` is about to change again.

8. ***Removing the watch on the variable.*** Type `info break` to display the current breakpoint and watchpoint. Notice that the watchpoint on `local-Time.second` is given number 2 because breakpoints and watchpoints share the same numbering sequence. Remove the debugger's watch on the variable by typing `delete 2` (Fig. A.36). Type `continue`—the application will continue executing without re-entering break mode.

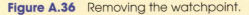

Figure A.36 Removing the watchpoint.

9. ***Closing the running application.*** Close your running application by pressing and holding *Ctrl* while pressing *C*. The debugger will stop running the application (Fig. A.37). Type `quit` and enter y at the **Exit anyway?** prompt to exit the debugger.

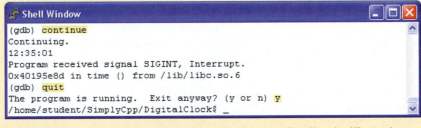

Ctrl-C sends an `Interrupt` signal, stopping the application execution

Figure A.37 Exiting the debugger while the application is still running.

10. ***Close the shell window.***

APPENDIX

Operator Precedence Chart

n Fig. B.1, operators are shown in decreasing order of precedence from top to bottom.

Operator	Type	Associativity
::	binary scope resolution	left to right
::	unary scope resolution	
()	parentheses	left to right
[]	array subscript	
.	member selection via object	
->	member selection via pointer	
++	unary postincrement	
--	unary postdecrement	
typeid	run-time type information	
dynamic_cast< *type* >	run-time type-checked cast	
static_cast< *type* >	compile-time type-checked cast	
reinterpret_cast< *type* >	cast for non-standard conversions	
const_cast< *type* >	cast away const-ness	
++	unary preincrement	right to left
--	unary predecrement	
+	unary plus	
-	unary minus	
!	unary logical negation	
~	unary bitwise complement	
(*type*)	C-style unary cast	
sizeof	determine size in bytes	
&	address	
*	dereference	
new	dynamic memory allocation	
new[]	dynamic array allocation	
delete	dynamic memory deallocation	
delete[]	dynamic array deallocation	

Figure B.1   Operator precedence chart. (Part 1 of 2.)

Operator	Type	Associativity
.* ->*	pointer to member via object pointer to member via pointer	left to right
* / %	multiplication division modulus	left to right
+ -	addition subtraction	left to right
<< >>	bitwise left shift bitwise right shift	left to right
< <= > >=	relational less than relational less than or equal to relational greater than relational greater than or equal to	left to right
== !=	relational is equal to relational is not equal to	left to right
&	bitwise AND	left to right
^	bitwise exclusive OR	left to right
|	bitwise inclusive OR	left to right
&&	logical AND	left to right
||	logical OR	left to right
?:	ternary conditional	right to left
= += -= *= /= %= &= ^= |= <<= >>=	assignment addition assignment subtraction assignment multiplication assignment division assignment modulus assignment bitwise AND assignment bitwise exclusive OR assignment bitwise inclusive OR assignment bitwise left-shift assignment bitwise right-shift assignment	right to left
,	comma	left to right

Figure B.1 Operator precedence chart. (Part 2 of 2.)

APPENDIX

ASCII Character Set

The digits in the left column of Fig. C.1 are the left digits of the decimal equivalent (0–127) of the character code, and the digits in the top row of Fig. C.1 are the right digits of the character code. For example, the character code for "F" is 70, and the character code for "&" is 38.

Most users of this book are interested in the ASCII character set used to represent English characters on many computers. The ASCII character set is a subset of the Unicode® character set used by Java to represent characters from most of the world's languages.

	0	1	2	3	4	5	6	7	8	9
0	nul	soh	stx	etx	eot	enq	ack	bel	bs	ht
1	lf	vt	ff	cr	so	si	dle	dc1	dc2	dc3
2	dc4	nak	syn	etb	can	em	sub	esc	fs	gs
3	rs	us	sp	!	"	#	$	%	&	'
4	(	)	*	+	,	-	.	/	0	1
5	2	3	4	5	6	7	8	9	:	;
6	<	=	>	?	@	A	B	C	D	E
7	F	G	H	I	J	K	L	M	N	O
8	P	Q	R	S	T	U	V	W	X	Y
9	Z	[	\	]	^	_	'	a	b	c
10	d	e	f	g	h	i	j	k	l	m
11	n	o	p	q	r	s	t	u	v	w
12	x	y	z	{			}	~	del		

Figure C.1 ASCII character set.

C++ Standard Library Reference

This appendix contains a listing of C++ Standard Library header files and the corresponding predefined functions, objects and classes that are used in the text. Each header file, function, object or class includes a description of its purpose.

Tutorial 1: Car Payment Calculator and Guess the Number Applications (Introducing Computers, the Internet and C++ Programming)

No new elements.

Tutorial 2: Welcome Application (Introduction to C++ Programming)

iostream Provides access to the basic services required for all stream-I/O operations.

■ *Object*

cout—Displays text on the screen. Text is displayed using the stream insertion operator (<<).

Tutorial 3: Inventory Application (Introducing Variables, Input, Memory Concepts and Arithmetic)

iostream Provides access to the basic services required for all stream-I/O operations.

■ *Objects*

cin—This object reads characters entered at the keyboard. Text is sent to the application when the user presses *Enter* and placed in a variable using the stream extraction operator, >>.

cout—Displays text on the screen. Text is displayed using the stream insertion operator (<<).

■ *Stream manipulator*

endl—This object places a newline into the output stream and flushes the stream's buffer so that all text stored in the output stream object is displayed immediately.

613

Tutorial 4: Wage Calculator Application (Introducing Algorithms, Pseudocode, and Program Control)

iomanip Provides access to parameterized stream manipulators.

■ *Stream manipulators*

fixed—This stream manipulator specifies that floating-point numbers should be printed using fixed-point notation (as opposed to scientific notation).

setprecision—This stream manipulator specifies that numeric values should be printed using the specified number of digits to the right of the decimal point. The argument to setprecision determines the number of digits that are displayed to the right of the decimal point when a floating-point value is printed.

Tutorial 5: Dental Payment Application (Introducing Logical Operators, chars, and strings)

string Declares classes and functions that store and manipulate strings.

■ *Object*

string—This object stores a string of characters.

■ *Functions*

size—This function returns the number of characters (as an int) in the string on which it is called.

getline—This function places characters from the specified input stream into the specified string object until a newline is reached. For example, the statements

```
string string1;
getline( cin, string1 );
```

cause the application to read from cin an entire line of text and store it in string variable string1.

Tutorial 6: Car Payment Calculator Application (Introducing the while Repetition Statement)

iostream This header file provides access to the basic services required for all stream-I/O operations.

■ *Objects*

cin—This object reads characters entered at the keyboard. Text is sent to the application when the user presses *Enter* and placed in a variable using the stream extraction operator, >>.

cout—This object displays text on the screen. Text is displayed using the stream insertion operator (<<).

■ *Stream manipulators*

endl—This object places a newline into the output stream and flushes the stream's buffer so that all text stored in the output stream object is displayed immediately.

fixed—This stream manipulator specifies that floating-point numbers should be printed using fixed-point notation (as opposed to scientific notation).

left—This object causes values to be left justified in a field. The stream into which left is inserted remains left justified until the application terminates or until the stream's justification is changed, whichever comes first.

iomanip This header file provides access to parameterized stream manipulators.

■ *Stream manipulators*

setprecision—This stream manipulator specifies that numeric values should be printed using the specified number of digits to the right of the decimal point. The argument to setprecision determines the number of digits that are displayed to the right of the decimal point when a floating-point value is printed.

setw—This stream manipulator indicates that (only) the next value should appear in a field of the specified width. If the value to be output is less than the specified width, the value is right justified in the field by default. If the value to be output is greater than the specified width, the field is expanded to the right to the appropriate width.

Tutorial 7: Class Average Application (Introducing Sentinel-Controlled Repetition)
No new elements.

Tutorial 8: Interest Calculator Application (Introducing the for Repetition Statement and the Math Library)
cmath This header provides access to functions that perform common arithmetic calculations.

- **Function**

  pow—This function performs exponentiation. The first argument specifies the value that will be raised to a power, and the second argument specifies the power to which the first argument will be raised.

Tutorial 9: Income Tax Calculator Application (Introducing the switch Multiple Selection Statement)
No new elements.

Tutorial 10: Enhancing the Wage Calculator Application (Introducing Functions)
cmath This library provides functions that perform common arithmetic calculations.

- **Functions**

  pow—This function performs exponentiation. The first argument specifies the value that will be raised to a power, and the second argument specifies the power to which the first argument will be raised.

  sqrt—This function returns the square root of a numeric argument.

algorithm This library provides functions that implement common algorithms, such as searching and sorting.

- **Functions**

  max—This function returns the larger of two numeric arguments.

  min—This function returns the smaller of two numeric arguments.

Tutorial 11: Fundraiser Application (Introducing Scope and Function Prototypes)
No new elements.

Tutorial 12: Craps Game Application (Introducing Random Number Generations and Enumerations)

cstdlib   This header file provides access to functions that convert numbers to text and text to numbers, generate random numbers and perform other utility capabilities.

■ *Functions*

   rand—This function generates an int value selected from 0 to RAND_MAX.

   srand—This function seeds the rand function, which determines the sequence of numbers that the application will generate. The srand function typically is used with an argument of time(0) to ensure that an application generates a different sequence of random numbers each time it is run.

ctime   This header file provides access to functions and types for manipulating and storing the time and date.

■ *Function*

   time—This function returns the current time, in seconds. The time is determined by calculating the number of seconds that have passed since midnight on January 1, 1970 (using UTC—Universal Time, also called Greenwich Mean Time).

Tutorial 13: Salary Survey Application (Introducing One-Dimensional Arrays)

   No new elements.

Tutorial 14: Student Grades Application (Introducing Two-Dimensional Arrays and References)

iostream   This header file declares basic services required for all stream-I/O operations.

■ *Objects*

   cin—This object reads characters entered at the keyboard. Text is sent to the application when the user presses *Enter* and can be placed in a variable using the stream extraction operator, >>.

   cout—This object displays text on the screen. Text can be displayed using the stream insertion operator, <<.

■ *Stream manipulators*

   endl—This object places a newline into the output stream and flushes the stream's buffer so that all text stored in the output stream object is displayed immediately.

   fixed—This stream manipulator specifies that floating-point numbers should be printed using fixed-point notation (as opposed to scientific notation).

   left—This object causes values to be left justified in a field. The stream into which left is inserted remains left justified until the application terminates or until the stream's justification is changed, whichever comes first.

   right—This object causes values to be right justified in a field. The stream into which right is inserted remains right justified until the application terminates or until the stream's justification is changed, whichever comes first.

Tutorial 15: Digital Clock Application (Building Your Own Classes and Objects)

`ctime` This library header provides function prototypes and types for manipulating the time and date.

- **Function**

    `time`—This function returns the current time, in seconds. The time is determined by calculating the number of seconds that have passed since midnight on January 1, 1970 (using UTC—Universal Time, also called Greenwich Mean Time).

- **Type**

    `time_t`—This type can be used to create variables that store a number of seconds. `time_t` values are typically represented by `long`s because the value returned by the `time` function can be larger than an `int` on some systems.

`iomanip` This library header is used to format stream input and output.

- **Stream manipulators**

    `setfill`—This stream manipulator specifies the character that fills unoccupied positions in a field.

    `setprecision`—This stream manipulator specifies that numeric values should be printed using the specified number of digits to the right of the decimal point. The argument to `setprecision` determines the number of digits that are displayed to the right of the decimal point when a floating-point value is printed.

`iostream` This header file declares basic services required for all stream-I/O operations.

- **Objects**

    `cin`—This object reads characters entered at the keyboard. Text is sent to the application when the user presses *Enter* and can be placed in a variable using the stream extraction operator, `>>`.

    `cout`—This object displays text on the screen. Text can be displayed using the stream insertion operator, `<<`.

- **Stream manipulators**

    `endl`—This object places a newline into the output stream and flushes the stream's buffer so that all text stored in the output stream object is displayed immediately.

    `fixed`—This stream manipulator specifies that floating-point numbers should be printed using fixed-point notation (as opposed to scientific notation).

    `flush`—This stream manipulator flushes the output buffer so that output is displayed on the screen immediately.

    `left`—This object causes values to be left justified in a field. The stream into which `left` is inserted remains left justified until the application terminates or until the stream's justification is changed, whichever comes first.

    `right`—This object causes values to be right justified in a field. The stream into which `right` is inserted remains right justified until the application terminates or until the stream's justification is changed, whichever comes first.

Tutorial 16: Shopping List Application (Introducing Pointers, References and Dynamic Data Structures)

`iostream` This header file declares basic services required for stream-I/O operations.

- **Function**

    `cin.ignore()`—Removes the next character from the input stream.

■ *Objects*

cin—Reads characters entered at the keyboard. Text is sent to the application when the user presses *Enter* and can be placed in a variable using the stream extraction operator, >>.

cout—Displays text on the screen. Text can be displayed using the stream insertion operator (<<).

■ *Stream manipulators*

endl—This object places a newline into the output stream and flushes the stream's buffer so that all text stored in the output stream object is displayed immediately.

fixed—This stream manipulator specifies that floating-point numbers should be printed using fixed-point notation (as opposed to scientific notation).

flush—This stream manipulator flushes the output buffer so that output is displayed on the screen immediately.

left—This object causes values to be left justified in a field. The stream into which left is inserted remains left justified until the application terminates or until the stream's justification is changed, whichever comes first.

right—This object causes values to be right justified in a field. The stream into which right is inserted remains right justified until the application terminates or until the stream's justification is changed, whichever comes first.

Tutorial 17: Payroll Application (Introducing Inheritance and Polymorphism)

No new elements.

Tutorial 18: Ticket Information Application (Introducing Sequential-Access Files)

cstdlib This library contains function prototypes for conversion of numbers to text and text to numbers, generation of random numbers and other utility functions.

■ *Functions*

exit—This function causes the application to terminate. An argument of 0 to the function notifies the system that the application terminated normally; an argument of 1 indicates that the application terminated due to an error.

rand—This function generates an int value selected from 0 to RAND_MAX.

srand—This function seeds the rand function, which determines the sequence of numbers that the application will generate. The srand function typically is used with an argument of time(0) to ensure that an application generates a different sequence of random numbers each time it is run.

fstream This header file contains functions and classes that access files.

■ *Constructors*

ifstream—This constructor takes a file name as an argument and opens that file for reading. The resulting ifstream object can read data from the specified file. The following code demonstrates the use of this constructor.

```
ifstream inputFile( "current.txt" );
```

ofstream—This constructor opens the file corresponding to the name specified by the string in the first argument using the file-open mode specified as the second argument. The second argument indicates whether new data should be appended (ios::app) to the end of the file or replace the existing data (ios::out). If the second argument is not specified, the file is opened in ios::out mode. The following code demonstrates the use of this constructor.

```
ofstream currentFile( "current.txt", ios::app );
```

■ *Function*

eof—This function returns true if the ifstream has reached the end of the file and false otherwise.

---

string This header file declares classes and functions that store and manipulate strings.

■ *Object*

string—This object stores a string of characters.

■ *Functions*

c_str—This function returns an array of characters containing the text stored by a string.

getline—This function places characters from the specified input stream into the specified string object until a newline is reached. For example, the statements

```
string string1;
getline( cin, string1 );
```

cause the application to read from cin an entire line of text and store it in string variable string1.

size—This function returns the number of characters (as an int) in the string on which it is called.

Tutorial 19: Screen Scraping Application (Introducing string processing)

cstdlib This library contains function prototypes for conversion of numbers to text, and text to numbers, generation of random numbers and other utility functions.

■ *Functions*

atof—This function converts its argument—an array of ASCII characters that represents a floating-point number—to a double value. If the array of characters cannot be converted, the atof function returns 0.

exit—This function causes the application to terminate. An argument of 0 to the function notifies the system that the application terminated normally; an argument of 1 indicates that the application terminated due to an error.

rand—This function generates an int value selected from 0 to RAND_MAX.

srand—This function seeds the rand function, which determines the sequence of numbers that the application will generate. The srand function typically is used with an argument of time(0) to ensure that an application generates a different sequence of random numbers each time it is run.

---

string The string class represents a sequence of characters treated as a single unit.

■ *Functions*

at—This function returns the character located at a specific index in a string.

c_str—This function returns an array of characters containing the text stored by a string.

compare—This function compares the contents of two strings and returns 0 if the two strings are equal. In the expression string1.compare(string2), the compare function returns a negative number if string1 precedes string2 in alphabetical order or a positive number if string2 precedes string1 in alphabetical order.

empty—This function returns true if the string does not contain any characters, and returns false otherwise.

find—This function returns the index of the first occurrence of its string argument in the string, and −1 if the string argument is not found.

find_first_not_of—This function returns the index of the first occurrence in a string of any character not in its string argument, and returns string::npos if all of the string argument's characters are contained in the string.

find_first_of—This function returns the index of the first occurrence in a string of any character in the function's string argument, and returns string::npos if none of the string argument's characters are contained in the string.

getline—This function places characters from the specified input stream into the specified string object until a newline is reached. For example, the statements

```
string string1;
getline( cin, string1 );
```

cause the application to read from cin an entire line of text and store it in string variable string1.

length—This function returns the number of characters in a string. Same as size.

replace—This function replaces in a string a number of characters (the second argument) beginning at the specified index (the first argument) with the specified string (third) argument.

rfind—This function returns the index of the last occurrence of its string argument in a string. It returns –1 if the string argument is not found.

size—This function returns the number of characters in a string. Same as length.

substr—This function creates a new string object by copying part of an existing string object.

■ *Constant*

npos—A value returned by the string find-related functions to indicate that a string or character was not found in the string.

Tutorial 20: Enhanced Car Payment Calculator Application (Introducing Exception Handling)

exception This header file contains the definition of the base class that represents most exceptions.

■ *Class*

exception—A class that represents an exceptional situation occurring in a C++ application that should be caught and handled by the application.

---

iostream This header file declares basic services required for all stream-I/O operations.

■ *Data member*

failbit—A bit that is set when a format error occurs on a stream.

■ *Exception*

ios_base::failure—Exception thrown when the error bit specified by the exceptions function call is set.

■ *Functions*

clear—Restores a stream's state to "good," so that I/O may proceed on the stream.

exceptions—Causes a stream object to throw an exception of type ios_base::failure when the specified error occurs.

fail—Returns true if an error has occurred, such as when failbit is set.

ignore—Removes the next character from the input stream.

■ *Objects*

cin—Reads characters entered at the keyboard. Text is sent to the application when the user presses *Enter* and placed in a variable using the stream extraction operator, >>.

cout—Displays text on the screen. Text is displayed using the stream-insertion operator (<<).

■ *Stream manipulators*

`endl`—This object places a newline into the output stream and flushes the stream's buffer so that all text stored in the output stream object is displayed immediately.

`fixed`—This stream manipulator specifies that floating-point numbers should be printed using fixed-point notation (as opposed to scientific notation).

`flush`—This stream manipulator flushes the output buffer so that output is displayed on the screen immediately.

`left`—This object causes values to be left justified in a field. The stream into which `left` is inserted remains left justified until the application terminates or until the stream's justification is changed, whichever comes first.

`right`—This object causes values to be right justified in a field. The stream into which `right` is inserted remains right justified until the application terminates or until the stream's justification is changed, whichever comes first.

Tutorial 21: Grade Book Application (Introducing Templates)

No new elements.

Tutorial 22: Phone Book Application (Introducing Operator Overloading)

No new elements.

E APPENDIX

Keyword Chart

T he table in Fig. E.1 contains a listing of C++ keywords. Many of these keywords are discussed throughout the text.

C++ Keywords

Keywords common to the C and C++ programming languages

auto	break	case	char
continue	default	do	double
enum	extern	float	for
if	int	long	register
short	signed	sizeof	static
switch	typedef	union	unsigned
volatile	while		

C++ only keywords

asm	bool	catch	class
delete	dynamic_cast	explicit	false
inline	mutable	namespace	new
private	protected	public	reinterpret_cast
static_cast	template	this	throw
try	typeid	typename	using
wchar_t			

Figure E.1   C++ keywords.

Symbols

 # (preprocessor operator)—An operator that must begin each statement that is processed by the C++ preprocessor.

* operator (unary version)—The dereferencing operator, which, when applied to a pointer, returns a synonym for the object to which its pointer operand points.

.. directory—A shortcut to the parent directory.

A

abstract class—A class that cannot be used to instantiate objects. It is often called an abstract base class because it is usable only as a base class in an inheritance hierarchy. These classes are incomplete; they are missing pieces necessary for instantiation that concrete derived classes must implement. The missing pieces are pure `virtual` functions.

accessor—A function that retrieves the value of a data member; a *get* function.

action expression (in the UML)—An expression used in an action state within a UML activity diagram to specify a particular action to perform.

action state (in the UML)—An action (represented by an action-state symbol) to perform in a UML activity diagram.

action-state symbol (in the UML)—A rectangle with its left and right sides replaced with arcs curving outward that represents an action to perform in a UML activity diagram.

action/decision model of programming—Representing control statements as *actions* to be performed and *decisions* to be made. In a UML activity diagram, actions are represented by action-state symbols and decisions are represented by diamond symbols.

activity diagram (in the UML)—A UML diagram that models the activity (also called the workflow) of a portion of a software system.

Ada—A programming language, named after Lady Ada Lovelace, developed under the sponsorship of the U.S. Department of Defense in the 1970s and early 1980s.

addition assignment operator (+=)—An operator that adds the value of its right operand to the current value of its left operand and stores the result in the left operand.

address operator (&)—A unary operator that returns the memory address of its operand.

algorithm—A procedure for solving a problem, specifying the actions to be executed and the order in which these actions are to be executed.

argument—Data that a function call sends to the called function. That data is passed to the corresponding parameter in the called function's header.

argument coercion—A feature of function prototypes that forces the arguments in a function call to the appropriate types specified by the parameter declarations.

argument list—A comma-separated list of the arguments sent to a function. The number, order and type of arguments must agree with the parameters in the function's parameter list.

arithmetic and logic unit (ALU)—The "manufacturing" section of the computer. The ALU performs calculations and makes decisions.

arithmetic operators—The +, -, *, / and % operators, used for performing calculations.

array—A data structure containing elements of the same type. Elements of an array are accessed by specifying an integer index in the range 0 to one less than the number of elements in the array.

array initializer—A comma-separated list of constant expressions enclosed in braces—{ and }—which is used to initialize the elements in an array. When there are fewer initializers than elements in the array, C++ explicitly initializes the elements corresponding to values in the initializer list and implicitly initializes the remaining elements to zero. When there is no initializer list, the elements in the array are not initialized.

arrow operator (->)—An operator that accesses a class member using a pointer to an object.

ASCII (American Standard Code for Information Interchange)—A character set, popular in personal computers and data communication systems, that stores characters as one byte.

assembly language—A type of programming language that uses English-like abbreviations to represent the fundamental operations of the computer.

assignment operator—The assignment operator, =, copies the value of the expression on its right side into the variable on its left side.

asterisk (*)—An arithmetic operator that indicates multiplication.

at function of the `string` class—A function that returns the character located at a specific index in a `string`.

atof function of the `<cstdlib>` library—A function that converts its argument—an array of ASCII characters that represents a floating-point number—to a `double` value. If the array of characters cannot be converted, the `atof` function returns 0.

attribute—A characteristic of an object that corresponds to a data member; another name for a property of an object.

Autos window—A feature of the Microsoft Visual C++ .NET debugger and other popular debuggers that allows you to view the values stored in an object's data members.

B

bandwidth—The information-carrying capacity of communications lines, typically expressed in bits per second.

base class—A class that is extended by another class to form a derived class. The derived class inherits from the base class.

base-class initializer syntax—A technique for initializing a base class's `private` data members from a derived-class constructor. A base-class initializer is formed using the base-class name, followed by a set of parentheses containing the base-class constructor arguments. In a constructor for a derived class, the base-class initializer appears between the constructor's parameter list and the left brace that begins the constructor's body. The base-class initializer is separated from the parameter list with a colon.

BASIC (Beginner's All-Purpose Symbolic Instruction Code)—A programming language developed in the mid-1960s by Professors Kemeny and Kurtz of Dartmouth College as a language for writing simple programs. Its primary purpose was to familiarize novices with programming techniques.

behavior—A characteristic of an object that corresponds to a member function.

binary digit—A digit that can assume one of two values (0 or 1).

binary operator—An operator that requires two operands.

binary scope resolution operator (::)—The operator that ties a member to a particular class. When a member function is defined outside its class's definition, the name of the function must be preceded by the name of the class followed by the binary scope resolution operator.

bit—Short for "binary digit," this is the smallest data item a computer can support.

block—A set of statements enclosed in curly braces ({ and }).

block scope—The scope for a local variable or a function parameter. Block scope is from the variable's definition (or declaration) to the terminating right brace (}) of the block in which the variable is defined (or declared).

body of a function—The group of statements contained inside a function. The body of a function begins with a left brace, {, and ends at the corresponding right brace, }.

"bombing"—Occurs when an application encounters a fatal logic error, causing the application to terminate unexpectedly.

bool type—A type that stores either the value `true` or the value `false`.

boolean expression—An expression with a true or false value that is used to make a decision.

break mode—The debugger mode the application is in when execution stops at a breakpoint.

break statement—The statement that typically appears at the end of each `case`. This statement immediately terminates the `switch` statement, and program control continues with the next statement after the closing right brace of the `switch`.

breakpoint—A marker that can be set in the debugger at any executable line of source code, causing the application to pause when it reaches the specified line. One reason to set a breakpoint is to be able to examine the values of variables at that point in the application's execution.

bug—A flaw in an application (sometimes called a logic error) that prevents the application from executing correctly.

busy waiting—This occurs when an application repeatedly tests a condition that will allow it to proceed eventually.

byte—A piece of data typically composed of eight bits.

C

c_str function of the string class—A function that returns the text contained in a `string` as an array of characters.

callee—The function being called.

caller—The function that calls another function. It is also known as the calling function.

calling a function—An action that causes a function to perform its designated task. It is also called invoking a function.

case label—The label that precedes the statements that will execute if the `switch`'s controlling expression matches the expression in the `case` label.

case sensitive—A property of a programming language that distinguishes between uppercase and lowercase letters in code.

cast operator (unary)—The unary operator (`static_cast`) that converts its operand to the type placed within its associated angle brackets.

catch an exception—Execute an exception handler when the application detects an exceptional situation and throws an exception of the type specified by the exception handler.

catch block—Also called an exception handler, this block executes when the corresponding `try` block in the application detects an exceptional situation and throws an exception of the type the `catch` block declares as its exception parameter.

central processing unit (CPU)—The part of the computer's hardware that is responsible for supervising the operation of the other units of the computer.

chaining stream insertion or extraction operators—Occurs when multiple stream insertion (<<) or extraction (>>) operators are used in a single statement.

char type—The primitive type used to store character values.

character—A digit, letter or special symbol. (Characters in C++ are normally composed of one byte. Characters represented by the `wchar_t` type are composed of multiple bytes.)

character constant—Another name for a character literal.

character literal—The value of a variable of the `char` type, represented by a character within single quotes, such as `'A'`, `'d'`, `'*'`, `'.'`, `' '` and the like.

character set—The set of all characters used to represent data items on a particular computer. C++ uses the ASCII character set by default.

checked access—This ensures that an application can access only data made available by a variable. For example, range checking prevents an application from accessing data outside the range of values contained in a variable.

cin (the standard input stream)—An object that has the ability to retrieve keyboard input from the user.

class—The type of a group of similar objects. A class specifies the general format of its objects; the properties and actions available to an object depend on its class. An object is to its class much as a house is to its blueprint.

class hierarchy—A definition of the inheritance relationships among classes. It is also known as an inheritance hierarchy.

class keyword—The keyword that indicates that what follows is a class definition.

class template—A placeholder for a class that is defined using the `template` keyword and that specifies at least one formal type parameter. A class template is defined generically to allow several different class-template specializations to be created from one class template definition.

class-template specialization—A class that the compiler generates and compiles using the corresponding class template. For example, when a client of a class template instantiates an object, the client specifies the type for each of the class template's type parameters. The compiler then associates each specified type with the corresponding type parameter in the class template to produce the source code for the class-template specialization.

class's body—Code that is included in the { and } of a class definition.

clear function of class ios—Restores a stream's state to "good," so that I/O may proceed on the stream.

client—When you create and use an object of a class in a function, you and the function are known as clients of that class.

<cmath> header file—This header file provides access to functions that perform common arithmetic calculations.

COBOL (COmmon Business Oriented Language)—A programming language developed in the late 1950s by a group of computer manufacturers in conjunction with government and industrial computer users. This language is used primarily for business applications that manipulate large amounts of data.

code reuse—Using pre-existing code to save time, effort and money; reusing carefully developed code can result in better programs than if you write all the code yourself.

column—In referring to an element of a two-dimensional array, the second index specifies the column.

comment—Text in a source code file that increases code readability by explaining the code. Comments are ignored by the compiler.

compare function of the string class—A function that compares the contents of two strings. It returns 0 if the two strings are equal. In the expression string1.compare(string2) the compare function returns a negative number if string1 precedes string2 in alphabetical order or a positive number if string2 precedes string1 in alphabetical order.

compilation error—An error detected by the compiler, such as a syntax error. Also called a compile-time error.

compiler—A translator program that converts high-level-language programs into machine language, so the programs may be executed on a computer.

complex condition—A condition that combines multiple simple conditions.

compound assignment operator—A symbol used for abbreviating assignment expressions that contain the same variable on both sides of the assignment expression.

computer—A device capable of performing computations and making logical decisions at speeds millions and even billions of times faster than the speeds at which human beings carry out those same tasks.

computer program—A set of instructions that guides a computer through an orderly series of actions to solve a problem.

computer programmer—A person who writes computer programs in programming languages.

concatenating stream insertion operators—Occurs when multiple stream insertion operators (<<) are used in a single statement. The operands do not have to be of the same type because the stream insertion operator "knows" how to place values of different types into the output stream. Also called chaining, or cascading, stream insertion operators.

concatenation of two strings—This occurs when one string is appended to another string.

concrete class—A class that can be used to instantiate objects.

condition—A bool expression (that is, an expression that evaluates to either true or false) that is used to make a decision.

consistent state—A description of an object whose data members contain values that are valid. Classes typically provide *get* and *set* functions to ensure that objects of the class remain in a consistent state.

const keyword—The keyword that precedes the data type in a definition of a constant.

constant—A variable whose value cannot be changed after its initialization in its definition.

constant expression—An expression whose value cannot be changed. A case label consists of the case keyword, followed by a constant expression, followed by a colon. This constant expression must be a character literal or an integer literal.

constructor—A function of a class that initializes the class's variables and has the same name as the class that contains it. A constructor cannot have a return type.

Continue debugger command—The debugger command used to execute until the next breakpoint is reached or until main terminates, whichever comes first.

control statement—A program statement (such as if, if...else, switch, while, do...while or for) that specifies the flow of control (that is, the order in which statements execute).

control variable—A variable used to control the number of iterations of a counter-controlled loop.

controlling expression—The expression in a switch statement whose value is compared sequentially with each case until either a match occurs, the default case is executed or the closing right brace is reached.

control-statement nesting—Placing one control statement in the body of another control statement.

control-statement stacking—Setting control statements in sequence. The exit point of one control statement is "connected" to the entry point of the next control statement in sequence.

counter—A variable often used to determine the number of times a block of statements in a loop will execute.

counter-controlled repetition—A technique that uses a counter variable to determine the number of times that a block of statements will execute. It is also called definite repetition.

cout (the standard output stream)—An object that has the ability to display text.

.cpp file—The type of file in which programmers write the C++ code for an application; also called a "C++ source code file."

"crashing"—*See* bombing.

<cstdlib> Standard Library header file—A header file that enables access to functions for conversion of numbers to text and text to numbers, generation of random numbers and other utility functions.

<ctime> Standard Library header file—A header file that enables access to functions and types for manipulating and storing the time and date.

cursor—The current screen-position indicator. When an application displays text, the next character is displayed at the cursor, and the cursor is advanced to the position just after the end of the character. When the user inputs text at the keyboard, the next character that is entered is typically displayed at the cursor, and the cursor is advanced to the position just after the end of the character.

D

data hierarchy—The collection of data items processed by computers, which become larger and more complex in structure as you progress from bits to characters to fields to files to databases.

data member—A variable defined within the body of a class.

data structure—An entity that groups and organizes related data.

database—A group of related files; an organized collection of information.

database management system (DBMS)—A collection of programs designed to create and manage databases.

debugger—Software that allows you to monitor the execution of your applications to locate and remove logic errors.

debugging—The process of locating and correcting errors in an application.

decimal digits—The digits 0, 1, 2, 3, 4, 5, 6, 7, 8 and 9.

decision symbol (in the UML)—The diamond-shaped symbol in a UML activity diagram that indicates a decision is to be made.

declaring a function—Using a function prototype to tell the compiler the name of a function, the type of data returned by that function, the number of parameters that function expects to receive, the types of those parameters and the order in which the parameters of those types are expected.

decrementing a variable—The process of subtracting one from an integer variable.

default case—The optional case whose statements execute if a switch statement's controlling expression does not match any of the cases' values.

default constructor—A constructor that accepts no arguments.

default precision—The precision with which C++ prints floating-point values by default. Normally, these values are displayed with six digits of precision.

#define preprocessor directive—A preprocessor directive that defines the name that appears immediately after the directive.

defining a variable—Specifying the type and name of a variable to be used in an application.

defining a function—Creating a function, which includes a function header followed by a left brace, the statements that execute when the function is called and a right brace.

definite repetition—*See* counter-controlled repetition.

definition of a variable—Code that specifies the name and type of a variable.

delete operator—An operator that deallocates memory allocated with the new operator. The delete operator calls the destructor for its operand.

delimit—Terminate. For example, the stream extraction operator delimits (i.e., terminates) input at whitespace characters.

dereferencing a pointer—Using the * operator on a pointer to create a synonym or alias for the variable to which it points.

dereferencing operator—*See* * operator.

derived class—A class that is derived from (inherits from) another class (called a base class).

destructive operation—The process of writing to a memory location in which the previous value is overwritten or lost.

destructor—A function that executes just before an object is removed from the system.

diamond (in the UML)—The symbol (also known as the decision symbol) in a UML activity diagram that indicates a decision is to be made.

diamond symbol (in the UML)—The UML symbol that represents the decision symbol or the merge symbol, depending on how it is used.

direct base class—The base class from which the derived class inherits.

disable a breakpoint (Visual Studio .NET)—Action that prevents the debugger from breaking at a breakpoint. A disabled breakpoint is displayed as a hollow maroon circle in the margin indicator bar, enabling you to reenable the breakpoint easily by clicking inside the circle.

divide-and-conquer technique—The technique of constructing large applications from small, manageable pieces to make development and maintenance of those applications easier.

do...while repetition statement— A control statement that executes a set of body statements while the loop-continuation condi-

tion is true. The condition is tested after the loop body executes, so the body statements always execute at least once.

dotted line (in the UML)—A UML activity diagram symbol that connects each UML-style note with the element that the note describes.

double type—A type that is used to store floating-point numbers (i.e., numbers with decimal points).

double-selection statement—The if...else statement; it selects between two different actions or sequences of actions.

dummy value—*See* sentinel value.

dynamic data structure—A data structure that can grow and shrink at execution time, such as a linked list.

dynamic memory allocation—Technique that allocates memory for objects at run-time (as opposed to compile-time). When that memory is no longer needed by the application, the memory can be released so that it can be allocated to other objects in the future.

E

element—An item in an array.

else clause—The block of code that is executed if the condition specified by the if part of the if...else statement is false.

empty function of the string class—A function that returns true if the string does not contain any characters, and returns false otherwise.

empty string ("")—A string value that does not contain any characters.

#endif preprocessor directive—A preprocessor directive that specifies the end of a block of code that begins with the #ifndef directive.

endl stream manipulator—A stream manipulator that places a newline in the output stream and flushes the buffer so that any text in the output stream object is displayed immediately.

end-of-file marker—A special character that marks the end of a file.

end-of-line comment—A comment that appears at the end of a line, following a statement or definition.

entry point—The location in an application's source code where execution begins. In C++, the entry point for an application is the main function.

enum keyword—The keyword that begins an enumeration.

enumeration—A user-defined type containing a group of related, named constants.

enumeration constant—A named constant representing a possible value for an enumeration type.

eof function of the ifstream class—A function that returns true if its ifstream object has reached the end of a file and false otherwise.

equality operators—The == (is equal to) and != (is not equal to) operators, which compare two values.

escape character (\)—The character that begins an escape sequence.

escape sequence—The combination of an escape character and the character that immediately follows. An escape sequence temporarily changes the way a stream of characters is processed, causing characters such as tabs, newlines and carriage returns to be printed or causing actions such as sounding the system bell.

exception—An indication of a problem that occurs during an application's execution.

exception class—Represents a type of exceptional situation occurring in a C++ application that should be caught and handled by the application.

exception handler—A `catch` block that executes when the application detects an exceptional situation and throws an exception of a type that matches the handler's exception parameter.

exception handling—A technique that enables you to separate error-handling from your application's logic by treating errors as exceptional situations. A function can throw an exception when an error occurs and provide one or more exception handlers that execute when the matching exception occurs.

`<exception>` header file—The C++ Standard Library header file containing class definitions and function prototypes that support exception handling.

exception object—An object that is thrown by a `throw` statement.

exception parameter—Identifies the exception type that the exception handler can process.

exceptions function of class `ios`—Causes a stream object to throw an exception when a stream error occurs.

`.exe` file—A Windows executable file. A `.exe` file is created by compiling the application's `.cpp` file and linking the compiler's output.

executable statement—A statement that has its effect, such as performing an action or making a decision, when the statement is encountered as the program runs. Comments are not executable statements; assignment statements, input/output statements, `return` statements and control statements are executable statements.

exit function—A function declared in the `<cstdlib>` header file that causes the application to terminate. An argument of 0 to the function notifies the system that the application terminated normally; an argument of 1 indicates that the application terminated due to an error.

explicit conversion—The type conversion that occurs when the programmer uses the cast operator to change the type of a value. An operation that converts a "larger" type to a "smaller" type can be dangerous because information can be lost.

extensible language—A language that can be "extended" with new classes.

F

`fail` function of class `ios_base`—Returns `true` if a stream error has occurred, such as when `failbit` is set. For example, the function call `cin.fail()` returns `true` if the user enters a non-numeric character when the application attempts to input an integer from the standard input stream.

`failbit` of class `ios_base`—A bit that is set when a format error occurs on a stream. This occurs, for example, if the user enters a non-numeric character when the application attempts to input an integer from the standard input stream.

`false`—One of the two possible values for an expression of type `bool`; the other is `true`.

fatal logic error—An error that causes an application to terminate unexpectedly—for example, division by zero.

field—A group of characters that conveys some meaning. For example, a field consisting of uppercase and lowercase letters might represent a person's name.

file—A collection of bytes. Applications often organize those bytes into records. Files often are used for long-term persistence of data, even after the application that created the data terminates.

file-open mode—The mode that specifies how a file is to be opened. For example, a file-open mode can enable an application to write new data starting at the beginning (`ios::out`) or the end (`ios::app`) of the file, or the file-open mode can enable the application to read data from the file.

file processing—Creating, reading from and writing to files.

file scope—The scope for a global variable. File scope is from the variable's definition to the end of the file.

fill character—A character that will appear in unoccupied positions in a field.

final state (in the UML)—A solid circle surrounded by a hollow circle (a "bull's-eye") in a UML activity diagram. It represents the end of the workflow after an application segment performs its activities.

final value of a control variable—The last value a control variable will hold before a counter-controlled loop terminates.

`find` function of the `string` class—A function that returns the index of the first occurrence of its `string` argument in a `string`, and returns `string::npos` if the substring is not found.

`find_first_not_of` function of the `string` class—A function that returns the index of the first occurrence in a `string` of any character not in a particular `string` argument, and returns `string::npos` if all of the argument `string`'s characters are contained in the `string`.

`find_first_of` function of the `string` class—A function that returns the index of the first occurrence in a `string` of any character in a particular `string` argument, and returns `string::npos` if none of the argument `string`'s characters are contained in the `string`.

`fixed` stream manipulator—Stream manipulator that causes floating-point values to be displayed using fixed-point notation (rather than scientific notation).

fixed-point format—The format that displays floating-point values with a decimal point after the value's ones digit, followed by the specified number of digits to the right of the decimal point.

flag value—*See* sentinel value.

floating-point number—A number with a decimal point, such as 2.3456, 0.0 and –845.4680.

`flush` stream manipulator—A stream manipulator that flushes the output buffer so that output is displayed on the screen immediately.

`for` keyword—The keyword that begins each `for` statement.

`for` repetition statement—A repetition statement that conveniently handles the details of counter-controlled repetition. The `for` statement header specifies all four elements essential to counter-controlled repetition.

`for` statement header/`for` header—The first line in a `for` statement. The `for` header specifies all four essential elements of counter-controlled repetition—the name of a control variable, the initial value, the increment or decrement value and the final value.

formal type parameter—A placeholder for a built-in or user-defined variable type. The type parameter is specified as an identifier, preceded by the `class` keyword, inside angle brackets following the `template` keyword. For example, in the expression `template < class T >`, the formal type parameter is T.

formatting—Modifying text's appearance for display purposes.

Fortran (FORmula TRANslator)—A programming language developed by IBM Corporation in the mid-1950s to create scientific and engineering applications that require complex mathematical computations.

forward slash (/)—The arithmetic operator that indicates division.

forward slash character (/)—Two consecutive forward slash characters indicate that the remainder of the line is a comment.

Framework Class Library (FCL)—A powerful library of reusable software components developed for Microsoft's .NET platform. The FCL provides capabilities similar to the Java class library.

<fstream> standard library header file—A C++ Standard Library header file that provides access to functions and classes that enable you to perform file stream I/O.

full-line comment—A comment that starts at the beginning of a line.

function—A portion of a C++ program that performs a task and possibly returns information when it completes that task. A function consists of a name, return type, comma-separated list of parameter declarations (if any) and executable statements enclosed in curly braces. Functions are used to divide an application into smaller, more manageable pieces that can be called from multiple places within an application.

function body—The braces, definitions and statements that appear after the function header. The function body contains statements that perform actions, generally by manipulating the parameters from the parameter list.

function call—Invoking a function, by specifying the function name and providing data (arguments) that the callee (the function being called) requires to perform its task.

function definition—The function header followed by the function body.

function header—The beginning portion of a function (including the return type, the function name and the parameter list).

function name—The identifier for a function, which when combined with the argument list, distinguishes one function from another. The function name follows the return type, can be any valid identifier and is used to call the function.

function prototype—A declaration that tells the compiler the name of a function, the type of data returned by that function, the number of parameters that function expects to receive, the types of those parameters and the order in which the parameters of those types are expected. The compiler uses function prototypes to validate function calls.

function signature—The portion of a function prototype that includes the name of the function and the types of its arguments. It is also called the signature.

function template—A placeholder for a function that is declared using the `template` keyword and that specifies at least one formal type parameter. A function template is a means for describing a function generically. When the compiler encounters a call to a function template, it creates a function-template specialization, replacing the formal type parameter(s) with the corresponding argument type(s).

function-template specialization—A function that the compiler generates and compiles using the corresponding function template. When the compiler encounters a call to a function template, it creates a function-template specialization, replacing the formal type parameter(s) with the corresponding argument type(s).

functionality—The tasks or actions an application can execute.

G

generic programming—A technique that uses templates to describe classes and functions generically by describing data types using formal type parameters. Generic programming enables the programmer to specify a family of solutions with a single code segment, thus speeding the program-development process.

get **function**—A function used to retrieve the value of a data member.

getline function—A function that places characters from the specified input stream into the specified `string` object until a newline is reached.

global variable—A variable defined in a file outside any functions in that file. The scope of a global variable is from the point at which its definition appears to the end of file.

guard condition (in the UML)—A condition contained in square brackets that must be associated with a transition arrow leading from a decision symbol in a UML activity diagram. The guard condition associated with a particular transition must be true for the workflow to continue along that path.

H

hardware—The various devices that make up a computer, including the keyboard, screen, mouse, hard drive, memory, CD-ROM and DVD drives and processing units.

header—A line of text at the top of a table that clarifies the information being displayed.

hidden variable—A global variable with the same name as a local variable is hidden while the local variable is in scope. Hidden variables can lead to logic errors.

high-level language—A type of programming language in which a single program statement accomplishes a substantial task. High-level language instructions look almost like everyday English and contain common mathematical notations.

HyperText Markup Language (HTML)—A language for marking up information to share over the World Wide Web via hyperlinked text documents.

I

identifier—A series of characters consisting of letters, digits, underscores or dollar signs used to name application units such as variables and functions.

if statement—The `if` single-selection statement performs an action (or sequence of actions) based on a condition.

if...else statement—The `if...else` double-selection statement performs an action (or sequence of actions) if a condition is true and performs a different action (or sequence of actions) if the condition is false.

#ifndef preprocessor directive—A preprocessor directive that specifies the start of a block of code that is passed to the compiler only if the name directly following the directive has not been defined. The specified block of code ends when the `#endif` preprocessor directive is encountered. Pairs of `#ifndef` and `#endif` directives are often used to prevent the same header file from being included multiple times.

ifstream object—An object that enables an application to input data from a file stream.

ignore function (of the cin object)—A function that removes a single character of input from the input stream.

implementation—The code that provides the functionality for a particular task.

implicit conversion—The type conversion that occurs when the compiler performs promotion. For example, when a `double` value is divided by an `int` value, the compiler will implicitly convert the `int` value to a `double`. Implicit conversions are "safe" in the sense that no information is lost when a value is converted.

increment (or decrement) of a control variable—The amount by which the control variable's value changes during each iteration of the loop.

incrementing a variable—The process of adding one to an integer variable.

indefinite repetition—*See* sentinel-controlled repetition.

index—An array element's position number, also called a subscript. An index either must be zero, a positive integer, or an expression that evaluates to zero or a positive integer. If an application uses an expression as an index, the expression is evaluated first to determine the index.

indexed array name—The array name followed by an index enclosed in square brackets. The indexed array name can be used on the left side of an assignment statement to place a new value into the array element. The indexed array name can be used in the right side of an assignment to retrieve the value of that array element.

indirect base class—A base class that is two or more levels up in the class hierarchy from a derived class.

indirection—The technique of referencing a value through a pointer.

indirection operator—*See* * operator.

infinite loop—A logical error in which a repetition statement never terminates.

inheritance—A form of software reuse in which a class absorbs an existing class's data members (attributes) and member functions (behaviors) and extends them with new or modified capabilities.

inheritance hierarchy—The inheritance relationships among classes. It is also known as a class hierarchy.

initial state (in the UML)—The beginning of the workflow in a UML activity diagram before the application performs the activities. The initial state is represented by a small solid circle.

initial value of a control variable—The value a control variable will hold when counter-controlled repetition begins.

initialization value—The beginning value of a variable.

input unit—The "receiving" section of the computer that obtains information (data and computer programs) from various input devices, such as the keyboard and the mouse.

input/output stream header file `<iostream>`—A file that provides basic stream input/output services. This file must be included to use objects such as `cout` and `cin`.

instance of a class—This is also known as an object of the class.

instantiate an object—Create an object of a class.

`int` type—A type that stores integer values.

integer—A whole number, such as 919, –11 or 0.

integrated Development Environment (IDE)—An application that allows a programmer to create, run and debug applications.

***Intellisense* feature**—A Visual Studio .NET feature that aids the programmer during development by providing windows listing available functions and pop-up descriptions of those functions.

interface—The names of a class's variables and functions that are available to clients of that class.

Internet—A worldwide computer network. Most people today access the Internet through the World Wide Web.

interpreter—A program that executes high-level language programs directly without the need for compiling those programs into machine language.

`invalid_argument` class—A derived class of `logic_error` that indicates that an invalid argument was passed to a function.

invoking a function—Calling a function.

`<iomanip>` header file—The header file that declares parameterized stream manipulators, such as `setprecision`, that enable the programmer to manipulate displayed text.

`ios::app` file-open mode—A file-open mode that specifies that data is written to the end of the file.

`ios::out` file-open mode—A file-open mode that specifies that data is written to the beginning of the file. If the file already con-

tains data, that file is truncated, so the original contents of the file are lost.

`ios_base::failure` class—A derived class of `exception` that is used to create an exception object that is thrown when a stream object encounters an error. This can occur if the application encounters non-numeric characters when attempting to input an integer.

***is-a* relationship**—A relationship in which an object of a derived class also can be treated as an object of its base class.

`istream` class—The class that is used to create input stream objects, such as `cin`.

K

keyword—A word that is reserved for use by C++ and cannot be used to create your own identifiers. *See also* reserved word.

L

Lady Ada Lovelace—The person credited with being the world's first computer programmer, for work she did in the 1840s.

left brace ({)—A symbol that indicates the beginning of a block of code, such as a function body.

left-justified output—Output that is aligned to the left side of a field.

left operand—An expression that appears on the left side of a binary operator.

`left` stream manipulator—A nonparameterized stream manipulator that causes output to be left justified in a field specified by stream manipulator `setw`.

`length` function of the `string` class—A function that returns the number of characters in a `string`.

letter—An uppercase letter A–Z or a lowercase letter a–z.

`<limits>` header file—The C++ Standard Library header file containing constants and functions for accessing numeric limits.

link—In a self-referential class, the data member that is a pointer to an object of the current class. This pointer can be used to "tie" one object of the class to another object of the same class.

linked list—A collection of data items "lined up in a row." Insertions and removals are made anywhere in a linked list. Specifically, a linked list is a series of nodes connected by pointer links.

linker—A program that packages compiled code into a single executable file.

literal—A sequence of characters within double quotes.

literal `string` object—A string constant written as a sequence of characters in double quotation marks (also called a string literal).

local variable—A variable defined inside a block. The scope of a local variable is from the point at which the definition appears in the block to the end of that block.

Locals window (in the debugger)—A debugger window that can be used to change the value of a variable at a breakpoint while an application is running.

logic error—An error that does not prevent your application from compiling successfully, but does cause your application to produce erroneous results.

`logic_error` class—The base class of several standard exception classes that indicate errors in program logic.

logical AND (&&) operator—A logical operator used to ensure that two conditions are *both* `true` before choosing a path of execution. It performs short-circuit evaluation.

logical negation (!) operator—A logical operator that enables a programmer to reverse the meaning of a condition: A `true` condition, when logically negated, becomes `false`, and a `false` condition, when logically negated, becomes `true`.

logical operators—The operators (`&&`, `||` and `!`) that can be used to form complex conditions by combining simple ones.

logical OR (||) operator—A logical operator used to ensure that either *or* both of two conditions are `true` before a path of execution is chosen. It performs short-circuit evaluation.

long type—An integral data type having a minimum range of values of –2,147,483,648 to 2,147,483,647.

loop—Another name for a repetition statement. A loop repeatedly executes its body until its continuation condition becomes false.

loop-continuation condition—The condition used in a repetition statement (such as `while` or `do…while`) that enables repetition to continue while the condition is `true`, but that causes repetition to terminate when the condition becomes `false`.

lvalue—Something to which a value can be assigned, such as a variable name. The operand of the address operator must be an *lvalue*.

M

machine dependent language—A programming language that can be executed only on certain types of computers.

machine language—A computer's "natural" language, generally consisting of streams of numbers (1s and 0s) that tell the computer how to perform its most elementary operations.

magic number—A number (such as the size of an array) that repeatedly appears in an application. A magic number takes on an artificial significance and can unfortunately confuse the reader when, for example, the application includes other instances of that number that have nothing to do with the size of the array.

main—The function that every C++ application executes first when started. Every C++ application must have exactly one `main` function.

margin indicator bar (Visual Studio .NET)—A margin in the IDE where breakpoints are displayed.

math library—A standard library that provides functions to perform common arithmetic calculations.

max (in the algorithm C++ library)—A function that returns the maximum of two `double` argument values.

m-by-*n* **array**—A two-dimensional array with *m* rows and *n* columns.

member-access operator (.)—An operator that enables access to data and functions that belong to the object to the left of the operator.

member-access specifier—A keyword, such as `public` or `private`, that can be used as part of a label that determines whether a class's members are accessible to non-member functions.

member function—A function declared within the scope of a class.

member initializer—A set of values that is used to initialize a class's data members. Member initializers appear between a member function's parameter list and the left brace that begins the member function's body.

members of a class—Functions and variables defined within the body of a class.

memberwise assignment—Assigns the values of the data members in the object in the right operand of an = operator to the data members of the object in the left operand. This is the default behavior of the = operator.

memory unit—The rapid-access, relatively low-capacity "warehouse" section of the computer, which stores data temporarily while an application is running.

merge symbol (in the UML)—A symbol (in the shape of a diamond) in the UML that joins two flows of activity into one flow of activity. A merge symbol has two (or more) transition arrows pointing to the diamond and only one transition arrow pointing from the diamond to indicate multiple activity flows merging to continue the activity. None of the transition arrows associated with a merge have guard conditions.

modulus operator (%)—An arithmetic operator that calculates the remainder after an integer division.

multiple-selection statement—A statement, such as a `switch` statement, that chooses among many different actions (or sequences of actions) by evaluating an integer expression.

multiplication operator—The asterisk (`*`) used to multiply its two numeric operands, calculating their product as a result.

multiprocessor—A computer that contains more than one CPU.

mutator—A function that alters the value of a data member; a *set* function.

N

name of a control variable—The identifier used to reference the control variable of a loop.

name of a variable—The identifier used in an application to access or modify a variable's value.

nested loop—A loop (such as a `for` statement) which is enclosed in another control statement.

nested statement—A statement that is placed inside the body of another control statement.

new operator—An operator that allocates memory dynamically for a new object. The operator takes as an argument the class of the object being created and returns a pointer to an object of that type.

newline character (\n)—A character that moves the cursor to the beginning of the next line. This character can be used to prepare the application to display text on the next line or to insert blank lines into an output stream (when several newlines appear back to back).

node—A self-referential class object. A linked list is composed of nodes tied together by pointer links.

nondestructive operation—The process of reading from a memory location, which does not modify the value in that location.

nonparameterized stream manipulator—A stream manipulator that does not specify any parameters, such as `endl` and `fixed`.

note (in the UML)—An explanatory remark (represented by a rectangle with a folded upper-right corner) describing the purpose of a symbol in a UML activity diagram. A dotted line connects each note to the item it describes.

NULL constant—A symbolic constant that is defined in the `<iostream>` header file (and in several other standard library header files) to represent the 0 pointer value. C++ programmers prefer to use 0 directly.

numeric_limits< streamsize >::max() constant—The maximum number of characters in a stream.

O

object—A reusable software component that models a real world entity.

object technology—A packaging scheme for creating meaningful, reusable software units that focus on particular application areas. Examples of objects include date objects, time objects, paycheck objects and file objects.

off-by-one error—The kind of logic error that occurs when a loop executes for one more or one fewer iteration than is intended.

ofstream object—An object that enables an application to write output to a file stream.

one-dimensional array—An array that uses only one index.

operand—An expression that is combined with an operator (and possibly other expressions) to perform a task (such as addition, comparison or stream insertion).

operation—A property of an object that corresponds to a member function.

operator—A symbol (or pair of symbols) that causes an application to perform a task by applying the operator to its operands.

operator overloading—A technique that allows the programmer to make C++'s operators work with objects (that is, any types that are not built in). To overload an operator, write a function definition (with a header and body) as you normally would, except that the function name now becomes the keyword `operator` followed by the symbol for the operator being overloaded. For example, the function name `operator+` would be used to overload the addition operator (+).

operator precedence—*See* rules of operator precedence.

ostream class—The class that is used to create output stream objects, such as `cout`.

out_of_range exception—An error that occurs when an application uses the subscript operator to access a `string` element that is not part of the `string`.

output device—A device to which information that is processed by the computer can be sent.

output unit—The section of the computer that takes information the computer has processed and places it on various output devices, making the information available for use outside the computer.

overflow_error class—A derived class of `runtime_error` that indicates an arithmetic overflow error occurred. Such errors occur when an application attempts to store a value that is larger than the maximum value that a particular numeric data type can store.

override—Supersede a base-class `virtual` function with a new implementation defined in the derived class.

P

parameter—A variable declared in a function's parameter list. Values passed as arguments to a function are copied to that function's corresponding parameters and can be used within the function body.

parameter list—A comma-separated list in a function header in which the function declares each parameter.

parameterized stream manipulator—A stream manipulator that requires an argument, such as `setprecision( 2 )`. Programs that use parameterized stream manipulators must include the `<iomanip>` header file.

parameterized type—A class template, so named because it requires one or more type parameters to specify a class-template specialization.

parent directory—The directory containing the current directory.

Pascal—A programming language named after the 17th-century mathematician and philosopher Blaise Pascal. This language was designed to teach structured programming.

pass-by-reference—A technique that allows a called function to access directly the argument in the caller. The original data in the caller can be modified by the called function. In C++, arrays are always passed by reference, while arguments of primitive types are, by default, passed by value. Because the array is passed by reference, the function can access the original array elements in the caller's memory.

pass-by-reference with pointer arguments—A form of pass-by-reference that uses pointer arguments. The caller must pass a pointer of the appropriate type to the function. The function must use the dereferencing operator (*) or arrow operator (->) to access the data or object to which the pointer points.

pass-by-reference with reference arguments—A form of pass-by-reference that uses reference parameters. To pass a reference argument, the caller simply specifies the variable name for the data that should be passed to the function for each reference argument. When the function call executes, each reference parameter becomes a synonym for its corresponding argument in the function call.

path name—A string that identifies a file by a series of directories separated by a forward slash (/) or a backslash (\).

persistent data—Data that exists even after the application that created the data terminates and even when the computer is turned off.

pointer—A variable that contains a memory address.

polymorphism—A concept that allows you to write applications that handle in a more general manner objects of a wide variety of classes related by inheritance.

position number—An alternate name for an array index. A value that indicates a specific position within an array. Position numbers begin at 0 (zero).

pow function—A function of the `<cmath>` standard library that performs exponentiation. The first argument specifies the value that will be raised to a power; the second argument specifies the power to which the first argument will be raised.

precision—The accuracy with which a number is printed to a display or stored in memory.

preprocessor—A program that performs manipulations on the application's source code file(s), such as including C++ Standard Library files, before the compiler's translation phase begins.

preprocessor directive—A message to the compiler's preprocessor. Preprocessor directives can be used, for example, to include source code from other files. This enables you to incorporate functions and services provided by those files in your applications.

primitive type—A type already defined in C++. The primitive types are `bool`, `char`, `int`, `short int`, `long int`, `float`, `double`, `long double`, `signed char`, `unsigned char`, `unsigned short int`, `unsigned int`, `unsigned long int` and `void`.

private member-access specifier—A member-access specifier that specifies that a class's data members or functions are accessible only to members of that class.

procedural programming language—A programming language (such as Fortran, Pascal, BASIC and C) that focuses on actions (verbs) rather than things or objects (nouns).

program control—The task of determining the next program statement to execute.

programmer-defined class—A class that a programmer defines, as opposed to a class predefined in the C++ Standard Library.

programmer-defined function—A function created by a programmer to meet the unique needs of a particular application.

programmer-defined type—*See* user-defined type.

project—The group of files containing source code and any instructions for building your application.

promotion—A type conversion where the value of a variable is stored in an equal or larger number of bytes to perform a calculation. Promotion changes only the type and size of the variable, not the value of the variable.

property—An object attribute, such as size, color or weight.

pseudocode—An informal language that helps programmers develop algorithms.

pseudorandom numbers—A sequence of values produced by a complex mathematical calculation that simulates random-number generation. Note that the calculation will produce the same sequence of numbers for a given seed value.

public member-access specifier—A member-access specifier that specifies that a class's data members or member functions can be accessed by clients of the class.

pure virtual function—A member function that is declared but not defined. A pure virtual function uses an initializer of = 0 (representing a NULL pointer) in its declaration. Any class with a pure virtual function is an abstract class.

Q

Quick Info box (Visual Studio .NET)—The box that displays the value of a variable when the mouse pointer hovers over that variable.

R

rand function—A function that generates an int value selected from 0 to RAND_MAX, when called with no arguments. An application that uses the rand function will generate the same sequence of values if the seed value does not change each time the application runs.

RAND_MAX constant—The largest possible value that the rand function will return. The value must be at least 32,767—the maximum positive value for a two-byte (16-bit) integer.

randomizing—Conditioning an application to produce a different sequence of random numbers for each execution.

range checking—This prevents an application from accessing data outside the range of values contained in a variable. For example, range checking prevents an application from using the subscript operator to access an element that is not part of an array.

record—A collection of related fields. A record is usually represented as a class in C++.

record key—A unique field used to identify a record and distinguish that record from all other records.

redefine—Supersede a base-class function that is non-virtual with a new implementation defined in the derived class.

redundant parentheses—Extra parentheses used in calculations to clarify the order in which calculations are performed. Such parentheses can be removed without affecting the results of the calculations.

reference parameter—A function parameter that specifies a synonym for the corresponding argument in a call to its function. A reference parameter is declared by placing an ampersand (&) after the type name in the parameter list.

relational operators—The < (less than), > (greater than), <= (less than or equal to) and >= (greater than or equal to) operators, which compare two values.

remainder operator (%)—An arithmetic operator that calculates the remainder after an integer division.

repetition statement—A control statement that might cause an application to execute statements multiple times. C++ provides the while, do...while and for repetition statements. A repetition statement allows the programmer to specify that an action or actions should be repeated, depending on the value of a condition.

replace function of the string class—A function that replaces in a string a number of characters (the second argument) begin-

ning at the specified index (the first argument) with the specified string (third) argument.

reserved word—A word that is reserved for use by C++ and cannot be used to create your own identifiers. *See also* keyword.

rethrow an exception—A catch block can use throw to defer the exception handling (or perhaps a portion of it) to another catch block associated with an enclosing try block.

return statement—The statement that returns a value from a function. A return statement begins with the keyword return, followed by an expression, which is evaluated to determine the value to return.

return type—Type of the result returned from a function to its caller.

rfind function of the string class—A function that returns the index of the last occurrence of its string argument in a string, and returns string::npos if the string argument is not found.

right brace (})—A symbol that indicates the end of a block of code, such as a function body.

right-justified output—Output that is aligned to the right side of a field.

right operand—An expression that appears on the right side of a binary operator.

right stream manipulator—A nonparameterized stream manipulator that causes output to be right justified in a field created by stream manipulator setw. Values output in fields continue to be right justified from the point at which right is inserted into the output stream until left is inserted into the output stream or the application exits.

row—In referring to an element of a two-dimensional array, the first index specifies the row.

rules of operator precedence—The rules that determine the precise order in which operators are applied in an expression.

runtime_error class—The base class of several standard exception classes that indicate errors that occur at execution time.

S

scientific notation—A numeric format that represents a floating-point number as the product of a value between 1 (inclusive) and 10 (exclusive) and a power of 10. For example, the value 12345.67 is written as 1.234567×10^4 in scientific notation.

scope—The portion of an application in which an identifier (such as a variable name) can be referenced. Some identifiers can be referenced throughout an application, while others can be referenced only from limited portions of an application (such as within a single function or block).

screen scraping—The process of extracting desired information from the HTML that composes a Web page.

secondary storage media—Devices such as magnetic disks, optical disks and magnetic tapes on which computers store files.

secondary storage unit—The long-term, high-capacity "warehouse" section of the computer.

seed—The value that the application uses to begin calculating random numbers. If an application uses the same seed each time it executes, the application will produce the same sequence of "random" values. By supplying the current time (which changes each time the application runs) as the argument to srand, your application will produce a different sequence of random values each time it runs.

selection statement—A control statement that selects among alternative courses of action. C++ provides the if, if...else and switch selection statements.

self-referential class—A class that contains a pointer member that points to an object of the same class. A node class for a linked list is an example of a self-referential class.

semicolon (;)—The character used to indicate the end of a C++ statement.

sentinel value—A special value that indicates that the application should terminate repetition.

sentinel-controlled repetition—A technique that causes an application to repeat an action until it encounters the sentinel value. This technique should be used when the number of repetitions is not known before the application runs.

sequential execution—This occurs when an application's statements are executed in the order in which they appear.

sequential-access file—A file that contains data that is read in the order that it was written.

set **function**—A function that sets the value of a data member and validates the value to ensure that it is appropriate for the variable that is being set to keep the object in a consistent state.

setfill parameterized stream manipulator—A stream manipulator that sets the character that is displayed in unused positions in a field.

setprecision stream manipulator—The parameterized stream manipulator that sets the number of digits of precision when displaying floating-point values.

setw stream manipulator—A parameterized stream manipulator that indicates that (only) the next value should appear in a field of the specified width. If the output value is less than the specified width, the value is right justified in the field by default. If the value to be output is greater than the specified width, the field is expanded to the right to the appropriate width.

short type—An integral data type having a minimum range of values of –32,768 to 32,767.

short-circuit evaluation—The evaluation of the right operand in && and || expressions occurs only if the condition to the left of the && in an expression is true or the condition to the left of the || in an expression is false.

signal value—*See* sentinel value.

signature—*See* function signature.

simple condition—A condition that contains one boolean expression.

single-entry/single-exit control statement—Each control statement has one entry point and one exit point.

single-selection statement—The if statement; it selects or ignores a single action or sequence of actions.

singly linked list—A list that begins with a pointer to the first node; each node contains a pointer to the next node "in sequence."

size function of the string class—A function that returns the number of characters (as an int) in the string on which it is called.

size of a variable—The number of bytes required to store a value of the variable's type. For example, an int is typically stored in four bytes of memory and a double is typically stored in eight bytes.

small circle (in the UML)—A UML activity diagram symbol that represents either the activity's initial or its final state.

software—The programs that run on computers.

solid circle (in the UML)—A UML activity diagram symbol that represents the activity's initial state.

solid circle surrounded by a hollow circle (in the UML)—A UML activity diagram symbol that represents the activity's final state.

solution—A file containing one or more projects.

solution file—A file with the .sln extension. These files are created by Visual Studio .NET when you create a solution, and they store information about your solution.

source code file—A file with the extension .cpp that stores C++ code written by a programmer.

special symbols—Characters such as $, @, %, &, *, (,), -, +, ", :, ? and /.

sqrt (in the cmath C++ library)—A function that returns as a double the square root of the double argument value.

srand function—A function that sets the seed for the rand function to the value passed as its argument. When the argument is the value returned by the time(0) function call (that is, the current time), srand will cause rand to produce a different sequence of random values each time the application executes.

statement—Code that instructs the computer to perform a task. Most statements end with a semicolon (;) character. Most applications consist of many statements.

static_cast operator—*See* cast operator.

<stdexcept> header file—The C++ Standard Library header file containing base class for representing runtime errors.

Step Into debugger command—The debugger command used to execute the next statement in an application. The **Step Into** command steps into function calls, allowing the programmer to execute the called function's statements line by line.

Step Out debugger command—The debugger command used to execute the remaining statements in the current function and transfer control to the location where the function was called.

Step Over debugger command—The debugger command used to execute the next statement in an application. The **Step Over** command executes function calls in their entirety.

straight-line form—The manner in which arithmetic expressions must be written so they can be typed in C++ code.

stream—A sequence of bytes. C++ reads from and writes to files using streams.

stream extraction operator (>>)—An operator that obtains data from the left operand (a stream input object, such as cin) and places that data in the variable to the right of the operand. When cin is the left operand, the stream extraction operator reads data entered at the keyboard.

stream input—Occurs when the stream of characters that the user types at the keyboard is sent to the application.

stream insertion operator (<<)—The operator that sends characters to a stream object such as cout. The stream object must be specified to the left of the operator; the characters must be placed to the right of the operator.

stream manipulator—An object that modifies a stream object (such as cout). The endl stream manipulator places a newline character in the output stream and flushes the stream buffer.

stream of characters—A sequence of characters passed to a stream object such as cout or input from a stream object such as cin.

stream state—A series of bits whose values indicate which stream I/O errors, if any, have occurred. For example, the failbit is set when the application encounters a stream format error (that is, encounters unexpected characters when inputting a value).

string—A sequence of characters.

string constant—A sequence of characters within double quotes.

<string> header file—The header file that declares classes and functions that store and manipulate strings.

string literal—A sequence of characters within double quotes.

string object—An object that stores a string of characters.

string::npos constant—A value returned by the `string` find-related functions to indicate that a `string` or character was not found in the `string`.

structured programming—A technique for organizing program control to help you develop applications that are easy to understand, debug and modify.

subscript—Another name for the term index or position number.

substr function of the string class—A function that returns a new `string` object by copying a specified part of an existing `string` object.

substring—A sequence of characters that makes up part or all of a `string`.

supercomputer—A computer that can perform hundreds of billions of calculations per second.

switch statement—The multiple-selection statement that selects one of many actions (or sequences of actions), depending on the value of the controlling expression.

syntax error—A compilation error that occurs when code violates the grammatical rules of a programming language. Syntax errors are detected by the compiler.

T

table—A two-dimensional array used to contain information arranged in rows and columns.

template—A C++ code unit that enables programmers to specify, with a single code segment, an entire range of related functions or classes.

text file—A file containing human-readable characters.

this pointer—In a member function, `this` is an implicitly defined pointer to the object for which the function is called.

throw an exception—A function throws an exception if the function encounters a problem that it cannot handle.

throw list—Appears after the parameter list and before the function body. It specifies the exceptions the function throws, but does not handle it. It contains a comma-separated list of exceptions the function will throw if a problem occurs when the function executes.

throw statement—A statement that throws an exception, so that it can be processed by an enclosing `try` block. A `throw` statement can specify zero or one operand, which can be of any type.

throw statement in a catch block—A statement that rethrows an exception from a `catch` block, so that it can be processed by an enclosing `try` block.

time function—A function in the `ctime` library that returns the current "calendar time" in seconds elapsed since January 1, 1970. This function is useful for seeding `srand` so that it produces a different sequence of random numbers each time you execute a program.

time_t type (in the ctime C++ library)—A type designed to contain a number of seconds. `time_t` values are typically represented by `long`s because the value returned by the `time` function can be larger than an `int` on some systems.

transfer of control—This occurs when the next statement to be executed in an application does not come immediately after the currently executing statement.

transition (in the UML)—A change from one action state to another that is represented by a transition arrow in a UML activity diagram.

transition arrow (in the UML)—A UML activity diagram symbol that represents a change from one action state to another.

Transmission Control Protocol/Internet Protocol (TCP/IP)—The combined set of communications protocols for the Internet.

true—One of the two possible values for a `bool` type; the other is `false`.

truncating in integer division—Any fractional part of an integer division result is discarded.

truncation (of a file)—Discarding all of the data in a file. This occurs when a file is opened with the `ios::out` file-open mode.

truth table—A table that displays the truth value of a logical operator for each possible combination of `true` and `false` values of its operand(s).

try block—A block that consists of keyword `try`, followed by braces (`{}`) that contain statements that might cause exceptions and statements that should not execute if an exception occurs. If an exception occurs inside a `try` block, the application executes the corresponding `catch` block, if one exists.

two-dimensional array—An array requiring two indices to locate an element. These arrays are often used to represent tables of information with values arranged in rows and columns.

type name—A name that identifies a type. Built-in type names include `bool`, `int` and `double`. An example of a user-defined type name is the identifier following the `enum` keyword.

type of a variable—Specifies the kind of data that can be stored in a variable and the range of values that can be stored.

U

UML (Unified Modeling Language)—An industry standard for modeling software systems graphically.

unary cast operator—*See* cast operator.

unary operator—An operator (such as unary + or unary -) with only one operand.

unary postdecrement operator (--)—Subtracts one from an integer variable. The variable is used to evaluate the expression containing the variable, then is decremented.

unary postincrement operator (++)—Adds one to an integer variable. The variable is used to evaluate the expression containing the variable, then is incremented.

unary predecrement operator (--)—Subtracts one from an integer variable. The variable is decremented, then is used to evaluate the expression containing the variable.

unary preincrement operator (++)—Adds one to an integer variable. The variable is incremented, then is used to evaluate the expression containing the variable.

uncaught exception—An exception that does not have an exception handler. Uncaught exceptions terminate application execution.

underflow_error class—A derived class of `runtime_error` that indicates that an arithmetic underflow error occurred. Such errors occur when an application attempts to store a value that is smaller than the minimum value that a particular numeric data type can store.

Unicode character—A character that can be stored using multiple bytes. The `wchar_t` data type can be used to represent members of the Unicode character set.

Unicode character set—An internationally recognized standard that is popular in Internet and multilingual applications. Its goal is to use a unique number to represent every character in all the world's languages.

user-defined type—A named collection of one or more values, each of which is also named. For example, an enumeration is a named collection of constant integer values, and each member value is named. A user-defined type can contain multiple values of different built-in data types.

using directive—A directive that notifies the compiler that the application will use services from the specified namespace.

V

value of a variable—The piece of data that is stored in a variable's location in memory.

variable—A location in the computer's memory where a value can be stored for use by an application.

virtual function—A function that can be overridden by a derived class. A function is made virtual by preceding its return type with the `virtual` keyword.

virtual keyword—A keyword that declares that a function can be overridden by a derived class. If the function is a pure `virtual` function, it *must* be overridden by a concrete derived class.

Visual C++ project file—A file with the `.vcproj` extension. These files are created by Visual Studio .NET, and they store information regarding your project.

void keyword—A return type that specifies that the function does not return any information.

W

Watch window (in the debugger)—A debugger window that is used to examine the values of variables and expressions.

wchar_t data type—A data type that stores characters using more than one byte, often to represent characters in the Unicode character set.

what function (of the exception class)—The exception class member function that typically returns a string describing the error. If the `exception` object was created by passing a string to the `exception` class's constructor, the `what` function typically returns this value.

while repetition statement—A control statement that executes a set of body statements while its loop-continuation condition is `true`.

whitespace character—A newline, space or tab character. Whitespace characters generally are ignored by the compiler.

workflow—The activity of a portion of a software system.

World Wide Web (WWW)—A collection of hardware and software associated with the Internet that allows computer users to locate and view multimedia-based documents (such as documents with text, graphics, animations, audios and videos).

World Wide Web Consortium (W3C)—A forum through which individuals and companies cooperate to develop and recommend technologies for the World Wide Web.

Y

yellow arrow in the debugger (Visual Studio .NET)—The arrow that appears in the margin indicator bar to the left of the next statement to execute.

Z

zeroth element—The first element in an array.

INDEX

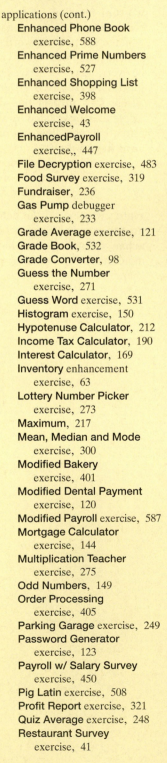

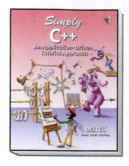

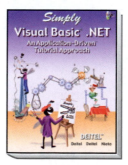

HOW TO PROGRAM BOOKS

The Deitels' acclaimed *How to Program Series* has achieved its success largely due to the innovative pedagogy used to teach key programming concepts. Their signature *LIVE-CODE Approach,* icon-identified programming tips and comprehensive exercises form the backbone of a series of books that has taught over one million students the craft of programming.

C++ How to Program Fourth Edition

BOOK / CD-ROM

©2003, 1400 pp., paper (0-13-038474-7)

Designed for beginning through intermediate courses, this comprehensive, practical introduction to C++ includes hundreds of hands-on exercises and uses 267 *LIVE-CODE* programs to demonstrate C++'s powerful capabilities. This edition includes a new chapter—Web Programming with CGI—that provides everything readers need to begin developing their own Web-based applications that will run on the Internet!

Java™ How to Program Sixth Edition

BOOK / CD-ROM

©2005, 1500 pp., paper (0-13-148398-6)

This text is up-to-date with J2SE™ 5.0 and includes comprehensive coverage of the fundamentals of object-oriented programming in Java. It features a new early classes and early objects approach; a new interior design including new colors, new fonts, new design elements and more; and a new optional automated teller machine (ATM) case study that teaches the fundamentals of software engineering and object oriented design with the UML in Chapters 1-8 and 10. Integrated case studies appear throughout the text including GUI and graphics (Chapters 3-12), the **Time** class (Chapter 8), the **Employee** class (Chapters 9 and 10) and the **Grade-Book** class in Chapters 3-8.

Small Java™ How to Program, Sixth Edition

BOOK / CD-ROM

©2005, 700 pp., paper (0-13-148660-8)

Based on chapters 1-10 of *Java™ How to Program, Sixth Edition, Small Java, How to Program, Sixth Edition* is up-to-date with J2SE™ 5.0. It also features a new early classes and early objects approach and comprehensive coverage of the fundamentals of object-oriented programming in Java.

Visual Basic® .NET How to Program Second Edition

BOOK / CD-ROM

©2002, 1400 pp., paper (0-13-029363-6)

This book provides a comprehensive introduction to Visual Basic .NET. *Visual Basic .NET How to Program, Second Edition* covers introductory programming techniques as well as more advanced topics, featuring ASP .NET, ADO .NET, Web services and developing Web-based applications. This book also includes extensive coverage of XML.

Visual C++ .NET® How To Program

BOOK / CD-ROM

©2004, 1400 pp., paper (0-13-437377-4)

This comprehensive book thoroughly examines Visual C++® .NET. Readers learn the concepts of object-oriented programming then explore such essential topics as networking, databases, XML and multimedia. Graphical user interfaces are also extensively covered, giving students the tools to build compelling and fully interactive programs.

Advanced Java™ 2 Platform How to Program

BOOK / CD-ROM

©2002, 1811 pp., paper (0-13-089560-1)

Expanding on the world's best-selling Java textbook—*Java™ How to Program*—*Advanced Java™ 2 Platform How To Program* presents advanced Java topics for developing sophisticated, user-friendly GUIs; significant, scalable enterprise applications; wireless applications and distributed systems. Primarily based on Java 2 Enterprise Edition (J2EE).

C# How to Program

BOOK / CD-ROM

©2002, 1568 pp., paper (0-13-062221-4)

C# How to Program provides a comprehensive introduction to Microsoft's C# object-oriented language. C# enables programmers to create powerful Web applications and components—ranging from XML-based Web services on Microsoft's .NET platform to middle-tier business objects and system-level applications.

C How to Program
Fourth Edition

BOOK / CD-ROM

©2004, 1328 pp., paper (0-13-142644-3)

C How to Program, Fourth Edition—the world's best-selling C text—is designed for introductory through intermediate courses as well as programming languages survey courses. This comprehensive text is aimed at readers with little or no programming experience through intermediate audiences. Highly practical in approach, it introduces fundamental notions of structured programming and software engineering and gets up to speed quickly.

Getting Started with Microsoft® Visual C++™ 6 with an Introduction to MFC

BOOK / CD-ROM

©2000, 163 pp., paper (0-13-016147-0)

Internet & World Wide Web How to Program
Third Edition

BOOK / CD-ROM

©2004, 1250 pp., paper (0-13-145091-3)

Teaches the fundamentals needed to program on the Internet. This text provides in-depth coverage of introductory programming principles, various markup languages, and relational databases—all the skills and tools needed to create dynamic Web-based applications.

Wireless Internet & Mobile Business How to Program

©2002, 1292 pp., paper (0-13-062226-5)

Wireless Internet & Mobile Business How to Program offers a thorough treatment of both the management and technical aspects of wireless Internet applications development, including coverage of current practices and future trends.

Python How to Program

BOOK / CD-ROM

©2002, 1376 pp., paper (0-13-092361-3)

Python How to Program provides a comprehensive introduction to Python—a powerful object-oriented programming language with clear syntax and the ability to bring together various technologies quickly and easily.

e-Business & e-Commerce for Managers

©2001, 794 pp., cloth (0-13-032364-0)

This comprehensive overview of building and managing e-businesses explores topics such as the decision to bring a business online, choosing a business model, accepting payments, marketing strategies and security, as well as many other important issues (such as career resources).

XML How to Program

BOOK / CD-ROM

©2001, 934 pp., paper (0-13-028417-3)

This book is a comprehensive guide to programming in XML. It teaches how to use XML to create customized tags and includes chapters that adress markup languages for science and technology, multimedia, commerce and many other fields.

Perl How to Program

BOOK / CD-ROM

©2001, 1057 pp., paper (0-13-028418-1)

This comprehensive guide to Perl programming emphasizes the use of the Common Gateway Interface (CGI) with Perl to create powerful, dynamic multi-tier Web-based client/server applications.

e-Business & e-Commerce How to Program

BOOK / CD-ROM

©2001, 1254 pp., paper (0-13-028419-X)

e-Business & e-Commerce How to Program explores programming technologies for developing Web-based e-business and e-commerce solutions, and covers e-business and e-commerce models and business issues.

Visual Basic® 6 How to Program

BOOK / CD-ROM

©1999, 1015 pp., paper (0-13-456955-5)

This text was developed in cooperation with Microsoft to cover important topics such as graphical user interfaces (GUIs), multimedia, object-oriented programming, networking, database programming, Script®, COM/DCOM and ActiveX®.

The DEITEL® DEVELOPER SERIES

Deitel & Associates is recognized worldwide for its best-selling *How to Program Series* of books for college and university students and its signature *LIVE-CODE Approach* to teaching programming languages. Now, for the first time, Deitel & Associates brings its proven teaching methods to a series of books specifically designed for professionals.

THREE TYPES OF BOOKS FOR THREE DISTINCT AUDIENCES

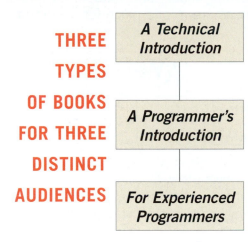

A Technical Introduction books provide programmers, technical managers, project managers and other technical professionals with introductions to broad new technology areas.

A Programmer's Introduction books offer focused treatments of programming fundamentals for practicing programmers. These books are also appropriate for novices.

For Experienced Programmers books are for experienced programmers who want a detailed treatment of a programming language or technology. These books contain condensed introductions to programming language fundamentals and provide extensive intermediate level coverage of high-end topics.

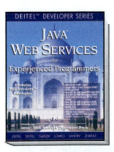

Java™ Web Services for Experienced Programmers

©2003, 700 pp., paper (0-13-046134-2)

Java™ Web Services for Experienced Programmers covers industry standards including XML, SOAP, WSDL and UDDI. Learn how to build and integrate Web services using the Java API for XML RPC, the Java API for XML Messaging, Apache Axis and the Java Web Services Developer Pack.

Web Services A Technical Introduction

©2003, 400 pp., paper (0-13-046135-0)

Web Services: A Technical Introduction familiarizes programmers, technical managers and project managers with key Web services concepts, including what Web services are and why they are revolutionary. The book covers the business case for Web services, the latest Web-services standards and Web services implementations in .NET and Java.

ORDER INFORMATION

SINGLE COPY SALES:
Visa, Master Card, American Express, Checks, or Money Orders only
Toll-Free: 800-643-5506; Fax: 800-835-5327

GOVERNMENT AGENCIES:
Prentice Hall Customer Service
(#GS-02F-8023A)
Tel: 201-767-5994; Fax: 800-445-6991

COLLEGE PROFESSORS:
For desk or review copies, please visit us on the World Wide Web at www.prenhall.com

CORPORATE ACCOUNTS:
Quantity, Bulk Orders totaling 10 or more books. Purchase orders only — No credit cards.
Tel: 201-236-7156; Fax: 201-236-7141
Toll-Free: 800-382-3419

CANADA:
Pearson Technology Group Canada
10 Alcorn Avenue, suite #300
Toronto, Ontario, Canada M4V 3B2
Tel: 416-925-2249; Fax: 416-925-0068
E-mail: phcinfo.pubcanada@pearsoned.com

UK/IRELAND:
Pearson Education
Edinburgh Gate
Harlow, Essex CM20 2JE UK
Tel: 01279 623928; Fax: 01279 414130
E-mail: enq.orders@pearsoned-ema.com

EUROPE, MIDDLE EAST & AFRICA:
Pearson Education
P.O. Box 75598
1070 AN Amsterdam, The Netherlands
Tel: 31 20 5755 800; Fax: 31 20 664 5334
E-mail: amsterdam@pearsoned-ema.com

ASIA:
Pearson Education Asia
317 Alexandra Road #04-01
IKEA Building
Singapore 159965
Tel: 65 476 4688; Fax: 65 378 0370

JAPAN:
Pearson Education
Nishi-Shinjuku, KF Building 101
8-14-24 Nishi-Shinjuku, Shinjuku-ku
Tokyo, Japan 160-0023
Tel: 81 3 3365 9001; Fax: 81 3 3365 9009

INDIA:
Pearson Education Indian Liaison Office
90 New Raidhani Enclave, Ground Floor
Delhi 110 092, India
Tel: 91 11 2059850 & 2059851
Fax: 91 11 2059852

AUSTRALIA:
Pearson Education Australia
Unit 4, Level 2
14 Aquatic Drive
Frenchs Forest, NSW 2086, Australia
Tel: 61 2 9454 2200; Fax: 61 2 9453 0089
E-mail: marketing@pearsoned.com.au

NEW ZEALAND/FIJI:
Pearson Education
46 Hillside Road
Auckland 10, New Zealand
Tel: 649 444 4968; Fax: 649 444 4957
E-mail: sales@pearsoned.co.nz

SOUTH AFRICA:
Pearson Education
P.O. Box 12122
Mill Street
Cape Town 8010 South Africa
Tel: 27 21 686 6356; Fax: 27 21 686 4590

LATIN AMERICA:
Pearson Education Latinoamerica
815 NW 57th Street Suite 484
Miami, FL 33158
Tel: 305 264 8344; Fax: 305 264 7933

ONEKEY IS ALL YOU NEED

Convenience. Simplicity. Success.
Powered by CourseCompass, Blackboard and WebCT.

OneKey is Prentice Hall's exclusive new resource for instructors and students. OneKey gives you access to the best online teaching and learning tools—all available 24 hours a day, 7 days a week. OneKey means all your resources are in one place for maximum convenience, simplicity and success.

Convenience
Prepare more effectively, present more dramatically and assess more easily. All our best online resources have been combined into one easy-to-use site. Also, an abundance of searchable presentation material together with practice activities and test questions—all organized by chapter or topic—make course preparation easy.

Simplicity
With OneKey there is no longer any need for instructors or students to go to multiple Web sites to find the resources they need. All of our best resources can be accessed with one simple login.

Success
Thousands of test questions—in multiple formats—let instructors create and assign tests for automatic grading. More review and assessment tools let students practice, explore on their own or create study programs to fit their own personal learning style. OneKey is all you and your students need to succeed.

Additional features of CourseCompass, Blackboard and WebCT

Intuitive Browser-Based Interface
Your students will love our browser-based interface, designed to be user-friendly and easily accessible.

Our use of full-text searching and hyperlinking makes it easy to navigate.

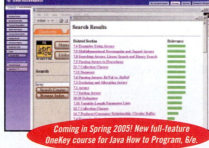

Coming in Spring 2005! New full-feature OneKey course for Java How to Program, 6/e.

Further Enhancements to the DEITEL® Signature *LIVE-CODE* Approach
Hours of detailed, expert audio descriptions of thousands of lines of code help reinforce concepts. OneKey includes an innovative learning environment for your introductory programming students called CodeKey. CodeKey allows your students to run and modify the programming projects at the end of each chapter, and provides them with meaningful feedback about the structure and function of their programs. Additionally, you can use CodeKey for submission of programming projects for course credit within the OneKey environment.

DEITEL® Course Management content available in CD-ROM based Complete Training Courses

An Abundance of Self-Assessment Material

Practice exams offer students hundreds of test questions with immediate feedback in addition to those found in the main text. Hundreds of self-review questions are drawn from the text, all with answers. Hundreds of programming exercises are drawn from the text, half with answers. (The main text does not contain answers to these exercises.)

These Course Management Systems offer you:

- **Features to create and customize an online course** such as areas to post course information (e.g., contact information, policies, syllabi, announcements, assignments, grades, performance evaluations and progress tracking), class and student management tools, a gradebook, reporting tools, page tracking, a calendar and assignments.

- **Testing programs** allowing for you to create online quizzes and tests from questions directly linked to the text, and automatically grade and track results.
- **Design tools** and pre-set designs that help you create a custom look and feel for your course.
- **Support materials** that are available in print and online.

Also Available:

CD-ROM based Complete Training Courses

Many *How to Program* texts can be ordered as *Complete Training Course* packages, each containing the main text and the corresponding *Cyber Classroom*—an interactive, multimedia, tutorial version of the book. The *Complete Training Courses* are a great value, giving students additional hands-on experience and study aids for a minimal additional cost.

Each* *Complete Training Course* is compatible with Windows 95, Windows 98, Windows NT, Windows 2000, Windows ME and Windows XP and includes the following features:

- Intuitive browser-based interface designed to be easy and accessible for anyone who's ever used a Web browser.
- Each *Cyber Classroom* contains the full text, illustrations and program listings of its corresponding *How to Program* book.
- Hours of detailed, expert audio descriptions of thousands of lines of code help reinforce concepts.
- An abundance of self-assessment material, including practice exams, hundreds of programming exercises and self-review questions and answers.
- In most *Complete Training Courses*, students can load programs into specific compilers or software (usually on the books accompanying CD), allowing them to modify and execute the programs with ease.
- * The *Complete Visual Basic® 6 Training Course, Student Edition* is not compatible with Windows 2000 or Windows XP. The *Complete C# Training Course, Student Edition, The Complete Visual Basic® .NET Training Course, Student Edition* and The *Complete Python Training Course, Student Edition* are not compatible with Windows 95.